BLUE G

D1139553

For Vronwy who loved Crete

Please write in with your comments, suggestions and corrections for the
next edition of the Blue Guide. Writers of the most helpful letters will be
awarded a free Blue Guide of their choice.

BLUE GUIDE

CRETE

Pat Cameron

A&C Black • London
WW Norton • New York

914.959

Seventh edition May 2003

Published by A & C Black Publishers Ltd
37 Soho Square, London W1D 3QZ

www.acblack.com

© Pat Cameron 2003
Maps by Mapping Company Ltd, © A & C Black Publishers Limited.

ISBN 0–7136–4676–4

All rights reserved. No part of this publication may be reproduced or used in any form or by any means—photographic, electronic or mechanical, including photocopying, recording, taping of information and retrieval systems—without permission of the publishers.

The rights of Pat Cameron to be identified as the author of this work have been asserted by her in accordance with the Copyright Designs and Patents Act, 1988.

'Blue Guides' is a registered trademark.
A CIP catalogue record of this book is available from the British Library.

Published in the United States of America by
W W Norton & Company, Incorporated
500 Fifth Avenue, New York, NY 10110

Published simultaneously in Canada by
Penguin Books Canada Limited
10 Alcorn Avenue, Toronto
Ontario M4V 3BE

ISBN 0–393–32134–7 USA

276C552

The author and the publishers have done their best to ensure the accuracy of all the information in Blue Guide Crete; however, they can accept no responsibility for any loss, injury or inconvenience sustained by any traveller as a result of information or advice contained in the Guide.

Cover photograph: the Phaistós disk, Archaeological Museum, Herákleion, by permission of the Hutchison Library; spring flowers at Spakhiá by permission of the Robert Harding Library.
Title page: Marine Style flask from Palaíkastro, now in the Archaeological Museum, Herákleion.

For permission to reproduce illustrations in the *Guide* the publishers would like to thank the following: Ashmolean Museum, Oxford, p 43; Christopher Helm Publishers (*The Handbook of Bird Identification*), p 57; British School at Athens, pp 112 and 270 (the latter photograph taken by Alexander MacGillivray); Ministry of Culture, Greece, pp 3, 78, 79, 88, 90, 365; Archaeological Museum, Ayios Nikólaos, p 216.

Pat Cameron has an MA from Oxford University where she read English at Somerville College. In 1979, after gaining the London University Diploma in Archaeology, she joined the staff of the British School at Athens to catalogue material in the School's Stratigraphical Museum at Knossós. She lived for five years on Crete working on this project and had time to acquire a detailed knowledge of the island to which she now regularly returns.

A&C Black uses paper produced with elemental chlorine-free pulp, harvested from managed sustainable forests.

Printed and bound in Great Britain by Butler and Tanner Ltd, Frome and London.

Contents

Maps and plans

Introduction

The island of Crete, in Greek Κρητη (Kríti), is by far the largest in the Greek archipelago, and as the major link in a chain of smaller islands it forms the southern
boundary of the Aegean Sea. The territory includes the most southerly point in
Europe, further south than Algiers or Tunis.

The island was the birthplace of the Minoan civilisation, the earliest civilisation of Europe, which was at the height of its power in the second millennium BC.
Visitors are attracted to the archaeological sites and the museums that preserve
the evidence and the evocative artefacts of this prehistoric culture. Others are
drawn by the natural beauty of the island, an ideal territory for walkers and of
great potential interest for botanists and ornithologists.

The history of Crete has clearly been influenced by its geographical position at
a crossroads for trading routes through the Mediterranean. The Minoans were in
touch with Egypt as well as the islands to the north. The city-states of the Iron
Age and Hellenistic times were submerged in the Roman Empire, and Roman
rulers were succeeded in due course by Arabs, and then by the forces, both military and cultural, of Byzantium, of Venice and of the Ottoman Empire. Crete
became part of Greece only at the beginning of the 20C. The varied remains of
many periods can add to the interest of a visit.

The Orthodox Church has played a major part in the history of the island.
Crete's surviving monasteries are sorely depleted as religious institutions, but
they remain for the most part havens of tranquillity and retain architectural surprises. Many Byzantine churches have survived, often with at least part of their
wall-paintings preserved, sometimes in isolated locations where the beauty of
their native setting is an integral part of their appeal.

Two hundred and fifty kilometres long, nearly 60km at its widest point but
only 12km at its narrowest, the island is dominated geographically by its great
spine of mountains; these slope gently to the north and very steeply to the southern coast, and so the centres of population have grown up in the bays along the
north coast. Herákleion with nearly a quarter of the island's population of something over half a million is the fifth largest and one of the most prosperous cities
in the whole of Greece. Khaniá and Réthymnon flourish, but on a smaller scale;
they retain strong hints of their past and seek to preserve them.

During the last part of the 20C the hotel industry has done no favours to
Crete's north coast, but across the still largely unspoilt interior improvements in
the road system are benefiting those exploring by car and the nature of the territory makes it ideal for walkers. The profits from tourism are largely responsible
for the island's prosperity, with Greece's membership of the European Union
leading to increased investment from abroad. The long-distance walking route
(E4) which traverses the island is only one of the conspicuous EU projects.

Crete has been known since antiquity as a fertile island and nowadays prof-
itable agriculture and horticulture provide the other plank on which prosperity
is founded. Huge numbers of sheep and goats are moved between the summer
pastures in the mountains and winter quarters at lower levels. The climate
favours the two main crops, the olive and the vine, but also many varieties of
fruit and vegetables. Since Minoan times olive oil has been an important source
of Cretan wealth, and wine production is already well documented during

Venetian rule. Hothouse cultivation, especially along the south coast with relatively higher winter temperatures, has become economically significant.

Crete came relatively late to heritage concerns such as the conservation of landscape and vernacular buildings, related to the pursuit of what has become recognised as sustainable tourism. But now a movement is gathering momentum all the time, encouraged by enlightened directors of historical and ethnographic societies and the showplaces of their museums. Visitors to the island can only enjoy and applaud.

Blue Guides have an unrivalled reputation for their reliable and informative approach to the cultural aspects of travel. This revised edition of Crete follows A&C Black's recent policy of carefully preserving that tradition while now also incorporating some elements of a companion guide to the opportunities offered within any particular location for full enjoyment of a varied holiday. A good travel agent specialising in Crete can make all the necessary travel arrangements but for planning a holiday and exploring the island a guidebook can contribute a great deal. Whether the search is for signed walks through remote unspoilt countryside, for unspoilt beaches, for accommodation within sound of the sea, or for communities dedicated to preserving the best of the traditional way of life Blue Guides aim to show the way.

Acknowledgements

This is the fourth time that I have undertaken a revision of Blue Guide Crete. I want to thank Gemma Davies who with her colleagues at A&C Black has supported and encouraged me at every turn as we produced this new edition, but I have been helped over the years by more people than it is now possible to record or thank individually. Critically important has been the advice and information that I have been able to count on from academics, and others who love Crete, who have patiently answered my questions and done their best to keep me on a straight path. The books of the experts which figure in the list of Recommended reading in this edition indicate the rich vein of information and the many sources of that help. In addition a large proportion of the academics happen to have contributed to the recent millennium publication *Cretan Quests: British Explorers, Excavators and Historians* published by the British School at Athens. In a spirit of gratitude I should like to recommend this book to Blue Guide readers who want to pursue in depth their interest in the island of Crete.

How to use this Guide

The guide begins with **practical information** which is designed to help with the planning of a visit to Crete whether it is to be a package holiday based in one place or a touring holiday with the aim of getting an initial overall view of the island. Following this there is **background information** which includes an outline of the history of Crete from earliest (prehistoric) times until 1913 when the island became part of Greece. This section is intended to provide a framework for some understanding of the various influences on Crete's antiquities, art and architecture in order to reduce repetition within the subsequent text.

The **main part of the guide** has been organised on the basis of the four *nomes* which are the Greek equivalent of counties or provinces. The first section covers the *nome* of Herákleion, with the capital city and Crete's airport, and the second takes the reader east to Ayios Nikólaos, still the best-known tourist resort and the principal town of the *nome* of Lasíthi. Then moving west the third section covers the city of Réthymnon and its *nome*, arguably the least discovered province, and finally to the city of Khaniá favoured by a colony of discerning expatriots and the hub of the province which covers all the western end of the island.

Each section starts with a short introductory overview of the particular province. Then there is a description of the main town followed by practical information dealing with the logistics of a short visit: car parking, arrival by bus, cultural objectives such as museums, churches and other places of interest as well as suggestions about where to look for a meal. It is inevitable that many details of practical information quickly become out of date so it is useful to check whenever possible.

For a longer stay in or near a town there is advice about sources of help and information about the choice of accommodation. After that the text describes possible excursions into the surrounding province indicating the principal features of interest along the way as well as distinctive landscape and any environment likely to appeal to naturalists and birdwatchers. The excursion can be handled selectively according to the particular interest of the reader, or touring motorists can build up a continuous itinerary.

Abbreviations

c circa (about)	EOT (GNTO) Greek National Tourism Organisation
C century	OTE Telecommunications Organisation of Greece
€ Euro	Leoph. (Léophóros) Avenue
EOS Greek Alpine Club	

Transliteration

The difficulty of achieving consistency in the transliteration of Greek into English has long been recognised. The process is still in a state of flux and for scholarly historical reasons several parallel systems of transliteration continue to exist side by side. The chief guiding principle here has been to help the reader to pronounce the Greek words in the text, especially the place names, in a manner recognisable to a Greek speaker. Attempts at absolute pedantic consistency do not always fulfil this objective, and sometimes produce unnecessarily ugly words without assisting pronunciation. Some well-known words already have an accepted spelling in the English language, for example Herakleion or Zeus. In practice the tourist soon learns that the transliteration of place names on signposts or notices, or in museum cataloguing, will not always follow the system used in this Blue Guide and quickly grows comfortable with Xania, Chania and Hania as well as Khania for Χανια, or Agios and Hagios beside Ayios, Ayia, etc. for saints' names. For further help with pronunciation see the Language section on p 33.

PRACTICAL INFORMATION

 Planning your trip

When to go

Crete enjoys a typical 'Mediterranean' climate with long hot dry summers and a winter rainy season with snow in the mountains. The best months if you want to explore the island are May, June, September and October. Between late June and early September a temperature of 30°C is no surprise, and there is the likelihood of at least one heatwave with readings up to 40°C. In midsummer you may also encounter the force 7 or 8 *meltémi* winds which make sandy beaches and the sea inhospitable places, although they do help to moderate the temperatures.

April (average maximum 20°C) is the time for ornithologists to observe the spring migration. February to May is ideal for botanists keen to search out Crete's renowned displays of wild flowers; orchids are at their best in the lowlands in March but continue into April, especially in the higher regions. However, the weather early in the year is unpredictable: wild storms and glorious mild spring days can occur within the same week while snow still lies in the high mountains and the nights are often cold. May is best for walking holidays, though there is still an outside chance of rain, especially in the western half of the island, and the high mountains may still be snow-covered. At the end of summer the temperatures relent but by then most of Crete's streams, fed by the melting snows in spring, will have dried up and an arid landscape waits for the first deluge of autumn.

As for swimming, hardy northern Europeans may enjoy the sea in April, but beach life does not begin in earnest on Crete until May. Along the south coast consistently higher temperatures make the Libyan Sea noticeably more inviting than the Aegean at both ends of the winter.

It is worth knowing that half-term holiday weeks in northern Europe (in May and October) have become a popular time for family holidays on the island. Flights and resort accommodation may be unexpectedly full. However, the interior of the island is not much affected during these periods.

If you have no choice but to go in July or August, you should be warned that there is competition for accommodation, flights and boat tickets from Greeks fleeing the furnace of Athens, as well as from foreign visitors. It is wise to make arrangements well in advance or be prepared to camp. The return to the mainland begins immediately after the feast of the Assumption on 15 August.

The winter season is very quiet, with no charter flights to the island. All the resort hotels close at the end of October as do tavernas geared to tourism. Many Cretans return to the traditional winter work of harvesting the olives. Some hotels remain open, but tourists contemplating a winter visit should make enquiries in advance from the Greek National Tourism Organisation.

Sources of information

The **Greek National Tourism Organisation** (GNTO), in Greek *Ellinikós Organismós Tourismoú* (EOT, pronounced ay-ot, accented on the second syllable) can provide information on travel to Crete and on planning a holiday on the island. The GNTO does not make travel arrangements and operates a strictly neutral policy that prevents employees offering recommendations.

UK and Republic of Ireland 4 Conduit Street, W1S 2DJ (off Regent Street), open Monday to Thursday 09.30–17.00, Friday 09.30–16.30, ☎ 020 7495 9300 or fax 020 7287 1369, email info@gnto.co.uk
USA Olympic Tower, 645 Fifth Avenue, New York, NY10022, ☎ (212) 421 5777, fax (212) 826 6940, email gnto@greektourism.com
Canada 1300 Bay St, Main Level, Toronto, Ontario M5R 3K8, ☎ (416) 968 2220, fax (416) 968 6533, email grnto.tor@sympatico.ca
1170 Place du Frère André, 3rd floor Montreal Quebec H3B 3C6, (514) 871 1535, fax (514) 871 1498
Australia and New Zealand 51–57 Pitt Street, Sydney, NSW 2000; PO Box R203 Royal Exchange NSW 2000, ☎ (00612) 9241 1663/4/5, fax (00612) 9235 2174, email hot@tpg.com.au
Netherlands Griekse Nationale Organizatie voor Toerisme, Kerkstraat 61, 1017 GC Amsterdam, (20) 625 4212/3/4, fax (20) 620 7031, email gnot@planet.ni

Web sites

www.gnto.gr	the English-language website for the Greek National Tourism Organisation
www.travelling.gr.	general Greek travel website
www.gtpnet.com	Greek Travel Pages
www.interkriti.gr	a Crete travel site, including general information, accommodation, car and bicycle hire
www.gogreece.com	general travel and information site
www.dilos.com	for accommodation and car hire
www.greekislands.gr	ferry schedules, hotels, camp sites and car hire
www.ferries.gr	ferry schedules
www.cretetracel.com	details of flights, ferries, and bus routes
www.ktel.org	bus routes around Greece
http://stigmes.gr/br	website of a Crete magazine; it also lists other useful websites

Where to stay

It is an important consideration for many visitors to Crete that the western part of the island is least affected by mass tourism. Walkers and naturelovers may choose to be within reach of the hills and moutains in the west, perhaps from a base around Réthymnon or Khaniá, or on the south coast in Palaiókhora, or they may prefer the still unspoilt extreme east around Siteía which has a drier and more temperate climate early and late in the year. However, it is important to remember that the island is 250km from one end to the other as the crow flies and if you are keen to visit the principal Minoan sites you will face a long haul to Herákleion and Knossós or Phaistós. If you depend on buses you will need to consider that services out of the south coast villages are often limited. Splitting the holiday between two centres has become a popular solution. There are further suggestions about where to stay in the introductory sections to each of the four provinces.

Tour operators in the UK

Specialist tour operators to Crete include:

Island Holidays, Drummond St, Comrie, Perthshire PH6 2DS, ☎ 01764 670107, fax 01746 670, email enquiries@islandholidays.net

Pure Crete, 79 George St, Croydon, Surrey CR0 1LD, ☎ 020 8760 0879 fax 020 8688 9951, www.purecrete.com

Simply Crete, Simply Travel, Kings House, Wood St, Kingston-upon-Thames, KT1 1SG, 020 8541 2201, fax 020 8541 2280, www.simplytravel.co.uk, email crete@simply-travel.com

Sunvil Holidays, Sunvil House Upper Square, Old Isleworth, Middx TW7 7BJ, ☎ 020 8568 4499, fax 020 8568 8330, www.sunvil.co.uk, email greece@sunvil.co.uk

Travel Club of Upminster, Station Rd, Upminster, Essex RM14 2TT, ☎ 01708 225000, fax 01708 229678

For guided cultural tours:

ACE Study Tours, Babraham, Cambridge, CB2 4AP, ☎ 01223 835 055, fax 01223 837 394, www.study-tours.org, email ace@study-tours.org

Martin Randall Travel, Voysey House, Barley Mow Passage, Chiswick, London, W4 4GF, ☎ 020 8742 3355, fax 020 8742 7766, www.martinrandall.com, email info@martinrandall.co.uk

The British Museum Traveller, 46 Bloomsbury St, London WC1B 3QQ, ☎ 020 7436 7575, fax 020 7580 8677, www.britishmuseumtraveller.co.uk

Walking tours:

Headwater, 146 London Road, Northwich, Cheshire CW9 5HH, ☎ 01606 720033, fax 01606 720034, www.headwater-holidays.co.uk

Island Holidays and *Simply Crete* (see above) offer special interest tours for birdwatchers and wild flower enthusiasts.

Travellers with disabilities

Crete has come late to an understanding of the particular needs of the disabled. It has to be accepted that the nature of some of the terrain, for example in hill villages, is not helpful for anyone with restricted mobility. In the towns special toilet facilities are rare and provision for wheelchair access is limited though the number of pedestrianised streets is growing. However, the position is changing annually and around the coast an increasing numer of hotels of Class A–C offer accommodation which presents no problems to wheelchair users; many of these are noted in the Blue Guide's advice on where to stay. Where EU funds have been used to improve public access to archaeological sites you can rely on there being a convenient route for wheelchairs. The site of the Minoan palace of Knossós is a shining example to others. For further information ask first for anything relevant from a GNTO office.

Useful contacts in the UK

RADAR (Royal Association for Disability and Rehabilitation), 12 City Forum, 250 City Road, London EC1V 8AF, ☎ 020 7250 3222, fax 020 7250 0212, www.radar.org.uk. An organisation of and for disabled people. It provides infor-

mation, campaigns for improvements and supports disability organisations.
Holiday Care Information Unit, 7th Floor Sunley House, 4 Bedford Park,
Croydon, Surrey CR0 2AP, 0845 124 9971, www.holidaycare/org.uk. A
national charity which acts a source of travel and holiday information for disabled and older people, their families and carers.

Useful contacts in the USA

Mobility International USA, PO Box 10767, Eugene, Oregon USA 97440, ☎
(541) 343 1284, fax (541) 343 6812, www.miusa.org. A non-profit organisation whose mission is to empower people with disabilities through international
exchange, information and technical assistance.
Society for Accessible Travel and Hospitality, 347 Fifth Ave, Suite 610, NY
10016, ☎ (212) 447 7284, www.sath.org. a non-profit educational organisation that campaigns on behalf of disabled and older travellers.

Passports

As Greece is a member of the European Union the only travel document required
by citizens of the UK and the Republic of Ireland to enter the country is a valid
passport. Foreign nationals from outside the EU will have their passports
stamped on entry (and exit). Permission to stay as a tourist is limited in the first
instance to three months; for longer periods of residency, visitors should contact
the Greek Embassy.

Money and currency regulations

The Euro (€) replaced the drachma as the official unit of currency in Greece on
1 January 2002. The Euro is subdivided into 100 *leptá* (cents). There are notes of
value 5, 10, 20, 50, 100, 200 and 500 euros, and coins of 1, 2, 5, 10, 20 and
50 *leftá* as well as for 1 and 2 euros. Small denominations are useful on arrival to
cope with airport trolleys, taxis, buses, telephone calls, etc.

The advice to anyone passing through Customs with large amounts of foreign
currency is to declare it on entry, to avoid problems about taking any substantial
amount out again when leaving the country. If there are special circumstances
consult your bank before you leave home.

Customs regulations

Valuable items (especially electronic equipment) may be entered in your passport
to ensure that you take them with you when you leave the country (otherwise
they might be subject to an import tax). Greece's drug regulations should be
strictly observed, and note that they include a total ban on codeine. If you are
taking any prescribed drugs a doctor's letter in clear English is a wise precaution.

Antiquities

Regulations to protect Greece's heritage are strictly and comprehensively
enforced; even picking up sherds (scraps of pottery) on an ancient site is prohibited. The use of metal detectors is also prohibited. Permits for diving and underwater photography are hedged about with restrictions. Except with special
permission, it is forbidden to export antiquities and works of art dated before
1830 which have been obtained (whether bought or found) in Greece. If a traveller's luggage contains antiquities not covered by an export permit (supplied
with bona fide purchases) the articles are liable to be confiscated and prosecution
may follow.

Health

The UK Department of Health issues a comprehensive and well-indexed booklet *Health Advice for Travellers*, obtainable from any post office and from their website, www.doh.gov.uk. The booklet includes an application for the Form E111 which entitles UK citizens to free or reduced-cost emergency medical treatment within the state system in Greece. (Readers in the USA might consult their government's Travellers' Health website, www.cdc.gov/travel.) However, it cannot be too strongly emphasised that visitors should also take out a travel insurance policy which covers the costs of accident and emergency treatment in the Greek private sector and includes, in the last resort, repatriation by air. In the event of a need to claim on the policy for medical or pharmacy costs, obtain and keep clear receipts (the word is *apódeixi*). It should be noted that bills, perhaps large fees, will need to be paid on the spot and can only be reclaimed later. A credit card is invaluable in the case of such unforeseen expenses.

What to take

People who use binoculars will certainly want them on Crete. A pocket compass can help in understanding inland site plans and directions. A torch is useful, especially for frescoed churches and caves, but also for paths through villages dark at night. Basic picnic equipment does double duty on rent room terraces.

Protection from the sun is clearly necessary, but anyone on a touring holiday in the early part of the year (March–April) should remember that in the mountains the weather may still be wet, and, at least at night, distinctly chilly.

A mosquito repellent such as Autan is advisable. Small electrical devices vaporise insectsidal tablets or you can burn mosquito coils (which do not require electricity); both systems are available locally in chemists and minimarkets. (Mosquitoes are *kounoúpies* in Greek.)

Maps

You will find maps of a sort in many tourist shops all over Crete. Good maps are now stocked by the half-dozen serious bookshops on the island, but initial supplies can sell out long before the end of the season. Dedicated explorers are recommended to equip themselves before leaving home. In the UK, maps may be obtained by post from *Stanfords*, 12–14 Long Acre, London WC2E 9LP, ☎ 020 7836 1321, fax 020 7836 0189, www.stanfords.co.uk.

Reliable maps include Freytag and Berndt's sheet 14 (1:200,000), in their series covering Greece, and *Kreta*, 1:150,000, by Marco Polo. *Road Editions 6: Kríti Crete* 1:250,000 (also stocked by Stanfords) has been produced with the cooperation of the Hellenic Army Geographical Service; on this map an 'unsurfaced road of good quality' or a 'scenic route' may still need to be treated with caution by the driver, but these 'scenic routes' will take you into magnificent walking country.

The best map for walkers and for the E4 is the Harms-Verlag touring map (1:100,00) which covers Crete in two sheets for the western and eastern halves of the island. A Cretan mapmaker Giorgis N. Petrakis produces the *Trekking and Road* map (1:100,00 in four parts). A recent addition to the walking maps is from Freytag and Berndt. This map, with a brief guide, selects five areas of the island which, with routes of varying difficulty, could be explored in depth.

Getting there

Direct flights to Crete from the UK

A direct flight to Herákleion or Khaniá (c 4 hours from the UK) is desirable and the only direct flights to the island from outside Greece are charter flights. These operate for the tourist season, late April (depending on the date of Easter) until October. The majority leave from Gatwick but there are some departures from other UK airports. There is a range of options and prices, and it is worth shopping around or asking a travel agent to do so.

A firm specialising in low cost charter flights to Crete is **Greek Tourism-Travel Ltd** at 255–256 Linen Hall, 162–168 Regent St, London W1B 5TG ☎ 020 7437 0218, fax 020 7494 1251, www.greektourismtravel.co.uk. This agency issues a leaflet with summer timetables and prices for Greek holiday destinations, and for late bookings acts as a clearing house for surplus flights from a wide range of agents and tour operators.

Scheduled flights via Athens

To reach Crete by scheduled services (and there may be no alternative early in the year) the normal route is to fly to Athens (Elefthérios Venizélos) and there transfer to a domestic flight of **Olympic Airways** or the competitor **Aegean Cronus Airlines**. If Olympic Airways is used for both flights luggage can be booked through from point of departure to final destination. There are eight Olympic flights daily to Herákleion (Níkos Kazantzákis airport) and five to Khaniá. Olympic also flies to Herákleion from Rhodes. There is a twice-weekly service from Athens to Siteía in eastern Crete; the new international airport being built at Siteía is behind schedule but it is hoped that it will be operational in 2004, the year of the Athens Olympic Games. For up-to-date information check with Olympic Airways or the Greek National Tourism Organisation. **Aegean Cronus Airlines**, ☎ 0030 210 998 8300, www.aegeanair.com, operate flights between Athens and both Herákleion and Khaniá.

Flights from the UK

Olympic Airways, from London Heathrow and Gatwick, and from Manchester, 11 Conduit St, London W1R 0LP, ☎ 0870 606 0460, www.olympic-airways.com, email@olympicairways.co.uk
British Airways, ☎ 0845 773 3377, www.britishairways.com.
easyJet, ☎ 0870 6000 000, www.easyjet.com

Direct flights to Athens from the USA

Olympic Airways, ☎ 800 223 1266, www.omogenia.com
Delta Airlines, ☎ 800 241 4141, www.delta.com

Direct flights to Athens from Canada

Olympic Airways, ☎ 800 223 1226, 416 964 7137, www.omogenia.com
Air Canada, 1 888 247 2262, www.aircanada.com.

By sea

There are three overnight car ferry services between Piraeus (port of Athens) and Crete. Boats run every night all the year round to Herákleion, Réthymnon and Soúda (for Khaniá); departure is 20.30 or later, whether to or from Crete; the journey time is 6–8 hours depending on the vessel.

To Herákleion there are two overnight sailings run by rival companies, *Minoan Lines* (in Herákleion, ☎ (0030) 2810 399 800, fax (0030) 2810 330 308; agent in UK *Magnum Travel*, 747 Green Lanes, Winchmore Hill, London N21 3SA, ☎ 020 8360 4244) and *ANEK* (in Herákleion, ☎ (0030) 2810 222 481, fax (0030) 2810 346 379; agent in UK *Viamare Travel*, ☎ 020 7431 4560, www.viamare.com). The Réthymnon and Khaniá services are run by ANEK. Accommodation on the overnight ferries is priced in five classes: de Luxe to Deck. Fares for a berth in a First Class cabin remain comparable with domestic air fares. The basic deck-class ticket covers travel in Pullman-type seats, or in the open air on summer nights, and costs roughly € 20. All ships have a restaurant (Second Class and above) and a café. At busy times (in July and August and for festivals such as Easter) it is advisable to book well ahead.

In addition to the long-established overnight services new daytime sailings between Piraeus and Herákleion were introduced in 2001, for July and August, and at weekends and festivals during the winter. *Minoan Lines* runs high speed ferries leaving in both directions around midday with the journey time reduced to six hours. The *Palaeologus travel agency* (p 65) will arrange first night accommodation.

For sea travel to Crete by less direct or less frequent services the GNTO distributes Greek Travel Routes (Domestic Sea Schedules); make sure you are referring to the current edition. *Lane Lines* (p 266) is experimenting with a regular service from Piraeus (via Mílos) to Ayios Nikólaos and Siteía, continuing twice a week to Rhodes. Kísamos (Kastelli Kisámou) in western Crete is linked by ferry (p 426) via the island of Kýthera to mainland harbours along the southeast coast of the Peloponnese.

There are currently no direct ferry services to Crete from outside Greece, but consult the annual publication *Ferries of Southern Europe* or their website www.ferrypubs.co.uk. International shipping schedules change frequently.

Cars, camping vans and motor cycles

These can be brought to the island on the ferries from Piraeus or Gýthion (southern Peloponnese). You should consult well in advance an office of the GNTO and ask about current formalities. Membership of the AA or RAC is an advantage, for in case of breakdown it ensures free assistance from the Greek equivalent ELPA (ΕΛΠΑ).

Useful websites

Minoan Lines www.minoan.gr
ANEK www.anek.gr
www.greekislands.gr
www.ferries.gr

Accommodation

Hotels

Hotels on Crete are inspected annually by the national tourist organisation (EOT) and graded in six categories: de Luxe and A–E. Prices are fixed accordingly and notice of the approved rate, inclusive of service and taxes, should be displayed in the room. There may be surcharges for short stays (less than three nights) and during the high season (July and August). A small reduction (20 per cent) can be expected for single occupancy of a double room if no single is available.

De Luxe and **class A** hotels, usually located in the main towns or beach resorts, are comparable with their counterparts elsewhere around the Mediterranean. The rooms have private bath or shower, balconies, and a full range of tourist facilities. Half-pension terms are usually obligatory. Many of the resort hotels are in effect holiday villages with bungalow accommodation, shops, a variety of bars and a nightclub, tennis courts, minigolf, agencies for hire of cars, motor bikes, mountain bikes, boats, windsurfers (where appropriate) and every kind of watersport equipment that may be required. Resort hotels should be booked in advance. It is possible to make the arrangements independently but you will usually find it more economical, and certainly easier, to use the advice and services of a good travel agent. Since these hotels are geared to package tours and block bookings by agencies from all over Europe and beyond, the independent traveller should not, at least in the high season, rely on rooms being available. Beach resort hotels close from towards the end of October till Easter, some till early May.

Many readers looking for a hotel on a touring holiday will find categories B and C better suited to their needs. **Class B** hotels are above-average comfortable establishments (classified as B rather than A on the basis of size, number of public rooms and so on). The management will usually advise on local tour agencies or hire shops but does not offer all such tourist facilities under one roof. There will be a breakfast room and probably a bar, but not necessarily a restaurant. Many hotels in this category provide an ambitious, self-service breakfast.

Class C hotels can be expected to provide simple rooms, usually with balconies, almost always with private shower and toilet. Frequently they have no restaurant, and thus no compulsory half-board terms. This grade of hotel is often family-run and offers good value as a functional base for a mainly outdoor holiday. The firms specialising in Cretan holidays (see p 13) make it their business to know about good small hotels in desirable locations. For the independent traveller touring the island this Guide offers suggestions where a hotel might make a convenient base for a few nights' stay. These suggestions are given in good faith but should not be taken to imply the personal recommendation of the author.

Classes D and E (increasingly rare on Crete) are old-fashioned hotels for those who are prepared to put up with spartan conditions for a bed in a chosen location. At this price level you will do better with a traditional rent room.

Rent rooms

Rent rooms are a time-honoured and characteristic feature of touring on Crete. In place of the traditional Cretan hospitality in family homes, inexpensive rooms, often nowadays in purpose-built modern blocks, are available for a single night or a longer period. The standard of these rooms can vary from the primitive to some of the most satisfactory accommodation on the island, providing a friendly, economical and unconstricting base in the local community.

On-the-spot inspection is essential. You should be able to check the room rate displayed inside the door. In case of doubt you might want to flush the toilet, have a look at the shower, enquire about the supply of hot water or use of a fridge or the nearest telephone. This is expected of you and a negative decision will be (regretfully) respected. If all is well you can ask the best price which will depend on location, length of stay, local circumstances and the time of year.

Advice on where to look for rent rooms will be found in the text, but a large proportion of villages on the island can provide a room of some description. Rooms are commonly advertised on boards and in windows, but in case of difficulty ask in a *kapheneíon*, minimarket or a post office if there is one. The English phrase is usually familiar, otherwise *ena domátio* is a room.

In coastal villages the traditional rent room has often evolved into what is known as a studio apartment, that is to say open-plan accommodation with cooking facilities and a terrace for outdoor living. These studios cater for inexpensive family holidays. Outside July and August many often stand empty and the owner may be happy to let for a two or three night stay, or longer.

Youth hostels

There are several hostels on Crete that belong to the **Greek Youth Hostels Oragnisation**, 75 Dhamáreos St, Athens (☎ (0030) 210 751 9530, email yhostels@otenet.gr). These are currently the *Herákleion Youth Hostel*, 5 Vironos St, ☎ (0030) 2810 286 281, email hostel@heraklio.forthnet.gr; the *Réthymnon Youth Hostel*, 45 Tobazi St, ☎ (0030) 28310 22848, email yh_rethymnon@yahoo.com; *Plakiás Youth Hostel*, (0030) 28320 32118/31560, www.yhplakias.com, email info@yhplakias.com.

Camping

Camping on Crete is officially restricted to designated camping sites. A current list should be available from tourist information offices (on Crete and abroad); you can expect more than a dozen widely distributed sites, all by or near the sea. During busy periods it is advisable to make reservations ahead of time.

Getting around

Sources of information

The **Greek National Tourism Organisation** (EOT) maintains regional offices in Herákleion and Khaniá but the latest news is that responsibility for the tourist information aspect of their work is to be passed to the local municipal authorities, perhaps involving a period of transition during 2003. (For the best advice currently available see under practical information for each city.) In case of diffi-culty the first port-of-call should be the tourist police. Other locally funded tourist information offices (also noted in the text) operate in the season in a number of towns and resort villages; their staff are usually knowledgeable about their dis-trict and go out of their way to be helpful.

Tourist police

The tourist police service is run by specialist members of the ordinary police force (recognisable by the shoulder flash Tourism Police on their uniforms) who staff information desks in police stations and act as a back-up to the official tourist information offices. They deal with reports of theft (for insurance claims). They act as interpreters and handle complaints about any aspect of the tourist trade. They are a useful sanction if you are concerned about overcharging or poor ser-vice from, for example, taxi drivers, restaurants or tourist shops. Contact details for local offices are given in the text. 24 hour emergency helpline, ☎ 171.

Travel agencies

Commercial agencies are found in all the towns and in resorts (down to quite small village resorts). Most agents offer currency exchange, and many will help with finding accommodation. They can also arrange car hire and book excur-sions or boat trips. Guided excursions on offer are likely to include the main archaeological sites, the Gorge of Samariá, the mountain plain of Lasíthi, and many other places of interest or natural beauty on the island. Travel agencies can often provide information on guided walks or similar local initiatives.

By car

Nearly all visitors driving on Crete use rented vehicles. The fly-drive arrange-ment, with a hire car waiting at the airport on arrival, is extremely popular. If you prefer to hire locally for the odd day or days during the holiday the official rate per day may be higher than when the hiring is part of a package paid in advance from abroad, but out of season, substantial discounts are often avail-able. (All rates, including any optional insurance costs, are subject to VAT.)

Cars, jeeps, motor cycles and scooters can be hired from agencies in all the towns and resort villages as well as from the large hotels and at the airports. Be sure to check the condition of the vehicle, especially the tyres, and that you under-stand the range of the rescue service in case of a breakdown, and the small print in the insurance policy; look carefully at the 'collision damage waiver' clause.

Of the household names *Hertz* is long-established on Crete and generally pro-vides a reliable service. You can book in advance from abroad (☎ 0870 599 6699) at favourable prepaid rates. On the island the firm has a dozen or so agen-cies, including desks at the airports, with the main office in Herákleion at Leoph. 25th Avgoústou 34, ☎ 2810 341 734. (Check when you hire but usually their insurance covers damage to tyres and the underside of the vehicle, claims which many local policies exclude.)

All car hire firms require a full driving licence, in most cases held for at least one year. Age restrictions may operate (also for motor bike hire). A deposit will be required.

Petrol

There are plenty of petrol stations along the north coast, and they operate on a par with anywhere else in Europe except that payment by credit card (increasingly common every year) should not be taken for granted. In the outlying areas, especially where tourists are not expected, there may be a rota system for opening evenings and weekends and it is sensible not to depend on being able to fill up after 19.00 (Saturdays 15.00) or on Sundays.

Roads

There are improvements every year in the island's road system and overall it is now more than adequate for exploring even the remotest parts. All main roads, and those to the most popular tourist centres, have an asphalt surface, and upkeep is generally good. Work continues on minor roads in remote rural areas, primarily for the benefit of isolated communities but also nowadays in an attempt (greeted with mixed reactions) to open up to tourism areas which used to be wilderness. Non-asphalt surfaces are generally noted in the text, though this information can quickly become out of date. Driven with reasonable caution short stretches of hard-packed dirt roads need present no problems.

It is customary to use the horn on blind corners. In the mountains, rock falls are a hazard, and subsidence or the torrential winter rains may produce unexpected pot-holes or gaps at the edge of the road. Drivers not used to Mediterranean conditions should take particular care after the first rains of autumn; greasy road surfaces catch out the unwary every year.

The north coast highway is the main artery running the length of the island. It was built in the 1960s and began life as the New Road. The last decade has seen a major construction programme. The highway has evolved into the New National Road (officially the E75) running between Kísamos in the west and Siteía in the east. Roadworks are set to continue, providing for the greatly increased traffic flow behind the main cities or realigning tortuous stretches through the hills, for example near Gourniá or on the descent to Siteía. The older sections of the highway still need to be driven with care. They were not designed for the fast business traffic, tourist coaches and European Union trucks that they now have to carry. Overtaking can be hazardous because the makeshift inside lane for slower traffic often runs out without much warning when it has to cope with a bridge or a minor junction. Local traffic often follows its own private rules rather than official road signs. The New National Road is a great boon for travelling from one end of the island to the other but it is worth remembering that the Old Road which it replaced provides meandering alternatives.

Roads to the south have always radiated in the natural historical pattern from the north coast capitals of the four *nomes* or provinces. Now the upgraded section of the south coast road across the Mesará plain (from Agii Déka to Pýrgos and on to Ano Viánnos) provides an easy route between the central region around the Minoan palace at Phaistós and the coast of southeastern Crete. The bus companies have not yet tackled this new route; you need private transport.

On all the main roads signposts are duplicated, the second one helpfully transliterating the Greek alphabet. (The result does not always match exactly the transliteration used in this Guide.) On minor roads the convention is to sign the chief destination once, and then to signpost the turnings off the road without repeating the original destination. It is assumed that you continue straight ahead unless directed otherwise.

By bus

Country bus travel on the island is efficient and inexpensive. The information desks, or windows, at the bus stations will have English speakers among the staff, and prominent noticeboards are designed to answer the most common questions. (The Greek word for ticket is *eisitípio*.)

Long-distance buses run to schedule fairly frequently between the main towns of the four *nomes* (provinces): Khaniá, Réthymnon, Herákleion and Ayios Nikólaos. Further details are given in the practical information sections for each of these towns. Because these services are operated (as they are throughout Greece) by a Joint Pool of Bus Owners (**KTEL**) journeys via Herákleion may involve a change of bus station. There are services within each *nome* between the provincial capital and the chief villages of each *eparchy* (district) but the timetable designed for the needs of local people is not always convenient for tourist excursions. Villages supplement the bus service with a communal taxi (marked ΑΓΟΡΑΙΟ) (*agoraío*) and sometimes a taxi may bridge the gap to the nearest long-distance bus route. At country stops, you must hail the bus; it will not halt automatically. It is important to note that Sunday bus schedules are almost always reduced. Summer (end of April–mid-October) and winter schedules differ markedly, so early or late season holiday-makers should check in advance especially carefully, at a bus station itself if possible. The companies publish a timetable (*dromolóyio*), also available from tourist information offices.

Taxis

Taxis are widely used on Crete. Those from the official rank at the airports are prepared to go anywhere on the island. Prices to the most popular destinations are listed beside the rank and the charge should be confirmed in advance. Town taxis should carry a note of fare rates beside the meter. You are advised to ensure at the beginning of the trip that the meter is running. Town ranks have a clearly displayed contact telephone number.

Basic taxi fares incur a surcharge for luggage weighing more than 10kg, for hire from airport, bus station or port, for waiting time, and for night work (00.00–05.00). Long-distance journeys are charged at double tariff.

A village taxi (*agoraío*) does not usually have a meter but approved charges apply and, again, should be confirmed before the journey. If the taxi is shared with strangers, the fare will be shared.

Radiocabs are a feature of life on Crete. If you are without private transport it is a good idea soon after your arrival to ask locally for a reliable number.

If you have a problem with a taxi driver, take the registration number and suggest that you will consult the local tourist police. This is a sanction taken seriously. In the last resort carry out the threat, but remember that local witnesses will not be biassed in your favour.

Coastal boats

There is a well-established boat service operating to schedule on a route along the south coast between Khóra Sphakíon and Palaiókhora (for further information see pp 387 and 411). As well as transporting from Ayiá Rouméli the many people who now walk down the Gorge of Samariá from the Omalós mountain plain to the Libyan Sea, the service offers opportunities to explore parts of this coast which are not accessible by road. The boats also serve the island of Gávdos.

Walking

The pleasure of walking on Crete has been given a new dimension by the arrival of the **E4 long-distance path**, more elegantly in Greek the **Epsilon Téssara**. These cross-frontier E-paths have been established on the initiative of the European Ramblers Assocation. The Cretan section (the last leg of a hiking route which starts in Gibraltar) runs the length of the island from Kastélli Kisámou in the west to Káto Zákros on the extreme east coast. The path should be marked the whole way (either on metal poles or painted on to rocks or fences) by yellow diamonds framing the black logo E4. It is equipped where necessary with footbridges, picket gates and steps of split logs, and at strategic points information boards indicating what to expect on the stretch ahead.

The main path is designed to tackle the island's conspicuous peaks of the Lévka Ori (White Mountains), the Psilorítis (Ida) range, the surroundings of the mountain plain of Lasíthi and the hills to the east around Ornó and Thriptí. Alternative routes (branches for access or subsidiary paths) take in many of the walks that tourists have traditionally enjoyed, such as the Sphakiá long-distance coastal path or the climb to the Kamáres cave.

Good maps of Crete (p 15) now indicate the route of the E4. You can leave a vehicle at any one of the places where the path crosses the road system (many of which are noted in the Blue Guide) and explore as much or as little as you wish. With good advance planning you may be able to walk a stretch between two bus routes.

The remote mountain areas are relatively unpopulated, and are a terrain only suitable for experienced (or guided) walkers. Consult the *Greek Alpine Club* (Ellinkós Oreivatikós Sýllogos, EOS) in Herákleion, Réthymnon or Khaniá (see the practical information sections for those towns) for any local maps or other guidance; in case of difficulty enquire at a tourist information office.

The kalderími system

Until the 1930s Crete's road system consisted of thousands of kilometres of paved trackways designed for mule transport. These were and still are known as *kalderímia*, a Turkish word for road. Some were built by the Turks to help control a rebellious countryside, but others, maintained and added to in the Turkish period, are thought to follow the line of the earlier Venetian (or even perhaps in some cases Roman) roads.

Rackham and Moody (see p 60) describe the trackways as on average 4.5m wide, carefully paved with flat stones, often with a row of larger stones down the middle. The tracks were stepped where necessary (which ruled out their use for wheeled traffic). They zigzag to cope with gradients and have retaining walls or parapets where they traverse steep slopes or cliffs. At river crossings the remains of paved fords have been detected.

Despite extensive road building since the Second World War the age-old routes between villages remain. They are often very overgrown but some are still used as local footpaths to fields, vineyards or chapels. Now stretches of *kalderími* have taken on a new life where the trackways are incorporated in the E4 long-distance footpath system. Many walkers find that recognising the old trackways, their meticulous and variable construction, their patterns across the landscape, is one of the particular pleasures of a day in the Cretan countryside.

Useful information

Banking hours

Banks are open Monday–Thursday 08.00–14.00, Friday 08.00–13.30. In high season, at tourist centres such as Ayios Nikólaos, one foreign exchange till may reopen at 17.30. (The word for bank is *trápeza*.)

Traveller's cheques are a safe and easy way of carrying funds; those from American Express and Thomas Cook are a good choice. Remember that a passport is required for identification and queues and delays are a fact of life in banks. Cash dispensers (ATMs) are generally available. All the main branches of the National Bank (**Ethnikí Trápeza Elláthos**) operate an Automatic Currency Exchange.

Credit cards are increasingly accepted in the towns and tourist areas on Crete but probably not by hotels below Class C, nor by rent room establishments nor tavernas. Mastercard and Visa are well recognised. Credit cards can be used to obtain cash and experienced travellers top up their credit card accounts before leaving home to avoid incurring interest. Mastercard is handled by the National Bank of Greece and Visa and American Express by the Commercial Bank (**Emborikí Trápeza**).

Outside the main centres post offices offer a useful exchange service (for cash only). Almost anywhere on the island where tourists are expected there is some facility for obtaining cash, at a municipal tourist information office or at one of the many commercial travel agencies which have proliferated in the resorts. Hotels of any size provide this service for their guests. Where there is a choice, tourists are advised to check what commission is charged.

Electricity

The voltage on Crete is 220v and the current is AC. A universal plug adaptor is useful and visitors from North America should check that any small electrical appliances are compatible.

Newspapers

Foreign-language newspapers are obtainable (at a price) in the main towns and resort hotels, usually on sale the day after publication.

The *International Herald Tribune* contains a pull-out section which is an English edition of the respected Athens newspaper *Kathemeríni* (literally *The Daily*). This is the paper to buy if you are interested in the politics, arts, regional news, business affairs and gossip of Greece (including Crete).

Postal services

The main **post office** (*takhydromeío*) in the principal north coast towns will be open for normal postal business Monday–Friday 07.30–19.30 (check under sections of practical information for each major town). In other towns and the larger villages the hours are Monday–Friday 07.30–14.00. Subsidiary post offices in temporary caravans are now common in popular tourist areas. In addition to the above weekday hours they may also open mornings on Saturdays and even on Sundays as well as in the high season. Staff generally speak some English.

Letter-boxes (ask for *grammatokivótio*) and the caravans are painted bright yellow. (At post offices there are also red boxes for express mail.) **Postage stamps** (*grammatósima*) can be bought at kiosks and at many shops which sell postcards, but a small premium is charged for the convenience and you need to know the correct stamps.

Parcels posted to Crete must be collected from a parcels office, where they are subject to handling fees, customs charges, and often to delay. The bus companies operate an efficient parcel delivery service between their own booking-halls.

Main post offices operate a **currency exchange** at rates on a par with the banking system. In conventional post offices (Monday–Friday) the hours for this are 08.00–13.30 but the caravans will help whenever they are open. The extensive network of post offices in villages across the island, and the extra opening hours in the bigger cities and tourist areas make this a particularly useful service.

Public holidays

The official public holidays in Greece are:

1 January	New Year's Day
6 January	Feast of Epiphany
Kathará Dephtéra	(literally Clean Monday), the Orthodox Shrove Day before the beginning of Lent
25 March	Greek Independence Day
1 May	May Day parades
Orthodox Good Friday, Easter Sunday and Monday, also Ascension Day	
15 August	Feast of the Assumption of the Virgin (*Panayía*)
28 October	*Okhi* day marking Greece's entry into the Second World War in 1940
25 December	Christmas Day
26 December	Feast of St Stephen (*Ayios Stéphanos*)

Carnival after a three-week period of festivities reaches its peak on the last Sunday before Lent with processions and student revels; on **Clean Monday** families take to the countryside and fly kites; on **May Day** there is an exodus to the countryside to pick wild flowers; **Good Friday** is marked by the procession of Christ's shrouded bier (*Epitáphios*) and the burning of Judas in the graveyard. The vigil preceding Easter Sunday includes the ceremonial lighting of the Paschal Candle during mass and then at midnight the '*Khristós anésti*' (Christ is risen) celebration with the light passed from the celebrant, candle by candle, to everyone taking part, which traditionally would have been the entire community. This is accompanied by the release of fireworks in front of churches and is followed on the morning of Easter Day by the cracking of red-painted Easter eggs and the ritual roasting of Paschal lambs.

On **Okhi Day** Greeks remember with pride the single word 'No', the blunt refusal to accept the Italian ultimatum of 1940 (see section on modern history). They celebrate with remembrance services and military processions.

If you are interested in the many other traditional festivals you should ask at your local tourist information office. In Asi Goniá, southwest of Réthymnon, the **sheep-shearing festival** is held on St George's day, the feast of Ayios Yeóryios (23 April unless this falls in Holy Week). In Khaniá there are festivities in late

May (**Anniversary of Battle of Crete**). In Sphakiá on 26 May and in Ierápetra on 3 October the community observes the **Anniversary of the 1821 revolution**, which led to the independence of mainland Greece. At the Arkádi monastery 8–9 November there is commemoration of the heroic episode during the 1866 revolt. Herákleion celebrates on 11 November the feast of the city's patron saint (**Ayios Minás**).

Shopping

Shop opening hours are usually 08.00–13.00 (most categories of food shop 13.30), also Tuesday, Thursday and Friday, 17.00–20.00 (winter 16.00–19.30). On Monday, Wednesday and Saturday they do not reopen, but the morning session is extended to 14.00 (Saturday 15.00). Souvenir shops and food shops in designated tourist areas may remain open all day, including Sundays. The old regulations were exceedingly complicated and are gradually changing. Butchers in particular (for historical reasons from before the age of refrigeration) keep different hours; enquire locally if you are in self-catering accommodation. Chemists take turns to offer a 24-hour service; the rota is posted on the shop door. Supermarkets (increasingly common) are allowed to remain open all day (08.00–21.00) but may close on Sundays.

The *períptero* or pavement kiosk is a characteristic feature of Greek urban life. Selling newspapers, postcards and stationery, stamps, cards for telephone boxes, cigarettes, chocolate, toilet articles, film and a great deal else, kiosks are open for up to 18 hours a day.

Telephones

The Greek telephone services are run by a public corporation, *OTE* (*Organismós Telepikinonión Elládos*, telecommunications of Greece), always referred to by its acronym pronounced o-tay, accented on the second syllable. All towns have a central office of the company, with call-boxes and arrangements for making domestic and international calls and sending faxes. The calls are metered, and payment is made to the cashier once the call has been made, cutting out the need for correct change. OTE offices in the cities are open 07.00–22.00. All villages have a (signposted) OTE centre, even if, in the smallest places, it is the local *kapheneíon*, in which case opening hours are likely to be much shorter.

This is the most economical way of making calls from Crete. The same metering system (*metrití*, a meter) is used, with a small surcharge per unit, for payphones which are found at kiosks (*períptera*) and in cafés, bars, some travel agencies and other public places across the island. Beware that telephone bills in hotels incur a high surcharge.

Operating alongside this traditional metering system public phone boxes accepting phone cards are now commonplace in towns and all resort areas. You can buy cards (*telekárta*) in units of 100, 200, 500 and 1000, at kiosks, at supermarkets or at an OTE office.

Dialling Crete from abroad

Dial 00 30 (for Greece) + area code + local number.

Dialling within Greece

Always dial the full area code plus the local numbers which should total ten digits.

Athens 210   Khaniá 28210

Ayios Nikólaos 28410
Herákleion 2810
Ierápetra 28420

Kísamos (Kastélli Kisámou) 28220
Réthymnon 28310
Siteía 28430

Dialling abroad from Crete

UK: dial 00 44 + area code (omitting first digit) + local number.
USA: 001 + area code (omitting first digit) + local number.

Off-peak rates are 15.00–17.00 and 22.00–08.00. Transferred-charge calls from Crete can be arranged through the operator (domestic 132, international 161). Directory enquiries (domestic) 131, (international) 161.

Time

All movable festivals are governed by the fixing of Easter according to the Orthodox calendar. Greece uses Eastern European Time (in summer 3 hours ahead of GMT, in winter 2 hours). Note also that πμ (pm) is English am and μμ (mm) is English pm.

Weights and measures

The French metric system, adopted in Greece in 1958, is used with the terms substantially unaltered. Thus *kiló*, pl. *kilá*, *misó kiló* (half a kilo), *grammária* (grams), etc. Some liquids such as wine from the barrel are measured by weight rather than in litres.

Food and drink

Where to eat

Hotel menus on Crete usually keep to a bland international cuisine with only an occasional touch of local colour. If you are travelling out of season you can often avoid a half-board arrangement or you might choose a hotel without a restaurant.

Eating out is one of the special pleasures of Crete. Formal restaurants (*estiatória*) are rare on the island and restricted to the main centres. Instead there is the **tavérna**, often family-owned and run, characterised by a relaxed, friendly atmosphere and (at its best) an uncompromisingly Greek cuisine. It has to be said that the best is no longer the universal rule; keeping an eye open for places where local people are eating is the best way to guard against tourist traps. In summer taverna tables are likely to be out of doors.

The dishes vary according to season, using local produce when it is plentiful and keeping prices down accordingly. Cretan produce has a deservedly good reputation; even in the smart markets of Athens the cry 'fresh from Crete' is a recommendation.

A **psistariá** (the name originally indicating a charcoal grill) is a specialised taverna offering meat (including chicken) spit-roasted or grilled with a limited choice of simple accompaniments. For meat eaters these establishments usually provide an economical meal in unpretentious surroundings. A take-away counter is almost always part of the service, with queues forming in the late evening and especially at weekends. Visitors with self-catering accommodation should ask for a recommendation in their neighbourhood.

An **ouzerí** is a traditional bar which serves *mezédes*. This selection of small dishes, often compared to hors d'oeuvre that originated in France, makes a starter (*oretiká*) for a serious taverna meal, but an *ouzerí* will if required produce sufficient for a light meal, with wine and soft drinks available as well as oúzo. There will be *taramosaláta* (a paste of smoked cod's roe), and perhaps little pieces of octopus (*ktapódi*) grilled or marinated, prawns (*garídes*) or baby squid (*kalamarákia*) or whitebait (*marídes*). Snails (*salingária*) are prized in the Lenten season. Other staples are olives (*eliés*), *tzatzíki*, yoghurt with cucumber and garlic, *melidzanosaláta*, a purée of aubergine, also stuffed vineleaf parcels (*dolmades*, or the diminuitive *dolmadákia*), served cold, or warm in an egg and lemon (*avgolémeno*) sauce. Courgettes and aubergines are sliced and crisply fried (*kolokithákia tiganitá, melidzánes tiganités*). Pulses may be represented by a dish of butter beans (*yigántes*) or by a yellow lentil purée (*fáva*). Beetroot (*pandzária*) can be a delicious speciality eaten with a thick garlic dip (*skordaliá*) which resembles a French *aïoli*.

A **zakharoplasteíon**, or patisserie, sells elaborate pastries and confectionery (and gift wraps if you are buying them as a present). *Baklavá, galaktoboúreko, kataïfi* and *bougátsia* are only the best known from a wide range to delight the sweet-toothed; they are combinations of filo pastry layered or shredded with fillings of nuts and honey or almond paste or vanilla custard. *Rizógolo* is a creamy rice pudding. There are a great variety of little fritters and tarts and pies and parcels filled with sweetened *mizíthra* (a sheep's milk cheese), many of them regional specialities. These cafés, almost always in an urban setting, serve tea (*tsái*) and coffee (including the popular chilled *frappé*) as well as freshly squeezed fruit juices and alcoholic drinks, and for the younger generation are replacing the quintessentially Greek *kapheneíon* (see below). Larger establishments in the towns may serve light meals, but in general their prices are not cheap.

Snacks are easy to find in all the main centres, where places selling pizza and hamburgers probably now outnumber those offering a *souvláki*, little pieces of meat grilled on a skewer, or a *tirópitta*, a flaky-pastry cheese pie. These pies or similar spinach ones (*spanakópittes*) are sold fresh from the oven at bakeries. *Kallitsoúnia* are an Easter treat.

The traditional Greek **kapheneíon**, the café of the villages, is an austere establishment usually thronged with male patrons for whom it is both a local club and political forum. Casual customers generally feel more comfortable at the tables outside. The *kapheneíon* serves Greek coffee, bottled and canned soft drinks, ice-creams, and alcoholic drinks such as *rakí* (also known as *tzikoudiá*) or *koniák* (Greek brandy).

Finally there is the **exokhikón kéntron**, literally a rural centre, which combines the functions of café and taverna in some particularly delightful countryside location or at the beach. At a successful establishment, especially on weekend evenings, the spontaneous conviviality, including Greek dancing, may be memorable.

Eating in tavernas

Tavernas which serve meals both at midday and in the evening (and, especially in the towns, not quite all do) usually cook their prepared dishes (*étimo fayetó*, literally ready food) at lunchtime. Cretans expect much of their food to be tepid rather than hot. If you mind about this you can try asking for it hot (*zestó*).

In the most popular tourist resorts you will often find that tavernas use refrigerated cabinets to display sample dishes. A menu ought to be displayed near the taverna entrance, and by law it must give for each dish first the basic price and then the final charge, which includes taxes and service (15 per cent). It is customary (especially in the case of foreigners) to leave a little extra in recognition of friendly service unless you are looked after in a small place by the owner. By convention tips left on the bill plate are for the waiter, and those on the table for the *mikrós* (literally the young one) who has done the fetching and carrying, but nowadays people round up the bill by something under 10 per cent. The menu will usually be translated and many of the waiters will speak some English (note that *kat.* on the menu means ingredients previously frozen). However, the correct way to order a taverna meal is still to go to the kitchen to inspect the food, and in the traditional taverna you will be respected and helped if you indicate that you understand this. Even in the larger restaurants in Herákleion and Khaniá Cretans (or one or two of the party) will expect to visit the kitchen or serving counter to see for themselves and discuss what is offered.

Mezédes and vegetable dishes There will always be *mezédes* (see *ouzerí* above) to start with. Then, depending on the size of the establishment, there may be from two to a dozen dishes probably including a substantial soup of beans (*fasólia*), lentils (*fabés*) or chickpeas (*revíthia*), and a pasta dish such as the usually excellent *pastítsio*, a baked macaroni layered with mince, sauce and cheese, or *khorís kréas*, without meat. There will be at least one vegetable dish which may be stuffed vegetables, tomatoes (*dómates*), aubergines, peppers (*piperiés*) or courgettes filled (*yemistés*) with a rice and cheese mixture or *briám*, chunks of these vegetables stewed gently in olive oil (similar to the French ratatouille). Such dishes using olive oil are known as *laderá*, and Greeks point to the fashionable popularity of the Mediterranean diet in a health-conscious world.

A salad is likely to be the ubiquitous *khoriatikí saláta*, village or country salad, traditionally including olives and cubes of féta cheese. However, it is possible to order only (*móno*) tomatoes or, for example, sliced cabbage.

Many types of herbs and wild greens are highly prized and still gathered from uncultivated ground early in the year (as they have been for centuries) for home use and now for tavernas and markets. The Greek word is *hórta*. Artichokes (*anginátes*) grow easily on Crete in the spring; for a seasonal speciality, known as *ala políta*, they are cooked with young broad beans (*koukiá*) and new potatoes (*patátes*) in an opaque lemon and dill sauce. *Yigántes* (butter beans) are simply cooked and served with a herb dressing. Green beans (sometimes cooked with chopped tomato) are *fasolákia fréska*; fried potatoes are *patátes tiganités*.

Aubergines cut in half lengthways are presented as *papoutsákia* (little slippers) with a stuffing and a layer of melted cheese. Both aubergines and courgettes are thinly sliced, deep fried and brought straight to the table. Marrow or courgette flowers are prized; they should enclose a delicate stuffing, with or without meat, and are usually deep fried. Vine leaves are eagerly awaited for stuffing at the right time of year (though preservation in barrels and tins extends the season).

Cretans often eat cheese with their *mezédes* or with vegetable dishes: *féta*, a salty sheep or goat's cheese is served with an oil, lemon and herb dressing; for *saganáki*, hard cheeses such as *kasséri* or *kephalotíri* are dusted with flour and fried. *Graviéra*, the Cretan equivalent of Swiss gruyère, is often available but more expensive. Pasta (*macarónia*) and rice dishes are part of the staple diet; plain rice (*piláfe*) with lemon juice is the favourite remedy for an upset stomach.

Meat dishes It is almost always possible to order plain grilled meat and fried potatoes, or an omelette (*omeléta*; with ham, *jambon*; with potatoes, *me patátes*) and salad. One speciality is the island's own lamb (*arní*) from the hills, although in this hot climate it is not always hung sufficiently for western tastes. In the first half of the year *païdákia* should be tender cutlets of young lamb. Baby goat, kid (*katsíki*), is perhaps the most highly prized seasonal meat. Rabbit (*kounéli*) is sometimes the kitchen's speciality. Pork chops (*brizóles khirinés*) are nearly always available and reasonably priced. A sucking piglet is roasted on special occasions. A beef steak is *filéto*. *Stifádo* will be translated as a stew, but at its best is a rich, lovingly flavoured concoction of beef or pork with baby onions, slow-cooked to the point when it can be eaten with a spoon. Meat balls in egg and breadcrumbs or with a sauce (*keftédes* or *tsoutsoukákia*) are popular and usually an economical choice as are *souvlákia*, pieces of meat, usually pork, cooked on a skewer. Apart from the spit roast the staple method of serving chicken (*kotópoulo al phoúrno*, in the oven) harks back to the days when big flat metal oven dishes were carried to the village baker. The jointed birds are basted and cooked with diced potatoes, in plenty of olive oil, often on a bed of rosemary.

psitó roasted	*tin katsaróla* cooked on top of the stove
tis skáras grilled	*tiganitós* fried

Fish dishes There are many specialist fish tavernas around the coast of Crete, often signed *Psarotavérna*. Your choice from the fish stored on ice is weighed to determine the price before you finally decide. For special occasions you will be recommended, if the fishing has gone well, one of the sea breams; *tsipoúra* or *synagrída* are generally regarded as the best but *fangrí* is close behind. Red mullet (*barboúni*) is also prized for grilling, and foreigners are often suprised at the cost of these fish. Baby red mullet (*barbounákia*) not large enough to grill but delicious fried, or a grilled swordfish steak (*ksifías*) are widely available and less expensive alternatives. Prawns are in season only October to May; in summer they will have been frozen. Fish from the grill is traditionally served with a separate jug of an olive oil, lemon and herb dressing. Various fish soups (*psarósoupa*) are often on the menu at these specialist tavernas; a lovingly prepared *kakaviá* is the Greek equivalent of a French bouillabaisse.

aláti salt	*pipéri* pepper
ládi oil	*xídi* vinegar
lemóni lemon	*zákhari* sugar
psomí bread	

Although traditional tavernas used not to serve a dessert course or coffee, and the *zakharoplasteíon* is still the place to go for pastries and speciality ice-cream, many tavernas do now offer fresh fruit (*froúta*), Yoghurt (*yiaoúrti*) or ice-creams (*pagotá*) and coffee are almost always available (see below, non-alcoholic drinks).

Drink

Non-alcoholic drinks
lemonáda lemonade
neró water, with ice (*pagoméno*)
ellinkós kafés Greek coffee is served black on the grounds in small cups: *glykós*

sweet, *métrios* medium sweet, *skétos* without sugar; *diplós* means a double. Instant coffee (referred to as Nescafé) is also available, but more expensive.

Alcoholic drinks

International drinking habits (whisky, gin and tonic and so on) are now commonplace on Crete. However, many visitors like to investigate local tastes and traditions and these drinks are comparatively inexpensive. The most widely known Greek aperitif is **oúzo**, a strong aniseed-flavoured drink made from the residue left when grapes have been pressed for wine. For Cretans **rakí** (also known as *tzikoudiá*) takes the place of *oúzo*; this is a stronger distillation without aniseed flavouring. As aperitifs both will be served with *mezédes*, titbits consisting of anything from a slice of cheese with a piece of tomato or some olives, to small pieces of salami sausage or grilled octopus or a dip of *taramasaláta*. You may be offered rakí at any time of the day as a gesture of hospitality. Many tavernas bring a complimentary glass at the end of a meal. To be correct you should wish good health (*eis iyeía*) to your host, for example the taverna owner, tapping the table with your glass before you drink. There is a Greek version of brandy from the firm *Metaxas* ordered as a *koniák*. Beer and lager (brewed on the island as well as imported) are very popular; the local product *Mythos* is widely available.

Cretan wine (**krasí**) can be excellent. At most tavernas and in supermarkets the principal mainland varieties (*Cambás*, *Demestiká*) are available, but the local bottlings are just as good and cheaper. They are steadily gaining respect among the wines of the Mediterranean basin. *Minós*, *Górtys* and *Lató* are widely known. Relative newcomers, recommended, are *Logádo* and *Olympiás*. The Arkhánes cooperative ranks high (and has won awards) in assessments of Greek wines. For a celebration calling for sparkling wine you might like to try the label *CAIR* of Rhodes.

Most tavernas have their own inexpensive 'house' wine. This used to be ordered as *khíma*, meaning loose as opposed to bottled; it was often the proprietor's or host's own wine. Now a request for a carafe (*karápha*) is normal. Traditionally, too, wine was ordered not by the litre or half litre, but by the equivalent kilo (*ena kiló, ena misó kiló*) and this thinking still prevails. 'House' wine is typically a brownish rosé but some tavernas are beginning to take a pride in offering a choice and you can taste from barrels on display before you order.

In Greek red wine is *mávro*, literally black to distinguish it from rosé or *kókkino* (literally red), the traditional brown-tinged wine of Crete; white is *áspro*. (In some tourist areas you may now find *kókkino* used for red.)

Retsína, the resinated white wine (flavoured with resin from pine trees) deriving from the Attica region of mainland Greece, has for a while been bottled on the island. It is worth acquiring a taste for retsína because it goes particularly well with grilled fish, and also is still remarkably cheap. The initiated have always known that bottled *retsína* and *retsína* straight from the barrel (as it is drunk along the coast of Attica) are two different experiences. Now enterprising merchants are bringing the wine in the barrel to tavernas on Crete and to traditional local stores which sell wine. The practice will surely spread, so it is worth asking whether *retsína apo to varéli* is available so that you can try it.

The wines of Crete

The reputation of Greek wine goes back to Classical times, and Crete was a respected source of wine again in the Venetian period when the centre of production for the widely traded *malvasía* wine (known in Britain as malmsey) moved to the island from Monemvasía on the Greek mainland.

Decline set in after the 17C but today, with technical advice and financial help from the European Union, the island's vineyards are again carving out a niche within the trade for table wines. By the 1990s around 20 per cent of all Greek wine was made on Crete. At the top end of the market the finest dry red wines are now held in high regard by connoisseurs. Some wines have been authorised to bear geographical place names (the widely recognised 'appellation of origin' system). The category, not necessarily a certificate of quality, regulates yields, alcohol content (higher in Cretan than in for example French wines), also soil standards and the choice of grape varieties. This step towards standardising winemaking practices, and the character of individual wines, is enjoying a measurable success. The new framework includes a category labelled TOPIKOS OINOS (pronounced *topikós ínos*), literally local wine. The special status (derived from the French *vins de pays* for some approved country wines) may be a useful guide for something better than 'house' wine.

Commercial wine-making on Crete has been organised, for historical reasons, very largely within cooperatives. Now a few privately owned wineries are beginning to make their mark.

Specialist wine merchants are found in all the big towns but also nowadays in some small resorts such as Kalýves east of Khaniá; look for the word *káva*/KABA, a wine cellar. Many supermarkets have discovered the appeal of a wide choice of Cretan wines and are a good place to browse.

The best wine-growing areas along the north coast enjoy the advantage of a climate usually free of extremes. Cretan wines from three groups of vineyards can be singled out for the attention of the interested visitor. Two areas, **Arkhánes** and **Pezá**, occupy adjacent valleys to the south of Knossós, and the third is in the extreme east of the island around the town of **Siteía**. All three have gained the coveted 'appellation' status.

The dominant grape for the red wines bottled under the Arkhánes label and those from Pezá is the *kotsifáli* blended with some *mandilariá* familiar across the southern Aegean. The Pezá white wines use the *vilána* grape recorded in Cretan vineyards as far back as Venetian times. Names to look for in the taverna or supermarket are *CAVA 33* (the date of the founding of this cooperative), with a red wine entirely from the *kotsifáli* grape and a white blending *vilána* and *rosakí*. *Logádo* from the same area offers notably reliable everyday wines: red (*kotsifáli* and *mandilariá*), rosé (*kotsifáli* alone) and white (the *vilána* grape).

The privately owned Miliarákis firm bottles its best wines under the *Sant'Antonio* label, but also puts out the less expensive red *Castello* and a white, *Minos Cava*, this perhaps an acquired taste but made from a historic combination of grape varieties descended from the Malvasía blending.

The wines of Siteía, the third area under consideration, are for many critics the most highly regarded on the island. This is one of Crete's oldest wine-making districts. The vineyards are planted with the early-ripening *liátiko* grape which can be traced back to ancient (Classical) times. One Zíros grower makes his own single-vineyard wine under the label *Oikonomoú*. The red (on sale in the Siteía supermarket opposite the archaeological museum) is particularly successful. For everyday drinking look for the label *Kritikós*, with the assurance Topikós Oínos (see above) of Siteía.

Wine drinkers travelling in the extreme west of the island will want to try the distinctive Kísamos wines, in paticular a red country wine made from the *roméïko* grape. There (confusingly) the name *Kritikós* is also used. (The vines for the *roméïko* were brought south to the area by the Venetians, though not from Italy.) In recent years French grape varieties have been blended with the time-honoured one, with considerable success.

Language

A knowledge of ancient Greek is a useful basis but no substitute for the study of modern Greek. Apart from the unfamiliarity of modern pronunciation, many of the commonest words (e.g. water, wine, fish) no longer come from the same roots. On the main tourist routes it is possible to get along comfortably enough without any knowledge of Greek but a foreigner's smattering of Greek is appreciated by Cretans and will lead to greater contact with local people. It is worth knowing that raising your voice at the end of a phrase can turn a couple of words into a question and avoid tangling with unfamiliar verbs. Asking *to mousío*; or *Plateía Venizélou*; on a rising inflection is the equivalent of where is the museum?, or please tell me how to get to the plateía? It is useful to be familiar with the Greek alphabet since names which are not transliterated, for example on shops or bus destination plates, may otherwise be puzzling.

The Greek alphabet now as in later classical times comprises 24 letters: Α α, Β β, Γ γ, Δ δ, Ε ε, Ζ ζ, Η η, Θ θ, Ι ι, Κ κ, Λ λ, Μ μ, Ν ν, Ξ ξ, Ο ο, Π π, Ρ ρ, Σ σ ς, Τ τ, Υ υ, Φ φ, Χ χ, Ψ ψ, Ω ω

Vowels There are five basic vowel sounds in Greek to which even combinations written as dipthongs conform: α is pronounced very short, ε and αι as e in egg (when accented more open, as in the first e in there); η, ι, ει, οι, υι have the sound of ea in eat; ο, ω as the o in dot; ου as English oo in pool. The combinations αυ and ευ are pronounced av and ev when followed by loud consonants, af and ef before mute consonants.

Consonants are pronounced roughly as their English equivalents with the following exceptions: β = v; γ is hard and guttural before a and o like the English g in hag, before other vowels approaching the y in your; γγ and γκ are usually equivalent to ng; δ = th as in this; θ as th in think; before an i sound λ resembles the lli sound in million; ξ has its full value always, as in ex-king; ρ is always rolled; σ (ς) is always hard, never like z; τ is pronounced half way between t and d; φ = ph or f; χ, akin to the Scottish ch as in loch, a guttural h; ψ = ps as in lips. The English sound b is represented by the Greek double consonant μπ, d by ντ.

The above are the equivalents commonly given for the Greek language, but in fact the pronunciation of the Cretan dialect is considerably softer than that of mainland Greece. In Αγιος, for example, the γ is nearer to 'j' than to the transliterated 'y' of this Guide or the alternative 'gh' of signposts, and χ (here written kh) approaches the 'ch' of church, or even 'sh', rather than the 'ch' in loch.

The 20C transition of Greek as the state language from *katharévousa*, the purist, consciously backward-looking language to a *demotikí* (colloquial) form is officially complete but in practice simplification continues and many spelling variations are still encountered: Knossós and Knosós, Mállia and Mália. In the neuter termination *-on* (*kapheneíon*) the n sound has disappeared in speech and is often omitted in writing.

To complicate matters all place-names decline like other nouns and this often produces a change of stress as well as of inflection. Some places have their more modern spoken form in the accusative, for example Zákro, though they appear on maps and signposts in the nominative, Zákros.

Street names are usually in the genitive: literally Street of 25 August, Square of Freedom. As in English a church may be referred to by the name of its saint in the nominative or genitive. The genitive is particularly noticeable in the case of monasteries: Moní Arkadíou, the monastery of Arkádi.

Stress accents

In the demotic language all Greek words of two syllables or more have one accent to mark the stressed syllable. The correct stress is crucial to the understanding of the spoken word in place-names and in numerous examples such as *trápeza* which means bank in contrast to *trapéza*, a table. Upper case characters are not accented, so in unmarked words starting with a vowel (Ayios, Embaros) the initial syllable carries the stress.

Manners and customs

Visitors may like to respect the more formal conventions of Greek people. In Crete, it is usual to shake hands at meeting and parting, and enquiries about health are taken seriously. The correct reply to *kalós orísate* (welcome) is *kalós sas vríkame* (glad to see you). To the enquiry *ti kánete;* (how do you do?) or *pos eíste;* (how are you?) the reply should be *kalá efkharistó, ke sis* (well, thank you, and you?), or *étsi ke étsi, ke sis;* (so-so, and you?). Note that in Greek the question mark is written as a semi-colon.

It is still customary to greet shopkeepers or the company in, for example, a kapheneíon, with *kaliméra* (good day) or *kalispéra* (good evening). Goodnight is *kaliníkhta*. *Khaírete* is greetings, or less formally is *yía sas*, hello. *Sto kaló* (keep well, the equivalent of godspeed) is used when bidding farewell to one who leaves, not when you are leaving yourself. *Sas parakaló* (please) is used when asking for a favour or for information, but not when ordering something which is to be paid for, when *tha íthela* (I should like) is more appropriate.

The Greek for yes is *nai* (né) or, more formally, *málista* (certainly). For no it is *ókhi*. *Endáxi* is all right, okay.

Kalí orexi (enjoy your meal) is conventional when people are about to eat. When drinking in company glasses are often touched with the mutual toast *eis iyeía sas* (your health) which is generally shortened in speech to the familiar *yá sas*, or *yiásou* (to you, a single individual) or *yámas* (to us).

Perastiká is a useful word of comfort, meaning 'may things improve'.

In direct contrast to English custom, personal questions showing interest in a stranger's life, politics, and money are commonplace conversation in Greece, and travellers should not be offended at being asked in the most direct way about their movements, family, relationships, occupation, salary, politics.

The **volta**, a structured evening stroll to and fro after the heat of the day, is still practised in many places across Crete such as along quaysides or the main village street, and visitors enjoy sharing the experience.

If you are on Crete during the Orthodox Lent (which may continue over the western Easter) it is good to remember that fasting is often taken seriously, and for the faithful is rigorous in Holy Week.

Museums and archaeological sites

The best known Minoan sites have become major tourist attractions and the palace at Knossós in particular is often frustratingly crowded at peak times. As a result the opening hours there are sometimes extended to 08.00–20.00 in high summer (see advice in the section about access to the palace).

Ancient remains of any significance are marked by a Ministry of Culture sign. The sites are all enclosed but some minor sites may not be locked. Most museums and all the major sites charge for admission. It has to be accepted that the position may change from year to year.

Opening hours have become more standardised over the years but the final details still depend on the results of annual negotiations, and accurate information cannot be guaranteed ahead of the (early spring) announcement. These hours differ quite markedly according to the season, and are not uniform throughout the island. The summer season runs from some time in April (depending on the date of Easter) to mid-October and winter hours are considerably reduced.

The smaller archaeological sites employing just one guardian usually close on Mondays. The palace sites vary and it is advisable to check in advance with the tourist information office. (In most cases you can now get through to the site office direct and expect to be able to use English; see information about the site for telephone numbers.) If state-run museums have a closing day (which the Herákleion Archaeological Museum does not, only variable morning hours) it is probably Tuesdays.

It should be expected that both museums and guarded archaeological sites will be closed on 1 January, 25 March (Greek Independence Day), Good Friday afternoon, Easter Sunday, and Christmas Day. Sunday opening hours will probably apply to other public holidays and festivals (see p 25). To avoid disappointment visitors on the island for the Greek Easter weekend should make particularly careful enquiries about the opening arrangements for the current year.

In general photography is accepted on archaeological sites, and in museums is permitted (without the use of flash) except where unpublished material is on display. Set fees (not cheap) are charged for using tripods, etc., and a permit may be required.

If directions to sites are needed beyond the detailed instructions given in the text, the following vocabulary may be useful; if you lift your voice after the word you signal an enquiry.

ta arkhaía ancient things	*to phroúrio* medieval castle or fort
to kástro any fortified height	*to tápho* tomb
tis anaskaphés excavations	

Ask for a church by its saint's name with Ayios (m) Ayía (f) Ayii (pl).

Many of the frescoed churches are nowadays kept locked. As far as possible, advice is given in the Blue Guide about the whereabouts of the key (*to kleidí*), but if the arrangement has been changed local help is often forthcoming. There is increasing interest in these churches, and the Service for Byzantine Antiquities is keen to make them more easily accessible. However, the search for a key can be a time-consuming business, and is still not always successful.

The majority of active monasteries close their gates during the afternoon (sometimes 13.00–17.00). Monastic communities are in steady decline. Decorous clothing is always requested, sometimes required; shorts are particularly disliked. In Orthodox churches women are not permitted to enter the sanctuary (bema).

BACKGROUND INFORMATION

A history of Crete

Neolithic period, c 7000–3500 BC

The earliest settlers of Crete arrived from the east or south, probably from Anatolia (now Turkey). Their economy was already based on farming, with domesticated animals and cultivated crops, and they spun and wove cloth. They lived in villages in the open, often on low hills as at Knossós and Phaistós, and sometimes for part of the year in caves. They built simple rectangular houses, at first entirely of sun-dried mudbrick and later of mudbrick on a stone socle. Their burial places, frequently in caves or rock shelters, were outside the settlements, which suggests a relatively advanced culture. Cave sanctuaries evidently played an important part all through the Neolithic period.

The first settlers at Knossós did not use pottery but this stage was short-lived and Neolithic pottery reached a high standard in dark burnished wares, sometimes with incised decoration of simple geometric patterns filled with white paste. Other characteristic artefacts were stone and bone tools, bone arrowheads, stone vessels and maceheads. There are female figurines in both stone and clay, typically modelled with exaggerated buttocks. Blades made from obsidian (volcanic glass) were of particular interest in that the source of the material was the island of Mélos in the Cyclades. By the end of the fourth millennium BC settlement had spread throughout Crete, and as far as some relatively remote offshore islands.

The Bronze Age, 3500–1100 BC

The Englishman Sir Arthur Evans, excavating the archaeological site at Knossós at the beginning of the last century, was confronted with evidence of a previously unsuspected Bronze Age civilisation. In the absence of written history for the Aegean Bronze Age he named the civilisation and its people Minoan after King Minos, a legendary ruler of Crete in the distant past according to the 8C BC Greek poet Homer.

Evans devised a tripartite system of relative chronology, the **Early Minoan** (EM), **Middle Minoan** (MM) and **Late Minoan** (LM) periods with each subdivided into three parts (as in EMI, EMII and EMIII) and sometimes further refined (LMIA, LMIB) to reflect the evidence of stratigraphy and pottery styles. This chronological framework for the Bronze Age on Crete became generally accepted and with minor modifications as the archaeological evidence has unfolded, it remains valid today (see p 38).

More recently the eminent Greek archaeologist Dr N. Platon proposed a system of chronology based on major events in the time-span of the Minoan palaces. He divided the Bronze Age into four periods: **Prepalatial** (the approximate equivalent of Evans's Early Minoan), **Protopalatial** (the period of the Old Palaces), **Neopalatial** (the period of the New Palaces) and **Postpalatial**. The majority of Minoan sites were destroyed at the end of LMI. However, the Palace of Knossós was re-occupied after that LMIB destruction and there is increasing evidence for

Dates BC	Minoan periods	Palace sequence
3500	Early Minoan (EM) EMI EMII EMIII Middle Minoan (MM) MMIA	Prepalatial
1900	MMIB MMII	Protopalatial Old Palace period
1700	MMIII Late Minoan (LM) LMIA LMIB	Neopalatial New Palace period
1450 1100	LMII LMIIIA LMIIIB LMIIIC	Postpalatial except Final Palace period at Knossós

Chronological outline for the Cretan Bronze Age

use as late as the 13C; so-called postpalatial dates during the final years at Knossós have to be viewed in that context.

These two dating systems are not incompatible and both are attempts to establish a relative chronology or intelligible sequence within the Bronze Age of Crete. For an absolute chronology, or calendar dates, archaeologists beginning with Evans painstakingly built up correlations with the world outside Crete, especially Egypt, using foreign artefacts excavated in a reliable context on the island, and Cretan artefacts similarly found abroad. Absolute dating of the Egyptian sequence was possible because the civilisation left written records and its hieroglyphic script had been deciphered in 1822. The scientific method of radiocarbon dating has provided a valuable complementary system for correlation with what are in effect historical dates from Egypt.

Further inter-disciplinary study of increasingly sophisticated scientific evidence continues to lead to revised interpretations in the realm of absolute dates and in the refining of the relative chronology of the Minoan civilisation in relation to the rest of the Aegean world.

The Prepalatial period, 3500–1900 BC, Early Minoan I–III and Middle Minoan IA

The transition from Neolithic to Early Minoan c 3500 BC was associated with a gradual infiltration of new settlers, again probably from an easterly direction, bringing with them the technique of copper-working. Many new settlements date from this time.

The **pottery of the EMI period** is marked by innovations in technique and style. It is still hand-made, but much more skilfully fired than before and there are distinctive new shapes such as the beak-spouted jug or tall pedestalled chalices with a patterned surface achieved by burnishing. Also seen at this time is the earliest painted decoration on pottery, consisting of narrow stripes (of red or brown on a buff or cream ground) grouped in a variety of designs, sometimes intersecting for a cross-hatched effect.

Burial in caves continued, but the first **built tombs** are recorded; there was a primitive *tholos* at Krási on one of the routes up to Lasíthi, and a huge cemetery of pit graves of Cycladic type at Ayía Photiá in eastern Crete. At Mókhlos in EMII house-like tombs were cut into terraces along a cliff.

The first evidence is recorded during EMI for the **communal tombs** of the Mesará plain. Tombs of this type, which occur elsewhere on Crete but less frequently, are large circular structures, free-standing, with a single low east-facing entrance formed of monolithic jambs and a heavy lintel. The walls were stone-built but it is doubtful whether, at least in the case of the larger ones, these tombs would have been completely vaulted in stone. They were in use for many generations during the third millennium, and some continued during the following period contemporary with the Old Palaces.

The EMII period marked the appearance of pottery in a mottled red, orange and black ware named after the site of Vasilikí in eastern Crete where it was first found. The striking effect over the entire surface of the vase was achieved by a combination of uneven firing and the use of several different-coloured slips on the same vessel.

Two sites of this period have been thoroughly excavated. Phournoú Koriphí near Mýrtos on the south coast is a close-knit settlement with defined living areas, kitchens, store-rooms and workrooms, but without separately defined houses. At Vasilikí the settlement plan suggests a less communal social structure and archaeologists point to features such as a paved courtyard and internal walls finished with hard red-painted plaster which perhaps foreshadow the mode of life of the palace civilisation of the next millennium. A more centralised society was encouraging specialised craftsmen who produced the bronze daggers, gold jewellery, ivory carving, seals and stone vases, often of superb refinement, which are known from the tombs of this Prepalatial period. Foreign contact increased and with it foreign influence; a Minoan colony was founded on Kýthera, an island off the southern Peloponnese.

The Old Palace or Protopalatial period, 1900–1700 *BC*, Middle Minoan IB–II

This period is marked by the emergence of the great centres which, following Evans, came to be known as **palaces**. The best explored and understood are at **Knossós**, **Phaistós**, **Mália** and **Zákros**, but others are now being excavated. The terminology reflects the scholarly approach at the end of the reign of Britain's Queen Victoria when the Minoan civilisation was discovered, but nowadays archaeologists think in terms of complex administrative centres and the religious, economic, social and cultural aspects of life within them.

Alongside the development of the palaces there is evidence of town life at the main sites, and individual houses have been identified, for example at Mália. Sacred caves and cult areas in high places (known as peak sanctuaries) began to play an important part in Minoan religious life, for instance on Mount Júktas above Knossós, at Petsophás above Palaíkastro, and at the sacred cave above Kamáres overlooking Phaistós. The Early Minoan tombs continued in use, but in many places a new method of burial was introduced with the body placed in a clay storage jar (**pithos**), as at the cemetery at Pakhiá Ammos near Gourniá.

In the potters' workshops of the palaces the new technique of the fast wheel made possible the production of fine polychrome vases, known as **Kamáres ware** from the sacred cave where it was first discovered.

Great strides were made in all forms of **metalwork**; bronzesmiths mastered elaborate castings in two-piece moulds, and understood the lost-wax (*cire perdue*) process. Some of their best work was reserved for the daggers, other weapons and tools exemplified in finds of this period from the Mesará tombs. The superb jewellery on display in the Herákleion Archaeological Museum includes examples of the goldsmiths' work, showing a free use of granulation and filigree techniques, with decorative patterns in minute grains of gold, or designs using fine gold threads.

The art of the **seal engraver** also developed rapidly with harder stones used for new shapes and vigorous, life-like designs. The remains of a sealcutter's workshop, found at Mália, included tools and unfinished seals, while a deposit of nearly 7000 sealings at Phaistós greatly enlarged the corpus of known designs. The so-called Hieroglyphic Deposit at Knossós (sealings, labels and tablets) testifies to the connection between seals and writing.

Evidence for **foreign contacts** comes from Egyptian scarabs appearing in Crete and MMII pottery in Cyprus, Egypt and the Near East, while both pottery and stone vases have been found on the Greek mainland and in the islands. At the end of the MMII period a great catastrophe almost certainly caused by earthquake left the palaces in ruins.

The New Palace or Neopalatial period, 1700–1450 BC, Middle Minoan III–Late Minoan IB

After the destruction at the end of MMII the palaces were rebuilt, though yet another major earthquake in MMIII was a temporary setback. The huge blocks hurled from the south façade at Knossós into Evans's 'House of the Fallen Blocks' are evidence of the strength of that upheaval. To the duration of these new palaces belong most of the elaborate Minoan buildings whose remains are now visible, including the large houses in the towns that surround the palaces, and those found elsewhere in rural settings across the island, sometimes referred to as villas on the Roman analogy. Fresco paintings decorated the walls of major rooms; efficient plumbing and drainage systems were installed. The extensive areas filled with huge storage jars bear witness both to the economic prosperity of the age and to the sophisticated redistribution system on which its economy was based.

Foreign contacts were wide-ranging. Crete exercised a strong influence on the mainland of Greece and indelibly stamped its character on the Mycenaean culture. Influence on the Cycladic Islands was even more profound; it is suggested that there were Minoan colonies on some of them, for instance Kéa and Mélos, and the clearest example yet excavated of a provincial Minoan town is the Akrotíri site on Théra (Santorini). Strong influence, if not actual settlement, has been noted on Rhodes and Kos, while sites in what is now Asiatic Turkey (e.g. Miletus and Troy) were well within the Minoan trading orbit. Further afield Minoan products reached west to the Lipari islands off Sicily and east to Cyprus and Egypt. At this point Crete commanded apparently unlimited supplies of copper and tin; copper ingots were found at Ayía Triáda and Zákros, and palatial-style hoards of bronze vessels at Knossós, Mália and Týlissos. Scientific research suggests that much copper came from deposits in the Lávrion area in Attica (also an important source of silver) as well as from the better-known source in Cyprus. The source of tin, a vital constituent of bronze, is less certain: Cornwall, Bohemia and Sinai have all been suggested.

It is a mark of the prosperity of the times that decorated pottery was no longer the leading artistic medium (despite the excellence of the so-called Marine Style). The innovative artists may have turned to **fresco painting**, and craftsmen were working in stone (vasemakers, gemcutters) or metal (weapons as well as vessels). Pottery ornament and shape, in many cases based on metalwork, became highly repetitive, in marked contrast to the great diversity of the earlier polychrome Kamáres ware. Technically, however, the best pottery of the New Palace period is excellent.

The Minoans had developed a cursive syllabic script (**Linear A**) to write a language which, despite intensive study and some limited progress, is not yet deciphered to general satisfaction. Still the most useful analogy is with a picture-book without text. A number of its signs are derived from the hieroglyphic script used from Early Minoan times and influenced by contemporary Near Eastern writing, but most of them are probably of local origin. The development seems to have taken place within the Minoan culture (though with a degree of external inspiration) and evidently to satisfy the new record-keeping needs of the emerging palace economy. The script is found on sun-dried tablets, interpreted as administrative records, but also on artefacts such as libation tables and ladles, miniature double axes, rings or pins in precious metals, and pots including large clay pithoi, as well as the potter's wheel. A significant number of these artefacts come from sacred caves or peak sanctuaries and it seems probable that in those cases the inscriptions have a religious connotation. Linear A writing has been recognised at more than a dozen sites, but by far the greatest number of finds so far come from Ayía Triáda and Khaniá.

The **decline of the Minoan civilisation** is not as well understood as is its development. The end of LMIB is marked by a horizon of major destruction by fire recognised at the palace sites and in other Minoan excavations right across Crete. Many attempts have been made to link this destruction with the volcanic eruption which is known to have destroyed the island of Théra (Santorini) and its settlements. However, the evidence from the Minoan town buried beneath layers of pumice at Akrotíri on Théra, and especially the study of its pottery, establishes beyond any doubt that the eruption occurred not at the end of LMIB but well before the end of the LMIA period. Crete cannot have been unaware of this catastrophe only 150km to the north, but some other explanation must be sought for the widespread destruction on the island that took place perhaps as much as a century later. Moreover the type of damage then is consistent with warlike activity rather than destruction by natural causes such as earthquake or tidal wave.

With the relative dating on an increasingly secure basis, there has been continuing refinement of **absolute dates**. The original chronological outline of Evans and his contemporaries, placed the LMIB destruction and thus the beginning of the end of Minoan civilisation at around 1450 BC. Under this conventional chronology the Théra catastrophe would have occurred only a few years before 1500 BC. However, during the last twenty years a formidable body of interested scientists, from the disciplines of geology and seismology among others, has added a new dimension to the researches of Aegean and Egyptian archaeologists. The new dating techniques make use of evidence from ice and lake-bed cores as well as dendrochronology (tree-ring dating).

As a result of this research proposals for the date of the great volcanic eruption range from 1650 to 1628 BC, alongside suggested modifications to many of the conventionally accepted dates for mid-second millennium Minoan Crete which may place the LMIB destruction around 1500 BC. Currently the two interpretations, the conventional and the revised chronology, coexist.

The last years of the New Palace at Knossós, Late Minoan II–Late Minoan IIIA1

For reasons imperfectly understood, Knossós was less affected by the LMIB destruction than other sites. Its damage was soon repaired and its life continued for several generations, apparently under the direction of Mycenaean Greeks who were either responsible for or took advantage of the events that had brought low the rest of Crete. The Minoan Linear A script had been supplanted by **Linear B** which in 1953 was deciphered by Michael Ventris and John Chadwick as Mycenaean Greek (see Recommended reading). The Linear B archives show that at this period Knossós was the administrative centre of the island. Sometime early in LMIIIA there is evidence of yet another major destruction, but even then parts of the palace continued to be used into LMIIIB (13C BC).

Linear B tablet from Knossós, now in the Ashmolean Museum, Oxford

The Postpalatial period, 1450–1100 BC, Late Minoan II–Late Minoan IIIC

After the widespread destruction at the end of LMIB at least some of the sites were not reoccupied. There were cases of reoccupation on a reduced scale during LMIII, where individual houses or rooms were cleared and re-used, but there were also substantial new buildings as at Ayía Triáda and Týlissos. Occasionally new settlements were established, for instance at Khóndros near Viánnos. The town at **Khaniá** flourished and had become a main centre of power on the island.

Shrines from this Postpalatial period have been found; characteristic furnishings include tubes associated with the **cult of the sacred snake** and **clay female figurines** with raised arms and cylindrical skirts. Examples noted in the text are at Knossós, Gourniá, Ayía Triáda and Mitrópolis near Górtyn. A new and distinct method of burial was introduced, with rectangular clay chests (**lárnakes**) placed in chamber tombs.

The epics of Homer, written down about 700 BC, set events which can be dated as contemporary with the LMIIIB period against the background of a heroic age. Sadly these tantalising hints of life in prehistoric times have to be accepted as the romantic embroidery of succeeding generations of storytellers, rather than a completely reliable account of that period.

The Subminoan period 1100–1000 BC

This was a troubled time of transition, marked by a movement of population to inaccessible mountain refuge sites such as Karphí above Lasíthi. There is evidence for some continuity of cult from the Late Bronze Age to the Iron Age provided by deposits of objects in sacred caves (such as the Idaian Cave on Mount Ida and the Diktaian cave above Psykhró), and a number of Iron Age settlements have traces of Late Minoan III occupation; Górtyn, Praisós, and Vrókastro are examples. A rich cemetery near Priniás in central Crete was in continuous use from Late Minoan times to the Greco-Roman period. But in retrospect it can be seen that a new era was beginning. The cultural traits of the Minoan and Mycenaean civilisations lost their dominance, and gradually the elements emerged which would shape Crete in the Hellenic world.

The Early Iron Age, 1000–650 BC. Geometric and Orientalising periods

Increasing familiarity with the technique of working **iron**, and its potential strength as opposed to bronze for agricultural tools and for weapons, were a basis for future economic development. At Knossós the appearance of new cultural influences had been marked by an abrupt break in tomb usage as well as in the non-Minoan features of the new Subminoan pottery. Late Minoan chamber tombs were methodically cleared before receiving the new burials. There was some local variation in burial practices across the island, but during the 10C **cremation** became the common rite, the urn containing the ashes often being placed in a rock-cut or stone-built family tomb which remained in use for several generations.

The detailed chronology of the Early Iron Age is still based on pottery sequences largely built up from cremation urns and the vases which accompanied them as grave gifts; outstanding examples are displayed in Herákleion's Archaeological Museum (Rooms XI and XII). The pottery decoration after which the Geometric period is named was based on increasingly elaborate arrangements of linear patterns and concentric circles. One Knossian workshop incorporated into its designs a range of fan-tailed birds with raised wing, and though Mycenaean pictorial decoration virtually disappeared there are rare but important portrayals of figures, such as the divinity known as the Mistress of Animals.

From around 850 BC there is evidence for intensification of **foreign contacts**, and pottery styles began to reflect influences from the eastern shores of the Mediterranean. There grew up on Crete one of the earliest Orientalising cultures of the Aegean. The island's geographical position on an east–west trade route was an important factor in shaping its cultural development.

This oriental influence is strikingly demonstrated in the **metalwork** of the period, for example in the figured relief work on beaten bronze for the votive shields from the Sanctuary of Zeus in the Idaian cave; these remarkable pieces (also exhibited in the Herákleion Museum, Room XIX) are attributed to a guild of itinerant craftsmen from the Near East. The same technique is used for spectacular jewellery (in Room XII) from a tomb within the Knossós North Cemetery, and it has been plausibly argued that this was the goldsmiths' family tomb. The characteristic burial urns of the fully developed Orientalising period were decorated with appropriate motifs in vivid polychrome of red and blue on a white ground.

Changes in social institutions were associated with the emergence of the **polis** or **city-state**. Homer speaks of the island's mixed population, including Dorians from the mainland and Eteocretans. The latter adhered to Minoan traditions, and inscriptions show that their language was pre-Greek. At Praisós and Dréros an apparently peaceful assimilation can be traced.

The island was divided among a great number of small city-states, each built in an easily defendable position usually on a hill-top with a water supply and agricultural land available nearby. Territory was jealously guarded and feuds were common. The cities were ruled by the **Kosmoi**, a body numbering less than ten, elected annually as administrators and, if necessary, as leaders in war. By the mid 8C Dréros had an *agorá* (or city-centre) and beside it a small temple, a sanctuary of Apollo Delphinios. In the following century an oath administered to the young men of Dréros lays down an exacting code of behaviour, with the civic virtue of loyalty to the *polis* already pre-eminent.

In the late 7C archaeologists recognise an emphatic full stop in the Cretan record. All Early Iron Age cemeteries were suddenly abandoned; burial in chamber tombs ceased and with this the diversity of grave gifts which had contributed significant evidence about the societies of the Geometric and Orientalising period. Round about 750 BC a **semitic script** was adopted for the Greek language and from this time inscriptions, as the earliest recorded history, are a useful aid to archaeological interpretation.

The Archaic, Classical and Hellenistic periods, c 650–67 BC

The **Daidalic style of sculpture**, named after the legendary architect and craftsman Daidalos, played a seminal part in the development of Archaic Greek sculpture. The style seems to have originated in Crete. Daidalic figures adopt Egyptian conventions, such as the rigidly frontal posture and wig-like hair. A bust from Eléftherna and the goddesses from above the transom of the Priniás Temple A doorway (well displayed in the Herákleion Museum, Room XIX) are good examples, as are the collections of terracottas in the museums at Ayios Nikólaos and Siteía.

Politically Crete remained detached from the mainstream of Greek history, from the impact of the Persian Wars and the short-lived brilliance of 5C Athens. The conservative and hierarchical pattern of a society focused on city-states continued to prevail. Despite this detachment the conquests of **Alexander the Great** of Macedon, and the imperial aspirations of his successors, brought new prosperity to the island. The warlike character and traditional bravery of the Cretans became a marketable commodity; they were in demand as mercenaries, and payment for their services enriched the island. Piracy was also a well-documented source of income.

On a wider scale the extensive trade patterns of the Hellenistic world in the wake of Alexander's conquests gave added importance to control of the sea routes. On the island the petty wars and fluctuating alliances continued, as Knossós, Lýttos, Górtyn and Kydonía (Khaniá) gradually emerged as the main contenders for supremacy. The rivalry was complicated by the involvement of foreign powers exploiting their influence on Crete in their own power struggle for control of the Aegean. Against a background of Macedonian expansionism, the Spartans intrigued in west Crete, the Egyptians gave garrison support to Itanos, Rhodes cultivated Oloús, and Eumenes of Pergamon contracted an alliance with 13 of the Cretan city-states. Gradually Rome became involved in Crete, first as a peacemaker between warring city-states, and then to reduce the menace of piracy from bases on the island.

The Greek mainland became part of the Roman Empire in the mid 2C BC. There was an abortive expedition against Crete in 71 BC, and two years later the Roman general **Q. Caecilius Metellus** (later Creticus) invaded with three legions. It took him nearly three years to subdue the island.

The Roman and First Byzantine Periods, 67 BC–AD 824

With its capital at Górtyn, Crete became, with Cyrene in North Africa, part of a joint praetorian province. It was administered by a proconsul who governed with a provincial council and a system of magistrates again known as Kosmoi. Knossós was made a Roman colony at a date still disputed, but not later than 27 BC. The island lay on the route which linked Rome with her Empire in the east. It shared the eastern Mediterranean culture transmitted along the trade routes and enjoyed from the conquest until the 7C AD an unusual period of peace and prosperity. This was reflected in large, spread out settlements in low-lying or coastal areas such as Górtyn, Knossós or Ierápytna (Ierápetra). Significantly, Lató on its almost impregnable hill near Kritsá gave way in importance to Lató pros Kamára at modern Ayios Nikólaos on the Bay of Mirabéllo. The settlement pattern came to include isolated villas and farms unknown in warlike Hellenistic times. Many sites such as Mókhlos were inhabited for the first time since the Bronze Age. It speaks volumes for the skill of the Roman Empire's colonial administration that, for perhaps the only time in Crete's history, foreign rule was not accompanied by a perpetual state of rebellion.

After AD 330 historians refer variously to a **Late Roman** or **Early Byzantine period**. The triumph of Christianity and the foundation of Constantinople by the Emperor Constantine the Great mark the beginning of the Byzantine era in Greece. With the division of the Roman Empire in 395 it was natural for Crete to become part of the eastern sphere of influence, looking to the new imperial capital on the Bosphorus, a beacon of European civilisation during the centuries when the western empire was in decline.

The architects of the **earliest churches** on Crete followed the prevailing practice by adopting the form of the basilica, a standard Roman public edifice divided into three aisles by interior colonnades; one or three apses were added at the east end to form the sanctuary, while at the west end a portico (narthex) extended across the whole width of the building. The sites of some 70 of these churches are known or suspected, and the great majority are dated to between the mid-5C and mid-6C. The best preserved, and architecturally the most sophisticated, is Ayios Títos at Górtyn, but many other basilica sites have been excavated, for example at Pánormos on the north coast, Vizári in the Amári valley and high in the hills above Gouledianá, south of Réthymnon; the church at Vizári is interesting because it dates from the late 8C, not long before the Arab conquest.

The Arab Occupation, 824–961

During the 7C the decline of the Roman Empire affected the security of the eastern Mediterranean, and in 674 the main Arab fleet wintered on Crete. From then on the island was under constant threat from Arab raiders based in North Africa, and there are indications at a number of sites of renewed attempts at fortification. But in 824 a band of Arab adventurers (originally from Spain, but by then based at Alexandria in Egypt) captured the island and held it, against several relief expeditions from Constantinople, until 961. Sicily also was lost to Christendom at this time.

The Arabs laid waste the capital city of **Górtyn** (which never recovered its grandeur), ravaged the whole island and destroyed every one of its basilica churches. There is little positive evidence of Arab occupation apart from a scattering of their coinage. The major exception is the foundation, on the site of the modern city of Herákleion, of **Rabdh el Khandak** which was for a while the slave-trading capital of the eastern Mediterranean.

The Second Byzantine Period, 961–1204

In 961 Rabdh el Khandak was recaptured by the Byzantine general (later Emperor) Nikephóros Phokás and the Arabs left Crete. When Cyprus too was seized by Phokás (in 965) Byzantine control of the sea allowed regular communication between Crete and Constantinople, the centre of the Greek world. With the island restored to Byzantium, the first priority was to reinvigorate the much-depleted Christian community. The monk **Nikon the Repenter** led a band of missionary clergy to the island. Many basilica churches were built or rebuilt, some to serve as episcopal churches for the twelve reestablished diocese (*episkpés*). Early in the 11C **Ayios Ioánnis Xénos**, St John the Stranger, also known as Ermítis (the hermit), who came from a village on the edge of the Mesará plain, was celebrated as an evangelist all over western Crete, and is still revered by Cretans today.

The fortified hilltop of Témenos, inland of Herákleion, is all that remains of an abortive attempt to move the capital to a less vulnerable position inland, and the administrative centre was soon re-established on the ruins of Rabdh el Khandak, thereafter **Khándakas**. In the 12C it became necessary to strengthen the Christian ruling class, and the tradition is that 12 noble families, the *Arkhontópouli* (or aristocrats, the lordly ones) were sent out to Crete from Constantinople. Their names, such as Kallérgis, Skordílis, Khortákis, have been conspicuous throughout subsequent Cretan history. Many of the small churches and chapels that these families built on their estates survive today, with in some cases the remains of the original decoration (or the redecoration of the following centuries). Gradually prosperity seems to have returned, based on an agricultural economy rather than piracy. This regime of the Second Byzantine period was to last until 1204.

The death of the Emperor Basil II (1025) is usually taken as the zenith of the Byzantine Empire; with benefit of hindsight the next 400 years can be seen to have been a period of slow but inevitable decline. The Great Schism of 1054 effected the final break between Rome and Constantinople. The Crusades, which began as a movement to rescue Christianity's holy places from the Moslems, ended in a thinly-veiled power struggle between the forces of the West. Venice, originally a vassal of the Byzantine Empire, became first an independent ally and then an implacable foe. In 1081 the Emperor Alexius I made trading concessions to Venice which were eventually to result in her commercial dominance in the eastern Mediterranean, but these concessions also caused much bitterness, which came to a head with what is known as the Massacre of the Latins at Constantinople (1182). In 1204 Venice succeeded in diverting the fourth Crusade to Constantinople in order to put the young Alexius IV on the imperial throne. But his failure to fulfil his obligations to Venice led to the sack of Constantinople not by Moslems, but by the forces of Christendom.

The Venetian period, 1204–1669

In the subsequent division of the Empire, Crete was apportioned to Boniface of Montferrat who, preferring mainland territory, sold the island to Venice reputedly for 1000 silver marks. Meanwhile, rival forces from Genoa landed on the island under the command of the notorious pirate Enrico Pescatore and, often with Cretan support, fortified isolated settlements from Canea (Khaniá) to the Castle of Mirabéllo (now Ayios Nikólaos). But Venice was not to be trifled with. In 1210, a Venetian Governor, Giacomo Tiepolo, was appointed **Doge of Candia**, as Khándakas, and indeed the whole island came to be known. This was Venice's first formally constituted overseas colony, with the Doge serving (as for the Republic itself, but only for a two-year term) with a Signoria and a Great Council. The Republic's new acquisition produced grain, wood for shipbuilding, oil, hides and wine; but more importantly it had an unequalled strategic position for trade to the east with the coastal ports of Asia Minor and Syria. Harbours and dock-yards were a priority.

Venice set about imposing a feudal administration with Venetian colonists as the ruling class. Castles were built, or strengthened, to control the countryside. But this formidable power found itself in conflict with the implacably indepen-dent character of the native Cretans, and the inevitable strife became a tale of ferocious revolts and harsh repression. The new taxes and labour obligations were a heavy burden. In 1363 even the Venetian nobility on Crete was divided. One faction, incensed by excessive demands from Venice, went so far as to declare the short-lived Republic of Saint Titus. The rebellion was eventually crushed by an expedition sent from Venice, and punitive measures were applied. The upland plain of Lasíthi, which had become a refuge for the rebels, was forcibly depopu-lated and cultivation and pasturing were banned.

Throughout this period of oppression Cretan links with Constantinople were cemented by a common language and the doctrines of eastern Christendom. The Venetians imported their own ecclesiastical hierarchy, and built many Latin monasteries; 376 were recorded by the 16C. Pope Alexander V (1409–10) was born in the Mirabéllo district (not far from modern Ayios Nikólaos) and educated by the Franciscans in Candia (Herákleion) before he set out for Italy. The Orthodox clergy, at first ordained outside the island, were officially subject to Latin bishops, but there was little active proselytising by Venetian Catholics. The Cretan ruling families continued to build and decorate their churches and chapels for worship within the eastern tradition.

The Italian scholar Giuseppe Gerola, in his great work on Venetian architec-ture, *Monumenti Veneti nell'Isola di Creta*, published in 1905, listed more than **800 frescoed churches** on Crete (the majority decorated in the 14C or 15C). A remarkable concentration of 600 or so still retain at least fragments for special-ist study. All the wall paintings are strongly conservative; against a background of foreign occupation and uncertain economic conditions they scrupulously pre-serve the hagiography of Byzantine art. Orthodoxy was always a strong thread in the fabric of Cretan nationalism.

Gradually an uneasy co-existence was established between Venetians and Cretans, and by the 15C there was a degree of intermarriage (sometimes with adoption of the Orthodox faith) and much less overt hostility. With the capture of Constantinople by the Turks in 1453, Crete became an important staging-post for Greeks fleeing to the West, and the manuscripts and works of art that they brought with them gave a new impetus to Byzantine culture on the island. The larger monasteries (Arkádi, Goniá, Ayía Triáda, Angárathos) became centres of Greek learning and built up great libraries. In the 16C the college in Herákleion attached to Ayía Aikateríni, a daughter foundation of the important Orthodox monastery on the slopes of Mount Sinai, was renowned for fostering both Greek scholarship and religious art. Fresco painting continued, but Crete also produced many notable **icon painters**, among them Mikhaíl Damaskinós; six of his icons can be seen today in the Ayía Aikateríni collection in Herákleion. Some of these artists left Crete to work abroad, as did Doménicos Theotokópoulos, who moved to Venice probably in 1567, was in Rome in 1570 as a disciple of Titian, and then went on to Toledo in Spain where he became famous as El Greco. One of his paintings has returned to the island and is now on display in Herákleion's Historical Museum.

Travel between Crete and Venice was a natural progess, and with it the transmission of the elements of Byzantine thought and art that nourished the Italian Renaissance. Members of the Cretan community in the mother-city contributed to the renewed interest in this learning. Márkos Mousoúros published Greek authors at the Aldine printing press, one of the earliest (1492) examples of this new and influential Venetian technology.

Poetry and drama flourished on the island during the 16C and 17C. One enormously long heroic poem, *Erotókritos* by Vitzéntzos Kornáros, remains popular today, as much for its use of the Cretan vernacular as for its romantic sentiments. It is read, sung and quoted wherever Cretans gather.

The discovery of the passage to the Far East around the Cape of Good Hope diminished the importance of the Mediterranean trade-route on which Venice's wealth and prestige depended. As Venetian power gradually declined, the Ottoman Turks pressed westward. They landed on Crete in 1645 and two years later laid **siege to Candia**. The city held out for 22 years, making this one of the legendary sieges of history. Help from the Christian world came too little and too late, and in 1669 this last bastion of Christendom in the eastern Mediterranean fell into Turkish hands.

The Turkish Occupation, 1669–1898

This time the overlords came not from a different rite within the Christian church, but from a different faith. The island was divided into three *Pashaliks*, and was ruled from Herákleion, known after the long siege as **Megálo Kástro**, the great fortress. The Ottoman rule was not at first particularly destructive, but was totally indifferent to the economic conditions of the countryside, thereby causing great hardship and deprivation. The Turkish administrators favoured urban life both for security and because it better suited their traditions; and their mosques (without exception converted churches), fountains, and a few houses preserved in the towns along the north coast are the only visible reminders of this foreign occupation which lasted for more than 200 years.

There was ruthless discrimination against Christians, especially insofar as taxation and property were concerned; survival frequently depended on compromise, and tactical conversions to Islam were understandably frequent. There was a sharp contrast between the vulnerable lowland districts and the remote and inaccessible mountain areas where sporadic rebellion and scheming in the cause of independence became a way of life. Unfortunately the people of the lowlands often had to endure the reprisals when the warriors withdrew to their mountain strongholds.

In 1770 a major revolt was led by the legendary Daskaloyiánnis from the proudly independent Sphakiá district of western Crete; he was encouraged by the

Russians as part of a diversionary move to further their own strategy on the mainland. The revolt collapsed, its leader surrendered and was executed, and Sphakiá suffered accordingly.

Throughout the island, leadership was provided, often covertly and in dangerous circumstances, by the monasteries. Their efforts were directed not only to protecting the Orthodox church but also to preserving through education the Hellenic cultural tradition, the ultimate aim being Cretan independence.

On the wider scene Crete had once again become a pawn in international power politics, this time in the world of the Great Powers of post-Napoleonic Europe, at that time Britain, France, Italy and Russia. The Revolt of 1821, triggered by the outbreak of the **Greek War of Independence**, was crushed with Egyptian help, and when, in 1832, the Greek state was established it did not include Crete, which had to undergo the humiliation of ten years of Egyptian rule.

The Greek throne was given to Prince Otto of Wittelsbach and placed under the protection of Britain, Russia and France; but this attempt to establish stable constitutional government was unsuccessful, and in 1862 Otto was deposed. A Danish Prince became King George I of the Hellenes, a hint of concession to the idea of a broader-based Greek state. In Crete the renewed outcry for **enosis**, union with Greece, resulted in the **uprising of 1866**, when the women and children killed in the taking of the Arkádi monastery attracted widespread sympathy for Crete's plight.

Greece's attention was taken up with problems on her northern frontiers, and her relationship with the Great Powers was often strained to the point of hostility. Uprisings continued on Crete until 1898 when the Powers finally took the opportunity of peace negotiations between Greece and the Ottoman Empire over mainland territory to impose a settlement on the island. Crete was granted autonomous status under Ottoman suzerainty, and a High Commissioner was appointed, in the person of Prince George, second son of the Greek King, who governed from Khaniá.

In a further crisis in 1906 Prince George resigned. His eight years of rule had brought *enosis* no closer, and he was faced with the rebel **Cretan Assembly**, constituted as a rival government pledged to the cause of union with Greece. One of its leaders was **Elefthérios Venizélos**. Born in Khaniá in 1864 (but technically a Greek subject) he had been prominent as a young man in the struggle for the island's independence, and now was an influential member of the Assembly, which first raised the Greek flag on Crete, on the hill of Prophítis Ilías on the Akrotíri overlooking Khaniá. The crisis was temporarily resolved with the appointment of the veteran Alexander Zaïmis as High Commissioner, but two years later Venizélos was called to Athens in a climate of nationalist rebellion, and after a revision of the constitution he became Prime Minister of Greece for the first of many times.

In 1913 *enosis* was at long last achieved. At the Treaty of Bucharest, which ended the Balkan Wars, Greek sovereignty over Crete was accepted and amid scenes of wild rejoicing the island finally became an integral part of the Greek nation.

Modern history, from 1913

An understanding of the early part of this turbulent period is inextricably involved with the decline of the Ottoman Empire, which led in due course to the emergence of modern Turkey, and with Greece's struggle to come to terms with her northern neighbours in a multilateral conflict among the evolving Balkan states.

Political consciousness is essential to the Greek character, as is still evident in the passionate arguments of day-to-day conversation, so that despite physical isolation from the zones of conflict, Crete remained involved after 1913 in the decisions and events unfolding in Athens. For much of this period constitutional issues were in one way or another crucial, with the uneasy relationship between monarchy and elected government often at the heart of the matter.

The Cretan-born statesman Elefthérios Venizélos was a force in national politics and a central figure in this constitutional controversy for a quarter of a century. Venizélos came to be respected as a master of diplomacy abroad, and as a leader with the strength of an exceptional command over public opinion at home.

During the **First World War** his convictions, which led him to favour the cause of the western allies, often put him at loggerheads with King Constantine I whose wife was the sister of the German Kaiser. In September 1916 matters came to a head, and from his native Khaniá Venizélos issued a proclamation which led to his establishing a rival government in the mainland city of Salonika (Thessaloníki). After nine months of negotiations, the king left the country and was succeeded by his second son, Prince Alexander. In Athens Venizélos recalled the parliament which the king had dissolved in December 1915, and received an overwhelming vote of confidence after a speech lasting nearly nine hours. The country entered the war on the allied side and played a part in the eventual victory.

Between 1920 and 1922 Greece was involved in a disastrous campaign of expansionism on the mainland of Turkey for which Venizélos did not escape all blame. The political motives included the ancient **Megáli Idéa** (the great idea), the reconstitution of the Byzantine Empire with its capital at Constantinople. The trauma of defeat and the sack of Smyrna, the Greek city on the coast of Asia Minor, by Turkish forces under Mustapha Kemal is still a painful folklore memory in Crete today. The ensuing exchange of populations under the Treaty of Lausanne (1923) brought more than a million refugees to Greece. A considerable proportion of them (including some Armenian families) were resettled on Crete, taking over the redistributed property of Turks who had remained behind when their army departed in 1898. The upheaval caused great hardship on both sides, but in modern times it has resulted in a relatively homogeneous population spared any risk of the tensions suffered by Cyprus.

Constitutional questions continued to dominate Greek politics; for a period the country became a republic. Venizélos was in and out of office as Leader of the Liberal party, but his lasting achievements at this time were in the field of foreign affairs. In 1932 in a climate dominated by the insoluble problems and hardship of the years of world-wide economic depression, and faced with bitter opposition to measures which were seen as an attempt to restrict the freedom of the press, Venizélos was forced to resign. The following year he survived an assassination attempt, and then in a mood of frustration at the failure of the Republic he retired to Crete. In 1935, after a last unsuccessful republican coup, he fled into exile; condemned to death in his absence, he was pardoned under an amnesty declared by King George II after the restoration of the monarchy, but died in France in 1936. He is buried on the Akrotíri high above Khaniá.

The new figure at the centre of Greek politics was the fervent monarchist, **General Metáxas**; his solution for constitutional stalemate was to persuade the

King to dissolve Parliament and the Chamber did not sit again for ten years. Metáxas himself assumed power as a dictator. However, he foresaw that war in Europe was inevitable, and he has been given due share of the credit for the fact that Greece, alone among the countries of southeast Europe, was in a position effectively to resist aggression when it came.

Mussolini occupied Albania on Easter Monday 1939, and the threat posed by a fascist power on Greece's border led to a British and French guarantee of Greek territorial sovereignty. Metáxas reaffirmed neutrality early in August 1940. On 27 October he attended an evening reception at the Italian legation in Athens, but early next day the Italian Minister conveyed to him an ultimatum which he is said to have rejected with the single word 'No'. This legendary gesture of defiance is proudly commemorated by a national holiday (*Oxi* day) on 28 October each year. Mussolini's troops were even at the time of the ultimatum already invading Greece, which became the only country voluntarily to enter the war on the Allied side during that period when Britain stood alone against the Axis powers.

The Greek army drove back the Italians to a position of stalemate in the mountainous terrain of Albania, but the balance was to be altered by Hitler's decision to march into Greece to protect the southern flank of his planned Russian front.

Metáxas died unexpectedly at the end of January 1941. In March Greece accepted reinforcement by a small expeditionary force composed of British, Australian and New Zealand troops, and a frontline was established in northern Greece, but the combined forces were unable to halt Hitler's invasion, and despite Greece's proclaimed determination to fight to the last, the campaign became a series of rearguard actions. In mid April the new Prime Minister committed suicide; the King turned to a Cretan, Emmanuel Tsouderós, and it was to Crete that the inevitable evacuation was to be directed. Yet another time of trouble for the island lay ahead.

The Battle of Crete

The withdrawal of the expeditionary force from the mainland of Greece took place during the last week of April and the first week of May 1941. King George was evacuated with his Government and Prime Minister Tsouderós. He stayed briefly at the Villa Ariadne at Knossós and was then established at Khaniá. The island was defended from sea-borne invasion by the British Mediterranean Fleet. As the campaign on the mainland ran into difficulties during 1940, Churchill had continually insisted on the strategic importance of holding Crete, but the resources of General Wavell, Commander-in-Chief Middle East, were greatly overstretched and it was not feasible to create the fortress of Churchill's vision.

The terrain of the likely battlefield presented particular problems. All the main harbours, including the extensive anchorage of Soúda Bay, were on the north coast and exposed to enemy aircraft. The more protected fishing ports on the south coast were useless for supply purposes because of the inadequacy of the roads across the island; the one from Soúda over to Sphakiá had not been completed even though it stopped only some six kilometres short of the Libyan Sea. There were airfields at Herákleion and at Máleme, west of Khaniá (at that time the capital of the island), and a landing-strip between them at Réthymnon, all on the narrow north coast plain that left any movement by day exposed to enemy spotter planes.

Historians writing with the benefit of hindsight have been critical of the lack of preparation or of any defined policy at this time; there had been six changes of command on the island in the six months before 30 April, when Wavell appointed the eminent New Zealander General Bernard Freyberg VC as Commander-in-Chief.

Hitler's principal objective was to use Crete as an air base against British forces in the eastern Mediterranean. His commander was General Student (of XI Air Corps), whose strength included a crack assault regiment of glider-borne storm troopers, a parachute division, a specialised mountain division and squadrons of the dreaded Stuka dive bombers. The Luftwaffe, flying from rapidly constructed forward bases in the Peloponnese and the Aegean islands, had undisputed command of the air.

Freyberg's garrison consisted of 32,000 British, Australian and New Zealand troops (including 21,000 of the expeditionary force who had been evacuated from the mainland), and 11,000 well-trained but lightly-armed Greek troops. The Cretan division, to its lasting chagrin, had been cut off on the Albanian front. It proved impossible to operate planes from the exposed airfields, so the force was severely handicapped by lack of air cover.

General Freyberg's Creforce headquarters was located to the northeast of Khaniá in the Soúda sector. West of Khaniá was the New Zealand Division, with some Greek support including a unit out along the coast at Kastélli. The New Zealanders were thus responsible for the defence of the vital airfield at Máleme which was dominated by their command position at the end of a ridge running out from the White Mountains, named Hill 107. In the centre of the line, in the area around Réthymnon, were four Australian and two Greek battalions. The Herákleion sector was held by three British, two Australian and three Greek battalions, the airport being defended by a British force.

The airborne invasion began on 20 May. The landings concentrated as expected on the airfields and the main towns of the north coast. In the Máleme area the Germans established a toehold west of the river Tavronítis and south of Kolymbári. A detachment of parachutists attempted to land in the broad valley (nick-named Prison Valley) running south towards the Omalós plain and the White Mountains; their aim was to converge with the forces on the coast road to advance on Khaniá, but at the end of the first day most of the German troops in this sector were disorganised and not responding to central control. The assault on the Akrotíri, using gliders, failed entirely, and thus the threat from the rear to Khaniá and Freyberg's headquarters did not materialise.

The Réthymnon airstrip, important to the Germans for a flanking movement to capture the anchorage of Soúda, was successfully defended by the Australians, despite a heavy imbalance of troops and firepower. Around the Herákleion airfield the Germans were in considerable disarray, and in the town their initial success had developed into heavy street-fighting with the civilian population, which led to a position of stalemate.

The first wave of landings met much stronger resistance than had been expected by German Intelligence, which had also underestimated the hostile reaction of the local Cretan population. The invading forces suffered heavy losses which were particularly critical for their command structure. It is generally agreed that this first assault was very nearly defeated, that General Student's eventual success was by a narrow margin, and that at the end of the first day the outcome hung in the balance.

However, what turned out to be the crucial battle had developed to the south and west of Máleme, centred on the New Zealand position on Hill 107. With hindsight it can be seen that the position of the German assault forces was exceedingly precarious. However, in the confusion of battle, which was compounded by an almost total breakdown in communications due to a shortage of wireless sets, essential defence reinforcements did not become available in time. On the evening of the first day of the assault, the commanding height had to be evacuated, leaving the vital airfield undefended, and thus the fragile balance altered. Most historians agree that at this point the battle for Crete was lost and won.

German forces were quick to exploit the situation, and to use the airfield to bring in troops and supplies. A counter-attack, organised on the second day, was carried out during that night, 21–22 May, but despite the valiant efforts of the Maori battalion Máleme airfield remained in enemy hands. On the fourth day of the battle German fighter planes began operating from its runway.

At sea the German invasion fleet was routed on 21 and 22 May, but with appalling losses to the Royal Navy. Throughout the battle the navy was operating in waters which could only be reached through two narrow straits (c 50–60km), guarded in the west by the island of Kýthera, and in the east by Kásos and Kárpathos, all in enemy hands. Once into the Cretan sea, as the Greeks call this area south of Théra (Santorini), ships were in reach of the network of bomber airfields that crowded the islands of the Aegean. Over three days Admiral Cunningham lost two cruisers and four destroyers, and had a battleship and another two cruisers and four destroyers severely damaged.

On land the Máleme position had been given up, and the weary Australian and New Zealand troops fought a series of brave rearguard actions as they fell back on Khaniá. On 26 May, with the Luftwaffe fighters at Máleme within a 20km range, Khaniá and the Soúda sector were plainly indefensible, and early next day the order reached their garrisons for the long withdrawal south across the island to Sphakiá, a coast-to-coast distance of c 40km.

The retreat along this route over the eastern flank of the White Mountains was only possible at all because of the heroic obstinacy of a Greek regiment cut off at the south end of 'Prison Valley', in the area of the Alikianós river-crossing (on the modern road up to the Omalós plain). For two days (24–25 May) these troops, reinforced by gendarmerie and civilians, held up crack German mountain troops who otherwise, in an outflanking move by the Mesklá and Kerítis valley route, would have cut the Sphakiá road, the only possible line of retreat for Freyberg's army. (King George and his ministers had been escorted down the Gorge of Samariá to embark at Ayiá Rouméli.)

The shambles of this march over the mountains, by Stýlos, across the upland plain of Askýphou and down the precipitous Nímbros gorge, has been described in many records, including Freyberg's own official report. However, the column was successfully protected against constant enemy harrassment by relays of rearguard troops. Some 12,000 men were involved in the retreat, and during the nights of 28–31 May the navy evacuated about three-quarters of them from the beach at Khóra Sphakíon. The author Evelyn Waugh, who took part in the retreat, gives a vivid account of it in the second volume of his war trilogy, as, from the New Zealand viewpoint, does Geoffrey Cox (see Recommended reading).

At Réthymnon the Australians denied the Germans the use of the airstrip for the whole course of the battle, until they were at last overwhelmed on 31 May.

From the port of Herákleion the Royal Navy evacuated the garrison by sea through the perilous Kásos strait on the night of the 28–29, with horrific loss of men and ships; the episode symbolises the courage with which this campaign was fought. The bald figures at its conclusion were: 18,000 evacuated, 12,000 taken prisoner, 2000 killed.

A considerable number of men who had not been evacuated were hidden by the Cretans until they could later be helped to escape from the island. There are many accounts of the Resistance movement that developed during the German occupation of Crete. The guerilla warfare, coordinated by Allied undercover agents and supplied from North Africa, affected German morale, and tied down units increasingly needed on other fronts. The civilian population suffered appallingly in the inevitable acts of retribution. One extraordinary account of the Resistance, *The Cretan Runner*, is especially recommended because its author, G. Psychoundakis, who was part of the movement is himself Cretan. Available in translation (see Recommended reading) this book throws light not only on the progress of the guerilla war, and on the involvement of idiosyncratic foreigners as seen through native eyes, but incidentally on many essentials of the Cretan character.

The anniversary of the Battle of Crete is movingly celebrated at the end of May each year. May 1991 marking the 50th anniversary saw the publication of a comprehensive account, *Crete: the Battle and the Resistance* by Antony Beevor. His book follows the story on land, at sea and in the air, with material from both sides engaged in the conflict, and from the fall of Greece through to the end of the war in Crete. He was able to draw on the authoritative published accounts and on previously secret Military Intelligence reports, but the book also benefited from the first-hand recollections of a wide variety of the original participants. Along the way the story of the dedicated and often heroic involvement of Cretans is sympathetically told.

Natural history

Crete's flora

Crete enjoys a typical Mediterranean climate with long hot dry summers. The winter rain falls as snow in the mountains, but there is an extensive frost-free coastal zone. This climate and a geographical position close to Asia are among the factors responsible for Crete's astonishing variety of wild flowers; the many hundreds of known species include over 130 endemic to the island.

Botanists will not need to be reminded of the specialised flora of Crete's high mountain plains and deep shaded gorges, the terraced hillsides and the coastline. The gorges shelter the Cretan dittany (*Origanum dictamus*), an endemic with aromatic leaves valued by herbalists since ancient times. Guided botanical tours are arranged from all parts of the world, especially in spring to search for the fifty or more varieties of orchid and ophrys flowering at the different elevations between March and May.

However, the visitor with a more general interest can scarcely fail to be delighted by the island's spring show of wild flowers. Sheets of *Anenome coronaria* in early spring are followed by *Ranunculus asiaticus*, sometimes in a shining buttercup yellow. In damp ground under trees and bushes *Cyclamen creticum* flourishes. At the edge of the melting snow on Ida or the Omalós plain appear drifts of Crete's special crocus, *C. sieberi var. sieberi*, often mixed with *Chionodoxa cretica*. In April and May the endemic ebony (*Ebonus creticus*) is conspicuous along the way to Ayía Triáda. In May and June in western Crete the fortunate may notice the blue spikes of the endemic *petromarula* falling from Roman cisterns and Venetian walls. In their season there are scented narcissus, wild iris, lupins, gladiolus and specialised forms of tulip. There are asphodels and mandragora or mandrake, the stuff of legend. Hillsides are coloured by varieties of pink or white cistus. *Oxalis pes-caprae* was introduced from South Africa but Rackham and Moody (see Recommended reading) point out that it has naturalised so successfully that the carpets of yellow flowers show up in pictures taken from space. When the first oleanders flower in dried-up stream-beds, or planted along the roads, the summer heat has begun. There are autumn flowers too, as growth starts again after the first rains, but they are less profuse and conspicuous, a more specialised interest. An exception is the sea daffodil, *Pancratium maritimum*, which from a large bulb flourishes in the sand dunes behind some beaches from July to September, with delicate sweet-scented flowers.

Crete's original forest cover has been exploited since Minoan times. Until the 16C cypress trees were still abundant on Mount Ida but the forests declined drastically during the Turkish occupation.

Visitors on a tour of Crete will still come across localised areas of woodland, especially in Sphakiá, where native trees flourish. There are the distinctive Cretan cypress, the tree of the White Mountains, and flat-topped pines, *Pinus brutia*, along southern slopes, and junipers in the east of the island, in the southwest and on Gávdos. There are both evergreen and deciduous oaks, and plane trees conspicuous around springs and along streams. There are sweet chestnuts, citrus and mulberry but these, like the olives, are cultivated for their crops.

However, large areas consist of a scrub known elsewhere in the Mediterranean region as *maquis* (defined as shrub country) and *garigue* with the lower undershrubs, in Greek *phrygana*. This typical low tough-leaved evergreen vegetation can be uncomfortably spiny, but the all-pervading scent of herbs such as sage, thyme and oregano will provide ample compensation, and the undergrowth shelters a great many members of the orchid family.

The main archaeological sites are now sprayed with herbicides; unfortunately this has become the easiest way to protect architectural features from invasive roots and weed cover. But many of the less well-known sites have not been affected, and moreover are legally protected from cultivation and grazing, so that they are ideal refuges for all manner of plant life.

Birdwatching

Ornithologists who have chosen to visit Crete will want to have with them Stephanie Coghlan's *A Birdwatching Guide to Crete*, perhaps backed up by *Birds of Greece* (see Recommended reading). The island is on a migration route and especially in spring (March and April) when there is water in streams and pools it is likely to prove a rewarding choice for a birdwatching holiday. A number of group tours organised and guided by experts (p 13) are available at this time of year but the tourist season has not begun in earnest and independent travellers are advised to do some advance planning.

Birdwatchers heading for wetlands will find that although Crete has only one natural lake (Kournás west of Réthymnon) several new reservoirs rapidly begin to serve the same purpose for birds on migration as well as for the breeding population. In the east the best-known is the Bramianá reservoir near Ierápetra and in the west the well established one at Ayiá inland of Khaniá. Along the north coast the seasonal streams very often end in reedbeds surrounding river-mouth pools (some noted in the Blue Guide) and any of these may be a rewarding stop. Two areas especially recommended for birdwatching are the Almýros river in the west which reaches the sea at Yeoryioúpolis and the Aposelémis river mouth in the east, near Gournés. The Eloúnda salt-pans are always worth inspecting for wading birds and other waterfowl. In the south the seasonal streams may reach the sea through gorges which are inaccessible when the snow is melting in the mountains, but stretches of coastal plain south of Anó Viánnos, or around Plakiás or Frankokástello are good walking country early in the year when temperatures are likely to be warmer than in the north of the island; all along this coast birds may be resting before the next stage of the journey north.

Mountain plains are a feature of the Cretan topography; Lasíthi, Nída and the Omalós are the best known. Here the experts may concentrate on birds of prey, looking out for the bearded vulture or lammergeier, now a threatened species. The Greek government has made a start on protection measures and the National Park of Samariá, a major tourist attraction, is a step in the right direction. There are other huge vultures (usually the griffon) and eagles, buzzards and various falcons which include the peregrine. Eleonora's falcon hunts on the mainland east of Siteía from breeding grounds on the offshore islets. Above Zarós on the southern slopes of Mount Ida the Vótamos lake, dammed from a mountain stream, attracts a wide variety of birdlife.

A lammergeier

All across the island there is a chance of sighting or of hearing the call of spectacular birds which may be resident or on passage, among them hoopoes, bee-eaters and golden orioles, also large flocks or red-footed falcon. There are kingfishers near water, sometimes along the coast, but a different glimpse of blue and a voice unmistakable once heard is the blue rock thrush. A melancholy drawn-out note, rhythmically repeated at intervals, comes from the Scops owl; it is a characteristic sound of the Cretan dusk.

A visit to the Museum of Natural History (p 98) outside Herákleion on the Knossós road is highly recommended to anyone interested in the birds of Crete.

Loggerhead sea turtles

The loggerhead, *Caretta caretta*, the most common sea turtle in Greece and the Mediterranean, can weigh more than 100kg with an average shell length of up to 90cm. Turtles are an acquatic reptile of the tortoise family. They spend their lives at sea but mature females return every 2–3 years to bury their eggs in the beaches where they hatched. Three of Crete's most spectacular beaches, east of Réthymnon, west of Khaniá and along the Mesará bay north of Mátala are among the loggerheads' main nesting sites in the eastern Mediterranean.

Agile in the water turtles are vulnerable on land, their feet modified into paddles. The egg-laying females and later the hatchlings racing for the sea are easily disturbed or disoriented by lights or noise. Nests are easily damaged. The turtles' nesting season is June to September, at the height of the tourist season on Crete. With the resort hotels and bars drawn to these beaches and hazards for the turtles from sunbeds, umbrellas and water sports there was potential for a catastrophic conflict of interest. However, there is now legislation to protect sea turtles in Greek waters and on Greek nesting beaches, and the conservation lobby working to reconcile the needs of the turtles with the local need for sustainable tourism has met with remarkable success.

The *Sea Turtle Protection Society of Greece* (STPS) has played a major part. The society's information huts are noted in the Blue Guide; the aim is to increase public awareness about the problems and their suggested solutions. Many restrictions have been accepted, for example on the use of the beach during the hours of darkness, or the arrangements for cleaning, for sunloungers or floodlighting in the interest of the breeding turtles. Volunteers monitor the beaches and rescue nests.

Sea turtles are classified as 'vulnerable' in world conservation terms, as a species likely to become endangered in the near future if the underlying causes of their problems are not corrected. There is cautious optimism on Crete that efforts here in aid of turtle protection may have a successful outcome. Further information is available from STPS, PO Box 30, 74100 Réthymnon, Greece, ☎ (00 30) 28310 72288, www.archelon.gr.

Recommended reading

Some of these books are out of print, but should be obtainable from libraries. A number of reprints are published in Athens and may be bought locally from bookshops or museums on Crete. In case of difficulty, consult *Zeno Booksellers*, 57a Nether Street, North Finchley, London N12 7NP, ☎ 020 8446 1986, www.thegreekbookshop.com, email info@thegreekbookshop.com or the *Hellenic Book Service*, 91 Fortess Road, London NW5 1AG, ☎ 020 7267 9499, www.hellenicbookservice.com/.

Art and archaeology
K. Branigan, *The Tombs of the Mesara*, Duckworth, 1975.
A. Brown, *Arthur Evans and the Palace of Minos*, Ashmolean Museum, 1983.
G. Cadogan, *Palaces of Minoan Crete*, Routledge, 1980.

R. Castleden, *The Knossos Labyrinth*, Castleden, 1989; *The Minoans*, Routledge, 1992.

J. Chadwick, *Linear B and Related Scripts*, British Museum Press, 1989.

C. Davaras, *Guide to Cretan Antiquities*, Noyes Press, 1976.

J.M. Dreissen and C.F. Macdonald, *The Troubled Island*, Liège, 1997.

Sir A. Evans, *The Palace of Minos*, Macmillan, 1921–36.

ed D. Evely, H. Hughes-Brock and N. Momigliano, *Knossos A Labyrinth of History*, British School at Athens, 1994.

J.L. Fitton, *The Discovery of the Greek Bronze Age*, British Museum Press, 1995; *The Minoans*, British Museum Press, 2002.

R. Higgins, *Minoan and Mycenaean Art*, Thames & Hudson, 1997.

S. Hood, *The Arts in Prehistoric Greece*, Yale University Press, 1992; *The Minoans*, Thames & Hudson, 1971.

ed D. Huxley, *Cretan Quests: British Explorers, Excavators and Historians*, British School at Athens, 2000.

J.A. MacGillivray, *Minotaur. Sir Arthur Evans and the Archaeology of the Minoan myth*, Jonathan Cape, 2000; *The Palaikastro kouros*, BSA Studies, vol. VI, 2000.

ed. J.W and E.E. Myers and G. Cadogan, *Aerial Atlas of Ancient Crete*, Unviersity of California Press, 1992.

J.D.S. Pendlebury, *A Handbook to the Palace of Minos at Knossos*, Macmillan, 1933.

N. Platon, *Zakros*, Adolf M. Hakkert, 1985.

P. Warren and V. Hankey, *Aegean Bronze Age Chronology*, Duckworth, 1989.

P. Warren, *The Aegean Civilisations: from ancient Crete to Mycenae*, Phaidon, 1989

Byzantine art and architecture

R. Cormack, Byzantine Art, Oxford University Press, 2000.

K. Gallas, K. Wessel and M. Borboudakis, *Byzantinisches Kreta*, Munich, 1983.

K. Kalokyris, *The Byzantine Wall- Paintings of Crete*, Small Press Distribution, 1973.

N. Psilakis, *The Monasteries of Crete*, Bank of Crete, 1988.

I. Spatharakis, *Byzantine wall-paintings in Rethymnon*, Mitos, 1998.

History

R. Clogg, *A Concise History of Modern Greece*, Cambridge University Press, 2002.

Th.E. Detorakis, *History of Crete*, Iraklion, 1994.

J.J. Norwich, *A History of Venice*, Penguin, 1983; *Byzantium: The Early Centuries*, Penguin, 1990; *Byzantium: The Apogee*, Penguin, 1993; *Byzantium: The decline and Fall*, Penguin, 1996.

C.M. Woodhouse, *Modern Greece: A Short History*, Faber & Faber, 1999.

Battle of Crete

A. Beevor, *Crete: the Battle and the Resistance*, Penguin, 1992.

C. Buckley, *Greece and Crete 1941*, Efstathiadis Group, 1984.

A. Clark, *The Fall of Crete*, Cassell, 2001.

G. Cox, *A Tale of Two Battles: a personal memoir of Crete and the Western Desert 1941*, William Kindar, 1986.

X. Fielding, *The Stronghold*, Secker & Warburg, 1953.

G. Psychoundakis (trans. P. Leigh Fermor), *The Cretan Runner*, Penguin, 1998.

I. (McD.G.) Stewart, *The Struggle for Crete*, Oxford Paperbacks, 1991.

Travel writing

A. Hopkins, *Crete: Its Past, Present and People*, Faber & Faber, 1979.

E. Lear, *The Cretan Journal*, D. Harvey, 1984.

M. Llewellyn Smith, *The Great Island*, Allen Lane, 1973.

R. Pashley, *Travels in Crete*, Cambridge, 1837; reprinted Amsterdam, 1970.

D. Powell, *The Villa Ariadne*, Libri, 2002.

T.A.B. Spratt, *Travels and Researches in Crete*, 1865; reprinted Hakkert, 1984.

J. de Baker, *Across Crete, from Khaniá to Herákleion*, Logos Tekstproducties, 2001.

Walking and natural history

S. Coghlan, *A Birdwatching Guide to Crete*, Arlequin Publications, 1977.

L. Chilton, *Ten Walks in the Plakias area*; *Six Walks in the Georgioupolis area*; *Plant List for Plakias*, all Marengo publications, available locally and from Stanfords Ltd (p 15); see also www.marengo.supanet.com.

J. Godfrey, *Landscapes of Western Crete*, Sunflower Books, 2002; *Landscapes of Eastern Crete*, Sunflower Books, 2003.

G. Handrinos and T. Akriotis, *The Birds of Greece*, Helm, 1997.

G. Hirner and J. Murböck, *Walks in Western Crete*; Rother, 2000.

A. Huxley and W. Taylor, *Flowers of Greece and the Aegean*, Hogarth Press, 1989.

O. Rackham and J. Moody, *The Making of the Cretan Landscape*, Manchester University Press, 1997.

G. Sfikas, *Trees and Shrubs of Greece*, Efstathiadis Group, 2001; *Wild Flowers of Crete*, Efstathiadis Group, 1992.

L. Wilson, *Crete: the White Mountains*, Cicerone, 2000.

Fiction

E. Waugh, *Officers and Gentlemen*, Penguin, 2001.

N. Kazantzakis, *Zorba the Greek*, *Report to Greco*, *Freedom and Death*, *Christ Recrucified*, all published by Faber & Faber; *The Odyssey: A Modern Sequel*, Pocket Books, 1986.

Miscellaneous

A. Davidson, *Mediterranean seafood*, Ten Speed Press, 2002.

C. Fassoulas, *Field guide to the geology of Crete*; Herákleion, 2000.

R. Graves, *The Greek Myths*, Penguin, 1992.

M. Lambert-Gocs, *The Wines of Greece*, Faber & Faber, 1990.

HERÁKLEION PROVINCE

The *nome* or province of Herákleion occupies the centre of Crete stretching from the north to the south coast. All the natural routes across the province have traditionally radiated from the great harbour
city of Herákleion, the political capital of the island since 1971 and an increasingly prosperous commercial centre.

With the development of the modern highway along the north coast, built in the 1960s but still known as the New Road, it now takes no more than an hour to drive east from Herákleion to Ayios Nikólaos or west to Réthymnon. The recent improvement of country roads in the south of the province has opened up possibilities for motorists to explore the island on a circular tour, or to enjoy some of the markedly less developed parts of the south coast.

There is much in the province to interest the tourist keen to learn about the cultural and historical aspects of Crete. A visit to the **Herákleion Archaeological Museum** is recommended for anyone interested in the Minoan civilisation; items from its collection are almost never allowed off the island. The **Historical Museum** is a widely admired institution.

Three of the four most thoroughly investigated **Minoan palace sites** are located within the province. **Knossós** lies on the southern outskirts of Herákleion, **Mália** on the north coast to the east of Herákleion, and **Phaistós** overlooks the plain of the Mesará from the southern slopes of Mount Ida. An area of particular archaeological interest is centred on Arkhánes where remarkable discoveries relating to a palatial complex have come to light. **Górtyn**, the capital of Roman Crete, played a significant part in the later history of the island.

A number of Crete's finest **monasteries**, for example those of Angárathos and Epanosíphis, and in the south the Odiyítria monastery, are to be found in quiet rural locations. Vrondísi and the monastic church at Valsamóneros on the south slopes of Ida are renowned for their Byzantine frescoes. Near Herákleion, above the villages of Krusónas and Rogdiá, there are two prosperous (and welcoming) convents. Many of these institutions played important roles in the religious and intellectual history of the island and also in the long struggle for independence from Ottoman rule.

Out of season it may be convenient to stay in **Herákleion** itself, but in summertime more attractive choices for a holiday within easy reach of the city include (15km west) the coastal resort of **Ayía Pelagía**, or the adjacent, and much quieter, bay of **Lygariá**. Further west is the picturesque harbour village of **Balí**, technically in the province of Réthymnon but not much more than a half hour drive from Herákleion. 5km east of Herákleion the beach at **Amnisós**, on a good bus service, has several hotels as well as studio rooms and apartments to rent. Beyond Amnisós, until the far side of Mália, the character of the development along the coast catering for the demands of mass tourism means that accommodation should be booked ahead only when reliably recommended. In case of doubt it may be wise to avoid this stretch of coast.

Inland of Mália there is a small hotel in **Kastélli** in the Pediáda countryside. Inland of Herákleion, **Arkhánes** is within easy reach (by frequent bus) of the city and Knossós but in atmosphere a world apart; there is as yet no hotel, only a limited number of simple rooms to rent. Both these large villages lie on the northern branch of the E4 long-distance walking route (p 23).

Readers are encouraged to spend time in the south of the province. It is perfectly possible to visit **Phaistós** from the north coast in one day (using private or public transport) and to include the neighbouring site of **Ayía Triada** and the Minoan harbour town of **Kommós**. However, from **Zarós** in the foothills of Ida and on the southern branch of the E4, or nearer the sea in rooms to rent in villages such as **Vóri** or **Kamilári** (even in Ayía Galíni or Plakiás in the province of Réthymnon) it is easy to be at Phaistós early in the day ahead of the tour coaches arriving from the north coast. There will also be time to explore the unspoilt hill country between the mountains and the sea, which is unlikely to disappoint readers interested in wild flowers and birds, and to enjoy the beaches and cliff walks along this stretch of coast.

The province's south coast has a number of fishing settlements that have expanded to take visitors, most of them fully booked only during the midsummer season when unauthorised camping also flourishes. Access to the coast is interrupted by the mountains of the Asteroúsia range. East of these hills, in the southeast corner of the province, along the coast south of Viánnos, you are even further from the well-trodden tourist track. Development here is still on a small scale, partly because of the distance from mainstream sites. Outside the high season you can swim and walk and live very simply, and for the occasional excursion the stunning mountainside location of the sanctuary above Sými or the Minoan sites at Mýrtos along the coast in the province of Lasíthi are not far away.

Herákleion

The city of Herákleion (or Iraklion) lies midway along the north coast of Crete and is the island's administrative capital. With a ferry service every day all the year round from Piraeus (the port of Athens), and the principal airport of the island nearby, Herákleion is for many tourists their introduction to Crete. The modern city may come as a surprise. Its population of 120,000 makes it the fifth largest in Greece, and its income per head, based on the success of agriculture as well as tourism, is the highest in the whole country.

The two principal objectives for tourists visiting Herákleion are the site of the Minoan palace 5km to the south at **Knossós**, and the outstanding collection of treasures of the Minoan civilisation in the city's **Archaeological Museum**.

Herákleion itself is not a beautiful city. A history of damage from earthquake, marauding pirate raids, foreign occupation and internal conflict culminated in

1941 in the full horror of modern warfare. The results of the German bombing of Herákleion are strikingly illustrated by a collection of photographs in the city's highly regarded **Historical Museum** (p 70). After the war rebuilding was necessary and modernisation desirable, but aesthetic considerations carried little weight against functional and commercial ones. First impressions for a visitor today may be of a densely populated urban environment beset by noise, traffic congestion and pollution, hardly an ideal background for a Mediterranean island holiday. Recently the municipality has wherever possible encouraged the establishment of streets and open spaces dedicated to pedestrians, and has attempted (with limited success) to keep traffic flowing on a one-way artery system.

In recent years the quickest escape to the beach from Herákleion has involved a short journey by car or a town bus west on the Old Road out of the city. But these western outskirts are in the process of being transformed by the building of a stadium (capacity 28,000) for the 2004 Olympic Games, with all the necessary local infrastructure. From central Herákleion the nearest good swimming is now to the east at **Amnisós** (p 194), reached by town bus no. 7. With private transport, the bay of **Lygariá** is 15km west (p 186) before Ayía Pelagía.

Visitors spending time in Herákleion will discover that the impressive star-shaped fortifications of the Venetian city have been well restored, including the Rocca al Mare fortress which (reconstructed more than once) has protected the harbour entrance for nearly 800 years. Within the walls the medieval street plan endures, with occasional hints of former glories.

A picturesque market street in the centre of town survives as a colourful attraction but nowadays the numerous upmarket shops with international brand names are equally typical of modern Herákleion.

Practical information

 ### Travel and transport
By air

Níkos Kazantzákis airport is 4km east of the city. Details of services are given under Getting to Crete (p 16). City bus no. 1 (see under buses) runs from the airport to Plateía Eleftherías and on to the Khaniá Gate. Taxis wait outside Arrivals, with sample fares listed on a notice by the rank.

Olympic, 25 Avgoústou, 27; ☎ 2810 343316/289070, www.olympic-airways.gr.

Aegean Cronus Airlines, Democratias 11; ☎ 2810 344324, fax 2810 344330, www.aegeanair.com.

By car from the airport

A spur road leads straight out on to the north coast highway (New National Road) but for the centre of Herákleion it is easier to use the Old Road along the coast with the sea on your right. Continue through the suburb of Néa Alikarnássos (passing Hotel Asterion). For the through road along the waterfront watch for signs right for the port, but for the centre keep straight ahead until the road climbs (with car park, left) into Plateía Eleftherías.

By car from other parts of the island

Leave the bypass section of the north coast highway at the junction controlled by traffic lights (signed for Knossós as well as the city centre) and at the bottom of the slip-road turn left, away from Knossós, towards the sea. Keep straight on and a double carriageway will take you into Plateía Eleftherías. At the end of the big square you can turn right, sharp downhill to ticketed parking under the walls (signed Museum Parking but also convenient for the centre of town).

Parking

Car parking is strictly controlled on main roads in the city centre 08.00–22.00 (except Sun), and central Herákleion is no place for apprehensive drivers in unfamiliar vehicles. On some stretches of the coast road, in both directions from the harbour, parking is allowed and (especially outside business hours) you can often find a space. If in doubt you may prefer to use a ticketed parking area.

For the Archaeological Museum and the centre, there is car parking just out of and below Plateía Eleftherías; see directions above. Flat charge all day, except Sundays free.

For the market and the cathedral area: in the moat just outside the New Gate, on the right heading into town. Open daily 07.00–22.00. Flat charge; free after 14.00 and on Sundays.

Near the Historical Museum: 24-hour underground parking off the main coast road, just to the west of the museum, less than ten minutes' walk to the Venetian harbour. (From the main road you follow large signs in a circle to reach the garage entrance.) Charges based on length of stay.

By sea

Details of services are given under Getting to Crete (p 16). The ferries dock at the quays which lie to the east of the Venetian harbour. There is a café, and taxis meet the boats. Bus stations are 200m west of the dock gates. For port information ☎ 2810 244912.

Minoan Lines, 25 Avgoústou 78, across from Ayios Títos; ☎ 2810 229602, 229646,

ANEK, 25 Avgoústou 33; ☎ 2810 222481.

By bus

You will arrive either on the harbour or outside the Khaniá Gate. The bus stations both for long-distance services and for the no. 2 bus for the city centre (and Knossós) are 200m west outside the dock gates. Services on city routes use blue buses. Tickets are sold in advance from kiosks near the principal stops. In the centre there is an information kiosk at the stop outside the cinema in Plateía Elefthería.

The most useful routes are:

1 East to the airport terminal and west to the Khaniá Gate from bus stops in Plateía Elefthería.

2 To Knossós every 20 minutes from the port (near the long-distance bus stations) with convenient boarding points in Plateía Venizélou (near the Morosini fountain) and Plateía Kornárou (at the top of the market street). On the return route, the bus turns into Plateía Elefthería, for the Archaeological Museum, and then descends directly to the harbour.

6 For the beaches and hotels at Ammoudára west of the city: the stop is outside the cinema in Plateía Elefthería.

7 To the Amnisós beaches; the stop is on the north (harbour) side of the plateía.

Long-distance routes

The buses are green. Because separate companies operate the various routes there are three bus stations, all under the umbrella of *KTEL* (www.KTEL.org), the bus owners' association.

Two bus stations (1 and 2 below) are next to each other on the inland side of the road between the Venetian harbour and the port, just east of the roundabout at the bottom of Leoph. Doúkos Bófor down from Plateía Elefthería. The third is outside the Khaniá Gate at the western end of town.

1 Destinations in eastern Crete, ☎ 2810 245017/245019. Routes to:
Mália, Ayios Nikólaos and Siteía, the plateau of Lasíthi and Ierápetra (via

Ayios Nikólaos), also Viánnos in the southeast of the province continuing twice weekly by this route to Ierápetra; also Arkhánes and Ayía Pelayía.

2 Destinations westwards. ☎ 2810 221765.

North coast routes west to Réthymnon and Khaniá; Ayía Galíni via Réthymnon and Spíli, one service a day.

3 Outside the Khaniá Gate, 150m down the side street right. ☎ 2810 255965. Routes to: south of Herákleion province for Górtyn, the palace at Phaistós, Mátala (and on to Ayía Galíni); to Zarós; to Léndas; west to Phódele, Týlissos and Anóyeia.

Tourist information

The **Greek National Tourism Organisation** (EOT) has its headquarters on Crete at Xanthoudídou 1, opposite the Archaeological Museum. Open Mon–Fri 08.30–14.00; ☎ 2810 228225, fax 2810 226020. If the information office moves before 2004 you can expect a notice here giving directions.

Tourist police

The tourist police office is at Leoph. Dikaiosíni 10. ☎ 2810 289614/283190, near the crossroads at the bottom of the market street; open all day.

Travel agencies

A selection from a wide choice, especially along 25 Avgoústou.

Adamis Tours, 25 Avgoústou 23; ☎ 2810 246202, fax 2810 224717

Creta Travel, Epimenídou 20–22; ☎ 2810 227002-3, fax 2810 223749

Minos Travel, Epimenídou 3; ☎ 2810 346169, fax 2810 226416

Paleológos, 25 Avgoústou 5; ☎ 2810 346185, fax 2810 346208, email info@ferries.gr, specialist shipping agents for the Athens ferries but also for cruises to Théra (Santorini), for inter-island travel and international lines.

Greek Alpine Club (EOS), 53 Dikeosynis Ave., 71201. The office is on the 3rd floor, opening times are 20:30–22:30 weekdays. ☎ 2810 227609.

Where to stay

At busy times of the year, or for the first night on the island, advance booking is recommended.

A *Atlantis* (164 rooms), Igias 2 (off Leoph. Doúkos Bófor), ☎ 2810 229103, fax 2810 226265, email: atlantis@atl.grecootel.gr; in a central position below the Archaeological Museum with balcony views over the port; comfortable and modern with the facilities of an A-class hotel including private parking and a swimming pool.

B *Atrion* (65 rooms), I. Khronáki 9, ☎ 2810 229225, fax 2810 223292, www.atrion.gr; a family-run hotel with airconditioning, behind the Historical Museum; designated street parking area or underground car parking (charged) nearby.

B *Esperia* (54 rooms), Idomenéos 22, ☎ 2810 228534, fax 2810 228556; in a residential area inland from the harbour, convenient for the Archaeological Museum.

B *Kastro* (38 rooms), Theotokopoúlou 22, ☎ 2810 284185, fax 2810 223622; in a relatively quiet area near the El Greco Park.

B *Lato* (50 rooms), Epimenídou 15, ☎ 2810 228103 fax 2810 240350, www.lato.gr, email: lato@her.forthnet.gr; a delightful hotel with views over the harbour, recently modernised to the highest standards and airconditioned; suitable for guests with disabilities.

C *Daedalos* (57 rooms), Daidálou 15, ☎ 2810 244812/5, fax 2810 224391; on this fashionable (pedestrianised) shopping street off Plateía Eleftherías, and adjacent to Korái which has some of the city's liveliest tavernas and bars;

reception will advise on parking.

C *Irene* (59 rooms), Idomenéos 4, ☎ 2810 229703, fax 2810 226407; at the quieter (harbour) end of this street; suitable for disabled guests; garage parking.

C *Kris* (10 rooms), Leoph. Doúkos Bófor 2, ☎ 2810 223211; opposite the Hotel Lató at the narrow end of the road; some rooms with views over the port and self-catering facilities; small swimming pool.

C *Asterion* (46 rooms), Leoph. Ikárou 50, ☎ 2810 227913 fax 2810 244027; a no-frills hotel five minutes from Níkos Kazantzákis airport, in Nea Alikarnássos, a suburb of Herákleion, convenient for early or late flights; airconditioning; swimming pool.

For inexpensive accommodation in rent rooms and pensions the National Tourist Information office recommends the area behind the Historical Museum. Start in Khortatsón or Khándakos, which runs parallel.

Youth hostel

5 Vironos, ☎ 2810 286281, fax 2810 222947.

Eating out
Overlooking the harbour

Ippokambós, just into Marinélli off the coast road, 50m west of the roundabout at the bottom of 25 Avgoústou. This taverna is patronised by knowledgeable Cretans for well-cooked fresh fish at reasonable prices. Pavement tables look across to the backdrop of the harbour fortress, floodlit at night.

Ta Psariá, a long-established taverna at the bottom of 25 Avgoústou, popular with tourists for the harbour views from its raised terrace.

Central, near the market

Ionía, patronsied by customers of the market, is recommended for its wide choice of dishes and its dedication to traditional Cretan cooking. (This is a day-time taverna, closed in the evenings.)

Khóvoli (meaning embers, burning charcoal) is an excellent *psistaría* in the pedestrian precinct Plateía Daskaloyiánnis, an excellent *psistaría*.

Koukoulós, on Koraí, set back in a garden from this pedestrianised street, is one of the most up-market tavernas in the city, with prices to match. The menu leans to Italian-influenced dishes rather than traditional Cretan cooking. The regular clientele come to spend the evening over a good meal; do not expect fast service.

Inland from Plateía Eleftherías

Kyriákos, Dimokratías 52, ten minutes on foot from the Archaeological Museum, on the left side of the double-carriageway out of the plateía, is noted for sophisticated Cretan cooking served in a tranquil atmosphere.

Banks

National Bank of Greece, 25 Avgoústou, on the corner of the plateía in front of Ayios Títos. Has a cashpoint and automatic currency exchange. There is a second, smaller, branch (with cashpoint only) in Plateía Kornárou opposite the top end of the market street, Odós 1866.

Post office and telephones

The **main post office** is in Plateía Daskaloyiánni; open, including foreign exchange (for cash and traveller's cheques) Mon–Fri 07.30–19.30. Subsidiary offices in caravans are in El Greco Park and beside the harbour bus stations.

OTE (telephone company): head office in El Greco Park, open Mon, Wed, 07.30–13.00; Tues, Thurs, Fri 14.30–21.00; Sat 08.00–15.00; closed Sun.

Hospitals

Apollónion between Márkou Mousoúrou and Alber, two blocks west from Plateía Kornárou at the top of the market street (1866), the most convenient during daytime hours.
Venizéleion on the Knossós road, 1km before the Minoan palace site.
Panepisteimiádon, beyond the southern outskirts of the city, off Phaistós road. For Accident and Emergency, on a rota system out of hours, ☎ 106.

Consulates

British Consulate, Odós Papalexandroú 16, ☎ 2810 224012.
Netherlands Consulate, 25 Avgoústou, 23, ☎ 2810 246 202222.
American and Canadian visitors should contact their embassies in Athens:
USA ☎ 721 2951-9, 721 8401;
Canada ☎ 727 3400.
Republic of Ireland. Visitors should contact their representative in Athens, ☎ 723 2771-2.

History

In the Neolithic period there was at least one settlement on the high ground above the Kaíratos stream-bed to the east of what is now Herákleion. Here the modern suburb of Póros is built over the site of the Minoan harbour town and cemetery, currently the subject of an exciting excavation by the Greek archaeological service. By Roman times, we know from the Greek geographer Strabo that Heraclium was the harbour of Knossós. With the Saracen conquest in AD 824, the town was renamed Rabdh el Khandak, literally translated as the castle of the ditch, referring to a great moat dug around it; the Arab settlement became a centre of piracy and a base for attacks on Constantinople, as well as being the principal slave market of the Mediterranean. After a number of abortive attempts to liberate the island for Byzantium, the army of Nikephóros Phokás, which included Russian, Slav and Scandinavian mercenaries, laid siege to the town. The Byzantine general is famous for demoralising the defenders by catapulting over the walls the heads of his Arab prisoners. After ten months and much bloodshed, Crete was once again part of Christendom. During this second Byzantine period the city (now known as Khándakas) was contained within the semi-circle of what today are Khándakas and Daídalos streets.

When the Venetians eventually took control of Crete (1210) they made the city their capital, calling it (and the island) Candia. The city became the seat of government for the Duke of Crete and his councillors, and was laid out accordingly by Venetian architects, with a ducal palace across the piazza from the church of their patron saint, San Marco. To encourage the development of the city, both the new Venetian nobility and the Cretan aristocracy were obliged to build houses and to live on the island for part of the year. At first the new building adapted to the existing Byzantine fortifications but as the city flourished the enceinte was no longer adequate. The impressive defences that still stand today, a 3km star-shaped circuit of walls, bastions and fortified gates, were built over a long period (15C–17C), with an important phase of construction (after Turkish raids in 1538) under the supervision of Michele Sanmicheli (architect of the Palazzo Grimani in Venice). Candia is documented in Venice's archives as a major city of the empire.

From the early years of the Venetian occupation the harbour, guarded by the great fortress, Rocca al Mare, became one of the leading seaports of the eastern Mediterranean, vital for the control of the trade route to the Levant

Candia in 1651, a drawing by Marco Boschini,
Il regno tutto di Candia

which underpinned Venice's extraordinary wealth and prosperity.

But in due course the power of Venice declined. In May 1648 forces of the ascendant Ottoman Empire began the **great siege** of the city of Candia which was to last more than 21 years, making it one of the longest in history. (During the siege the Venetians and their allies lost 30,000 men, the Turks 137,000.) The Turkish camp was established 4km to the south on the slopes of the Fortétsa hill from where their cannon bombarded the city.

Candia was the last bastion of Christendom in the eastern Mediterranean. For a long time the Christian world only watched and waited, but then gradually, against a background of turmoil in Europe, the defence of Candia took on a pan-European dimension. Small forces were sent at various times from first Spain and then France. There were periods of stalemate, but Venice retained control of the sea throughout. Both sides wooed the Cretans with promises to restore the authority of the Orthodox clergy.

In 1661 the struggle was interrupted by an outbreak of the plague. In 1666 the Ottoman assault took on a new seriousness with a change of command. At the same time the experienced Francesco Morosini (the younger) was sent by Venice to take control of the defence which at last became a matter of concern to the whole of Christendom. Mercenaries were recruited in France, and forces sent by the Duke of Hanover, by the Grand Master of the Teutonic Order and by the Holy Roman Emperor, Leopold I, but they were greatly outnumbered by Turkish reinforcements (40,000 soldiers transferred from the Peloponnese) and the Christian generals never managed to create a single command. The city was steadily being destroyed by the Turkish bombardment.

A relief force under the Duc de Beaufort made a heroic but ill-judged sortie which ended in disaster and the French withdrew from the island. The end was near. On 5 September 1669 Morosini at last accepted the inevitable defeat; he negotiated the honourable surrender of the city and the Venetians were allowed to sail away from Crete unharmed. Under the terms of the treaty Morosini had ten days to leave. He evacuated the entire remaining Christian population to the island of Día. Many Cretans went on to build new lives in the Ionian islands. Morosini also had the foresight to carry away with him the state archives (an invaluable record for future historians). Three out of five ships loaded with books and papers reached the safety of Venice.

The Turks chose to rule the island from Khaniá, and Morosini's city, deservedly known as Megálo Kástro, the Great Fortress, became the seat of a Pashalik.

It is impossible to do justice here to the stirring history of Crete's struggle for union with Greece against the background of European powers motivated by their own political ambitions rather than concern for the relief of Turkish oppression on Crete. By far the best account is found in Professor Detorákis's *History of Crete* (Recommended reading, p 59).

Visitors often ask about the episode commemorated in the Herákleion street name **Odós 25 Avgoústou**, properly Martýron 25 Avgoústou, that is, the martyrs of that date. In 1898 the long struggle was nearly over. Union with Greece would have to wait for another 15 years but the principle of autonomy was granted and for the leaders of the struggle for independence this meant freedom. Detorákis refers to the massacre in Herákleion on 25 August that year as 'the last act of the Cretan drama'. A detachment of British soldiers was escorting officials of the new Executive Council up the main street from the harbour when they were attacked by an enraged mob of Turkish Cretans. In the ensuing massacre, burning and looting, many Christian civilians were killed, in addition to 17 British soldiers and the British Honorary Consul. At last the British took decisive action. They hanged 17 Turkish Cretan ringleaders and imprisoned or expelled others. The British navy sailed into Herákleion harbour. The city was cleared of Turkish forces and on 2 November 1898 the last Turkish soldier left Crete.

Khaniá was made the administrative capital of independent Crete, but after the Second World War Herákleion (renamed when Turkish rule ended) grew rapidly to become the chief commercial centre. Because of this pre-eminence, and the central location, the capital was transferred here in 1971.

To the harbour from Plateía Eleftherías

Plateía Eleftherías (Liberty Square) is in many ways the hub of modern Herákleion, and a popular meeting place surrounded by tavernas and cafés. Here you are close to the Archaeological Museum, which is just out of the square at the northwest corner. The seaward view reminds you that this was a walled city on a hill, commanding one of the major harbours of the Mediterranean. On the rampart there is now a huge statue of **Elefthérios Venizélos** (1864–1936), a native of Crete (p 50) who became a respected national statesman and one of the architects of modern Greece. From the public gardens which are inland of the plateía there is a good view of the Vitoúri Bastion and another fine section of moated walls.

Set off downhill under the garden wall round the Archaeological Museum. On your right the Old Road to eastern Crete descends through the ramparts, at the point controlled in Venetian times by the St George's (or Lazzaretto) Gate. A Turkish fountain has been set in the restored city wall. Follow Leoph. Doúkos Bófor as the rampart sweeps down to the sea. Above you, left, the Hotel Atlantis has superb views over the harbour.

The **Museum of the Battle of Crete and the National Resistance of 1941–45**, run by the municipality, is on the corner of Hadzidáki where the side-road climbs up to the hotel. Open daily 09.00–14.00, ☎ 2810 246554. The collection preserves documents, photographs, newspaper articles and other memorabilia of these traumatic years of Cretan history. Only the major items are labelled in English but much of the material hardly needs explanation.

On the last stretch of the ramparts, before you get down to sea level, there is a choice of routes, both ending at the Venetian harbour. You can continue ahead along the slope on what is still Doúkos Bófor, or descend to the roundabout in view on the coast road below. If you keep to the higher level you will see the *Hotel Lató* ahead uphill. The road becomes Epimenídou which runs through to 25 Avgoústou, the main street from the central crossroads down to the old harbour. Along it you will find banks, shipping offices and a choice of good travel agents, and at the bottom by the quays a number of fish tavernas and cafés.

From the slope before the Hotel Láto you can see the old harbour (below left). To the right along the coast road are the long-distance bus stations with the terminus for the blue city buses, and beyond them the quays for the Athens ferries, cruise ships and cargo operations.

The Venetian harbour is guarded by the **Rocca al Mare fortress** (also known by its Turkish name **Koulés**). Open 08.30–15.00 daily except Monday.

The original castle dated from the first years of the Venetian occupation, but was destroyed by earthquake in 1303. The building was completely reconstructed in 1523, the date given in the inscription over the northern gate. The restored interior, with 26 chambers, is an impressive example of its kind. A ramp leads to the upper level, which in summer becomes an open-air theatre. There is a commanding view from the battlements. On the external walls are three high-relief carvings of the Lion of St Mark, symbol of the Serenissima, the Serene Republic of Venice; the best preserved one now to seaward.

Along the road that now skirts the Venetian harbour are the partially restored 16C **arsenals**, remains of the great dockyard which was begun soon after Venice took control of the island. The arsenals now stand as two groups of echoing arcades. Here, on what was then a sloping shore, the Venetians built or repaired their ships, each vault holding one galley.

On Saturday mornings there is a popular outdoor market beside the dual-carriageway beyond the dock gates.

For the **Venetian harbour** now used by fishing boats and yachts you turn left from the big roundabout on the coast road under the echoing arches of the former Venetian arsenals or ship sheds. By the fish stalls at the bottom of 25 Avgoústou (and another roundabout) the long-established fish taverna *Ta Psariá* overlooks the harbour which is dominated by the Venetian fortress, Rocca al Mare. 50m past the roundabout (west of it) is another, simpler but well recommended, fish taverna, *Ippokambós*; this one is set back a little from the coast road but here, too, in the evening the backdrop is the floodlit fortress.

East of the Venetian Harbour are the Port Authority offices, and then the moorings for cruise ships. The Marina café is conspicuous along the east quay of the Inner Harbour, convenient for a pause at any time of day. From the roundabout east of the Venetian arsenals, take Leoph. Doúkos Bófor up on to the ramparts for the return to Plateía Eleftherías.

For the Historical Museum (p 93) walk west from the harbour along the esplanade. You pass the ruined walls of the priory church of **Ayios Pétros** (recently the subject of a major archaeological investigation), dating to the period of Venetian rule. The south chapel (locked) preserves remains of the only known Byzantine frescoes still in situ in the city. Westwards along the main road from the ruins of the church is a 19C Neo-classical building with a striking new glass frontage; this houses the Historical Museum.

A little west of the Historical Museum, an indent in the coastline, the Bay of

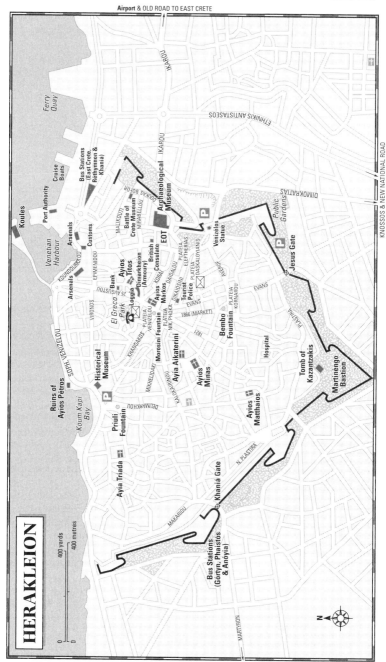

HERAKLEION

Dermatás to the Venetians, is now more often known by its Turkish name **Koum Kapí** after the Sand Gate, a postern in the Venetian sea wall between the bay and the city.

Due south from the centre of the bay (along Delimárkou directly behind the children's playground) is a **fountain** built by the Venetian governor, Antonio Priuli, in 1666 during the last phase of the great siege, in response to the destruction by the Turks of Morosini's aqueduct. The design of its façade, reflecting Palladian influence, is based on a Corinthian temple with pillars and columns supporting a pediment flanked by brackets in the form of decorated volutes. A Latin inscription with date commemorates Priuli; the tablet above was added by the Turks.

To the market from Plateía Eleftherías

The outdoor market (*agorá*) in **Odós 1866** is best visited during the morning shopping hours. From the plateía follow Leoph. Dikaiosíni. This busy one-way street runs down to the central crossroads at one end of Odós 1866. On the way you may notice an elegant marble doorway embellishing the main entrance to the **Nomarkheíon**, the administrative and legal headquarters of the province (nome) of Herákleion. Three coordinated blocks of offices use restored Turkish buildings (on the site of Venetian barracks). The portal was sent from Italy in 1409 by the Cretan pope, Alexander V, a member of the Franciscan order, for the friary which stood on the present site of the Archaeological Museum.

Between the office buildings a flight of steps takes you up to the **statue of Ioánnis Daskaloyiánnis** (an 18C revolutionary leader from Sphakiá) to get to the little plateía of the same name, with a row of tavernas and cafés including an excellent *psistaría*, **Khóvoli** with food from the grill. Across the plateía, right, is the central post office, and beside it, sharp right, the short street (Yiánnari) heads towards the market.

On the corner with Odós Evans is the *Taverna Ionía*, patronised by Cretans visiting the market, and open all day but closed in the evenings.

Odós Evans is parallel to the market street. You can cut through to it down an alley opposite the Ionía packed with taverna tables (an atmospheric place for a midday break) or loop round by the main road to the crossroads at the bottom of the market.

A visit to the lively **market street** is a traditional feature of Herákleion life, and Cretans from out of town, as well as local inhabitants, still come here to shop and do business. Many of the food products of the island are represented here. The fruit and vegetables are temptingly displayed. There are butchers and bakers, and a fish market at the top end of the street. Sheep and goat's milk cheeses and yoghurt in pottery bowls come straight from the mountain pastures in summer. All the year round there are local herbs, almonds, honey, nougat, olive oil, and olives, some imported from Kalamata in the Peloponnese and some cured in the traditional Cretan manner, recognisable by their wrinkled skins.

At the uphill end of the street the **Bembo fountain** (1588) was the first to supply the town with running water; it is composed of antique fragments, including a headless statue which the Italian architect Zuanne Bembo brought from Ierápetra (Greco-Roman Ierápytna) in southeastern Crete. The fountain is hidden behind a polygonal kiosk, itself adapted from a Turkish fountain and in use as a café, convenient for a pause to observe the market scene. Only occasionally now do you notice men of the older generation dressed for a day in town in the traditional Cretan costume of breeches or baggy trousers, tall leather boots, cummerbund and the *mavromándilo*, a long black scarf knotted round the head.

Conspicuous across the open space of Plateía Kornárou at the top of the market is the massive modern sculpture entitled ***Erotókritos and Aretoúsa***, by the Cretan sculptor Ioánnis Parmekéllis.

If you turn right (opposite a branch of the National Bank in the plateía, with a well-stocked bookshop next door to it) and follow the main road against the flow of one-way traffic (past the turning for the Apollonión Hospital) you will arrive in front of the modern cathedral, Ayios Minás, completed in 1895. The old church of **Ayios Minás**, the medieval predecessor of the cathedral, is tucked below the terrace at the cathedral's west front. At the northeast corner of the cathedral the Sinaite church of **Ayía Aikateríni** displays, among other ecclesiastical valuables, part of the Icon Collection of the Orthodox church of Crete (p 96).

To find the tomb of Níkos Kazantzákis you cross Plateía Kornárou from the top of the market street and walk up Odós Evans towards the city walls at the reconstructed Jesus Gate, now known as the **Kainoúria Pórta** or **New Gate**. The walls are over 40m thick at this point.

Outside the gate (to the right) is the entrance to the **outdoor theatre** which in July and August is the venue for many concerts and other events brought to Crete from the Athens Festival. In the shadow of the wall (the **Jesus Bastion**) there is a pleasant shaded café. Inside the gate Odós Plastíra leads west parallel with the walls. It is less than five minutes to the **Martinengo Bastion** and the **tomb of Níkos Kazantzákis**, the eminent Cretan author of, among many works, *Zorba the Greek* and *Freedom and Death* (see the museum at Myrtiá, p 134). Kazantzákis died in Germany in 1957. The inscription on the memorial here quotes one of his more famous lines: 'I hope for nothing. I fear nothing. I am free.'

Along Odós Daidálou to the city's historical centre

Daidálou is a pedestrianised street out of Plateía Eleftherías which runs north of and parallel to the main road, Leoph. Dikaiosíni. The street offers a good choice of popular tavernas with tables on the pavement and is otherwise lined by upmarket shops selling goods with internationally recognised brand names. You pass the Hotel Daedalos and one or two travel agencies. Near the bottom of the street on the left (Daidálou 6) is one of the best international bookshops in town, with an admirable stock of maps as well as a wide variety of travel books and literature relating to the island and its people.

Between Daidálou and Epimenídou (above the harbour) is an attractive residential area. Parallel with Daidálou, **Koraí** (opening into a little plateía) comes alive in the evenings with tavernas and bars popular with university students. *Koukoulós* is highly regarded, with prices well above the student range.

Daidálou emerges at the top end of 25 Avgoústou, opposite the **Plateía Venizélou**, a paved area around the **Morosini fountain**. The square has become a focus for tourists. This is the place to sample Cretan pastries with cafés open from breakfast-time on, bookstalls selling foreign newspapers and souvenir shops. The Knossós bus stop nearby is usually indicated by a milling crowd.

Plateía Venizélou lay at the centre of the Venetian city, the site of the ducal palace. Its fountain was built in 1628 by order of the Venetian governor

Morosini fountain, from Gerola, Monumenti Veneti nell'Isola di Creta, *1905*

Francesco Morosini (the elder, father of the legendary commander during the siege) and was supplied by an aqueduct from springs 15km away on the slopes of Mount Júktas. It was originally completed by a marble statue of Neptune, but this was demolished during the Turkish occupation. The lions are 14C work, probably from an earlier fountain elsewhere. Below the basins marine scenes are carved in relief.

Across the road from the Morosini fountain stands the restored Venetian church of San Marco, now (as **Ayios Márkos**) used as a hall for concerts, lectures and exhibitions. These events are advertised in the portico. A triple-transept basilica was built here in 1239, damaged by earthquake in 1303 and again (after restoration) in 1508. The bells of a campanile played their part in rallying the population during the great siege. During the Turkish period the church became a mosque. The campanile was replaced by a minaret; the stump can still be seen to the right of the façade.

A little towards the harbour from Ayios Márkos is the reconstructed **Venetian loggia**, a careful copy of the original arcaded design (1626) which provided an elegant meeting-place for the Venetian nobility. Adjoining the loggia, the restored Venetian armoury has become the City Hall (**Dimarkheíon**). Set in its north wall is a relief from the **Sangredo fountain** (1602) which originally decorated the northwest corner of the loggia; Sangredo was one of the Dukes of Crete. The sadly defaced female figure is believed to represent the nymph Crete, holding in her left hand a shield and in her right a club. In mythology Crete was the mother of Passiphaë (wife of Mínos) who gave birth to the Minotaur. 25 Avgoústou will take you down to the harbour.

On the left of this street you notice a public garden planted with orange trees, Párko Theotokópoulou. This was the family name of the painter El Greco so the square is known to most foreigners as **El Greco Park**. There is a post office caravan here, and on the west side of the gardens the head office of the telephone company (*OTE*).

On the right side, towards the sea from the Venetian loggia, the church of **Ayios Títos** is set back in a tree-lined plateía. St Titus, Bishop of Crete, was the friend and companion of St Paul who consecrated him the first Bishop of Crete. The original Byzantine church, which had been converted into a mosque, was destroyed by earthquake in 1856. However, the mosque was rebuilt, and this, rededicated to Ayios Títos, is substantially what you see today. A reliquary containing the saint's skull is revered in the church. It had been carried away to safety by the defeated Venetians in 1669 at the end of the great siege, but was returned here in 1966 to much rejoicing

The Archaeological Museum

• The museum is at Xanthoudídou 1, at the northwest corner of Plateía Eleftherías; ☎ 2810 224 630/226 092.

Open summer Mon 12.00–19.00, Tues–Sun 08.00–19.00; winter 08.00–17.00; closed Good Friday (until 12.00), Easter Sunday, 1 May, 25 and 26 December. The entrance ticket is valid for any number of return visits on the day of purchase. To avoid the overcrowding during the tourist season, caused by the popularity of guided tours, a visit in the late afternoon is recommended.

There is a good bookstall in the museum entrance hall and a coffee shop (with toilets) on the terrace behind the main building.

Two good catalogues are available from the bookstall. The more up-to-date (1999) publication is by Andonis Vasilakis but the older work by Professor J.A. Sakellerakis is still a valuable guide to the legacy of the Minoan civilisation.

The museum stands on a hill overlooking the sea, on the site of the Latin monastery of St Francis which dominated the skyline of Herákleion during the Venetian period. An excavation, now covered by the garden, revealed part of the foundations of the friars' church, which was destroyed in the 17C by Turkish bombardment during the Great Siege. The present building (1937–40), designed on functional anti-seismic principles rather than aesthetic ones, provides 20 rooms on two floors.

A major project is underway to extend and modernise the existing buildings. The changes must be expected to lead to some rearrangement of the collection with the opportunity for drastic improvement of the mounting and labelling using the best modern practices of museum display.

This museum houses a vast collection of material, amassed since 1883, from the Neolithic to Roman periods of Cretan history. A large proportion of the exhibition space is devoted to the Minoan civilisation with a display of particular interest because so few Minoan artefacts have found their way from Crete to museums elsewhere in the world. In the early days of the discovery of the Cretan Bronze Age, material from all excavations around the island was brought to Herákleion. In the last 30 years regional archaeological museums have been established in Ayios Nikólaos, Siteía, Khaniá and Réthymnon, and the Herákleion archaeological authorities usually handle new material only from within their *nome* (province). This is still a formidable task.

The arrangement of the collection The Bronze Age collection occupies Rooms I–X on the ground floor, the vestibule at the foot of the staircase (clay coffins) and three rooms on the upper floor where the remains of the Minoan fresco paintings are displayed. Visitors may notice that dates in the museum catalogues, and in this Guide, do not always correspond exactly with those on the labels in the cases. The problems of dating the Neopalatial period, taking into account both the traditionally accepted chronology and refinements suggested by recent research are discussed in the History of Crete (p 37).

After the Minoan exhibits on the ground floor, Rooms XI and XII contain superb examples of material from excavations dating to the Early Iron Age on Crete (Protogeometric-Orientalising periods). Upstairs rooms XVII and XVIII are used for special exhibitions.

On the ground floor opposite the bookstall are two further rooms (XIX and XX) often closed but sometimes accessible on request. Room XX offers Roman sculpture and epigraphy, probably of interest only to specialists, but Room XIX, easily missed at the end of the itinerary, is strongly recommended. It houses some major artefacts, and pieces of Archaic (pre-Classical Greek) sculpture in stone, bronze and clay, from sites across the island.

Room I Neolithic period (from 7000–3500 BC) and Minoan Prepalatial period (Early Minoan I–III and MMIA, c 3500–1900 BC)

Starting on the right of the door two cases contain the Neolithic material: pottery, bone and stone implements and a variety of figurines, including one with exaggerated buttocks, probably a female deity. The hand-made pottery was decorated by burnishing, or with incised patterns filled with a chalky paste.

The other cases are devoted to artefacts of the Early Minoan (EM) period, the Early Bronze Age, which preceded the emergence of the palace civilisation on Crete. The EMI pottery (c 3000–2600 BC) includes red-on-buff painted wares and tall pattern-burnished cups and vessels in grey wares on rounded bases.

Much of the evidence for the Prepalatial period comes from the communal tombs of the Mesará but the sites at Vasilikí, on the islet of Mókhlos and the cemetery of Phourní at Arkhánes are also represented. The display illustrates the prosperity and the level of technical achievement of the craftsmen who produced these spectacular artefacts.

The distinctive **Vasilikí ware** (EMII in **Case 6**) appears in characteristic shapes such as beak-spouted jugs and horizontally spouted 'teapots' with a mottled, semi-lustrous surface. The effect was achieved by uneven firing.

The carving of **stone vases** was a highpoint of achievement in this period. Some of the finest of these come from the cemetery on Mókhlos (**Case 7**). Materials such as the banded marbles and various limestones are superbly adapted to the shapes of the vases. These were carved by hand using a reed or copper drill with an abrasive powder. A style of pottery with white decoration on a dark ground (EMIII, **Case 8**) replaced the Vasilikí mottled ware.

Among artefacts in this room which throw light on the society which produced them are a boat from Mokhlós in Case 8, and another, from Palaíkastro in eastern Crete (**Case 10**), also the **four-wheeled cart** which is among the earliest (c 2000 BC) evidence for wheeled transport on the island. Libation vessels (in the free-standing **Case 12**) include a bull figurine with tiny acrobats clinging to the horns, and bird-shaped vases. **Case 15** shows clay models of animals including an *agrími* (the Cretan ibex) and vessels known as *kérnoi*, with multiple receptacles for offerings.

There is an important display of sealstones, many from Mesará tombs, including the ivory cylinders with designs cut at each end, and the Babylonian haematite cylinder of the period of Hammurabi.

Central cases display elegant jewellery, from Mókhlos, the Mesará tombs and the Arkhánes cemetery (Phourní), as well as exquisite examples of the Minoan ivory-carver's art.

Room II Protopalatial period (Middle Minoan IB–II, c 1900–1700 BC)

This room displays examples of the finds from the first Minoan palaces (the Old Palaces) at Knossós and Mália, from peak sanctuaries (Minoan holy places usually on mountain tops) and from cemeteries.

The free-standing case near the door contains the **Town Mosaic** from Knossós. These polychrome faience plaques of house façades may have decorated a wooden chest. The buildings (of two or more storeys) seem to be of masonry strengthened by wooden beams. Window-panes painted scarlet suggest oiled parchment or some other anticipation of glass. A gold-hilted dagger is from Mália. Nearby are examples of the Middle Minoan hieroglyphic script which is still not fully deciphered though the numerical signs are clear.

Important material comes from early levels at Mália, including from Khrysólakkos (the Gold Pit). The much-illustrated gold bee pendant is in Room VII, but here there is a mother-goddess figure and a table for offerings, also moulds for double axes.

Among figurines found in shrine deposits (see **Case 20**) the enigmatic objects resembling sheep-bells may represent horned masks used for ceremonies. **Case 23** has the only one known in faience, from Póros-Katsambás, harbour of Knossós.

A selection of the material dedicated at **peak sanctuaries** such as Kóphinas, Júktas and Petsophás, includes figurines of the worshippers as well as a wide variety of other votive offerings; there are models of animals and ships, altars and shrines with libation vases and other equipment for ritual as well as some exquisite jewellery.

Among the pottery in this room the polychrome vases in the distinctive **Kamáres style** rank among the outstanding achievements of the Minoan potters' art. Kamáres ware, one of the most decorative of Bronze Age pottery styles, took its name from the cave high on Mount Ida (overlooking the palace at Phaistós) where it was first excavated. The exhibits range from delicate, thin-walled vases (eggshell wares) to large pots such as the pithos decorated with palm trees. The ware is admired because of the harmony between the design of the decoration and the shape of the vessel with patterns brilliantly adapted to the form. Popular shapes are bridge-spouted jars and several types of cup, often with carinated (angular) profiles imitating work in metal. (Further examples are found in the next room.)

The display is completed by bronze artefacts and a collection of seals, including some from the seal-engraver's workshop at Mália.

Room III Protopalatial period (Middle Minoan IB–II, c 1900–1700 BC) at Phaistós

The **Phaistós disk**, prominently displayed, is a renowned enigma. Found in MMIII levels (17C BC) in the palace, it is handmade from clay, and stamped in a spiral with characters in an unknown script which are framed and divided up by incised lines. The inscription, running from the outside to the centre, is thought to constitute a form of syllabic writing.

This room continues the superb display of **Kamáres ware**. Just inside the door are vases from the cave after which it is named. Among the more ambitious vessels (shown together in a free-standing case) are a krater with applied flowers, large jugs and a fruitstand with toothed hanging rim and elaborately painted interior.

There is an important exhibit demonstrating the variety of **sealings** in use this early in the development of palatial organisation. The archive, found in an MMII context, consisted of over 6500 seal impressions employing nearly 300 distinct motifs, chiefly abstract designs. Finally, the contents of a shrine (from the West Court of the palace) surround a red-burnished clay libation table decorated with a border of incised bulls and a spiral motif.

Room IV The Neopalatial period (Middle Minoan III–Late Minoan I, 1700–1450 BC)

This room includes material from the palaces at Knossós, Phaistós and Mália. In pride of place three pieces, all from Knossós, are individually displayed. The **Bull's Head Rhyton** from the Little Palace at Knossós has holes in the mouth and crown of the head for pouring libations. It is carved from serpentine, with eyes inlaid with jasper and rock crystal, and nostrils outlined in white tridacna shell; the horns (restored) were of gilded wood. A double axe is incised between the eyes.

The Bull's Head Rhyton, from the Little Palace at Knossós

The ivory figure, skilfully restored, is known as the **bull-leaper**, as in the much-illustrated fresco panel; it may have been partly covered with gold leaf. From the Central Treasury came the **Lioness Head Rhyton**, carved from alabaster.

Near the entrance, **Case 44** shows (from Knossós) examples of the Minoan Linear A script, incised on an amphora shoulder and on two silver pins, and written in cuttlefish ink inside two cups. **Case 52** contains ceremonial swords of MMIII date from Mália. One, nearly 1m long, has a pommel of rock crystal on an ivory hilt. Another, of rapier type, has a bone pommel, and on an encircling disk of gold leaf an acrobat is displaying his skill. Among the stone vase fragments with relief decoration and miniature work in ivory, rock crystal and faience, note the fragment of a relief with a scene interpreted as a procession of worshippers at a peak sanctuary.

Case 46 contains material relating to the sacred snake and associated cult practices, in particular the use of the snake as a symbol of the underworld. The tubes may have been shelters for the snakes, with cups for milk. One vase is in the shape of a honeycomb encircled by a snake.

On the opposite wall, in **Case 47**, a brown schist sceptre, one end a leopard, the other an axe, is outstanding among finds from the palace at Mália.

The **pottery** in this room is of superb quality. **Case 45** has the so-called **lily vases**, with white-painted lilies originally on a dull lilac-brown ground. A conical rhyton is painted with horns of consecration. Two new styles of pottery are in evidence, with decoration based either on floral or on marine patterns. The Floral Style incorporated leaves, grasses and reeds (including the papyrus motif from Egypt) as well as flowers. The Marine Style decoration uses, as the name suggests, various forms of sea creatures (octopuses, sea anemones, molluscs and starfish) against a background of seaweed, sponges and rocks, all naturalistically entwined around the pot and perfectly adapted to its shape. From the final destruction of the palace at Phaistós (**Case 49**) came the graceful jug with an all-over pattern of grasses and a rhyton decorated in the Marine Style with argonauts.

Case 57 displays the remarkable **gaming board** found in the East Wing at Knossós and dated c 1600 BC; the ivory frame is inlaid with rock crystal, faience, lapis lazuli, and gold and silver leaf.

Much of the outstanding material exhibited in this room comes from Evans's Temple Repositories in the West Wing of the palace at Knossós. The smaller objects from the two

Snake goddess from the Temple of Repositories, Knossós

sunken treasuries (sealed some time after the beginning of the Neopalatial period) are displayed in **Case 50**. They include the two faience **figurines of the snake goddess**, argonauts, flying fish and other decorative plaques (also of faience), banded limestone and marble libation vases, a rock crystal rosette for inlay, and painted shells. Other finds from the Temple Repositories are in **Cases 54, 55 and 58**. The large vases include a distinctive 'bird' jug, an import from the island of Mélos in the Cyclades, decorated with a type of partridge.

Room V The last years of the palace at Knossós (Late Minoan II–IIIA, 1450–c 1380 BC)

The material in this room illustrates the continuing life in the palace and town of Knossós before and after the destruction at the end of LMIB which at so many other Minoan sites across the island caused a complete break in the archaeological record. Alongside this Knossós material the room accommodates a selection of finds from the recent excavations at Arkhánes and in the Minoan harbour town now covered by the Herákleion suburbs of Póros and Katsambás.

The Knossós material came from excavations along the Royal Road, from the South House (silver vessels in **Case 62**), from the Little Palace (bronze figurines in **Case 61**) and Evans's Unexplored Mansion (vases and figurines in **Case 63A**) as well as from the site of the main palace itself.

The collection of pottery sherds (**Case 68**) illustrates the range of motifs and the styles of decoration in use at this time and seen on many pieces elsewhere in the room.

The work of stonecarvers is represented in vases and lamps, and (**Case 61**) in fragments of architectural decoration from the palace. Materials include antico rosso and porphyry (as for the pyramidal standard weight with relief decoration of an octopus in **Case 62**). Egyptian pieces from Knossós (in the same case) suggested datable contact between Crete and Egypt.

There are important exhibits of sealstones and sealings, and of Linear B tablets accidentally preserved by the heat of the catastrophic fire which finally destroyed the Knossós palace.

From Arkhánes there is a Minoan clay model of a house showing timber and stone construction. The house has a main room with a supporting pillar, small windows for insulation, a little court serving as a light-well, and a stepped ledge on the roof-terrace; there is also a pier-and-door partition arrangement (*polythýron*).

Case 70 contains miniature work with some exquisite examples of Minoan ivory carving. One stone fragment bears a relief of a captive bull.

Material of palatial quality is being introduced into the display from the harbour town of Póros-Katsambás, and its nearby tombs (18C–15C BC). There is jewellery of gold, semi-precious stones and faience, moulds for casting and the raw materials from a jewellery workshop. There is evidence (an air conduit and bellows) for a metal-working furnace, as well as fresco fragments and a selection of the finest pottery, ranging from Kamáres ware (from the tombs) to fine examples of the Neopalatial (LMIB) Marine Style.

Among free-standing exhibits a giant (unfinished) stone amphora in banded tufa with a decoration of shallow-relief spirals came from the Lapidary's Workshop in the palace. The large jars include a pithos from Galatás (the site of a newly discovered Minoan palace) and two examples (17C BC) from the sanctuary of Anemospília above Arkhánes. A jug from Póros-Katsambás has Marine-style decoration painted but (unusually) also in relief.

Room VI Neopalatial and Postpalatial cemeteries of Knossós, Arkhánes and Phaistós

The high quality of the grave gifts in this room contributes to an understanding of the wealth and splendour of the Knossós and Arkhánes region at this time, and the skills of the local artists and craftsmen. Much of the material displayed came from pre-1939 excavations of rich LMII–IIIA Knossós cemeteries down the Kaíratos river valley, and from tombs near the mouth of the Kaíratos at first inventoried under the place-name of Katsambás but now, after systematic investigation, recognised as an integral part of the harbour town (Póros-Katsambás).

Some of the artefacts provide evidence for contact with Egypt but weapons, helmets and other martial material, as well as quantities of bronze vessels and utensils, draw attention to the change of outlook associated with Mycenaean supremacy. Excavations of rich warrior graves in the Knossós North Cemetery (**Case 84**) and tholos tombs in the cemetery of Phourní at Arkhánes confirm this change.

Three clay models of cult scenes (**Case 71**) come from the tholos tomb at Kamilári, near Phaistós: a shrine shows two pairs of seated divinities (or revered dead) with worshippers placing offerings before them; the religious element of a banquet for the dead is emphasised by doves and horns of consecration, which also indicate a ritual setting for a ring of male dancers. A striking clay figurine in **Case 73** (from Knossós) has been interpreted as a goddess with child.

At **Phourní** in a side-chamber of Tholos Tomb A, a sealed larnax contained the burial of a young woman, princess or priestess (or perhaps both), with 140 pieces of gold jewellery among the offerings. From besdie the entrance to that side-chamber a ritual horse burial is shown exactly as it was found, the horse having been dismembered after the sacrifice.

The ribbon-handled gold cup with embossed decoration of double running spirals (**Case 77**) came from a tomb in the North Cemetery at Knossós. A remarkable ivory pyxis from Póros-Katsambás (**Case 79A**) is carved with a bull-catching scene strikingly similar to that on the famous gold cups from Vápheio in the Peloponnese, now in the National Archaeological Museum in Athens but long believed to be of Cretan workmanship.

In **Case 78** is a reconstructed boar's-tusk helmet of a type described by Homer. This came from the Zápher Papoúra cemetery but an amphora of LMII date from Póros-Katsambás, in **Case 82**, is decorated with four similar helmets. Also from Póros-Katsambás (in Case 82) is the important Egyptian alabaster vase with a cartouche of Tutmosis III (1504–1450 BC), the great king of the 18th Dynasty and (in **Case 80**) a Marine Style libation jug with stylised argonauts and spiked decoration.

Material from a Postpalatial (LMIII) cemetery in the south of the island, at Kalývia near Phaistós, is displayed in **Case 79**. Among the stone lamps and vases are an alabaster rhyton carved in the shape of a triton shell, and imported Egyptian 18th-Dynasty alabastra, as well as a faience amphora.

Jewellery and ivory toilet articles complete the display, with many of the finest achievements of the Cretan goldsmiths and ivory carvers. Outstanding (**Case 87**) are the gold ring from Isópata, engraved with an ecstatic dance of a goddess and worshippers on a flower-filled ground, and earrings in the shape of a bull's head, showing a masterly use of the technique of granulation. Phourní contributes jewellery and ivory carving of the highest quality, including the handle for a bronze mirror and a pyxis lid in ivory with figure-of-eight shield handles. A set of ivory plaques would have decorated a footstool.

Room VII Neopalatial settlements, sacred caves and cemeteries of central Crete

The bronze double axes on restored poles and painted bases came from the intriguing Neopalatial building at Nírou Kháni which contained quantities of cult objects such as painted plaster tripod tables and the stone horns of consecration exhibited here. The discovery of the three huge bronze cauldrons led to the excavation of the Týlissos site.

A superb selection of material from Ayía Triáda is dispersed around this room. Individually displayed and considered among the finest examples of the Minoan stonecarvers' art are three serpentine vases carved with relief scenes: the **Chieftain Cup** portrays a Minoan official receiving tribute of animal hides, and the much-restored **Boxer Rhyton** has scenes of boxing and wrestling matches, and of bull sports. The **Harvester Vase** with only the upper half is preserved has the shoulder carved with a procession of youths, the leader carrying a long rod, the rest pitchforks and scythes. They are accompanied by four singers; one, the sistrum player, is not wearing the customary tight belt. All three vases are believed to be products of a Knossós workshop.

Among finds from Nírou Kháni and Týlissos (**Case 89**) are bronze figurines of young male worshippers in the typical saluting position. One older man (from Týlissos) is portrayed (like the sistrum player) without the restriction of a tight belt.

The Ayía Triáda material includes (**Case 93**) figurines, pottery decorated with ritual motifs and an exhibit of carbonised beans, barley, millet and figs. **Case 102** displays stone artefacts including a vase in the shape of a seated monkey, a Hittite sphinx and a model of a boat. There are bronze tools and utensils in **Case 100**. A rare exhibit (in **Case 99**) is a hoard of raw material, a collection of copper 'talents' incised with signs, shown here with copper hammers. The unit of weight of these oxhide-shaped ingots is c 40kg, the same as similar talents from elsewhere around the Aegean Sea.

Figurines (human and animal) and other votive offerings from the Diktaian cave and various cave sanctuaries are shown in **Case 92**. The saluting figures are from Skoteinó. The miniature double axes of gold, silver and bronze (also in Case 100) came from a huge deposit of metalwork found in the sacred cave at Arkalokhóri in central Crete, as did the magnificent bronze swords in **Case 97**.

Case 101 displays exquisite gold and silver jewellery and miniature work from tombs across central and eastern Crete. Here is one of the great treasures of Minoan art, the **gold pendant** of Prepalatial (MMIA) date from the Khrysólakkos funerary precinct at Mália, consisting of two bees (or perhaps hornets) entwined over a honeycomb covered with granulation.

Room VIII The Minoan palace of Zákros

The material in this room, from the palace at Zákros in eastern Crete, dates almost entirely from the Neopalatial period (1700–1450 BC) and principally from the last (LMIB) phase before the palace's final destruction by fire. Two cases (108 and 110) contain artefacts found in the houses of the town overlooking the palace, and some of these pieces, for example Kamáres wares, are evidence for Old Palace period activity on the site. The palace ruins were never plundered so the exhibits that have been recovered illustrate particularly well the culture, and the wealth, of the Minoan civilisation.

Many of the museum collection's finest examples of pottery with marine and floral decoration, dating from the end of the Neopalatial period, are shown in this room. The two styles of decoration can be compared in **Case 106** which has rhytons (libation vessels) in conical and piriform shapes, also an elegant 'fruit-stand' with spiral and ivy-leaf decoration.

Case 104 displays unusual vessels believed to be for ritual use, one with plastic birds attached to it and others with figure-of-eight handles.

Case 113 has an elephant tusk from the palace storerooms (raw material, probably from Syria, for the ivory carvers), which was discoloured by burning in the great fire that destroyed the palace. The bronze talents in the shape of double axes were imported for the metalworkers from Cyprus. There are bronze utensils in **Case 105** and an incense burner with chased decoration of ivy leaves. **Case 112** displays a sword with gold rivets, and a ceremonial double axe with duplicated blades and decoration of stylised lilies. **Case 115** has large two-handled saws, inlay plates decorated with papyrus flowers, and a vase mounting (circular strip) with double axes.

A curiosity (in **Case 108**) is the conical cup containing olives, retrieved from one of the palace wells; the olives at first appeared perfectly preserved but shrivelled after only a few minutes of exposure to air.

An outstanding collection of stone vases includes the **Peak Sanctuary Rhyton** (**Case 111**), once covered in gold leaf, a superb piece of Minoan stone-carving that also provides valuable evidence for an understanding of Minoan cult practices. It depicts in relief a mountain shrine hallowed by the double axe, and with wild goats, birds and plants. The material is chlorite, turned brown in parts from the effects of fire. An exquisite **rock crystal rhyton** (**Case 109**) has a handle of crystal beads stained green by the bronze wire on which they are threaded. The museum's conservation staff restored this extraordinary work of art from more than 300 tiny fragments.

Case 116 displays a chlorite bull's head rhyton; it is smaller than the well-known one from the Little Palace at Knossós but of equally fine workmanship.

The stone vases from the unplundered **Treasury of the Shrine**, shown here in two cases (114 and 118), form the finest collection of such vessels yet known on Minoan Crete. In **Case 114** there are conical and fluted rhytons, among them one of *lapis Lacedaemonius*, a basalt imported from the only known source near Sparta. **Case 118** has a group of chalices that include examples in white-spotted obsidian, gabbro (an igneous rock) and in the banded polychrome limestones also used for an amphora with high curving handles. Thre are two Old Kingdom Egyptian vases in porphyritic rock, adapted for use by the Minoans by adding bridge-spout and bronze handles, and an 18th Dynasty imported alabastron. In the same case are three faience rhytons with animal heads.

Case 117 has miniature work from the palace and from houses in the town; there are ivory double axes and a butterfly discoloured by fire, also a faience rhyton in the shape of an argonaut.

Several large painted vases and five coarse-ware pithoi are free-standing exhibits. One of these, with an inscription in Linear A, including the sign for wine, comes from the country house just outside Ano Zákros; it was found beside a wine press now on display in the Siteía Museum.

Room IX Neopalatial settlements of eastern Crete (MMIII–LMI, c 1700–1450 BC)

The Palaíkastro material is to the right of the doorway. Stone vases and lamps are displayed, with a clay bull rhyton and bronze figurines. The pottery includes fine LMIB vases such as the octopus flask and a jug with papyrus decoration. There are an eight-vesseled *kérnos*, two feline heads in clay and fragments from a cup in rock crystal. The free-standing **Case 125** has rhytons in clay and stone and two stone libation tables.

Case 161 displays finds from the excavations on the Pýrgos hill at Mýrtos: clay and stone vessels and utensils, seals and a bronze dagger. A thin-walled vase with fluted rim which contains a cluster of miniatures of similar shape is unique.

The Gourniá material on the far side of the room (**Case 121**) has LMI pottery (including a Marine-style stirrup jar and an unusual double vase), a small bull's head rhyton and a bronze figurine. A free-standing case shows a collection of rhytons with a fluted stone example in antico rosso and several large limestone lamps.

Case 129 exhibits pottery from Mókhlos and bull rhytons and bronze vessels, including a cup with ivy-leaf decoration, closely similar in shape to gold cups from Vápheio in the Athens Archaeological Museum.

In **Case 122** (near the door) are high-quality clay and stone vases and lamps from the island of Pseíra. A basket vase is decorated with double axes.

The remaining wall case (**Case 123**) has clay votive figurines, both human and animal, from the peak sanctuary at Piskoképhalo near Siteía. The beetles climbing on the human figures are *Rhinoceros oryctes*.

The two remaining central cases exhibit seals and seal impressions from various sites across the island, together with small objects, notably ivories and inlays, from Palaíkastro and elsewhere in eastern Crete. This is a highly important collection of LM sealstones; the craftsmen used Cretan materials such as steatite but also semi-precious stones (often imported) such as agate, carnelian, chalcedony, the jaspers, *lapis Lacedaemonius*, lapis lazuli and rock crystal. The large vases around the room include burial pithoi from the cemetery in the sand of the Pakhyámmos beach near Gourniá.

Room X Postpalatial period (LMIII, 1400–1100 BC)

The decline of the Minoan culture is reflected in the remains exhibited here from the Postpalatial age. It is noticeable that vase-painting has lost its vitality and that fine carving in stone no longer occurs.

Popular pottery shapes are the tall-stemmed kylix, tankard, krater and stirrup vase. The earlier LM patterns, such as the octopus, have now become stylised, but there are still interesting bird motifs. Pottery in **Case 132** from the LMIII settlement at Palaíkastro includes a group of figures dancing round a musician playing the lyre. The conspicuous clay goddess figurines with raised arms came from a shrine at Gázi, on the western outskirts of Herákleion; the central figure has attracted attention for her head-dress of poppies.

Case 135 has figurines and other cult objects from the domestic shrine of the Minoan villa at Mitrópolis near Górtyn.

There are displays of grave gifts from individual chamber tombs in eastern Crete. In **Case 137** the imported glass bottle is from Amnisós and the limestone horns of consecration from Póros-Katsambás. **Case 138** contains terracotta objects including *psí* figurines and a goddess mounted on a horse.

The central cases exhibit some semi-precious jewellery (**Case 139**) together with stone moulds for ornaments. There are furnishings (**Cases 140 and 142**) from a number of LMIII shrines including from the Shrine of the Double Axes at Knossós. Among the large vases on display, one, a krater from Moulianá has the earliest Cretan rendering of a warrior on horseback. Clay figurines both animal and human, from various sanctuaries include (**Case 143**) the much-illustrated figure on a swing found at Ayía Triáda. **Case 144** has tools and weapons of all kinds in bronze, the main series coming from the two LMIIIC tombs at Moulianá.

Room XI Subminoan, Protogeometric and early Geometric period (1100–800 BC)

The cases on the right contain Protogeometric and Geometric material from sites in central and eastern Crete. The new pottery shapes and the decoration with geometric motifs indicate that changes were occurring on the island. During the Cretan Geometric period, burial rites altered from inhumation, the habit of the Minoans and still prevalent in LMIII, to the practice of cremation. This was then the rule until the end of the Late Orientalising period (c 630 BC), except in the east of Crete where the older tradition sometimes persisted. The ashes were buried in large clay jars or vases, occasionally in a bronze vessel; the most usual pottery shape eventually became the spherical pithos, though many variations occur and are well represented here and in the next room.

Among grave gifts buried with the dead were (**Case 145**) a *kérnos* in the form of a ring with human figures as well as receptacles (miniature amphorae) and a rhyton in the shape of a duck (one of several bird vases in this room each with individual character in conformation and plumage).

Two cases (**146 and 147**) exhibit finds from Vrókastro and Kavoúsi overlooking the Bay of Mirabéllo. Among the pottery are examples of the *kálathos* (openwork basket vases) and *hydria* (three-handled vessel for carrying water), one decorated with a chariot scene. There are interesting bronze figurines, one of them a model of a lyre-player.

Pottery and ritual objects, including model clay huts (**Case 154**), are from the refuge settlement flourishing at the end of the Bronze Age at Karphí above the Lasíthi mountain plain. The larger model of a house sanctuary came from a Protogeometric tomb in the Knossós North Cemetery; interesting features are the interior ledge, small high-set windows, chimney, ventilation holes, a flat roof with a course edged with stones and the painted decoration on walls and door.

From the Karphí shrine are the clay goddess idols with birds perched in their head-dresses conspicuous on the end wall (**Case 148**). The feet are made separately and fitted into the aperture in the cylindrical skirt. A peculiar rhyton is in the form of a charioteer drawn by bulls, of which only the heads are represented.

In **Case 149**, votive offerings from the cave sanctuary of Eileithyia, goddess of childbirth, (at Inatos, now Tsoútsouros, on the Libyan Sea) include clay figures embracing, some in coital positions, and women pregnant or giving birth. There are bull figurines and double axes preserving the Minoan tradition, and models of boats. From this site also (**Case 158**) are an ivory figurine of a naked goddess, faience goddesses, scarabs and jewellery.

A majestic lidded pithos (free-standing) is one of the grandest examples of the new cremation urns.

Four cases contain important vases from Protogeometric and Geometric tombs in the Knossós North Cemetery. Typical shapes (**Case 150**) include: several types of *oinochoe* (jug) including trefoil-mouthed juglets; the *hydria*; the *skyphos* and bell-*skyphos* (two-handled drinking vessels). The pithos shape is represented with and without a defined neck.

Two bell-kraters with figured scenes are in **Case 155**. On one is a deer hunt; on the other, two lions attacking a man, with the reverse side showing facing sphinxes, a water bird to the right; this vase had been used as a cinerary urn before the pithos shape became customary.

Case 156 contains an imposing pedestalled krater. **Case 157** exhibits a globular pithos between two belly-handled amphorae, elaborately decorated with zones of typical geometric motifs: rosettes and chequers, hatched meander and filled concentric circles.

Grave gifts from rich tombs at Siderospiliá near Priniás (**Case 151**) include clay figurines in the Daidalic style. The wheels shown beside the galloping horses indicate they were probably harnessed to a cart. The bronze bit from a bridle was found on the skull of a horse skeleton in a ritual burial in this cemetery.

Case 153 exhibits metalwork from various sites.

With the new skill in smelting at high temperatures, bronze was gradually replaced by iron for the manufacture of tools and weapons, though bronze continued in use for figurines, bowls and ornamented pieces such as shields. Iron objects of this age on Crete are rarely well-preserved.

Room XII Late Geometric and Orientalising periods (8C–7C BC)

Apart from the main display five cases are accommodated in this room, out of strict chronological sequence, containing finds, chiefly votice offerings (Minoan to Hellenistic in date) from the Sanctuary of Hermes Dendrites at Sýme, on the south slopes of Mount Díkte. A 3C AD inscription between two cases on the right-hand wall affirms the sanctuary's dedication.

The Minoan material from Sýme (**Case 160**) includes bronze figurines of worshippers, stone vases and small altars, one with a Linear A inscription. There are finds from the succeeding period of Mycenaean influence, and from the Early Iron Age, including a bronze figurine of a woman with spear and shield.

Case 161 contains votive offerings from the Archaic and Hellenistic periods, with a figurine of Hermes playing a lyre. The nearby exhibit of openwork bronze sheets contributes graphic details of the contemporary pilgrims at the sanctuary. There are terracotta figurines and plaques, and, among the bronzes, miniature votive shields, and also three Minoan swords, two of them ivory-handled.

The rest of this room shows the finest pieces from the museum's collection of the **Geometric and Orientalising** (early Archaic) **periods**. The material comes almost entirely from tombs, and in particular from the North Cemetery at Knossós and from the Arkádes cemetery near Aphráti in the Pediáda. There are majestic cremation urns as well as a great variety of gifts to accompany the dead, including examples of superb craftsmanship in jewellery and metalwork. Simple geometric patterns such as concentric circles continue in the decoration, but pictorial scenes are well represented. The Orientalising influence is conspicuous where cremation urns, with looped feet and elaborate lids, have the distinctive polychrome decoration of curvilinear patterns of lotuses, lilies, papyri and rosettes. The *aryballi* (small jars with narrow neck, **Case 162**) show Protocorinthian influence; Crete was in touch not only with the East, but with many parts of the Greek world.

A bell krater in **Case 159** has on one side facing wild goats, the Cretan *agrími*, and on the other a scene of boats. This vase, used for a cremation burial, came from a tomb of the Protogeometric period, which puts its pictorial decoration among the earliest known examples. The grave gifts in it included a faience ring. On another funerary urn a goddess with raised arms has a snake coiled around her.

Panels of birds occur in the painted decoration on urns and lids; in **Case 165** a smaller bird is shown carried on the parent's wing. Here too is an *olpe* (jug) with scale pattern and an animal frieze which includes griffins. The tail of a bird vase (**Case 166**) is in the form of a *hydria*. In **Case 167** are two *lekythoi*, vases with the elongated slender neck of the so-called Praisós type. The shoulder of an urn is painted with a pair of human figures.

Case 162 exhibits some of the most outstanding clay, bronze and faience objects from the same Knossós tombs. Exquisite small vases include a feeding bottle and a double flask. There are unusual models of birds and monkeys, a double horse and trees with birds perched in their branches. One lid has Zeus before a cauldron, with birds; in one hand he holds an eagle and in the other a thunderbolt.

Cases 163 and 168 contain material from the important cemetery of **Arkádes**. Straight-sided tub vases were favoured at this site for cremation burials. Floral and plant decorative motifs as well as figures with mythical associations such as sphinxes, griffins, winged horses and feline heads were influenced by eastern traditions. One vessel (in Case 168) is painted in added white with a bearded man controlling a long-legged horse, one of the early examples (mid-7C) of man and horse depicted together. On a similar vase is a winged male figure between two sphinxes. Orientalising influence is again reflected in a scene on a *situla* (bucket), where a goddess (the 'mistress of the animals') holds aloft a tree between two tall birds. On the lower shelf are two vessels, one bronze, the other clay, which still contain the charred bones buried in them; in each was a single grave gift, an *aryballos*.

The Arkádes material in Case 163 includes a lyre player, owl figurines, an anthropomorphic *hydria*, a crouching lion with a dish between its paws (said to be a clay imitation of eastern faience figures) and a cylindrical cremation vessel with a grieving woman as one of a pair of mourners. Especially notable is the *oinochoe* with, depicted on its neck, two figures interpreted (on slender evidence) as Theseus and Ariadne.

Two cases (**169 and 164**) display metalwork from the **Knossós cemetery**, and also from other sites such as the great cave sanctuary on **Mount Ida**. There are fragments of cast bronze which once decorated tripod cauldrons; one scene shows a couple in a boat propelled by oarsmen (perhaps also a reference to the abduction of Ariadne). A bronze quiver is embossed with sphinxes and a figure, in this case the 'master of the animals' between lions and fragments of body armour with a chariot. The bronze greaves (leg armour) are from Kavóusi. On a bronze girdle from Fortétsa (Case 164) three divinities in a sanctuary are protected from a chariot attack by a file of archers.

In the **central case** is a magnificent collection of **9C–7C jewellery**, much of it from a single tomb in the Knossós cemetery. This tholos tomb, originally constructed in the Bronze Age, was cleared for reuse under the new rites at the height of the Protogeometric period, and remained in use until early Orientalising times; the jewellery was found in two small plain Orientalising vases sunk into the ground just inside the tomb doorway. One gold pendant has crystal and amber inlays on a plaited gold chain with snake's head terminals. A second one is fashioned as a crescent ending in human heads and framing birds; the circular compartments (cloissons) on the crescent would have held inlays, and both they and the birds are delicately enhanced using the granulation technique. A gold band shows a hero subduing a lion, each panel impressed from the same matrix. The string-holes of a necklace of rock crystal beads are lined with gold, and two silver pins with gold bird heads are linked by a gold loop-in-loop chain. It has been proposed that the superb craftsmanship of this material points to a guild of metalworkers at Knossós whose origins lay in the Near East, and that this tomb may have been their family vault.

In this same case there are pieces of gold, silver and electrum. The near-uniformity of the gold bars looks deliberate, and they have been considered by some to be forerunners of Greek coinage, but they may have been the raw material for the goldsmiths in the form in which it was usually handled.

The huge relief pithoi between the doors range in date from Subminoan (nearest Room XI, from Priniás), to the Archaic period; the one with Orientalising motifs of sphinxes and leopard-headed spirals is from Lýttos, the others from Arkádes and Dréros.

Room XIII Minoan coffins

During the Bronze Age burials were often in clay chests or larnakes. Those displayed here (from various sites) are of two periods: there are MM tub-shaped examples, painted with abstract designs, and LMIII rectangular chests on four feet, often with gabled lids. The most common designs on these chests consist of octopuses or stylised flowers, but several here are more unusual; decorative elements include birds, fish, a boat (from Gázi), an animal suckling her young (Gourniá) and griffins with the sacred horns of consecration (Palaíkastro). Sometimes elliptical bathtubs with marine designs were used for burials, and examples can be seen with a plug-hole to let the water escape. From occasional remains of wood in tombs and the panelled form of the Postpalatial chests it is considered that this design was based on a wooden prototype.

In one corner of this room there is a burial, transported from a Postpalatial tomb at Sellópoulo, one of the cemeteries of Knossós. A second skeleton (complete with bronze finger ring) is from Phourní at Arkhánes.

A staircase leads to the museum's upper floor where the restorations of the Minoan frescoes are displayed.

Room XIV The Hall of the Frescoes

The Minoan frescoes are displayed in Rooms XIV, XV and XVI. Only fragments of the original wall-paintings remain, much restored after the collapse of walls and sometimes discoloured by the fires which destroyed the buildings they adorned. The scenes hint at aspects of the religious and secular life of the Minoans, now thought to revolve around the worship of the Minoan goddess. They illustrate the involvement of the Minoans with the natural world around them.

The artists used the true fresco technique: the paint was applied to the plaster while it was still wet, though in some cases the area of the picture seems to have been prepared by impressing with a tool or with taut string. Sometimes the plaster was moulded, before painting, into figures in low relief.

The surviving pieces are mostly from Knossós and Ayía Triáda, but there are also examples from Amnisós, Nírou Kháni, Pseira and Týlissos. The majority of them date from the Neopalatial period (mainly LMI). Some from Knossós are from the final period of presumed Mycenaean control, and the floor with marine scenes from the shrine at Ayía Triáda belongs to the Postpalatial period.

At the top of the stairs there is a fragment of a **Bull Fresco** (1) from the Upper Hall of the Double Axes at Knossós. Next comes the restoration of the **Procession Fresco** (2 to 5), with its best-preserved figure the Cup-Bearer, who

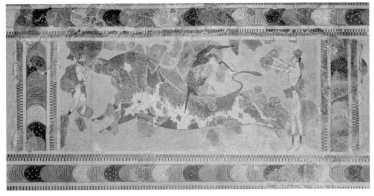

The Bull-leaper fresco from Knossós

wears a seal on his wrist; these frescoes decorated the walls of the long ceremonial approach from the West Court to the Central Court of the palace.

The **Fresco of the Griffins** (6) is from the palace Throne Room in its final phase. Next on this wall are scenes (18 to 24) recovered from Ayía Triáda: a kneeling female figure, perhaps picking flowers; a seated goddess beside a building that is identified as a shrine by the horns of consecration; a cat stalking a pheasant in a landscape of rocks and plants where the cat arches its back to spring but the pheasant struts about, not suspecting danger. A ritual procession (21) of figures bearing offerings and led by a musician playing a lyre is very similar to one that appears on the sarcophagus in the centre of the room and was probably painted by the same artist. A second procession (22) has women approaching a shrine, and in another fragment (23) a woman leads a deer towards an altar, presumably for sacrifice. At the end of the room is a **frescoed plaster floor** (24) from the LMIII shrine at Ayía Triáda. It consists of a colourful marine scene showing dolphins, an octopus and small fishes.

Exhibited here is an elaborate **model** of the palace of Knossós. The reconstruction greatly helps to illustrate the layout, especially in the West Wing (facing the museum staircase) with the Tripartite Shrine, and in the Hall of the Double Axes (King's Hall) at the bottom of the Grand Staircase in the East Wing.

Along the opposite wall, all except the last two frescoes are from Knossós. First there is the restored **Shield Fresco** (7) from the Hall of the Colonnades off the Grand Staircase; the markings on the shields represent the sewn animal hides from which shields were made. The rosette spirals are a clue to the LMII date of this work. Similar shield frescoes have been found in mainland Greece. Next comes the familiar figure known as the **Priest King** or Prince of the Lilies (8), wearing his plumed lily headdress and collar of fleurs-de-lis and leading an animal, perhaps a griffin, as shown on sealstones.

The remains of the **Charging Bull** (9) executed in stucco relief are from the portico above the North Entrance Passage. There follows the scene of the **Ladies in Blue** (10) from the East Wing of the palace and the fragments of a **Dolphin fresco** (11) found in the Queen's Hall. Two colourful **spiral friezes** (12 and 13) decorated wooden roof beams. Then (14) comes the frieze of **partridges and hoopoes** standing among coloured stones, from the Caravanserai on the south approach to the palace. Next is the much-illustrated scene known as the **Toreador Fresco** (15), the best-known representation of bull-leaping in Minoan art. Red is known to be the convention for male figures, white for female, and here both sexes are participating.

The last two frescoes on this wall are the decorative panels of graceful **lilies** (16) **and irises** (17) from the Neopalatial House of the Lilies at Amnisós. The lilies were separately modelled in white plaster.

At this end of the room there is a scale model of the Little Palace at Knossós. A nearby case contains fresco fragments, from Knossós, reconstructing a scene entitled **The fountain**.

The Ayía Triáda sarcophagus

The prominently displayed stone sarcophagus found in a Postpalatial context at Ayía Triáda is carved from a single block of limestone, covered with a layer of plaster and painted (as with the wall-paintings) while the plaster was still damp. Both long sides portray funeral ceremonies: the one with processions of figures bearing offerings consists of two scenes, distinguished by background colour and

The Ayía Triáda painted sarcophagus

the direction in which the figures are facing. On the left the female figure pouring the contents of a vase into a krater is conducting a purification rite for the deceased. The sacred surroundings are symbolised by double axes with birds perching on them. On the right the procession conveys gifts, including a model boat, towards a figure in front of a richly decorated building. This figure used to be interpreted as the spirit or personification of the deceased in front of his tomb. However, considering the similarity between the long robe and the kilts in the procession, it is now thought more likely to represent a priest in charge of the rite.

On the other side, female figures are officiating at the sacrifice of a trussed bull, to an accompaniment on a flute. Ritual significance is seen again in the double axe with a bird, the tree and the altar with sacral horns.

On the ends of the coffin are shown a procession (not well preserved) and chariots driven by pairs of females and drawn by horses and griffins.

Room XV

All of these frescoes are from Knossós except where otherwise stated.

In Room XV are panels of the **Miniature Frescoes** found on the upper floor of the palace's West Wing; in the first panel (25), crowds of spectators, both men and women, attend some ceremony, including a dance, while another part of the composition (26) is the best illustration yet known of a tripartite shrine (aiding the reconstruction of those identified at Knossós and Vathýpetro); the columns display the sacred symbol of the double axe. The central case contains a fragment of a miniature fresco from Týlissos. Also here is a diagrammatic representation of a labyrinth, from Knossós, a motif common at a later date on that city's coins.

On the wall is the well-known panel (27) named by Evans's workmen **La Parisienne**; the neckline of her garment is finished with the symbolic sacral knot. Beside her (28) are the fragments of the **Camp Stool** or **Libation Fresco** with priests and priestesses seated on stools holding chalices and goblets. La Parisienne may have been associated with this group though she is on a larger scale.

The **Spiral Cornice Relief** was a ceiling decoration. The relief fragments (numbered 6–8) of athletic games, and the two griffins tied to a column tail to tail seem to have been part of a frieze from the East Hall of antithitically placed pairs of animals in high relief. It is now recognised that this hall beside the Grand Staircase was an important shrine area of the palace at Knossós.

Room XVI

Again, all of the pieces are from **Knossós** except where otherwise stated.

A central case has scraps of the **Palanquin Fresco** with a figure carried in a litter and another bull-leaping scene. In the corner left of the entrance from the main hall is the original restoration of the **Saffron-Gatherer Fresco** done when the main figure collecting saffron flowers was thought to be a boy. Later it was reinterpreted as a blue monkey, as shown in the adjacent revised version.

Next is the often illustrated **Captain of the Blacks** (33), found near the LMI House of the Frescoes along the Royal Road. A Minoan officer with two spears leads a troop of black soldiers, perhaps Nubian mercenaries. A **Dancing Girl** comes from the Queen's Hall in the East Wing, a fragment of a tri-columnar shrine from the West Magazines of the palace and scenes of **olive trees** in relief from the North Entrance Passage.

Opposite are three panels from the House of the Frescoes, some of the finest examples of the Minoans' involvement with nature. First is the fresco of the **Blue Bird** (38), similar to a roller. Next are two panels of monkeys perhaps looking for eggs among crocuses, ivy, irises and other wild flowers.

Finally, from houses on the island of Pseíra in eastern Crete, there are two wall-paintings using stucco relief, of a scene of women or goddesses, elaborately attired. The so-called sacral knot, understood as a religious symbol, came from Nírou Kháni.

Rooms XVII and XVIII

This area used to house a private collection given to the museum in its early days (the Giamalákis collection) and antiquities from the Archaic, Classical, Hellenistic and Roman city-states of the island. Nowadays the rooms are used for temporary exhibitions. It is hoped that in an enlarged museum the original exhibits will be on show again.

The staircase behind the model of the palace in Room XIV leads down to the ground floor near the bookstall.

Room XIX Archaic sculptures and bronzes (700–550 BC)

This room opposite the foot of the stairs may be locked but often one of the guardians in the hall will open it. Above the entrance there is a 7C Gorgoneion from Dréros. In pride of place in the centre of the room, from the sanctuary of Apollo Delphinios at Dréros, are **three bronze statuettes** (7C BC) made by the *sphyrelaton* techinique (the sheet bronze hammered on a wooden core and then pinned); they are believed to represent Apollo with his sister, Artemis, and his mother, Leto.

Nearby are the remarkable **bronze shields** from the Idaian cave, which have lion's head bosses and repoussé decoration of battle and hunting scenes, with an eagle gripping a sphinx. A bronze cymbal, also from the Idaian cave, shows Zeus between two Kourétes; in the myth they protected him as a baby from his father, Cronus, by clashing cymbals, or swords against shields, to hide the sound of his crying. The superb workmanship is attributed to craftsmen from the East who may have settled on Crete. Other shields are from Palaíkastro and Arkádes (modern

Aphráti). The clay crouching lion (c 600 BC) is from Praisós.

In the corner to the left of the entrance door a lion's head in poros (a quartz-rich sandstone) came from Phaistós. On the left wall are examples of the Daidalic style of sculpture: the remains of a seated goddess and two large reliefs of three deities which were recovered from the Archaic temple on the acropolis of Górtyn.

The frieze of horsemen high up on the left wall is a part of the important sculpture which decorated one of the two mid-7C temples at Priniás (ancient Rizenía). Seated goddesses from the doorway into the cella of one of the Priniás temples here frame the doorway to Room XX; their thrones are placed over a frieze of lions and deer, suggesting that the divinity may be the Cretan Britomartis (Artemis).

Two grave steles, of a warrior and a woman spinning, are also from Priniás. An eagle and a hawk, of poros, on pedestals with Ionic volutes came from the sanctuary of Zeus Thénatas at Amnisós, and, also of poros, the torso of an Archaic *kouros* from Eléftherna.

To the right from the entrance door are large Archaic period pithoi from Phaistós, decorated in relief. A terracotta *sima*, or waterspout, showing a stylised chariot scene with a running dog is one of the few remaining traces of the 6C temple of Diktaian Zeus at Palaíkastro. A stele from Palaíkastro, carved in Roman times, preserves an inscription from the Archaic Hymn to Diktaian Zeus.

Room XX Classical, Hellenistic and Roman sculpture

Almost all the exhibits date from the Late Hellenistic period and the succeeding centuries (1C BC–4C AD) when Crete was part of the Roman Empire; they include good copies of Classical works. Much of the material is likely to appeal only to specialists. The numbering of the pieces (see below) helps with idenitification but satisfactory labelling has to wait unitl the new mounting of the collections gathers pace. In the meantime by far the most detailed listing is to be found in the museum catalogue by A. Vasilakis.

The principal behind the arrangement is that material from the region of Knossós and ancient Herákleion is shown to the left of the room as you enter. Exhibits from Górtyn, capital of Roman Crete, are on the far wall and nearby in that part of the room. This leaves the right-hand side for sculpture retrieved from other Greco-Roman city-states. Along the wall either side of the doorway are various relief carvings including grave steles, some dating back to the 5C BC.

From Knossós (to the left of the entrance) came the portrait head of Homer (220) and two statues of Dionysos (46 and 315). There are two doorways of a house in the Classical style, one with lion's mask mouldings. The 2C AD mosaic floor near the centre of the room, also from Knossós, is by an artist named Apollinaris (see inscription). Poseidon is drawn by sea horses, accompanied by tritons and dolphins.

The sarcophagus inscribed 'polybus' (8), found in Herákleion and tentatively dated to 1C AD, depicts a flute player and an orator who harangues the dead; the basket below an offering table is a symbol associated with the Eleusinian mysteries.

The colossal statue of Hadrian (5) with decorated corselet showing the she-wolf suckling Romulus and Remus and two Victories crowning Roma is from Górtyn. A bearded philosopher (1) has books at his feet. On the far wall the statues from Górtyn are mainly Roman copies of earlier works; by the pillar is a 2C AD copy (347) of the Athena Parthenos of Pheidias, the cult statue of the Parthenon.

Among the cult statues from the temples at Górtyn are Apollo Kitharoidos (326) from the Temple of Apollo Pythios, and from the Temple of Isis and Serapis the group of Egyptian deities (259 and 260), Isis, Serapis, Certberus and Hermes Anubis. The goddess Aphrodite with a bowl (154) came from the Górtyn Nymphaion.

There are numerous portraits of Roman Emperors and their families, brought from Górtyn, and also, mostly shown on the right side of the room, from many other Cretan city-states. The Attic sarcophagus (317) found at Mália is dated to the 2C AD.

Among the relief carvings to the right of the entrance are two early pieces: a temple metope (363), late 5C BC from Knossós with a labour of Hercules, who brings the Erymanthian boar to the terrified King Eurystheus taking refuge in a large jar, and an Attic 4C BC funeral stele (145) showing a hunter, a notable piece from Ayía Pelayía (ancient Apollonia), west of Herákleion.

The Historical Museum

The Historical Museum has a well deserved reputation both for its work in preserving the evidence of Crete's past, and as a progressive institution admired throughout Greece. A visit is strongly recommended to readers interested in the history of Herákleion as well as the evolution of modern Crete.

• Leoph. Soph. Venizélou, on the seafront five minutes' west of the Venetian harbour, beyond the imposing ruins of the Venetian cathedral of Ayios Pétros.
    Open April–Nov Mon–Fri 09.00–17.00, Sat 09.00–14.00, closed Sun and public holidays; ☎ 2810 283219, www.historical-museum.gr. There are books and postcards for sale. The labelling and wall information panels are in English as well as Greek.

The museum was opened in 1953 in the spacious Neo-classical family house of Andréas L. Kalokairinós, a notable benefactor of Herákleion. Restored in 1903, the building was originally entered on its inland side through a hall decorated with Doric columns and friezes of scenes from the *Iliad* and the *Odyssey* (still in situ). With the help of the Kalokairinós bequest, a collection of major importance was built up by the Society for Cretan Historical Studies. To increase the exhibition space, a wing was added at the west side of the house in similar Neo-classical style. In 1991 the passage linking the original building and the wing was transformed into a bridge on two levels executed in glass and aluminium designed by the Cretan architect J. Pertselákis. In 1996 further construction in the same materials and designed by the same architect provided additional rooms and an elegant new entrance hall with frontage on the main coast road.

Kalokairinós room

On the right of the entrance a permanent exhibition commemorating the original founder of the museum provides an invaluable introduction to the history of Crete from the First Byzantine period (AD 330) to the island's integration into modern Greece. The exhibition is organised chronologically. It describes the changing patterns of power in the eastern Mediterranean and how, at each successive period, these changes affected intellectual, religious and practical aspects of life on the island. It emphasises Crete's pivotal role in preserving the artistic and intellectual traditions of a waning Byzantine empire and revitalising them through contact with Venice and the values of the western Renaissance.

The story of the 21-year siege of Herákleion (1645–69), treated today as one episode of the Cretan war, is particularly well covered, and is set in the perspective of the European powers who, even if hesitantly and too late, felt it their duty to send aid to this last outpost of Christendom in the eastern Mediterranean. The commentary makes the point that this was perhaps the first time in the history of European politics that rulers tried to collaborate against a common enemy.

The exhibition is supplemented by a large (4m x 4m) model of 17C Candia (Herákleion), with spotlights on locations referred to in the information panels.

Ceramics room

Across the hall another permanent exhibition is devoted to the history of ceramics on the island. The displays, dating from the Roman to the Ottoman periods, allow comparison between contemporary wares, some local and some imported.

The sculpture collection

Take the stairs down from the new entrance. Over the years the Society for Cretan Historical Studies has rescued a random collection of architectural and art historical remains (sculpture, inscriptions, dedications and epitaphs, coats of arms and elements of ruined monasteries, churches and secular buildings). These pieces form a record of Crete's heritage from the Byzantine and Venetian periods. They are the more to be valued on account of their scarcity, the result of an unremitting history of conquest, revolt and attendant destruction.

The new display selects rigorously so that (with the help of background text in English) chosen pieces build up a picture of various aspects of the social history of Herákleion, for example the role of hierarchy or the existence of ethnic diversity. In short this is a superb teaching exhibition.

Exhibits include an elegant double doorway from the Latin monastery of St Francis, a tall tiered fountain from a Venetian palazzo in the city, a marble medallion carved in high relief from the St George's Gate in the ramparts, and an analysis of the three main types of representation of the Lion of St Mark.

The old ground floor

Upstairs, at ground level in the original house, a small room has been airconditioned to house a painting by El Greco.

El Greco

Born Doménico Theotokópoulos (1541–1614) in or near Herákleion, he served his apprenticeship in an artistic community rooted in the Byzantine traditions of the Cretan School of icon painting. He was already recognised as a master painter in Cretan documents of 1566. He left the island to study in Venice in 1569. There he came under the influence of Titian and Tintoretto. He was in Rome for several years before he moved to Spain in 1576, to Toledo, where he lived and worked for the rest of his life.

The painting hung here, *Mount Sinai and the monastery of St Catherine*, is believed to date to c 1570. The monastery, one of the most symbolic and influential Byzantine religious institutions, lay at the foot of the sacred mountain where according to the Old Testament Moses received the tablets with the Law of the Prophets. The Sinaite monks were in contact with Crete and at least by the mid-16C had established a dependency in Herákleion.

The work is not thought to be painted from life; it is likely that the artist was familiar with one of many engravings available to him in Italy at that time. The painting, in tempera and oil on wood, is unsigned, but an article on the wall opposite where it hangs deals with its provenance, building a case through the well-authenticated El Greco triptych in Modena.

Next door to the El Greco room a reconstruction of a typical single-aisled and vaulted Byzantine chapel has been lined with 14C frescoes, rescued from a church destroyed during the German occupation (1941–44); they are said to be good examples of the style of the Macedonian School, a major influence on the Cretan fresco painters.

Two cannons standing in the original hall are from Venetian galleys sunk in Herákleion harbour during the great siege. The hall is hung with a collection of 17C maps and views of the island's cities, fortresses and harbours. The coloured engravings are by Marco Boschini (an official Venetian cartographer) published under the title *Il regno tutto di Candia* (Venice, 1651).

Medieval and Renaissance collection

On the far side of the hall a double room is devoted to material which complements the exhibits (architectural fragments, sculpture, inscriptions) already encountered on the lower floor. The earliest items, dating back to the First Byzantine or Early Christian period, before the Arab invasion, are in the cases in the smaller of the two areas at the far end of the room; the ecclesiastical valuables include pieces from the 6C basilica of Ayios Títos at Górtyn.

The display in both areas is dominated by works from the Historical Society's collection of portable icons, many rescued from destroyed or disused Byzantine churches. To the left of the entrance one group of icons consists of examples painted in the style of the Cretan school, with the modelling of flesh achieved with dense highlights on dark brown underpaint. Painted sanctuary doors and part of a carved wooden iconostasis (late 16C) are from the church of the Panayía Gouverniótissa at Potamiés on the road up to Lasíthi.

Further down the room a carved wooden lectern and a 17C ecclesiastical throne came from the former monastery church of Valsamóneros on the south slopes of Mount Ida. Richly embroidered vestments (17C and 18C) belonged to the former Asómatos monastery in the Amári valley. Pottery, gold and bronze coins, and elaborate Byzantine and Venetian jewellery complete the exhibits in this room.

Other portable icons held here for security include a magnificent **Virgin as Fountain of Life** (1655) from Savathianá, now a nunnery in the district of Malevísi. An interesting comparison is offered because the same theme is treated in an icon painted for the former Armenian church of Candia.

The Struggle for Independence

In the room across the hall is the collection of material, chiefly from the time under Turkish rule (17C–19C), entitled the Struggle for Independence. Exhibits range from Venetian armour to memorabilia of the Independent Cretan State (1898–1913) under two successive high commissioners for the Great Powers (Britain, France, Italy and Russia), first Prince George of Greece up to 1906 and then Alexander Zaïmis. (When the Mouréllos photographic archive is on display it covers this same brief period of autonomy. See also the stamp collection in the Tsouderós room upstairs.)

Left of the doorway, documents from the Turkish period include *firmans* relating to the position of the Christian church at that time; one is illustrated with a view of the Mount Sinai Monastery of St Catherine (the subject of the El Greco painting, see above). Beside this is a satirical interpretation of Turkish rule over Crete.

On the theme of the long and proud struggle for independence from foreign rule, there are portraits of the Cretan chieftains and a lithograph of the leaders of ten revolts between 1770 and 1897, also a fine collection of their intimidating weapons. The tattered 1912 banner of a chieftain from Argyroúpolis (in the hills behind Réthymnon) proclaims the slogan of the struggle: 'Freedom or death'. Contemporary cuttings from foreign newspapers emphasise the support from abroad for the Cretan national cause. There is a case of commemorative china.

One section is devoted to Elefthérios Venizélos (1864–1936) who became an internationally respected statesman and served on a number of occasions as prime minister in Athens.

The glass extension forming a bridge to the museum's west wing provides display areas on two levels. Across the bridge on the upper level the passage walls are lined with evocative photographs taken during the Battle of Crete (1941).

Kazantzákis room

On the left a room is furnished as the study of the Cretan-born author Níkos Kazantzákis (1883–1957), with desk, library and other personal possessions from his home on the island of Aígina. Paintings and engravings inspired by his books are hung nearby. Katzantzákis has his own museum at Myrtiá, not far from Herákleion. Kazantzákis died in Germany in 1957. In line with his somewhat unconventional views was his request for burial on the Martinengo Bastion of the Herákleion city walls.

Tsouderós room

A dais is furnished as the study of the Cretan statesman Emmanuel Tsouderós, a native of Réthymnon, who became prime minister of Greece on 18 April 1941, after the German invasion of Macedonia and only days before the evacuation of the Allied forces from the Greek mainland to Crete. Faced with the imminent occupation of Athens by the Germans, King George II and his government under Tsouderós left on 23 April for Crete, the only remaining free territory in Greece. Examples of the Historical Society's collection of rare maps are hung at the entrance to the room.

Folk arts

The top floor houses an important collection of Cretan folk art, including exceptionally fine textiles and needlework of all types, as well as traditional Cretan costume, jewellery, musical instruments and furniture such as dowry chests. A reconstruction of a house interior of c 1900 concludes the exhibition.

Icon Collection of the Orthodox Church on Crete

- Open Mon–Sat 09.30–13.00, and Tues, Thurs, Sat 17.00–19.00 (winter 16.00–18.00). Closed Sun and public holidays.

The Orthodox Church on Crete houses some of its collection of icons, old manuscripts and other valuables in the former monastic church of Ayía Aikateríni of Sinai, which is across the plateía on the north side of the cathedral of Ayios

Minás. You can find Plateía Ayía Aikateríni and the churches from Leoph. Kalokairinoú (running out from the centre to the Khaniá Gate), or from Plateía Kornárou at the top of the market, or by cutting through from halfway up the market using Odós Odiyítrias.

The church of Ayía Aikateríni dates from 1555, with 17C alterations. The foundation was a dependency of the great monastery of the same name on Mount Sinai, and in the 16C and 17C its college here became a famous centre of the arts and learning, and played an important part in preserving and disseminating Byzantine culture after the fall of Constantinople. Only one church in Herákleion still remains in the monastery's possession, Ayios Matthéos of the Sinaites, five minutes away from the plateía of Ayía Aikateríni, which also contains important icons (see below).

Icon painting and Mikhaíl Damaskinós

The first portable icons documented on Crete (1025) were brought to the island from Constantinople, the Byzantine capital. There is evidence of artists travelling in both directions between Crete and Constantinople before it fell to the Turks in 1453, but it is after this date that Crete's particular political and social circumstances (as a fervently Orthodox community within the Venetian Empire) gave the island a special importance in the field of icon painting.

The painters working on Crete at this time inherited the iconographical traditions and strict conservative technique of the style that was revived under the Palaiologan emperors (1261–1453), the last Christian rulers of Constantinople. However, the Venetian regime on Crete facilitated contact with the considerable Greek community in Venice, and the Cretan painters were therefore open to the influence of the art of Renaissance Italy.

Production on the island is known to have been organised in workshops staffed by large numbers of apprentices, and there are records of substantial orders to satisfy demand from western Europe as well as from the remaining Hellenic world. There was also a demand at this time from Catholic customers for icons painted on Crete in the Latin style. The versatility of the Cretan icon painters of the 15C and 16C is conspicuous.

Only a small proportion of the icons of this period have survived, and few remain on Crete. It was not customary for artists to sign their work, but one who did so was Mikhaíl Damaskinós. Many of his icons show the conservative Byzantine traditions of iconography enriched, within the limits of religious painting, by influences from Renaissance art .

Damaskinós (active 1555–91, an older contemporary of El Greco is recognised as one of the major icon painters of the period. He studied at Ayía Aikateríni and then, like so many other Cretan artists at that time, sought employment abroad. He worked in Venice 1577–82 where he is known to have been involved in the decoration of San Giorgio dei Greci. He was responsible for the fresco decoration of the apse, and the individual panels on the tier of the iconostasis where according to the conventions icons portrayed the 12 great festivals of the church.

Today the art of Damaskinós is widely dispersed but six major works can be seen here in the Ayía Aikateríni collection. These icons are paintings of his mature period (late 16C) after his return from Venice. They were held in the Vrondísi monastery on the south slopes of Mount Ida until 1800, and then brought for safety to the old Ayios Minás church in Herákleion. Now they are displayed on the south wall of the Ayía Aikateríni nave. From left to right as you look at them they are as follows.

The First Ecumenical Council held at Nicaea in AD 325, at which the Emperor Constantine conferred with his bishops to settle the Aryan controversy. This work was painted in 1591.

The Divine Liturgy, with Christ celebrating Mass in the midst of the encircling hosts of angels.

The Virgin and the Burning Bush, showing Moses on Mount Horeb, and the bush which burned but was not consumed, a symbol of the virginity of the Mother of God.

'Noli me tangere', where Christ appears to the Holy Women.

The Last Supper.

The Adoration of the Magi, the work said to show most clearly the influence of western art.

You will notice a **Christ Pantokrátor** (17C), and on the north wall the ***Ayios Phanoúrios*** icon is the early 15C work of the admired artist Angelos. At the east end of the cruciform church a variety of religious art of high quality is on display, including an illustrated *Gospel* from the monastery of Epanosíphis and other manuscripts, sacred relics, furnishings, eight icons from the screen of the monastic church of Kerá Kardiótissa on the way up to Lasíthi, with behind them a beautiful miniature version of the *Birth of Christ* (late 16C). There are sanctuary doors from Arkhánes and fragmentary 13C and 14C wall-paintings rescued from abandoned chapels.

In the church of **Ayios Matthéos**, five minutes' walk from Plateía Ayía Aikateríni (sometimes open mornings only) are two more icons now fairly confidently attributed to Damaskinós. Check access with the guardian at Ayía Aikateríni.

If you start from the big paved space outside the west door of the cathedral, and cross the busy road, a short street (at an angle left) opens into Taxiárkhou Markopoúlou; the church is halfway along that street on the right.

The two narrow panels by Damaskinós are *Ayios Symeós Theodókhos* (Receiver of God), *St Simeon with the Christ Child*, which conveys the message of the Presentation in the Temple, and *Ayios Ioánnis Prodrómos* (the Baptist). In this latter work the wings are an innovative feature, and the scene lacks the traditional severed head at the saint's feet, but otherwise he is portrayed in the iconographical tradition of the Palaiologan style, wearing a sheepskin, and with one hand raised in the act of blessing, the other holding an open scroll.

Museum of Natural History of the University of Crete

- Knossou 157. ☎ 2810 324711. Open 09.00–19.00 daily during the main summer months (out of season you can check by telephone and hope at least for the morning hours).

This collection has been built up over a period of 20 years by the University of Crete, but the exhibition was only opened to the public in 1998.

The museum is scheduled to move to a purpose-built complex in Herákleion, near the Historical Museum, but in the meantime it is housed in a former school building in the suburb of Ayios Ioánnis along the road out to Knossós. The site is less than 1km after the bridge carrying the north coast highway over the road; watch for signs on the left.

The collection is presented in two separate areas: the first occupying the ground floor of the main building as you go in, and the second on the upstairs floor in an annexe across the garden at the rear. To reach it go past the bookstall, through a pleasant café and across the attractive botanical garden which incorporates a serious study collection.

The displays are explained by informative text (translated into English) with the aim of raising public awareness of the natural environment of Crete and its diversity. The various cases cover the wildlife and vegetation of the mountains, of forest and shrubland, of the micro-environment of gorges and caves, of the wetlands and the coast. Particular attention is paid to species that are endemic to Crete, and also to those that are threatened or in need of protection, such as the wild goat, loggerhead turtles and bearded vultures. The ornithology section stresses the importance of the island to birds on migration, and the exhibit of birds of prey is outstanding.

The upper floor across the garden provides an introduction to the geology of Crete in the context of the southeastern Mediterranean area, with special reference to the history of earthquakes in the region.

A main theme running through the whole exhibition is the interdependence of nature and the activities of mankind, and appropriately one ambitious display is given over to the Minoans in their Bronze Age environment.

The university department plays an important part in all aspects of environmental conservation, and is involved in LIFE programmes under the auspices of the European Union. You can be confident that you will find information in this museum on any current project.

Knossós

The Minoan palace at Knossós lies 5km south of the centre of Herákleion.

- Open daily 08.00–19.00 mid-June to mid-September, closing one or two hours earlier outside the high season, and in winter 10.00–15.00. To check opening times ☎ 2810 231940 or enquire at any tourist information office. There is good wheelchair access. The site attracts huge numbers of visitors but tour groups are usually less in evidence late in the day. Knossós online: www.bsa. gla.ac.uk/knossos

  At present admission is only to the palace site and the Minoan town house excavations in the immediate vicinity (see area plan on p 105). Outside the site fence all the main dependent buildings, the Little Palace, the Royal Villa, the Caravanserai and the Temple Tomb are closed to the public. However, a project for an archaeological park on the western side of the main road from Herákleion is in an advanced stage of planning.

Travelling by bus

Town bus no. 2 leaves its Herákleion terminus near the harbour every 15 minutes with a convenient stop in the city centre at Plateía Venizélou. The journey time is about 30 minutes, with the palace at the end of the line. The return route runs through Plateía Eleftherías, passing the Archaeological Museum.

By car from Herákleion, leave Plateía Eleftheriás along the dual-carriageway, Leoph. Dimokratiás, which outside the centre of the city becomes Odós Knossoú. From the New National Road use the exit at the junction (with traffic lights) at the eastern end of the bypass, following signs down a short one-way system to join the same road. After undistinguished suburbs you pass, c 4km from the city centre, a turning to Fortétsa and opposite it the Venizéleion hospital. From the later phases of the Minoan period until Early Christian times this was an important cemetery area (now known as the Knossós North Cemetery).

Once across the stream-bed beyond the hospital the road enters the settlement area which spread out around the Knossós palace in the Bronze Age. In later times the Roman city had its centre here but almost nothing remains above ground. Where the stone wall begins, right, the Hadrianic **Villa Dionysos** (first investigated in the mid-1930s and excavated in 1971) is undergoing a major programme of conservation to prepare the site for opening to the public. This peristyle building took its name from the subjects portrayed on its high-quality 2C mosaic pavement floors. The polychrome mosaics are said to be among the finest on the island and the equal of contemporary work anywhere across the Roman Empire. They depict the god and his circle of followers framed in elaborate geometric designs with motifs appropriate to the Dionysiac cult. Amphorae and lamps with erotic decoration were recovered, as well as fragments of wall plaster painted with scenes of women and satyrs.

Further along the roadside wall a private driveway leads to the Villa Ariadne, built by Sir Arthur Evans in 1906 as his dig-house on a hillside overlooking the site of the palace and the great dependent buildings that he was uncovering. Between 1926 and 1955 the house belonged to the British School at Athens and then (in a rearrangement of responsibility for the whole archaeological area) it became the property of the Greek government. It sheltered King Paul of the Hellenes for a brief period after the evacuation of mainland Greece in 1941, and during the German occupation it was the residence of the military commandant. The final surrender of German forces on the island took place in May 1945.

Now cafés and tavernas, souvenir shops, coaches and car parks (both official and unofficial) mark the approach to Knossós.

Mythology

In classical Greek mythology Knossós was the home of King Minos, one of the three offspring of Zeus and Europa; his wife was Passiphaë, daughter of the nymph Crete. Central to the story was the Minotaur (half man, half bull), the monstrous result of Passiphaë's infatuation with a white bull sent by the god Poseidon. According to legend the Minotaur was incarcerated in the labyrinth built for Minos by his architect Daidalos, and at regular intervals seven youths and seven maidens, tribute owed to Minos from Athens, were sent to Crete to be sacrificed to the monster. Eventually Theseus, son of the Athenian king Aegeus, determined to destroy the Minotaur and volunteered as one of the seven youths. Minos's daughter Ariadne fell passionately in love with Theseus. She gave him a sword and a ball of woollen thread to unwind so that, after killing the Minotaur, he was able to retrace his steps out of the labyrinth. The lovers sailed triumphantly from Crete, departing from the harbour of Knossós, but Theseus soon abandoned Ariadne on the island of Náxos. His punishment was swift. On his return to Athens he neglected to hoist the prearranged signal of success, a white sail, and his father watching from the cliffs threw himself into the sea in despair. Thus the Aegean Sea got its name.

History of the Knossós area

There was a Neolithic village on a low hill known as Kephála in the valley of the Kaíratos river as early as 7000 BC. Although the first phase of habitation predated the use of pottery, the settlers built with mud bricks and practised mixed farming. Fired pots soon appeared in the record, as did houses with stone foundations. By the Late Neolithic period the settlement covered 5 hectares and occupation debris had accumulated so that at the beginning of the Bronze Age, c 3500 BC, the Neolithic strata were up to 7m deep. From the Late Neolithic material came a copper axe, one of the earliest metal objects known from Crete.

Through the third millennium BC, the Early Minoan period (Chronology, p 38), the Prepalatial settlement expanded and buildings became more substantial. Prosperity and links with the world outside Crete are demonstrated by the artefacts from the Greek mainland, the Cyclades and the Levant on display in the first room of the Herákleion Archaeological Museum.

The cemeteries for the Knossós settlement lay on the surrounding hillsides. The earliest known Minoan tomb (dated to Middle Minoan IA) was discovered on the height to the west known as the Acropolis hill. By the end of this Prepalatial period traces of a monumental building in a northwest area of the settlement (near the later Throne Room) may indicate a predecessor of the known palaces. The first of these two palaces (the Old Palace in Knossós terminology) was built in Middle Minoan IB, soon after the beginning of the second millennium. A Central Court was the focus of the Old Palace and rooms on the west side opened on to it. Outside the palace a West Court was laid out, on a terrrace over houses of the Prepalatial period. On the east side of the palace a great cutting into the slope of the hill had within it rooms that were later remodelled into the Domestic Quarter. Other building included storerooms, some containing giant pithoi, on both west and east sides of the main court; the so-called Royal Pottery Stores held fine Kamáres wares. Already the rapidly increasing Minoan prosperity depended on sufficient storage space for the redistribution of commodoties, and tablets with signs in the hieroglyphic script suggested a system of administration.

Cemeteries of this Old Palace (Protopalatial) period have been excavated on the Aílias ridge across the river, around the Mávro Spélia cave, and on the hill of Gypsádes to the south, where a tholos tomb was found.

The Old Palace was destroyed by fire at the end of Middle Minoan II (c 1700 BC). The palace was rebuilt almost immediately during the following period (MMII) but this New Palace then suffered damage by earthquake, a frequent phenomenon throughout Cretan history. Evidence of the severity of the destruction on this occasion is preserved where elements of the South Front remain displaced in the House of the Fallen Blocks. The damage necessitated rebuilding and restoration, and this second phase of the New Palace forms the basis (in part reconstructed in the 20C) of the remains visible today.

During what came to be known as the Neopalatial period the town of Knossós expanded greatly, to the north and west of the palace. Elegant town houses were built in the immediate vicinity of the palace: the Royal Villa, the South House, the South East House among others. The Little Palace dates from this time, as well as the building (named by Evans the Unexplored Mansion) which was connected to it by a bridge. The Little Palace displayed all the sophistication of the finest Minoan architecture. The famous **Bull's Head Rhyton** was found here (with other objects for ritual) in a tiny walled recess in a pillar crypt at the south end of the building.

The tantalising fragments of fresco decoration from Knossós, now preserved in the Herákleion Archaeological Museum, mostly date from this same phase of the Neopalatial period (LMIA) which marked the artistic climax of the Minoan civilisation. It is suggested that the slowing of this expansion in LMIA may have been associated with the great eruption of Théra.

As is the case in the rest of Crete, few Neopalatial tombs have come to light though the last burials took place in the Aílias cemetery and the Gypsádes tholos. The Temple Tomb on the Gypsádes (south along the main road) is an intriguing exception, with the burial chamber enclosed by a two-storey building with courtyard and pavilion.

One find from Late Minoan IB levels of an excavation west of the palace, under the auspices of the British School at Athens, has caused much speculation in archaeological circles for it involved the unburnt bones of children showing knife-cut marks suggesting that the flesh had been deliberately cut away. The most likely explanation seems to involve some form of sacrifice for an offering to the gods, possibly even preparations for a ritual meal.

At the end of this LMIB period there was a major break in the history of Knossós. A certain amount of physical damage occurred and parts of the town suffered severely in a fire but there was not the wholesale fire destruction found at this date at other excavated sites throughout Crete. Both the palace and at least some of the great dependent buildings continued in use though changes in culture are noticeable.

The Late Minoan II and Late Minoan IIIA periods are classified as Postpalatial elsewhere on the island, but here at Knossós this terminology is confusing, for they cover the last years of the palace. The archaeological record points to three particular changes. New burial customs appeared. Graves for single or family use replaced communal tombs and burial with weapons, as in the so-called Warrior Graves in the Knossós North Cemetery, was a practice not seen before on Crete. Secondly, there were developments in pottery decoration. The naturalistic vase painting of the previous period gave way to a formalised handling of motifs (often the same motifs as before) in a style which is akin to mainland decoration of this period. Thirdly, there was the appearance on Crete of a new script. Sometime during LMIII (there is still controversy about the exact date) the palace was destroyed by a catastrophic fire. Large numbers of clay tablets were accidentally baked in the fire and thus preserved for posterity. The tablets were inscribed in **Linear B** which has been deciphered as an early form of Greek. The Little Palace was destroyed at the same time and similar tablets were found in the debris. The script is also known from Mycenaean centres in the Peloponnese. This combination of cultural changes has led most archaeologists to accept that LMII–IIIA Knossós was inhabited by mainland Greeks, and became for a time the administrative centre for the Mycenaeans on Crete.

After the great fire very limited reoccupation was noted, for example in the LMIIIB Shrine of the Double Axes in the palace and at various points in the town, but the centre of power on the island seems to have moved to Kydonía, modern Khaniá.

Later remains lie thick all over the Knossós region, but it has been suggested that a tradition of sacred ground grew up around the palace site, possibly fostered by the myth of the Minotaur and the labyrinth; both became standard symbols on the coins of later Knossós. Near the staircase up from the propylaeum in the palace evidence has recently been found for a possible hero cult dating back to the Protogeometric period (10C BC). In the same area Evans had cleared what he thought was a small Classical temple. South of the palace on the lower slope of the Gypsádes hill the Sanctuary of Demeter, goddess of the fruits of the earth, was an important place of worship from the late 8C down to the 2C AD; the dedication was established by an inscription on an Early Hellenistic silver ring.

Material from the North Cemetery (now in Herákleion Museum, Room XII) provides some of the most spectacular evidence from Knossós from the end of the Bronze Age and through the Early Iron Age. Late Minoan chamber tombs, conveniently available, were methodically cleared before re-use, in some cases as early as the Subminoan period. The richest burials, with some remarkable cremation urns, were from the Geometric and Orientalising periods (8C and 7C). Grave offerings included bronze and iron artefacts and superb jewellery, as well as luxury items of faience from the eastern Mediterranean region. Pottery imports were identified from Athens, eastern Greece, the Cyclades and Cyprus.

Knossós emerged as the principal city of Hellenistic Crete, but it opposed the successful Roman invasion in 67 BC and suffered a defeat. Górtyn was made the capital of the Roman province but 40 years later, under the Emperor Augustus, Knossós became a Roman colony, *Colonia Julia Nobilis Cnossus*. The usual large public buildings are recorded, including an aqueduct, temples and houses embellished with mosaic floors and statuary.

Christian churches were built at Knossós. Two basilicas have been exca-

Coins of Greco-Roman Knossós, from Pashley, Travels in Greece, *1837*

vated to the north of the Roman city, one a large mortuary church (5C) and the other a martyrion (early 6C) built over Christian graves. The bishop of Knossós was present at early councils of the church in 431, 451 and 787.

As the threat of Arab raids increased the city's apparently undefended (and not easily defensible) position near the sea may have contributed to a decline in its importance. After the Arab conquest in 824, the fortified Rabdh el Khandak (modern Herákleion) became the principal settlement on the island and henceforth dominated the Knossós area.

History of the excavations

The palace of Knossós with its surrounding town and cemeteries was thoroughly explored in the early part of the 20C. Mínos Kalokairinós, a member of a respected Herákleion family, had investigated the Kephála hill in 1878. Heinrich Schliemann, discoverer of ancient Troy, sensed the site's importance but failed to reach agreement with the owners. It was left to the Englishman Arthur Evans (later Sir Arthur) to persist with negotiations in the difficult political climate at the end of Ottoman rule until he was able to buy a large parcel of land in 1900 and begin the great work.

A major part of the site was exposed by 1906 but supplementary work continued until the excavation of the Temple Tomb in 1924. The work is enshrined in Evans's four-volume *The Palace of Minos*, and summarised in *Sir Arthur Evans and the Palace of Minos*, by Ann Brown (see Recommended reading). Sir Arthur's interest in the site passed to the British School at Athens. Exploration continued on a small scale until 1940 and resumed after the Second World War along the Royal Road. In 1952 responsibility for the former Evans estate was transferred to the Greek government. Selective tests within the palace have addressed specific problems about the stratigraphy and successive architectural phases, especially where Evans's original conclusions were a matter of dispute. In the Minoan town excavation has concentrated on areas to the west of the palace, contributing greatly to an understanding of occupation levels through the Middle and late Minoan periods and on into the Early Iron Age.

During the late 1990s a programme of conservation was started by the Greek Archaeological Service. Changes in the arrangements for visiting the site had become necessary to meet the needs of more than one million tourists who come to Knossós each year and to protect the fabric of the palace for future generations.

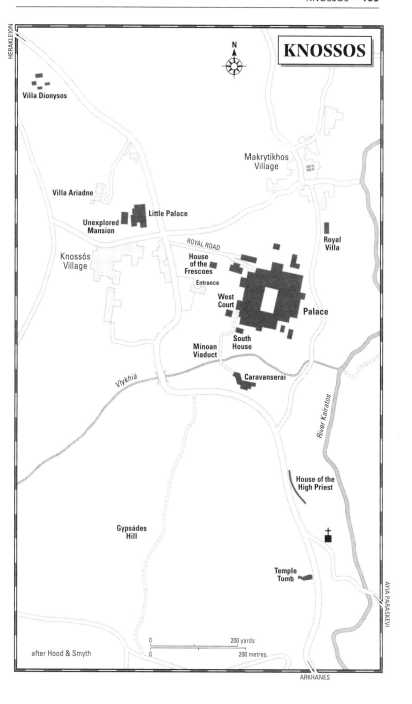

The palace

Facilities just inside the site entrance include a café, toilets, a bookstall and a shop under the auspices of the Ministry of Culture selling authorised replicas of museum pieces.

The modern approach to the palace (see plan p 108) leads by a path under a trellis of vines and bougainvillea to the paved West Court; the last stretch of the Minoan ramp is visible in the cutting to the right of the trellised path. A bust of Sir Arthur Evans, the gift of the municipality of Herákleion, surveys his formidable achievement. His work has always been controversial for archaeologists. Those who value his achievements concede that sometimes he allowed his own preconceptions undue weight and was often selective in his interpretations. His detractors look for conjecture in his restorations, but it is generally accepted that his Knossós reconstructions, as he himself called them, have fired the imagination of generations of visitors to the Bronze Age remains.

However, you are visiting the palace a century after Evans's great work and where his concrete and steel have suffered it has become necessary to attend to the early 20C restorations as well as to the conservation of the Bronze Age fabric. Positive results of this programme are seen in practical measures such as timber walkways round the site and the new viewing points which replace unregulated access. There is a project to insert presentation panels near main features.

Sir Arthur Evans

Arthur John Evans was born in Hertfordshire, England, in 1851, into a family whose money came from a successful papermaking business. His father, Sir John Evans, was a scholar and antiquarian of repute. Arthur was educated at Harrow and Oxford. After graduating, he spent time in the Balkans, including an eventful period as Balkans correspondent for the *Manchester Guardian*. He was able to pursue his archaeological interests, acquiring sealstones and coins and even embarking on the excavation of a Bronze Age barrow. In 1877 he met Margaret Freeman whom he married in 1878.

In 1882 Evans returned with his wife to Oxford and prepared his archaeological researches in the Balkans for publication. In the following year the couple travelled in Greece, including visits to Mycenae and Tiryns, and met Heinrich Schliemann, who had already made enquiries about excavating at Knossós.

In June 1884 Evans was made Keeper of the Ashmolean Museum in Oxford, a position he retained until 1908. He expanded the collection to cover all areas of European archaeology, and supervised the construction of a building to house the new material. During his time as Keeper, Evans was able to continue his travels in Greece. He was convinced that the early civilisation of the Aegean must have used a system of writing, and clues such as signs engraved on sealstones suggesting a pre-Phoenician script pointed him in the direction of Crete.

Evans first visited the island in March 1894. He was taken to Knossós (already known as an ancient site) and on the Kephála hill inspected the trenches which Minos Kalokairinós had opened in 1878–79. He visited antiquities dealers who showed him sealstones and evidence of scripts. His mind became set on acquiring the Kephála site to excavate, although other foreign archaeologists were also interested. However, at this politically sensitive time the Cretan Assembly was committed to delaying tactics to protect Cretan antiquities until the Ottoman rulers were removed. Evans was sympathetic to the Cretan cause. On a practical level there were problems with the owners of the land; Evans purchased one part in 1894 and then waited four years until Turkish forces left Crete and he could acquire the rest.

On 23 March 1900 the digging began. To further the cause of reconciliation on the island Evans insisted on a team of Cretan workers from both Christian and Muslim faiths. He was an inexperienced excavator but he employed as his site director Duncan Mackenzie who was fresh from a major excavation on the Cycladic island of Mélos. Mackenzie's meticulous day-books of the excavations at Knossós were to prove invaluable to Evans as he wrote up his reports for publication, and they have been used as a mine of accurate information for scholars ever since. Evans also included an architect in his team, a commonplace practice now but not at that time.

The importance of the site was soon recognised, with excavation required on a far larger scale than had been expected. Evans's detailed tripartite chronology of Bronze Age Crete became the framework which his successors have adopted. The major part of the enormous task (which included work on areas in the town, the harbour, roads and surrounding cemeteries as well as the palace) was completed by 1906. Protection had to be provided for the fragile building materials which the work was exposing to the weather, and Evans also decided to restore features of the palace wherever possible.

Evans saw ancient history through the perspective of the Classical authors, and prehistory in terms of mythology. When he wrote and lectured to raise money for a Cretan Exploration Fund he related these myths to the physical reality (the great buildings, the evidence for wealth and sophisticated craftsmanship) that he was uncovering. He was knighted for his work in 1911 and in 1914 was made president of the Society of Antiquaries, and *ex officio* a trustee of the British Museum. He worked for many years on his widely admired publication, *The Palace of Minos at Knossós (1921–36)*. On his last visit to Crete in 1935 he was honoured by the city of Herákleion and the bronze bust overlooking the entrance to the palace was unveiled. He died in Oxford in 1941.

The tour starts in the **West Court**, which was first laid out on a terraced area under the Old Palace walls as part of the entry to the palace from the town. It was probably designed as a place for public assemblies. The court's paving is crossed by raised walks (part original stone, part restored) which are a typical feature of Minoan architecture. You are directed to the walk to the right (south) side of the court, towards the West Entrance to the palace. Here you join the new system of built timber walkways.

Before you cross the court you pass (left) three **walled pits**, known as *kouloûres* (from the Greek word meaning hollow or circular). When the court was extended at the end of the Old Palace period they were filled with rubbish, including much broken pottery of high quality, and were paved over. At the bottom of the central pit were the remains of a house of Middle Minoan IA date, the period

PALACE OF KNOSSOS

Theatral Area

ROYAL ROAD

36

37

N

33

35

31

34

Altar

9

8

Throne Room

7

12

10

Central

13

11

Court

West Court

6

Altar

5

Entrance

West Porch

1

4

14

2

3

17

38

South House

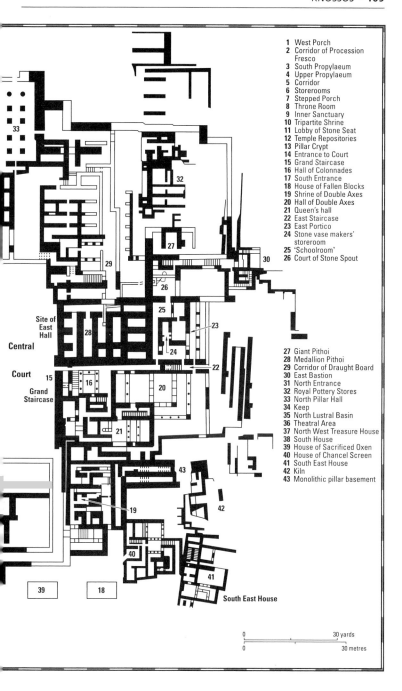

1 West Porch
2 Corridor of Procession Fresco
3 South Propylaeum
4 Upper Propylaeum
5 Corridor
6 Storerooms
7 Stepped Porch
8 Throne Room
9 Inner Sanctuary
10 Tripartite Shrine
11 Lobby of Stone Seat
12 Temple Repositories
13 Pillar Crypt
14 Entrance to Court
15 Grand Staircase
16 Hall of Colonnades
17 South Entrance
18 House of Fallen Blocks
19 Shrine of Double Axes
20 Hall of Double Axes
21 Queen's hall
22 East Staircase
23 East Portico
24 Stone vase makers' storeroom
25 'Schoolroom'
26 Court of Stone Spout

27 Giant Pithoi
28 Medallion Pithoi
29 Corridor of Draught Board
30 East Bastion
31 North Entrance
32 Royal Pottery Stores
33 North Pillar Hall
34 Keep
35 North Lustral Basin
36 Theatral Area
37 North West Treasure House
38 South House
39 House of Sacrificed Oxen
40 House of Chancel Screen
41 South East House
42 Kiln
43 Monolithic pillar basement

Site of East Hall

Central

Court

Grand Staircase

South East House

0   30 yards

0   30 metres

immediately before the construction of the Old Palace, so this feature is one of the earliest (c 2000 BC) now visible on the site. A flight of steps leads down to the foundations of a room. Both the floor surfaces and the walls had been rendered with red plaster.

The court extends to the **West Façade** of the palace in front of which is an altar base. Behind it a recess in the façade would have held a window in the storey above. It has been suggested that these windows were used for ceremonial appearances. The massive wall of the palace building rests on a levelling course, and is faced with gypsum blocks now severely weathered. There are gypsum quarries that were worked in Minoan times on the appropriately named hill of Gypsádes immediately to the south of Knossós. The signs of burning on the façade indicate that at the time of the great fire which finally devastated the palace the wind was from a southerly direction.

In the corner of the court a designated viewing point overlooks the **West Entrance and Porch** (1 on plan). The gypsum base of the porch's single column is preserved, and an inner room with a red plaster floor. The walls of the West Porch bastions were frescoed, and Evans found fragments painted with bulls' hooves which indicated that in Minoan times the visitor entered between representations of stampeding animals. From the porch, huge wooden doors opened into the **Corridor of the Procession Fresco** (2). The sockets for the doorposts remain, and between them a small hole for a central bolt. The corridor was paved with gypsum flagstones (the remaining fragments now very worn) which were flanked by blue schist set in red plaster.

Part of the imposing processional way into the palace is lost owing to the erosion of the hillside. Originally the Corridor of the Procession Fresco led south before turning left and left again, describing three sides of a rectangle to reach either the main ceremonial rooms of the West Wing, or the Central Court. The modern walkways reconstruct this route to the Central Court.

Where the coloured floor of the corridor falls away and the timber walk makes the first left turn, there is a fine view of the South House (**38**) down in the valley below. This house lay on another of the main approaches to the palace, named by Evans the Stepped Portico. The South House (p 118) can be reached by a modern stairway (nearby, right) but to continue the tour of the palace, turn left towards the Central Court across the South Front.

One branch of the Corridor of the Procession Fresco turned left to enter the **South Propylaeum** (3), a monumental roofed gateway supported by four huge columns. One corner has been restored and column bases indicate the ground plan. (Where columns at Knossós are reconstructed they are given the downward taper which is a typical feature of Minoan architecture.)

The fresco copy here is a detail from the *Procession Fresco*, which includes the so-called Cup-bearer. The figures in the procession strikingly resemble those of the Keftiu (Minoans) bearing offerings to the Pharaoh on the walls of 18th-Dynasty tombs at Thebes in Upper Egypt. Where copies of wall-paintings occur in the palace, the original fragments can be seen in the restored frescoes exhibited in the Herákleion Archaeological Museum.

The Corridor of the Procession Fresco continued along the south façade of the palace to turn left directly into the Central Court (p 111), and a branch of the modern walkway does the same, passing the large (restored) Horns of Consecration which would originally have adorned this south front.

From the gateway with the Cup-bearer fresco a monumental staircase ascends to the **Upper Propylaeum** (4).

Evans restored this upper level of the West Wing and, on an Italian analogy, because he believed that this was where the grand state apartments and reception halls lay, he named it the *Piano Nobile*. He relied on the evidence of architectural elements such as column bases, door jambs, paving slabs and steps which had collapsed into the level below. The thickness of the walls of the lower storey also helped to indicate where the upper walls should be.

The reconstruction has an Upper Long Corridor running north with columned halls opening from it on both sides. A gap allows you to look down into the impressive storeroom block below where the passage named by Evans the **Long Corridor of the Magazines** (5) has **eighteen storerooms** (6) opening off it; fresco fragments showed that the walls of the complex were painted, and decorated with simple linear motifs. The large jars, or pithoi, indicate the palace's storage capacity for such commodities as grain, oil and wine; the blackening of the gypsum slabs at the entrance to some of the storerooms is a reminder of how fiercely the oil must have burned at the time of the destruction. To increase the capacity during the period of the New Palace, cists or chests were sunk in the floor. The pyramidal stone stands in the corridor would have held double axes on poles, as portrayed in a scene on the Ayía Triáda limestone sarcophagus displayed in the main fresco room of the Herákleion Museum.

A **staircase** (7) leads down to the Central Court but if you now keep straight ahead on the upper level, following the line of the corridor, you can turn right through a group of small rooms to a covered area where modern copies of some of the best known of the palace frescoes are hung. From the left inside the door: 1. Two panels of the *Miniature Frescoes* with a tripartite shrine portrayed on the upper one; 2. *The Ladies in Blue*; 3. *The Bull-leaper*; 4. *The Captain of the Blacks*. The other four are from the House of the Frescoes: scenes from the *Blue Monkey fresco*, and the much-illustrated *Blue Bird*.

These reconstructed rooms are above the Throne Room and the feature beside it known as a Lustral Basin. From the corner terrace a narrow private staircase used to give access to the Central Court. Nowadays you have to return to the imposing stairway (7) noted above (perhaps still undergoing restoration). The twelve steps have two central columns one at a higher level than the other which led Evans to give the name **Stepped Porch** to this descent to the court.

The area for the **Central Court** was levelled at the time of the construction of the Old Palace in MMIB. The top of the existing mound was in effect sliced off, and much of the earlier material, which included demolished buildings, was dumped to raise and extend the northwest part of the site. The court, c 50m by 25m and aligned north-northeast by south-southwest as at Phaistós and Mália, was originally paved and fragments of that paving are preserved near the entrance to the Throne Room. Here the rounded corner, at the bottom of a narrow private staircase, is one of the surviving elements of the Old Palace's ground-plan. In this northwest angle of the court a section of its drainage system is exposed under grilles.

The Stepped Porch stairway (7) brings you down to ground level in front of the **West Wing** and areas given over to shrines and storage. North of the stairway is the **Throne Room** (8) which may have been the principal shrine. You can enter the Antechamber which has gypsum benches along two walls (and replica throne in wood). Part of the original floor remains. The Throne Room itself is railed off but from the threshold you can see the gypsum throne flanked by benches and by copies of the original painted griffins. The crazy paving of the floor is bordered by regular gypsum flagstones. Opposite the throne, at the bottom of the light-well, steps lead down into a **Lustral Basin**, probably used for ritual cleansing and purification.

At the back of the Throne Room is the entrance to a small enclosed **Inner Sanctuary** (9) where Evans found overturned jars and large flat gypsum alabastra which he interpreted as evidence of a dramatic scene during the final moments of the palace.

Although the Throne Room was remodelled during the period of Mycenaean influence, its history goes back to the time of the Old Palace (MMII). Over the years the special fame of this room has been that it contains the oldest throne in Europe. However, modern thinking about the function of Minoan palaces, building on evidence from the subject matter on Minoan seals, vase carving and wall-paintings, emphasises the religious and cult aspects of this set of rooms, even envisaging an epiphany ritual, with a priestess appearing robed from the inner sanctuary to represent the Minoan goddess.

Tripartite Shrine, Knossós. Reconstruction by M.A.S. Cameron from the Temple Grandstand Miniature Fresco

Immediately south of the Stepped Porch staircase the **Tripartite Shrine** (10) pointed to the sanctity of the West Wing. Pairs of columns on the façade flanked a block supporting a single column, all shielding the sanctuary behind. Besides appearing in the Miniature Frescoes, this type of shrine is also recognisable on a gold ring from Arkhánes and a steatite vase from Zákros, both in the Herákleion Museum.

On the south side of the shrine and immediately behind it is a group of rooms devoted to storage and administration as well as to the associated cult rituals. Access to this area is restricted, but the archaeological evidence from these rooms is crucial to an understanding of the function of Minoan palaces. At the bottom of a flight of five steps is the **Lobby of the Stone Seat** (11), a small paved court (sometimes known as the Room of the Column Bases). The little court leads, right, into the **Room of the Tall Pithos** and then to the **Temple Repositories** (12). (The adjacent Stepped Porch staircase is useful as a viewpoint.) Two large stone-built cists, or containers, were sunk under the floor here in the early days of the New Palace. (A smaller box between them was a later addition.) When the area of the Temple Repositories was first excavated the cists were not found, and only when the floor began to sag the following year was their presence suspected. These containers have peg holes for fixing shelves and a careful construction suitable for the storage of precious objects.

In the repository nearest to the court Evans found the two faience figurines of snake goddesses, acknowledged masterpieces of Minoan art, together with other furnishings of a shrine that are now on display with these pieces in the Herákleion Museum (Room IV). The other large cist had been robbed, but traces of gold leaf remained and Evans believed that its precious objects had been taken to the mainland, perhaps to find their way into the Mycenae shaft graves where many of the artefacts recovered have long been considered to be of Cretan workmanship.

From the Lobby of the Stone Seat there was access to the outer of the two **Pillar Crypts** (13). These were enclosed rooms without natural light, each with a central pillar. Double-axe incisions on the pillars are taken as signs of religious significance, and troughs in the floor beside them could have received liquid offerings. Pillar crypts, dark and mysterious, seem to have played an important part in Minoan ritual connected with shrines and sacred treasuries. In the **Vat Room**, opening north out of the east crypt, there was a further small treasure hoard of MMIA date (the end of the Prepalatial period), which pointed to the sanctity of this area even at such an early time.

A gypsum-paved passage led through from the Lobby of the Stone Seat, along the south side of the crypts to join the Long Corridor (5) serving the Storerooms (6) already seen from above. The layout of this central area of the West Wing emphasises the close association for the Minoan civilisation between the wealth derived from commodities and one of the most sacred areas of the palace.

In the later, Mycenaean (LMIIIA), period the Linear B archives recovered from ths area throw light on the administrative functions. One deposit of tablets found towards the north end of the Long Corridor deals with the arrival and despatch of olive oil; others refer to textile production and aromatics. The **Room of the Chariot Tablets** (south of the Lobby of the Stone Seat) provided evidence for wooden boxes in which the tablets had been stored, together with a number of seal impressions.

In debris south of the gypsum-paved passage Evans found a number of Minoan stone vases of ritual type, including the magnificent *Lioness Head Rhyton* now prominently displayed in the Herákleion Museum. He believed that the vessels had fallen from a treasury above when the upper floor collapsed in the LMIIIA fire destruction. However, it is now thought more likely that they had been stored where they were found, as a valued collection of rarities of superb quality, antique already in Mycenaean times.

The **southern entrance** to the court (14) was from the Corridor of the Procession Fresco (noted above). Fragments of the original floor pattern seen in the West Porch at the start of the corridor are preserved again at the end of it. Here Evans set up a restoration of the fresco of the Prince of the Lilies (sometimes called the Priest-King); this is one of the most well known of all Minoan figures but the restoration is controversial.

The view from this southern end of the court takes in, to the left (east) across the valley of the Kaíratos river, the limestone ridge of **Aílias** rising to a height of 350m. The lower ridge to the west is known as the **Acrópolis hill**. To the south, beyond the little that remains of the South Entrance to the palace, the foreground is filled by Gypsádes, the hill where the Minoans quarried gypsum for their buildings, but the court is aligned on the sacred **Mount Júktas** conspicuous on the horizon. On a spur just below the summit, in sight from the palace, was one of the most important peak sanctuaries on the island, known to have been a place of pilgrimage at least from the Early Minoan period.

You cross the court to the **East Wing** of the palace (past a gypsum block which was the base of an observation tower used during the original excavation). The Grand Staircase (**15**) descends from the court to the heart of the East Wing, which Evans interpreted as the **Residential** or **Domestic Quarter**. Below the level of the court two storeys are preserved, built into the slope of the hill, and there would have been at least one more storey above the court.

Immediately to the north of the Grand Staircase a flat concrete area is the presumed location of the East Hall which would have been an imposing structure at the level of the court. There was evidence for decoration with relief frescoes of male and female bull leapers, and remains of a large wooden idol indicated an important palatial shrine. The massive foundations for this building will be seen later in the tour.

The Grand Staircase, for which there are several viewing points at the level of the court, is one of the masterpieces of Minoan architecture. During the excavations Evans found that the hillside had partially retained the stairs and the supporting elements as they collapsed, and this assisted greatly with an authentic reconstruction. Two double flights of broad shallow gypsum steps are preserved, with landings on the return, and there was evidence for a fifth flight going up to a floor above. The staircase was built with a stepped parapet supporting columns on its outer side where it gave on to a light-well.

From the court you can see the gallery round the stair-well at the first level on the way down, and the entrance to the Upper East–West Corridor off which was the so-called Hall of the Royal Guard. Evans restored the Shield Fresco depicting ox-hides stretched and sewn on figure-of-eight frames which he thought hung in the equivalent position at the lower level.

The staircase ended at the bottom of the light-well in the impressive **Hall of the Colonnades** (**16**), named for its four massive weight-bearing columns. Another east–west corridor from the foot of the stairs gave access to the Hall of the Double Axes (**20**) which you will be able to see later in the tour.

With the Grand Staircase closed off you now use the new timber walkway which leaves the court by the southeast corner to take you round to these lower levels of the Domestic Quarter. First you pass an area of the palace that is not well preserved. On your right are the remains of the South Front of the New Palace. Viewing the façade from below you can identify the bastions of the **South Entrance** (**17**) which has masons' marks clearly visible on the walls of the passage leading to it.

As you return to the walkway and turn east at the bottom of the slope, you will notice (below right) that enormous ashlar blocks from an earlier South Front, toppled by an earthquake at the end of MMIII, still lie in the foundations of the building named by Evans the **House of the Fallen Blocks** (**18**).

At this south end of the site you are within reach of several excavations of dependent buildings (p 118) but most visitors prefer first to complete the tour of the palace.

On the walkway heading north again, parallel with the Central Court, you will pass on your left (roofed and gated for protection) the Postpalatial **Shrine of the Double Axes** (**19**). This tiny domestic shrine dates from the period of limited reoccupation (LMIIIB, 1300 BC) following the great fire which destroyed the palace. A ledge against the back wall held miniature horns of consecration and terracotta figurines on drum-shaped bases. Immediately west of the shrine is the **Corridor of the Sword Tablets** named after an important find of clay tablets of this shape inscribed in Linear B.

Beside the pathway you notice two types of drainage channel. One length of piping supplied water brought by an aqueduct system from springs on Mount Júktas; it is crossed by a drainage channel taking rainwater away from the buildings higher up the slope.

Approaching the lowest level of the Domestic Quarter you arrive at the terrace of the **Hall of the Double Axes** (**20**). The name is taken from the distinctive symbol carved on the ashlar blocks of the light-well at the hall's west (inner) end. The scale and elegance of this grand set of rooms led Evans to conclude that they were designed for the ruler or rulers of the palace. At this outer end a broad L-shaped portico overlooking the Kaíratos stream has a south and east aspect sheltered from Crete's prevailing winds.

Looking into hall you will immediately notice that the balance of pillars and columns is architecturally effective. The piers of the *polythyron* have been reconstructed to show how the folding doors operated. The arrangement allowed for variations between an enclosed, well-protected, inner room and a large open area where a current of fresh air would be drawn through to the shaft of the light-well at the rear. On the north wall of the inner hall scorched remnants are preserved of what may have been a plaster-backed throne.

The Hall of the Double Axes communicated, via a dogleg passage south, with the set of rooms known as the **Queen's Hall** (**21**). If you walk round to the left you should be able to see into these rooms. Here Evans restored the main room with benches round the wall and decorated it with fresco paintings of a scene with dolphins, a frieze of spirals and another of rosettes, also panels of dancing girls. (Current thinking is that the dolphins were probably part of the floor decoration from a shrine on the level above.) Below the paved floor of this restored room, near a LMI clay jar, some of the irregular stonework of an earlier floor was found in situ and left uncovered.

The Queen's Hall had its own terrace area, sheltered by a light-well on the east side; its drainage system is visible under a grille. Separated from the main room by a balustrade is a small area which Evans reconstructed as a bathroom but the clay bath tub now placed there was found in pieces nearby, not in situ. Beside Evans's bathroom a narrow corridor leads west to a **toilet** with drainage system. Light is provided from the **Court of the Distaffs** adjacent to the north (named for the masons' marks on its wall) through which there was a circuitous private route back to the well of the Grand Staircase. A corridor continued, past a little secret room which may have been a treasury, to a narrow staircase up to the floor above. In the cupboard space under its return was found (in many pieces) the much-illustrated ivory figure of a bull-leaper which is prominently displayed in the Herákleion Museum.

If you now continue north (past the terrace of the Hall of the Double Axes) you notice on the left a narrow flight of steps, the **East Staircase** (**22**), that led up to the floor level of the Domestic Quarter above this lowest complex of rooms. (A fresco fragment in low relief found there, part of a larger than life leg and foot of a bull, is dated to the period of Mycenaean influence.)

This flight of steps in from the east could have provided convenient access to and from the Domestic Quarter for dealings with the outside world. It would have led into the upper East–West Corridor on the way to the Grand Staircase at the heart of the East Wing. Linear B tablets found in the corridor were named by Evans the percentage tablets because the figures on them mostly added up to 100. They have since been deciphered as records of large flocks of sheep and the administration of the wool industry. (Over 400 loomweights from the Proto-palatial period, found in the nearby Loomweight Basement, added substantial evidence for weaving.)

If you carry on in a northerly direction from the foot of the staircase, you come to the **East Portico** (**23**), on a terrace looking out across the river valley to the slopes of Aílias. (In the foreground are the pine trees planted by Evans a century ago.) The designated path leads straight ahead, to the north, in the direction of the East Bastion (**30**).

Behind the portico, parallel to the walkway, a corridor passes a small **store-room** (**24**) still containing blocks of Spartan basalt (*lapis Lacedaemonius*, a raw material used by Minoan stonecarvers for vases and seals) which must have been imported from its sole source near Sparta in the Peloponnese. The corridor opens into an area with a bench along the wall which Evans named the '**School Room**' (**25**). It was probably a craftsman's workshop, with a basin which could have been used for kneading the clay for tablets.

You come to the **Court of the Stone Spout** (**26**) with high up left part of the palace's drainage system (see below). Ahead of you, north, the **Storerooms of the Giant Pithoi** (**27**) are conspicuous, with mighty vases dating from the Old Palace period.

Uphill, on the Central Court, is the presumed location of the East Hall. At this basement level you can see the hall's massive foundations, including (nearest the court) the immensely strong walls and supporting piers of the **Corridor of the Bays**, and also the **Storeroom of the Medallion Pithoi** (**28**). (A similar pithos in stone came from the Tomb of Klytemnestra at Mycenae.) Here you can follow, below the paved surfaces, the drains carrying storm water from the East Hall down the slope towards the Court of the Stone Spout. The same system dealt with the drainage of open lightwells at various points around the palace.

The faience plaques known as the *Town Mosaic* were found in the debris of the East Hall and just outside it, in the **Corridor of the Draught-Board** (**29**), the magnificent inlaid gaming board (both now in the Herákleion Museum). In this corridor, under a grille, you will notice the fresh water supply system; a channel carries interlocking clay pipes which are tapered to produce a greater head of water.

On the slope between the foundations of the East Hall and the Court of the Stone Spout you can follow, below the paved surfaces, the drainage system for storm water (see plan). The stone channels carry clay pipes which are tapered in order to produce a greater head of water. (Similar systems dealt with the drainage of open light-wells at various points around the palace.)

From the Storerooms of the Giant Pithoi a staircase leads down to the **East Bastion** (**30**) above the East Entrance. A stone water channel, a continuation of the drainage system noted above, descends beside the steps in a series of para-bolic curves and small settling basins to break the flow of rainwater and debris down the steep slope.

At the bottom of the slope the easily defended gate would have controlled access to and from the town and to houses such as the Royal Villa, also the way out to the north coast along the east bank of the Kaíratos.

Climbing back up again, past the Giant Pithoi and an area which may have been stalls for animals, you could take a stairway up into the Central Court beside the East Hall, and cross the court diagonally to the **North Entrance Passage** (**31**). This is dominated by Evans's reconstruction of part of the **porch** with the relief of a charging bull. Alternatively the timber walkway from the Storerooms of the Giant Pithoi continues north. It passes a viewing platform level with the bull fresco, and Old Palace storerooms, Evans's **Royal Pottery Stores** (**32**), which contained fine Kamáres wares, on its way to the external approach to the North Entrance. Here the **North Pillar Hall** (**33**) has a double row of gypsum pillars which are thought to have supported a dining hall above.

This hall was added when the New Palace was built, and at the same time the ramp ascending the North Entrance Passage was altered to create a narrow (perhaps more easily guarded) approach to the court between bastions decorated with intimidating frescoes. The lower courses of the bastion walls in the North Entrance Passage preserve further examples of masons' marks (in this case tridents and double axes) carved in the ashlar blocks. This would have been the entrance from the direction of Póros-Katsambás, the principal harbour of Minoan Knossós. Evans interpreted the North Pillar Hall as a customs house.

On the west side of the North Entrance Passage was a complex of rooms of especially massive construction named by Evans the **Keep** (**34**). The stone-lined pits of early date, from the Protopalatial or even perhaps the end of the Prepalatial period, may have been granaries rather than dungeons as Evans thought. In Neopalatial levels here, the *Saffron Gatherer Fresco* and the *Miniature Frescoes* were found.

A walkway leads from the northwest corner of the Central Court (near the Throne Room) to the **North Lustral Basin** (**35**), which you will also pass if you stay on the path past the North Portico outside the palace buildings. The careful restoration of this lustral basin has provided a fine example of these features so typical of Minoan architecture. Signs of burning on the gypsum facing and the oil jars found in the destruction material suggest a ritual of purifying and anointing before entry to the palace.

The stepped **Theatral Area** (**36**) (Neopalatial as you see it now, but built in two phases) is superimposed on the Royal Road and looks west along it. It has been suggested that the area had a role in the welcoming of important visitors, but many other types of assembly or performances (even legal judgements) can be envisaged. There is a paved courtyard at the foot of shallow steps (similar in design to the terraces above the West Court of the Old Palace at Phaistós). An intriguing feature is the small raised platform to one side.

The **Royal Road**, with central flags (largely original) bordered by drains, continues west into the Minoan town of Knossós and a branch turns north into the Little Palace. Another stretch was picked up in an important excavation in an area of the town further west, 200m from the modern Herákleion road.

The Bronze Age road was lined with buildings, some perhaps similar to the houses portrayed on the faience plaques of the *Town Mosaic* (p 116). These Royal Road houses seem to have been built above ground floor workshops. On the left was the **House of the Frescoes** dating to MMIII, where Evans discovered a stack of fragile slabs of painted plaster. Many of these have been pieced together in the Herákleion Museum to include the striking *Blue Bird* scene and a landscape with *Blue Monkeys*. The right (north) side of the road was the site of the **Arsenal** or Armoury. At the far end, before the site fence, there are traces of another similar road leading off south. Built at the same time as the Old Palace, around 1900 BC, these Knossós roads are among the earliest urban roads in Europe.

From the Theatral Area you can make your way back to the West Court outside the northwest corner of the palace and its imposing West Façade, past the broken gypsum Horns of Consecration and the scant remains of the excavation of the **North West Treasure House** (37) where a rich hoard of bronze vessels was found.

If you now intend to visit the excavations of dependent buildings below the South Front you keep straight on across the West Court, into the Corridor of the Procession Fresco (2) and ahead again down the timber steps. Below them the South House is in view. Otherwise the modern walkway directs you from the lower end of the theatral area to the trellised exit from the site.

Town houses and other excavations south of the palace

From the Corridor of the Procession Fresco (2 on palace plan) a modern stairway takes you down the southern slope of the Kephála hill to the **South House** (38), which is best viewed from its downhill side. The house stood beside the Minoan road on the southern approach to the palace, encroaching on the **Stepped Portico** (see area plan, p 105).

Dating to the first phase of the New Palace period, the house was set in a deep cutting (down into EM and even Neolithic levels) which has preserved up to eight courses of its back wall. It is partially restored on three levels and illustrates features typical of Minoan domestic architecture.

The original entrance led from the southeast corner, through a porch and anteroom into a light-well in front of a main hall. This hall had a window out to the east, and a floor with central paving bordered by gypsum flagstones; on its west side was a small lustral basin. West of the staircase was a room with a central pillar and evidence for ritual around it included a conical stone stand for a double axe. The basements of the house were constructed as pillar crypts. Silver vessels, now on display in the Herákleion Museum, were found in the destruction debris, and a hoard of bronze tools.

South of the South House, on the far side of the Vlýkhia stream (inaccessible, see area plan) are the remains of buildings named by Evans the **Caravanserai**, which could have served as a resting-place below the imposing southern entrance to Knossós. A shallow trough or footbath was fed by springs and the adjacent hall was decorated with the *Partridge and hoopoe fresco*, much-illustrated and now to be seen in the Herákleion Museum. The **Spring Chamber** nearby was frequented for cult purposes in the Subminoan period until votive offerings ceased when the water from the spring dried up. Finds, which included a goddess with raised arms and a hut-urn, suggest a continuation of Minoan cult.

From the Caravanserai, travellers in Minoan times would follow the road over the Vlýkhia stream on the great viaduct, a Protopalatial construction using monumental stone blocks, and then up the ramp to the imposing Stepped Portico beside the South House.

From the South House you can cross the South Front of the palace, parallel to the perimeter fence.

The **House of the Sacrificed Oxen** (39) was built during the first (MMIII) phase of the New Palace period, destroyed by earthquake at the end of that phase and not rebuilt; only basement levels are preserved. The name comes from the two heads of sacrificed oxen found implanted in front of portable altars. It has been suggested that the cult practices may have been intended to propitiate the deity of earthquakes who according to Homer's *Iliad* took delight in the roaring of bulls.

The **House of the Fallen Blocks** (18) was noted during the palace tour for the massive blocks of masonry hurled into it from the palace's south façade by earthquake forces.

The **House of the Chancel Screen** (40), from the first phase of the New Palace period, preserves the feature which gave it its name. The screen has a door between two columns with, behind it, a platform for a seat or altar. The Royal Villa has something similar and there are parallels with the Tripartite Shrine of the Miniature Frescoes (p 112).

The **South East House** (41) preserves the remains of a particularly elegant Neopalatial house. The original approach was down the double flight of stairs, but now you walk round to the lower level. On the north side is a pillar room with two double-axe stands and a wall niche, also a cist let into the floor. A tall purple-stone lamp was found in this room so the niche may have been for offerings rather than light. The main room on the south side shows good ashlar masonry, an interior wall of gypsum slabs set on end and a gypsum floor. The room opened to the south on to a peristyle court (a miniature cloister) which could be shut off on two sides by folding doors. The court's covered walk was paved with gypsum, the open centre with more weather-resistant stone.

North of this excavation you will find the remains of an **LMI kiln** (42), enclosed for protection, and the basement of the **House of the Monolithic Pillars** (43), one of the earlier buildings on this site, perhaps dating back to the end of the Prepalatial period (MMIA). The basement has four bays divided by piers notable because it is unusual to find tall gypsum pillars (in this case two of them) hewn in one piece.

A view over palace and valley

This recommended walk or drive of less than 2km offers a bird's-eye view of the excavations. You start out on the busy road south from Knossós. Not far beyond the bridge over the Vlýkhia there is a minor road left which circles round the palace site to the hamlet of Makrytíkhos past the remains of the so-called Royal Villa.

On the main road you notice a sign to another Minoan building, the **House of the High Priest**, named on account of its stone altar between stands for double axes behind a columnar balustrade. 1km from the village watch for an awkward drop on the left into a narrow side-road signed for the churches of Áyios Yeóryios (100m) and Ayía Paraskeví (1km). The road crosses the Kaíratos stream and climbs the limestone ridge of Aílias to a broad terrace below the little church of Ayía Paraskeví. From here the view of Knossós sets the palace with its surrounding buildings in the context of its natural environment.

The palace extends over a low hill at the junction of the Kaíratos and its tributary the Vlýkhia; both streams were fed by springs which under natural conditions would have ensured a year-round water supply. The river valley stretches away to the north, 5km to the sea. The Minoans used the higher ground for their cemeteries. One of the Minoan roads followed the east bank down to the harbour of Knossós at Póros-Katsambás under the headland to the east of the modern port of Herákleion.

From this new perspective on the remains of the palace you can see the formidable North Entrance as the approach from the sea. To the south is the Vlýkhia crossing (near the modern bridge) on the ancient road across the island from the harbours on the south coast. In this direction also was the Minoan peak sanctuary on Mount Júktas. You can appreciate the need for the viaduct between the Caravanserai and the Stepped Portico beside the South House.

From the palace's North Portico the paved Royal Road ran west past the Theatral Area. It served the **Little Palace**, which is now hidden in trees west of the modern road, and continued out to the west into the Minoan town.

Beyond the palace excavation you can make out the modern road to Herákleion crossing the protected archaeological area as far as the hospital (also partly concealed by trees). The rising ground here would always have hidden Knossós from the direction of the sea.

The idea of the palace set in open country is misleading, for around it in the second millennium BC there was a sizeable town. The archaeologists envisage a densely occupied central zone, and then, since there is no evidence that the town was surrounded by defence walls, a gradual merging of town with countryside, with the houses on the outskirts separated by gardens or cultivated ground. Beyond this isolated farmsteads have been identified. At the most flourishing period of the Minoan civilisation a conservative estimate puts the population of the Minoan town at about 12,000 and the settlement area has been calculated at approximately 75 hectares, only slightly smaller than that of medieval Candia (Herákleion).

Inland from Herákleion

Arkhánes

Arkhánes is a large and prosperous village lying 380m above sea level across a valley below Mount Júktas, 15km inland from Herákleion. Most of its visitors come up from the coast and spend only one day in the area. Although there is currently no hotel and no great number of rooms to rent the village is within easy reach of Herákleion and Knossós for sightseeing purposes, and also at the centre of a rewarding part of the island to explore either by car or on foot.

The land here is chiefly given over to the cultivation of vines, and dominated by the summit of Júktas, its profile interpreted as a reclining bearded head. Since antiquity a persistent tradition has associated the mountain top with the tomb of Zeus.

For those interested in the Minoan civilisation Arkhánes has a great deal to offer. The modern village is built over a Bronze Age settlement. The burial ground for the settlement, on the hill of Phourní, is regarded as one of the most important prehistoric cemeteries in the Aegean. A Minoan peak sanctuary overlooks the village from the summit of Mount Júktas, and on the flank of the mountain at Anemóspilia an isolated shrine destroyed by an earthquake left behind evidence pointing to an act of human sacrifice. A small museum in the village provides an introduction to the archaeological sites, and directs the visitor to the major finds on display in Herákleion.

4km south of Arkhánes the excavation of a Minoan country house at Vathýpetro enjoys a panoramic view typical of central Crete. The valley road continues 3km to Khoudétsi on a main route south where walkers can use the Pýrgos or Khárakas buses for the return to Herákleion. With private transport you can continue (11km) to the tranquil Epanosíphis monastery, and a choice of ways back to the north coast.

Travelling by bus

Buses to Arkhánes (via Knossós) run approximately hourly, except Sundays, from the harbour bus station in Herákleion, with a convenient stop in the city centre at Plateía Venizélou.

Leave Herákleion on the Knossós road (p 100) or join it from the New National Road. 2km beyond Knossós a fine aqueduct supported by two tiers of arches spans a ravine. It was built to improve the Herákleion water supply during the brief interregnum (1832–40) when Egyptians replaced Turks in control of the island. The aqueduct had a Roman predecessor. The road climbs through **Spília** where there are agreeable tree-shaded tavernas. You pass a turning left with a short-cut signed through Skaláni for the Kazantzákis Museum (p 134). Continuing on the main road keep right for Arkhánes. Beyond Patsídes you need to slow for an acute right turn at a T-junction. In 1944, towards the end of the German occupation of Crete, this was the scene of a daring exploit, the kidnapping of General Kreipe (see box, below), still hallowed in Cretan folk memory.

The kidnapping of General Kreipe

In April 1944, the Cretan resistance movement, which was in contact with the Allied High Command in Cairo, planned to strike a blow intended to demoralise German troops and to encourage forces sympathetic to the Allies. It was decided to kidnap the divisional commander of the German forces on the island as he was being driven from his headquarters in Arkhánes to his residence in the Villa Ariadne at Knossós. The operation was carried out by Major P.M. (Paddy) Leigh Fermor and Captain W.S. (Billy) Moss from the British Military Mission with a band of their Cretan colleagues. They halted the general's staff car on the Arkhánes road, concealed him and then, disguised as general and driver, drove him straight on past the Villa Ariadne, through checkpoints at the heavily guarded gates into and out of Herákleion, and on west towards the foothills of Mount Ida below Anóyeia. In an attempt to minimise reprisals the car was abandoned near the shore with evidence carefully incriminating a British contingent rather than the Cretans.

The general spent 18 days in hiding with his captors, and the crossing of the Ida mountain range by mule and on foot, eluding intensive German searches, became the stuff of legend. After a number of hitches in the plans and narrow escapes the party was at last picked up by a Royal Navy submarine from a cove at Rodákino on the south coast. Reprisals followed, but not, it seems, solely on account of this episode, and its propaganda value for the islanders was beyond question.

The story was told by Moss in his book *Ill Met by Moonlight* (which was made into a film) and later by Antony Beevor in the definitive *Crete: the Battle and the Resistance*, published in 1991 to coincide with the 50th anniversary of the German invasion of the island.

You pass through the hamlet of **Káto Arkhánes** before reaching the main village of **Arkhánes** (strictly Ano or Epáno, upper, Arkhánes). At the beginning of the main street you will notice (right) a war memorial and beside it a three-aisled church and a free-standing clock tower. The church dedicated to the Panayía Vatiotissa merits a visit (key from the *Papás*, the local priest, ask at the museum) but it is also a landmark on the way to the archaeological sites described below.

As you continue into Arkhánes a one-way system sweeps you round anticlockwise, past a sign left for the **museum** and up into the triangular plateía, a paved and planted central area surrounded by good tavernas at the top of the village. The post office is in the plateía, and the bus station just below it. (The return section of the one-way system is the old main street.) Arkhánes is a place of narrow streets on a steep hillside, often with awkward access for cars.

Where to stay and eating out

If you are looking for accommodation the plateía is the place to start, with *Taverna Spitimo* acting as agents for **Orestes Rooms to Rent**. *Stavros*, next to the *períptero* (kiosk), sometimes advertises rooms.

As well as these two popular tavernas on the plateía, there is *Myriophito* with a shady courtyard, and on the uphill side, near the start of the main street, a modernised *psistariá*, with a wood-fired oven. *Tavérna Rodakinies*, opposite the three-aisled church noted on the way in from Herákleion, is more expensive but has a good reputation and may be crowded on summer weekends.

Arkhánes prides itself on its local **wine** which is generally regarded as some of the best on Crete. There is a co-operative bottling plant just outside the village, but several of the tavernas offer a good choice from the barrel.

The **Archaeological Museum** is open 08.30–15.00 daily except Tuesday. From the plateía walk down the main street following the one-way system. Watch for a sign to the left. This small museum aims to create a detailed picture of the Arkhánes area in the Bronze Age. A visit is strongly recommended before you set off for the sites.

The museum layout uses presentation panels as well as the impact of the artefacts themselves, in replica where necessary because much of the material from the excavations is in the collection of the Archaeological Museum in Herákleion and contributes some of its most outstanding exhibits. The display here in Arkhánes covers a number of themes such as aspects of ritual, tomb architecture and the evidence for foreign relations. There are reconstructions, drawings and photographs, and reports on the work of specialists such as anthropologists and forensic scientists.

Artefacts are grouped in an illuminating way, for example a replica of a *sistrum* found at Phourní is related to an illustration of the famous Harvester Vase from Ayía Triáda carved with a scene where the instrument (a type of rattle) is being played.

Minoan excavations in and around Arkhánes

Sir Arthur Evans was the first to uncover Minoan remains in Arkhánes. While excavating the massive ashlar masonry of a monumental well-head or spring chamber, he noted that Minoan walls had been incorporated in some neighbouring houses. Since the early 1960s there has been a major programme of excavations in the locality, under the direction of the husband and wife team of J. and E. Sakellarákis. They have written a well-illustrated guide book to the sites of Arkhánes (particularly useful for Phourní). An English version is available in shops in the village but not at the sites.

At **Turkogeitoniá** (meaning Turkish neighbourhood), among the houses of the modern village of Arkhánes, the Sakellarákis team has been uncovering parts of a large palatial-style building of the Neopalatial period which in scale and quality of architecture is comparable with the known Minoan palaces. The site is not open to the public but a certain amount can be seen from vantage points around it.

The main excavation is less than five minutes on foot from the three-aisled church and clocktower noted above. Leave a vehicle near the war memorial and start towards the centre against the one-way traffic flow, almost immediately turning left (with an orchard on the corner) into a short, narrow street. At the end go right to the gates for the best view over the excavation.

Turkogeitoniá has produced information of exceptional archaeological interest. Building materials were found to include marble, schist and gypsum as well as hewn ashlar blocks. There was evidence for wall decoration of frescoes and painted shallow reliefs. Finds included Marine Style pottery, faience, stone vases, sections of tusk and a lump of imported red jasper for which the most likely source is modern Iran. Particularly notable among the discoveries were fragments of five chryselephantine figurines (of ivory finished with gold leaf). A large rectangular altar, of a type known from numerous artistic representations, is the first to be found complete in an excavation.

From the palatial building there was evidence for two distinct destruction levels, both within Late Minoan I, in the middle and at the end of the Neopalatial period. (Mycenaean artefacts were also noted.) An intense fire destroyed the LMIA building and its upper floor collapsed, leaving evidence for two shrines. Walls on both levels had been decorated. One particular area is cited as an example of the architectural sophistication of the building: a *propylon* gave access, along a corridor, to an L-shaped peristyle from which a monumental staircase led to an upper floor. Here the peristyle colonnade was repeated on a smaller scale. The floors were paved with irregular slabs, in varying colours, and pointed with red and yellow plaster. With such a clear understanding of the original building the excavators believe that in due course an attempt at reconstruction will be justified.

Phourní

The cemetery of Phourní lies on the hill of the same name to the northwest of the village of Epáno Arkhánes. Open 10.00–14.30 daily except Monday.

From Epáno Arkhánes follow signs on the Herákleion side of the three-aisled church and clock tower noted as landmarks at the entrance to the village. After 1km there is room to park where the track ends by a sheepfold. A roughly paved path, an overgrown *kalderími*, starts uphill between two walls probably following the original Minoan route. (To the left a ravine separates the cemetery hill from Mount Júktas where telecommunications masts below the white church overlook the Minoan peak sanctuary.) It is a ten minute climb to railings round the cemetery and you keep right to find the entrance; the guardian's hut is at the centre of the site. The cemetery can also be reached by vehicle on a 2km track, rough but passable, intermittently signed from Káto Arkhánes. This track, a recommended walk, brings you to a car park at the uphill (north) end of the site.

Excavation has been going on here on the hill of Phourní since 1964 when what had been considered an old stone-built hut was recognised as the upper part of Tholos Tomb A. Its domed roof, formerly visible from the valley, may have influenced the name of the hill: *phoúrnos* means an oven.

The cemetery was in continuous use from the Early Minoan II period, mid third millennium BC, to near the end of the Bronze Age (Chronology, p 38). The earliest Prepalatial burials spread out from the south, the downhill end, but individual tombs were sometimes in use for hundreds of years, perhaps with modifications and additions, and, in some areas, later tombs were cut into these Prepalatial levels.

The numbering on the site plan relates to the order in which the structures were excavated, not to a chronological sequence, so it is suggested that the best way to tackle this complicated site is to start at its uphill (north) end and work downhill from there.

Walking up from Epáno Arkhánes you enter through the lower gate from the east on a level with the excavations around Tholos Tomb B, but a broad, worn path right, under olive trees and cypresses, will lead you north to Tholos Tomb A. On your right almost immediately is **Building 4** (dating to the Neopalatial period), a complex layout on different levels which probably included a second storey. Intriguing finds showed evidence for secular activities such as weaving and wine-making as well as a great variety of implements and a large bronze ingot. The excavators concluded that Building 4 had been used by the living in the course of caring for the dead. They drew parallels with Egypt where the living (in that case priests) were installed near funerary buildings to attend to the practical as well as the ritual aspects of the veneration of the dead.

Along the path north you come to **Building 21**, a horseshoe-shaped tholos below ground level with an internal staircase recalling those of the Minoan lustral basins. However, the main use of this structure dated to near the end of the Bronze Age (LMIIIB). Here again there was no suggestion of burial use and the function of this tholos remains uncertain.

Tholos Tomb A, with a long east-facing *dromos*, is one of the best preserved tombs of its type in the Aegean area. The small rock-cut side chamber opening out of the circular tholos contained a single burial, the first unplundered royal burial found on Crete, dated by the excavators to early in the 14C BC (LMIIIA), around the time that the palace at Knossós was destroyed, when Crete is thought

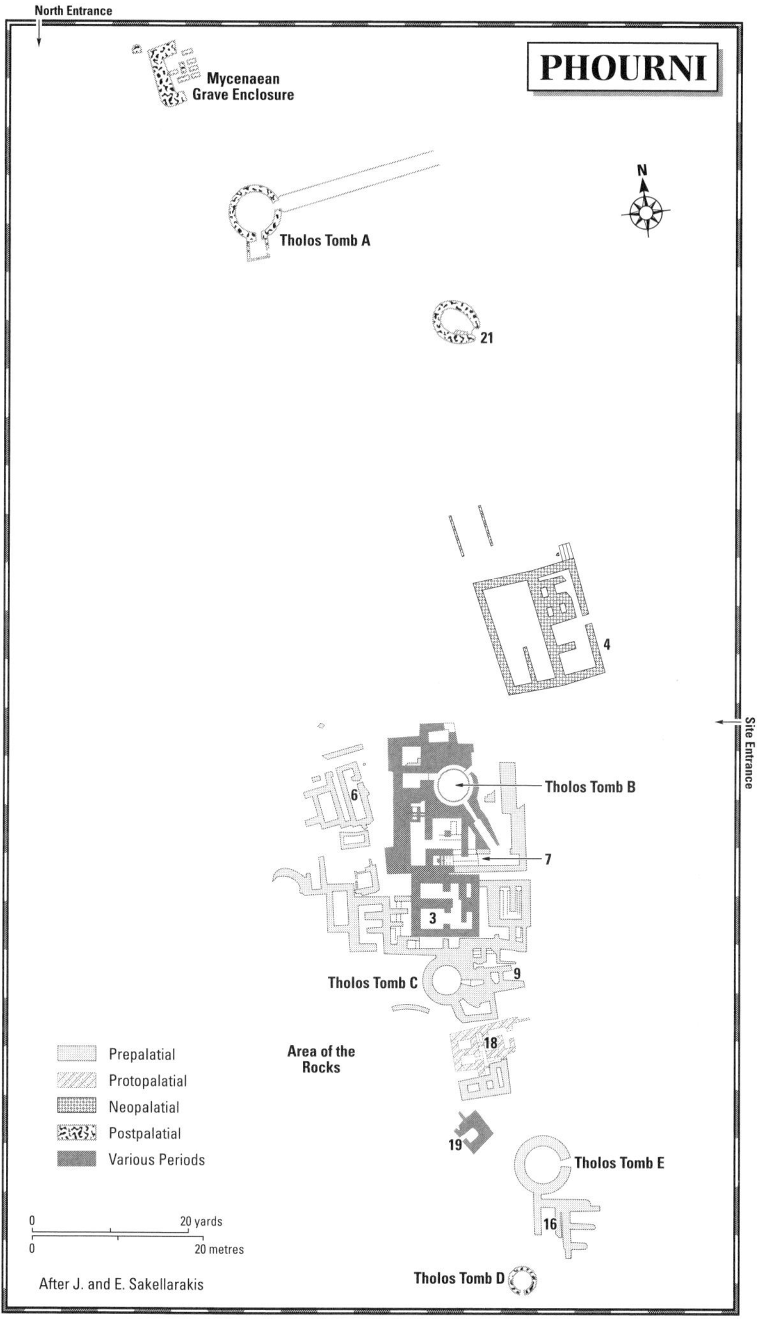

North Entrance

PHOURNI

Mycenaean
Grave Enclosure

N

Tholos Tomb A

21

4

Site Entrance

6

Tholos Tomb B

7

3

Tholos Tomb C

9

18

Area of the
Rocks

Prepalatial
Protopalatial
Neopalatial
Postpalatial
Various Periods

19

Tholos Tomb E

16

0   20 yards
0   20 metres

After J. and E. Sakellarakis

Tholos Tomb D

to have been controlled by Mycenaeans. The evidence pointed to a burial of a high-ranking female who was also closely involved with cult practices.

A sealed *lárnax* (clay burial chest) held a body in the foetal position with 140 pieces of gold jewellery, many of which are now displayed in the Archaeological Museum in Herákleion. Some of the goldwork would have adorned a long burial garment. On the floor of the side-chamber next to the *lárnax* were ten remarkable bronze vessels, also clay vases and 87 pieces of ivory inlays which had decorated a wooden footstool. To the right of the door to the side-chamber the remains of a horse sacrifice were found; the body had been dismembered. In the blocking wall of the side-chamber there was also the skull of a bull. This evidence for animal sacrifice associated with a rich burial is of particular interest in connection with the scene of a bull sacrifice on the frescoed sarcophagus from Ayía Triáda (now on display in the Herákleion Museum).

Immediately north of Tholos Tomb A is the burial complex known as the **Mycenaean Grave Enclosure** (also dated LMIIIA). Only the uphill part has survived, with seven shaft graves. Each grave had contained a *lárnax* with painted decoration but these were found broken and empty. Many rich burial offerings remained in the graves and the archaeologists suggested that the damage was not the work of robbers but that at some time after burial the dead were ritually exhumed and the bones placed back in the shafts on the *lárnax* bases. The importance of these burials is indicated by the quality of the offerings and by the funerary steles placed above them as grave markers within the built enclosure. These markers are interesting in relation both to mainland Mycenaean practices and to the development of the stele in later Greek funerary rites.

Just to the north of the Mycenaean Grave Enclosure a circular pit produced evidence for libations, recalling for the excavators the funerary cult rituals described by Homer.

The main path from the north entrance takes you back (past the guardian's hut) to the complex around **Tholos Tomb B**. This is the most complicated structure in the cemetery. The tholos was built over what was already, towards the end of the Prepalatial period, an important funerary area (**Funerary Building 7**). The archaeologists were able to date the foundation of the tholos to later in that same period (MMIA), and they found evidence for continuous use during more than 600 years (to LMIIIA). By then, after many modifications, a large rectangular complex (of two storeys in places) stood here, with the tholos at its centre reached by a *dromos* from the southeast. Several side-chambers were added, of which the western one, rectangular with a small *dromos* leading from the tholos, is the best preserved today. During the early history of the complex a pillar crypt was added to the south, carefully constructed against what was then the outer wall of the tholos. The crypt with the room above it became an integral part of the funerary rituals of Tholos Tomb B and remained so all through its period of use. Among many spectacular finds were a gold ring depicting a goddess and a griffin, and a silver pin inscribed in Linear A.

A paved road leads west from the Tholos Tomb B complex to a sequence of four rooms set at an angle to it and associated with open paved areas and a stairway. Named **Funerary Building 6**, and dating back to late in the Prepalatial period, this is cited as one of the best examples yet uncovered of a Minoan ossuary, an essential part of the ritual of clearing funerary buildings to allow room for further burials. Dense deposits of skulls and bones were found, at first laid on the floor and then later in *lárnakes*, pithoi or vases. The deposits were accompanied by rich offerings including jewellery and an important series of seals. Imported ivory, an Egyptian scarab and the use of the Linear A script were among evidence for trading activities and foreign contacts at this early date.

To the south of Tholos Tomb B, adjacent to its pillar crypt, is **Funerary Building 3**, which consisted of six rooms in a carefully built square structure. There was further indication here of the process of clearing to make way for later burials. Among the finds were ivory artefacts and an agate sealstone, pointers to the wealth and status of the deceased, but also tripod offering-tables for use in funerary rites. A globular diorite vase was recognised as an Egyptian import many centuries older than the Minoan burial with which it was here associated.

A path circles the southern half of the cemetery; care is needed in places. Out to the west is what is known as the **Area of the Rocks**, where the broken surface of the ground was found to contain a large amount of debris probably cleared from nearby Prepalatial burials. Further west (50m from Tholos Tomb C) are traces of the quarry which produced building stone for the cemetery.

Sufficiently well-preserved to be easily identifiable, **Tholos Tomb C** dates back to the Prepalatial period. It was built above ground with a low east-facing entrance, as was accepted practice for this type of tomb, familiar across the Mesará plain of southern Crete at this period. The tholos was found to contain an undisturbed burial level securely dated to EMIII. The excavators identified 45 burials, 18 in the foetal position in *lárnakes*, the remainder at ground level between them. A rich assortment of artefacts had been carefully deposited as funerary offerings among a layer of stones arranged on the tholos floor. One of only five clay vases contained 80 sea shells; 11 ivory seals were particularly valuable archaeological evidence with the benefit of this securely dated context. Three bronze daggers are the only Prepalatial examples so far found in the cemetery. There was a wide range of precious jewellery, but rarest among the finds were figurines of Cycladic type, with evidence for 15 in all from this tomb, most of marble but also of schist and quartz, and one of ivory. The excavators point to the importance of the Cycladic connection at this time. Finds of pottery of the LMIIIA period indicate that nearly 1000 years later the tholos tomb was still standing intact.

South and east of Tholos Tomb C, against its wall, are the remains of **Funerary Building 9**. Skulls found here were covered with a fine layer of earth, a mark of the attention paid to mortal remains at this date towards the end of the Prepalatial period. Offerings included miniature bull figurines and two bull rhytons. This funerary building is particularly notable for the number of infant and child burials grouped together (172 in all). Among the great variety of associated grave goods a remarkable find was a clay model of a *sistrum* or rattle; the Arkhánes museum (see above) sets this artefact in a wider Minoan context.

Continuing south, the chief importance of **Funerary Building 18** is that it produced Kamáres ware and other finds dated to the Protopalatial period and thereby provided the missing link for a continuous series of Minoan burial rites on the hill of Phourní. **Funerary Building 19** is the only apsidal funerary building at present known on Crete; the curved wall was contained in a square structure.

On the slope to the southeast **Tholos Tomb E**, built above ground but now damaged by erosion, is the earliest funerary building yet uncovered in the cemetery.

The lower of two burial levels could be securely dated to EMII. The great wealth of offerings (117 items in all, which included eight seals) pointed to a considerable number of burials. However, evidence from the EMII burials was erased when the tholos was reused 200 years later. Adjacent to the south and not well preserved is **Funerary Building 16** (dating to MMIA, c 2000 BC), a complex of two wings where many of a considerable number of burials were in pithoi or *lárnakes*; offerings included seals and a bronze earring.

In complete contrast **Tholos Tomb D**, the last building at the south end of the hill, with its entrance from the south, contained only one burial, that of a wealthy female, perhaps as the archaeologists suggest of royal blood, certainly a member of the ruling class. This burial was dated to LMIIIA, shortly after that in Tholos Tomb A (described above) and during the final years of the cemetery's use. The tholos roof appears to have collapsed before the end of the Postpalatial period but the arrangement of the body, the position of the offerings (for example the bronze mirror near her face) and of her spectacular jewellery including the decoration of her garments and hair could be documented by the excavators in the greatest detail.

In the soil of the collapsed roof were three burials which could be dated to the Subminoan period c 1000 BC. This concluded the 1400-year history of burials in this remarkable cemetery site.

Anemóspilia

The sanctuary of Anemóspilia, 3km northwest of Arkhánes, was discovered in 1979 and interpreted by its excavators as a Minoan temple. It lies across the ravine to the west of Phourní, on the flank of Mount Júktas.

To find the site from the Herákleion end of the village continue past the war memorial and three-aisled church (see p 122) into the start of the one-way system. Where the road widens turn right following signs. Leaving the village the road climbs steadily (past the local rubbish dump) and then more steeply as it nears the site. The excavation (fenced but usually open) is up a bank, left of the road at a curve. The panoramic view is magnificent, and towards the coast, in the valley away to the right, a dark splash of cypress and pine trees marks the palace at Knossós.

The Minoan shrine, within an enclosure wall, had three rooms preserved along the uphill side of a wide central corridor. Two of them contained a great quantity of fine artefacts including a chalice, other ritual vases and a large stone basin, as well as pithoi for storage. On a bench at the back of the central room there were clay feet that had belonged to a wooden cult statue, and in the room to the west there was a free-standing altar. The shrine was destroyed by earthquake, probably at the time of the destruction of the Old Palace at Knossós at the end of Middle Minoan II, and, unusually for Crete, human skeletons were found in the debris. The evidence for ritual at first pointed to animal sacrifice, but the bones on the altar with a long bronze knife were those of a young man. Three other skeletons, presumably of people involved in the ritual, were found nearby; one was crushed outside the doorway of the central room with a fine Kamáres ware vase beside him, and two (a man and a woman) were on the floor of the room with the altar. The man had been wearing an agate seal and a ring of silver coated with iron. Taking account of forensic evidence, the excavators concluded that the youth on the altar had been sacrificed minutes before the building was destroyed by the earthquake disaster which the ritual was perhaps designed to avert.

To Mount Júktas

South from Arkhánes the valley road runs directly below Mount Júktas and then, 5km from the village, passes the excavation of a Minoan country house at Vathýpetro.

Just out of the village a short detour takes you to the frescoed church of **Ayios Mikhaíl Arkhángelos**. **Asómatos**. The key is held in Arkhánes at the *Taverna Myriophíto* on the plateía. (Be prepared to deposit a passport as security.) You take the Vathýpetro road which leaves the triangular plateía at its top end (by the post office) and immediately bears right. 1km from the plateía a turning left is signed to Asómatos. Soon curving right, the side-road runs between vineyards for 1.5km. At a sharp bend across a stream-bed, the trees down to the left hide the little church, all that remains of the Venetian settlement of Asómatos.

The well-preserved frescoes (dated 1315–16 by inscription on the south wall) include scenes from the life of the Archangel Michael. There is a stern *Pantokrator* in the half-dome of the apse, a remarkable *Crucifíxion*, and among Old Testament scenes the *Fall of Jericho* where soldiers are portrayed in 14C armour contemporary with the painting. On the west wall (bottom left) the donor Mikhaíl Patsidiótis, with his wife, reverently offers a model of his church to his patron saint the archangel.

Back on the valley road to Vathýpetro, the view to the right is dominated by the bulk of Mount Júktas. The 19C traveller, Robert Pashley, climbed the mountain in search of 'the tomb of Zeus' and the notion lingers on Crete even today. The church of Aphéndis Khristós (Christ the Lord) is conspicuous on the summit (at a height of 811m). Griffon vultures are a common sight around the peak.

One of the most important of the **Minoan peak sanctuaries**, high on the northern shoulder of the mountain, Mount Júktas was a place of pilgrimage for the Minoans for more than 1000 years. The sanctuary site (marked today by the telecommunications masts) commanded a fine view over the surrounding countryside but, perhaps more importantly, was conspicuous from far away, in particular from the palace at Knossós.

3km out of Arkhánes a narrow asphalt road climbs the hill (signed, keeping right at the first fork) or you may decide to walk from the turning, 4km to the summit. (There is a direct path up from Arkhánes which is shorter but very steep.) On the last bend before the church a footpath leads off right, along the flank of the hill, ten minutes to the derelict relay station which encroaches on the archaeological area. The main area of the excavation blocks the path just before you reach the masts.

The peak sanctuary was first investigated by Sir Arthur Evans who found substantial structures and a *temenos* wall of Cyclopean masonry built of large close-fitting but irregular stones, a method unusual on Crete. He also traced stretches of a Minoan road from the direction of Knossós.

In 1977 the Greek Archaeological Service returned to the site for a major programme of work which has established that the peak sanctuary was in use as a cult place at least from the Prepalatial period (EMII) through to Mycenaean times (LMIIIB).

The excavation is fenced but the sure-footed can scramble up to vantage points on the hillside above it. Here, at the upper (south) end of the *temenos* is the distinctive feature at the heart of this peak sanctuary, a natural cave-like cleft or chasm 10m deep into the bedrock. The cleft, reached by a ramp, was defined on its east and south sides by a retaining wall, two terraces with buildings and a rectangular enclosure clearly designed for cult practices. The features that were still distinguishable date from the New Palace period but contemporary with the Old Palace there was terracing here on a simpler plan and down the north slope a *temenos* covering c 200m x 100m. On the west side of the cleft a stepped altar was constructed and next to it was a large stone *kérnos* with around 100 depressions presumably for offerings. A hoard of bronze double axes was found nearby. Associated with this cult area round the cleft were rich finds of offerings, vessels for libations, materials for building pyres and the remains of sacrifices.

Offerings cleared from the cleft itself dated back to the EMII. They included hundreds of terracotta figurines, both human (the majority male but also women squatting in labour) and animal, and body parts in clay such as heads, hands, torsos and phalli. There were many artefacts (vessels, figures, seals, jewellery) in more precious materials such as stone, bronze, faience, gold leaf and rock crystal. The majority of the offerings can be dated to the Old Palace period, but fragments of numerous offering tables, many with Linear A inscriptions, definitely came from LMI levels. It used to be thought that peak sanctuaries were a Protopalatial phenomenon, but these finds pointed conclusively to the importance of cult practices here in the Neopalatial period. A (headless) model of a sphinx established the continuity of the sanctuary into Mycenaean times.

Beyond the telecommunications equipment the north end of the *temenos* extends apron-like over a lower slope to what was the northern entrance in the wall. Here there was evidence for workshops and a potter's kiln of the Neopalatial period.

Before leaving the hill you may like to take the rocky path along the precipice, beyond the four-naved church of Aphéndis Khristós, for a bird's-eye view stretching from the Lévka Ori (White Mountains) in the west to Mount Díkte in the east, and south across the island to the Asteroúsia range. If you are on the ridge in the company of local people you may find that they will remind you that you are walking on the burial place of the Cretan Zeus.

Vathýpetro

The valley road continues to the archaeological site of Vathýpetro, signposted 200m right of the road at a water point. Open 08.30–14.30 daily except Monday.

This large country house, excavated at the beginning of the 1950s but never fully published, was built in Late Minoan I, the Neopalatial period. The architecture incorporated ashlar masonry, pillar basements, a tripartite shrine and other typical Minoan features. The house seems to have been destroyed by fire in the LMIB period. Interesting evidence for self-sufficiency was discovered; as well as weaving equipment there were both wine and olive-oil presses, and a kiln among the outbuildings pointed to the existence of a potter's workshop.

To the west the site commands a superb view across one of the natural north–south routes from the coast through to the Mesará plain. In the middle distance to the northwest you can distinguish the twin-peaked hill of Prophítis Ilías where the Byzantine general Nikephóros Phokás built a fortress (p 132).

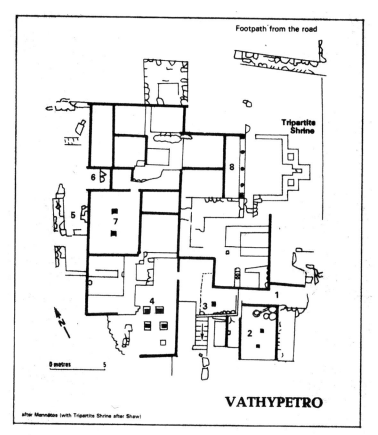

You enter the house at the southeast, along a corridor (**1** on the plan). On the left are storerooms (**2**) where wine-making equipment is on view in a good state of preservation. At the end of the corridor the staircase (**3**) led to an upper floor over the storerooms. The main room (**4**) has four central pillars and a paved floor. Along the west façade a paved area forms a miniature West Court (**5**) with drains running out of the house wall; an olive press with basin was found here. The façade has a deep recess (**6**) which may have held a shrine. The roofed area (**7**) is a pillar basement, a storage area with 16 giant pithoi emphasising the importance of the agricultural produce (chiefly wine and oil) on which the prosperity of this estate was based. To the north is a set of rooms (poorly preserved) which are thought to have been the private living quarters. The entrance to this part of the house was through a three-columned portico (**8**); to the east of it, across a small court, the excavator identified a tripartite shrine with a central recess flanked by two square niches, recalling both the shrine in the **Miniature Frescoes** found at Knossós and the sanctuary carved on the **Mountain Shrine Rhyton** from Zákros. A grander version, but on the same principle, is the tripartite shrine beside the Central Court of the palace at Knossós.

You can continue from Vathýpetro 3km to Khoudétsi on the main Herákleion–Pýrgos road for the direct route (c 20km) back to the north coast. If you turn right in Khoudétsi a circular tour could include the Epanosíphis monastery. One of the possible return routes on country roads passes the hill above Prophítis Ilías which has a long history as a fortified site.

Moní Epanosíphi

The Epanosíphis monastery Moní Epanosíphi is thought to have been founded towards the end of the period of Venetian rule, c 1600; the original church, dedicated to Ayios Yeóryios, was destroyed in an earthquake in 1856. This was a particularly wealthy foundation with valuable land and property, and the community still flourishes, now under the jurisdiction of the cathedral in Herákleion. During the Turkish period it was a centre of learning, and, like so many other religious houses on the island, gave constant support to the cause of Cretan nationalism, for which it suffered severely.

There is a fine view from the terrace below the church over fertile but sparsely populated countryside typical of this area of central Crete. You are looking south across the eastern end of the Mesará plain to the coastal ridge of the Asteroúsia mountains. The isolated hill rising from the plain marks the village of Ligórtynos.

The 19C traveller Robert Pashley came here and remembered the cypresses and palm trees of a 'retreat from the busy hum of men'. The monastery is still deeply revered and valued by Cretans and on Sundays is often the objective of an *ekdromí*, or family outing. The feast of Ayios Yeóryios is celebrated on 23 April (unless that date falls in Holy Week, when it is transferred to the Monday after Easter); if you are in the area you may like to plan a visit to coincide with the celebrations. At other times this is usually a tranquil place, with a fountain contributing the constant background noise of running water.

From the monastery it is 9km on a country road to **Rukáni**. On the edge of the village a picturesque domed cruciform church dedicated to Ayios Ioánnis dates to the Second Byzantine period (11C–12C). 4km further, at Kypárisos, a left turn will bring you out (after 6km) at Veneráto for the Palianí convent (see p 145) and the main Herákleion–Phaistós road.

The alternative is to keep right towards **Prophítis Ilías**. Above the village is a twin-peaked hill once the site of the **fortress of Témenos** though nothing remains except parts of the circuit wall. The climb is rewarded with stunning views of the surrounding countryside.

After the Byzantine general Nikephóros Phokás had driven the Saracens from the island in 961, he built a great fortress on the hill here and called it Témenos. He planned to establish a new capital inland, away from the danger of pirate raids, but the move failed to gain popular support, and in 968 when Phokás was recalled to Constantinople as emperor, only the fortress had been completed.

The first Venetian Duke of Crete, Giacomo Tiepolo, took refuge here (in what was referred to as the *oppidum fortissimum*) at a time of rebellion in Candia (Herákleion). The fortifications were restored after an earthquake in 1303, and again in the 16C when the Turks began to threaten the island.

Until recently the village was known as Kanlí Kastélli (Bloody Castle) in memory of a battle here in 1647 when the Venetians inflicted a great defeat on invading Turks.

From the top of the village (near the church of Prophítis Ilías) there is an easy track running left, along the northern flank of the double hill, to the ruins of the old main entrance to the fortress and the church of Ayía Paraskeví. But to climb directly from the village church to the west summit ask for the path up to the Panayía which is out of sight immediately above you. (Gesture uphill because there are two chapels with this dedication.) The steep path will bring you in ten minutes to the *Rocca* or stronghold on the summit where Phokás built his castle.

More than 1000 years earlier this was the site of the Greco-Roman city-state of **Lýkastos** and near the chapel of the Panayía there is a well-preserved double cistern, probably Roman in date.

On the summit nothing is preserved except traces of rock cutting. The panorama includes the craggy southwest slopes of Mount Júktas, and the Minoan site at Vathýpetro (see above) discernible to the southeast across the valley below the quarry scar. You can walk across the Témenos saddle to the eastern high point, **Apáno Kastélli**. In the dip a good stretch of the southern curtain walling still stands. As you climb east you pass the church of Ayios Nikólaos (rebuilt on old foundations) and beside it the remains of substantial buildings, probably Venetian. The defended saddle, designed as a haven in times of trouble in the surrounding countryside, slopes down to the north to the old main entrance where formidable overlapping defence walls are excellently preserved. In places the walls reuse Hellenistic material, presumably from Lýkastos. Inside the entrance **Ayía Paraskeví** has only tantalising indications of the frescoes which the Italian scholar Giuseppe Gerola admired at the beginning of the last century. The track from that church leads back to the village.

It is worth walking south into the village round the foot of the hill to the Venetian fountain known locally as the great spring, **Megáli Piyí**. A precipitous rock-cut stairway climbed from this water source to the fortress above it; up the rock face the remains of the old guard posts are marked by brick courses conspicuous in their walling.

The valley road back to the coast past the vineyards of Phinikiá (on record already in Venetian times) will bring you out in Herákleion by the Khaniá Gate. Turn left for the junction with the north coast highway.

The Pediáda district

The district of Pediáda (a word meaning flat country) is a prosperous agricultural region between Herákleion and the mountains surrounding the upland plain of Lasíthi. This expedition, which offers the chance to explore an unspoilt landscape, is described as a circular drive of c 80km from Herákleion, inland to **Kastélli Pediádas** the traditional centre of the region, returning north to the coast road at Khersónisos. There are opportunities to visit the **Kazantzákis Museum**, the **Angárathos monastery** and the potting village of **Thrapsanó**, as well as a number of frescoed churches. Above Kastélli, which lies on the E4 long-distance walking route, is the site of the Greco-Roman city of **Lýttos**. Part of this circular itinerary could be combined with a morning visit to the Minoan palace at Mália (p 200).

Travelling by bus

There is a bus service from Herákleion to Kastélli Pediádas. It is possible to enjoy a strenuous 18km walk on quiet country roads, using an early bus up to Kastélli, climbing 6km to Lýttos and continuing to Avdoú (p 234).

You can then catch the afternoon bus down from Lasíthi or take a local taxi back to the north coast. Alternatively you could stay in Kastélli and walk sections of the E4.

Leave Herákleion on the Knossós road, or join it from the New National Road as for Arkhánes (p 121). After Spília there is a sign, left, for a cross-country short cut through Skaláni to the Kazantzákis Museum in Myrtiá (see below). The main road to Kastélli keeps left when the Arkhánes road forks right, and continues south. **Pezá**, 18km from Herákleion, has one of the largest processing plants on the island for olive oil, and is at the centre of a prosperous wine-growing region. In recent years serious efforts have been made to improve the quality and expand the export of Cretan wine. At the end of the village keep left at a fork and you will soon pass, set back on the left, an exhibition centre and museum run by the **Pezá Union of Wine Producers**. Open Easter–mid-Oct, 08.00–15.00 Mon–Fri. There are promotional events and opportunities to taste and buy wine and olive oil, and related products such as olive oil soap. The consistently reliable wines of Pezá are available in many tavernas and supermarkets. They are marketed as *Logádo*, *Viglinós* and *Líktos*, with *Minos Palace* at the top of the range.

From Pezá you continue to the edge of Ayiés Paraskiés, and then left into the village when the main Viánnos road to the south curves sharply right signed for Arkalokhóri. The Kastélli road runs east from Ayiés Paraskiés through the intensively cultivated Pediáda countryside. After 3km signs point left for a short detour (c 2km) to the museum in the village of **Myrtiá** in honour of the distinguished Cretan writer Níkos Kazantzákis (1883–1957). He is most widely known as the author of *Zorba the Greek*, a work said to be fashioned out of nostalgia for the island of Crete as well as for the character of Zorba himself. Myrtiá was the home village of Kazantzákis's father.

The **Kazantzákis Museum** is open March–October Mon, Wed, Sat, Sun 09.00–13.00 and 16.00–20.00; Tues and Fri mornings only; Thur closed. To find it follow signs to the far end of the village street before turning right to park around a little plateía.

The display is well arranged to illustrate Kazantzákis's personal, literary and political life in Greece and abroad, with extensive background notes (translated into English). Kazantzákis was born on Crete in 1883; he took a degree in law at the University of Athens, and afterwards continued his literary and philosophical studies in France, Germany and Italy. Between the two world wars he worked from his home on the island of Aíyina. His study from that period is reconstructed in the Historical Museum in Herákleion (p 93). Briefly in 1945 he was Minister of Education in the Greek government.

Among his most admired works are *Freedom and Death*, *Christ Recrucified* and *The Odyssey: A Modern Sequel*. Some of the novels have been made into films and plays, but Kazantzákis also wrote specifically for the theatre. On display are contemporary photographs and documents, personal articles, theatrical memorabilia and editions of his books, including a great number in translation. One room is devoted entirely to Zorba.

Back on the main road and 3km beyond the Myrtiá turning, a broad byroad to the left crosses a stream and brings you after 4km to the tranquil **Angárathos monastery**, traditionally one of the most respected religious houses on the island. The monastery is now also one of the rewards for walkers following the E4 path.

The exact date of the monastery's foundation is not known, but it is mentioned in 16C manuscripts in the British Museum and St Mark's Library, Venice, and the records of its abbots go back to 1520. After the fall of Constantinople, Angárathos rivalled the Sinai College in Herákleion as a seat of learning. The monastery flourished during the first half of the 17C, but at the time of the Turkish invasion of 1645 its valuables and documents were taken for safety to the island of Kýthera, where the abbot's family had estates. Among the objects rescued was a treasured icon of the Panayía (the Virgin Mary); the name Angárathos enshrines the belief that the original church was built on the spot where this icon had been found, under a bush of the tall herb *agkaraviá* (Jerusalem sage).

The present church, dedicated to the Assumption of the Virgin (Feast Day 15 August), dates only from 1894, but it is surrounded by a triangular courtyard of picturesque buildings which preserve many early features. Several of these are dated by inscription: the gateways at both north and south entrances (1583 and 1565 respectively), a sarcophagus built into the north side of the court (1554), and a lofty barrel-vaulted storeroom opposite the west end of the church (1628). The old north gate is to the left of the modern approach.

Galatás and Thrapsanó

Back again on the main road, you could continue straight ahead to Kastélli, but a turning is signed (right) to Thrapsanó, a village famed for its pottery, in particular the plain earthenware which includes the traditional large jars or *pithária*, little changed from the storage jars of Minoan times.

For Thrápsano you pass the edge of **Vóni** and here readers with an interest in archaeology may choose to make a 2km detour (right) to visit a hilltop site above **Galatás** where Greek archaeologists are excavating a newly discovered Minoan palace and part of a sizeable settlement. There is no public access but you can get a fair impression of the site from outside the fence. The panoramic view alone is worth the climb.

Through the hamlet of Galatás your objective is across the valley, on a bluff marked by a lone wild fruit tree. Beyond the second rise in the road, tracks join it from both left and right. Leave a vehicle and walk right. (Further along the road there is a double-naved unpainted chapel, a useful landmark on the approach from the south, from Arkhalokhóri.) In spring, with the snow still lying on the peaks around Mount Díkte, the track uphill is lined with the Cretan iris (*Iris cretica*), asphodel and a variety of orchids. The area is protected as an archaeological site; this is not the place to pick flowers. Walk to the top of the hill until the track leads round, right, towards the excavation.

The palatial buildings at Galatás were laid out around a paved central court (37m x 16m) aligned north–south. The small plateau does not seem to allow room for a west court. At the north end of the court the impressive façade is built of ashlar blocks; many masons' marks were noted. Best preserved was the East

Wing where the excavators have uncovered a pillar hall in which they found a built hearth, a pier-and-door partition feature (*polythýron*) and storerooms with pithoi. There is evidence for frescoes with pictorial decoration in miniature, recalling the **Miniature Frescoes** of Knossós. Fresco fragments were also found in houses of what is believed to be the surrounding settlement.

There was occupation on this site as far back as Prepalatial times and in the Protopalatial period substantial buildings, with evidence for grain processing on a scale that seems to exceed domestic needs. But the palace buildings recently uncovered around the court were constructed in MMIIIB or LMIA, the early part of the Neopalatial period. They had a short life, for the excavators found that they had been gradually abandoned, with frescoes removed from the walls, and were in ruins before they were destroyed by an earthquake which is tentatively associated with the LMIA eruption of Théra. It is suggested that the centre of power moved to Kastélli.

Back on the main route and continuing from Vóni you come to the potting village of **Thrapsanó**. A Cretan monk, Agápios Lándos, whose work was published in Venice in 1642, commented that all the men of Thrapsanó were potters, and the tradition has endured. Potting is a seasonal occupation. As soon as the weather is suitable in early summer, the potters work a seven-day week. There is a primitive production line through potting, drying and firing, and each pot may take up to a week from start to finish. Most of the potteries welcome visitors, and their products are everywhere for sale.

Thrapsanó is a long village set on a hillside. On the way in you pass one of the workshops for the large jars. Others are below the village and you can walk downhill from the little triangular plateía. Otherwise drive through the village and turn left in front of a clock-tower at the end (for the Kastélli road). Downhill, almost out of Thrapsanó, double back on the first road to the left, past a prominent modern domed church, and along a stream-bed. There are pottery kilns and workshops in the fields along this road. You can ask for potters specialising in the large *pithária*. The road bends right and crosses the stream towards the village lake, a recently enlarged reservoir which often shelters waterfowl, especially during the spring migration.

The road from Thrapsanó to Kastélli continues through three small villages, two of which, **Evangelísmos** and **Sklaverokhóri**, have Byzantine churches decorated with wall-paintings.

The first you come to, in the middle of its village, is the domed cruciform church of **Ayios Evangelísmos** with 14C frescoes uncovered in 1981 in the west arm of the cross. They were found to include Old Testament scenes, rare on Crete, of the **Creation of Adam and Eve**, the **Garden of Eden** and the **Expulsion from Paradise**. The church key is kept at the *kapheneíon* across the street. (In the hot months avoid the siesta hours.)

4km further, in Sklaverokhóri, the frescoes in the church of **Eisódia Theotókon** are unusually well preserved. (There is a graffito date of 1481.) If you turn right off the village street before it bends left, the church is ahead on the right. You should find the guardian in one of the houses on the same side just before the church. In the customary position in the apse is a portrayal of the **Panayía Platytéra**, the Virgin Mary framed by angels, hierarchs and deacons, and 'wider than the heavens' in Orthodox iconography. On the arch above is the

Ancient of Days. In the nave are the ***Birth of Mary*** and the ***Presentation in the Temple*** (on the vault), as well as scenes from the life of Christ, including a baptism with male and female river gods. The south wall has a scene of ***St George slaying the dragon***, and rescuing a princess (the daughter of the King of Alassia) while her parents watch from the city walls with God's hand outstretched from above. The figures opposite include St Francis, one of only three examples on Crete of the portrayal of this subject, one of the saints of the western church.

Ahead, past the church, you rejoin the main road. Turn right for Kastélli. On the way in to the village there is a sign left for the former **Kallérgis monastery** where a tall, elegant chapel with bellcote, showing strong influence of Venice in its architecture, now stands at the centre of a thriving farmstead. The (slow) drive to it, of 4km across empty countryside, is often rewarding to both flower and bird enthusiasts.

Kastélli Pediádas

As the busy centre of an intensively cultivated agricultural region Kastélli is remarkably little affected by the world of mass tourism prevailing less than 20km away on the north coast. The place has a long history. Recent archaeological excavations ahead of new building have shown that there was a sizeable Minoan settlement here. The modern place-name refers to a Venetian castle which survived until the early years of the 20C.

The direct route back to the coast from Kastélli keeps left through the centre and then turns north following signs for Khersónisos and Herákleion. Readers with an interest in old churches should consider two short detours described below, the first south from Kastélli to Lilianó, and the other off the Khersónisis road before Piyí, in an idyllic setting above a stream. In the hills to the east of Kastélli is the site of the Greco-Roman city-state of Lýttos, and from there you can cut across on minor roads to Avdoú and one of the main routes up to the Lasíthi plain.

Staying in Kastélli, walkers could explore the first (marked) stretches of the traditional paths into Lasíthi, from Kastamónitsa on the E4 or further afield from Embaros (p 179).

Where to stay

C *Hotel Kalliópi* (10 rooms), ☎ 28910 32685, fax 28910 32273/32685, a recently opened block of rooms near the centre of Kastélli but with views over open countryside, and run by a Cretan family eager to make your stay a success.

Kastélli offers a good choice of tavernas aiming to serve traditional Cretan food.

For the intriguing church of **Ayios Ioánnis**, **Lilianó**, take the road south from the centre of Kastélli signed for Viánnos. After 2km watch for a guardpost opposite a road (right) to a military airfield. Shortly after this the church (and village) are signed right, with the church partly hidden in an olive grove. It is usually open but if not ask in the village for the key.

Ayios Ioánnis presents a puzzling mixture of Venetian influence and features more often associated with much earlier churches. The ground-plan of three aisles ending in apses and divided by two pairs of columns (Ionic with plain abacus capitals) indicates a basilica, though the short square nave is not typical; it was probably designed to support a dome. The church now has a wooden saddle roof, and across the west end a barrel-vaulted narthex supporting a bellcote. Material reused from older buildings (perhaps from Lýttos, see below) is particularly noticeable outside the church in the lower courses of both north and south walls. The block serving as a bench against the west wall has an inscription in ancient Greek, and a fragment of an Early Christian altar is let into the threshold at the church door. The basilica plan (with floor lower than that of the narthex and c 1m below the present level of the cemetery) combined with the antiquity of the building material suggests an early date. However, the roof construction, other architectural details, such as corbels, and the narthex all show unquestionable Venetian influence. On the south wall the remains of a pulpit (five stone steps and part of a column) suggest the practice of the Latin rite, which would put any adaptation of a Byzantine church at least no earlier than the 13C.

To find **Ayios Pandeleímon** near **Piyí** (meaning a spring) which is a Second Byzantine period church with 13C–14C frescoes, take the main road north from Kastélli to Khersónisos, and after 1km watch for a byroad to the right signed to the church and a taverna. After 2km the church almost blocks the way, shaded by two spreading oak trees, in an area kept green by nearby springs which used to feed the Roman aqueduct supplying ancient Khersónisos. The taverna occupies the slope to the stream below the church, and the church key is kept here. If the taverna is closed, ask in Piyí.

The church stands on the foundations of an Early Christian basilica, and Hellenistic inscriptions as well as architectural fragments suggest an earlier sanctuary. Ayios Pandeleímon is the patron saint of healing, and this, together with the health-giving waters of the spring, makes it likely that there is continuity on the site from a temple dedicated to Asklepios. Almost a ruin when Giuseppe Gerola saw it at the beginning of the last century, Ayios Pandeleímon was carefully restored in 1962. The three-aisled church is an unconventional structure incorporating many reused architectural fragments and decorated blocks, as well as inscriptions of Hellenistic and Roman date. One of the interior columns is made up of four superimposed Corinthian capitals resting on a square abacus plate. The partially restored blind-arcading in the south wall is thought to relate to a previous building phase, perhaps a larger cruciform domed church. Frescoes are preserved in the apse and on the walls of the nave, dated stylistically to the late 13C–early 14C; on the north wall (at its east end) there is a rare scene of *St Anne nursing the infant Mary.*

There is a choice of routes for the return to the north coast. You can continue on the Khersónisos road due north, or you can climb east from Kastélli into the hills to Lýttos, and on across country under a wall of mountains to Avdoú, on the main road between the coast and the mountain plain of Lasíthi.

Lýttos

Lýttos is signed (3km) from the centre of Kastélli, straight ahead when the main road to the coast turns left. The village, formerly Xydás, has been renamed after this important city-state of Greco-Roman times which spread over these hills.

Approaching the village its modern church is visible ahead for some distance. Across the valley to the left the tiny chapel of **Ayios Yeóryios** (recently restored) is set among cypresses and orange trees. Remains of frescoes preserved in the apse and on the south wall are dated by inscription to 1321. To visit Ayios Yeóryios stop by the war memorial below the modern church. The chapel is in sight in the valley, and steps lead down to a path which passes it. Ask at the *kapheneíon* above the steps whether you need a key.

At the end of the village of Lýttos a road ahead takes you down to Kastamónitsa in the valley, and the start of the traditional mule path from the west up into the mountain plain of Lasíthi. This is the route for walkers using the E4. For the archaeological site of Lýttos you turn left, signed for Avdoú, to climb for 2km to the hilltop site. Two white chapels stand out on the skyline, right, and near the watershed the path to the antiquities is signed to the first of them, Tímeos Stavrós. There is not much above ground of the Greco-Roman city, but a walk along the ridge is recommended, to enjoy the majestic position of the site against the wall of the Lasíthi massif and with a splendid view back over the Pediáda countryside. It is worth keeping a lookout for birds of prey ranging out from the mountains.

Some accounts say that it was to Lýttos that Rhea came to give birth to Zeus at a safe distance from Kronos (see Cave of Zeus on Mount Díkte). Homer spoke of 'broad Lýttos' and the exploits of the Lyttian force under Idomeneus, leader of the Cretan contingent in 'eighty black ships' at Troy. Koiranus, leader of the Lyttians, gave his own life to save Idomeneus from Hector's spear.

Lýttos was one of the most powerful and warlike of the city-states, and a deadly rival of Knossós, at least from the 4C BC. Its territory extended from the north to the south coast, with a port at Khersónisos. In the war of 221–219 BC Lýttos resisted the alliance between Knossós and Górtyn which aimed to control the whole island. The Lyttian army embarked on an expedition against Ierápytna (now Ierápetra), unwisely leaving the city unguarded, and Knossós seized the opportunity to destroy Lýttos utterly. Around 150 years later the rebuilt city put up strong resistance against Quintus Metellus Creticus (the commander of the 67 BC Roman invasion), but survived to flourish under Roman rule and into the First Byzantine period. Statue inscriptions dedicated to Trajan (AD 98–117) and Hadrian (AD 117–138) are particularly numerous.

Archaeological evidence for the historical record at this huge site used to depend largely on these inscriptions, the reports of early travellers (who noted the largest theatre known on the island) and chance finds. Now systematic investigation by the Greek Archaeological Service is under way.

A Hellenistic house has been excavated where four column bases and a built altar were preserved in a main hall, as well as storage and workshop areas. The house was destroyed by fire in 221–220 BC, presumably in connection with the events described above.

The chapel of **Tímios Stavrós** (The Holy Cross) is built over the foundations of a large 5C basilica; the area around it was the *agorá* or centre of the ancient city. The second church, **Ayios Yeóryios** on the southern peak, lies on a 2C AD building in which painted wall plaster was found. Built into the church's southeast corner are architectural fragments from ornate piers, with crosses set in delicately carved acanthus foliage. Nearby, part of the city's *bouleuterion* or council chamber has been excavated, revealing an area with built platforms or benches. This building was destroyed by earthquake c 200 AD.

The hilltop area between the two churches was enclosed by a formidable wall which can still be traced in places, most easily along its outer side. It is of rubble faced with squared stones in the Roman style, and has been compared with the fortifications of the acropolis at Górtyn. Its probable date is 7C AD.

Crossing the narrow valley to the southeast are traces of an aqueduct which brought Lasíthi water to Lýttos from springs near the Kerá convent. From away to the left the road from the north coast climbs into the mountains past the convent (p 234), and directly across the valley, a mule track or *kalderími*, one of the eight ancient ways up to the Lasíthi mountain plain, snakes up towards the Tsoúli Mníma pass (now the route of the E4). Like similar mule tracks all across the island this one has been subjected to the attentions of the bulldozer for the benefit of shepherds' vehicles.

For the main route back to the north coast you return to Kastélli but the road past Lýttos continues beyond the site and at the watershed begins a long descent to Aski. Turn left there on to an unpaved road connecting the villages in the valley below which will bring you (in 12km from Lýttos) to the frescoed churches and the tavernas of Avdoú (p 234).

Priniás and Krousónas

This is a leisurely excursion on minor roads with opportunities to explore the countryside southwest of Herákleion, and the eastern foothills of the Ida mountain range. There is access to the E4 long-distance walking route at Ano Asítes. Above Priniás is the hilltop site of the Archaic city-state of Rizenía from which came temple sculpture now on view in the Herákleion Archaeological Museum. Krousónas lies at 460m on what was in former times a main route from the east over to the Nída mountain plain and the Idaian cave. The climb (by the direct road from Gázi) to the village and the nearby convent of Ayía Eiríne could follow a visit to the excavations at the Minoan site of Týlissos (p 189).

Travelling by bus

The itinerary assumes that you have your own transport, but using buses from Herákleion, from the bus station outside the Khaniá Gate (p 64), you can get to Priniás, either direct through Asítes or by walking (7km) along the road from Ayía Varvára which is on the main Phaistós route. There is also a bus service to Krousónas. You will need to consult the timetables in advance.

For Priniás you leave the north coast highway, the New National Road, at the Míres junction, at the start of the Herákleion–Phaistós road across the island. Then, on the outskirts of Herákleion, watch for a turning right signed to the university hospital and Ayios Mýronas and Asítes (20km). Beyond Voútes you are in open country. About 10km after leaving the Phaistós road a turning right is signed for Kitharída and Krousónas (see below).

The Priniás road continues to **Ayios Mýronas**, conspicuous from a distance on its hilltop, the site of ancient Rávkos. The village's name derives from the 3C martyr saint born here who went on to become bishop of Knossós. If you keep right, on the lower road through the village, you pass his grotto, and behind it steps lead up to a big 13C–14C church. This is cross-domed in plan with the later addition of a domed narthex; the drum supporting the main dome is designed with eight linked arches framing slender windows. (If necessary you can enquire about access at the *kapheneíon* opposite on the upper road.)

5km further, at the north end of the village of **Káto** (Lower) **Asítes**, there are signs for a steep 2km climb to Moní Gorgolaíni (closed 13.00–16.00). There was a monastery here in the time of Venetian rule, but except for the two-aisled church of Ayios Yeóryios the buildings are of no great age. The detour is recommended because what is now a convent, standing on a terrace shaded by cypress trees at a height of 400m, offers a grandstand view over central Crete.

Very soon after Káto Asítes comes **Ano** (Upper) **Asítes** where you cross the route of the E4. To the west this sets off on the climb to the Nída plain by way of the Prinós refuge hut run by Greek mountaineering club, EOS. This is a stretch of trail suitable only for serious long-distance walkers, but there is a loop left along a stream-bed. In the other direction from the village a gentle path heads east, cutting across through Kerásia to Veneráto on the main north–south road (and the Phaistós bus route).

The Priniás road climbs from Ano Asítes across uncultivated country (promising for wild flowers, especially orchids in spring) and soon, 2km before the modern village, the distinctive rock formation known as the **Patéla** meaning 'naked expanse', dominates the view, with the chapel of Ayios Pandeleímon perched on its eastern brow. You pass through the cemetery area of Siderospiliá (see below).

Priniás

The Patéla of Priniás is a flat-topped hill (686m) which became the acropolis of the ancient Greek city of Rizenía. This is a naturally defended position, accessible only from the west, and of strategic importance overlooking the easy route across the island using valleys between the north and south coasts.

A track from the crest on the road now allows you to drive most of the way up the hill, and then a path along the north side of the acropolis out to Ayios Pandeleímon affords access (across spiky undergrowth) to areas of archaeological interest on the site. The Patéla hill is highly recommended to bird-watchers.

Italian archaeologists first excavated on the Patéla at the end of the 19C and returned here in 1969. Their best known work was concerned with the two Archaic temples on the flat summit but on the eastern side they identified a refuge site with an associated sanctuary dating to the end of the Bronze Age (c 1200 BC) and comparable with the LMIII sites of Karphí or Vrókastro (p 236, 242). From the sanctuary came a goddess figurine with cylindrical skirt and raised hands similar to those from Gázi and Karphí (all on display in Herákleion's Archaeological Museum). There were also numerous votive terracottas including snakes, and curious tubes with columns of loop handles known as snake tubes thought to be associated with the cult of the sacred snake. The sanctuary continued in use until the Archaic period.

At the southwestern edge of the hill are the remains of what has been called a splendid toy fort. It dates from the Hellenistic period and was square, a formidable construction with corner bastions. The most evocative features now visible on the acropolis are the remains of the excavated foundations of two Archaic period temples. Along the path from the car park to the chapel you first notice (right) excavations of a residential quarter, and then (at a fig tree) you can turn off to the location of the temples, fenced in the middle of the plateau. Viewing is restricted but it is easy to envisage the impact that in their prime these east-facing buildings must have created.

Temple A, the more northerly and the better preserved of the two, produced evidence relevant to the evolution of the Greek temple. The ground plan of this 7C BC building is said to reflect the influence of Minoan architecture. There was a central pillar between the side posts of the porch (dividing the entrance in two) in place of the pair of columns that would be expected in the simplest form of Greek temple, the *templum in antis*. In line with this pillar, inside the temple on the long axis of the cella, there were two wooden columns on low stone bases with a hearth between them; ashes and burnt bones of animals were found on the hearth. The arrangement recalls the temple at Dréros near Ayios Nikólaos.

On the east side of the Priniás temples archaeologists uncovered a courtyard with buildings round it; the court had been levelled with a mixture of volcanic ash and crushed pottery.

Some of the sculptures which embellished the entrance to Temple A are displayed in Room XIX of the Herákleion Museum. They include two seated female deities in the Daidalic style, from above the doorway into the cella, and fragments in low relief from friezes depicting panthers and a procession of mounted spearmen. The archaeologists point out that this sculptural assemblage decorating a Cretan temple predates the emergence of the Classical Greek orders of architecture.

The road south continues through the village of Priniás, and, 7km from the site, rejoins the main Herákleion–Phaistós route in Ayía Varvára (p 145). However, to continue on the circular excursion to Krousónas on the western slopes of the Ida mountains, you must retrace part of the route you took to the Patéla of Priniás.

500m back along the road north you pass the location of the cemetery of **Siderospiliá**, on a slope facing southeast across to the acropolis. Its 680 excavated tombs yielded important evidence for a sequence of burial rites and grave goods that was continuous from the late 13C to the middle of 6C BC, the first burials thus being contemporary with that of the settlement on the Patéla. The Italian archaeologists found that burial practices covered pit-graves, inhumation in tholos tombs and cremation burials. Outside the main sequence a number of crouch-burials, without grave gifts, were thought to be associated with a nearby Minoan Prepalatial settlement. Roman tombs of the 1C and 2C AD were also found. Two particularly well-preserved examples of these **rock-cut Roman tombs**, with niches and benches, and cists in the floor, are conspicuous at a bend in the road in a cutting on the left (west) verge.

Eighteen animal burials were found in the cemetery, associated with inhumation in tholos tombs. Twelve of them contained horse skeletons arranged in pits in a careful manner suggesting ritual significance, one with a bronze bit laid across his head. For the excavators these animal graves alongside human burials of the Early Iron Age recalled the horse sacrifices frequently mentioned in ancient literature. You continue north, back through Ayios Mýronas, and then watch for a sign on the left, to Kitharída and (7km) to Krousónas.

Krousónas

The village is laid out with theatrical effect across the head of a valley at an altitude of 460m. The main access road from the north coast (c 15km, see below) winds up the valley through vineyards before turning towards the peaks, so that the village is hidden until the final approach. On this side-road from Kitharída you come in at the top of the village, where an acute-angled turn uphill at the beginning of habitation is signed (3km) to the Ayía Eiríne convent. If you pass the turning you continue till the main street sweeps round in front of the church at the heart of the village.

A visit to the **Ayía Eiríne convent** above Krousónas at a height of 700m in the eastern foothills of the Ida range is strongly recommended.

The religious foundation of Ayía Eiríne dates back at least to 1589 when it benefited from Venetian patronage. It continued to thrive under Turkish rule and played an important but unobtrusive role as a centre of Hellenic education. The Venetian buildings were destroyed by the Turks in 1822 during the Cretan rebellion at the time of the war of independence on the mainland. This was an act of revenge for the slaughter of 370 Albanian soldiers (in the service of the Turkish rulers), who had been trapped by the Cretan rebels in one of the Krousónas churches. The Albanians met with no mercy despite the fact that they were holding hostage a Cretan child. The convent buildings were only reconstructed towards the end of the Second World War. Four nuns took up residence in 1944 (see plaque on the main doorway) and have established a thriving, self-supporting community.

The convent gate is usually kept open all day, and the nuns welcome visitors with generous hospitality. You are quite likely to find a Cretan family chatting over coffee and rakí or pastries. The nuns are also keen to sell their needlework. As it is not always easy to discuss prices after enjoying the hospitality, you may like to look at the craft work before you sit down.

The convent's isolation may soon come to an end for surfacing is threatened along the rough track climbing west beyond it. This is the traditional route to upland pastures and eventually over to the road between Anóyeia and the Nída mountain plain. In antiquity it was the approach from the direction of Knossós to the great sanctuary of the Idaían cave. While this is still an area of wilderness and fine mountain views, readers in search of upland flowers and birds of prey will enjoy exploring on foot.

Returning from Krousónas to the north coast you come to a junction with the Old Road (Herákleion–Réthymnon). To the left you are 6km from the Minoan excavations at Týlissos (p 189). For Herákleion turn right under a bridge carrying the highway.

From Herákleion to Phaistós

The site of the Minoan palace at Phaistós is 65km from Herákleion with the intriguing excavation at **Ayía Triáda** only 3km further, and the Minoan harbour at **Kommós** 7km down the road towards Mátala. This excursion from the north coast can be a day-trip to include a brief stop at **Górtyn**, once the capital of Roman Crete, and perhaps a visit to **Vóri** for its ethnographic museum, regarded as one of the best of its kind on the island. To explore the huge site at Górtyn, you might choose to return on another day and combine the visit with the drive over the Asteroúsia mountains to the coastal village of **Léndas**. Readers interested in Byzantine churches can take the road from Ayía Varvára to visit the monasteries along the south slopes of Mount Ida (but note that the Valsamóneros church is closed in the afternoons). An alternative return route from Phaistós takes you east across the Mesará plain from Ayii Déka.

From a base in the southern half of the province visitors are within easy reach of Phaistós and the other Minoan sites as well as having the chance to explore off the beaten track the unspoilt countryside and coastline south of the Mesará plain.

Travelling by bus

There are seven or eight buses a day for the visit to Phaistós and Ayía Triáda (via Górtyn) from the bus station outside the Khaniá Gate in Herákleion. (There is also a decent service to Phaistós from Ayía Galíni.) Some buses continue from Phaistós to Mátala but using public transport it may be difficult to include a visit to Kommós in a single day.

Where to stay

Above **Zarós** (p 145), in the foothills of Mount Ida, there is the secluded Class C *Hotel Idi* which, with an atmosphere in complete contrast to the coastal resorts, appeals to both Greeks and foreigners; advance booking is desirable. **Mátala** is perhaps not a place to stay for long except out of season but for a night or two there is a good choice of hotels for people who like to book ahead, and waterfront tavernas well placed for relaxing evenings. Travel agencies on the north coast will advise (or see p 65). You can also book ahead in **Léndas** (p 173) on the coast, a 30km drive south from Górtyn. The larger resort of **Ayía Galíni** (p 330) in the province of Réthymnon is only 20km from Phaistós.

For accommodation in **rent rooms** and studio apartments in the south look under **Zarós** and **Vóri** (p 147). South of Phaistós you could make for **Kamilári** (p 160) or for **Pitsídia**'s rooms to rent near the turning for Kommós.

The direct road from Herákleion to Phaistós follows the natural long-established route dictated by the topography of the island. It climbs from the coast using the north–south valleys on its way to cross the spine of hills which are a continuation of the mountain chain between the peaks of Ida and Díkte. It then drops in spectacular fashion to the Mesará plain where it runs through the Roman site of Górtyn.

From the centre of Herákleion you leave to the west by the Khaniá Gate, and after 2km watch for signs left for Míres. Then keep straight ahead, passing under the New National Road. From other starting points on the north coast you will join the road across the island at this Míres junction. On the edge of town is the turning for a minor road (right) for Ayios Mýronas and the Archaic site above Priniás (p 141). Staying on the main road you climb gently through a valley planted with vines and olives, the Italian cypresses scattered with picturesque effect. Daphnés, off to the left, is the centre of one of the main wine-producing areas on Crete.

The road continues through Síva to **Veneráto**, 20km from Herákleion, where a well-signed detour left leads in 2km to the ancient religious house of **Palianí**, now flourishing as a convent. Here there is the reward of a wide view back towards the coast, with Ayios Mýronas conspicuous on the summit of a hill away to the north. The Palianí convent is on the route of the E4 long-distance footpath which continues east to Prophítis Ilías and Arkhánes.

Moní Palianí was documented as an antiquity (*palaiá*, meaning old) even in 668. The nuns are hospitable and will point out interesting features of the old buildings. This is a self-supporting community and their fine needlework is for sale.

The 13C church (the narthex is a 15C–16C addition) retained the plan of the underlying three-aisled 6C basilica, but in the 19C it was much restored after Turkish destruction and earthquake damage. Some of the Early Byzantine (6C) capitals and impost blocks are preserved; two capitals are in situ, four support the altar, and others lie outside in the courtyard.

The Phaistós road continues through Veneráto and **Avyenikí**, and then gains height through olive groves. On a sharp bend (25km from Herákleion) you pass left the turn for **Ayios Thomás**, offering a short detour. The village, 4km off the main road, lies at 530m above sea level among curious rock formations which in geological terms are part of the spine of the island. The church of Ayios Thomás (recently restored) is a fine example of a Second Byzantine period building, three-aisled with its dome raised on a tall drum over the narthex. The key is held by the *papás* in the next village, Megáli Vrýsi, but you can get an impression of the interior through a narthex window. Across the main street from the church you can climb up under the pine trees, signed (five minutes) to Roman tombs, the best way to get a view of the village on the saddle between two pillars of rock.

Edward Lear passed this way on 16 May 1864 and sat down to sketch soon after dawn. His journal reads: 'I sit to draw among the great rox [sic], which at Ayios Thomás are magnificently picturesque', and then: '5.45 Have made a drawing; position very superb and rox vastly grand.' He was looking down on the village from this vantage point with the church of Ayios Thomás at the centre of the view.

You can continue ahead to rejoin the main road on the southern outskirts of Ayía Varvára. If you have kept to the main road rather than turning off for Ayios Thomás you will notice on the skyline, right, a white chapel marking the acropolis of the Archaic city-state above Priniás. In the valley between the main road and the acropolis hill, curious circular rock formations, a strong erosion feature, are known locally as the 'old lady's cheeses'.

30km from Herákleion is **Ayía Varvára**. On the approach to the village the little church of Prophítis Ilías, perched high on a rock called Omphalos (navel), is said to mark the centre of Crete. At the beginning of the long village you could turn off for Priniás.

At the far end of the village of Ayía Varvára you pass a second turning (right) which is the start of a scenic drive (p 175) across the southern foothills of Mount Ida to Zarós, the frescoed churches of the Vrondísi monastery and Valsamóneros, and Kamáres at the foot of the climb to the sacred cave. The road continues to the Amári Valley (p 336) or you can turn south to drop down to Míres, or to Vóri near Phaistós.

Shortly after Ayía Varvára on the main road south, the **Mesará plain** is suddenly in view. Beyond it are the Asterousia mountains which hide the Libyan sea.

The lowland plain is an alluvial basin consisting of rich silts and clays brought down to it by rivers, probably in the Pleistocene period. From the foothills of the Díkte range to the bay of Mesará, it lies parallel to the south coast, watered now, at least in the early part of the year, by two rivers, the Anapodáris (at the east end of the plain) and the Yeropótamos which, joined by a tributary from Górtyn (the Mitropoliános), flows into the sea below the Minoan site of Ayía Triáda. The fertile soil and benign climate in the shelter of the island's mountain spine have favoured settlement through the ages, and the region is nowadays one of great agricultural prosperity.

First settled at the end of the Neolithic period, the Mesará saw rapid population growth during the Early Bronze Age, with a number of settlements on the rising ground of the Asteroúsia foothills, and the first appearance of the great collective tombs on a circular plan with the entrance from the east, which have become known as the Mesará type. By the beginning of the second millennium, Phaistós had begun to emerge as the palatial centre and economic focus of the region. At a later period the city of Górtyn on the northern edge of the plain became the capital of Roman Crete, and retained a position of power until the second half of the 7C.

The road winds down from the hills and in summer the temperature increases at every bend. On the outskirts of Ayii Déka an acute left turn is signposted for Pýrgos (p 184), one of the settlements at the eastern end of the plain. (This road offers an alternative route for the return to the north coast, c 60km to Herákleion.)

Ayii Déka

Continuing towards Phaistós into Ayii Déka, the village (44km from Herákleion) is an agreeable place to break a journey. There are café-bars and tavernas along the main street. The name, the Holy Ten, commemorates ten Christian martyrs of the Persecution of Decius (AD 250) and the martyrs' church is signposted below (south of) the through road in the older part of the village.

The much restored 13C–14C church incorporates reused material from the nearby Greco-Roman city of Górtyn as do many of the old houses around the attractive tree-shaded square in front of it. In the nave of the church an icon portrays the martyrdom, and below in a glass case is a stone at which the ten are supposed to have knelt to be executed. A signed path leads (five minutes) to the southwest outskirts of the village, and to a crypt beside the portico of a modern chapel where six tile graves are venerated as the tombs of the martyrs.

Ayii Déka is on the edge of the archaeological area of Górtyn. A back road leads on from the graves, deep into the huge site, to the Roman Praetorium, but a visit to Górtyn (p 166) usually starts near the basilica of Ayios Títos (with parking and ticket office) 1km further along the main road.

Continuing beyond Górtyn towards Phaistós you come to **Míres** c 50km from Herákleion, not a picturesque place but the busy centre of this agricultural region. On Saturday mornings the wide main street is taken over by the weekly market. A minor road to the left is the direct way (18km) to Mátala, but for Phaistós and Ayía Triáda keep straight on.

About 3km beyond Míres, the site of the Minoan palace at Phaistós comes into view left of the road ahead, at the end of a low ridge jutting into the Mesará plain. You pass on the right the **Kalyvianí convent**, one of the most flourishing ecclesiastical establishments on the island, where the nuns run an orphanage and school. An avenue of clipped bougainvillaea leads to the big modern church with Italianate campanile and behind this is the 14C **frescoed chapel** of the Panayía Kalivianí.

Vóri

From the direction of Míres you would pass the well-signed turning left for Phaistós and then almost immediately turn right into Vóri, a village with an attractive plateía on a minor road up to Kamáres.

The well-signed **Museum of Cretan Ethnology** lies less than 1km off the main road and a visit is strongly recommended. Open daily 10.00–18.00. The museum was established to promote the study of Cretan culture after AD 1000. An old courtyard building near the church has been converted to house the comprehensive and imaginatively arranged collection relating to the arts, crafts and social history of the island. The exhibits are clearly labelled and explained in English as well as Greek, and there is a helpful illustrated catalogue.

Where to stay and eating out

Pension Margit, with a reputation as a well-run establishment, is near the top of the village, clearly signed from the museum. There are three tavernas, including a *psistariá* with spit, with tables under trees on the plateía.

For Phaistós you take the turning noted above off the main road and cross the tree-lined Yeropótamos river to climb steeply to the car park for the Minoan palace site.

Phaistós

- Open May and Sept 08.00–17.00; June 08.00–18.00; July and August 08.00–19.00; winter 10.00–15.00. It is always wise to consult a tourist information office or telephone the site, ☎ 28920 42315. If you are planning to visit Ayía Triáda as well, note that this site may close at 15.00 all the year round.

  From the Phaistós car park (and bus stop) a paved path to the archaeological site leads up to the ticket office and a tourist pavilion with a self-service café and bookshop.

The Minoan palace, according to literary tradition the home of Rhadamanthys, brother of King Minos, occupied a magnificent position looking out over the Mesará plain. To the north, beyond the valley of the Yeropótamos, is Mount Ida, snow-capped for half the year, and to the south the Asteroúsia range running parallel to the coast.

History of the site

Begun in 1900, the excavations at Phaistós have been the work of Italian archaeologists. Returning to the site in the second half of the century they uncovered a considerable area of the Old Palace (First Palace in the Phaistós terminology) and of the surrounding Minoan town. Exploration and study continue. Evidence from this Protopalatial period is better preserved here than elsewhere on Crete so this work has contributed significantly to an understanding of the achievements of Minoan architecture and administration during that time.

Phaistós was inhabited in Late Neolithic times (end of the fourth millennium; see Chronology, p 38) and during the Early Minoan period; pottery deposits are found beneath the earliest palace floors, and scattered traces of structures have been uncovered. The Old Palace, built in Middle Minoan IB (c 1900 BC), marked a great leap forward in the life of Phaistós, suggesting a growth in prosperity that would have been based on an agricultural economy. The Old Palace developed around a main central court, but had in all five paved courts including a west court with terracing to one side and raised walks across it.

Settlement extended all around at this time, downhill towards what is now the village of Ayios Ioánnis and west along the slope where the Venetian monastery church still stands. Interesting and important finds from this Protopalatial period include Kamáres ware pottery, the enigmatic Phaistós disk and a great archive of clay sealings, as well as tablets in Linear A.

This Old Palace was probably destroyed, like Knossós, at the end of MMII. The ruins were levelled and consolidated to provide foundations for its successor, the New or Second Palace, which except in the west court area is what visitors mainly see today.

Archaeologists are puzzled that from Neopalatial levels at Phaistós, where buildings are certainly complex and monumental, there was little sign of the rich finds which might have been expected. Portable items of value could have been removed by their owners or pillaged, but the almost complete absence of fresco decoration or clay sealings and tablets, which could not or would not have been removed, is harder to explain. The comparisons must be with Neopalatial Knossós or Zákros where evidence for the richness of Minoan invention is strikingly apparent and the same is true at Ayía Triáda (p 154), neighbour of Phaistós. It seems that during the Neopalatial period Ayía Triáda became somewhat more important at the expense of Phaistós, with the two sites complementing each other in a way that is far from fully understood.

The New Palace at Phaistós was itself destroyed, along with the majority of settlements on the island (including Ayía Triáda) at the end of Late Minoan IB. There was some reoccupation in LMIII, towards the end of the Bronze Age, and in the Geometric period (8C BC). The remains of a temple and some substantial houses date to the Classical-Hellenistic era. The city is mentioned in Linear B tablets and by Homer (*Iliad*, II, 648 where it is described as 'fair to dwell in'). Phaistós was the birthplace and home of the Cretan poet and prophet Epimenídes who was called to Athens (c 596 BC) by the renowned leg-islator, Solon, to conduct purification ceremonies in the city after a debilitat-ing pestilence. Phaistós retained some importance in the later periods and minted its own coins, until it was destroyed by Górtyn in the 2C BC.

From the modern entrance to the site, you cross the **Upper Court** diagonally to a flight of stairs. (On your right are the remains of Hellenistic buildings.) A stair-case takes you down to the **Theatral Area** (1 on the plan) and the **West Court**. To the right of the staircase, along the north side of the West Court, is an elabo-rate retaining wall for the Upper Court, and below it tiered rows provided seats for whatever events took place here. The court would have provided a place of assembly outside the palace.

From the West Court two successive palace façades can still be identified. When the New Palace was built its west front was set back about 8m behind that of its predecessor, and the level of the new West Court was raised accordingly. Its new paving was laid above more than 1m of cement-like fill, in the process cov-ering the lower tiers of the Theatral Area. During excavation this paving and fill were removed leaving the West Court of the Old Palace as you now see it, with its raised paths a distinctive Minoan feature, and (outside the fence) *kouloúres* similar to those at Knossós and Mália.

To the south and west of the Theatral Area, beyond a fine Minoan paved road (also outside the fence), lies part of the Minoan town with substantial houses that were destroyed at the same time as the Old Palace. From this complex has come an astonishing number of polychrome vases in the Kamáres ware, named after the sacred cave where it was first identified but believed to have been made only at the palace workshops of Knossós and Phaistós.

> ### Kamáres ware
> Kamáres ware provides some of the finest examples of the Minoan potter's art which include substantial vases as well as the thin-walled (eggshell) wares made possible by the development of the potter's wheel. Ceramics spe-cialists speak of the artistry of the distinctive decoration in white, red, orange and yellow on a black ground, and the inventiveness of the curvi-linear motifs flowing over the whole surface fo the pot. Kamáres pots have been found in Egypt and Cyprus, and along the Syrian coast.

At the northeast corner of the West Court, a group of small rooms (2) is a **shrine complex** of the Old Palace; two adjoining areas have benches round the walls. These rooms contained a large clay offering-table, stone vases, a triton shell and other cult objects now forming an exhibit of major importance in the Herákleion Museum. In a sacrificial pit (adjacent to the north of the shrine) charred animal bones indicated burnt offerings.

To the south of the shrine the **West Façade** (3) of the Old Palace is recessed, as was the later version, for the windows of the storey above. Behind this the excavated rooms of the Old Palace have been covered over to form a level surface in front of the New Palace façade. These rooms ended to the south at a corridor which provided a west entrance for the Old Palace. Down the hill south of the corridor (fenced off and roofed for protection) work continues on the wing where the New Palace did not extend over the ruins of its predecessor. This has allowed

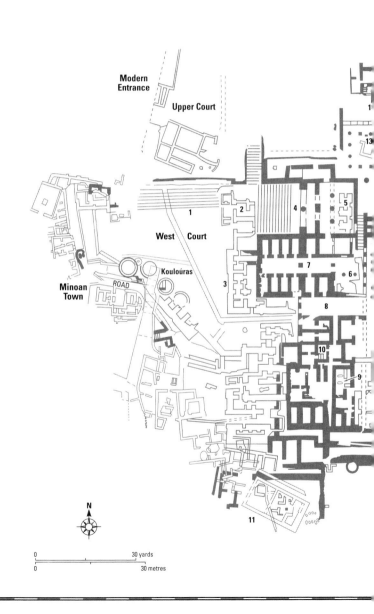

PALACE OF PHAISTOS

Modern Entrance

Upper Court

West Court

Kouloúras

Minoan Town

ROAD

N

1
2
3
4
5
6
7
8
9
10
11
13

0   30 yards
0   30 metres

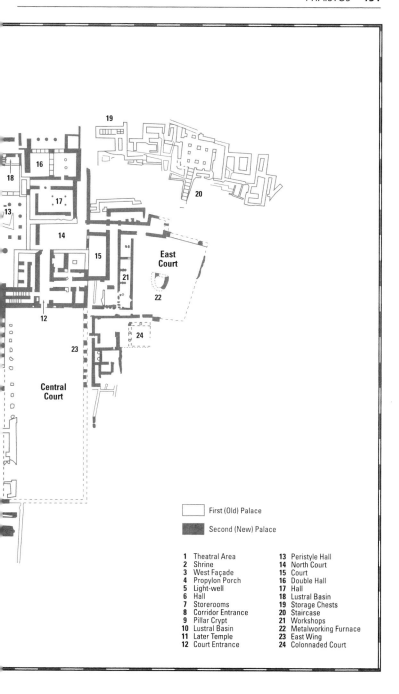

East
Court

Central
Court

First (Old) Palace

Second (New) Palace

1	Theatral Area	13	Peristyle Hall
2	Shrine	14	North Court
3	West Façade	15	Court
4	Propylon Porch	16	Double Hall
5	Light-well	17	Hall
6	Hall	18	Lustral Basin
7	Storerooms	19	Storage Chests
8	Corridor Entrance	20	Staircase
9	Pillar Crypt	21	Workshops
10	Lustral Basin	22	Metalworking Furnace
11	Later Temple	23	East Wing
12	Court Entrance	24	Colonnaded Court

archaeologists a unique opportunity to investigate Old Palace remains.

You now climb the broad **staircase** which is generally agreed to be one of the most memorable features of Minoan architecture. It leads from the Theatral Area of the West Court into the New Palace and, walled in fine ashlar masonry, it formed part of a monumental **Grand Entrance** through the **Propylon** (4). This was a porch with a massive central column, in front of a pair of double doors leading to a narrow anteroom and a large colonnaded **light-well** (5). This imposing entrance changes character at this point, for from the light-well only small unimposing exits led left by a roundabout route to the reception rooms, or right to the great paved **Central Court** (51.5m by 22.5m). You should take the staircase which descends, right, to the level of the court.

You find yourself at the north end of the Central Court. The overall view is most impressive from the southern end of it, but this wing on the west side of the central court rewards attention. Of particular interest is the close proximity of areas connected with religious ritual and the sophisticated storage of wealth-producing goods. (A similar arrangement is noted in the West Wing at Knossós.)

On the right, at the foot of the stairs and under the propylon light-well, are **storerooms** of the Old Palace where large pithoi have been left in position on their stands. The **square hall** (6) was built with two internal columns, and there is an **oval column base** (unusual in Minoan architecture) extending the same line and between two pillars in the colonnade on the court; massive doors would have closed from both sides on to the column that rested on this oval base. The hall seems to have controlled access to the double row of storerooms behind it, as well as being associated in an administrative capacity with them. Beneath the floor of the building, and dating to the earlier palace, the archaeologists found tablets in the Linear A script, and the important archive of clay sealings referred to above. From more than 7500 seal impressions some 300 different motifs have been identified. A display in the Phaistós room of the Herákleion Museum illustrates the wide variety of subjects.

Behind the columned hall, the **storeroom block** (7) is still a tangible reminder of the importance of storage and redistribution to the Minoan palace economy; the solid construction and the central pillars would have supported an upper floor from which gypsum slabs, dadoes and column bases found in the storerooms had fallen. At the end of the row (right) giant pithoi of the New Palace period are visible behind a grille.

Adjacent to the south was a **corridor** (8) walled with massive stone blocks; it formed an impressive entrance in the vicinity of the storerooms and could be closed at both ends by double doors. The area south of this is poorly preserved and has been fenced off, but several of the rooms here are believed to have had ritual purposes. There is a **pillar crypt** (9) with a bench round it as at Knossós, and behind this a **lustral basin** (10).

Down the slope at the southwest corner of the site, at an oblique angle to the Minoan remains, are the lower courses of the walls of a **temple** (11) of the Classical period (on 8C foundations), thought to have been dedicated to the Great Mother, Rhea. A hut dating to the Neolithic period was recognised in the same area. The palace buildings to the south and east have been lost owing to the erosion of the hillside but part of the drainage system survives in the southwest angle of the court and is exposed near the site fence.

Looking north at this point, the spectacular view is dominated by the distant mass of Mount Ida. One of its southern bluffs has distinctive twin peaks with a shallow saddle between them, and a little below the right-hand peak a large dark spot (especially dramatic when snow lies on the mountain) marks the Minoan sanctuary, the sacred cave of Kamáres.

Both long sides of the Central Court had porticoes along their frontage, and some of the stone bases for wooden columns or pillars still survive; those on the west side, and at a lower level, belong to the portico of the earlier palace. The foundations of the buildings on the east side of the court have survived only at their northern end; they are described later on the tour.

The **north façade** of ashlar blocks is designed with a formality known only at Phaistós. A **central doorway** (12) into the North Quay is framed by half-engaged columns (originally wood) and by recesses which are understood as sentry boxes. The plaster which lined them was decorated with a lozenge-pattern fresco of dark lozenges on light ground. Sockets can be seen in the threshold block for the double doors which opened into a **paved passage**. Just inside the passage there is a further recess for a sentry (also showing traces of the lozenge-pattern fresco) and next to it a staircase (with a pithos under it) which would have given access to important reception rooms on the upper floor. Perhaps, as has been suggested in similar positions at Mália and Zákros, these included a dining hall.

The staircase was one of the routes to the important **Peristyle Hall** (13). This could also be reached from an ante-room of the Propylon (4), or by the staircase from the Central Court, as well as from the grand private quarters to the north (identified by their protective cover). To take the stairs from the northwest corner of the Central Court you pass pithoi placed here by the excavators and (dating from the Postpalatial period) a stepped stone block with a double-axe mason's mark which has been compared with the altar shown on the painted sarcophagus from Ayía Triáda (p 89).

At the top of these stairs from the court, an ante-room leads into the Peristyle Hall, an architectural design so far recognised only at Phaistós. Part of the foundations of an earlier (Prepalatial) building have been left uncovered in the centre, but the colonnade of the New Palace hall would have produced an effect similar to a cloister, with the north side open to the mountain view from an elaborately paved verandah.

You can make your way back to the central paved passage behind the entrance (at 12) from the Central Court. A drain running down the centre of this passage suggests that it was unroofed and took rainwater from the buildings on either side. It leads to the **North Court** (14) which separates the main block of reception rooms on the Central Court from the grand private quarters ahead towards the trees on the slope of the hill. Over to the east is a large **open area** (15), its well-preserved ashlar masonry similar to that of the North Court; it may have been a walled garden.

The **private quarters**, fenced and roofed for protection, can be viewed from several vantage points. Here the **double hall** (16), nearest the edge of the hill, has an elaborate plan similar to that of the Hall of the Double Axes at Knossós. Pier-and-door (*polythýron*) arrangements on the north and east sides of the main inner area allowed this space to be securely enclosed or to be thrown open to the verandah with mountain views to the north, or to the portico giving on to a sheltered light-well to the east. This light-well has a drain for rainwater through the wall at its northeast corner. Across a passage to the south (with staircase up to the Peristyle Hall) the **hall room** (17), a smaller room with four columns, gypsum bench and dado, has been compared with the Queen's Hall at Knossós.

From the southwest corner of the larger hall, a dogleg passage leads to a **lustral basin** (18) which has been relined with gypsum slabs from nearby quarries at Ayía Triáda. The original choice of this soluble material supports the belief that these basins were not intended to contain water. West of the lustral basin the outer of two small rooms was a **lavatory** where a hollowed stone was connected to a drain.

Continuing east round the flank of the hill you come to a series of **chests** (19) built of mudbrick and originally faced with plaster. In one of them, in 1903, the excavators found the mysterious **Phaistós disk**. The disk (prominently displayed in the Herákleion Archaeological Museum's Room III) is of baked clay, c 16cm in diameter, and is stamped on both sides in an unknown ideographic script. The signs (241 in all) are set in a spiral thought to run from circumference to centre. Despite many ingenious attempts to decipher the script, the disk remains an enigma.

On the northeast edge of the hill lies a further complex of rooms reached by a long **staircase** (20). The underlying levels visible here date from the Old Palace, and the area with columns at the foot of the staircase may have been a peristyle anticipating the plan of the hall (13) described above.

Returning by the stairs towards the centre of the site, you pass **craftsmen's workshops** (21) along one side of the East Court. In the middle of it (fenced) are the remains of a large **furnace for metalworking** (22); scraps of copper and bronze were found still adhering to its walls.

A ramp connected this court to the northeast corner of the Central Court, and the foundations of a set of rooms known as the **East Wing** (23). This self-contained complex demonstrates all the delights of Minoan domestic architecture: a versatile main hall, a peristyle court, a bath, even a bench outside the door to the Central Court. The finds here included LMI vases, an offering-table and bronze double axes. The **colonnaded court** (24) was surely designed to benefit from the uninterrupted prospect of the Mesará plain, to the Asteroúsia mountains and the distant Lasíthi range, and 3500 years ago this must have been the rewarding view that it remains today.

Ayía Triáda

The archaeological site of Ayía Triáda, 3km from Phaistós, is beautifully situated, overlooking the plain at the mouth of the Yeropótamos where it runs into the bay of Mesará. The ancient name of the place is unknown (although tentatively identified with *da-wo* on a Linear B tablet from Knossós), so archaeologists adopted the dedication, Ayía Triáda, the Holy Trinity, of the double-naved Venetian church lower down by the river bank (in view from the car park) 250m southwest towards the sea. A gypsum quarry found near that church was probably in use by the Neopalatial period.

• Open daily 08.30–15.00. For information ☎ 28920 91360.

Leave the Phaistós car park at the far end towards the picturesque church, recently restored as all that remains of the Venetian monastery of **Ayios Yeóryios Phalándras**. Keep right at the fork here along the south-facing slope where in April and May the hillside is covered with pink drifts of the endemic ebony (*Ebonus cretica*).

History of the site

The site was first explored in the early 20C by Italian archaeologists under Federico Halbherr, better known for the discovery of the Górtyn Law Code (p 168). Work started again in 1977, and is still in progress.

There is evidence here of continuous occupation from the Neolithic period to the 13C BC. Part of an Early Bronze Age settlement has been excavated beyond the cemetery area to the north where two Prepalatial tholos tombs were found (see below). However, the chief interest for visitors to Ayía Triáda centres on two periods of its history: the Late Minoan I phase contemporary with the New Palace at Phaistós, and the Late Minoan III phase of reoccupation after a major fire characteristic of the widespread destruction found at other Minoan sites across Crete at the end of LMI. Ayía Triáda was exceptional in that it regained its importance and flourished in this Postpalatial period. For a time the settlement seems to have become the focus of economic and political power in the western Mesará.

At Ayía Triáda the architecture of the LMI buildings was of palatial quality, with details such as alabaster facings, fresco decoration and paved roads, though the layout does not conform to the conventional palace plan; there were buildings on only two sides of a courtyard. As at Zákros these Neopalatial buildings escaped systematic ransacking, even though the later foundations were dug into the ruins. Finds included carved stone vases which are among the masterpieces of Minoan art, bronze figurines and a hoard of 19 copper ingots (a total weight of 556kg) as well as one of the most important archives of tablets inscribed in Linear A so far known on the island.

With the architectural evidence and the level of skilled craftsmanship indicated by the finds, the excavators at first identified what they were uncovering as a Royal Villa, variously described as a country seat of the rulers of Phaistós or a seaside villa of the lords of the Mesará. Now, after study of the archive and the large numbers of sealings and storage jars, more importance is attached to the evidence for economic and administrative functions on the site. This points to a major operation for the collecting and recording of goods and produce, which would complement the role of the political seat of power at that time, the palace at Phaistós.

In the Postpalatial period there is evidence for significant rebuilding dating to the early decades of the 14C, at a date shortly after the final destruction of the palace at Knossós (the second half of LMIIIA). The architecture inclines to a new monumental style suggesting Mycenaean influence from mainland Greece.

The principal buildings of note in this context were a rectangular hall in the style of a megaron (the earliest of this type known on the island), a shrine with frescoed floor and a large stoa in front of what may be shops or storerooms along one side of a court. The smaller of the two Prepalatial tholos tombs was reused at this time and to the same period is dated the tomb immediately south of it where the famous painted limestone sarcophagus was found.

In later times part of the site seems to have had cult associations, with finds of clay and bronze figurines of the Geometric period. There was a Hellenistic shrine dedicated to Zeus Velkhanós. The little Byzantine church above the excavation, **Ayios Yeóryios Galatás** (key with site guards), has remains of frescoes (1302) including, sadly worn, a rare scene in the apse with the Christ child representing the elements of the Eucharist.

You can get a preliminary understanding of the site by viewing it from the mound by the Byzantine church, looking out across the excavation to the broad river valley and Mount Ida away to the north.

The irregular remains of paving immediately in front of you indicate the position of the **Upper Court** (see plan). The palatial-style Minoan buildings (contemporary with the New Palace at Phaistós) occupied an L-shape consisting of two wings along the north and west sides of it. There was evidence for an upper storey. Beyond (in the direction of the mountains) is the **Lower Court** with its surrounding buildings, and beyond that the excavated remains of the settlement or town. The **cemetery area** is on the slope to the northeast of the settlement.

At the eastern end of the L-shape (under the protective roofing) is a set of rooms where the quality of the architecture suggests an important reception area, with its own adjoining storerooms. The grandest apartments, named the *signorile* quarter by the Italian excavators, lay in the northwest corner (in the angle of the L). To the south of this (level with the west end of the church) was a more modest block which included **storerooms** and a **kitchen**.

The **main storeroom block** of the Minoan complex, where many of the large clay pithoi were found, was centrally placed in the wing to the north of the Upper Court. Superimposed on this wing the excavators found substantial rectangular structures from the LMIII reoccupation phase. The principal building, known as the **Megaron**, unshaded on the plan, is built over (but on a different axis to) the Minoan storerooms. Associated with it was a **loggia** (indicated by the remains of rectangular flagstones and a column base) which faced on to the Upper Court.

From the eastern end of the Upper Court, two short flights of a narrow **staircase** (1) lead you down into the **North Wing** of the L-shape described above. In the Minoan period this area, which was open to the east on to a forecourt, consisted of a set of **rooms** (2) with windows on to light-wells, gypsum stairs, dadoes, benches and a drainage system; the remains hint at the refinement of the architecture. (The raised levels of the drainage system belong to the later reoccupation in LMIII.) In Minoan times the Lower Court was a private open space, the broad staircase now leading down to it being a later adaptation. The court was bounded on its east side by a five-columned portico, and on the north by a massively built structure (3) known as the **Bastion**, possibly a warehouse.

The paved Minoan road (the *Rampa dal mare* of the Italians) led out of this court, along the north façade of the Neopalatial buildings. (The stepped section was a Postpalatial alteration.) The sea may have been nearer in Minoan times but the hypothesis that it came right up to the foot of the hill is now discounted, and Kommós (see below) is seen as the harbour site for both Phaistós and Ayía Triáda.

The main **storerooms** (4) contain a number of pithoi, and one, up stone steps, has five gypsum pithos stands, all severely burnt, as is the threshold itself, providing a vivid reminder of the fire which destroyed this Minoan phase of Ayía Triáda.

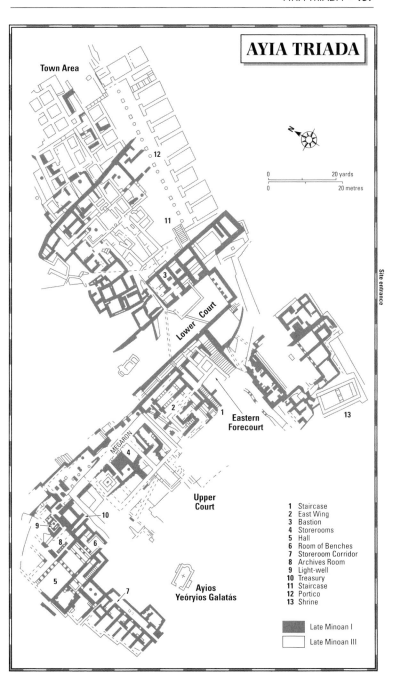

AYIA TRIADA

Town Area

N

| 0 | | 20 yards |
| 0 | | 20 metres |

Site entrance

12

11

3

Lower Court

2

1

Eastern Forecourt

13

MEGARON

4

Upper Court

10

9

8

6

5

7

Ayios Yeóryios Galatás

1 Staircase
2 East Wing
3 Bastion
4 Storerooms
5 Hall
6 Room of Benches
7 Storeroom Corridor
8 Archives Room
9 Light-well
10 Treasury
11 Staircase
12 Portico
13 Shrine

Late Minoan I

Late Minoan III

At the point where the excavated stretch of the paved road comes to an end, turn left up into the **West Wing** where the *signorile* quarter, in what was surely a deliberate choice, enjoyed the view to the sea. (A second paved street runs along the west façade below the retaining wall.)

The largest room of the Minoan (LMI) phase of building (c 6m by 9m) is the **Hall** (**5**) with a pier-and-door (*polythýron*) arrangement on two sides. The inner doors lead into two columned porticoes (a scheme unusual in Minoan architecture) with breccia column bases and a black-and-white pebble floor with a sunk rectangular basin. You cross a narrow light-well to a small **inner chamber** (**6**) with benches round the walls. These were covered with a gypsum facing (now restored), with red stucco filling between the slabs; you can see the recesses for wooden beams. This room leads on the left to a smaller chamber which also had access to the light-well. The huge, slightly raised gypsum slab in the paved floor has been interpreted as a divan base; it could have held a wooden bed similar to one found in the excavation of the Minoan town at Akrotíri on Théra. Both rooms were lit by tall pedestal stone lamps (originals in the Herákleion Museum).

This suite would have provided the public rooms for entertaining while those to the north were used for administrative purposes. There was an upper floor over both sets of rooms where valuable artefacts were kept. Found fallen from above in the destruction debris were scattered pieces of the ***Harvester Vase*** and the ***Boxer Rhyton*** carved in relief from serpentine. These vases are among the most important examples of Minoan stone-carving yet discovered, valued both for the skill of the craftsmen and for the scenes of Minoan life that they portray. The conical beaker known as the ***Chieftain Cup*** came from an upper room a little to the south; the carving is thought to show a Minoan official receiving tribute of animal hides. All three vases, now prominently displayed in the Herákleion Museum (Room VII), are believed to be products of a Knossós workshop.

The block to the south, adjacent to the reception rooms, is seen as service quarters and storerooms. The **paved area** (**7**) has been plausibly interpreted as a kitchen with the built-in platforms with circular depressions serving as mortars for the preparation of food. Six pairs of rooms open on to a long north–south **corridor** (**8**) which leads in from a south entrance. One storeroom held pithoi and other coarse-ware vessels, clay sealings and loomweights.

North of the reception rooms, in the block of rooms apparently given over to administration, is the **archives room** (**9**). Here, in a gypsum chest, was found a deposit of over 200 clay sealings (out of 700 in all on the site). The walls of the inner part of this room were covered with exquisite frescoes (now in the Herákleion Museum) including a woman seated in a garden and a cat stalking a partridge. Fragments of a different fresco found below the paving showed that this room had remained sufficiently important to need redecoration. There are stairs to a little porticoed **light-well** (**10**) equipped with a central bowl for rainwater. On the stucco plaster of the walls were scored graffiti in Linear A script.

Behind this group of rooms, and not apparently connecting with it, is the **Treasury** (**11**), a small narrow space from which came the 19 copper ox-hide ingots now exhibited in the Herákleion Museum alongside the stone vases described above.

The paved ramp leads back to the Lower Court, passing on the left the remains (**12**) of structures of an earlier date (MMIA). Beyond the Bastion a **staircase** (**13**) descends towards the excavated part of the town. Both staircase and much of the town are of LMIII date, a number of the houses being built over or adapted from Neopalatial buildings.

On the right at the foot of the staircase, opposite the town houses, was what may have been a row of **shops**, of a regular size, and each with a large threshold block preserved. Along the front was a columned **portico (14)** similar in design to later stoas. If this was an *agorá* (rather than another row of storerooms) it is a feature which has as yet no exact parallel in Bronze Age excavations on Crete. To the north of this is the cemetery area, but while work continues there is no access (see below).

Finally, returning across the Lower Court and up the broad staircase out of it, you pass near parts of a substantial Minoan **house** cut into by the cella and vestibule of a **shrine** of the Postpalatial period (**15**). The shrine floor was decorated with a fresco seascape of octopus and dolphins, remains of which are in the Herákleion Museum.

To view the **cemetery area** turn left on to the path outside the site gate. You pass the covered excavation of a LMI **potters' kiln**, rectangular in plan with the fire-chamber at the front and a series of hot-air conduits.

The path leads (in less than five minutes along the contour of the hillside) to vantage points outside the fence on the slope above the remains of the two Prepalatial circular stone-built tombs. The better-preserved (eastern) one, **Tholos Tomb A**, was in use for communal burials between EMII and MMI, and had annexes outside it used as ossuaries as well as for offerings. The chamber and annexes held in all about 150 individuals; the grave goods included bronze daggers, jewellery and stone vases, as well as many small clay pots. An important deposit of 100 sealstones included some carved from ivory and faience. The smaller **Tholos Tomb B**, approximately contemporary, had been cleared out and reused in the Postpalatial period. Immediately south of it is the rectangular **chamber-tomb** that contained the famous **painted limestone sarcophagus** which is displayed as the centrepiece of the main room showing Minoan frescoes in the Herákleion Museum. This tomb was recently re-excavated, for the fourth time, to establish precisely the date (LMIIIA2), which is contemporary with the main Postpalatial buildings at Ayía Triada. Another tomb in this cemetery, with four rooms cut out of the rock, produced an Egyptian seal of Queen Tyi (1411–1375 BC), wife of Amenhotep III, and also a Hittite sphinx.

Early Minoan buildings northeast of Tomb A now in the process of excavation and study are presumed to be part of the settlement for which the tholos tombs were the cemetery.

From the Ayía Triáda car park an unpaved road continues ahead to rejoin the main Timbáki road. It is less than ten minutes on foot down to the river. If you are prepared to ignore the rubbish dumps this is often a rewarding place to search for birds or wild flowers.

From Phaistós to Kommós and Mátala

The excavation of the Minoan harbour town at Kommós, a major piece of work by American archaeologists, is less than 2km off the Mátala road from Pitsídia. Before that there are opportunites for short detours to the Kamilári tholos tomb and the Odiyítria monastery. Walkers with time to explore the area can continue from the monastery to the Ayiophárango gorge running down to the sea.

Where to stay and eating out

Suggestions are given earlier in this section (p 144) and here, on the way from Phaistós to Mátala, there is a good choice of pleasant rent rooms and studios. The attractive village of **Kamilari** offers various alternatives but you could start at *Pension Phaestias* in the centre. **Sivas** has the *Lofos Rent Rooms*. At **Pitsídia** *Níkos Apartments* and *Agápi* rooms to rent are signed and in view at the turning to Kommós.

1km south of Phaistós on the Mátala road, in the village of **Ayios Ioánnis**, there is a popular taverna of the same name; its speciality is rabbit, a traditional delicacy on the island. Both **Kamilári** and Pitsídia have several good tavernas and at **Kommós** and **Mátala** you can eat overlooking the sea.

Just beyond Ayíos Ioánnis the church of **Ayios Pávlos**, hidden among cypresses (left) in a cemetery surrounded by an old wall, reflects in its architecture a long period of Cretan history. Restored in the recent past it is the product of three building phases. The oldest part, now the sanctuary (bema), may date from the pre-Christian period; originally it consisted of no more than a cupola supported by four massive piers between open arches, on a square ground plan. This design recalls the spring chambers of Late Roman times, and it is notable that there is still a well behind the church. The nave was added later, with a dome resting on a drum, and the open arches under the cupola were blocked where necessary. (The narthex, with open pointed arches in the Venetian style, is a later addition. 15C–16C.)

A frieze round the dome above the nave carries a painted inscription dated 1303–04 which may refer to the time of construction or of subsequent redecoration. The Latin inscription describes the church as: 'dedicated to the Apostle Paul in a village called Baptistiras restored and surrounded by a wall'; the name is taken to mean Ayios Ioánnis, the village of St John the Baptist. The inscription adds that the decoration of a venerable historic building was at the command of the Emperor Andronicos II Palaiologos (1283–1328), his Empress Irene and their son Michael. The dedication to St Paul may have been inspired by his brief stay at Kalí Liménes, on the coast less than 10km away, after which he commissioned Titus to convert Crete. There are remains of frescoes dated by the inscription: best preserved are the *Punishments of Hell* on the west wall, and on the pendentives the *Evangelists Matthew* (southwest) and *Luke* (northwest). If a spring chamber of antiquity came to serve in due course as a Christian baptistery that would make this 'venerable historic building' one of the earliest ecclesiastical buildings still in existence on the island.

The Kamilári tholos tomb

For the village of Kamilári stay on the main road as far as the Sívas crossroads, but for a detour (c 3km) to one of the best preserved examples of the great communal tombs of the Mesará, the Minoan tholos of Kamilári, take the narrow road opposite Ayios Pávlos. After 2km you reach a crossroads by a fountain near isolated houses; the village is up to the left from here. From the crossroads the way is signed for the tomb, ahead and then right and left through the olive groves to find the Greek Archaeological Service's notice.

The large communal tomb was built on a low hill here at the beginning of the Protopalatial period (MMIB) and remained in use for many centuries into Postpalatial times. Its thick stone walls still stand 2m high, and the evidence from the excavation suggested a roof structure of wooden beams supporting masonry, the best evidence yet found that such tombs originally had stone roofs. Outside the entrance, a complex of five small rooms associated with a paved area was used for funerary cult purposes, and in the later periods also as ossuaries.

The Kamilári tomb was robbed in antiquity, but three interesting clay models were found by the archaeologists and are prominent in the Herákleion Museum, Room VI. Belonging to the last (LMIIIA) burials, they illustrate different aspects of a precise funerary rite. Two are connected with banquets or ritual offerings for the dead; on one of them offerings are being placed on small altars in front of four figures seated in a shrine. The third model shows a group of dancers in a circle, reminiscent of Cretan dance today, with horns of consecration and doves to emphasise the ritual setting of the events.

Kalamáki, 3km away on the Mesará bay, is a rather characterless place but you can walk north along the coast to the mouth of the Yeropótamos river, often rewarding for birdwatchers. It is important to take seriously any warning notices associated with the Timbáki military airfield.

Kommós

7km south of Phaistós the Mátala road skirts the centre of the village of Pitsídia. Here the short detour down to the coast at Kommós is strongly recommended. A major programme of excavation and study by archaeologists from the American School of Classical Studies at Athens has been under way since 1976. Their work has uncovered a harbour town of the Minoan period and a later Greek-period sanctuary with evidence for a series of temples of the first millennium BC which were superimposed on the civic buildings of the Bronze Age settlement. The remains occupy a magnificent sweep of beach looking out to the west over the Bay of Mesará.

There are two access roads. The first turns right towards the sea halfway along the stretch of main road through **Pitsídia**. You keep straight on following the asphalt surface down to the car park for the site. The second road to the beach is signed, 1km on the Mátala side of the village, at the crest of a hill. The excavation is soon in view far below, down by the shore. You can fork right aiming for the guardian's hut or continue straight ahead along the contour (1km) to a cliff-top taverna. From the adjacent chapel a path drops down to the beach for the five-minute walk to the site, north along the sand under tamarisk trees. (Swimmers should beware of ancient remains under the surface.)

At first sight, when the prevailing northwesterly winds of Crete are whipping up the sea along this coast, Kommós may seem an inhospitable place for a harbour town. However, 350m offshore, waves break over a reef that is now only just visible. In Minoan times the sea level was 2m lower so the shoreline was perhaps 50–100m nearer what was then a much more substantial reef ensuring relatively calm water for vessels on its leeward side. Six huge **galleries**, Postpalatial in date, which faced the sea in the harbour complex, could have been shipsheds for the storage of ships during the winter months, outside the sailing season.

The harbour at Kommós must surely have been a trading outlet for Phaistós and Ayía Triáda, and one of the major points of entry to south-central Crete. The variety of imported pottery found in the excavation, especially from the Neopalatial and first half of the Postpalatial periods, suggests widespread international connections. Fragments of short-necked amphoras were found on the floors of the galleries. On the assumption that they may have come from a type of pot used for transporting commodities, similar pots are being searched for around the harbours of the eastern Mediterranean in the hope that they may throw light on the trade routes of that Postpalatial time. Two large stone anchors (also Postpalatial) from the site were found to originate in the Ugarit area, on the Syrian coast, which was already known to have had contact with the Mycenaean world.

There is at present no public access to the site though plans are well advanced for funding to open it; in the meantime you can get a good impression from outside the fence. If you stand with your back to the sea where the excavated remains are at beach level, the Minoan town would have covered the slopes of the low hill to your left at the north end of the site. You can see that two areas have been investigated, one on the hilltop and one lower down. The settlement was founded in MMI and by the height of the Neopalatial period densely packed houses built of rough stone covered the hilltop.

Down by the shore where you are standing, at the south end of the site, there were **grand civic buildings** presumably linked to harbour activity. In contrast to the majority of Minoan sites (including Phaistós and Ayía Triáda), Kommós showed no signs of destruction by fire at the end of LMIB and there was continuity on the site which flourished in the Postpalatial period. The **sanctuary** of the Greek period (with a series of temples dating from Protogeometric to Roman times) was superimposed on this Bronze Age complex; only the remains of the latest sanctuary (4C–1C BC) are now visible.

In the Minoan levels the archaeologists uncovered two adjoining **monumental buildings** dated to LMI, aligned east–west. They were constructed using ashlar masonry and enormous orthostats, some of which (up to 3.46m long) are the largest cut blocks recorded from Minoan Crete. The smaller of the two buildings, the one next to the shore, had been damaged by the sea, but the larger of them was laid out on a palatial plan, with four wings set round a central court, those on the north and south sides colonnaded. This complex (**Building T**) covered 6000 square metres, more ground than the palace at Zákros, though less than that at Phaistós. At least part of the building seems to have gone out of use before the end of the Neopalatial period and a large pottery **kiln** with a fire pit adjoining four sloping flues was constructed within the south stoa. Pottery was found inside the kiln, with a dump of wasters nearby; it is exceptional for such specific evidence of a Minoan kiln's use to be preserved.

Running up from the beach along the north side of these harbour buildings is a broad slab-paved **Minoan road** (2.5m wide) which probably continued inland to link Kommós with the neighbouring centres of Phaistós and Ayía Triáda. The scale and architectural sophistication of the civic buildings at Kommós inevitably raise intriguing questions about the political and administrative relationship between the three sites at the height of the Minoan period. At Kommós the settlement and its civic buildings were not finally abandoned until the 12C (sometime in LMIIIB).

The sanctuary of the Greek period

The temples superimposed in the area of the Greek sanctuary during the first millennium BC cover the period from the Protogeometric through to Roman times. A small **10C temple**, probably a rural shrine, was built over the Minoan walls and is among the earliest temples known in Greece.

Within the **second temple**, founded in the 8C BC, the archaeologists recognised Phoenician inspiration in a shrine perhaps established by Phoenicians who landed at the harbour. In both these early temples animal bones were interpreted as evidence of ritual sacrifice. A large proportion of the temple offerings throughout the sequence consisted of animal figurines.

The **third temple**, superimposed in the 4C BC, was similar in plan to those known from Dréros and Priniás (both of which preceded the building at Kommós) and the one at Líssos which was of slightly later date. This ground-plan, with a central hearth and benches round the walls, helped to consolidate understanding of a major temple type unique to Crete. Here at Kommós double doors to the east led out to a courtyard and open-air altars. In later phases this courtyard acquired four altars. Ancillary buildings to the north of the court were for storage and perhaps residence as well. On the basis of evidence for feasting, a hall to the northwest was interpreted as a dining-hall. By the end of its life c 150 AD the building on the temple precinct was the only one in use on the site; the excavator believes it may have become a residence rather than a shrine.

Mátala

Mátala is a small resort on the coast 11km southwest of Phaistós (75km from Herákleion). The village has grown up around a beautiful west-facing cove with good swimming under cliffs spectacularly honeycombed with rock-cut Roman tombs. These date back to the 1C or 2C AD but they have been exploited through the ages, sometimes as a refuge from pirates, but most recently by young people from abroad who set up camp in them, a practice which is no longer permitted. The caves are now the subject of a study project.

Mátala has adapted itself to cope with the trade from the tour coaches to Phaistós which continue to this picturesque spot on the coast for lunch and a swim or some souvenir shopping in the waterside market. The beach is packed with sun loungers and straw umbrellas. There is a post office van near the car park and the two travel agencies change money. Out of season the village grows calmer in the evening when the coaches have departed. You can watch the sun setting into the sea from a well-placed bar or taverna, or in tranquillity along one of the cliff paths which lead to quieter beaches. The beaches of the Mesará bay

Eating out and where to stay

There is not much to choose between the dozen or so modern B and C class hotels but both these are within easy walking distance of the cove.

C *Frangiskos* (45 rooms), ☎ 28920 45380, 28920 45728.

C *Matala Bay* (55 rooms), ☎ 28920 45100, 28920 45301.

To find something suitable among the large number of **rooms** and **studio apartments** to rent you could start in the side-roads running south immediately across from the main car park. The back of the beach is lined with a variety of cafés and tavernas. The recommendation is to walk out (left) to the southern end of the waterfront, under the cliffs, and make a choice there.

are one of the three main nesting habitats on Crete of the loggerhead sea turtle (p 57); during the summer months there is an information hut in Mátala staffed by the *Sea Turtle Protection Society of Greece* (STPS).

The Odiyítria monastery and the Ayiophárango

This recommended detour leaves the Phaistós–Mátala road and uses minor roads for the c 9km to the monastery (officially closed 14.00–16.30). You can continue (4km towards the bay of Kalí Liménes) for a walk, less than an hour to the sea down the Ayiophárango, Holy Gorge. In high summer the number of campers in the gorge may spoil the sense of remoteness, which, for the rest of the year, is one of the principal attractions of these western foothills of the Asteroúsia mountains.

From the crossroads serving Kamilári and Sívas less than 5km from Phaistós take the road into **Sívas**. For the monastery keep straight on across the plateía with the village church on your left. The road winds through olive groves interspersed with cypresses, and climbs steadily into the hills towards the south coast. After about 3km the White Mountains of western Crete (60–70km away) are in view on a clear day, with in the foreground the distinctive angular Mount Kédros, and the Paximádia islands in the Bay of Mesará. In **Lístaros** turn right downhill in front of the church. The country road climbs to a less fertile level, technically garigue (in Greek *phrýgana*), the scrubby herb-scented upland typical of so much of the island's landscape; groups of beehives are scattered about the hillside.

The **Odiyítria monastery** is in view from some distance away. The dedication to the Panagía Odiyítria (showing the way) refers to the icon type where the Virgin points to the Christ Child in her arms as the way of salvation. The monastery, founded before the end of the 16C in this remote corner of Crete, commands a ridge high above a tributary of the Ayía Kyriakí river, which flows to the sea through the Ayiophárango. The position set back from the coast afforded some protection from the pirate raids of medieval times. The rambling buildings, whitewashed and only partly surrounded by a wall, are dominated by a massive rectangular stone-built tower.

The Italian Giuseppe Gerola came here at the beginning of the 20C, researching his treatise on Venetian monuments, and remarked on the familiar pattern: quadrangular enclosure, a large courtyard around a church, but the enclosing wall substantial only on the north and west sides. The flat-topped hill drops steeply on the other two sides. Gerola noted the three gates, a gravestone with an inscription of 1564 and the kitchen garden, and was much impressed by the **tower of Xopatéras**. This was the name, meaning ex-priest, given to a disgraced monk who achieved fame as chieftain of a local band active in the 1828 revolution. The avenging Turks pursued him to the refuge of the monastery tower where he perished with all his family. Legend has it that the attackers had to contend with beehives hurled from the roof of the tower. The climb up the tower is worthwhile for the view from the roof. A giant key to unlock the door is held by the guardian monk who also opens the church.

In the church the remains of frescoes have been uncovered on the vault of the nave, with scenes from the life of the Virgin. The Odiyítria has a highly regarded collection of **icons**. There is a fine *Deisis*, and both the *Embrace of Peter and Paul* and the depiction of *Christ with the twelve apostles* in the branches of a vine are said to be the work of the 15C painter Angelos. An icon of *Ayios*

Phanoúrios by the same artist has been removed to become part of the collection (no. 4) in Ayía Aikateríni in Herákleion.

150m north of the monastery (left as you approach the entrance), two **communal tombs** have been excavated; these were circular stone-built Minoan burial chambers of the Mesará type, in use in the Prepalatial period (EMI–MMIA). Both tombs had been looted but they still contained interesting finds of artefacts which had accompanied some 150 burials. There were stone vases, pottery, seals and much jewellery including three gold diadems and a bracelet. Stone axes and obsidian blades indicated the early date of some of the burials. There were rectangular rooms on the east side of the larger tholos and in an ossuary between the two tombs an undisturbed deposit which included 22 seals.

For the walk through the **Ayiophárango** (the Holy Gorge) to the Libyan Sea first take the fork left outside the monastery, towards Kalí Liménes. The road descends c 2km to cross the river-bed. 1km further, with room to park before a left bend, a track turns back at an acute angle (right) and drops down to the river and the footpath to the gorge. (On foot from the monastery you should be able to get down to the river-bed before this.) At first there is a clear path, but further towards the sea it is necessary to follow the stream-bed, so this expedition is not advisable in early spring or after heavy rain. This is a good hour's walk from the parking place and you must be prepared to retrace your steps because there is no easy path along the coast.

Gradually the valley narrows, and then vertical walls loom ahead, to a height of 100m for a 600m stretch of gorge. At the far end, with the sea almost in sight, the substantial domed church of **Ayios Antónios** is built into the rock wall (left), enclosing the grotto **chapel of Ayios Ioánnis Xénos**, St John the Stranger, the 11C evangelist who came from this region (he was born in Sívas in 970), although he is principally associated with the monasteries in the northern half of the island; he died at the Katholikó on the Akrotíri near Khaniá.

The road continues 7km from the monastery to the coast. The beautiful bay of **Kalí Liménes** has one of the few long sweeps of beach on the south coast of the island, but it is not much visited because the idyllic view has been radically altered by the building of an oil bunkering station on one of the offshore islands. Kalí Liménes may appeal to some as a quiet base for walking or watching sea-birds.

There are tavernas and a few rooms to rent in the harbour village and along the bay to the east where the road from Pómbia comes down to the sea, and also on the low headland (with a grey, rather gritty beach) by the site of ancient Lasaía.

The bay has been used since antiquity as a sheltered anchorage for ships of passage, 'secure for ten galleys' according to a Venetian document, and was the Fair Havens of St Paul (Acts 27,12). St Paul knew that 'the harbour was unsuitable for wintering', but in the strong southerly winds that are a feature of the weather along this coast there is some shelter in the lee of the two offshore islands, Megalónisi and Ayios Pávlos. St Paul's ship left here to sail westward in the lee of the land to the safe winter harbour of Phoínix (modern Loutró), but with a change of wind it was driven by the unfavourable 'Euroclydon' (probably a strong northerly *meltémi*) south of the island of Gávdos and onward to shipwreck on Malta. Not surprisingly the double-naved church on the western headland is dedicated to Ayios Pávlos.

In the Greco-Roman period the anchorage was controlled by the city-state of **Lasaía**. The centre of the city was on the cliffs above an islet 100m offshore at the eastern end of the beach. The breakwater, built of loosely piled stone blocks, running out from the shore to the islet, is likely to be an ancient structure. A narrow channel was left at the southern end before the islet, allowing boats to be moved to sheltered water either side according to changes of wind. Nothing of the city has been excavated officially (though considerable damage has been caused by illicit activity), but a survey of the headland has identified the site of a temple and a probable basilica church, as well as house walls, cisterns and an aqueduct. There is also evidence for Minoan settlement on the acropolis as well as associated chamber tombs in the vicinity. It has been suggested that nearby copper-workings could have been exploited in antiquity.

The dirt road winds inland (7km) before coming down to the coast again at **Platía Perámata**, where there are tavernas. You can then turn into the hills to Andiskári for Moní Apezanón (p 172) or continue on a rough road along the coast c 10km to Léndas (p 173). The main road connecting Kalí Liménes directly with the Mesará plain runs north, via Pigaidákia and Pómbia, 25km to Míres (p 147).

Górtyn

Górtyn or Górtyna (modern Greek Górtys) was the most powerful city on the island during Greco-Roman times and during the first years of Roman rule the capital of the province of Crete and Cyrene (on the north coast of Africa). The remains of the city now lie spread out in olive groves where the eastern foothills of Mount Ida meet the Mesará plain. A river, the Mitropoliános, runs out of these hills to join the Yeropótamos down on the plain.

Travelling by bus

The bus service from Herákleion or Ayía Galíni will set you down at the entrance to the fenced part of the site.

The main road from Herákleion to Phaistós cuts through the centre of Górtyn (area plan, p 169). 1km on the Míres side of the village of Ayii Déka (146), a small part of the huge site is fenced to enclose the ruins of the basilica church of Ayios Títos as well as the area of the Greco-Roman *agorá*. Here you will find the exhibit of blocks inscribed with one of the earliest law codes of the ancient world. There is a parking area and the guardian's ticket office marks the entrance.

- Open 08.00–18.00 every day in the summer months; winter 10.00–15.00. Closing time is 17.00 in mid-season. For enquiries ☎ 28920 31144.
    Near the guardian's office there is a helpful large-scale plan of the excavations which is also displayed at other strategic points around the site.

The site was first explored in the 1880s by the Italian archaeologist Federico Halbherr, whose primary interest was epigraphy. He was drawn here by earlier travellers' tales of fragments of inscribed blocks and almost immediately located the major part of the Law Code inscription.
    A team of Italian archaeologists is engaged in the formidable task of uncover-

ing antiquities from the Early Iron Age to the Late Roman or Early Byzantine times, with additional evidence for a Minoan presence which includes the substantial remains of a farmstead near the modern village of Mitrópolis. Material from each of these periods is on display in Herákleion, in the Archaeological Museum, except for some stone carvings and liturgical furnishings from Ayios Títos which are shown in the Historical Museum.

The small **museum** in a loggia near the guardian's office houses examples of Górtyn's sculpture. There are also photographs (labelled in Greek and Italian) taken at the time of the earliest excavations.

History

There was a settlement on the acropolis hill from the end of the Bronze Age (Subminoan c 1000 BC) until the 7C BC, during which time it became a place of religious and military significance. The *Iliad* refers to Górtyn as walled, and archaeologists have confirmed that the acropolis was fortified as early as the Geometric period. (Parts of a bastioned wall still stand but this dates to c 670 AD when the Saracens were threatening the island.) The city spread on to the plain below the acropolis hill and was flourishing by the first half of the 5C BC, the date of the Law Code. Expansion continued during the Hellenistic period. After the defeat of Phaistós (2C BC), Górtyn added to its strength and importance with the acquisition of the two harbours of Mátala and Lebéna. There is a record of internal conflict with other major city-states such as Knossós and Lýttos, but this was also a time of increasing influence from external powers. In particular it saw the beginning of Roman involvement in Cretan affairs and Górtyn emerged as, and remained, the centre for pro-Roman sentiment on the island.

In 189 BC the Carthaginian general Hannibal, in flight after the battle of Magnesia, visited Górtyn where he was pursued by influential Romans including his old enemy Scipio. At the time of the Roman invasion (65 BC) the city put up no resistance to Quintus Metellus, and while Knossós was destroyed, Górtyn went on to flourish as the capital of the new Roman province. Many of the great public buildings date from the Imperial period, particularly from the 2C AD. St Titus, commissioned by St Paul to convert the island, was installed here as the first Bishop of Crete.

The Early Byzantine city spread over the plain to the south during a period of great expansion; six basilica churches existed contemporaneously in one small area (1km long and 500m wide) beside the river between the Odeion and the position of the modern village of Mitrópolis. The region suffered a number of severe earthquakes, and at last, towards the end of the 7C, Górtyn was destroyed by Arab raiders. The basilica of Ayios Títos was rededicated in the 10C and there was a Venetian monastery on the Praetorium site, but the great city was never rebuilt.

The basilica of Ayios Títos

The basilica of Ayios Títos, by tradition the burial place of the saint, is by far the best preserved Early Christian church on Crete. Its foundation is attributed to the Justinianic period (early 6C), but it underwent many reconstructions. Architectural fragments dating from the 2C suggest a previous building, probably a temple, on the site or nearby. After a study by the Italian Giuseppe Gerola in

A reconstruction of the basilica of Ayios Títos by Giuseppe Gerola, from Monumenti Veneti nell' Isola di Creta, 1905

1900, Ayios Títos was excavated by Greek archaeologists. Originally it was an imposing three-aisled basilica church, built of unusually large limestone blocks, and elaborated by the addition of a cross-dome plan, reflecting the influence of Eastern architecture. The ruins of the chancel are still impressive. The ground-plan of the church remains intelligible: the central cross with side-arms which end in apses, the nave with side-aisles and the narthex. Around the central dome, the nave and the arms of the cross were barrel-vaulted.

The basilica stands beside the largely unexcavated **Agorá** of the Classical and Hellenistic periods. A path leads north to the **Odeion**, a theatre used for musical performances or contests. The excavated remains now visible are those of a 1C BC structure restored (under Trajan) after earthquake damage in the early 2C AD. The stone blocks inscribed with the famous 5C BC **Law Code of Górtyn** were discovered in an earlier building on this site; they had survived because they had been reused in a building of Hellenistic date. Originally the blocks would have lined a circular assembly building, setting out the city's laws for meetings of council and citizens under the direction of magistrates (*kosmoi*).

The Law Code

The inscription, now displayed beyond the Roman Odeion, is written in a dialect dating to the first half of the 5C BC. The inscription is divided into 12 columns, with 600 lines in all and 17,000 letters. It is written by the method known as *boustrophedon*, a Greek word describing the pattern of oxen ploughing a field, so alternately one line reads from left to right, the next from right to left, and so on.

The inscription codifies in great detail the laws relating to property in respect of marriage and divorce, the sale and mortgage of property, the rights of heirs and the division of property among children, including adopted children. It deals with the procedure for adoption. It covers cases of seduction, rape and adultery, as well as general assault, also the position of slaves, and much else besides.

If you walk to the back of the fenced area you can see the ruins of a Venetian water-mill; there is an old photograph of it showing the Odeion and associated reconstructions, in the museum at the site entrance. Some of the blocks of the great inscription were found close to the artificial water channel powering the mill. In 1884 when Halbherr was trying to rescue the inscription, the owner of the mill registered strong objections which were only overcome when the eminent Cretan archaeologist Dr Joseph Khatzidákis arranged for the purchase of the property.

You will also notice nearby a plane tree, *Platanos orientalis*. According to Greek

GORTYN

N

Acropolis — Kastro — Altar

Temple

Aqueduct

Theatre

Odeion and Law Code

Agora

Ayios Titos

Aqueduct

PHAISTOS

River Mitropolianós

Temple of Apollo Pythios

Temple of Isis and Serapis

Nymphaeum

Theatre — Praetorium

Ayii Déka

Basilica

Basilica

Megáli Pórta Baths

Mitropolis

Minoan Villa ans Shrine

Amphitheatre

Cemetery Area

Stadium

0 — 200 yards
0 — 200 metres

PLATANOS & LENDAS

mythology Europa lay with Zeus under a plane tree here and conceived Minos. In the 4C the Greek philosopher and botanist Theophrastus referred in his *History of Plants* to the ancient plane at Górtyn which had remained evergreen in memory of the occasion.

Across the Mitropolianós stream from the Odeion, and cut into the lower slope of the acropolis hill, the outline of the **Larger Theatre** can be detected; in Roman times the stream ran through a culvert. The plan of the theatre is known from the drawings by the Italian antiquary Onorio Belli, physician to the Venetian Proveditor General of Candia from 1583. During a tour of the island with him (designed to 'rectify disorder') Belli recorded invaluable information about Roman monuments still surviving at that time.

The **acropolis** (outside the main fenced site) is reached from the bridge on the main road by a track along the west bank of the stream. Beyond the theatre a gate marks the start of the path uphill, and the easiest route gains height across the south slope, to reach the flat summit at its southwest corner (ten minutes from the gate, a recommended climb if only for the view).

The acropolis was fortified as early as the Geometric period (see history section above). Parts of the Hellenistic circuit, a bastioned wall of concrete with good stone facing, can still be traced. It was destroyed by earthquake and defences were not needed again until Byzantine times.

On the southern brow of the hill are the excavated foundations (fenced) of the 7C BC **Temple of Athena** (a rectangular building with cella and central *bothros* or circular pit) which continued in use, restored on several occasions but not basically altered, into early Roman times. Below the temple, terraced into the east slope, was an associated **altar of sacrifice** (8C–3C BC), which stood on a wide platform supported by a massive ashlar wall. The cult statue from the temple, remains of decoration including relief carving of the naked feminine triad, and Geometric and Archaic finds from the rich votive deposit at the altar site are on display in the Herákleion Museum; they include notable exhibits in the Daidalic style. In the 4C the temple was succeeded on this site by the first of two Christian churches.

These fenced remains are dwarfed by an unexcavated but well-preserved Roman building known as the **Kástro**, which consists of a spacious hall sunk up to 6m into the rock. Its function, probably as some official building, is uncertain.

The rest of the site of interest to visitors lies across the main road, east of the turning to Plátanos and Léndas. Paths from the main road are signposted. On either side of the road (notably opposite the sign to the Praetorium) remains can be traced of the various branches of the great **aqueduct** that brought water to the city from springs at Zarós on the slopes of Mount Ida.

Walking along the main road from Ayios Títos the first path (at c 500m) leads into the centre of the site past the **Temple of the Egyptian Divinities**. This is a simple rectangular cella with its south side understood as a crypt complex for initiation ceremonies. The cella has a tripartite podium in the east wall for the statues of the Egyptian divinities; those of Isis and Serapis were recovered and the third was probably Hermes Anubis. A stylobate of six Ionic columns fronted the west façade. This temple is dated 1C–2C AD from the dedication to Flavia Philyra and her two sons.

To the south along the path are the excavated remains of the **Temple of Apollo Pythios**, the most venerated sanctuary of pre-Roman Górtyn and known in its day throughout the Greek world. The original 7C temple was a simple cella with four wooden columns supporting the roof and a rectangular treasury just inside the doorway (right). The external surfaces were covered with inscriptions. In the Hellenistic period a pronaos was added with six half-engaged columns of the Doric order. Between the columns, four inscribed steles displayed Górtyn's 2C BC treaties with other Cretan cities and with Eumenes II of Pergamon. The stepped monumental altar in front of the temple and the small heroön just to the northeast were built at this period. During the time of the empire (2C AD) the temple was converted, with the addition of an apse and arcaded Corinthian columns, into a three-aisled Christian basilica, which continued as the religious centre of the city until c 600 and the construction of Ayios Títos.

Nearby (to the southwest) are the remains of the **Smaller Theatre**, the best-preserved Roman theatre on Crete, built in brick-faced concrete with a double-tiered cavea, seating arrangement; it was used for competitions associated with the cult of Apollo Pythios.

To the east along the track (or reached on the signed path off the main road) is the **Praetorium**, the grand palace complex of the Roman governor of the province, which can be viewed from outside the fence. (Along the north side there is a fine stretch of part-Roman, part-medieval road.) Excavations have revealed several phases of building. The early 2C AD construction, contemporary with the rebuilt Odeion of the Trajanic period, probably replaced an Augustan palace, and then was itself enlarged and rebuilt in the 4C after earthquake damage. The architectural fragments on the site include marble columns, and capitals of both the Ionic and Corinthian orders. The 4C reconstruction created the large basilica audience hall (27m x 12m) in the northwest corner of the site; it was built of concrete, faced here with stone, and the floor was paved. Along the outer wall the dedicatory bases intended for statues of prominent citizens of the Roman world are preserved. East of this was the bath suite. The 2C **Nymphaeum** to the north was supplied by a branch of the city's main aqueduct (see above). The Praetorium building survived in part as a monastery during the Second Byzantine period, and the Nymphaeum became a public fountain.

Southeast of the Praetorium (c 150m) are the remains of the **Amphitheatre** (late 2C AD). Further south the Stadium is scarcely discernible under cultivation. If you work your way south from the Praetorium you will pick up a well-trodden path crossing the site from Ayii Déka to the Mitrópolis road.

To the west of the Amphitheatre are the ruined walls, standing to 7m in places, of the Roman building which was given the name **Megáli Pórta** or Great Gate. This has not been excavated but is now recognised as a 2C AD public baths complex, the arch being part of a large hall.

Mitrópolis

Opposite Ayios Títos is the turning for the road south to Plátanos and Léndas (see below). The modern village of Mitrópolis has grown up within the Górtyn archaeological area (see plan) and a footpath from the Praetorium brings you out on the road just to the north of it. On the right of the road as you go south a major excavation is under way (the work of Italian archaeologists and the Cretan authority for Byzantine Antiquities) to uncover a large basilica church.

A highly recommended detour from Mitrópolis takes you in less than 2km (by car or on foot) southwest to the substantial remains of a Minoan villa or farm near **Kanniá**. To find the site you leave the Léndas road where it widens slightly in the village into a small plateía. Take the narrow street west, continue till you cross the stream, the Mitropolianós, and turn left along it. After 600m you pass on the left a white chapel (Ayios Phanoúrios) and 500m beyond it watch for a sign right. The road bears right and the roofed excavation is in view ahead. The site is fenced but there is a good vantage point on the far side.

This was a farmhouse of the Late Minoan I period with a large number of storerooms containing pithoi (many still in situ). It was destroyed, like so many other Cretan sites, at the end of LMIB but was inhabited again in the Postpalatial period. A household shrine from this time (LMIIIB) had clay goddesses in the typical posture with raised arms.

From Górtyn to Léndas

Léndas, site of ancient Lebéna and now a small resort village in an isolated position on the south coast, can be reached from the main Herákleion–Phaistós road turning off either at Ayii Déka or at Górtyn, but the more interesting of the two routes (c 30km) starts south opposite the church of Ayios Títos at Górtyn (p 167).

Travelling by bus

There are two buses a day from Herákleion (via Górtyn), from the bus station outside the Khaniá gate. From Léndas you can get by bus to Phaistós, Mátala and Ayía Galíni; you may have to change in Míres.

From Górtyn the road crosses the Mesará plain to the Yeropótamos river. On the far side, in the village of **Plátanos**, two excavated examples of the great communal tombs of the Mesará are signposted, right and right again. These circular stone-built Minoan burial chambers, linked by a paved area, date to the third millennium BC, although they remained in use over a long period. There are numbers of similar tombs throughout the Mesará, and a few elsewhere on Crete, but **Tombs A and B** at Plátanos are the largest yet known; the internal diameter of Tomb A is 13m, and its wall is nearly 3m thick. This type of tomb is always freestanding, with a single low doorway, usually on the east side. The antechamber before the entrance was a common feature and sometimes, as here, further groups of rooms were added. It has been suggested that these annexes provided space for rituals once the tombs themselves had become congested, but there was also evidence for periodic clearance of the chambers, and fires, perhaps for ritual or for fumigatory purposes. For the smaller tombs the vault may have been completed in stone, but these at Plátanos were probably roofed in a lighter material, such as mud-brick or small stones on a framework of wooden beams, brushwood and thatch.

A walled trench outside Tomb A (the first you come to on the site) contained a quantity of small stone vases, presumably for ritual use. In Tomb B was found the Babylonian haematite cylinder seal of the period of Hammurabi (1792–1750 BC) which is on show in Room I of the Herákleion Museum, along with much of the finest Early-Middle Minoan material found in the Mesará tombs.

The Léndas road continues 2km to **Plóra**, and on the far side of the village keeps left at a fork towards Apesokári.

For a detour 10km to the isolated **Moní Apezanón**, you should take the right fork on the far side of Plóra towards Ayios Kýrillos. You climb to a less cultivated level with rewarding views across the foothills of the Asteroúsia range. Through Ayios Kýrillos (where there is a short cut on a good dirt surface back to the Léndas road) watch for signs right. From a long way off, a line of cypresses marks the monastery buildings. The original north entrance is a little beyond the modern gate into the courtyard.

The monastery was founded in the Venetian period. Its church is dedicated to Ayios Antónios of the Ayiophá006 (p 165s) and there is a tradition that the monks were forced to retreat inland, from the original foundation at the mouth of that gorge, in search of safety from pirates. Giuseppe Gerola, in his five-volume survey of Crete's Venetian monuments (published 1901–04), described the pentagonal wall enclosing the monastic buildings, with its towers, a defended gateway, and turreted and loop-holed battlements. Enough remains (despite modern additions and restoration) to convey some of the original effect.

On the Léndas road from Plóra you arrive at an oblique T-junction just short of **Apesokári**, and turn sharp right for the steep climb south into the Asteroúsia mountains. As you gain height towards a ridge there are magnificent views back over the Mesará plain. The excavation at Phaistós stands out on a spur of the foothills of Psilorítis.

You continue through **Miamoú**, where a cave (now under village houses) was excavated at the end of the 19C; it produced evidence for human occupation as far back as the Final Neolithic period.

The road winds down the hillside, with coastal views. You look east to the prominent conical hill of **Kóphinas**, highest point (1231m) of the Asteroúsia mountains. On the summit the Minoans established one of their most important peak sanctuaries. (The climb, from Kapetanianá, can be recommended only to fit and experienced walkers; the last stretch is as precipitous as it appears from a distance.)

Léndas

Ahead you have a bird's-eye view of the long sweep of bay and the fishing village of Léndas. The promontory beyond the village, sheltering it from the west, is Cape Léndas, the name derived from the Greek for lion, the cape being seen as the profile of a lion crouching.

Here, in the same sheltered position, was the site of ancient Lebéna. Therapeutic springs were the focus of a renowned sanctuary for healing, with a temple of Asklepios dating from the 4C BC. (The Hellenistic sanctuary was apparently superimposed on the site of a cult of water deities.) Lebéna was one of the harbours of Roman Górtyn and the temple complex near the sea was restored in the 2C AD, the great building period at Górtyn.

You reach the coast a little to the east of the modern village. A dirt road, left, runs east along the shore of the 5km bay of **Loutrá** to a summer taverna of the same name and ends at Cape Trakhoúlas. (Energetic walkers from Léndas can continue up the **Trakhoúla gorge** to **Krótos**, in time for a bus or taxi for the 10km return to Léndas.)

At the edge of the village of Léndas the bus terminates within sight of the restored Byzantine church of Ayios Ioánnis and you walk on into the village. By car you follow the road round to the little plateía behind the main cove. Ayios Ioánnis is set in the foundations of a late 5C/early 6C basilica church which was built just to the southeast of the temple of Asklepios (see below) and was probably intended to uphold the sanctity of the place.

Modern Léndas has expanded from the original cluster of beach tavernas, but on the whole in a simple style, with rooms or studios available in the village or close to the neighbouring beaches. Around the plateía there are a couple of mini-markets and a travel agency where you can ask about accommodation and change money.

The road loops inland to continue west, or there is a 15-minute walk on a path over the promontory. Either way you drop down to what is now called **Dytikós beach** (the name meaning western), a long stretch backed by the shade of tamarisk trees. This beach offers magnificent swimming, especially early and late in the year under the influence of the benign south coast temperatures, but to enjoy it you need to be comfortable with nudity. In summer the whole area is taken over by campers.

Where to stay and eating out

Léntas (12 bungalows just above the village plateía), ☎ 28920 95221, fax 28920 95222, is probably the most comfortable choice.

There are **rooms to rent** on the plateía and above the tavernas along the cove. At the start of the **Dytikós beach** there are a number of places to stay and to eat, also bars playing music in the evenings.

Hotel Léntas is a modern complex of studio rooms around a garden. The taverna on the terrace immediately below (with steps to the beach from its terrace) offers traditional cooking as well as rooms to rent right on the sea.

Taverna Nikólaos is popular with Cretans for Sunday lunch.

Further (up to 1km) west, in the area known as **Yerókambos**, there are scattered and (outside the camping season) quieter blocks of rooms or studios.

The Minoans had a settlement (not yet excavated) on the inland slope of Cape Léndas and in the vicinity five large Early-Middle Minoan tombs of the circular Mesará type (similar to those at Plátanos, see above) were excavated 40 years ago. One lies east at **Zervoús**. Two (belonging to the settlement on the promontory) are just west of Léndas at **Papoúra**; finds included a gold diadem, two Cycladic figurines, beads and seals, and an Egyptian scarab. Another pair of tombs (with four small annex rooms) lies c 2km to the west behind the beach at **Yerókambos**. One of these produced a great deposit of vases of Early Minoan I date, as well as later offerings similar to the Papoúra finds, including another scarab.

The guardian for the local archaeological sites will if necessary help with directions. He is often at the sanctuary site but otherwise ask in the village for the *phýlax*.

The **Sanctuary of Askelpios** lies to the left of the road as you drive into Léndas from the east. Open in the summer 08.00–19.00 except Monday. The site was excavated by Italian archaeologists early in the 20C but recent work (bringing to light areas which had been backfilled at that time) has left the ground plan easier to make out.

The **temple**, on an artificial terrace, consisted of a simple cella (12m x 13m) with a podium for the statue of the god against the inner (west) wall. Two granite columns still stand in front of the podium area. In the Hellenistic period the walls were of stone, but in the Roman restoration they were given a lining of brick. Near the statue base dedicated by Xenion (inscription on loose fragment) is a scrap of Roman mosaic. At the northeast corner of the temple was the treasury, which has a Hellenistic (3C BC) pebble mosaic floor executed in black, white and red, depicting a sea horse framed in a scroll of waves, with two delicate palmettes. The floor, now protected by a roof, was damaged in antiquity by the sinking of a shaft (to hold offerings) which was subsequently looted.

Leading north from the treasury was the colonnaded **West Stoa**, a free-standing portico, and along the whole length of the east side of it a broad flight of marble steps gave access to the raised level of stoa and temple. To the northeast of this stood the **North Stoa**. 15m to the east of the flight of steps there is a brick-tiled arch which the excavators recognised as part of the building above the Asklepieíon's therapeutic spring. The stream flowed down beside it. (On the hillside a little below the temple were two great basins, perhaps for the total immersion of the sick.)

The sanctuary complex originally included lodgings for the pilgrims. The building had texts inscribed on its walls, and the ritual of healing apparently included the reading of votive tablets in a local Doric dialect. The therapeutic powers of the god are vividly described: one sufferer from sciatica was cured while he slept.

From Léndas a dirt road, slow and still rough in places for vehicles, highly recommended as a walk, leads west along the coast through Platiá Perámata (with tavernas) 12km to Kalí Liménes (p 165).

South slopes of Mount Ida ~ Zarós to Kamáres

A road west from Ayía Varvára (30km from the north coast on the main Herákleion–Phaistós road) runs through the beautiful country of the southern foothills of the Ida massif on its way across to the Amári valley. Along this road there are some notable churches with well-preserved fresco decoration: the monasteries of **Vrondísi** and **Ayios Nikólaos** should be open all day except during the siesta hours, but the remarkable church at **Valsamóneros** is only open in the morning, until 13.00. A beautifully sited hotel above Zarós makes a convenient base for visiting the Minoan sites to the south and is also a good choice for a walking holiday. High in the mountains above Kamáres is the sacred cave which gave its name to a distinctive style of Minoan pottery.

You leave the main north–south road at the southern end of the long village of Ayía Varvára (p 145) at the signpost for Yérgeri and Kamáres. There will be glimpses of the Libyan Sea ahead, and beyond Yérgeri a fine view of the Paximádia islands in the Bay of Mesará. (The **Rouvás forest** can be reached on a well-signed track north from Yérgeri.) After 15km you come to Zarós, and the junction with a road from the south which climbs into the hills (10km) from the main road between Ayii Déka and Míres.

Zarós is a large, attractive village with abundant water; the springs here used to feed the aqueduct that supplied the numerous fountains of the great Roman city of Górtyn. **Lake Vótomos**, an artificial lake 1km up the mountain on the road past the hotel towards the gorge of Rouvás, is a recommended detour for birdwatchers. Herons come to fish and colonies of alpine swifts to drink.

Where to stay and eating out

B *Idi* (59 rooms), ☎ 28940 31301, fax 28940 31511. A well-signed turning, right, in the middle of the village takes you (1km) up to a secluded location beside a mountain stream. The hotel has a swimming pool and air-conditioning.

Taverna Votomos, beside the Hotel Idi, attracts diners from some distance to enjoy the speciality of trout fresh from the lake.

Keramos rooms offer simpler but welcoming accommodation below the main village street.

To the north of Zarós is the **monastery of Ayios Nikólaos** where a curious little church has frescoes of two periods (14C and 15C). You can reach the monastery by car: 500m beyond the end of the village take a side-road right that climbs 2km up a valley. On foot there is a short cut (c 20 minutes), starting up the stream-bed, or a (longer) marked path from Lake Vótamos. The church of Ayios Nikólaos is at the centre of a flourishing monastic community. The north aisle was the original chapel, and has the earlier (14C) paintings, including a tender scene, on the north side of the sanctuary, of the ***Birth of the Virgin***.

The monastery lies at the foot of the **Gorge of Rouvás**. You may be directed to the cave church of **Ayios Eftímios** (also frescoed) c 30 minutes up the hillside, but the alternative is to follow the (marked) path up the gorge, a walk of a little under 2 hours to the chapel of **Ayios Ioánnis** at the top, where you join the main east–west route of the E4.

Around 20km on the road from Ayía Varvára, the **monastery of Vrondísi** is signed right. (On foot you can use the low-level option of the E4 footpath from Zarós; the path continues to the Valsamóneros church.)

Outside Vrondísi, shaded by two great plane trees, there is a 15C Venetian fountain with figures (damaged) of Adam and Eve. The terrace commands a splendid view across foothills to the Mesará plain. The main gateway was destroyed in 1913, but an inscription from it dated 1630–36 has been set above one of the cell doors. By the end of the Venetian period Vrondísi was one of the most influential monastic communities on the island, renowned as a centre for scholars and artists. The six icons by Mikhaíl Damaskinós, now in the Ayía Aikateríni collection in Herákleion, remained in the church here until the early years of the 19C.

In the monastery courtyard is the two-aisled church with bell-tower. The older south aisle, dedicated to Ayios Antónios, preserves some important frescoes dating from the first half of the 14C, early examples of the style known as the Cretan School, a specific trend in Palaiologan painting. The scene of the ***Last Supper*** appears here in the vaulting of the apse and occurs in this position at no other church on Crete; below it is the ***Apostle Communion***. On the right of the Hierarchs the figure of Simeon holds the Christ Child.

Back on the road you continue 3km to the village of Vorízia (if walking see above). On the way look left across the valley to the red roof and triangular gable of the bellcote of the church of **Ayios Phanoúrios**, **Valsamóneros**, which contains some of the finest and best-preserved examples of fresco painting on the island.

Towards the end of the village a side street (signed to the Byzantine church) drops awkwardly downhill left. It immediately bends left and after 150m passes on the left the house of the guardian. He opens the church between 08.00 and 13.00 daily from around Easter to early October. Out of season you may find him in the village.

At the bottom of the village street you cross a bridge over a stream shaded by plane trees, and follow a well-signed surfaced minor road along the contour as the valley opens out ahead, until after 2km the church comes into view. A new car park does little for the romance of the place. (If you are using the E4 footpath from Vrondísi you will approach from the opposite direction.)

The church of **Ayios Phanoúrios** (a Rhodian saint) is all that remains of the once influential Valsamóneros monastery. Its exterior is one of the best examples on the island of Venetian influence on the detail of Byzantine church architecture; on the south façade the main doorway has carved rosette decoration and over the door into the narthex is a Venetian coat of arms with a wreath and inter-woven leaf motif. As a result of several building phases Ayios Phanoúrios has acquired a highly unusual ground-plan: there are two parallel naves or aisles on the usual east–west axis, and a third at right-angles across their western end forming a transept. Alongside the transept there is in addition a narthex. The original nave along the north wall, erected in 1328, is dedicated to the Panayía (Virgin Mary) who was depicted in the sanctuary above the Apostle Communion. On the barrel vaulting of the nave there is the most complete set of scenes from the life of the Virgin (the *Hymns to the Mother of God*) known in Cretan fresco painting.

The south aisle (just inside the main door) is dedicated to Ayios Ioánnis Prodrómos (literally the forerunner, St John the Baptist). The new addition was completed by 1406–07 but was not decorated until 1428. The frescoes include a scene of *Ayios Ioánnis in the desert*, where the elongated figures have been com-pared with the work of El Greco.

The transept honours Ayios Phanoúrios. The frescoes were painted by Konstantínos Ríkos in 1431 (inscription next to the doorway through to the narthex). At the south end of the transept, in the east wall, there is a miniature apse with the *Pantokrátor* in the vaulting, and below this the *Communion of the angels* with Christ as high priest offering communion to the richly clad angels in heaven. This rarely found scene here replaces its more usual counterpart in the theme of the Divine Liturgy, the Communion of the Apostles. Scenes of the mir-acles of Ayios Phanoúrios are preserved on the east wall, and on the pillar he is depicted as soldier-saint.

From Vorízia it is 4km on along the road west to Kamáres. Just out of Vorízia the track into the mountains has been widened and surfaced for some 3km to telecommunications masts, at the start of the old route round the flank of Mount Ida to the Nída plain above Anóyeia. For now this chiefly benefits local shepherds and beekeepers (and walkers looking for a change from the E4), but those who value the Cretan wilderness view with foreboding any suggestion of extending the upgrade.

A walk to the Kamáres cave

From the village of **Kamáres** a very steep path climbs (4–5 hours) to the Kamáres cave which gave its name to some of the finest polychrome pottery of the prehistoric world (p 77). The cave, at 1524m, was discovered by a shepherd only in 1890. It was investigated in 1904 by Italian archaeologists who found the first examples of the distinctive Kamáres ware and dated it to the Protopalatial period. In 1913 the site was fully excavated by the British. There was evidence for occupation during the Neolithic period, after which the cave became a sanctuary.

The climb to the cave is now marked for the benefit of users of the E4 but this is an expedition only for fit and experienced walkers. There is simple overnight accommodation in the village, but you would do much better in Zarós.

At the Herákleion or eastern end of Kamáres, the start of the walk to the cave is marked by an outsize sign; then watch for the paint splashes and yellow E4 signs. The path climbs steeply up the watercourse following a pipeline. The first landmark (after about 1 hour) is a group of water troughs. Then you strike east to the edge of the trees, looking for marked rocks which lead up to a second water point: troughs and a spring. From here it is a further hour's climb to the cave which is soon in view. For many years the cave-mouth has been the home of a noisy colony of alpine choughs.

There are time-honoured paths from the cave, northwest to the summit of Psilorítis (2456m) and east and north around the shoulder to the other great sanctuary on the mountain, the Idaian cave (p 323). Now that these paths have been incorporated into the long-distance European trekking route they may become more commonplace expeditions, but still Mount Ida, Psilorítis (the High One) needs to be treated with respect. Consult the **Greek Alpine Club** (EOS) in Herákleion, ☎ 2810 227609.

From the village of Kamáres a minor road, newly asphalted, runs down to Vóri (for the Museum of Cretan Ethnology) and 20km to Phaistós. If you stop to look back there are dramatic views of the rock wall of Mount Ida. Alternatively, you can continue from Kamáres into the province of Réthymnon, to Apodoúlou (c 12km) at the southern end of the Amári valley.

Ano Viánnos and the coast

It is 65km from Herákleion to the large village of Ano (Upper) Viánnos under the Lasíthi mountains in the southeastern corner of the province. You could make the return trip in one day to the south coast beaches between Tsoútsouros and Mýrtos, or you might stay in one of the relatively undeveloped coastal villages and explore the beautiful country along the southern foothills of Mount Díkte. This is also the first stage of the journey to eastern Crete by the south coast route.

Travelling by bus

The service is limited. There is one bus a day from Herákleion (harbour bus station) to Viánnos, which continues twice weekly to Ierápetra.

The main road sets off across the island past Knossós and Pezá (p 134). At Ayiés Paraskiés you continue south to Arkhalokhóri where you turn towards the mountains of Lasíthi. From the coast around Mália you can join this route by striking inland on the Kastélli road west of Khersónisos (c 55km from the coast road to Viánnos).

From Ayiés Paraskiés the main road runs south through vineyards, where the vines for the *rosakiá* table grapes are trained on tall wire trellises. Around 30km from Herákleion you come to **Arkalokhóri**, the busy centre of this agricultural region, but still retaining a delightful old world atmosphere. The nearby sacred cave of **Prophítis Ilías** (no longer accessible) was an important cult centre from the Early Minoan period to Neopalatial times. From rich deposits of votive offerings came a quantity of Late Minoan I bronze rapier blades suggesting worship here of a warlike deity. With them were miniature double axes in bronze, silver and gold (on display in the Herákleion Museum), some intricately decorated with traced ornament and one with a vertical inscription in Linear A. Altogether this was one of the largest deposits of metalwork to come to light in the Aegean area.

From Arkalokhóri it is possible to make a detour north 5km on an upgraded road to **Galatás**, where archaeologists are excavating a newly discovered Minoan palace (p 135).

The evocative ruins of an episcopal church of the Second Byzantine period may also merit a detour, in this case south 5km on the Pártira road. Just before the village watch for a track signed right which will bring you (in 1km) to the ruins of the church of **Sotíros Khristós** (Our Saviour Christ) at a place still known as **Mikrí Episkopí**. There are fragments of fresco decoration preserved (early 14C, and 15C in the side-chapel) but the chief interest lies in the architectural sophistication of the design which incorporates columns and Corinthian capitals from an Early Christian building. In 1599 both Latin and Greek orthodox liturgies were celebrated here.

From Arkalokhóri you can keep straight on for Skiniás and Tsoútsouros (see below) on the Libyan Sea, but the Viánnos road turns sharp left near the end of the village towards the Lasíthi range, where Mount Díkte may be snow-capped till May. After 6km, at a meeting of five roads, turn right for Viánnos.

You will pass a sign for a turning right to Afráti where the road skirts a hill which was the site of the Classical city-state of **Arkádes**. Nothing remains above ground today. Early in the 20C Italian archaeologists excavated an important Iron Age cemetery; some cremation urns of the Orientalising period, painted with figurative scenes, are on display in the Herákleion Museum.

A detour to the village of **Embaros** less than 1km left of the main road is recommended. The church of Ayios Yeóryios has much admired frescoes of 1436–37 by Manuel Phokás, who also worked at Avdoú in the Pediáda and Epáno Sými southeast of Viánnos. You can walk into the mountains southeast from the village, or northeast from Xeniákos (1km further along the minor road). This is one of the old traditional routes up into the mountain plain of Lasíthi.

Remaining on the Ano Viánnos road you come to a turning right to Khóndros (and Keratókambos, see below). 3km from the main road is the Bronze Age site above **Khóndros** which is important in that it is one of the few excavated settlements known to have been founded in the Postpalatial period (LMIIIA), after the widespread destruction of Minoan sites across the island at the end of LMI. The excavation comes into view on a saddle immediately above the village. At the first group of houses watch for signs right; after less than 1km the site is three minutes on foot uphill left. In early spring the orchids around it may prove a distraction.

The (poorly preserved) buildings of the settlement are in two groups along the saddle, separated by a double wall, each complex consisting of a number of house units perhaps for a community of several extended families. The architecture is typical of the LMIII period, with walls up to 1m thick, stone-flagged floors, low benches and fixed storage places. Loomweights suggested the weaving of wool from the community's own sheep. The western complex (away from the modern village) had a grander area reached by steps and with a room with a dais, perhaps the house of the local ruler. In the nearby debris a group of ritual objects, including fragments of an offering table decorated with lions in relief, provided evidence of a shrine on the upper floor. The settlement appears to have had a short life. It was destroyed by fire, but whether as a result of earthquake or hostile action is unclear. Certainly it was not reoccupied.

Viánnos

On the way into Ano (Upper) Viánnos you pass the **Museum of Historical Folklore**. Open April–October only; hours are variable. Out of season you can rely on Sun–Wed 09.30–13.30. In summer the museum may open daily and reopen in the evenings 17.00–19.30; ☎ 28950 22801. There is easy parking and a coffee shop (open museum hours) with a fine view over the fertile plain of Khóndros.

The comprehensive collection is well arranged to illustrate aspects of traditional everyday life in this region as well as the impact on it of the history of the island during the last 200 years. There is some labelling in English, especially for the 1940–45 wartime material, but the guardians are available to add interest to unusual exhibits such as the obsolete Cretan bagpipes or the rakí still.

Where to stay and eating out

The success of the new museum may encourage the renting out of rooms in Viánnos. You could enquire here or in the central plateía. Otherwise there is a choice of accommodation at Keratókambos (via Khóndros, see below) or, if you continue 20km further east towards the province of Lasíthi, at Arvi (p 182).

There are several café-bars around the plateía and an *ouzéri* just below it towards the police station. The taverna ***O Menios*** is about halfway along the main street.

Viánnos is a large, unspoilt and picturesque village laid out on a hillside like the classical city-state of the same name. It has several interesting Byzantine churches, notably **Ayía Pelayía** with well-preserved frescoes dated by inscription to 1360. Follow the brown Ministry of Culture signs from the plateía up the stepped side-streets to the church on a high terrace with another splendid view. On the way up ask for **Ayios Yeóryios**, a 14C–15C church with fine doorways and bellcote. Local people may encourage you to return along the high terrace to a main flight of steps down to a huge plane tree by a fountain. You will find yourself on the uphill side of the main street at the eastern end of the village; you turn right for the plateía.

The plateía has a post office and a taxi rank. There is a bank at the other end of the main street on the way out to eastern Crete.

A rough road due south from the plateía in Viánnos (not recommended as a vehicle road to the coast) is signed (c 2km) to **Ayía Moní** (the Holy Monastery), an ancient foundation with an interesting collection of icons. Two (including a fine *St John the Baptist*) are credited to the 15C Cretan master, Angelos.

Keratókambos and Tsoútsouros

A decent road descends via Káto Viánnos and Khóndros (see above) to the bay of Keratókambos and the Libyan Sea. This stretch of coast between Arvi and Tsoútsouros is at the time of writing little affected by organised tourism. Threatened development at Tsoútsouros has been restricted, if only temporarily. If you are looking for coastline off the beaten track where the fishing boats are still pulled up in time-honoured fashion on the long pebble beach you should investigate **Keratókambos**.

Where to stay

The *Taverna Creta*, in a prominent position on the seafront, acts as a clearing house for rent rooms and apartments (many with sea views) and you have a good choice of simple tavernas along the beach.

From Keratókambos there is an unsurfaced road east, which winds inland and back to the coast (after 12km) at Arvi; for the surfaced road to Arvi, see below. To the west you can walk or drive, close to the shore all the way, 10km to **Tsoútsouros**.

The improved dirt road (serving the familiar plastic hot-houses) crosses the broad riverbed of the Anapodáris on a functional modern bridge. There is a good beach on the west side. Despite horticultural activity the wading birds that use this area during the spring migration still seem to be regular visitors. The road climbs over headlands and down to the tamarisk-lined beach and strikingly clear sea at Tsoútsouros. Deep water is close inshore, which made this bay a favoured landfall during the Second World War for Allied submarines maintaining links between Cairo and the Resistance movement on Crete.

Along the coast is the most attractive approach to Tsoútsouros. Development, which began a few years ago to transform the coastal hamlet into a resort, has run into planning restrictions. Behind the beach there are many shells of buildings, few completed, and the future is uncertain.

In the meantime old-style tavernas flourish here and the swimming from the steeply shelving cove is some of the best on the island. From a base along this coast you can walk on west, along the coastal track, and up into the Asteroúsia mountains dominated by Mount Kóphinas (p 173).

Where to stay and eating out

On the way in from Keratókambos you come to a row of waterfront tavernas catering on summer weekends to Cretan families on a day trip from the north coast. *Taverna Inatos* serves traditional food and the owners will find you a room to rent. *Taverna Venetia* has rooms on the sea.

The haven where the fishing boats tie up is at the far end of the bay under the cliffs. This was the harbour of the Greco-Roman city state of **Inatos**, famous for the important **cave sanctuary of Eileíthyia**, goddess of childbirth. The cave (at the back of the beach 200m before the end of the road) was excavated in 1970 after illicit digging, but then sealed up. The remarkable votive offerings were mostly dated to the Geometric and Archaic periods but the Minoan tradition persisted in numerous bull figurines and double axes. Finds included clay figurines invoking the blessing of children and women pregnant or giving birth. There was some Egyptian material and a model boat, perhaps a reminder of pilgrimages to this bay. Some of the material is exhibited in the Herákleion Museum (Room XI).

The road north from Tsoútsouros climbs 11km to Káto Kastelliraná on the main east–west route across the Mesará plain (Viánnos–Pýrgos, p 184). It runs high above a narrow valley where in summer the river-bed glows with oleander. At the ridge you pass a traditional double-naved chapel, completed in 1991 to watch over the new road.

East of Viánnos to Arvi

The road down to the coastal village of Arvi (20km from Viánnos) starts from **Amirás**, c 6km east of Viánnos and on the south side of the main road to Mýrtos and Ierápetra. There is a choice of turnings: the one nearest to Viánnos (not the most direct) is beside a **war memorial**. This striking monument commemorates the victims of German reprisals after an uprising of the local Resistance band in September 1943, towards the end of the Second World War. Six villages were burned and some 500 civilians shot by the Germans.

From Amirás, it is 11km down to the coast where you could turn west to Keratókambos (see above), but left, east, takes you into **Arvi**. This is still a relatively unspoilt village welcoming visitors to simple accommodation and tavernas, the best all within earshot of the sea rattling on a narrow pebble beach. There are lively cafés in the small plateía halfway along the one main street. There is little sign so far of any significant attempt to transform the village into a tourist resort, perhaps because local prosperity depends chiefly on the favourable microclimate of this narrow strip of land sheltered by mountains, and on the hothouses growing bananas that exploit it. A monk from the monastery above the village is credited with the introduction of banana cultivation from Egypt to Crete soon after the end of the First World War.

Where to stay and eating out

C *Ariadne* (14 rooms), ☎ 0895 71300, a small hotel in a good location at the western end of the village street, but perhaps still due for modernisation.

For **apartments** or **rooms** you could start with *Livykón* or *Pension Gorgóna*, but several of the tavernas along the seafront also rent out rooms on their upper floor. *Taverna Diktynna*, at the far end, is quieter in the evenings than

some, and friendly. New developments on a small scale even further east, just before the cliffs close off the plain, includes *Arvi Villa Apartments*.

1km outside the village along the coast in the other direction, west of the road down from Amirás, is the *Pension Kolybi* with sea-view rooms, and taverna tables under the acacia trees at the back of the stony beach.

From the plateía in the middle of Arvi you can turn inland for the monastery of **Áyios Antónios** overlooking the foot of the dramatic gorge which is in view from the village. The monastery's buildings are of no great age (late 19C) but its position is memorable and the one monk in residence cares well for the church and maintains an atmosphere of prayer and devotion. You can drive, but this is a highly recommended walk (allow half an hour) to enjoy the cultivated valley where tall trees stand out to striking effect among the vines and orchards against a background of jackdaw activity at the bottom of the gorge.

A narrow coastal track continues east from Arvi, never for long far from the shore, all the way to Tértsa and Mýrtos.

The Sanctuary at Sýme

High above the village of **Káto Sýme**, at 1130m on the southern slopes of the Dikte range of mountains, an important **sanctuary of Hermes and Aphrodite** has been thoroughly investigated in recent years by Greek archaeologists. A rough road climbs up to the site, c 5km from the village, or allow an hour for a recommended walk. The excavation has to be viewed from outside the protective fence.

From Viánnos take the main road east to Mýrtos and Ierápetra. Soon after the village of Pévkos (9km from Viánnos, c 30km on a pine-scented road from Mýrtos) there is a turn for (2km) Káto Sýme, clearly signed to a war memorial and the sanctuary. The valley follows a stream lined with plane, walnut and fig trees. The war memorial (on the right before the village) commemorates the battle between German troops and the Cretan Resistance which provoked the terrible reprisals recorded on the monument at Amirás (see above).

Káto Sýme has two attractive tavernas. If you want to visit the frescoed church of Ayios Yeóryios, Epáno Sýme, ask here whether the key is available. At a fork beyond the village, where there is a house hidden in the angle of trees, the road right leads (2km) to the picturesque church; the frescoes (dated by inscription to 1453) are by Manuel Phokás (compare Embaros and Avdoú, pp 179 and 234 respectively). If the key is not forthcoming you can see a certain amount through a window.

For the **sanctuary site** keep left at the fork mentioned above and climb for c 3km till a rougher track comes in from the right (from Epáno Sýme) across a ford below a waterfall. 1km further the site is above the road right, often surrounded by beehives, always securely fenced (a useful landmark) and locked. There are several vantage points.

The site, at a place known as Krýa Vrýsi (cold spring), lies in a natural bowl at the foot of the cliff by a perennial gushing spring of ice-cold water. The water descends through channels to a valley now filled with deciduous trees alive with song-birds. The mountain wall above shelters eagles and vultures. The sanctuary associated with this source of water occupies a series of platforms across the natural amphitheatre on the mountainside. Particular importance is attached to the evidence that this isolated spot was a place of worship from the Bronze Age Protopalatial period to the 3C AD. The excavation has provided an example, rare if not unique on Crete, of continuity of religious practice from Minoan to Postminoan times. The open-air sacred enclosure of the Neopalatial period with a paved approach road was extended in the Geometric period to include a monumental altar, and by Roman times there was a temple (near the northeast corner of the current excavation).

Great quantities of votive offerings were brought to the sanctuary over the centuries. From the Minoan period, evidence has been recovered for large numbers of stone offering tables, many inscribed in Linear A script. There are stone vases, clay and bronze figurines and, of Postpalatial date, three bronze swords with incised decoration. In the later periods, at the end of the Iron Age, deposits included a series of remarkable bronze cut-out plaques, now well displayed in Room XII of the Herákleion Museum. The worship of Hermes Kendrites and Aphrodite is attested by votives and by graffiti on the roof tiles of a house shrine of the Hellenistic and Roman periods, and confirmed by a stone inscription. This continuity of architectural remains and votive deposits has led to the suggestion that the worship of Aphrodite and Hermes may have contained elements of the ritual associated with the Minoan goddess and her young consort.

From Viánnos west to Pýrgos

The road between Viánnos and Pýrgos, only recently upgraded, carries traffic east–west c 40km across the southern part of the province, and makes possible a circular tour of the island. It runs for much of the way along the slopes above the Mesará plain, and this raised level, where the villages were traditionally sited above the fertile ground, offers superb long-distance views.

Travelling by bus

There are services from Herákleion to Viánnos and to Pýrgos but at the time of writing there was no bus service between these two southern villages.

From Viánnos take the main road north for 9km and then at Mártha watch for a turning left, signed for Tsoútsouros (26km) and Skiniás. The route leads south-west down a valley towards the Asteroúsia mountains. You cross the main river, the Anapodáris, at Demáti. At Káto Kastelliná, pass the major junction for Tsoútsouros (p 181) and continue along the southern edge the plain.

Pýrgos

Pýrgos is a large village with a mountain stream channelled through it on a slope where the foothills of the Asteroúsia range rise steeply from the plain. It flourishes as the centre of this prosperous agricultural region and there is a bank, post office, rooms to rent and a good choice of tavernas. The old heart of the village, uphill from the through road, has an interesting frescoed church dating from the Venetian period when the settlement was the fief of the Latin clergy in Candia. Pýrgos can be considered as a base for a night or two off the tourist track from which to explore, either by car or on foot, the villages and upland along this south side of the Mesará plain.

Where to stay and eating out

Rent Rooms Saridakis, pleasantly modern, are in a quiet location at the top of the village. They are signed straight uphill from a group of tavernas including *O Minas* and the *psistariá* (grill) *To Spitiko* which you find on the main street across the upper level.

The **church of Ayios Yeóryios and Ayios Konstantínos** is at the eastern end of the main street not far from the stream; ask for the key at the laundry next door. This used to be a triple-naved church but the third aisle, dedicated to Ayía Eléni (Constantine's mother), had to be sacrificed during widening of the village street. In the surviving decoration at least three phases of wall-painting can be detected within a relatively short period, the earliest in the north aisle of Ayios Yeóryios. The Constantine cycle is in the south aisle with a donor inscription in the apse dating it to 1314–15. In depicting episodes from the life of the Emperor Constantine the Great (commonplace in the iconography of western Christendom) these frescoes are unique in the Byzantine world. Extant (lower registers of the eastern half of the vault) are: the birth of Constantine; his parents with the young Constantine on horseback with his father; the crowning of Constantine's son; the battle of the Milvian bridge when Constantine's vision of the Cross is believed to have determined the future religion of the Roman Empire. These frescoes are in the conservative linear style with no sign of the influence of the Palaiologan art recognised in Constantinople by that time. Stylistic features typical of that movement, and its more generously moulded figures, can be compared in the remaining (slightly later 14C) panels in the west bay of this same aisle.

From Pýrgos a main road runs due north 50km to the coast at Herákleion. If you are staying with the southern route across the island turn left after 5km, on the edge of Protória, to head for Ayii Déka (through Asími and Stóli) c 20km across the intensively cultivated plain, to link up with the main Herákleion–Phaistós road (p 144) which continues to the south coast in the province of Réthymnon.

The scenic drive back to Herákleion sets off from Protória along an avenue of gum trees and up the fertile valley of the River Anapodáris to climb to **Ligórtynos**. It winds through the cultivated uplands of central Crete, often with wide views east to the Lasíthi mountains, and ahead to the profile of Mount Júktas.

A 3km detour to Moní Epanosíphi (p 132) is signed left, before you pass Khoudétsi, Pezá and Knossós to join the north coast highway.

West of Herákleion

There is a choice of roads between Herákleion and Réthymnon, a distance of c 80km. The route along the New National Road takes little more than an hour and provides access to the resort villages which have grown up in the coves along the coast, and to Phódele a short distance inland.

In contrast, the Old Road, which runs further south, follows the route which has traditionally linked the rural settlements on the north slopes of the Ida range with the cities of the two provinces, Herákleion and Réthymnon. The road is still narrow and winding in places, and inevitably slow as it accommodates local traffic. From it you can make short detours off the beaten track to the villages of **Rógdia** or **Krousónas**, both with flourishing convents nearby, and to the Minoan excavations at **Týlissos** (13km from Herákleion). If you intend to climb into the mountains to Anóyeia and the cave of Zeus on **Mount Ida**, explore the site of ancient **Eléftherna**, or visit the monastery of **Arkádi** (all in the province of Réthymnon) you will need to allow most of a day.

Travelling by bus

There is a frequent bus service on the New Road between Herákleion and Réthymnon, and four or five departures a day using the Old Road, all from the harbour bus station in Herákleion. From Herákleion to Anóyeia, there are five buses daily from the bus station outside the Khaniá Gate, also a limited service to Týlissos, Krousónas, Rógdia and Phódele.

Where to stay and eating out

Lygariá (Lygariá Akhládas, of the parish of Akhláda) has a choice of up to a dozen good tavernas side by side along the beach; many offer rooms to rent. *Taverna Anatoli*, halfway along the shore at the bottom of the western approach, is rightly popular and outside the high season one of its modern studio apartments may be available.

In complete contrast to Lygariá, **Ayía Pelayía** has one of the few hotels on Crete in the luxury class, and the only one within a short distance of Herákleion.

L *Capsis Beach* (660 rooms and bungalows), ☎ 2810 811112, fax 2810 811076, www.capsis.gr, email: capsis-kriti@capsis.gr. This entirely self-contained, exclusive and expensive resort hotel occupies a fine position on a headland. The complex provides all expected facilities, including watersports and a private bus service to Herákleion. Arriving by car use the western of the three minor roads signed to the hotel on a bend at the top of a hill.

A *Peninsula* (240 rooms), ☎ 081 811313, fax 081 371600, www.peninsula.gr, email: peninsula@her.forthnet.gr. Situated on the rocks immediately above the sea, this complex has all the usual facilities of a Class A hotel and is good for family holidays.

The New Road towards Réthymnon

The north coast highway bypasses Herákleion. From the city centre you reach it most easily from the Knossós road, or otherwise 3km out along the Old Road which leaves town to the west through the Khaniá Gate. Watch for the Míres turning signed left at traffic lights and then for access to the highway towards Réthymnon. Nearly at the end of the bay, opposite the Herákleion power station, a slip road inland (a legitimate exit only if you are driving east) takes you on to the Old Road to Réthymnon (see below) for Týlissos and Anóyeia.

Towards the end of the Herákleion bay you will notice a Greek Orthodox seminary beside the Pantánassa bridge, and soon after, at **Palaiókastro**, the walls of a Venetian fort stand to seaward of the road. The fort was built in 1573 to protect the city of Candia against Turkish pirate raids. High up left Rógdia (see below) clings picturesquely to the hillside. The highway makes the long climb out of the bay and cuts across a cape.

On the rocky coast west of the cape is the fast-growing tourist resort of **Ayía Pelayía**, built around coves to some extent sheltered by headlands from the *meltemí*, the prevailing north (or west of north) wind of the summer months.

There are three by-roads to the sea in a 4km stretch of the highway. Just over the crest as you leave the Herákleion bay a minor road is signed down to **Lygariá**, a particularly beautiful cove (less developed than the ones further west), which (c 15km from the city) offers a practical alternative to the town beaches after a morning's sightseeing. It is not usually over-crowded except in the high season and on Sundays, a time for Cretan outings. (If you are approaching from the opposite direction you have to use a slip road right, signed for Lygariá, and then branch right by a chapel high above the sea.)

Ayía Pelayía is built on the site of the ancient city-state of **Apollónia**. Excavations, now scattered among the terraces and gardens of the Capsis Beach Hotel, have revealed extensive remains of the Classical and Hellenistic periods including what is probably the ancient *prytaneion*. The city was destroyed in 171 BC by the people of Kydonía (modern Khaniá), in one of the most treacherous attacks ever recorded on a friendly city-state. The Apollonians went down to the harbour to welcome their allies who came streaming out of the boats to slaughter them. After this destruction the site was fought over by Górtyn and Knossós, and these squabbles led to one of the earliest diplomatic interventions by the Romans in a Cretan border dispute.

Phódele

22km from Herákleion, Phódele lies a short distance inland surrounded by orange groves, stunning at blossom time around Easter. On the drive into the village you catch glimpses, across the valley to the right, of a domed Byzantine church (see below).

Traditionally Phódele was accepted as the birthplace of Doménikos Theotokópoulos (1541–1614) the painter better known as El Greco, but scholars now believe that he was born in Herákleion (p 94). At the far end of the main street, past the ubiquitous souvenir shops, there is a popular taverna as well as pleasant shady cafés beside a stream where water runs for most of the year. Under the plane and chestnut trees here the University of Valladolid in Spain erected in 1934 a bilingual inscription in honour of El Greco; it was carved on slate from Toledo where he lived and worked for the last 38 years of his life.

To find the picturesque church noted above, the **Panayía Loubiniés** (dedicated to the birth of the Virgin, festival 8 September), take the signed side street that crosses the stream by the larger bridge in the village. The carefully restored cross-in-square pillared church, with the dome supported on a drum lit by 11 narrow windows, is built into the central nave of an 8C (pre-Arab) basilica. Traces can be seen of the basilica apses, and of the medieval village which surrounded the church. Remains of several layers of frescoes have been uncovered, in contrasting styles. The oldest paintings, in the sanctuary, date back to the early years of the Venetian occupation (13C); those in the south cross-arm include a donor inscription of 1323.

4km inland from Phódele, in unspoilt countryside, is the former **monastery of Ayios Pandeleímonos** which dates to the period of Venetian rule. The church is still consecrated, although its finest icons have been removed to Herákleion's Historical Museum. The surrounding buildings now serve as a farmstead. You can drive there straight on south out of the village. However, this makes a highly recommended walk, either out from and back to Phódele or downhill all the way on the same (partly unpaved) road from the Old Road bus route to Réthymnon (p 188).

Soon after the Phódele turn, continuing west on the New Road, you enter the province (nome) of Réthymnon. (A recently improved road could sweep you inland to Alóides on the eastern slopes of the Kouloúkonas hills, to connect with the Old Road.) You will notice the picturesque harbour village of **Balí** (p 310), and above it (signed left from the highway) you can visit the flourishing monastery of Ayios Ioánnis (closed Fridays). 10km beyond Balí is **Pánormos** (p 309), just off the road, with cafés and good tavernas on the harbour; there is an excavated basilica site south of the highway.

The Bay of Réthymnon comes into view, with the Levká Ori (White Mountains) in the distance as you cross the river Yeropótamos. Australian forces fiercely defended an airstrip on the flat land here, at the time of the German invasion in 1941; 6km beyond the river bridge you pass close to their war memorial (p 308) at **Stavroménos**, inland (east) of the junction signed for the Old Road to

Herákleion. Going west the Old Road follows the coast, now serving resort hotels. From it you can turn inland for the historic monastery of **Arkádi** (p 312) or a short-cut on back roads is signed from the highway.

The New National Road bypasses **Réthymnon**. For the city centre use the bypass as far as the junction for Spíli, then watch for signs which bring you out at the Municipal Gardens (and car parking) near the gate into the old city (plan on p 303). Alternatively remain on the bypass to its western end, to the only junction with traffic lights, where you can turn down to the coast and then left (near the bus station) following the shore under the fortress walls for the direct approach to the harbour.

The Old Road to Réthymnon

From the centre of Herákleion the Old Road to Réthymnon and western Crete leaves by the Khaniá Gate, and keeps straight on past the junction with the New National Road. Major disruption has to be expected along this coastal strip where a 28,000-seat stadium is being built for the 2004 Olympic Games. You are heading for the suburb of **Gázi**, probably the site of the Minoan harbour of Týlissos (see below) and associated with a shrine of the Late Minoan (Postpalatial) period from which came impressive clay figures now displayed in Room X of the Herákleion Museum. One goddess, 75cm tall, in the typical position with arms raised, attracts particular interest for the three poppy-heads in her crown.

At the end of Gázi you pass under a bridge carrying the highway over the Old Road and ahead are spectacular views of Psilorítis (Mount Ida) where in the high crevasses the snow often lies until June. At the junction just beyond the bridge you would leave the Réthymnon road for the recommended excursion to **Krousónas** (signed left, p 142) and the Ayía Eiríne convent high above the village. Continuing towards Réthymnon from the underpass, a by-road right, c 8km from Herákleion, loops back towards the highway and then climbs (6km) to Rogdiá and the Savathianá convent set in a lovingly tended garden.

Rogdiá

The village clings to the hillside 300m above the sea with coastal views and taverna terraces from which to enjoy them. This was part of a Venetian feudal estate, and the ruined façade of a grand house survives near the church. You can continue (signed, sharp uphill left at the beginning of the village, 5km northwest into cultivated uplands, to **Moni Savathianás**, founded during the Venetian period; open 08.00–13.00 and 16.00–19.00, daylight permitting. A community of more than 20 nuns now flourishes here and they proudly welcome visitors to one of the most delightful gardens on Crete, in the shade of trees alive with songbirds. The road ends at the gates of the nunnery with a red-roofed church in view against the cliffs across the valley.

The nunnery's main church, dating from 1635, is dedicated to the Panayía (the birth of the Virgin, festival 8 September), but c 200m along a path through the garden, the red-roofed Ayios Antónios protects the grotto which was the original nucleus of the monastery. The path crosses an old bridge (inscription 1535) where springs feed a stream.

In 1991 the nuns brought to light an important icon documented in old records but believed lost. It takes its title from the prayer used in the Orthodox liturgy on the feast of the Epiphany which begins 'Thou art Great, O Lord', and traditionally depicts each of the 61 phrases of the prayer. After cleaning, this icon is believed to be by Ioánnis Kornáros (1745–1806), best known for his masterpiece on the same theme, painted in 1770, which is treasured in the monastery church at Toploú in the far east of Crete.

From Rogdiá village the road continues (still unsurfaced for part of the way) to the north coast highway for Ayía Pelayía by the sea, or to Akhláda and Phódele (p 186).

Continuing on the Old Road, past the Rogdiá turning and on towards Týlissos, there is a fine view east across vineyards on the fertile slopes of the district of Malevísi, famous in Venetian times for the strong sweet wine known as malvesey or malmsey which found its way in great quantities to western Europe.

Malmsey

It appears that the name for this sweet dessert wine came originally from Monemvasía at the southern tip of the Peloponnese, but by 1420 it had become associated with wine shipped from the Malevísi district of Crete. Venetian records of the trade to England indicate that by the end of the 15C the island had become the main source of supply and an English consul to Candia (Herákleion) was appointed for the first time in 1522. In 1478 the Duke of Clarence, a prisoner in the Tower of London, was put to death by drowning in a butt of malmsey wine. This wine, relatively stable because it was heated during the making, was highly prized in the time before the introduction of glass bottles and corks (c 1600) which made it possible to keep wine drinkable for a longer period. The trade was disrupted after the Turkish invasion in the mid 17C and gradually declined thereafter. Sherry took the place of Cretan wine.

11km from Herákleion you come to a left fork signed for Týlissos and here you leave the main road if you intend to visit the Minoan excavations (2km) or climb into the mountains to Anóyeia and the Idaian cave.

Minoan excavations at Týlissos

Týlissos, an attractive village at the heart of the Malevísi district, retains the pre-Hellenic name which occurs on Linear B tablets as *tu-ri-so*. The excavated Minoan houses are on the edge of the modern village, signposted from the main street left and left again. Open Tues–Sun 08.30–15.00; closed Monday and public holidays.

History of the site

The original excavations (1909–13) took place, during the brief period of the island's independence, after Cretan archaeologists had been alerted by the chance find of the huge bronze cauldrons now on display in the Herákleion Museum's Room VII.

There are traces of buildings at Týlissos dating back to the third millennium BC but of the excavated remains interest centres on three large Neopalatial (MMIII–LMIA) houses. These should be thought of not as an isolated group, as they now appear, but as part of the wealthy area of a prosperous town flourishing at the height of the Minoan civilisation. The finds from the site were numerous and of the same high quality as material from the contemporary Minoan palaces; they included a bronze figurine of an older man in the typical votary position, and inscriptions in Linear A as well as large clay storage jars. Fragments of miniature frescoes were evidence for the palatial-style refinements of these Týlissos buildings.

After the destruction of the Minoan buildings in Late Minoan IB there was considerable reoccupation of the site in the Postpalatial period, including the construction of a large circular cistern at the northeast corner. There was also later Greek Classical period occupation when Týlissos was an independent city-state with its own coins.

The excavated remains of the three Neopalatial buildings (see plan) are complicated by vestiges of the earlier and later construction work. **House A** is the most easily intelligible of the three. Its plan (maximum dimensions 35m x 18m) consists of two blocks or wings, linked by a partially covered court. From the site entrance you can walk to the right round the south edge of the fenced area, to appreciate the finely dressed ashlar masonry and to reach House A's entrance, an angled passage leading into a small paved **court** (1 on plan). The passage, now restored, had been cut into by LMIII reoccupation walls. On two sides of the court (west and north) was an L-shaped **peristyle** (2); notice the central column base, pithos stand and a window lighting the staircase on the west side. North of the peristyle are two large **storerooms** (3). The pillars would have supported the upper floor, and fallen fragments of painted plaster indicated important rooms at that level; by analogy with the palace at Mália it has been suggested that they included a banqueting hall. Food could have been prepared in the small ground floor rooms west of the storerooms, where there is a convenient second staircase. Some of the storage jars still in situ (in 3) are set on stone slabs and have holes near their bases for tapping the liquid contents.

A passage south from the peristyle court leads to the heart of the south wing. Here the **main hall** (4) with an irregularly paved floor has a **lustral basin** (5) at one corner. This hall is designed, in accordance with the flexible (*polythýron*) arrangement typical of Minoan architecture, with double doors opening out on to a colonnaded **light-well** (6) which has a window in its west wall. The drain at the southwest corner of the light-well can be followed on the other side of the wall. The portico to the north of the light-well leads to a **pillar crypt** (7), where the excavator found a pyramidal stand for a double axe similar to those in the so-called Corridor of the Magazines in the palace at Knossós. Two small **rooms** (8 and 9) which may have been treasuries are reached from the pillar crypt. From hereabouts came the three huge bronze cauldrons, the chance find which led to the discovery of the site. The storerooms also held tablets with Linear A inscriptions and a copper ingot similar to those found at Ayía Triáda.

The small rooms in the southwest corner, with a short passage from the central room and a private staircase nearby, have suggested parallels with the layout of the presumed women's quarters in the palaces.

House B, set on traces of earlier walls, is a rectangular building with few recognisable architectural features except a staircase in the northeast corner. Its function may have been associated with administration and storage.

House C is basically square but with a characteristic irregular outline, and the

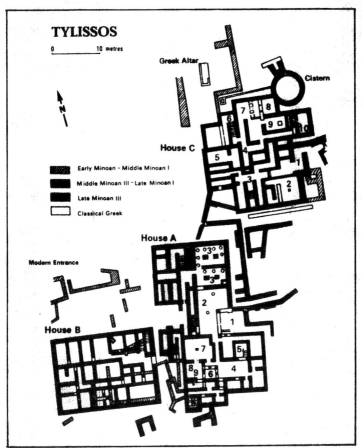

Minoan walls of Neopalatial date are preserved almost to the second storey in places. This house was cut into and overlaid by later construction work. Still in situ above the Minoan levels is evidence for the Postpalatial house (which perhaps resembled the megaron building at Ayía Triáda) and the cistern complex which is contemporary with it (see below). There are also bases for columns or statues, and an altar stone from the Classical levels.

The entrance of House C (partly destroyed, like that of House A, by later walls) is on the east side (1), and a clear system of corridors connects the various parts of the house. On the left as you enter is a supposed cult area including a room with a central pillar (2); at the staircase (3) the corridor turns right (4), under the paving of a later floor. On the west side of the house is a block of storerooms (5); the raised column base here is from the LMIII reoccupation level. Off the corridor is a staircase (6); the lower flight dates from the original Neopalatial house, and the upper one from the later Classical period building. Across the corridor from the staircase, at the north end of the house, is the residential quarter, where a main room with paved floor (7) opens east through a pier-and-door arrangement on to a large porticoed light-well (**8**). The big window, now restored, lit the adjacent room (**9**). A corridor ran east to west outside this room to reach a staircase (**10**) to an upper floor, and a toilet equipped with a drain through the outer wall. To the northeast of the house, and built over its corner, is a circular cistern of later (LMIII) date entered by a staircase from the north. The water reached the cistern by a stone channel on the west side, having first been decanted in a basin or trap at the west end of this channel.

North of the channel are scanty remains of foundations of a large early (Prepalatial period) structure, as well as an altar stone from the Classical period. Part of a fine paved Minoan road is preserved along the west façade of House C.

The modern road southwest out of Týlissos climbs steadily inland, and the landscape becomes wilder. Beyond a war memorial you pass through a rocky defile, and into a long valley with the village of Goniés (on a hill of chloritic and serpentine rock) spread out across the head of it. Soon the road cuts across the façade of a **Minoan country house** overlooking the small open plain of **Sklavókambos**. This Neopalatial building, though substantial, did not exhibit the architectural refinements of Týlissos. It is more crudely built, of partly worked boulders, and the floors were apparently unpaved, but the quality of the pottery and the number of seal impressions found here show that the life of the occupants was far from crude.

The house is aligned north to south. The main entrance was on the east side and there was a pillared verandah at the north end with the view over the valley. Behind the verandah there were storerooms where pithoi were found. The rooms to the south included a small open court with three pillars to support the peristyle roof. In the passage from the entrance several clay sealings with bull-leaping scenes were found. The same seal impression has been recognised at Zákros, Gourniá and Ayía Triáda, which suggests an extensive trading system.

The road, dominated to the south by the mountain range of Ida (in Greek *Psilorítis*, the High One) continues through **Goniés** to a crest at the *nome* boundary, and (less than 35km from Herákleion, 55km from Réthymnon) reaches the mountain village of **Anóyeia**. For Anóyeia and Mount Ida in the province of Réthymnon turn to pp 321 and 323.

From Týlissos, the Old Road towards Réthymnon gains height round the seaward flank of the conical **Mount Stroúmboulas** a conspicuous 800m peak. The domed building in ruins on the right of the road (signed Koumbédes) was in Turkish times an inn for travellers unable to reach the city before the gates were closed at nightfall. To the east is Mount Júktas, the isolated peak behind Knossós and legendary burial place of the Cretan Zeus; from this view the profile strikingly resembles the head of a reclining bearded god. On a hairpin bend you pass a curious geological feature signed *voulisméno alóni* (sunken threshing floor), which would have been an impressive cave before the roof collapsed. Near the 15km post, where the landscape is wild and strewn with boulders, a cleft between two outcrops of rock briefly affords a dramatic view back over the bay of Herákleion. A café is perched on a terrace at the head of the valley, and just beyond it the way up to the conspicuous radar station also allows you to pull off the main road.

1km after the village of **Márathos** a partly unpaved road runs downhill, right, 7km to Phódele. This connection between the Old and New roads makes a recommended walk which passes the former monastery of Ayios Pandeleímonos (p 187). The bus should stop at the turning, but in case of doubt get off it in Márathos. The gradual 7km descent brings you to Phódele and then it is another 3km to catch a main road bus on the north coast highway. Here the stop is 500m east of the junction, at the end of the bay.

On the Old Road, the next village after Márathes is **Damásta**, and you cross the boundary with the province of Réthymnon. You continue through a number of small villages, several with café-bars shaded by pollarded mulberry trees. Carved memorial stones are a reminder of the sufferings of the population during the Second World War.

Soon after the turn for Alóides (and a well-engineered short-cut down to the north coast highway) the Old Road leaves the foothills and descends gradually between vineyards. After the junction with the road down from Axós and Anóyeia (below Garázo), you follow the east–west Mylopótamos valley.

55km from Herákleion you reach Pérama, the busy centre for this agricultural region. You can turn north to (7km) Pánormos on the coast, or you can continue west on the Old Road to the junction of the two roads at Stavroménos. For rewarding excursions aournd the Pérama, north to Melidóni or inland to Eléftherna, turn to p 315.

East of Herákleion

The north coast highway (officially the New National Road) takes you east from Herákleion 70km to Ayios Nikólaos in the province of Lasíthi, passing at about halfway the site of the Minoan palace of **Mália**. Places to visit just off the road include the excavations of Minoan sites at **Amnisós** and **Nírou Kháni**, and the **Lychnostátis open-air museum** of traditional Cretan life at Khersónisos. Short detours will take you to the sacred caves of **Eileíthyia** and **Skoteinó**.

The first stretch of the Old Road, the original road east from Herákleion, runs between the highway and the coast, past the airport, to beaches which are conveniently close to the city; Amnisós, on the coast, could be a base for visits to Herákleion and Knossós.

Travelling by bus

There is a good bus service from the main bus station near the harbour in Herákleion, covering both the New and (much less often) the Old Road routes to Mália and Ayios Nikólaos. The Minoan palace is 3km beyond the resort of Mália, but Ayios Nikólaos buses stop on the highway only 500m from the site.

In summer, the no. 7 blue city bus runs every 20 minutes from Plateía Eleftherías in the centre of Herákleion to the Amnisós beaches. Out of season, long-distance buses on the Old Road will stop on request.

To take the New National Road to Mália you set off from the eastern end of the Herákleion bypass. The airport is soon in view, below left, with the island of Día in the distance. It is 7km to the exit for Amnisós (perhaps still signed only for Goúrnes). 10km further a c 10km loop inland has created a bypass for Khersónisos. An exit halfway along this stretch is signed for Kastélli but this is also one of the main routes up to the mountain plain of Lasíthi. If you plan to visit the great cave at Skoteinó, or look for birds at the mouth of the Aposelémis river, you should watch for the start of the new bypass and follow signs off it for Goúves and the Old National Road.

To Amnisós

The Old Road leaves Plateía Eleftherías in the centre of Herákleion, downhill past the car park for the Archaeological Museum. Keeping straight on you cross, after 2km, the Kaíratos stream which runs down from the Knossós valley. At its mouth the modern suburbs of **Póros** and **Katsambás** cover the principal harbour town of the Minoan palace of Knossós. (The Archaeological Museum shows finds from the current excavations.)

You continue through the suburb of Néa Alikarnássos, passing the Hotel Astérion, useful if you need to be at the airport at an awkward hour. Soon the Old Road to Ayios Nikólaos forks right skirting the airport and a military establishment, and runs parallel to the highway before descending, beyond the airport, to the bay of **Amnisós**.

The first of several tracks to this long sandy beach, only 6km from the city centre, is opposite a small cave church near the mouth of the Karterós river and its reedbeds. There is some small-scale development along this bay, but access to the beach is not restricted, and it is popular in summer with both local people and tourists. Far out the currents can be treacherous and even strong swimmers should be aware of this. Out of season the beach is usually deserted. You could allow half an hour to stroll from one end of it to the other, and the area is strongly recommended to birdwatchers, especially during both spring and autumn migrations.

From the road behind the beach several side-roads run down to the sea. One is signed to the organised public beach where the cleanliness of the facilities is unreliable. Another turning to the sea (with convenient bus stop) is before the low hill towards the eastern end of the bay, signed to the Sanctuary of Zeus Thénatas. On the further (eastern) side of the hill there is a sign to Minoan antiquities (an excavated Minoan house). Where there is access to the New National Road, a minor road inland for Episkopí passes after 1km a cave sacred to the goddess Eileíthyia.

Where to stay and eating out

A *Minoa Palace* (130 rooms), ☎ 2810 380404, fax 2810 380422, email: minoaplc@iraklio.hellanet.gr. This resort hotel may have rooms free outside the high season and as long as you accept the level of noise from the airport flight path it can provide a comfortable retreat from visits to Knossós and afterHerákleion. Swimming pools; suitable for wheelchair users; good for family holidays.

B *Karteros* (55 rooms), ☎ 2810 380402, fax 2810 380523; on the coast road 200m back from the beach near the eastern turning to the sea; swimming pool.

B *Prince of the Lilies* (30 rooms, including studio apartments), ☎/fax 2810 225822, in the same area as Hotel Karteros.

Hotel Amnisos and the *Ariadne*

Apartments are close by, and along at the turn to the Karterós public beach the apartment blocks **Knossós** and **Minos Bay**.

Tavernas and café-bars cluster near the apartments. At the extreme east end of the bay an area known as **Tobroúk** has the popular taverna *Acapulco* and just beyond it tables on a terrace above the beach are served from a kitchen on the inland side of the road.

Amnisós was a second harbour for Minoan Knossós and was mentioned in Bronze Age Linear B tablets. According to the *Iliad* it was from here that Idomeneos, leader of the Cretan contingent in the Trojan war, set sail. It is tempting to speculate that some of the fleet, specified as 80 black ships, might have sheltered from the prevailing northerly winds in the three natural harbours along the south coast of the island of Día.

The **House of the Lilies** is an excavated Minoan villa of the Neopalatial period named on account of the graceful floral frescoes (now in the Herákleion Museum) that decorated its walls. The site under the eastern side of the low hill is fenced, but there is a vantage point on the seaward side where the villa's flagged terrace is immediately in front of you. Behind the terrace there was a spacious room which, with six sets of piers-and-doors (a *polythýron*), could be a cool retreat open to the sea view or an enclosed hall protected from winter storms. The frescoes were found in the southwest area of the house, the main room with bases for two columns. The west façade was built of massive ashlar blocks, some of which were toppled out of place, presumably by earthquake action. Burnt patches on the stones are a reminder of the fierce fire that destroyed the villa at the end of the Late Minoan I period.

The site was first excavated in the 1930s by Spyridon Marinátos (and re-examined in 1983 by German archaeologists). Marinátos found a quantity of the laval by-product pumice, which led him to relate the LMIB destruction level here and at many other sites on Crete to an eruption on the volcanic island of Théra (Santorini) only c 100km away to the north. After years of academic argument revolving around the dating evidence of pottery styles it is now agreed that the Late Minoan period IB destruction on Crete occurred later, perhaps as much as a century later than the eruption which engulfed the Bronze Age sites on Théra.

If you walk west from the excavation of the House of the Lilies along the Amnisós beach to the other side of the hill, you will notice the (fenced) remains of the Archaic **sanctuary of Zeus Thénatas** dating to the 6C BC. Two life-size eagles in stone, found here associated with a large round open-air altar, are displayed in Room XIX of the Herákleion Museum. The massive foundation wall reuses blocks from a Late Bronze Age building. A little further west, where the rocks run down into the sea, there are traces of substantial constructions below the shore line, indicating the Minoan harbour works.

The cave sacred to **Eileíthyia**, goddess of fertility and childbirth, and revered as her birthplace, is on the hillside overlooking Amnisós. This was an important place of worship from Late Neolithic to Roman times, and was known to Homer (*Odyssey* XIX 188). The site is locked; the guardian at the nearby Minoan site of Nírou (see below) holds the key, but usually requires notice if he is to arrange access.

To reach the cave take the road under the highway which climbs inland, signed for Episkopí. After 1km (with the drop to seaward on your left) watch for a sign, just before a gully. The entrance is below the road under a fig tree. On foot you can approach straight up the gully, from where the tree is also visible. The cave was excavated in the 1920s. Two stalagmites, associated with a low wall and a primitive altar, seem to have been the focus of ritual. Finds extended to the small terrace in front of the cave mouth.

From Amnisós you can continue on the Old Road which follows the coast to the next sandy bay, another popular place to swim. At the far end of it, below the Hotel Arina Beach, the chapel of **Ayii Theódori** is a landmark for the remains of a Minoan harbour and dockyard. Swimmers may notice traces of the installations under water.

Nírou Kháni

In Nírou, 5km from Amnisós on the Old Road, a bridge crosses a gully just before (signed right) the excavation of a large Minoan building named by archaeologists the **House of the High Priest**. Open 08.30–15.00; closed Monday.

This was a house from the Neopalatial period of at least two storeys, and the remains are among the best preserved of their kind on the island. The interior of the building (see plan) is railed off, but all points of interest can be viewed from outside it. The paved courtyard (**1**) has raised paths across it and a stepped platform (**2**) where a fragment of horns of consecration (stylised bulls' horns) was found. The main entrance (**3**) was between two columns, and then through a

NIROU KHANI

Modern Entrance

After Xanthoudídes

typically Minoan pillar-and-door (*polythýron*) scheme to a hall (**4**) with gypsum dado and decorative floor paving. Out of this a corridor (**5**), originally frescoed, led west to the central block of the house. To the left of the columned entrance, there is a room (**6**) where four large thin bronze double axes were found; their size and delicacy implied a ceremonial usage, with a heap of ashes suggesting a shrine with a hearth for burnt offerings. West of this are the foundations of a staircase (**7**).

Towards the centre of the house is the Room of the Benches (**8**) with its integral light-well (**9**); there was a room above, also with benches, and also opening on to the light-well, creating a sheltered environment here at all seasons. Behind the Room of the Benches, and accessible only from it, is a room (**10**) where four stone lamps were found. The rooms numbered **11** and **12** contained about 40 tripod tables for offerings, stacked in piles. Across the central corridor one room (**13**) has a built seat, and the one next door (**14**) contained a further three tables for offerings. The quantity of these finds, with their implications for ritual, has led to speculation about the export of such artefacts from the harbour of Ayii Theódori. On the way out you will notice five storage bins (**15**) built of mudbrick, with steps up to them, and next to them a deposit of large storage jars. Finds from the building are in Room VII in the Herákleion Museum where the double axes are strikingly displayed on reconstructed poles and bases.

Soon after you leave the site the Old Road joins the direct road from Herákleion to Khersónisos. Turn left for Káto Góuves but for the nearest access to the New National Road's Khersónisos bypass, turn right.

The sacred cave of Skoteinó

In Káto Góuves, 18km east of Herákleion, there is a turning right (to Góuves) where brown Ministry of Culture signs direct you on a 7km detour to the Skoteinó cave. If you are staying in the area this makes a recommended walk; consult locally about any new marked footpaths.

After less than 2km **Góuves** offers tree-shaded tavernas in an attractive plateía. Beyond Góuves watch for a right turn to the village of Skoteinó. Keep left through it and about 2km further, on a bend, branch right at a sign for the cave and church of **Ayía Paraskeví**. At the final rise the sea is in view (right), with behind you a panorama across the centre of the island to the Lasíthi mountains. Ahead, on bare upland, the white church marks the mouth of the cave.

The site now has conspicuous fencing and a car park, which combined with the amiable gossip of guards echoing in the cavern may reduce the awe-inspiring impact of the place. Nonetheless, through antiquity this was one of the most important sanctuary sites on Crete.

The huge cave of Skoteinó (the name means dark) is 160m deep, with four levels and steeply sloping galleries. It was first investigated by Sir Arthur Evans and then was excavated in 1962 by the Cretan archaeologist Costis Daváras. His finds ranged in date from Middle Minoan I to Roman times; the church dating to the Venetian period suggests continuity of worship. From the Neopalatial period three bronze statuettes of male votaries were of outstanding interest. These figures, now in Room VII of the Herákleion Museum, are modelled wearing only a loin-cloth, in the typical pose with the right hand raised to the forehead.

Continuing east on the main road the end of Káto Góuves is marked (in Greek) at a narrow bridge over the Aposemélis river bed. A path following the river down to the sea offers a walk that is likely to reward birdwatchers, especially during the spring migration. It leads to a short stretch of lagoons and saltmarsh behind the beach (also reached across a waste area from the grounds of the Creta Sun hotel). The wildlife conservation lobby faces an uphill struggle here for this is prime development land.

Where to stay

A *Creta Sun* (295 rooms) ☎ 0897 41103, fax 0897 41113, email: cretasun@hrs.forthnet.gr. This hotel, signed off the main road east of the Káto Goúves turn to the Skoteinó cave, is part of the well known Grecotel chain. It usually opens in March to accommodate birdwatching enthusiasts.

East of the river bridge you soon come, 23km from Herákleion, to the turn for Kastélli Pediádas and the mountain plain of Lasíthi (p 232). Inland there is access to the bypass round the holiday resort of Khersónisos, a great improvement for through traffic to Mália and Ayios Nikólaos.

Khersónisos

The coast road continues down into Khersónisos, strictly Limín Khersonísou (harbour of Khersónisos) because the original village lies a short distance inland. (A minor road right climbs 2km to Piskopianó for the village folk museum.) The main street through the resort is lined with souvenir shops and motor bikes for hire. A sign to the port leads to the waterfront, but this is noisy with bars and clubs.

Where to stay and eating out

There are a number of resort hotels along the coast. The *Creta Maris* (grade A), ☎ 28970 27000, fax 28970 22130, www.maris.gr, email: reserv@maris.gr, is a long-established, entirely self-contained complex, but most readers would prefer the surroundings at Ayios Nikólaos.

Koutoulouphári, uphill and quieter at the back of Khersónisos, has tavernas on or near an attractive little plateía. Out of season the *Koutoulouphari Apartments* (Class A), ☎ 28970 22688, fax 28970 21487, email: tvhck@hrs.forthnet.gr, or *Villa Medoussa* (Class D), ☎ 28970 22624, fax 28970 21080, may have rooms.

Khersónisos manages to retain traces of its interesting history as an important Greco-Roman harbour town, with secure anchorage sheltered and defended from the north by the rocky headland of Kastrí, creating the safest harbour on the north coast between Herákleion and Oloús (Eloúnda). This was the port of the mighty city of Lýttos 15km inland, but it must have been autonomous at least by the 4C when it issued its own coinage. A temple on the headland dedicated to Britomartis was known to the 1C BC Greek historian, Strabo. The city continued to flourish in the Roman period.

Halfway along the waterfront the road bends round a much restored Roman fountain, in the form of a pyramid, with a stepped channelling system and remains of 2C–3C AD mosaics of a fishing scene. Off the little point here are vestiges of ancient harbour works, below water because the sea level has risen by about 1m since the Roman period. The Roman harbour was formed by a southerly mole (at right-angles to the shore in front of you) and an L-shaped quay on the line of the modern one east across the water. Along the shore north of the mole are remains of a concrete quay. On the shore just to the south of the mole large dressed stone blocks are the remnants of Hellenistic harbour works.

The headland of Kastrí, marked by the white chapel of Ayía Paraskeví, was fortified in the Late Roman period. Up a flight of steps are the excavated remains of an early 6C triple-aisled basilica church, one of the largest basilicas known on Crete and probably once the seat of the local bishop. Its spectacular position must have made it an impressive landmark for shipping. The mosaic floors are not well preserved, but a 2C AD Attic sarcophagus lid was reused as an altar base, and the apse is unusual in being included in a rectangle.

On the seaward side of the basilica, the headland meets the sea in a flat rock-shelf, and at the east end of the shelf, just submerged, are three rectangular tanks (the largest 4m x 3m) cut in the Roman period to hold fish kept alive in sea water. The tanks were enclosed by a wall and had a system of cut channels to ensure a fresh water supply.

Lychnostátis Open-air Museum

You may be reluctant to pause in the centre of Khersónisos, but readers interested in the traditional life and rural economy of Crete are strongly recommended to look out for the Lychnostátis Open-air Museum of Cretan Traditional Life, an outstandingly successful enterprise which gained a European Museum of the Year award in 1996. The museum is on the coast road, well signed a short distance towards the town centre from the eastern end of the bypass (bus stops on the coast road).

• Open April to October, 09.30–14.00; closed Monday. The museum entrance charge includes a return visit on another day and the complex has a café bar and an audiovisual facility. There are excellent guided tours at hourly intervals; ☎ 28970 23660 for the starting times of the English-speaking guides or for information about the many special events such as performances of Cretan music and dancing or opportunities for wine tasting. The museum is designed to accommodate wheelchair users.

This is an ambitious project in tune with the principles of the ecological movement which is gaining strength on the island. The aim is to preserve Crete's heritage and give visitors an insight into the fast disappearing traditional ways of life. The collection was begun by a professor of ophthalmology, and the museum has been laid out around his family's former summer home. You can learn about traditional architecture, furnishing and domestic equipment, and many of the customs and occupations of an earlier way of life. A picture gallery promotes local artists and craftsmen. Out of doors the numerous exhibits record aspects of the rural economy and set them within a framework which informs about the natural environment of Crete. The gardens identify indigenous plants, herbs, vines and fruit trees.

From Stalída east of Khersónisos, a road inland climbs steeply 9km to **Mokhós**, an attractive village around a large shady plateía. There is a good choice of tavernas and rent rooms (booked up from abroad in high season). This is recommended as a direct route from the Mália area up to the Lasíthi plateau, with the newly constructed (shorter) way from Krási down to Mália more suitable for the return (p 234).

Mália, 34km from Herákleion, is another of the major resorts along this coast. It sits at one end of a fine long sandy beach, but its particular appeal is made clear on the road down to the sea which is a kilometre of bars, pubs and discotheques. The archaeological site is to the east of the resort.

The palace of Mália

The site of the Minoan palace and town at Mália (ancient name unknown) lies 3km to the east of the modern resort, signed towards the sea from the main road. Past the site entrance the surfaced road continues (less than ten minutes on foot) to a simple taverna on Mália's long sandy beach, which though crowded in summer offers good swimming after a visit to the archaeological site.

The Bronze Age settlement at Mália grew up on the narrow strip of coastal plain to the north of the Lasíthi mountains, on the natural lowland route between central and eastern Crete. A chapel of Prophítis Illías marks the spur level with the site, and rising steeply behind (to 1559m) is the dominating bulk of Mount Seléna.

Travelling by bus

Long-distance buses on the main road will stop at the turning, 1km from the site (and at busy times some divert to the entrance).

- Open 08.30–15.00 including public holidays; closed Monday, ☎ 28970 31597. There is a café, a good bookstall, and a small, well-illustrated exhibition providing background information to complement what you can now see at the site.

History of the excavations

Mália was first explored in 1915 by Greek archaeologists but since 1922 both the palace and a series of large houses and administrative buildings, part of a Minoan town of considerable size, have been excavated by the French School at Athens which publishes the excellent *Guide des fouilles françaises en Crète*. Site plans at Mália use the Greek alphabet to distinguish the various *quartiers* or sectors.

Protective covers have been erected over areas specially vulnerable to weathering. The soaring translucent roofs, designed to avoid any echo of the original Minoan architecture, are a striking innovation. A bonus was that the digging of postholes for the supporting frameworks offered a valuable opportunity to re-examine the stratigraphy recorded by earlier archaeologists.

The remains left on view by the early excavators were largely those of the second (LMI) phase of the New Palace. More recently, work has concentrated on features dating to the Protopalatial period, with particularly interesting results in Quartier Mu, an excavation covering upwards of 4000 square metres. This complex is located 200m west of the palace, alongside the road out to the sea. Access is from inside the main site fence and usually restricted to the midsummer months. The current study of the nearby Quartier Nu is contributing to the knowledge of the Postpalatial (LMIII) period at Mália.

History of the palace and town at Mália

There was settlement in the Prepalatial (Early Minoan II; see Chronology, p 38) period at Mália. Only limited remains of an Old Palace were identified by the original excavators, although Protopalatial levels were encountered at various points; for example where the so-called Sword of the Acrobat was found under the later rooms in the northwest sector. The first convincing evidence for a town, which may have been walled (see below, near the coast) dates to this Protopalatial period when a system of paved streets was found to radiate from the Old Palace buildings.

In the town the main building phase of Quartier Mu occurred in Middle Minoan II, towards the end of the Protopalatial period. The complex consists of administrative buildings and craftsmen's workshops whose special importance is reflected in refined architecture and in the wealth of the finds. Economic functions included storage and record-keeping, but the excavator concluded that the chief function of this complex was bound up with cult and religious administration.

The Mália Old Palace suffered damage (as, probably, did Protopalatial buildings at Knossós and Phaistós) in a major earthquake at the end of MMII. After rebuilding, the New Palace flourished through the two phases of its life that have been identified. It exhibits the essential characteristics expected of Minoan palaces. There is a central court, and a paved west court with raised walkways outside the palace. The west façade is constructed in ashlar masonry, and all four exterior walls are designed with angular projections and recesses.

There were a number of entrances. The main one for official use was to the north, facing the sea. The southern entrance is associated with an area for cult purposes. The evidence for storage, the basis of the palace economy, is well-preserved and a tour of the site shows how the administration of this storage system was integrated with the political and religious functions of Minoan society.

At the end of LMIB both the palace and the main dependent buildings were destroyed. A few parts of the town site, notably House E (see below) were reoccupied in the Postpalatial period. Recent excavations adjacent to Quartier Mu (Quartier Nu; not on plan) are contributing to an understanding of this Postpalatial, or Mycenaean, phase; Linear B tablets have been found.

You approach the palace excavation from the paved **West Court** (see plan). The flagstone paths form raised walks which are a feature typical of Minoan town planning and also part of a recognisable system of paved streets radiating from the palatial buildings. One of these paths serves the **North Entrance**, and another runs along, though not exactly parallel to, the **West Front**. At the south end of this façade, and dating from the Old Palace period, is a double row of **circular structures** (1), eight in all, each 5m in diameter. These pits (*kouloúres*) were probably used as silos or granaries, and from the evidence for central pillars it is deduced that they were roofed.

From the West Court you can follow the palace's south façade towards the south entrance. You pass the narrow opening to a shrine which contained a concave altar with incised signs of a star and a cross. The flagged passage of the **South Entrance** (2) was probably cut off from the Central Court by an extension of the wall at its inner end, so that entry was effected indirectly. You would have turned left through a door into an **antechamber** (3), which gave on to a **paved terrace** (4) from which two steps led to the court. Set in the terrace floor is a circular limestone table usually referred to as the **Mália Kérnos**, with a large hollow at its centre and 34 smaller ones round the circumference. This may have played a part as a table for offerings in rituals associated with harvested first fruits, or the fertility of seed. Just to the north are the lower steps of a monumental staircase (5).

The rectangular **Central Court** (48m x 22m), which has been shown to date back to the Old Palace period, lies on the same north–northeast to south–southwest axis as those at Knossós and Phaistós. It is not certain whether the surface was paved all over, or only in certain areas. In the centre is a shallow pit which may have been an **altar** (6); it was found to be lined with mudbrick, with four mudbrick stands in it, and was perhaps associated with the cult of the pillar crypt in the west wing for it is aligned between the pillars in that area. It has also been suggested that its exact central position was of technical significance in the original survey for laying out the court and its surrounding buildings. Along the east side of the Central Court was a **portico** supported by alternate columns and pillars, a stylistic arrangement much favoured by the Minoans, presumably for decorative reasons. Pairs of round postholes between each pillar and column base indicate a balustrade.

Behind the portico, at its south end, is the **Southeast Entrance** and corridor (7) and north of it the **East Storerooms** (8) now displayed under an elegant roof protecting the mudbrick construction. These storerooms would have held oil and wine. The equipment includes raised platforms for storage vessels which had spouts for drainage near their bases, also separating tubs for oil and channels for collecting spilt liquid.

On the west side of the court the complex known as the **Loggia** (9) consisted of a small room raised on a platform reached by steps from the Court; it was perhaps intended for ceremonial purposes. The broad staircase (10) which would have led up to a set of large rooms above. The central part of the ground floor of this West Wing is occupied by a **Hall** (11) and its interconnecting rooms. The hall opens to the west into a flagged **pillar crypt** which would have been a dark enclosed room similar to those near the Temple Repositories at Knossós; there are double axes carved on the pillars. Behind this cult area are storerooms, indicating a juxtaposition of functions found also at Knossós and Phaistós. By the long **West Corridor** (12) you can return past a huge pithos to the area behind the Loggia. Here (13), on an Old Palace floor, were found the ceremonial stone axe in the shape of a leopard (dated to the first phase of the New Palace), and a great bronze sword with a rock-crystal hilt; both these exquisite examples of Minoan craftsmanship are on display with the Mália exhibits in the Herákleion Museum.

The **North Wing** lay behind a colonnaded portico, of which the column bases are preserved. It contained a **Pillared Hall** (14) with six internal pillars, possibly to support a grand room on the floor above. Cooking pots were found in the small room to the west and, by analogy with pots and food debris in a comparable position at Zákros, it has been suggested that the upper storey contained a dining hall. On the east side the start of a staircase to this upper storey is preserved and there is another further north.

The **paved corridor** (15) which sets off towards the North Entrance is partly

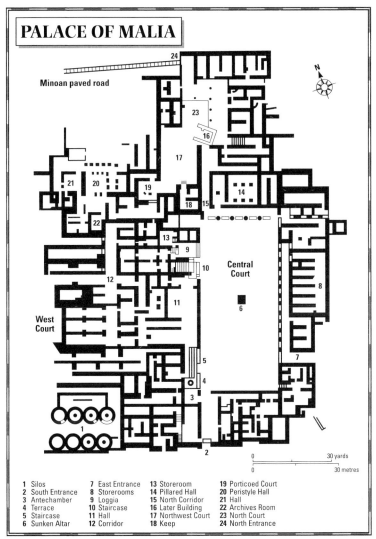

PALACE OF MALIA

Minoan paved road

Central Court

West Court

N

1 Silos	**7** East Entrance	**13** Storeroom	**19** Porticoed Court
2 South Entrance	**8** Storerooms	**14** Pillared Hall	**20** Peristyle Hall
3 Antechamber	**9** Loggia	**15** North Corridor	**21** Hall
4 Terrace	**10** Staircase	**16** Later Building	**22** Archives Room
5 Staircase	**11** Hall	**17** Northwest Court	**23** North Court
6 Sunken Altar	**12** Corridor	**18** Keep	**24** North Entrance

0   30 yards
0   30 metres

obstructed by a later building (**16**) on an oblique alignment. This is thought to be a shrine, but its Postpalatial dating to LMII is uncertain. The corridor led on into the **North Court** (**23**) but doubling back left takes you into the **North West Court** (**17**; also known as the Keep Court) at the south end of which, up three steps, is the solidly built structure of the **Keep** (**18**). West of this again is a small **court** (**19**) with a portico to the south from which a dogleg passage leads west to the **staterooms**, sometimes described as the royal apartments or private quarters. The **Peristyle Hall** (**20**) has a broad colonnaded verandah to the north which probably looked out over a garden; the wall footings now visible here are the excavated remains of the Old Palace. On its east and south sides this main hall of the private quarters gave on to light-wells which in the manner typical of Minoan architecture could be shut off by means of a pier-and-door (*polythýron*) arrangement. To the west is a smaller **paved hall** (**21**) (usually compared with the Queen's Hall at Knossós), and off this (south) is a lustral basin (or bath). West of these rooms, in a Protopalatial context, was found the famous **Sword of the Acrobat**, named for the figure arched across a gold disk on the pommel. The sword, on display in Herákleion Museum, is an important piece of evidence for the wealth and sophistication of Protopalatial society. The **Archives Room** (**22**) yielded tablets in Hieroglyphic as well as Linear A scripts.

From the light-well east of the main hall (**20**) a passage (now closed off) led back to the Keep Court. Returning as permitted to the North Court you will notice on its east side evidence for the columns of a Greek pi (π) shaped portico. You can leave the palace by its **North Entrance** (**24**), which was designed to impress with a double anteroom and dog-leg approach. You will notice two giant pithoi; the one inside the entrance shows dramatic evidence of burning. A fine Minoan paved way which serves this entrance will lead you west into the town.

Immediately to the northwest of the palace and set at an angle which aligns it exactly with the cemetery of Khrysólakkos near the sea (see below) lies the complex known as the **Agorá**. Excavated in the 1960s, this was found to have been in use by the Protopalatial period. You identify first, to the north of the Minoan paved road, what used to be a walled space. (The remains of houses on the east side date to the later, Neopalatial, period.) The courtyard, c 29m x 40m, was surrounded by a formidable stepped wall with three entrances. The northeast gate faced in the direction of the cemetery and the southwest one gave access to the upper floor of the part of the complex known as the **Hypostyle Crypt**; its fragile plastered walls are now protected by one of the elegant new roofs. The building is below ground level, approached by a flight of steps, and consists of two interconnected halls with benches round three sides and a series of storerooms. (The plans provided here on the site help to identify the various features.) The puzzling lack of finds from these halls has led to the suggestion that they served as some kind of council chamber for a political centre, during or perhaps before the existence of the Old Palace.

Quartier Mu is reached by a path which starts behind the Hypostyle Crypt. To allow access for visitors while conserving the fragile fabric of the remains, a system of modern high-level walkways has been constructed. Presentation panels at viewing points help to make sense of the site. At the time of writing access is restricted; the excavation may be on view during the summer months (July–September).

The archaeologists found two large buildings (Buildings A and B) and the rest of the complex consisted of smaller buildings including some with workshops (for a seal-engraver, a potter and metalworkers) on the upper floors and living quarters below. The main phase of construction dated to MMII, towards the end of the Old Palace period. The complex was destroyed by fire at the end of MMII and was not rebuilt.

Building A (the southern of the two) had a main entrance from the west and numerous staircases were evidence for an upper storey. The sophisticated architecture (often with stuccoed wall surfaces) included a *polythýron* (pier and door)

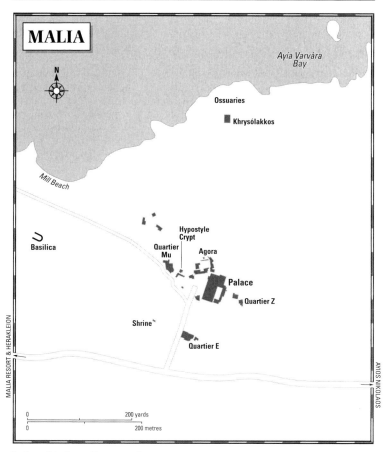

hall and light-well, a paved portico and an early example of a roofed lustral basin. At the northwest corner was a large square room with a sanctuary beside it, as well as small storerooms.

The west side of **Building B** consists of a basement with walls, doors and small windows unusually well preserved.

The wealth of the Quartier Mu complex is demonstrated by great numbers of prestigious finds (examples of which are on display in the Ayios Nikólaos Museum). An upper floor storeroom served as a treasury in Building B but together the two main buildings produced hundreds of stone vases as well as cauldrons and a bowl in bronze, ceramic reliefs (one of a sphinx) and ceremonial weapons such as a dagger with an openwork gold handle. The seal engraver's workshop contained 150 seals, as well as others unfinished and broken, worked raw materials (steatite and rock crystal) and also tools. The finds established a basis for identifying seals (found elsewhere) from this particular workshop, and already over 500 have been confidently attributed.

Particularly important was the find of a Hieroglyphic archive uncovered near an east entrance to Building A. Underlining the administrative functions of Quartier Mu were the numbers of Hieroglyphic inscriptions occurring on tablets, pottery, medallion and cone seals, and on sealing impressions.

The economic functions of Quartier Mu were defined as production, storage, record-keeping and the redistribution of goods, but the finds also pointed to the cultic associations of these functions. For instance, the stonemason's workshop contained an unfinished *kérnos*. In the potter's workshop numerous human and animal figurines were found, together with miniature vases and offering-tables, as well as shells and horns (from *agrímia*, the Cretan wild goat), all of which suggested furnishings for Minoan shrines. The archaeologists concluded that the principal purpose of this sector of the town in the Protopalatial period was the business of cultic or religious administration.

The cemetery at Khrysólakkos

The name of this site means 'pit of gold', as the area was known locally long before archaeologists began their investigations. Here was found one of the masterpieces of the Minoan goldsmiths' art, the much-illustrated **gold pendant of two bees** holding a berried fruit or honey cake.

It used to be thought that the so-called **Aíyina treasure** now in the British Museum, London, had been plundered from Khrysólakkos at the end of the 19C, but following research on the island of Aíyina this theory has become controversial.

To find the site you take the road past the palace and turn right where it reaches the sea on to the coastal footpath heading east. After 10 minutes, at a rise where the little bay and islet of Ayía Varvára are in sight, Khrysólakkos is just to the right of the path, fenced and signed.

The main period of use at Khrysólakkos is dated to the Middle Minoan period, early in the life of the Old Palace. The large rectangular enclosure, built of dressed limestone blocks, is divided into many compartments, with paved areas around the enclosure. Along the east side there was a long portico, an architectural feature unknown elsewhere on Crete at this early date.

The function of the enclosure is a matter of debate. A Prepalatial phase probably had a funerary use and Khrysólakkos has traditionally been thought of as an ossuary or cemetery, or even, because of the quality of the finds, a royal burial-place. However, the buildings of the Protopalatial phase (now visible in the excavation) resemble no other funerary structure known on Crete. The presence of clay figurines and a stuccoed altar indicates that some of the rooms on the east side (covered for protection) were used for cult purposes, and the enclosure may have served as a sanctuary.

On the rocky bluff immediately to the north of the excavated site are caves which were used as primitive ossuaries, while to the east around the Bay of Ayía Varvára, there are further known remains, including workshops of Protopalatial date. Swimmers here encounter underwater hazards suggesting harbour installations.

Walking east to the sea from Khrysólakkos the path follows the line of a defensive wall built at the beginning of the Neopalatial period. It is only recently that such walls have begun to be recognised in the Minoan record. This part of the coastline is constantly in demand for tourist development and the authorities fight an uphill battle to protect the archaeological area.

In Minoan times a larger harbour area lay behind the Mill Beach, named after a modern water mill now disappearing under the sand. (A sandstone quarry 100m southwest of the bay was probably used by the Minoans.) The sea level along this coast has risen since the Bronze Age, so the bay would then have included the hinterland where reedbeds are now an attraction for birdwatchers.

Due south of the Mill Beach the ruins of an Early Christian basilica (6C–7C) were found to cover a tomb which contained an imported Attic sarcophagus of the Antonine period (2C AD but re-used here) which is now displayed with the sculpture collection (Room XX) of the Herákleion Museum.

On the way from the palace car park back to the main road you pass, on your left side, **Quartier E**, lying to the south of an east–west town street. The large **House E** is of Neopalatial date. You can make out an entrance from the north, an angled portico, remains of a pier-and-door hall and a lustral basin with niches. There was evidence for painted plaster. In LMII a pillar room with bench and hearth was added on the east side. The building was reoccupied during LMIII, after the LMIB destruction of the palace. Just across the approach road from Quartier E remains have been uncovered of another building identified as a **shrine** on account of the horns of consecration, a Minoan symbol of sanctity, incorporated in its construction.

East on the highway you are 25km from Ayios Nikólaos. You come almost immediately to a turning left, signed for Vrakhási on the Old Road. This is also the turning for **Sísi** (less than 5km. just into the province of Lasíthi), with good tavernas round a picturesque cove (p 229).

Beyond the Sísi turning the New National Road climbs inland through the **Gorge of Selenári** and bypasses Neápolis (p 228). The foothills of the Lasíthi mountains provide a grand scenic background. Derelict windmills are a feature of the landscape before a tunnel brings the road out above the Bay of Mirabéllo. On the outskirts of Ayios Nikólaos a wide crossroads offers (left) the Eloúnda road and (right) the bypass leading on into eastern Crete. Ahead, in the busy resort of Ayios Nikólaos, a one-way system operates. For the town plan and directions turn to p 210.

LASÍTHI PROVINCE

The *nome* (province) is made up of four administrative districts, Mirabéllo, Lasíthi, Ierápetra and Siteía, and visitors will notice that the character of each district is recognisably different. Physical differences are pronounced. The deep Bay of Mirabéllo on the north coast, with a stunningly beautiful coastline of rocky coves between strategically placed islands is sheltered by the curve of Cape Ayios Ioánnis from the unremitting north–northwest winds of summer. Not long after the Second World War, visitors came to enjoy the picturesque harbour village of **Ayios Nikólaos** in these scenic surroundings. Development of the island for tourism began here and has never looked back. Today the town competes with holiday resorts around the eastern Mediterranean to balance the needs of an upmarket clientele in a number of the most luxurious and idyllically situated hotels on Crete with the different priorities of life in the waterfront cafés and late-night music bars. Even during a brief stop, the Archaeological Museum with exhibits from all over eastern Crete merits a visit.

The *Guide* has suggestions for readers with requirements between these two extremes, with a choice of places to stay (perhaps in or around **Eloúnda** or at **Istro** east of Ayios Nikólaos) which will provide an agreeable base on the sea for exploring the Mirabéllo district within easy reach of (for example) the well-preserved frescoes in the Byzantine church of the Panayía Kerá near **Kritsá**, the sites of hilltop city-states at **Lató** or **Dréros** and the Minoan excavation at **Gourniá**.

There is unspoilt countryside out on Cape Ayios Ioánnis north of Neápolis, in the mountains above Kritsá (the **Katharó plain**) and inland from Istro, with guaranteed displays of wild flowers in their season. The good bus services to Siteía and Ierápetra will suit those planning a walk on the route of the European long-distance footpath (E4), perhaps from the Minoan site of Vasilikí or from **Monastiráki** near the dramatic Gorge Khá above the isthmus of Ierápetra.

The administrative district of Lasíthi covers the high (850m) plain and the mountain range that surrounds it with Mount Díkte at 2148m. It is easy to visit the villages of the **Lasíthi plain** in a day trip from Ayios Nikólaos (best by private transport but also possible by bus), but an overnight stay up on the plain offers a different perspective on the traditional way of life of the mountain villages and simple but comfortable rooms to rent are now available. The E4 walking route crosses the plain.

The isthmus of Ierápetra is the narrowest north–south crossing on the island, not much more than 15km from coast to coast. In the past the short land route would always have been preferred to the sea passage round the inhospitable Cape Síderos, notorious then as now for its fierce gales. **Ierápetra**, the only town on the south coast, prospers by growing fruit and vegetable crops in a climate of high average temperatures and low rainfall; it has coped with tourism almost as an afterthought.

The hinterland in both directions from Ierápetra is good walking country, up the **Mýrtos** valley and in the foothills of Mount Díkte around **Málles** as well as to the east in the uplands towards Thryptí.

There are excavated Minoan sites at **Mýrtos** (two separate sites) and at **Vasilikí**. Early Iron Age settlements in beautiful empty country above **Kavoúsi** on the north coast east of the isthmus have for many years been the object of intensive study by teams of American archaeologists.

Coastal development immediately east of Ierápetra is increasing every year without any particular character. It is possible to stay in Ierápetra and out of season this may be a satisfactory solution, but the suggestion both for touring motorists and for those wanting a base for a walking holiday is to look for accommodation in the village of Mýrtos.

The district of Siteía covers most of the territory east of the isthmus of Ieráptera. The eagerly awaited Siteía airport, which is being upgraded to provide direct access to the region from outside Greece, is behind schedule but should completed by 2004. This eastern corner of the island is visited primarily, perhaps, because of the excavation by Greek archaeologists of the Bronze Age palace at **Káto Zákros**. Anyone interested in the Minoan civilisation who passes through Room VIII in the Herákleion Museum is likely to fall under the spell of the material retrieved from this unplundered palace. The romantic setting of the Zákros palace in a remote cove at the extreme far east of the island is rarely a disappointment. Visits to the Minoan sites at **Mókhlos**, **Khamaízi** and **Palaíkastro** fit neatly into the itinerary.

The town of **Siteía** on the north coast can be recommended as a base for getting to know the region or for a pause during a touring holiday. Both the Siteía museums are an enjoyable experience with their collections set in local context in a way which will contribute to an understanding of the area.

The relatively unspoilt coastal villages of Mókhlos, Palaíkastro and Zákros offer a choice of agreeable small-scale accommodation but development along the beaches on the Libyan Sea, around **Makriyialós**, is of patchy quality and sound advice is needed before making an advance booking.

As you go east from Mount Ornó (inland of Mókhlos) the countryside turns into rolling upland and valleys. Some of Crete's best vineyards flourish on these hillsides. The red wines of the Siteía region are developing an enviable reputation. Wildflower enthusiasts come for the stretches of uncultivated and unfenced land along the minor roads and around the rocky coast which in places is still isolated and difficult of access.

The E4 long-distance walking route across Crete reaches its end, fittingly for an island of such striking physical contrasts, in a dramatic stretch down the Pharángi ton Nekrón, the Gorge of the Dead at Zákros.

Ayios Nikólaos

Ayios Nikólaos is the administrative centre of the province of Lasíthi which covers the whole of eastern Crete. A harbour town beautifully situated on the west side of the Bay of Mirabéllo, it was the first of the north-coast settlements to develop into a popular tourist resort, and it managed to do so while still retaining much of its charm. The secret of its attraction is the combination of harbour and the picturesque **Lake Voulisméni** set against the backdrop of a steep cliff. The lake was traditionally regarded as bottomless, but is now known to be funnel-shaped to a depth of 64m. Lake and harbour are linked by a short channel dug in 1867–71 and crossed by a road bridge, now a natural meeting-place (and usually a source of congestion) at the centre of town. This is the obvious place to get your bearings (see plan).

Ayios Nikólaos could not be said to owe its success as a resort to its bathing beaches. You can swim from a strip of sand (Ammoúdi) along the road north from the centre. There is a popular pebble beach, crowded in summer, on the little **Kitroplateía cove**, and the long municipal beach stretches southeast beyond the marina. Another, attractively reed-fringed, is 10 minutes further on foot, just outside the town at the start of the road to Siteía; its name, **Almyrós**, the name implies an area of salt marsh.

Nowadays Ayios Nikólaos likes to cater for an upmarket clientele drawn here by a number of first-class hotels, good shopping and the tavernas and bars packed side by side along lake and harbour shores, creating (by day and on into the night) a lively cosmopolitan atmosphere. Prices in the resort are on the whole geared to the expensive end of the tourist range.

Practical information

Travel and transport
From the airport
Ayios Nikólaos is an hour's drive from the centre of Herákleion using the New National Road and a spur from Herákleion airport joins this road to the east of the city. Taxis are available outside the airport terminal; check the proposed fare with the notice near the rank.

Olympic Airways office, Plastíra 20, on the cliff above the lake, ☎ 28410 28929.

By car from other parts of the island

Arriving by car from other parts of the island you have a choice of exits from the highway, one at each end of the town bypass. A one-way traffic system operates in the centre and you need to watch for signs, but from both directions you will end up down on the crowded harbour front.

Parking

Car parking is not easy in the centre. For a short visit to Ayios Nikólaos use the northern exit, the first on the approach from Herákleion (also the junction for Eloúnda). You are very soon diverted right and then left, past the hospital, the bus station and a large municipal car park. From here you can walk (on Odós K. Palaiológou) directly downhill past the Archaeological Museum, in less than 10 minutes, to the bridge between lake and harbour. Approaching from the other direction, from the east of the island, watch for signs to parking near the entrance to the new marina.

By bus

There is a frequent express service from the harbour bus station in Herákleion to the Ayios Nikólaos bus station which is near the hospital at the north end of the town. Services to Mália and Herákleion run approximately hourly until early evening; to Eloúnda and to Kritsá frequently; to Siteía and to Ierápetra five or six times a day. Timetables are clearly displayed in the waiting room. Information desk, ☎ 28410 22234.

By sea

A car ferry service run by *Lane Lines* (a local company that is part of the *ANEK* group) operates through Ayios Nikólaos on the Athens–Rhodes route, with intermediate calls at various Cycladic islands to the north, and Siteía, Kásos, Kárpathos and Kos to the east. In recent years there has been an overnight service direct from Piraeus three times a week, but domestic boat schedules are liable to alter every year. All tourist information offices should have current timetables.

Port authority

Beside the tourist information office, ☎ 28410 82384.

Taxi ranks

Beside the lake, in the big Plateía El. Venizélou and near the bus station. To call for a taxi ☎ 28410 24000.

 ## Tourist office

The municipal tourist information office is in the ground floor of the Port Authority buildings overlooking the harbour at the north end of the bridge by the lake. Open daily April–Nov 08.30–21.30, ☎ 28410 22357, fax 28410 82534 (with foreign currency exchange at bank rates). There are advertisements for rooms and studios for rent.

Tourist police

A department of the regular police sta-

tion, ☎ 28410 26900, on Odós Latoús, the road into town from the southern junction on the bypass.

Travel agencies

Travel agencies are thick on the ground in Ayios Nikólaos, though the turnover is considerable. The tourist information office keeps an up to date list. Look along the waterfront on the Eloúnda road, Aktí S. Koundoúrou. As well as handling coach tours to all the main tourist attractions on the island, the agencies book tickets for boat excursions around the Mirabéllo bay (advertised on the harbour front), for example to Spinalónga, and day-trips further afield including to Théra (Santorini). They can arrange the hire of cars and bikes.

Buzz Travel, Aktí I. Koundoúrou 2 (above the ferry boat quay, specialising in boat trips), ☎ 28410 22608.

Creta Travel, Aktí S. Koundoúrou 3, ☎ 28410 28496.

Nostos Tours, R. Koundoúrou 30, ☎ 28410 22819.

 ## Where to stay

The GNTO lists nearly 100 hotels and furnished apartments of class C and above in Ayios Nikólaos, the majority geared to package holidays arranged from abroad; in high season the best in any price bracket are liable to be fully booked by agents from all parts of the world.

The luxury hotels or bungalow complexes are beautifully situated around the bay. If you need medium-priced accommodation for a few nights during a touring holiday, look along the shore road, Aktí Themistokleóus, with views over the bay, between the ferry quay and the Kitroplateía beach. If you want inexpensive accommodation, you could try the *Sunbeam Rooms to Let* above a simple café-bar at Ethnikís Antistáseos 23, parallel to K. Palaiológou.

In case of difficulty or if cheaper

accommodation is required at short notice, consult the tourist information office (see above). With the advantage of planning in advance (and for a tranquil base for longer periods) readers are urged to consider **Eloúnda** and **Pláka** or **Istro**, formerly Kaló Khorió, on the road east to Siteía.

Hotels

L *Minos Beach* (118 rooms), ☎ 28410 22345-9, fax 28410 22548, email: minosb@her.forthnet.gr. An old-established de luxe resort hotel, in well-kept grounds only ten minutes' walk from the centre of town along the esplanade towards Eloúnda. Accommodation is mostly in bungalows. A loyal clientele returns year after year.

L *Minos Palace* (148 rooms), ☎ 28410 23801-9, fax 28410 23816, email: minpal@otenet.gr. Sited on a promontory looking back across the bay near the Byzantine church of Ayios Nikólaos. Offers all the facilities expected of the best modern resort hotels.

B *El Greco* (49 rooms), ☎ 28410 28894, fax 28410 26836. On the seafront south of the harbour towards the Kitroplateía bay.

C *Lato* (37 rooms), ☎ 28410 24581-2, fax 28410 23996, email: niot@agn.forthnet.gr. On the seafront in the direction of Eloúnda.

C *Sgouros* (29 rooms), ☎ 28410 28931, fax 28410 25568. A comfortable well-run hotel on the Kitroplateía bay often open earlier in the season than its competitors.

 ## Eating out

The harbour front, seafront and lakeside offer an inexhaustible choice of cafés, bars and traditional tavernas mingled with fast food outlets both Greek and foreign. These are places from which to watch the world go by or enjoy the constant activity associated with the harbour. Prices may be higher than in comparable establishments elsewhere on Crete, and more geared to international notions of eating and drinking; you can check the menus posted outside all reputable premises.

If you are looking for a traditional taverna meal make for the Kitroplateía beach, where *O Faros* is one of several establishments on either side of the Hotel Sgouros. Close together towards the north end of the short road along this beach are *Taverna Trata* and *Ofou to Io*, both of which usually include Cretan specialities on their menus. In unsettled weather you might do better in the centre of town. Just to the north of the bridge (at the bottom of Palaiológou) *Pevko* has tables by the lake in summer but is a serious year-round taverna, and the *Café Must* is open all day.

A short walk downhill from the Archaeological Museum is the *Taverna Aouas*, with a garden shaded by a vine-covered trellis.

Among top-quality fish restaurants *Pelagos* (elegant and correspondingly expensive) enjoys a reliable reputation. You find it at the start of Koráka, one street back from the shore road (Aktí S. Koundoúrou) up a short flight of steps beside the agency Creta Travel.

Banks

National Bank of Greece, with an automatic currency exchange, is towards the top of R. Koundoúrou, on the corner with Polytekhníou.

Commercial Bank (Emporikí), just inland from the harbour with entrances in 28 Oktovríou and R. Koundoúrou.

Post office and telephones

The **post office** is on Odós 28 Oktovríou.

OTE for telephone, fax and email services on K. Sphakianáki, a left turn about halfway up R. Koundoúrou.

Hospital

The hospital is on Odós Knossoú at the north end of the town, across from the Archaeological Museum near the bus station, ☎ 28410 25224.

Shopping

The smarter shops are concentrated between the harbour and the central plateía. Running uphill from the harbour is the short, tree-lined street R. Koundoúrou (more often referred to by foreigners as the main street) and parallel to it, towards the lake, 25 Oktovríou. Here, among the ubiquitous souvenir shops, you will find the better-quality establishments for jewellery, leather goods, fabrics and rugs. Just back from the front on R. Koundoúrou there is an excellent bookshop (with English-language books and newspapers).

History

The modern town has grown up only since the second half of the 19C. In the early Hellenistic period the settlement here on the bay was the harbour of Lató (p 225), the city-state 10km into the hills near Kritsá, and was known as *Lató pros Kamára*, meaning 'towards the arch' and perhaps referring to the cliff overhanging Lake Voulisméni. The coastal settlement flourished in Roman times on the low hill jutting into the bay between the modern port and the sheltered south-facing shore of the Kitroplateía.

The Venetians used a cove a short way northwest along the bay towards Eloúnda for their harbour and named it the Porto di San Nicolo after the little Byzantine church (see below) on the headland overlooking it. Almost completely sheltered from the prevailing winds, the cove still provides a safe winter anchorage for fishing boats and the local ferries.

The Porto di San Nicolo was protected by the castle of Mirabéllo (built by the Genoese during their brief stay on the island after 1204 before the Venetians exerted control). This castle was sacked by a Turkish raiding party in 1537, more than a century before the Turks finally captured Crete, and nothing remains today. When the Turkish threat became even more serious, the Venetians assigned the defence of the region to the almost impregnable fortress of Spinalónga on a rock offshore to the north (p 221).

By the road-bridge at the harbour is the tourist information office. Next to it is a small **Folkore Museum**, open 10.00–14.00 daily except Sat. This contains (alongside textiles and an assortment of domestic exhibits) a good collection of old photographs and engravings which include (behind the big desk) a contemporary view of the old castle of Mirabéllo.

On foot from the harbour you can head uphill inland to the big Plateía Elefthériou Venizélou in front of the cathedral; for the view from the cliff above the lake turn off to the right along N. Plastíra before the plateía. From the harbour front, you can go south on M. Sphakianáki over the promontory to the Kitroplateía cove, so-called because of a historical association with the shipping of citrus fruits.

From the lake K. Palaiológou leads uphill to the Archaeological Museum (see below).

The Byzantine church of Ayios Nikólaos

To visit the frescoed Byzantine church of Ayios Nikólaos, take the busy Aktí S.

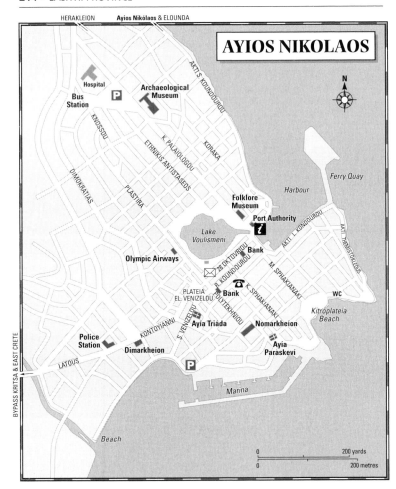

HERAKLEION   **Ayios Nikólaos** & ELOUNDA

AYIOS NIKOLAOS

Koundoúrou running north from the harbour (in the direction of Eloúnda) 15 minutes on foot to the headland where the Hotel Minos Palace has a view of the town. You pass the fishing-boat haven which was the Porto di San Nicolo of the Venetians.

From the coast road the picturesque church is half-hidden among trees out on the headland. There are signs for the hotel and the church is on the right of the approach road to it, with the key available from the reception desk in exchange for a passport as security.

This is a single-nave church with three bays, the central one supporting a dome. The building is said to be difficult to date architecturally. Restoration in the 1960s (and again recently) has uncovered two layers of frescoes: there is some 14C work including a (damaged) *Pantokrator* with a fragment of inscription in the conch of the apse, but unique on Crete (and rare in all Greece) are remains of much earlier wall-paintings, clearest in the eastern bay (south side) but also distinguishable opposite, across the nave. These go back at least to the early years of the Second Byzantine period (middle of the 10C) when the island had just been reclaimed for Christendom from the Arabs.

The formal geometric designs of these earlier fragments are consistent with the principles advanced in the 8C–9C by the Iconoclasts who banned the representation of the divine or saintly form in the religious art of the Byzantine Empire. The work in the church of Ayios Nikólaos adheres to this earlier tradition. The motifs include crosses, lozenges and interlocking circles, but also quatrefoils and blossoms in a free-flowing and imaginative design. The upper frieze on the south wall and the fragments remaining on the dome and its supporting arches are sufficiently preserved to hint at the effect that this system of decoration would have created.

The Archaeological Museum

The museum is uphill from the lake on K. Palaiológou. It houses finds from archaeological sites all over the province of Lasíthi, although nowadays material from the extreme east of the island is more likely to go to the museum in Siteía. Open 08.00–15.00; closed Mon and public holidays. There is an illustrated publication on sale with text by the museum's first director, the archaeologist Costis Daváras, in which he describes the major exhibits and sets them in context.

The museum consists of eight rooms around a central court. The clearly labelled cases are arranged roughly in chronological order, and the first three rooms contain Bronze Age material of exceptional quality. (As newly excavated finds join the display, changes may occur from time to time.)

Room I Neolithic and Prepalatial A stone idol is prominently displayed; it came from Pelekitá, a remote cave with Neolithic material on the seaward side of Mount Traóstalos, north of Káto Zákros. Five cases are devoted to finds from the huge cemetery of the Early Minoan period (EMI and EMII) at **Ayía Photiá** on the coast just east of Siteía; characteristic is the pottery's burnished surface (perhaps imitating wood) and incised decoration, often with white clay filling. Shapes include the biconical goblet or chalice and the cult vessels known as frying pans. Multiple vases (double, triple or quadruple) are also well represented; a lidded double vase on a tall foot is noteworthy. A bird-shaped vase with incised decoration (used here to suggest plumage) is one of the earliest in what became a long tradition for the Cretan potter. There are good displays of obsidian blades and bone tools. Among the bronze weapons one had been deliberately bent to render it harmless.

Room II Prepalatial and Protopalatial Pride of place belongs to the anthropomorphic libation vase known as the *Goddess of Mýrtos*. This highly unusual piece, with an Early Minoan II date, came from Phournoú Koriphí, near Mýrtos west of Ieráptera. The goddess cradles a small jug with beak-spout which is the rhyton's only opening. From the same site (lower shelf, free-standing case) are disks used as a primitive form of potter's wheel (the slow wheel), with other related finds, including seals and figurines, on the right-hand side of the room.

Left of the entrance to this room there is a good exhibit of **Vasilikí pottery**, named after the site where it was first recognised on the isthmus of Ierápetra. The effect of a distinctively mottled, slightly lustrous, surface was probably achieved by uneven firing combined with the use of different coloured slips on the same vessel. The teapot vase with exaggerated spout is a common shape.

The Goddess of Mýrtos, an Early Minoan rhyton; Archaeological Museum, Ayios Nikólaos

On the left wall are finds from the Prepalatial (EMII) cemetery at **Mókhlos**, now a small island just offshore between Ayios Nikólaos and Siteía. Here, from one of the built house-tombs, came delicate gold jewellery hidden inside a flattened silver vase. The treasure included bracelets, chains, hair ornaments, and a remarkable diadem decorated with three heads of the Cretan ibex in dot-repoussé technique and finished by three delicate V-shaped horns. Stone vases exhibited here show the veining of the material superbly exploited, for example the teapot vase in breccia also from Mókhlos.

The cases between giant pithoi from the palace at Zákros contain grave groups from the Myrsíni tholos (the first tomb of Mesará type to be excavated in eastern Crete) and from the Middle Minoan burial enclosures at Zákros.

Room III Protopalatial, Neopalatial and Postpalatial This room has an interesting display of votive offerings from peak sanctuaries. A large proportion of the known sites of this type, places of pilgrimage for the worship of the Minoan deity on mountain tops or other remote places, have been found in eastern Crete. Terracotta figurines, deposited to represent the worshippers themselves, throw interesting light on their physical appearance and attire, and on their needs and desires. Animal figurines are also found, which may have been substitutes for a sacrifice.

Petsophás above Palaíkastro was one of the most important of these peak sanctuaries, and continued in use into Neopalatial times. From this site came the double horns of consecration, with a second pair inside the larger one, an uncommon variation on this Minoan symbol of sanctity.

Other sites which have contributed some outstanding examples of Minoan workmanship to the exhibits in this room include the palace at Mália, the Neopalatial settlement at Mýrtos (Pýrgos) and a country house at Makriyialós (both on the province's south coast), the Postpalatial cemeteries at Mílatos (east of Mália) and Myrsíni (west of Siteía).

The prominently displayed **steatite triton** from the palace at Mália has relief carving of two facing genii, one pouring a libation from a double-spouted vase into the outstretched hands of his companion.

Right of the door, among a shelf of finds from Mílatos, are an ivory sphinx and a miniature crocodile, also in ivory, which was probably designed as a pendant. The crocodile is carved in relief, with some of its features borrowed from feline models.

The excavation at Makryialós produced artefacts which hint at the quality of life and the range of contacts of the large Minoan country houses and estates contemporary with the New Palaces (c 1550–1450 BC). The Marine Style alabastron with octopus decoration is thought to come from the Knossós workshop, and the fine marble chalice from Zákros.

This room displays a good collection of Minoan clay sarcophagi. These are of two types: chests (*lárnakes*) with low feet and gabled lids, and the oval bath-tub shape, often with drainage holes suggesting that they had functioned as bath tubs. The decoration includes birds, fish and the stylised octopus. With them are the large pithoi also used for burials.

The central cases contain seals, ivory work and jewellery. You will notice a gold pin superbly decorated with a bramble motif and an inscription of 18 Linear A signs. Nearby (from Mália) is a clay bar, unusual because it has Linear A inscriptions on each of its four sides.

At the far end of the room attention is drawn to the female figurine, a votary or priestess (from the Postpalatial cemetery at Myrsíni) which is modelled on a drum base with joined hands suggesting an attitude of worship.

Room IV Postpalatial and Early Iron Age The Bronze Age material is completed in this room with Late Minoan III exhibits. From the Myrsíni cemetery are the incense burners and conical clay rhytons pierced at the tip for use as libation vases. Among the pottery from cemeteries in the Siteía region and at **Kritsá** the straight-sided cremation urns are characteristic of the new trends, but the typically Minoan horns of consecration motif still occurs in the painted decoration, as on the vase from Apáno Zákros. The potter's wheel from Kritsá in the central case complements the display of clay disks (slow wheels) seen in Room II. An infant burial is displayed exactly as found in the transitional LMIII–Protogeometric cemetery at Kryá, in the upland interior south of Siteía.

The Early Iron Age covers the Subminoan, Geometric and Orientalising periods. During this time the pottery from the eastern part of the island is categorised as provincial, with a rustic charm when compared with contemporary pieces from central Crete shown in the Herákleion Archaeological Museum.

Room V Terracotta collection Geometric and Orientalising pottery from Siteía overflows into this room which is otherwise given over to a display of terracottas of the Archaic and Classical periods (7C–5C BC), mainly from the city-state of Oloús near Eloúnda (the collection of clay animals) and from a rich deposit, presumed to be associated with a shrine, discovered near the centre of modern Siteía. Many of the female figurines and heads are fine examples of the Daidalic style, spare and typically frontal (not three-dimensional) with stylized wig-like hair; some retain traces of the paint which originally adorned them. The widely admired Archaic head from Siteía (separately displayed) points to the part played by Crete in the early development of Greek sculpture. There is a fine collection of coins presented to the museum by a benefactor.

The anteroom (**VI**) completes the display of terracottas from Siteía, with some contemporary vases.

Room VII Greco-Roman period This room is largely devoted to material found in or around Ayios Nikólaos, especially from an important cemetery in the area known as Potamós. There is a display of well-preserved Roman glass (perfume flasks), various types of lamp, a number of interesting figurines and a hoard of Roman coins.

At the far end of the room is a remarkable exhibit, a skull still (after 2000 years) adorned with a gold wreath; the bronze *aryballos* in a nearby central case came from the same burial which is dated to the early 1C AD by the silver coin of Polyrrhénia that had been placed between the teeth of the dead.

Room VIII This last room is reserved for further material from the Hellenistic-Roman cemetery of Potamós. The centrepiece is an example of 1C AD superimposed burials, lifted intact as found.

North and west of Ayios Nikólaos

Eloúnda, Pláka and Spinalónga

Eloúnda is 12km north along the coast from Ayios Nikólaos. This fishing village at the base of a long inlet sheltered by the peninsula of Spinalónga has expanded to welcome visitors to an idyllic setting. The road follows the coast north from Ayios Nikólaos gaining height over a headland with superb views of the Bay of Mirabéllo.

Travelling by bus
There is a frequent service on the route between Ayios Nikólaos and Eloúnda.

On the coast road you pass through **Elliniká**. A side-road leads inland to the remains (excavated in the 1930s) of a 2C BC temple dedicated to Ares and Aphrodite which is on record as the subject of a lengthy territorial dispute between the city-states of Lató (p 225) in the hills and Oloús in the locality of modern Eloúnda. The small porticoed temple, built of the local limestone, consisted of two chambers each with a bench altar but with no communicating door between them. Mount Oxa (563m), conspicuous to the northwest, is a woodland conservation area.

   When the road begins the gradual descent from the headland to sea level there are designated stopping places (much favoured by photographers) offering a bird's-eye view of the Eloúnda coastline. You can make out the causeway built on what remains of the isthmus of Póros; it crosses from the village of Eloúnda to the peninsula of land stretching away to the north, known as Spinalónga. On a rock off the north end of the peninsula the Venetians built a fortress (see below) to counter the menace of the Turkish fleet. The isthmus marks the (now submerged) site of ancient Oloús, an important harbour in the Greek period.

Eloúnda
The resort village of Eloúnda has grown by amalgamating a number of separate settlements, but it has a comfortable air of permanence when compared with many seaside hamlets which have expanded rapidly during the last decade. The

exceptionally beautiful setting is exploited by several of the most select and luxurious resort hotels on the island.

On the road from Ayios Nikólaos you pass the turning for the site of Oloús and continue down to the harbour busy with fishing boats, ferries to the island fortress of Spinalónga and other tourist trips.

The waterfront plateía allows car parking, and three sides of it contain all the necessary facilities close together: tourist information office, post office, banks, telephone and fax centre (OTE), bookshop, a good bakery, a chemist, and travel agencies for car and bicycle hire, excursions and apartments to rent.

Practical information

Travel agency

Olous Travel ☎ 28410 41131, fax 28410 41132 is on the long side of the plateía opposite the sea, next to the post office.

Where to stay

The four resort hotels officially classed as de luxe are mainly geared to advance bookings from travel agents abroad; out of season they may have accommodation available.

L *Elounda Beach* (301 rooms in hotel and bungalows), ☎ 28410 41412, fax 28410 41373, www.eloudabeach.gr, email: elohotel@eloundabeach.gr. This hotel has set the standard for many years. Suitable for wheelchair users.

L *Elounda Mare* (108 rooms in hotel and bungalows), ☎ 28410 41102, fax 28410 41307, www.eloundahotels.com, email: elmare@agn.forthnet.gr. The restaurant has a high reputation for seafood.

C *Aristea* (33 rooms), ☎ 28410 41300, fax 28410 41302. On the main street just out of the plateía by the harbour waterfront.

For something simpler make for the junction at the far (north) end of the plateía; straight ahead, at the start of the climb to Phourní, there are several pensions and apartment blocks. The Pláka road turns right at this junction, keeping to the coast, and at the edge of Eloúnda watch for *Taverna Despina* with **rooms to rent** and fine views from terraces across the bay to eastern Crete. The hamlet of **Pláka** (5km; see below) also has studios and rooms to rent.

Eating out

The waterfront around the picturesque harbour at Eloúnda is lined with fish tavernas, and with a clientele from the luxury hotels in the immediate neighbourhood prices are not cheap.

Britomartis, conspicuous on a pontoon, and *Kalidon* nearby on the quay are at the top end of the market and their food has taken on an international character.

For less expensive eating there are two places back from the sea, side by side at the far end of the plateía, both specialising in simple grilled dishes. For a quieter location, take the road down to the isthmus towards Oloús (see below); there is a small car park. Here *Melisos* among others on the waterside keeps to a traditional Cretan menu.

The site of ancient Oloús

During the Greek period, this was an important harbour city in the lee of Cape Ayios Ioánnis out to the north. The isthmus of Póros, connecting the Spinalónga peninsula to the mainland, marks the site but because of the rise in sea-level most of the remains of ancient Oloús are now under water.

On the main street in Eloúnda, 500m towards Ayios Nikólaos from the harbour plateía, watch for signs and an awkward turning down to the seafront. The road leading to the isthmus (10 minutes on foot from the harbour) runs along the shore past salt-pans dating from the Venetian period, always a worthwhile stop for birdwatchers.

It was not until the end of the 19C that a narrow channel was cut through the isthmus by French sailors, part of the force occupying Crete for the alliance of European powers interested in Crete at that time. This canal opened up a short route from the southern end of the natural harbour of Eloúnda to the open sea and in the process cut in half the site of the Greco-Roman city-state of Oloús. The sea level has risen here but masonry can be seen in the water on either side of the isthmus, and along the shore to the east, level with a white chapel. It is known that there were great temples to Zeus Talaios and Britomartis here. In the Hellenistic period Oloús maintained close relations with Rhodes, and an inscription of 200 BC gives details of an agreement by which Rhodes could use anchorages here for her drive against piracy. Interesting inscriptions from the area include a dedication to Asclepiodotos, the 4C restorer of the Roman governor's palace at Górtyn.

Outside the main summer season the isthmus is a tranquil place with fishing boats chugging under the canal bridge overlooked by a restored windmill. Beyond the canal the foundations of an **Early Christian basilica** have been cleared. A sign by the windmill points to a fenced area, right, reached by a path beside a taverna. A black and white mosaic pavement over part of the nave suggests a two-phase building with the mosaic belonging to an earlier, smaller church. The unusual asymmetric design in a combination of geometric and natural motifs includes panels of lively dolphins. Two inscriptions name the donors; the mosaic was dated to the 4C from the style of the writing.

If you keep straight on at the bridge, along the waterfront, you come to a track inland which cuts across the peninsula of Spinalónga to its eastern shore. The surface is not suitable for normal hire cars, but a recommended 40 minute walk leads to a bay opposite the islet of **Kolokýthia** where a sandy shore offers some of the best swimming in the area. There are traces of a small basilica at what is now the water's edge, and an ancient road to it, of Roman or possibly Hellenistic date, can be picked up crossing the last ridge. The islet attracts a variety of birds during the spring migration, as well as large numbers of gulls in the breeding season. In the middle of the day excursion boats taking advantage of the sheltered water may disturb the peace but they do not usually stay long.

The hamlet of **Pláka** looks across a narrow strait to the island fortress of Spinalónga, at the northern tip of the peninsula of the same name. Usually, depending on the weather and the time of year, you can arrange to be ferried the short distance for a visit to the rock. (Guided tours leave from Ayios Nikólaos or Eloúnda.)

The approach road to Pláka, 5km north from Eloúnda, hugs the shoreline. This is a recommended walk, perhaps for a swim from Pláka's pebble beach where the cliffs start to shut off the coastal track, or for a taverna meal.

The hamlet can make a good base for some not too strenuous walking. There are paths out as far as the lighthouse on Cape Ayios Ioánnis, recommended to ornithologists during the spring migration, and the local road system is adequate for exploring all this unspoilt countryside north of Neápolis (p 228), by car though slowly in places, by mountain bike or on foot.

Where to stay and eating out

Development at Pláka is beginning but is still at an early stage and accommodation is in simple blocks of rooms, mostly owned by the waterfront tavernas. The place may be busy with visitors during the day, but when they leave all is peaceful.

There is a good choice of tavernas. *Delphini* has a reputation with Cretans for fresh fish served simply in the traditional manner.

The island fortress of Spinalónga

Built by the Venetians on a rock that commands the northwestern approaches to the Mirabéllo bay, this fortress later became a leper colony.

There are boat excursions lasting about 4 hours from Ayios Nikólaos every afternoon in summer (sea conditions permitting) to the partly ruined fortress. The rock can also be reached by smaller boat from the harbour of Eloúnda, or from Pláka the nearest point on the mainland. The Ayios Nikólaos boats pass close to the island **Ayii Pántes** (All Saints) which is maintained as a reserve for the *agrími*, the Cretan wild goat (*Capra aegagrus creticus*). The conditions of captivity may be a subject of controversy, but the protected herd has grown to some 200 animals, and the adult male is a fine sight.

The direct route follows the coast north, offshore of the peninsula of Spinalónga. Some boats divert to pass near the underwater remains of the ancient city of Oloús (see above), and some may include a stop for swimming. On the east side of the peninsula, especially passing the islet of Kolokýthia, bird-watchers will want to keep binoculars to hand.

The Spinalónga fortress was built in 1579 in response to the growing threats from the Ottoman Empire to Venetian possessions in the region. It was designed to defend the Bay of Mirabéllo and it also controlled the entrance to the Venetian fleet's anchorage of Eloúnda. Until 1715, 46 years after the fall of Candia to the Turks, the fort was allowed to remain nominally in the possession of Venice, as one of the last remnants of this once great colony. The Turks then took control and held the rock till 1903. At the end, with Cretan independence assured, the fort was for some Turks too a last refuge on Crete.

From 1903 to 1955 the fortress was notorious as a leper colony. Its establishment was one of the first public health measures of the new Cretan Assembly, and though the colony on the rock was in many ways a place of great sadness and tribulation, the authorities succeeded in reducing for the wider population the incidence of a disease which had become endemic on Crete.

A guided visit includes a tour of the Venetian fortifications seen both from the sea and from the battlements on the island, usually with a sympathetic account of the recent history. Most of the buildings within the enceinte, including the lepers' village, are in an advanced state of decay, and for reasons of safety independent exploring requires common sense and caution.

The quarry for the blocks for the Venetian ramparts is across from the islet on the northeastern shore of the Spinalónga peninsula.

Kritsá and Lató

Kritsá, a village with a long tradition of weaving and needlework, is 10km inland from the junction on the north coast highway where it bypasses Ayios Nikólaos. Along the road you pass the Byzantine church of the **Panayía Kerá** with one of the finest and most complete sets of frescoed wall-paintings on the island. Picturesque Kritsá, clinging to the wall of the Lasíthi mountains, is the starting point for a visit to the beautifully situated remains of the Greek-period city of Lató, less than 4km from Kritsá, or an expedition (16km) into the Lasíthi mountains to the high plain of **Katharó**. For walkers, the path through the **gorge of Kritsá** is signed from the Lató road. You can return to the coast from Kritsá by looping north, partly on unsurfaced roads, through Phlamouriáná, or south by Kroústas and Pýrgos.

Travelling by bus

There is a frequent service from Ayios Nikólaos to Kritsá, with a stop outside the frescoed church, and a few buses continue to Kroústas.

The church of the Panayía Kerá

The frescoed church of the Panayía (the Virgin) of Kerá is clearly signed on the right of the road up to Kritsá, 7km from the bypass. Open daily 08.30–15.00. On sale in the adjacent café-cum-shop is the authoritative and lavishly illustrated commentary *Panaghia Kera: Byzantine wall-paintings at Kritsa* by M. Borboudákis.

The domed three-aisled church, which was dedicated to the Assumption of the Virgin, dates from the early years of the Venetian occupation. Both fabric and frescoes have been meticulously restored. The central aisle or nave is believed to be the **original (mid-13C) structure**. Two phases of painting have been identified, both dated stylistically within the 13C. Remnants of the earlier decoration are preserved only in the apse and on the flat surfaces of the arches supporting the dome. On the south arch is the figure of a female saint, but better preserved, in the apse, is the *Ascension* above four hierarchs holding open scrolls and dressed in chasubles decorated with crosses. On the jambs are the deacons, *Stéphanos* and *Romanós*.

The **dome** and the **nave** are decorated in the later style (end of 13C). Instead of the conventional *Christ Pantokrátor* in the dome, there are four Gospel scenes (an arrangement perhaps dictated by the quadrating effect of the reinforcing ribs), but some expected elements are preserved: *four angels* in the apex triangles, the *twelve prophets* round the cylinder of the vault and the *four evangelists* on the pendentives. The four gospel scenes anti-clockwise from the west are: the *Presentation*, the *Baptism*, the *Raising of Lazarus* and the *Entry into Jerusalem*. Other scenes from the Gospel occupy their usual places on the vault of the nave. Many details are charmingly rendered in contemporary medieval terms, for example the Venetian glass and pottery on the tables laid for the *Last Supper* and for *Herod's Feast*. On the side walls are the worshipping saints, among them (on the northwest pillar) a rare *St Francis*, or Frantzískos, reflecting the influence of the Latin Church during this period of Venetian rule.

On the west wall are the remains of a portrayal of the *Crucifixion*; the centurion's soldiers wear 13C armour. Below are gruesome scenes of the *Punishment of the damned*.

The **south aisle** (early 14C) is dedicated to the Virgin's mother, *Ayía Anna*, who looks down from the quadrant of the apse. The vault of the aisle is decorated with scenes, largely inspired by the *Apocrypha*, narrating with much human tenderness the life of the Virgin. Arranged in pairs on either side of the vault they begin at the east end with the **House of Joachim**, the husband of Ayía Anna, and the Angel's answer to Joachim's prayers for his barren wife. After the rejoicing the story continues through the **Birth of the Virgin**, her **Presentation to Zacharias** in the temple, then scenes known as **Joseph's sorrow** (his early misunderstanding of his wife's pregnancy) and **The water of trial**, a test of the Virgin's chastity. Finally there is the **Journey to Bethlehem**, and **Mary triumphant with the infant Christ** encircled above a closed gate that, as in the vision of Ezekiel (who is shown with arms raised in prayer), would not exclude the Lord God of Israel.

The Embrace of Joachim and Anna, from the frescoes in the Panayía Kerá

On the west wall there is an inscription naming the donor, António Lámeras, and the village of 'Kritzea'. The date here is worn away but is recorded to translate as 'the century beginning 1292'.

The **north aisle** is dedicated to Ayios António (patron saint of the donor) and the frescoes, dated to the mid-14C, proclaim, in the most ambitious treatment of this theme known from Crete, Christ's Second Coming. Below the ascended **Pantokrátor** in the apse are the **Hierarchs** who pointed to the appropriate text. Towards the east end of the vault the enthroned apostles and the massed ranks of angels, with below them the saints, wait in prayerful readiness for the salvation of the world. On the reinforcing arch the angel holds a scroll of stars (*Book of Revelation*). Next in the vault (south side) is the depiction of paradise as a walled garden with fruit trees and birds; the four rivers of paradise (Tigris, Euphrates, Geon and Phison) are identified only by their initial letters. Beside the **enthroned Virgin**, the patriarchs, Abraham, Isaac and Jacob, protect the souls of the just. The gate of paradise is guarded by **Ayios Pétros** (St Peter) who admits the righteous thief. Across the vault is portrayed the **Dance of the female martyrs and saints entering paradise**. On the south side two panels showing the **Wise** and **Foolish virgins**, symbolised by candles lit and extinguished, are unusual in this context.

In the scenes at the **west end** of the vault the Earth (with snake) and Sea (with boat) are delivering up their dead on the **Day of Judgement**. And high up on the west wall, above the recording angel supervising the judgement scales, the **Archangel Michael** sounds the last trumpet call which proclaims the Second Coming.

Of exceptional interest on the wall in the northwest corner of this nave is the period treatment of the portrait of the donor, *Yeóryios Mazizánis*, with his wife and child.

If you are spending time in the region you could ask the guardian at the Panayía Kerá about access to several other churches with frescoes interesting to specialists. These include **Ayios Yeóryios Kavousiótis** on the edge of Kritsá, indistinctly signed downhill left from the Kroústas road (see also below), which has remains of frescoes by two painters (late 13C and mid-14C); **Ayios Ioánnis Theológos** (the Evangelist), beside the road further towards Kroustás; the cemetery church of **Ayios Ioánnis Pródromos**, with frescoes dated 1370 by inscription; and **Ayios Konstantínos** (1354–55). If the guardian is off duty, you will probably need to ask at tavernas in Kritsá for the local priest (*O Papás*). (Start at *O Plátanos* or *O Kástellos* in the tiny tree-shaded plateía on the main street.)

Kritsá

The streets of the large village of Kritsá are terraced across the hillside, with views down to the coast, and cafés and tavernas from which to enjoy them. The old streets are narrow, so to visit the village it is best to leave a vehicle in the car park (signed as you approach along the one-way system) and continue on foot.

Kritsá is renowned for its weaving, long considered among the finest on Crete. The work is everywhere displayed and looms are in operation at the back of some premises. The knowledgeable walk the length of the main street before considering a purchase. The most characteristic pieces are either in the natural wool colours of cream, grey and brown, or sometimes dyed to a strong red. Nowadays you may have to persist to find the traditional designs based on geometric patterns or natural variations in the wool.

Where to stay

The attractive *Pension Argyro* is set in a garden, on the left on the way into the village, just past the turning for the ancient site of Lató (see below).

At the beginning of the main street a good road forks left (passing Ayios Yeóryios, see above) to Kroústas. Less than 2km along it, the picturesque triple-aisled church of **Ayios Ioánnis Theológos** (mentioned above) dating back to the Second Byzantine period is superbly situated at the head of a valley. There are convenient buses up to Kroústas from Ayios Nikólaos (or you might take a taxi from Kritsá), and the gentle downhill stroll (5km) back to Kritsá, past this church, is recommended.

Kroústas is a starting point for a more ambitious walk east to Pýrgos on usually waymarked cross-country paths which incorporate *kalderímia*, the old paved donkey tracks predating the modern road system. Ask at Kroústas for the start of the path.

Less than 4km beyond Kroústas (on a well-maintained dirt road heading south to Prína), the isolated Byzantine chapel of **Ayios Ioánnis** is signed, c 500m along a track to the left. Frescoes are dated by inscription to 1347–48. The chapel is usually locked (key held by the *papás* in Kroústas). Anyone coming to Crete in search of rural tranquillity is unlikely to be disappointed in this locality scented by pine trees and disturbed only by the sounds of birdsong, running water and sheep bells.

You continue, whether in a vehicle or on foot, through the pine woods to Pýrgos and (7km from Kroústas) the coast road at Istro where walkers could use the Siteía or Ierápetra bus service for the return to Ayios Nikólaos.

The mountain plain of Katharó

For the road from Kritsá to the mountain plain of **Katharó plain** you make your way up the village's main street, and at the far (northern) end loop back left for the start of the climb, c 10km on a surface now asphalted all the way to the pass.

On foot what is left of the *kalderími* shortens the climb for part of the way; ask for the start of it out of the village or watch for signs along the road. The steep climb into empty hills is recommended for its panoramic views, for a fine area of woodland along the way and for the variety of wild flowers as the altitude changes. In April drifts of the yellow *Arum creticum* are a striking sight. The Katharó plain, inhabited only during the summer months, lies at an average height of 1100m under Mount Lázaros in the Díkte range of mountains. A stream meanders across it to drain into the Lasíthi plain to the west. Dirt tracks circle the plain which grows vines, cereals, almonds and various fruits; the slopes are grazed by sheep and goats. This is old-style farming; donkeys and mules are still fairly commonplace and drifts of vetch and poppies colour the summer crops.

Sometime in the Pleistocene the Katharó is thought to have been a lake. Mammal and reptile fossils have been recovered at various times (among them evidence for the dwarf hippopotamus) and quite recently a tooth and pieces of tusk of a medium-sized elephant, *Elephas creuzburgi*, were found by local people working on the plain who presented them to the Natural History Museum of Crete in Herákleion.

Beyond the pass you drop down to the hamlet of **Avdeliákos** where there is a choice of simple tavernas and a *kapheneíon*.

A right branch of the vehicle track ends near the start of the old *kalderími* over one of the eight traditional passes into the mountain plain of Lasíthi, to Mésa Lasitháki and on to the Kroustalénia monastery (p 239). There are rumours that developers have their sights on the Katharó plain, so if you have the opportunity you should go soon.

Lató

At the entrance to the village of Kritsá a turning is signed, right, for (3km) Lató and the surfaced by-road drops to cross a bridge over a river-bed. Here a walking route marked with blue arrows sets off upstream on its way to the gorge of Kritsá. Early in the year you can follow the parallel vehicle track c 1km and then descend to enjoy the river path; the walk through the gorge is only practicable in the dry season. Allow 2 hours from the bridge to reach Tápes on the Phamourianá road. The Lató road continues over the bridge and keeping right at a fork takes you up to the archaeological site. This area, at a height of 300–400m, is known locally as **Goulás** and covers two acropolis peaks and the saddle between them where the centre of the ancient city lay. Open 08.30–15.00, closed Mon; entrance free.

The city-state of Lató (*étero*, the other Lató) was founded in the Archaic period (7C BC) and flourished down to Hellenistic times. With hardly any evidence of Roman occupation, it is clear that there was a decline in importance before that time in favour of the harbour town *Lató pros Kamára* (see Ayios Nikólaos) and it is thought that the city here in the hills was abandoned some time around the end of the 2C BC.

Though securely identified by an inscription found during exploration by French archaeologists in 1899–1900, Lató was largely ignored in favour of Minoan remains until excavations were begun again in 1967. Now it is the best preserved and most thoroughly excavated site of its period on the island, with walls still in places several metres high. The principal interest lies in the detailed evidence for the town plan of a Classical city, and the light thrown on its character and organisation. The panoramic view from the north acropolis serves to explain the city's control over the main route from central to eastern Crete.

From the guardian's hut at the entrance to the site a rough path climbs to the remains of the **city gate** in the fortification wall; see plan. The gateway, designed for defence, led through two inner doorways into a small square **court** from which a long stepped **street** sets off at right angles. The street is bordered on the right by shops and workshops, which open from the steps and back on to the defensive wall itself. On the left a stout wall ascends the steep slope; it is interrupted by several narrow doorways leading into the northern sector of the town. This wall is given added strength by two towers, which were found to serve in a dual capacity as dwellings. The street bends right and then left to reach the **agorá**. This is a trapezoidal area with at its centre a small civic temple in front of a deep square **cistern**, a cube of 5.25m. (There is no spring at Lató, so cisterns were essential to conserve the water supply; in this case the builders made use of a natural depression.) In its present form the *agorá* dates to the beginning of the Hellenistic era, 4C–3C, but figurines dated to the 6C BC came from the temple (perhaps from an open-air shrine).

The west side of the *agorá* is bounded by a **stoa** that has stone benches round three walls behind a Doric colonnade. (The southern end is cut by a modern threshing floor.) To the south of the shrine, set at an angle, is an **exedra**, a rectangular shelter open to the court.

On the north side of the *agorá*, and flanked by two massive **bastions** or towers, an elaborate **staircase** consists of a triple flight of broad steps separated by narrow ones for easier ascent. The bastions buttressed the building above, and also contributed to the monumental effect of the design which looks back in time to the Minoan theatral area (a distinctive feature at Knossós and Phaistós) and forward to the seating arrangement of a Greek theatre.

The staircase gives access to an upper terrace on which stood the Hellenistic **prytaneíon**, essential to the administration of the city-state. These civic buildings are often compared with a modern town hall, with the added dimension of the fire kept burning continuously on an altar of Hestia as a sign of the city's continuity with its past.

The main **hall**, with a central hearth and couches for eight people, has access to the east to a **peristyle court**; the small rooms behind, on the north side, are interpreted as a **treasury** holding the city's archives. These buildings are dated to the end of the 4C and through the 3C BC. One of the inscriptions found, recording a treaty between Górtyn and Lató, was important for the identification of the *prytaneíon*.

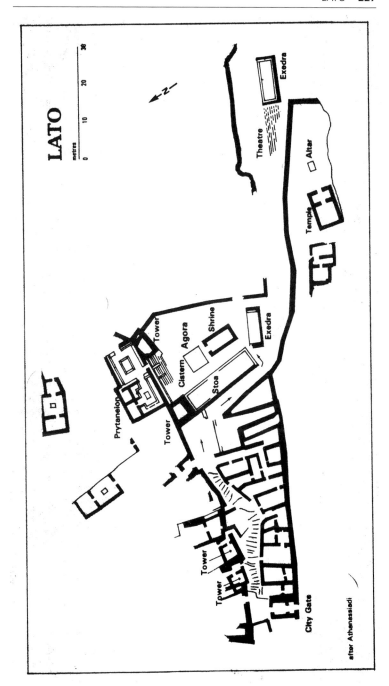

LATO

metres

0 — 10 — 20 — 30

←N→

Exedra

Theatre

Altar

Temple

Exedra

Shrine

Agora

Cistern

Stoa

Tower

Prytaneion

Tower

Tower

Tower

City Gate

after Athanassiadi

Across the *agorá*, above its southeast corner, is a **terrace** supported by a well-preserved retaining wall of rustic polygonal masonry capped by a slightly projecting course. On the terrace there are four courses preserved of a temple (known as the **Large Temple**, late 4C–early 3C) which had an almost square *cella* without columns but with remains of an inscribed base for a cult statue. The *pronaos* opened to the east and outside it stood a stepped altar. Further east still, below the temple terrace, there are traces of 10 or 11 steep, partly rock-cut, steps and a semi-circular area facing north, a complex understood as a small **theatre**, with beside it another **exedra** similar to the one on the edge of the *agorá*.

The summit of the northern acropolis is reached by a rough path and the view repays the effort required to climb to it. Vultures are a not uncommon sight.

To return to the coast by a different route you can follow the road down from the parking place to turn right very soon, signed for (2km on an unsurfaced road) Phlamourianá. On foot you can continue round the hill and across country to Khamiló; the site guardian will point out the path.

Neápolis and the surrounding countryside

A pleasant provincial town just off the New National Road c 15km northwest of Ayios Nikólaos, Neápolis retains its individual character partly because it is ignored by most of the tourist traffic speeding past. The town lies in a wide bowl-shaped valley known locally as the trough (*skáphi*) of Mirabéllo.

Travelling by bus
There is a bus service from Ayios Nikólaos which is also convenient for Dréros (see below).

Where to stay
C *Neapolis* (12 rooms), ☎ 28410 33966, fax 28410 33440. A recently refurbished small hotel, perhaps useful as a base off the beaten track for exploring this region. There are signs from the plateía along the Old Road west towards Herákleion, or from the highway if you are heading east.

Neápolis (literally the new town) was laid out by its Ottoman governor during the second half of the 19C with a spacious central plateía around gardens in front of the cathedral. The town is the administrative centre of the district of Mirabéllo and the seat of a bishopric.

At the top of the plateía there are Ministry of Culture signs to the Neápolis Archaeological Collection. A new exhibition of finds from local sites was prepared in 1999 but because of staff shortages there have been problems about opening it to the public.

Overlooking Neápolis from hills to the north of the highway is the site of Dréros, a city-state of the Archaic period where one of the earliest temples known in Greece was excavated in the 1930s (see below).

North towards Cape Drepáni the Mirabéllo countryside is unspoilt, and not much frequented apart from the two coastal village resorts: Sísi with recommended tavernas on a picturesque inlet, and Mílatos where a cave is a place of pilgrimage on account of a 19C Turkish atrocity.

Neápolis lies at the foot of Mount Seléna in the Lasíthi range and at the start of one of the main routes up to the Lasíthi mountain plain. Two kilometres into the climb south, inland from the plateía, you pass **Moní Kremastón**, now a convent where the nuns welcome visitors.

The 'Cretan Pope'

In the location now occupied by Neápolis, the village of Karés was the birthplace in 1340 of Pétros Phílargos, who became Pope Alexander V, the only Cretan ever to be elected to the papacy. His parents died of the plague and he was cared for by the Catholic friars of nearby Ayios Antónios. He went on to study at the renowned friary of St Francis in Candia (on the hill where the Herákleion Archaeological Museum now stands) and took orders in 1357. An academic career led him to many European universities including Padua, Oxford and Paris where he taught theology. He was appointed an ambassador at the court of the Duke of Milan, Giovanni Visconti. In 1405 he became a Cardinal and on 26 June 1409, at the Synod of Pisa, was proclaimed Pope. However, in 1410, before he reached Rome, he died in Bologna and was buried there in the church of St Francis. There were rumours of poison.

Sísi

The harbour village of Sísi grew up around a rocky inlet used by fishing boats which makes an attractive setting for a line of agreeable tavernas. The settlement has expanded on to the headland to the west and behind the good beach to the east, to exploit the tourist potential of holiday apartments and resort hotels. The tavernas may be crowded during the high season and on Sundays but they are recommended for being conveniently close (less than 5km) at the end of a visit to the Minoan palace site of Mália.

Sísi can be approached most easily from the north coast highway, but from Neápolis you could take the Old Road, winding but scenic, west through Latsída and Vrakhási. Before the Old Road turns north to the coast it runs alongside the highway to negotiate the **Selinári gorge**; griffon vultures have taken to nesting on a ledge not far up the cliff here, almost opposite the monastery buildings of Ayios Yeóryios Selinári which is off the New National Road.

When you reach the coastal village the main street runs down to the harbour cove. You pass signs (left) to a good bakery and (right) for the beach road where you will find a post office caravan and two travel agencies. There is car parking on the seafront, signed just before you reach the cove.

Where to stay and eating out

For inexpensive accommodation the Cactus Pub acts as agent for *Eleni's Rooms* which overlook the cove. *Pension Ergina*, probably quieter, is near the post office, a short way along the road to the beach. Outside the high season one of the travel agencies should be able to find an apartment to rent.

Taverna Miramare, out on the point where the cove and seafront meet, has an excellent reputation for seafood. There is a wide choice of less expensive alternatives.

Mílatos

The village of Mílatos, 2km inland of its new beach settlement, is c 5km east from Epáno (upper) Sísi.

There was a Bronze Age settlement at Mílatos and finds from Postpalatial tholos tombs are displayed in the Ayios Nikólaos Museum. The city-state of the Classical period, a contemporary of neighbouring Dréros, was destroyed by Lýttos in the 3C BC. According to Cretan tradition the great Ionian city of Miletus in Asia Minor was founded from here; in recent years Minoan influence has been identified in the archaeological record of that city.

A large **cave** in the hills behind the village is a place of pilgrimage for Cretans on account of a Turkish atrocity against the Christian populace in 1823. The cave is signed inland at a T-junction in Mílatos village; the last 500m is on foot. At the main entrance there is a modern chapel to honour the dead. In the cave a torch may be useful.

Cretans recount that during the years of revolution coinciding with mainland Greece's successful bid for independence, the cave became a place of refuge for 2700 Christians, mostly women and children, with a handful of armed menfolk. The hiding place was betrayed and a large force of Turks besieged the cave. Great privation ensued but when, after fierce fighting lasting two weeks, the Christians negotiated a surrender, the terms were not honoured by the Turkish commander and all the Christians were slaughtered or sold into slavery.

From the cave you can continue by country roads (mostly surfaced) across unspoilt uplands, through **Kounáli**, and then south, following a deep valley to rejoin the Neápolis road at Latsída. A recommended 3km detour (with extensive views between mountains and sea) takes a left turn at the T-junction in Kounáli, then 1km byond Tsámbi right at a stone-built farmhouse where the tranquil long-abandoned monastery of **Ayios Antónios** soon comes into view.

Dréros

Dréros was a typical small city-state in the Archaic period but it is exceptional in that excavations during the first half of the 19C uncovered one of the earliest temples to have survived in all Greece. The city occupied a saddle between two acropolis peaks with magnificent views of the countryside around.

To find the archaeological site, 3km from the centre of Neápolis, by car or on foot, leave the big plateía at its north end towards the New National Road. Cross the bridge over the highway and follow signs ahead to the archaeological site. Fork right after 2km and the road ends at the start of the path up the site.

There are views to enjoy to the south across the Neápolis valley towards Mount Díkte at 2148m above Lasíthi, but to climb to the site take the well-maintained path at the northern end of the parking area, on the left as you reach it. In around ten minutes, just before a crest, you will notice below the path a stone-built shed which now protects the excavation of the temple.

The city plan at Dréros was comparable with that of Lató (p 230): the square *agorá* with retaining wall and the essential cistern to conserve rainwater. Nearby public buildings probably included a *prytaneíon*, but here all is less well preserved than at Lató, and less easy to make out.

The **Temple of Apollo Delphinios** (dated to the Geometric period, second quarter of the 8C BC) consists of a simple cella orientated northeast–southwest. The north end, where the original entrance may have been through a porch, was unfortunately destroyed by the construction of a lime kiln. The temple overlooked the city's *agorá* on its eastern side and was reached by a still surviving short flight of steps up to its entrance.

Inside the temple, on the long axis, the archaeologists found a central rectangular sunken hearth (lined with small stone slabs and full of ash) and a base for a wooden column; it is believed that there were originally two columns. On a ledge in the southwest corner were an early 6C bronze *gorgoneion* (gorgon's mask), vases and terracotta figurines, and in front of this on the floor a stone offering-table. The most exciting find consisted of three important **bronze statuettes** (the largest 80cm tall) which would probably have stood on the ledge. Dated to c 650 BC, they are made by the *sphyrelaton* technique, hammering bronze plates over a wooden core, and are thought to represent Apollo, Artemis and Leto (worth searching out in Room XIX on the ground floor of the Herákleion Museum). Beside the ledge was a low altar in the form of a stone box filled with the horns of young goats, recalling the horn altar at Delos around which Theseus and the Delian maidens of mythology performed the crane dance after his triumphant return there from Crete.

The site had a long history of settlement. The majority of finds date to the Geometric and Archaic periods, when the city was flourishing, but a cemetery area had graves from the end of the Bronze Age (11C BC) and the huge cistern (13m x 5.5m x 6m) below the temple was constructed in the Hellenistic period (3C BC).

The city declined in importance before the end of the 2C BC but there are traces of occupation in the Second Byzantine period on the east acropolis hill which takes its name from the chapel of Ayios Antónios on the summit.

Interesting **inscriptions** are recorded from Dréros. An inscribed pillar (dated end of the 3C BC) was found here in 1855. It detailed an oath of civic loyalty taken by the young men of Dréros and incidentally confirmed the city's ancient name.

Another inscription, an early code of constitutional law, had been carved on blocks in Archaic times, making it the first such code known for a Greek city. The blocks had fallen into the great cistern, perhaps from the walls of the temple. Also from the cistern came a scrap of text using the Greek alphabet but for both the Greek and Eteocretan languages, the latter believed to be the language of the original pre-Greek population. This strengthens the impression here at Dréros of ancient Cretan traditions mingling with those of the post-Minoan population. A similar continuity has been recognised at Praisós, a powerful city-state in the extreme east of the island.

To return to the coast you can use a quiet country road which will bring you over the hills to Eloúnda, along the way offering stunning views of the Bay of Mirabéllo and eastern Crete. Leave Neapolis heading east on the Old Road, signed towards Ayios Nikólaos. In **Nikithianós**, watch for the left turn for Eloúnda. Leaving the Old Road there is a steep climb with the site of Dréros above left, where the chapel of Ayios Antónios can be seen as a landmark on the hill top. You continue through Kastélli and on along an avenue of gum trees to **Phourní**. You pass the Millstone Museum proclaiming itself the museum of cottage industry; the project is in its early stages and opening hours are uncertain.

Just beyond Phourní an acute left turn is signed for Doriés and Karídi. This offers a recommended detour (7km) to the recently restored **Moní Aretíou** (founded 16C), once the wealthy seat of the local bishopric but now peaceful and isolated among cypresses and cedar trees, at a height of 530m above sea-level.

On the way up there, in **Doriés**, the former monastic church of **Ayios Konstantínos** retains an icon of the *Panayía Odiyítria* which is of interest to experts. Dated to the end of the 14C (though somewhat restored and altered), this icon is said to be the earliest now remaining on Crete. The work became part of a double-sided icon, the reverse being a slightly later *Crucifixion*. (The church key will be with the *papás* who lives nearby.)

On the road from Phourní towards the coast, suddenly the Bay of Mirabéllo fills the view, with the island of Pseíra and the hills of eastern Crete in the distance. You descend steeply, several times crossing the old *kalderími*, and finally turn right into the centre of Eloúnda (p 218).

The Lasíthi mountain plain

This fertile and intensively cultivated mountain plain lies at the height of 817m to 850m, ringed by small villages and surrounded by a girdle of mountains. The plain (12km by 6km) used to be famous for the number of windmills drawing water for irrigation but in recent times this function has been performed more prosaically by electric pumps. At one time it seemed that soon only rusting wind-mill frames would remain, but with the support of grants from the EU there is now a move to halt this decline.

Just above the plain on **Mount Díkte**, a cave associated with the cult of Zeus has become one of the principal tourist attractions on the island, but there are a number of other good reasons to enjoy this still relatively unspoilt landscape. The Lasíthi area, traversed by the E4, is strongly recommended to walkers, and espe-cially to those with an interest in flowers of the mountains or in birds of prey. The excavated site of **Karphí**, a refuge settlement inhabited at the end of the Bronze Age and dramatically perched on the rim of the ring of mountains, can only be reached on foot.

Travelling by bus

There is a limited service to Psykhró (for the Diktaían cave) both from the Herákleion direction and from Ayios Nikólaos.

To the Lasíthi plain

There is a choice of several routes for the approach to the Lasíthi plain. The expe-dition is usually undertaken as a day trip, perhaps using different roads (from the Herákleion direction or from Ayios Nikólaos) for the outward and return jour-neys, but simple overnight accommodation is available in the mountain villages of **Tzermiádo**, **Ayios Yeóryios** and **Psykhró**.

The main route from central Crete sets off inland from the stretch of the New National Road that bypasses Khersónisos for a drive of some 35km to Tzermiádo, principal village of the plain (see below for further details). You can join this road up from the coast by a stiff climb through Mókhos, or on a new road direct from Mália to Krási. From Tzermiádo it is a further 12km to the Diktaian cave; a good road completes the circuit of the plain.

From Ayios Nikólaos

On the c 40km approach to Lasíthi from the east, you can start the climb south at Neápolis, or you can join this route at Drási. To do so either follow the Old Road inland from Ayios Nikólaos and turn off through Ayios Konstantínos or leave the Ayios Nikólaos–Kritsá road at the highway junction to run through Skísma, Phlamouriáná and Exo Lakónia. With funding from the EU the most difficult stretches of the road have been upgraded, but it is still narrow and winding in places. **Zénia**, a mountain village across the head of a valley with windmills on the nearby ridge, continues a tradition of craftsmanship in woodworking. **Exo Potámi** and **Mésa Potámi** lie along a beautiful well-watered valley at a meeting of mountain streams. (Both place-names incorporate the Greek word for river.) Fine trees stand out in the stretches of woodland here, usually prickly oaks, *Quercus coccifera*.

Mésa Potámi has two tavernas across the road from each other with rooms to rent above one of them, the *Marianna*, and alternative accommodation at the well-signed *Apolos*.

The pass of **Tou Patéra ta Seliá** (with parking by a big café-bar) brings the plain into view, stretching away to the west where the natural drainage occurs. You will descend to arrive in **Mésa Lasíthi**, one of the ring of villages above the cultivated land. The glint of water away to the left is a new reservoir, part of the island-wide conservation scheme also funded by the EU.

At the junction with the road around the plain you turn left for Psykró or right for Tzermiádo (see below).

From central Crete

25km from Herákleion the turning inland from the coast (or the bypass) west of the resort of Khersónisos, is signed for Lasíthi and for Kastélli in the Pediáda. The Kastélli road forks right after 5km; in the ravine below the road beyond the turning are the ruined piers of a Roman aqueduct which brought water to Khersónisos from springs around Piyí and Ayios Pandeleímon (p 138).

As you approach the village of **Potamiés**, a sign indicates the side-road (left) 1km up to the frescoed Byzantine church of the Panayía, all that remains of the **Gouverniótissa monastery**. You climb (1km) past the chapel of Sotíros Khristós (Our Saviour Christ, also frescoed) to the monastery church dedicated to the Assumption of the Virgin (festival 15 August) which looks out from the hillside over the Langáda valley. There has been an arrangement to open the church in the mornings, but if you draw a blank enquire for the *phýlax* (guardian) at the first *kapheneíon* right of the main street in Potamiés.

The cruciform church of the Panayía, with a ground-plan where three arms of the cross are of almost equal length, has a central dome resting on a drum that is lit by eight blind-arcaded windows. Venetian influence is seen only in the quatrefoil window and pointed arch above the entrance and in the window of the apse. The frescoes, dating from the second half of the 14C, are best preserved in the west arm, with a double tier of gospel scenes above the worshipping saints. The church is dominated by the *Pantokrátor* in the dome, above the four evangelists on the pendentives. A beautiful carved wooden iconostasis, the sanctuary doors and a group of 16C icons from this church can be seen in the Historical Museum in Herákleion.

Beyond Potamiés the road levels out as it approaches the dramatic wall of the Lasíthi mountains. The knob shape conspicuous on the skyline is Karphí (p 236).

Avdoú is an attractive and unspoilt village with two frescoed Byzantine churches well worth a visit. **Ayios Konstantínos**, 1km off the main road (key from the first *kapheneíon* on the right of the main street), has well-preserved frescoes painted by the brothers Mánuel and Ioánnis Phokás, dated by donor inscription to 1445. Manuel painted the churches at Embaros and Epáno Sými near Viánnos. This Avdoú church is signed, right, as you arrive from the north. Bear right and continue to a bridge; 500m beyond it the precinct is hidden among trees on the right. **Ayios Antónios** is in the middle of the village (signed, opposite the above *kapheneíon*, left and immediately left again). Its 14C frescoes of gospel scenes are interesting for their powerful draughtsmanship executed largely in tones of brown paint.

From **Goniés** the climb begins in earnest. You come to the junction with a road up from the coastal region between Khersónisos and Mália and 3km beyond that junction a loop (left) off the main road takes you through the delightful village of **Krási**. (Here is the new road up from the coast direct from Mália. Because of the formidable gradient, this route might be chosen for the downhill journey back to the coast.) On one side of the plateía in Krási spring water is harnessed through vaulted basins opposite an enormous ancient plane tree which is reputed to need 12 people with outstretched arms to girdle its trunk. The plane tree (*Platanus orientalis*) is a typical feature of village squares across Crete, growing alongside the spring at the heart of the settlement, but this tree is one of the oldest and finest that you are likely to see. There are two pleasant tavernas overlooking the scene.

Between Krási and Kerá you will notice (next to a new exhibition building) a signpost pointing to the archaeological site of Karphí. A less steep route starts from Tzermiádo (p 236).

On the right, just below the road, before **Kerá**, is the **monastery of the Panayía Kardiótissa**, now operating as a convent. The epithet *kard* implies a Cretan variation of the Virgin of Tenderness. The nuns tend a garden that benefits from the mountain climate (at 630m) and has a fine view from its terrace. They also run a small shop selling their handwork. The convent celebrates the Nativity of the Virgin on 8 September.

There was a foundation here at least as early as 1415 when the Florentine monk Cristoforo Buondelmonti noted the miraculous powers of the renowned Kardiótissa icon then revered in the church. Under the Turks the monastery acquired extensive property, and with its advantage as a look-out position became a favourite meeting-place of revolutionaries. During the revolt of 1866 the surrounding Pediáda and Lasíthi districts suffered systematic destruction at the hands of Omer Pasha, and the monastery was not spared.

The unusual ground-plan of the church is the result of four successive building phases, though care was taken with windows, stonework and decorative tiling in order to achieve a homogeneous exterior. The original three-apsed chapel serves as the sanctuary of the present convent church. An extended narthex was added, forming a triple transept (with steps needed to adjust to the slope of the hillside). Parallel to this transept is a conventional narthex now serving as the entrance to the church. The small chapel to the north is a further addition. Frescoes have been uncovered: those in the sanctuary are dated to the early 14C; those elsewhere in the church were painted later in the same century and are said to show the influence of the Macedonian school.

Beyond the hamlet of Kerá, the road climbs to the **Selí Ambélou pass** (900m) at a row of stone-built windmills. This first sight of the mountain plain is nowadays likely to come about in the company of crowds making for a café and souvenir shop beside the road. If you walk up along the line of the windmills (which were grinding corn until the early years of the last century) there is usually peace to enjoy the view which extends back to the coast and forward to Mount Díkte, at 2148m the highest peak in the range.

Descending from the Selí Ambélou pass, you join the road which makes a circuit of the plain. A right turn would take you in 8km to the Diktaian cave at Psykhró, visited as a traditional birthplace of Zeus. Turning left to circle the plain in a clockwise direction, you arrive at Tzermiádo.

The plain

Oropédio Lasithíou, the mountain plain of Lasíthi, is one of a number of fertile upland plains on Crete but Lasíthi is the only area above 800m that is inhabited all the year round. There is a strong sense of community among the 20 or so villages and hamlets around the edge of the plain. The winters are severe so seasonal preparations are still a serious business.

The cultivated land lies above the olive-tree line, but its apples and potatoes are valued in the markets of Athens as well as throughout Crete. Some cereals are still grown, also other fruit crops and an abundance of almonds, a splendid sight at blossom time. The fertility of the plain results from the rich alluvial soil brought down from the mountains by the melting snows. A river crosses the plain, flowing from east to west, to the lowest lying area in the northwest corner, near the village of Káto Metokhí, where it disappears to drain into a great cave, the Khónos. Through history the capacity of the cave has been crucial. Flooding has been a problem, and sometimes still, early in the year, the low-lying areas of the plain are under water. The Romans are thought to have tackled the drainage problem but the grid of ditches (known as *liniés*) which now gives much of the western half of the plain the appearance of a chessboard was installed by engineers from Padua, probably in 1631–33 when the success of the wheat crop was of particular importance to the Venetian Empire. The irrigation system employed countless picturesque windpumps, each with between four and eight triangular sails of white cloth revolving anti-clockwise to draw water to the surface during the dry season. Recently mechanised competition seemed to have prevailed, but now EU funding for projects on the plain comes with conditions about reinstating windmills, so the picture may change again.

There is evidence for Neolithic occupation on the plain with an important sanctuary at the Trapéza cave (see below). The Diktaian cave at Psykhró (see below) was a place of pilgrimage from Middle Minoan times to the 7C BC, a period of 1000 years. In Hellenistic times the area was under the control of

Lýttos, the powerful city-state to the west just outside the girdle of mountains, and there is plenty of evidence for Roman settlement exploiting the rich soil.

The Lasíthi plain, with only eight natural passes through the encircling mountains, has always been an easily defended refuge, and at many periods a centre of revolt. During the early part of Venetian rule the situation was so critical that in 1284, in spite of Crete's considerable contribution to the granaries of Venice, the authorities forcibly cleared the population from the plain, and forbade tillage or pasturage for nearly two centuries.

The principal village of the district of Lasíthi is **Tzermiádo** where there is a choice of places to eat and to stay for the night.

Where to stay
C *Kourites*, ☎ and fax 28440 22194. At the far end of the village the big taverna caters for tour groups in the middle of the day, but there are rooms above it looking out across the plain, and in an adjacent purpose-built block.

Karphí
In the last years of the Cretan Bronze Age a settlement was built 1100m above sea level on the northern rim of the mountains around the Lasíthi plain by a community still adhering to Minoan religious traditions 300 years after the collapse of Minoan power. The desolate site at Karphí (the Greek word for a 'nail' or 'spike') occupies a spectacular position clinging to the southeast slopes of a limestone knob that is conspicuous from far away and from all directions.

The easiest of several routes starts from Tzermiádo. On the approach to the village from the west a track beside the district health centre is signed for the church of Tímeos Stavrós and for the archaeological site; it climbs gently up to the little area of the Nísimos plain (20 minutes on foot or you can drive this stretch).

At the edge of the plain there is a choice of tracks. Right will take you up to the chapel and a panoramic view over to Mount Díkte to the south. The track ahead continues straight across the Nísimos plain to a paved *kalderími* through the hills towards the north coast. This is one of the eight traditional passes out of Lasíthi, and a recommended walk, but on this occasion your destination is in sight left, a saddle between two peaks at the top of a long narrowing gully. The track to the left will take a vehicle as far as a chapel at the edge of the rising ground where you pick up a footpath to gain height up the left incline of this gully. The path ascends in a fairly straight line until it crosses the gully near the top. You pass the Astividerós spring, one of the two known water sources for the settlement, and may notice a group of four small tholos tombs of the type where a circular vault covers a roughly rectangular chamber.

All this area is a delight for botanists; in April and May the wet gullies in the hills surrounding the Nísimos plain shelter the creamy white peony *P. clusii* which is endemic to Crete.

On the last stretch the direct path to the site leads between outcrops of rock up the slope from which the excavated remains are in view. The survey post on the (right-hand) peak of Mikrí Kopróna marks their eastern limit. When you step out on to the ridge all north central Crete is spread out below. The site was presumably chosen at least partly for defensive purposes for it commanded two of the entrances to the mountain plain, but it has also been suggested that this sizeable

Summit of Mikrí Kopróna

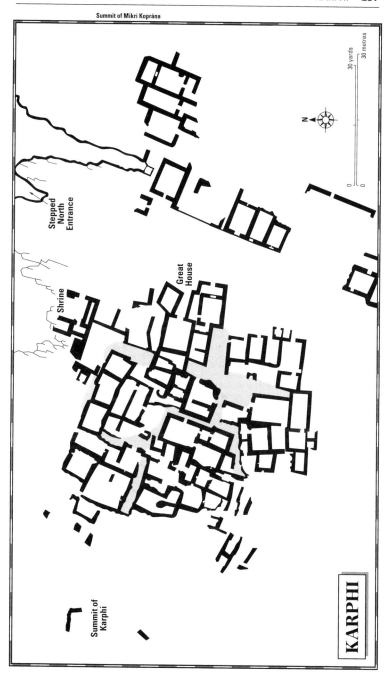

Stepped North Entrance

Shrine

Great House

Summit of Karphi

N

30 yards
30 metres

KARPHI

settlement with a population estimated at 3500 could have been a safe haven for brigands, as was the mountain plain of Lasíthi in historical times.

Karphí was excavated just before the Second World War by the British archaeologist John Pendlebury (p 373). There are indications for a Middle Minoan peak sanctuary on the knob at Karphí, but settlement dates from the Late Minoan IIIC period (12C BC). The site was occupied for some 150 years (perhaps into the Protogeometric period) and then peacefully evacuated, so that only limited evidence about its occupants was left behind. They are known to have had links with the outside world across the south Aegean and as far as Cyprus. They certainly worshipped Minoan gods some 300–400 years after the destruction of the political power of the Minoan palace civilisation.

The settlement spreads across the saddle between the two peaks (see plan). About a third of its area has been excavated. Houses were roughly built of stone without plaster, and only thresholds and doorjambs were of carefully cut blocks. Pendlebury's **Great House** can be identified by its superior construction; pottery and bronze ornaments confirmed its relative importance. The paved streets give shape to the town, but individual house plans, where clusters of rooms are huddled together in agglomerative fashion, are not so easy to make out. One notable feature was the number of house shrines identified by the excavators.

A **stepped entrance** was found at the top of the steep northern ascent. The temple or civic **shrine** was built at the edge of the precipice and part of it has been eroded away. The largest room with remains of an altar was entered from the east and had two small adjoining rooms opposite this doorway. Among the furnishings left behind in the shrine when the settlement was abandoned were clay goddesses with the traditional cylindrical skirt and hands raised in a gesture of blessing. One, nearly 1m high, has birds perching in her crown. A unique rhyton is in the form of a chariot drawn by three oxen represented only by their heads. All these are on display in the Herákleion Archaeological Museum's Room XI. If there was indeed a Middle Minoan peak sanctuary on the knob at Karphí, where the later shrine was built, a particular religious significance may have influenced the choice of this inhospitable site.

If you climbed on foot from Tzermiádo you have the choice of an alternative return route. Follow the path along the ridge west, passing a second water supply, **Vitsilóvrisis**, the Fountain of the Eagles. (The modern inscription commemorates the British archaeological team which excavated Karphí.) Another cemetery of 17 small tholos tombs is located nearby. A white chapel is in sight on the outer slope of the hills and a little further on you meet a main path crossing the ridge. Turning left on to it you very soon start the descent to the Lasíthi plain on a stepped stone-built *kalderími*, another of the eight ancient ways (the Asphendámi pass) through the girdle of hills. You reach the road less than 1km west of the health centre where you started the ascent.

The Trapéza cave

In the middle of Tzermiádo an awkward left turn is signed for this cave. By car you can continue through the village in the direction of Psykhró. Soon a side road leads off to the left (here misleadingly signed to Krónio) and 300m along it (signed right) is the start of the path for a steep ten-minute climb up to the terrace in front of the cave mouth.

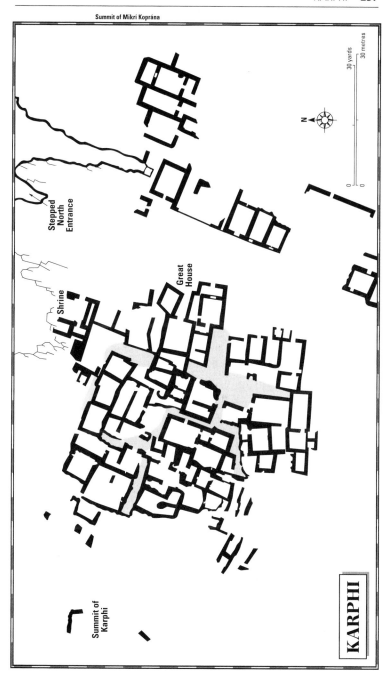

Summit of Mikrí Kopりána

Stepped North Entrance

Shrine

Great House

Summit of Karphi

30 yards
30 metres

KARPHI

settlement with a population estimated at 3500 could have been a safe haven for brigands, as was the mountain plain of Lasíthi in historical times.

Karphí was excavated just before the Second World War by the British archaeologist John Pendlebury (p 373). There are indications for a Middle Minoan peak sanctuary on the knob at Karphí, but settlement dates from the Late Minoan IIIC period (12C BC). The site was occupied for some 150 years (perhaps into the Protogeometric period) and then peacefully evacuated, so that only limited evidence about its occupants was left behind. They are known to have had links with the outside world across the south Aegean and as far as Cyprus. They certainly worshipped Minoan gods some 300–400 years after the destruction of the political power of the Minoan palace civilisation.

The settlement spreads across the saddle between the two peaks (see plan). About a third of its area has been excavated. Houses were roughly built of stone without plaster, and only thresholds and doorjambs were of carefully cut blocks. Pendlebury's **Great House** can be identified by its superior construction; pottery and bronze ornaments confirmed its relative importance. The paved streets give shape to the town, but individual house plans, where clusters of rooms are huddled together in agglomerative fashion, are not so easy to make out. One notable feature was the number of house shrines identified by the excavators.

A **stepped entrance** was found at the top of the steep northern ascent. The temple or civic **shrine** was built at the edge of the precipice and part of it has been eroded away. The largest room with remains of an altar was entered from the east and had two small adjoining rooms opposite this doorway. Among the furnishings left behind in the shrine when the settlement was abandoned were clay goddesses with the traditional cylindrical skirt and hands raised in a gesture of blessing. One, nearly 1m high, has birds perching in her crown. A unique rhyton is in the form of a chariot drawn by three oxen represented only by their heads. All these are on display in the Herákleion Archaeological Museum's Room XI. If there was indeed a Middle Minoan peak sanctuary on the knob at Karphí, where the later shrine was built, a particular religious significance may have influenced the choice of this inhospitable site.

If you climbed on foot from Tzermiádo you have the choice of an alternative return route. Follow the path along the ridge west, passing a second water supply, **Vitsilóvrisis**, the Fountain of the Eagles. (The modern inscription commemorates the British archaeological team which excavated Karphí.) Another cemetery of 17 small tholos tombs is located nearby. A white chapel is in sight on the outer slope of the hills and a little further on you meet a main path crossing the ridge. Turning left on to it you very soon start the descent to the Lasíthi plain on a stepped stone-built *kalderími*, another of the eight ancient ways (the Asphendámi pass) through the girdle of hills. You reach the road less than 1km west of the health centre where you started the ascent.

The Trapéza cave

In the middle of Tzermiádo an awkward left turn is signed for this cave. By car you can continue through the village in the direction of Psykhró. Soon a side road leads off to the left (here misleadingly signed to Krónio) and 300m along it (signed right) is the start of the path for a steep ten-minute climb up to the terrace in front of the cave mouth.

The local community hoped to arrange opening hours daily 10.00–18.00, but enquire in advance if possible. Access to the cave is cramped and awkward; be prepared for the guardian to be in close attendance.

The cave of Trapéza was cleared in 1936, also by John Pendlebury (see Karphí). The findings have been the subject of controversy but it appears that the cave was visited as early as the Late Neolithic period (fourth millennium) and then through the transition to the Bronze Age. By Early Minoan II (mid-third millennium) it was in use for communal burials, characterised by Pendlebury as 'a fashionable burial place' on account of the quality of the grave goods which included sealstones, rings and other jewellery, figurines, metalwork, stone vases and a glazed steatite scarab. The site seems to have been abandoned at the beginning of the Neopalatial period, Middle Minoan III. A settlement has been excavated nearby, just to the east of the cave on the hill of Kástellos.

The road turns south, passing **Moní Kroustallénias** on a rise at the junction where the road up from Ayios Nikólaos joins the circuit of the plain. The monastery has suffered on many occasions, sharing Lasíthi's turbulent history. If you are using only the northwestern approaches to Lasíthi you might want to make a short detour here through Mésa Lasíthi to climb to the eastern pass (Tou Patéra ta Selliá) for a different perspective.

Continuing the circuit you follow the eastern edge of the plain through Ayios Konstantínos to Ayios Yeóryios where you meet the E4 long-distance footpath.

Ayios Yeóryios

This village makes a good base for some serious walking. From Mésa Lasíthi you can cross the pass over to the Katharó plain above Kritsá. You can climb on paths that should be well-marked and maintained south to the summit of Mount Díkte, or southwest from Magoulás over to Embaros. These are expeditions for fit, experienced and well-equipped walkers. However, the paths do also enable the average enthusiastic walker to follow a marked trail a little way into the quiet of the mountains.

Where to stay and eating out

There are two long-established small hotels in the centre of the village, the **Dias** and the **Rea**, both welcoming but both with only basic facilities. On the edge of the village, overlooking the plain, there is modern, well-equipped accommodation in **Maria's Studio**

Rooms to Rent, purpose-built by the owners of the Hotel Rea, ☎ 28440 31209.

At the popular taverna below the Rea the main dish of the day is often a traditional Cretan speciality.

The well-arranged **Folklore Museum** is open daily 10.00–16.00. This is a 19C village house faithfully restored as an example of the vernacular architecture of Lasíthi as well as the traditional way of life. The building on a higher level at the back of the museum is given over to an exhibition dedicated to the life and times of the Cretan statesman Elefthérios Venizélos (1864–1936).

Diktaian cave

At the end of the village of **Psykhró** a turning (signposted Spileon) leads up to the official car park and ticket office for the cave (open daily 08.30–14.30, but confirm in advance at a tourist information office if possible).

There is a superb view over the plain. A stepped path ascends (15 minutes, donkeys available) to the cave itself, 1025m above sea level and 200m above the village. It is often slippery underfoot and chilly at the lower levels so sensible footwear and a sweater will be useful.

The Zeus myth

There are many rival versions of the Zeus myth but according to one Cretan tradition, as told in the Hymn of the Kouretes (see the Temple of Diktaian Zeus at Palaíkastro), this cave on Mount Díkte was the birthplace of Zeus, the greatest of the Olympian gods of Greece. An oracle had decreed that Kronos, the youngest of the Titans, would be dethroned by his son, so his wife Rhea contrived to give birth in a cave deep in the mountains of Crete (hence the title Zeus Kretagenes, Cretan-born). In the Greek poet Hesiod's 8C BC account Kronos had swallowed his five previous offspring, but on this occasion he was duped with a stone wrapped in swaddling clothes; meanwhile the infant Zeus was kept hidden in the cave, nursed by the goat-nymph Amaltheia, and protected by the armed demi-gods, the Kouretes, who clashed their swords against their shields and shouted to drown the infant's cries. In due course the boy was raised to manhood by shepherds on Mount Ida (see Idaían cave, p 323) and though all six children proved to be immortal, Kronos was succeeded by his third son Zeus.

This cave, one of Crete's most spectacular caverns, has chambers on two levels. The upper cave is a wide vestibule with natural light. The lower cave, accessible down a steep rock path (now equipped with a stairway) is a sloping chamber 80m long, up to 35m wide and 5–12m high. Groups of stalagmites and rock pillars create side-chambers and galleries. The deepest part is marked by a small pool of icy water. One small dark chamber is traditionally known as the birthplace of Zeus with a fine example of a sheet of stalactites compared to the baby's shawl.

The cave attracted the interest of archaeologists (including Evans) at the end of the 19C, and the wealth of votive deposits indicated that it must have been a cult centre of antiquity. Finally in 1900 it was thoroughly explored by British archaeologists with a team of 70 workmen using dynamite where necessary.

There was evidence for habitation from the Late Neolithic period, or Early Minoan I, and after that the cave was used for burial. There are Kamáres ware sherds from Middle Minoan II, but from then on overwhelming evidence for a religious function, with the finds including cult equipment such as offering receptacles, stacks of clay cups and great quantities of bronze objects. Continuity was seen in Geometric period vases, Roman lamps and even a Byzantine cross.

In the upper cave two particular features were investigated in the area to the right of the entrance. Against the rock there were the remains of an irregular enclosure, defined by a wall and roughly paved; this was understood as a sacred precinct. Beside it, 2m in from the cave wall, was evidence of an altar, roughly built and about 1m high, possibly decorated with painted stucco. It was close to a deep crevice in the rock which could have played a part in the ritual performed here. Round it were found many fragments of offering-tables (in serpentine or limestone) and pottery and animal bones consistent with sacrificial offerings. A similar stone fragment, purchased by Evans and now in the Ashmolean Museum, Oxford, is inscribed with Linear A signs.

In the lower cave, at the bottom between the spectacular rock formations, water now lies for most of the year; it would have been deeper in antiquity. Bronze votives were found in great numbers in the pool, in the vertical crevices formed by the fine stalactites and sometimes embedded in the stalactites themselves. Almost all the finds from this lowest level were of Neopalatial (Late Minoan I) date. This was the main period of use, but there was a revival of ritual activity in the 8C and 7C when open-work bronze plaques were the characteristic votive offerings.

About 4km from Psykhró, just beyond the village of Káto Metokhí, you come to the bridge over the river which has meandered across the plain and fed the artificial drainage system (the *liniés*). It is here about to disappear into the **Khónos**, the great cave in the hillside (left) which channels excess water into its limestone depths. However, the experts point out that nowadays the mountain plain suffers from too little water, not too much.

On the far side of the bridge is the start of a shepherd's track and the old *kalderími* over the girdle of mountains by the **Tsoúli Mníma** pass towards Lýttos. Allow about an hour to the pass where there is a magnificent view across the Pediáda countryside.

The road now completes the circuit of the plain, passing the deserted **Vidianí monastery**, a 19C foundation in the process of restoration. You arrive (8km from Psykhró) at the junction, below the windmills of the Séli Ambélou pass on the road up from Herákleion.

East of Ayios Nikólaos

The north coast highway east from Ayios Nikólaos follows the rocky shore around the bay of Mirabéllo. Though still winding and slow in places this is a scenic drive all the way to **Siteía** (70km). It is 20km to **Gourniá** where a Minoan town has been excavated. 2km beyond the archaeological site is the time-honoured parting of the ways at the start of the route across the island at its narrowest point coast to coast, to **Ierápetra** c 35km from Ayios Nikólaos. Now engineers are radically altering the scenery, carving a 5km stretch of road through the hills so that Ierápetra traffic will cut across south of Gourniá and Pakhiá Ammos.

Travelling by bus

There are good bus services to Siteía and Ierápetra; both routes pass Gourniá.

Around the bay to Gourniá

Leave Ayios Nikólaos following Siteía signs on the one-way system and join the bypass. On the left of the road the reed-fringed **Almyrós beach** attracts bird-watchers as well as swimmers according to the time of year. The road winds around the bay with fine views.

After 10km you come down to the waterfront at **Istro**, which has expanded from a beach settlement attached to the village of Kaló Khorió into a pleasant village resort strung out along the main road. At the eastern end a sandy bay is rightly popular for swimming; there is parking opposite the big Panórama taverna. If you are staying in the area you will find less frequented stretches of beach round the same bay.

Where to stay

L *Istron Bay* (117 rooms), ☎ 28410 61303, fax 28410 61383, www.istronbay.com, email: istron@agn.forthnet.gr. A self-contained resort hotel, with all the expected facilities, on its own cove 2km east of the village.

C *Elpída* (96 rooms), ☎ 28410 61403, fax 28410 61481. In the middle of the village, in a garden set back from the through road.

C *Golden Bay* (49 rooms). ☎ 28410 61202, fax 28410 61224. In the village on the seaward side of the through road, a five minute walk from the beach.

Traditional rent rooms are not a feature of the Istro developments but outside the main season **apartments** and **studios** should be available. You could start by asking next door to the Hotel Elpída or consult *Minotours Tourist Services* in the same block.

As you drop downhill on the approach to the bridge at the beginning of Istro the site of the Early Iron Age settlement of Vrókastro is on the seaward summit of the hills ahead, with a terraced gully pointing up to it.

At the bridge there are two roads inland: the first, signed for Pýrgos, is recommended for a peaceful day on country roads through pine woods back to Kroústas and Kritsá (p 224); the second climbs to Kalamávka on the spine of the island and a little used route over to the south coast. At **Prína** (7km from the coast, by taxi if necessary) you can join an east–west stretch of the E4 footpath.

Vrókastro

The inhabitants of the refuge settlement of Vrókastro chose an uncomfortably steep limestone spur 300m above the sea with obvious potential for easy defence and as a look-out position. The plan of the settlement is not easy to make out, but remains of houses cling to the hilltop. The site, partially excavated at the beginning of the 20C by Edith Hall, a pioneer American archaeologist, proved to have been occupied at least from the 12C (near the end of the Bronze Age) to the 7C BC (the Orientalising period).

You can tackle the stiff 20-minute climb on the seaward side and the walk is worthwhile if only for the view from the top. Turn off the main road just beyond the Golden Bay Hotel in Istro, and follow the side-street round left to pick up the rough track heading off in the direction of the gully noticed on the approach to the village. Once the climb begins you are aiming, with the help only of goat tracks, for the saddle which connects the highest peak on your left with the hills behind. After the first stiff ascent an easy path leads from the saddle to the peak.

To approach Vrókastro with a vehicle (or walk on a less steep gradient) continue for c 4km along the main road, past the Istron Bay Hotel. At a deep indent in the coast the natural route inland to loop back to the archaeological site follows a stream-bed, but road construction is affecting traffic here and the best advice is to watch carefully for signs.

Around the Vrókastro peak is a tangle of house walls, the irregular plan reflecting the nature of the terrain, with a second group down the terraced north slope. The rooms are huddled together, and separate houses are difficult to distinguish. All the floors were of trodden earth, but column bases indicated three possibly grander areas. Several shrines were identified. Traces of a town wall were found on the northern slope.

The archaeologists reported evidence for metalworking which included some of the earliest iron produced on Crete. Pottery and metal artefacts which originated in the Cyclades, the Dodecanese and Athens are taken to indicate direct links with these regions. There was evidence for a variety of burial practices during this time; rock-cut chamber tombs contained both inhumations and cremations, and walled enclosures were used as ossuaries.

The coast road continues towards Gourniá. 6km from Istro a turning is signposted at an angle right for **Moní Phaneroméni**. (On the seaward side of the road is the approach to a camping site, *Gournia Moon*, in an apparently idyllic position; but this stretch of coast is subject to sea currents which bring debris across the bay.) A steep climb of c 6km on a narrow road brings the reward of the austere monastic buildings on a rock ledge with extensive coastal views. There was a religious foundation here in the Second Byzantine period, before the island fell under Venetian rule. Nowadays worship in the church (dedicated to the Panayía, Assumption of the Virgin, feast day 15 August) revolves around a grotto with a tradition of a miraculous icon of the Virgin.

In March the roadside beyond the turn for the monastery is covered with *Ranunculus asiaticus*; the distribution of this brilliant yellow form is notably localised. Orchids also flourish in the uncultivated areas.

Gourniá

20km from Ayios Nikólaos the archaeological site of Gourniá is spread across a low hill (right) overlooking a sheltered cove of the bay of Mirabéllo. The total size of the settlement is known to have been up to four times greater than the excavation on the acropolis, and houses were located down by the shore where the harbour would have been. The geographical position was a major advantage for trade and communication with the south coast of the island; the alternative in ancient times to a hazardous sea voyage around the eastern capes was a mere 12km journey across gently undulating terrain.

- Open Tues–Sun 08.00–14.30, closed Mon and public holidays. The entrance is signposted 150m off the coast road.

The Minoan town, ancient name unknown, was intensively excavated (1901–04) by the American Harriet Boyd Hawes. There is evidence for occupation from the Early Bronze Age (3rd millennium). There were houses on the hill in the Middle Minoan period, with the street pattern already in place, but most of the remains now visible are of the Neopalatial period. Like so many other Minoan sites Gourniá was destroyed by fire at the end of Late Minoan IB. There was limited reoccupation in LMIII, the time of Mycenaean rule at Knossós.

The street-plan of the Minoan town and the ground floors or basements of houses are unusually well preserved. The narrow streets, which are wide enough for pack animals but not for wheeled transport, are cobbled and stepped, and equipped with an efficient drainage system. In places the houses still stand to a man's height, and there were certainly second storeys because five stone staircases were found as well as evidence for wooden steps. Stone was used in the building, but also mudbrick, often faced with plaster. The doorways were carefully constructed, with limestone thresholds level with the street. The grand scale of the largest palaces makes a strong impression, but it is here in the streets of Gourniá that for many of Crete's visitors the everyday domestic life of the Minoan civilisation comes alive.

The streets used to lead up from all directions to the top of the hill, where the palatial quarters are located. Archaeologists differ on whether this complex should properly be identified as a palace: it is smaller in area (less than half the size of the palace at Zákros) but may be sufficiently similar in design and function to be ranked with the other known Minoan palaces. Architecture and provision for cult practices compare well: there is a court, though it is not laid out as a central focus of the palatial-style buildings; there are storeroom blocks though not, perhaps crucially, the Linear A archive which would confirm beyond doubt the existence of a literate bureaucracy and influence in the locality.

Inside the modern entrance gate it is best to keep left on the street which runs round the outside of the excavated town, and to persist with it until it gradually gains height to bring you to the large open space which the excavator called the **Town Court** (1 on plan); it has been compared with an *agorá* or market place.

At its north end, in clear contrast to the domestic architecture of the town, the remains of two porticoes in the northwest angle of the court flank the entrance to the palatial quarters. The L-shaped staircase of the **Stepped Entrance** (2) recalls, on a miniature scale, the Theatral Area at Knossós. (North of the staircase there was access to an upper floor.) The west flight of the staircase leads up to the **North Portico**, which is paved with limestone slabs, one unusually large and pierced at its southeast corner. It has been suggested that this slab was the setting for the bull sacrifice connected with bull-leaping sports in the court, with the hole as a drain for blood. Fragments of the stylised bulls' horns which had fallen into the court from the pillars of the portico identified this as a cult area, and the room immediately to the west has a fixed stone *kérnos* indented with a ring of 32 hollows, another possible sign of ritual activity.

The **West Portico** (3), on the court and directly south of the *kérnos*, has been compared in design and function with the Tripartite Shrine at Knossós. Behind it is the **South Wing** of the palatial quarters.

Their central area with alternate pillar and column bases may have been an open court or a large hall giving on to an open lighted area (4), similar to the Hall of the Double Axes at Knossós. To the north were associated **storerooms**, and

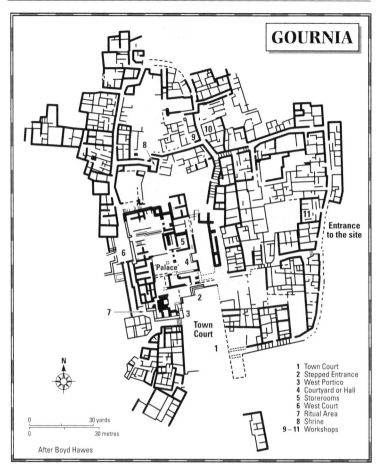

GOURNIA

8
9 10
11

Entrance
to the site

Palace
5
6
4
7
2
3

Town
Court

1

N

0   30 yards
0   30 metres

1 Town Court
2 Stepped Entrance
3 West Portico
4 Courtyard or Hall
5 Storerooms
6 West Court
7 Ritual Area
8 Shrine
9 – 11 Workshops

After Boyd Hawes

there are others behind the west façade at what was then basement level. There would have been grander rooms on the ground floor above this important west storeroom block.

In front of the west façade there is a narrow cobbled **West Court** (6); the façade itself, of imposing ashlar sandstone construction, is recessed for windows on a floor above. Ashlar is regarded as a sign of rank and wealth in Minoan architecture. A corridor, paved and originally roofed, leads south from the West Court ending (at the level of the south wing noted above, behind the West Portico) in a small square open space believed to be a **ritual area** (7). Here an irregular stone slab (of conglomerate) c 1m long by 0.75m high stands on a east–west orientation in a little court apparently designed to accommodate it. This is understood as a sacred stone for in association with it, just to the east, are a stone *kérnos*, a double-axe mason's mark and part of a terracotta channel.

To the southwest of the Town Court are houses of the LMIII reoccupation period. These show an architectural scheme influenced by the Mycenaean megaron of mainland Greece. Contemporary with these Postpalatial houses is a small **shrine** (**8**), reached by the cobbled street running north from the West Court. Off this, right, a sloping path is carefully paved with a central pattern of evenly matched cobbles. The shrine, up three steps, is a simple room (3m x 4m) with a ledge for cult objects. The finds (now in the Herákleion Museum, Room X) included a low tripod altar in clay, goddesses with raised arms and bell-shaped skirt, clay tubes with snakes modelled in relief, a sherd with a double axe in relief, and bird figurines and serpents' heads in terracotta.

The finds from the Neopalatial town increased understanding of economic and industrial aspects of Minoan life. There was evidence for the carving of stone vases, also a set of carpenter's tools (found at **9**), and workshops of a potter (**10**) and a bronze-smith (**11**). Near the entrance to the site a press was found with other equipment for the production of olive oil or wine. At the northeast corner of the site there were traces of a house of the MMI period, the earliest building recorded on the hill.

In 1910 the eminent American archaeologist, Richard Seager, excavated a cemetery at **Sphoungarás**, on a hill-slope at the eastern end of the cove directly below the site. He uncovered 150 pithos burials, the majority of Neopalatial (LMI) date, contemporary with the last phase of the Minoan town; the grave gifts included an important series of seals.

The road climbs away eastwards from Gourniá with a fine general view over the site. You descend sharply through several bends to **Pakheiá Ammos** (deep sand) on the coast, which has basic accommodation and waterside tavernas.

In 1914 a substantial Minoan cemetery was exposed on the beach here after a severe storm. Again it was Seager who directed the excavation. Apart from six chests, or *lárnakes*, he found upwards of 200 pithos burials mostly of Neopalatial date, with a few earlier, from the end of the Prepalatial period. The body was folded head down into the pithos which was then buried with the base uppermost. Seager found some of the jars below the water, and considering the difficulty of sinking them into wet sand, he took this as evidence of a rise in sea level along this coast since the Bronze Age.

Across the isthmus of Ierápetra

20km from Ayios Nikólaos and 50km from Siteía on the north coast highway, just to the east of Pakhiá Ammos, is the parting of the ways to Sitéia (p 265) in the northeastern corner of the island and Ieráptera on the south coast. The road south across the isthmus, the narrowest distance on the island, is 14km coast to coast. The archaeological site of Vasilikí is just off the road 3km inland. There is an alternative route through the hills from Istro via Kalamávka, longer (25km) and slower but with much to recommend it, perhaps as part of a round trip (see below).

The valley road south across the isthmus is dominated to the east by the massive Thryptí range cut by a spectacularly narrow cleft, the **Khá Gorge**, signed off the main road just to the north of the village of **Monastiráki** which is on the route of the E4 walking route. The gorge is formed by a crack more than 300m deep, and geologists note that where it cuts through the rock-beds and their folds these match exactly on the two sides. The gorge is more or less inaccessible for at its exit the riverbed is on a steep incline and, further in, the varying levels encourage waterfalls and pools.

Vasilikí

Level with the Khá Gorge is a right turn for (after 300m) the archaeological site of Vasilikí. The guardian's hut is a landmark up the hillside on the left of the road. Look out for the fence above the path; you should find the gate open. Vasilikí is renowned for its profusion of wild flowers in the spring.

The site occupies a superb position above the valley and would have commanded the north end of the isthmus route through to the south coast. It was first excavated early in the 20C, but in 1970 Greek archaeologists began a major programme of work to clarify the stratigraphy and look again at the material.

Vasilikí used to be known primarily as a Prepalatial site of two phases in the Early Minoan II period (middle years of the 3rd millennium BC) where the architecture of major buildings hinted at the evolution of the mature palatial style of later Minoan times. A type of pottery first found at the site, the distinctive mottled Vasilikí ware, can be seen in the Ayios Nikólaos and Herákleion museums.

The recent work has established that despite several episodes of destruction there was unbroken occupation at Vasilikí from the time of that important EMII settlement through to Late Minoan I, at the height of the Neopalatial period, as well as reoccupation in Roman times.

It has also thrown valuable light on the evolution of a Minoan village, on successive architectural techniques and on the social organisation and everyday activities of the community. There was evidence, for example, of the precise paving methods employed, and of the details of craft activities such as pottery production, wool working and the processing of grain.

Vasilikí is not an easy site to understand because of the repeated rebuilding through its history and also because of the recent stratigraphical work. The path from the hut, south along the flank of the hill, brings you first to the level ground of recent work where the foundations of a Neopalatial building (known as House M) are well preserved.

The important excavation of Prepalatial buildings lies at the south end of this path along the contour, an area up the slope identified from the depth of the excavated (basement) rooms; the house walls still stand in places to near a man's height. If in doubt you can climb for an overview to the high point marked by two carobs and an olive tree.

This complex (see plan) has been explained as two separate buildings which have been named the **Red House** and the **West House**, dated to two overlapping phases both the second half EMII. The conspicuously deep basement rooms belong to the Red House. The rough construction of the walls was concealed by a hard red lime plaster, which at other sites in later periods was to provide an ideal ground for Minoan fresco painting. Small patches of this red stucco are still preserved, as are channels for structural timbers.

Up the hill just to the west of the complex are the remains of paving for a **court** (in use for both Prepalatial houses) which is understood as an open space for communal use.

One exciting discovery from the recent work on ceramics was the recognition of five sherds (pre-dating Vasilikí ware) which are decorated with dolphins, a motif which was not found again till the height of the Neopalatial period when it occurs in the patterns of LMI Marine Style vases and in fresco decoration.

The upgraded main road sweeps on towards the south coast. The village of **Episkopí** is bypassed but anyone interested in church history and architecture should detour into it. Below the village street, on its east side, there is an intriguing medieval church, with double dedication to **Ayios Yeóryios and Ayios Kharálambos** (key with the *papás*, but access is often difficult).

The 19 blind arches round the drum below the dome are outlined with an elaborate decoration of tiles set upright in mortar and fringed with a band of rosettes, a scheme found only rarely on the Byzantine churches of Greece. (Similar decoration on mainland churches uses a glazed fabric.) The closest parallels occur in Bulgaria at the end of the 12C; in conjunction with the complete absence of Venetian influence here, the tiles help to date this church to the 12C–13C, the years just preceding or at the beginning of Venetian rule.

The unusual ground-plan of the little church consists of a south nave (Ayios Kharálambos) which was added to an earlier domed church (Ayios Yeóryios) with conch-shaped east and west cross-arms and a small, strictly rectangular, north aisle or inner room, now reached only from the main body of the church. (The existing doorway in the west conch was opened during the Venetian period.) The conch plan suggests that the church may have been designed as a martyrion, and according to the Service for Byzantine Antiquities a martyrion may have been associated with a system of Early Christian catacombs perhaps reached through the north room.

During road building in 1946, chamber tombs with burials of the Minoan Postpalatial period (LMIII, c 1300 BC) were found under the village street here. One much illustrated clay *lárnax* with remarkable painted decoration is now on display in the Ierápetra museum (p 252).

From Papadianá, just to the east of Episkopí, there is a good dirt road up to the high village of **Thryptí** (also accessible on foot from Kavoúsi on the north coast) with the chance to explore unspoilt mountain country across to Oreinó and down to the south coast near Makryialós.

Ierápetra

Ierápetra is the only sizeable town on the south coast of Crete and the southern-most one of Europe. It is the bustling commercial centre of a district which owes its prosperity first of all to the large-scale cultivation in hothouses of fruit and vegetables. The town has developed as a holiday resort rather as an afterthought, benefiting from its long beaches and a warm dry climate, exceptional even by Cretan standards. The coast around here claims the most hours of sunshine and the lowest rainfall in all Greece. The *Kýria festival* of cultural activities is an annual event in July and August.

To reach the centre of modern Ierápetra follow the *kéntro* signs on a ring-road and one-way street system which should bring you down to the seafront at a small plateía (Kanoupáki; see plan) with a single palm tree on a central island. On the seaward side is the Dimarkheíon or town hall. The small museum housing the archaeological collection of Ierápetra is here, and the covered market for fruit and vegetables is less than 200m inland.

From Plateía Kanoupáki the harbour is to the right and the new town to the left as you look out to sea. Turning left takes you into Plateía Eleftherías which leads to the one-way streets Kothrí and Koundouriótou, and on to Plateía Plastíra, all in an area behind a wide promenade, Markopoúlou.

From Plateía Kanoupáki along the waterfront to the right the narrow one-way street, Kýrva, is signed to the fort (*phroúrio*). This is the direction for what is left of the Old Town and the former Turkish quarter around the harbour.

Practical information

Travel and transport
Parking
At the far end of Kýrva there are spaces on the quay in front of the old Customs House, a plain unadorned building near the jetty for the excursion boat to Krýsi island (see below), or you can continue further along the front to an area beside the fort overlooking the harbour used by fishing boats.

By bus
The **bus station** is on Lasthénous, ☎ 28420 28337. There are services north to Gourniá and Ayios Nikólaos, east to Makriyialós and on to Siteía, west to Mýrtos and twice a week through to Herákleion via Viánnos.

Taxis

There is a taxi rank in each plateía.

Tourist office

The municipal tourist information office on Plateía Kanoupáki has been closed for some time; the position is reviewed annually.

Until the municipal information office reopens, the **tourist police** are supposed to help with visitors' queries. The entrance to their first floor office is from the southern end of the promenade, on the seaward side of the main police building on Plateía Eleftherías.

Travel agencies

Ierapetra Express, Plateía Eleftherías 24, ☎ 28420 28673.
Magic Tours, Kothrí 26, ☎ 28420 24323.
Zanadu, Kýrva 31, ☎ 28420 25470.

Where to stay

The resort hotels and apartments, popular for family holidays, are along the coast to the east, towards Koutsounári, 7km from the town centre.
Camping Koutsounari is a long-established site on a good beach.
Accommodation in the town centre may be useful on a touring holiday outside the peak season, when not all the smaller seaside places will be open (and when the town nightlife will be less overwhelming).
There is a choice of three hotels behind the town beach on Odós Kothrí.
B *Astron* (66 rooms), 5 Kothrí, ☎ 28420 25114, fax 28420 25917.
C *Camiros* (41 rooms), 15 Kothrí, ☎ 28420 28704, fax 0824 24104.
C *El Greco* (33 rooms), 40 Kothrí, ☎ 28420 28471/2.
D *Cretan Villa* (8 rooms), 16 Lakérdra, ☎ 28420 28522, www.cretan-villa.com. A family-run pension in an attractive traditional house a little inland towards the bus station.
D *Coral* (8 rooms), 106 Ioannídou, ☎ 28420 22743. Simple accommodation overlooking the sea near the harbour.

In this older part of town behind Samouíl and near the harbour, there are well-advertised pensions and rooms to rent.

For an extended stay, as a base for exploring this coast and the beautiful hill country inland, the coastal village of **Mýrtos**, 15km west, is recommended as an alternative to Ierápetra.

Eating out

Along the beach in front of Samouíl (between the Customs House quay for the excursion boats and the fort guarding the old harbour) is a long row of tavernas and cafés with a good variety of menus.
Taverna Konaki is usually reliable, and near the harbour *Napoleon* is always popular.

The tradition of the Cretan *ouzeri* remains strong in Ierápetra. There are several advertising themselves as such along the Samouíl promenade, and one of these might be a good place to try a range of *mezédes*.

Banks

Banks are on Plateía Eleftherías and along Kothrí.

Post office and telephones

The **post office**, open Mon–Sat 07.30–14.00, is on Plateía Kanoupáki. The *OTE* for telephone and fax is on Kóraka, inland of Plateía Eleftherías, open Mon–Fri 07.30–20.00.

Hospital

The hospital is on Kalimeráki, north of Plateía Plastíra; ☎ 28420 22488.

History

The Dorian city-state of Ierápytna destroyed neighbouring Praisós c 145 BC to become the main rival to Itanos at this extreme east end of the island. Ierápytna put up strong resistance to the Romans in 67 BC, but flourished later in the Roman period as a typical harbour city of the empire, on the route between Rome and Egypt and particularly well located for trade and communications when Rome established Crete as one province with Cyrene on the African coast. The ancient city covered a larger area than the modern one. Investigations have begun in recent years, in the harbour area and west of it, but little has yet been excavated and nothing remains above ground of the amphitheatre, two theatres, temples, baths and aqueducts mentioned by earlier travellers.

There has been a fort, called the Kalés, guarding the harbour at least since the early years of Venetian rule. It was twice rebuilt: in 1626 (after earthquake damage) by Francesco Morosini to counter the Turkish threat, and again during the Turkish occupation. Recently its walls have again been repaired.

Opposite the clock-tower near the restored fort you will notice a sign to a house where, according to a not very securely founded tradition, Napoleon Bonaparte is supposed to have spent a June night in 1798, breaking his voyage on the way to campaign in Egypt.

Some of the narrow paved lanes here are dedicated to pedestrians. If you walk westwards along the harbour quay, from the clock-tower and the fishing-boats, the road continues close to the shore, and curves round to a plateía with a Turkish fountain, well restored, in front of a former mosque (with a text from the Koran on the lintel over the entrance) now doing duty as a concert hall; there is a pleasant taverna here in this quieter part of town from which to contemplate the scene.

The **Archaeological Collection** of the Ministry of Culture is at the corner of Adrianoú on Plateía Kanoupáki. Open 08.30–15.00 daily except Mon and public holidays. The star exhibit of the collection, and a masterpiece of Minoan art, is the **larnax** of Postpalatial (Late Minoan III) date from a tomb at Episkopí on the road from the north coast. This clay coffin in the shape of a rectangular chest is decorated in 12 painted panels with scenes of hunting, a chariot procession and a stylised octopus; the gable of the lid has a bull's head modelled at one end with a human figure at the other.

The museum also houses antiquities from the Greco-Roman city of Ierápytna, with pride of place rightly given to a marble statue of Demeter (2C AD), a sheaf of corn in her left hand and in her headdress two snakes beside an altar.

Khrysí

The uninhabited islet of Khrysí (traditionally Gaidouronísi or Donkey Island) 15km offshore, is easily reached on a daily excursion boat from Ierápetra, leaving at 10.00, with return journey at 16.30. Tickets are sold only from the official office at the back of the quay. If you want to book ahead from a distance consult a travel agency. This has become a popular excursion chiefly for the chance to swim from quiet sandy beaches. There are tracks (without much shade) round and across the islet, and three places to get something to eat.

There has been a move to change the traditional name of the island to Khrysí (the Khryséa of ancient times) the associations with gold or golden sands being preferred, but you will find both names still in use.

> The Minoans settled here and in Roman times there was a village with a field system, tombs and probably a church, but after that there is no sign of occupation apart from a medieval chapel with traces of outbuildings which may indicate a monastery.
>
> The islet was cultivated till a few years after the end of the Second World War by people crossing from the mainland of Crete. Now it is browsed by rabbits (which do not occur wild on Crete). It may be relevant that Venetian documents suggest a rabbit warren on nearby Kouphonísi.

An interesting feature for botanists is that more than half the island is covered by low growth largely made up of lentisk and juniper, both the land and sea varieties. You may be told that the sea juniper is cedar (sea cedar is the Cretan name for it) but the experts insist that correctly it is *Juniperus macrocarpa*, rare on Crete itself, with its characteristic single trunk often elaborately gnarled or distorted; some specimens are more than 200 years old.

The hill country inland

Leaving Ierápetra to the west, the main road runs close to the shore. The scenery is not improved by the polythene hothouses for fruit and vegetables occupying every suitable space on the narrow coastal plain. **Mýrtos** (c 14km from Ierápetra) is a delightful village on the sea with two interesting Minoan sites nearby, just before the main road leaves the coast to climb along the southern slopes of **Mount Díkte**. Soon after leaving Ierápetra you could turn inland to explore a stretch of unspoilt upland country in the southeast foothills of the Díkte range.

For ornithologists a short detour is highly recommended. About 4km off the coast road north of **Bramianá** a dam has created a large reservoir designed to serve the needs of the hothouses. It is attracting an exciting range of waterfowl and wading birds both during the spring migration and as year-round residents.

Leaving Ierápetra watch for a newly built circular chapel with dome, an unmissable landmark on the inland side of the main road. The turning is signed for Bramianá and Kalamávka (12km). Where the hothouses begin to peter out you can see the dam ahead. The Kalamávka road sweeps left to run up the west side of the reservoir but if you continue ahead (on a concrete surface) you climb to the east end of the dam and can walk (or drive) across it. A track makes it possible to circumnavigate the reservoir. The best vantage points depend on water levels and on the position of the sun, but the west end of the dam is usually a good starting point. (If you are arriving from the north you will need to watch for a glint of water and a big lay-by where you can get your bearings.)

From the dam you can climb to **Kalamávka** sited in a cleft on the spine of the island. The village is surrounded by 20 or more curious spikes of rock where the hard limestone core of the massif is exposed. There are signs for the *Exotiko kentro Neraida*, a big outdoor taverna with charcoal grill, delightfully situated beside the mountain stream running through the village.

At the watershed just to the north of Kalamávka, on the way to Prína and the E4 walking route, there is a particularly fine view taking in both coastlines. A great variety of orchids flourishes early in the year in this hilly terrain.

The junction in Kalamávka offers a recommended road first south to Anatolí (the taverna *Dryres*, café-bars and a direct return route to the coast) and then west to Máles.

Moní Panayías Exakoústis (the Virgin Renowned), dedicated to the Nativity of the Virgin (feast day 8 September), lies 2km outside Máles on the Anatolí road. Now operating as a nunnery, this 19C foundation was twice dissolved before being brought back to life in the 1960s. Except for the original rock-cut chapel the buildings have no great age. The scented garden on a pine-covered hillside offers a memorable view of the Mýrtos valley.

Máles is a big rambling village spread out across the head of the valley at a height of 580m on the well-watered slopes of Mount Díkte. You can park on the main street by the sign for the post office and explore on foot. There are café-bars and the welcoming taverna **To Steki**.

There is a shepherds' track over the mountains from Máles to the Katharó plain above Kritsá (near Ayios Nikólaos) but for the marked route to join the E4 it is easiest to continue westward 2km from the village and leave a vehicle at the end of the asphalt at **Khristós**. The E4 then takes you up to the forested hillside around **Selakáno**, on the age-old traditional way to the summit of Mount Díkte (2148m). This is serious mountain walking.

To return to the coast near Mýrtos there is a choice of dirt roads down one of the most beautiful valleys on Crete; you are never far from the river. Or you can walk from Khristós through **Metaxokhóri**. A surfaced side-road descends to cross the Mýrtos river near **Mýthi** (c 10km from Máles) where you keep left for Mýrtos and the return to Ierápetra, or bear right to join the main road 5km northwest of Mýrtos to proceed west towards Viánnos in the province of Herákleion.

Staying near the coast west from Ierápetra, the main Viánnos road passes behind Mýrtos. Three kilometres before the village you come to **Néa Mýrtos** where a domed cruciform chapel is a landmark on a knoll at the edge of the pebble beach. Across the road, on the hill beyond the bridge, at the far west end of the bay, is the first of two Minoan sites.

Mýrtos Phournoú Koryphí

The Early Bronze Age settlement above Néa Mýrtos is known as Phournoú Koryphí, the traditional name of the summit on which it stands. There is no official access to the site but to view it from outside the fence the best route for the steep climb (about 10 minutes, not clearly marked) starts on the east side of the hill. From the road you can see the site fence on the cliff skyline. Take the path beside a gully past hothouses under the cliff. At the top cross the gully into an olive grove and then, still heading inland, make your way upwards, across the flank of the hill, to arrive at the fence.

The excavation, by British archaeologists in the 1960s, uncovered c 90 small rooms and passages forming a community of perhaps six family units with single storey houses joined to each other in a dense cellular structure. A circuit wall around the village was probably intended for defence.

The settlement which flourished in the Early Minoan II period (third millennium BC) yielded valuable information about the evolution of rural communities. Seals and sealings from the village could be securely dated to this early time. Study of the material from the site established evidence for the farming of cereals, olives, and vines and the herding of sheep, goats, cattle and pigs. There was equipment for weaving and potting, and for making wine and olive oil.

An area at the southwest corner of the site was recognised as a domestic shrine, one of the earliest yet known to exhibit elements of Minoan religion. The clay figurine of a goddess holding a miniature jug typical of the shapes found in the village is prominently displayed in the Ayios Nikólaos museum, with examples of the site's 700 clay vases and other objects relating to daily life, including a potter's wheel. The village was destroyed by fire at the end of EMII (c 2200 BC) and was not rebuilt.

Mýrtos Pýrgos

The second Minoan site is high above the road just before it reaches the village of Mýrtos. Excavations here, also by British archaeologists, uncovered a small provincial settlement of long duration during Minoan times. The elegance of its architecture reflected the prosperity demonstrated by the work of potters and other craftsmen now on display in the museum in Ayios Nikólaos.

A hill called Pýrgos (tower) on account of the watchtower built during the Turkish occupation overlooks the coast and the Mýrtos river valley with an arched Venetian bridge in the middle distance. The Minoan settlement now known as Mýrtos Pýrgos spread over the summit of this hill. The path to the top (well marked by whitewashed stones) starts near the bridge on the main road, striking uphill (for 10 minutes) from the track beside the river bed.

There was Prepalatial (EMII) settlement, contemporary with the village at Phournoú Koryphí, and destruction by fire at the same time but, unlike Phournoú Koryphí, Mýrtos Pýrgos was reoccupied and the Minoan village continued to develop on the slopes of the hill. The remains of a communal tomb and a stretch of paved road survive from this time.

By the Neopalatial (LMI) period (following another destruction by fire) the settlement was dominated by an elegant building on the summit which faced across a court to the sea. This house consisted of two or possibly three storeys; the lower one, cut into the rock of the hilltop, is what you see today. The design of the building makes clever use of the natural rock and the small space available, and there are decorative features such as gypsum and ashlar masonry and colour contrasts in the floors and courtyard.

MYRTOS PYRGOS
Minoan Villa

0 metres   5

after Cadogan

As you stand on the summit a stepped **street** (1 on plan) leads up the eastern slope of the hill from the area of the Minoan village along an ashlar façade to the paved **courtyard** (2). The plaster-lined **cistern** (3) with an estimated capacity of 23 tonnes dates from the Protopalatial period, but when the court was laid out it was filled with river pebbles, and acted as an ornamental soak-away for storm water. A raised **walk** (4) of flagstones bordered in purple limestone ran along the front of the house's gypsum-floored **verandah** (5) which had two wooden columns on purple limestone bases either side of a pillar. (The pits were cut in the 19C to quarry the ashlar masonry for reuse.) A column base and edging of purple limestone (6) indicates where a small pavilion or **shrine** would have completed an L-shaped façade for the courtyard.

The main entrance to the **house** (7) was from the court, at the west end of the verandah. It opened into a passage which led to a **staircase** (8) to an upper floor which would have been nearly at ground-level at the top of the hill. In the passage and the three rock-cut basements beside it the archaeologists found gypsum slabs which had fallen from this first floor, also the contents of a household shrine. With the slabs were a Linear A tablet (apparently recording 90 units of wine), two clay sealings, a conch shell of pink faience and four clay tubular stands for offerings. Typically these finds point to the close association in Minoan society between administration and religion.

Past the staircase the passage arrives at a **light-well** (9) and across from this there is a **bench** (10). At the bottom of the stairs was a stone basin. Both staircase and bench are of gypsum, a material susceptible to weathering, and both have been covered for protection. The staircase, which showed no signs of wear, was separated from the light-well by a stepped parapet with evidence for wooden columns in an arrangement recalling in a modest form the Grand Staircase at Knossós. The bench had gypsum back panels, and below the seat triglyph decoration imitating carved wood. Beside the bench a rock-cut **pantry** (11) held a large tub and a quantity of plain cups.

The floor of the light-well, of purple limestone set in white plaster, sloped to a central basin. Since the walls of the light-well were of gypsum rather than the more usual ashlar it is suggested that overhanging eaves directed rainwater straight into this basin. Also found hereabouts was a fragment of a stone vase, of interest because it was carved from obsidian from a source in the Dodecanese islands.

In the east wing of the house a second entrance opening from the street up from the village, led into a **passage** (12) and behind the ashlar façade to **storerooms** (13 and 14) which contained large pithoi; clay and stone vessels, found in the street among the debris resulting from the fire, pointed to the existence of a grander room above. The storerooms would have contained highly combustible material. The fire which destroyed the house at the end of the Neopalatial period (LMIB) was so fierce that it splintered the ashlar masonry, vitrified pottery and fired mud bricks (as well as the Linear A tablet), and yet it did not touch the houses of the surrounding settlement.

If you walk round the hill to the north side (starting down the stepped street (1), and then turning left along the contour of the east slope) you will come to a deep cistern dating from the Old Palace period, the largest of its kind known from Minoan Crete. When it burst over the edge of the hill it was not repaired, so that from then on all water had to be carried up from the valley below. Above the path are terrace walls and the lower courses of what may have been a defensive tower.

The site footpath (that takes you round to the west slope of the Pýrgos hill and eventually back down to the road) passes a well-preserved stretch of **paved street** which leads to the remains of a **two-storey communal tomb**. Both features date to the end of the Prepalatial period, but the tomb continued in use, probably intermittently, through to the Neopalatial (LMI) period. It opens on to a small paved courtyard reached by steps. Outside the tomb, north and south of it, there were two ossuaries; a large jar of bones surrounded by neatly stacked skulls was found in the southern one.

Mýrtos

The coastal village of Mýrtos is a recommended place to stay, especially outside the high season, during a tour around the island. It also makes a good base for a walking holiday in the Mýrtos valley and the mountains behind. You are in easy reach of the pine-scented countryside along the Viánnos road and around the sanctuary site high on Mount Díkte above Káto Sýme, just within the province of Herákleion.

Travel agency

Magic Tours, ☎ 28420 25135, in the centre of the village, will help with visitors' requirements, including currency exchange and, in case of difficulty, accommodation.

Where to stay

C *Mýrtos* (16 rooms), ☎ 28420 51227, fax 28420 512215, www.mirtoshotel.com, email: egp1@otenet.gr. This small, family-run hotel on the main street behind the beach was completely refurbished in 1998 to a high standard of comfort.

There are numerous establishments offering **rooms to rent** in the village and modern **self-catering apartments** on the main road cutting across inland of it.

Eating out

Tavernas line the short promenade recently built out from the shore, The old-fashioned *Katerina* on the way down to it keeps to a traditional menu. On the main street the taverna attached to the *Hotel Mýrtos* is rightly popular.

An unsurfaced road follows the coast west, rough in places for vehicles but a recommended route for walkers (especially bird watchers early in the year), through the hamlet of Tértsa and on to Arvi in the province of Herákleion.

From the isthmus of Ierápetra to Siteía

From Pakheiá Ammos on the Bay of Mirábello it is 45km east on the north coast highway to Siteía.

Kavoúsi

Kavoúsi is an attractive village with noteworthy Byzantine churches within its confines and two archaeological sites of major interest in the hills behind. It could make a base for a few days during a walking holiday to explore the paths to the south into the Thryptí mountains. Rooms to rent are advertised west of the crossroads on the main through road and there is a choice of tavernas.

To explore the village turn inland at the crossroads (near the big modern church) into a street leading uphill to the plateía. Ask here for directions, and keys if necessary, to **Ayios Yeóryios**, which has elegant 14C frescoes (quite well-preserved), and **Ayii Apóstoli** where particular interest attaches to frescoes illustrating the transition to the style known as the Cretan School of painting.

Up behind the village several archaeological sites were briefly excavated at the beginning of the last century by Harriet Boyd (later Boyd Hawes); her discoveries included two major settlement sites, on an intermediate ridge at **Vrónda** (meaning thunder) and high above that around the **Kástro**, the pinnacle conspicuous from the main road. In 1901 Boyd began to explore the Minoan town of Gourniá, and Kavoúsi returned to relative obscurity. In the last 20 years the area has been systematically re-examined by a team from the American School of Classical Studies in Athens, with attention centred on these two settlement sites which date from the end of the Bronze Age and the Early Iron Age.

The sites lie along and overlooking the old road up to the Thryptí plain, the pass between the southern part of the isthmus and the far east of Crete. Thanks to a millennium project organised by the American School, signs and presentation panels now help visitors find the excavations and to understand them.

Walking in the hills behind Kavoúsi

There is a choice of routes for the walk up to the two sites. The romantic route follows the old traditional *kalderími*, still roughly paved in places; allow 45 minutes to Vrónda and twice that to the Kástro. The *kalderími* would take you (in altogether more than five hours of strenuous walking) over from Kavoúsi to the upland valley of Thryptí, and on to Monastiráki (p 246) above the isthmus of Ierápetra.

The longer way is by a dirt track, not recommended for the average hire-car but kept in tolerable repair for shepherds' trucks or for reaching the chapels in the hills. The track leaves the main road just before the bridge at the eastern end of Kavoúsi. At the only doubtful fork (nearly at the site) keep right, past the Ministry of Culture sign; the excavation will be on your left. Flower enthusiasts will enjoy all this countryside and the great variety of orchids early in the year.

The traditional route from the top of the village is waymarked as it climbs into the hills crossed in places by the dirt track. When a church (Panayía Kardiótissa) is in view above left, with the Kástro pinnacle towering behind it, watch for a split in the path. The *kalderími* continues ahead, but for Vrónda follow signs right, uphill. In five minutes the church of **Ayía Paraskeví** comes into view, with the old cottages of the summer-pasturage village of Vrónda on the skyline to the right. A path between them leads over the hill (five minutes) to the excavation which is fenced but accessible.

At **Vrónda** there is archaeological evidence of activity as far back as the Late Neolithic, and again in Early and Middle Minoan times, but what you can make out now used to be a sizeable settlement (c 60m by 40m) of Postpalatial (Late Minoan IIIC, 12C BC) date. On the ridge the large building with a paved court on its south side, named by Boyd '**The House on the Summit**' and now known as Building A, appears to have been abandoned peacefully during the succeeding Subminoan period. In the north part of the court a flat stone *kérnos* has 24 small circular depressions set in an oval ring; similar objects at other sites (Gourniá, Mália) have usually been interpreted as cult-related offering tables, but a gaming use has also been suggested. A cobbled street ran west from the court, and structures on its southeast side are interpreted as basement storerooms, with one area for the preparation of meals. The massive wall here is a terrace wall rather than a defensive one. A kiln also belongs to this period.

On the southwest slope of the ridge a shrine building was uncovered, with some of the furnishings still in situ. Beside a bench along the east wall were six nearly complete snake tubes and seven *kálathoi* (vases in the shape of a basket), one decorated with horns of consecration, another with snakes modelled inside it. There were fragments of the torso of a goddess with upraised hands. The earlier discovery of similar fragments of Late Minoan IIIC goddess figurines had suggested the existence of a shrine; now the conservators have evidence for at least 17 such figurines.

On the north slope just below the settlement and associated with it were a number of small stone-built tholos tombs with chambers approached by a short trench or abbreviated *dromos*.

There has been some erosion of the ridge, and the picture is further confused by reuse of the area as a cemetery in the Late Geometric period. Study of these 8C BC burials has added new information about funeral ceremonies and burial practices. In some cases the Bronze Age tholos tombs were reused, but there are also cist graves, in two of which a cremation burial was followed by an inhumation. Remains of pyres showed that cremations sometimes took place in the abandoned Bronze Age houses, with the bones and grave gifts afterwards roughly covered; there were also secondary burials with the already cremated bones brought there to be covered by stones or a pithos.

In contrast to the sparse offerings in the earlier tholos tombs these 8C burials were accompanied by a surprisingly rich array of iron tools and weapons. The intriguing question remains as to whether these people lived in some as yet undiscovered settlement on the ridge. The Kástro was still occupied in the 8C but it is unlikely that the inhabitants came down this far to bury their dead.

To continue to the **Kástro**, the peak towering above Vrónda, you will need to retrace your steps to Ayía Paraskeví (or use the path back to the *kalderími* on the eastern side of the site). The main route to the Kástro passes in front of the chapel and rejoins the old paved way, climbing steadily. When this reaches the head of a cultivated valley it turns right, away from the site, on its way to Thryptí. Leave the *kalderími* and cross the valley, left, on a terraced path making for the saddle behind the pinnacle for the approach to the summit round the further flank. The view here at a height of 710m is stunning, and the strenuous walk from the village is highly recommended, quite apart from the archaeological interest.

The refuge site on the Kástro clings to a jutting pinnacle which commands one of the passes into the hills behind, and inevitably this provokes speculation about why such a precipitous position was chosen. Successive generations built and rebuilt here despite the structural problems compounded by earthquake damage.

There is evidence for settlement on the Kástro in the LMIIIC period (12C), and notable expansion during the Late Geometric period, especially on the saddle on the seaward side of the main peak; part of the site was still occupied in the Orientalising period (early 7C BC).

The original 1900 excavation on the main peak revealed houses occupying narrow terraces around the pinnacle, of much more regular construction than at Vrókastro (p 242). Each complex is carefully rectangular, and large blocks are employed in foundations and doorways; there were stone benches outside the houses either in the alleys or in small private courts.

The recent excavations have greatly enlarged the scope of the investigation, and have shown that the Kástro settlement extended across the saddle to the false peak to the northwest, and on terraces down the slopes overlooking the coast. Late Geometric buildings were found 100m inland (south) of the settlement on the summit.

On the west slope the earliest (LMIIIC) levels show that the occupants exploited the wide natural fissures there, using the inner rock wall for the back of their dwellings. On the terraces of the eastern slope interest attaches to a room where two centrally aligned column bases were found with a hearth between them, an arrangement recalling the temple at Dréros. A little to the north of this, on the most precipitous part of the east slope, movement between the various levels of the long narrow terraces may have depended on wooden ladders.

The many interesting finds included a number of small female figurines of an unusually crude unpainted type, also a stone *kérnos*. Scientific studies on the material are continuing so that contexts can be available for the study of bones, stone artefacts and shells which will contribute to an understanding of the sequence of activity at this remarkable settlement.

From Kavoúsi the main road climbs high above the coast. 4km towards Siteía at **Plátanos** a café and the taverna *Panorama* enjoy a superb view across to the island of **Pseíra** from tables on the seaward side of the road. To date there are no regular excursions to the island from Ayios Nikólaos. It is possible (but not cheap) to hire a fishing boat to visit the island from Mókhlos.

The American archaeologist Richard Seager excavated on the island in the first years of the 20C. He uncovered a prosperous Minoan settlement of Prepalatial date (founded in EMI with evidence for use in the Final Neolithic) and continuously occupied until its destruction in LMIB. The settlement overlooked an anchorage facing south-southeast which was well protected from the prevailing winds of late summer. It was built on terraces on the sheltering peninsula and the hill to the north of the harbour. In 1985, a Cretan and American collaboration recommenced and the work has resulted in a definitive plan of the town which by the end of its life (in LMIB) consisted of 60 buildings, some with many rooms on several terraced levels. These houses were divided into blocks by streets and stairs including a long flight of steps up from the harbour to an open court at the top. There was a town shrine with fine frescoes. In the cemetery 19 tombs were recorded. Finds from the site including imported pottery of high quality are in the archaeological museums in Herákleion and Siteía.

Mókhlos

There are several roads signposted down to Mókhlos, an attractive fishing village catering for tourists but still on quite a small scale. This was the site of a harbour settlement in the Bronze Age. You can detour to the coast for a meal on the waterfront and a swim from the pebble beach, or to be ferried across to the rocky islet to see the Minoan excavations, but Mókhlos can also be recommended for a longer stay.

Going east from Plátanos the first road left turns down by a gypsum quarry; another starts from the village of **Spháka** (c 30km from Siteía). On foot the 7km walk down to Mókhlos from the bus stop in Spháka can be shortened by using footpaths for part of the way. On the descent the coastal plain soon comes into view, with the modern settlement at the western end of the bay opposite the small island 200m offshore.

Getting to the island
There is often rough water and a current in the strait, but in calm weather a local boatman will ferry you across; ask at the taverna *Ta Kokhylia* on the harbour front.

Travel agency
Barbarossa, on the main street behind the harbour, will change money, hire bikes and help with finding a room. You could enquire here about organised walks with a botanist guide, or ☎ Anne Lebrun 0843 94725.

Where to stay and eating out
D *Sofia* (5 rooms) ☎ 28430 94554, fax 28430 94238. Simple but comfortable accommodation above one of the best tavernas on the harbour; ask for a sea view.

E *Mokhlos* (9 rooms), ☎ 28430 94205. Small hotel at the end of the village street known for its friendly welcome.

In the summer season, or when archaeologists are at work here, Mókhlos may be surprisingly full, but at other times there are plenty of **rooms**, well advertised.

For a taverna most visitors make for one of the four attractively sited on the waterfront looking across to the island.

Through the village and at the far end of the beach to the west of it, the taverna *Sta Limenaria* rents out well-equipped studio rooms.

History
Mókhlos was an important settlement in Minoan times. The island is believed to have been attached to the mainland by a narrow spit, and this would have made for a versatile harbour with particular shelter from the prevailing northwest winds. Along the shoreline to the east of the modern village, Roman fishtanks that are now fully submerged point to a considerable rise in sea level since the 3C AD.

In 1908 the American Richard Seager excavated settlement remains on the island which dated chiefly from the Neopalatial period, with evidence for earlier Prepalatial occupation, but his most exciting finds came from a cemetery area on the western side of the island. He found tombs of Prepalatial date (in use from Early Minoan II to Middle Minoan IA) built against the cliff and resembling house structures.

Burial gifts from the richest tombs, presumably those of the local rulers, included spectacular jewellery and sealstones, silver cups, the earliest faience as well as one of the finest collections of stone vases known from Minoan Crete. The materials include rock-crystal, marble, steatite and brecchia (see the displays in the Ayios Nikólaos and Siteía museums).

In recent years work has begun again at Mókhlos as part of a programme of collaboration between Greek and American archaeologists. The new excavations have opened further tombs in the cemetery (some reused in Neopalatial times) with particular attention paid to the associated funerary

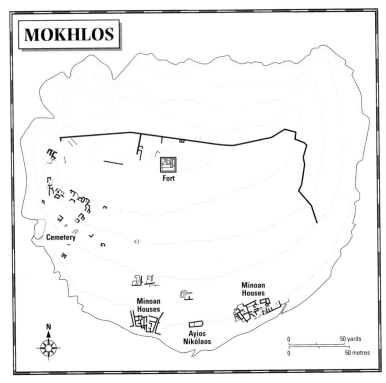

cult. The Prepalatial settlement on the island (beneath Seager's Neopalatial houses) has been investigated, revealing a paved street. The street system of the Neopalatial settlement has also been uncovered with at least three houses found with their contents still intact.

The discovery of a Late Minoan IB settlement on the mainland, behind the modern village, with a bench shrine and evidence for workshops for the production of bronze artefacts, stone vases and pottery is taken to indicate the arrival of new settlers at this time. Two kilns had stoking chambers full of olive pits, a fuel that, as the excavators note, is still used in Cretan kilns today.

All the new evidence (from the pottery sequence and the findings of volcanic ash in the stratigraphy) supports the argument that the Minoan civilisation continued to flourish on Crete during the LMIB period, long after the major volcanic eruption on the island of Théra. This settlement was destroyed by fire at the end of LMIB, as were so many other sites across Crete. The unusual factor at Mókhlos was that human skeletons were found in the destruction debris.

Some reoccupation took place in the Postpalatial period, the time of Mycenaean influence. A house has been identified on the island and there was a cemetery on the mainland. Among the 29 known tombs the variety in mortuary practices may reflect a socially mixed or a highly stratified population.

In later times there were fortifications above the island's northern cliff with evidence for towers behind an east–west curtain wall. The largest tower, at the high point on the island, has been shown to date from the 2C or 1C BC, shortly before the Roman occupation of Crete. Mókhlos was occupied in the Early Byzantine period and the wall may have continued in use as a defence against Arab raiders.

The white chapel of Ayios Nikólaos is a useful landmark on the island and presentation panels add interest to the visit. The excavations of the Neopalatial settlement lie on either side of the chapel, looking back to the mainland. The largest house exposed by Seager is on the east side: the main entrance to the south led to a lightwell with bench, a main room and stairs to an upper floor. West of the chapel, a building designed with ashlar façades is understood as the administrative centre of the settlement. It was terraced in three storeys against the hillside and had pillar crypts on the lowest floor.

The Early Minoan cemetery is signed on a path west from the landing place. On the terraces, in addition to two rock-shelter tombs, there are upwards of 20 house-tombs. Some have doorways which could be closed with large stone slabs, and they would have had flat roofs of reeds and clay. The most important group of tombs opened on to a paved court with an outdoor altar. The walk up to the remains of the fort is worthwhile for the view of the bay that it would have protected.

Beyond Spháka the highway, planted with cypress and oleander, continues past a number of villages along the foothills of Mount Ornón. The road skirts Myrsíni where the church terrace enjoys a splendid view.

On a hill near the sea, north of Myrsíni, 12 rock-cut chamber tombs of the Postpalatial period (LMIII) were excavated in 1960; the grave goods included a rich variety of vases, weapons and utensils now on show in the Ayios Nikólaos Museum, including the goddess figurine on a drum base shown in Room III.

Also on the slopes below Myrsíni a much earlier circular tomb, the first (and one of the few) of the Mesará type to be found in eastern Crete, contained over 60 burials dated by associated finds to the end of the Prepalatial period.

The road crosses a high spur to **Mésa Moulianá**. Two tholos tombs excavated nearby in the first years of the 20C were Late Minoan III tombs reused during the Protogeometric period. The rich LMIII grave offerings included a gold mask, bronze vessels and a sword reflecting the Mycenaean influence, but of particular interest was a Protogeometric (10C BC) bell-krater with on one side a scene of a huntsman pursuing two wild goats (probably the *agrími*), on the other a man on horseback, the first such representation known from Crete (Herákleion Museum, Room X).

Khamaízi

Ruined stone windmills are a landmark on the last crest before the Bay of Siteía comes into view. For a short detour to the Minoan site of Khamaízi (recommended as a 15-minute walk but possible by car) a signed track leaves the road, right, and keeps right again beyond the converted mill.

The fenced site is visible from a distance, on the flat top of a conical hill with panoramic views of the Piskoképhalo valley, a location with obvious advantages as a look-out post. The remains on view at Khamaízi, dated to MMIA, towards the end of the Prepalatial period, are intriguing because this is the only Minoan building so far discovered that is roughly oval in plan. First excavated in 1903 and rein-

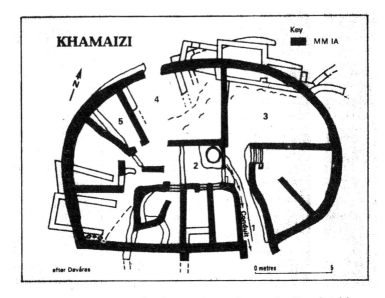

vestigated in 1971 it proved to be superimposed on earlier Prepalatial houses encircling the hilltop.

The complex had a **paved entrance** from the southeast (**1** on plan). The rooms are set around a small **courtyard** also paved (**2**), within a thick perimeter wall, an arrangement which no doubt offered some protection from the fierce winds which sweep across this eastern tip of the island. Raised in the northeast corner of the court is a deep circular cistern, or well, lined with masonry; the conduit system can still be traced.

Three figurines now in the Herákleion Museum, Room II, probaby furnished a small household **shrine** for an area (**3**) northeast from the court contained a movable hearth and fragments of a clay altar. A subsidiary **north entrance** leads into the room (**4**) where the walls were faced with schist and limestone, and adjacent (**5**) was a **staircase** to an upper floor.

In the village of Khamaízi there is a small **Folk Museum**; the display includes a rare type of loom. Opening hours are erratic: in theory 09.00–13.00 and in high season 17.00–19.00. It is best to park on the main road and follow the signs into the village on foot. You may have to ask for the guardian.

East of Khamaízi **Skopí** is below the road right and soon a turning is signed for a detour to **Moní Phaneroméni** near the coast (not to be confused with the convent in the hills behind Gourniá). The peace of the countryside has been disturbed by major engineering works on a new stretch of road to serve the enlarged Siteía airport but you can still walk or drive on tracks, surfaced in places, c 5km out to the coast. (Walkers based in Siteía can benefit from the Ayios Nikólaos bus service.) At the coast the track runs west below white cliffs and towards the western end of the bay the monastery is signed a short distance inland. The former monastic buildings are now disfigured by a huddle of modern ones but the dramatically sited church of the Venetian period, perched on the edge of a ravine looking down to the sea, is unscathed.

The little church dedicated to the Panayía Phaneroméni (the Virgin revealed or made manifest) is built on a north–south axis over a grotto traditionally associated with the miraculous appearance of an icon of Mary; the grotto is still revered. The remains of frescoes are preserved, one panel with a graffito date of 1465.

The main road comes to a wide junction where a newly constructed road sets off left to sweep round the airport and (avoiding the town centre) to approach the port of Siteía from the north. On the east side of the junction you will notice the bottling plant of a Wine Cooperative offering a tour of the premises and an exhibition of local products (with tasting sessions and the opportunity to buy). Keeping straight ahead on the old route you drop down into the town turning left at the waterfront into the main plateía.

Siteía

Siteía is the harbour town and the commercial centre for this extreme eastern end of the island. A much less hectic setting for a holiday than Ayios Nikólaos, it is recommended as a base for exploring the region.

The moorings for fishing boats and a new marina for private yachts are tucked into the western corner of a wide bay with the quays for larger vessels to the north under the sheltering headland. Stretching eastwards around the bay is a long beach of sand and shingle ending in smooth rocks.

The town centre is on the harbour around Plateía Iróon Polytekhníou (see plan). North of this the tree-shaded waterfront is lined with tavernas and attractively colour-washed houses rise steeply, tier on tier, behind. A broad stepped street (Metakháki) leads up the hillside to the red-domed **episcopal church** of Ayía Aikateríni on Gabr. Arkadíou. This street runs out to a small (much restored) Venetian **fort**, known as the Kazárma. From a terrace there are rewarding views of the bay and the hills of eastern Crete. In summer the fort is used as an outdoor theatre.

Siteía's excellent **Folklore Museum** is located in an old house straight uphill from Plateía Iróon Polytekhníou while the **Archaeological Museum** is a short distance inland (five minutes on foot) beside the main road into town. Beyond the taverna tables on the waterfront the Port Authority building and **Customs House** are conspicuous. Cretan sultanas have traditionally been exported through Siteía, but now the region is becoming known throughout Crete and beyond for the quality of its wine. A lively festival takes place on the quays in August.

The old waterfront walk north of the Customs House comes to a point where it has to divert a few paces inland. Among the rocks here, just below the present sea-level, are the remains of tanks cut during the Roman period to store live fish. Through a picturesque archway straight ahead you can make out the cuttings which are comparable with those at Khersónisos and Mókhlos. A stretch of road has been built out into the harbour to allow traffic to reach the cargo port area without negotiating the unsuitably narrow streets of the 19C town; the new layout avoided damaging the Roman tanks.

Leaving Siteía in this direction a fine new 5km swathe of highway runs in an arc across the cape to the north, linking airport and harbour, and creating a ring-road from a junction on the route from central Crete.

Practical information

Travel and transport
By air

The airport, ☎ 28430 24666, is less than ten minutes by taxi from the centre of town. Currently there are two flights a week from Athens. The construction of a new airport capable of handling international flights is behind schedule but it is hoped that it may open in 2004.

Olympic Airways, 4 Septemvríou, near the post office, ☎ 28430 22270.

By car

The main roads from central Crete by the north coast highway and from the south coast come together near the Archaeological Museum before you reach the sea. Follow signs down to the shore where turning left brings you into the central Plateía Iróon Polytekhníou. There is some **parking** here and on the quays. A municipal car park is signed from the coast at the start of the road east.

By sea

The ferry quay at the north end of the harbour is a good five minutes on foot from the centre. Taxis meet the boats. *Lane Lines*, the Lasíthi Shipping Company, ☎ 28430 25555 has started a regular service from Piraeus calling at Mílos and Ayios Nikólaos (five days a week) and continuing twice a week from Siteía to Kásos, Kárpathos and Rhodes.

By bus

The bus station, ☎ 28430 22272, is opposite the entrance to the Archaeological Museum at the junction of the roads from Ayios Nikólaos and across from Ierápetra on the south coast.

By taxi

Taxi rank in Plateía Iróon Polytekhníou.

Tourist information

Run by the municipality, the tourist information office is located on the coast road level with the yacht marina, ☎ and fax 28430 28300.

Tourist police

Just into Therisoú, the road out to Ayios Nikólaos, ☎ 28430 24200.

Travel agencies

Sitia Holidays, Kornárou 83, ☎ 28430 28555, fax 28430 22492.

Tzortzákis Tourism and Shipping Agency (for ferry services), Kornárou 150, ☎ 28430 25080, fax 28430 22731.

Where to stay

Siteía has a small resort hotel, the *Sitia Beach*, but also a number of pleasant, well-equipped hotels of C class, some right on the harbour front, some (perhaps quieter) a little further back from it.

C Castello (16 rooms), ☎ and fax 28430 23763 at Rousseláki 21. Out of the centre towards the ferry quay.

C Denis (13 rooms), ☎ 28430 28356, fax 28430 24953. In sight from Plateía Iróon Polytekhníou above the waterfront tavernas.

C El Greco (15 rooms), ☎ 28430 23133, fax 28430 26391. Uphill on the way to the fort.

C Itanos (72 rooms), ☎ 28430 22146, fax 28430 22915. A well run hotel on the waterfront plateía overlooking the marina. Completely refurbished in 2000 with terrace restaurant and air-condi-

tioning. Open year round.
C *Krystal* (41 rooms), ☎ 28430
22284, fax 28430 28644. Welcoming
and comfortable, just into Kápetan Síphi
(at 17). Open year round.

There are many places offering rooms
and studios to rent. Some of the most
desirable are around the Folklore
Museum on Kápetan Síphi, for example
Pension Anna or *Pension Venus*. Others
are out to the northeast above the ferry
quay on E. Rouseláki; you could start at
the family-run hotel *Pension Nora* (at
31).

Youth hostel

At the start of Therisoú near the outskirts of town on the right of the road in
from Ayios Nikólaos, this hostel has a
good reputation,

Eating out

In summer tourists naturally make for
the harbourside tavernas north of the
Hotel Denis.
Zorba is long-established but there is
fierce competition all along the front.
O Mikhos, just back from the front, on
Kornárou, is popular, especially for out-
of-season eating when good food is more
important than a waterside location.
Kalí Kardia, an *oúzeri* on Phoundalídou,
recommended for its *mezédes*, is uphill
from the main plateía, across Kornárou
and to the right.
Creta Beach taverna is along from the
Hotel Itanos (which itself has a pleasant
café).
Steki, round the corner on the double-
carriageway (A. Papandréou), is an
excellent *psistariá* for grilled meats.

Out of town in **Ayía Photiá**, 5km
east along the bay, *Taverna Neromylos*
is up the hillside in a picturesque
location with a fine view (not improved

by new buildings).
Taverna Panorama is on the main road
below the Neromylos. Cretans drive long
distances to enjoy the traditional cooking here, which is sufficient recommendation.

Banks

National Bank, Plateía Iróon
Polytekhníou, on the corner of Kápetan
Síphi, with automatic currency
exchange.
Commercial Bank, immediately across
the street from the National Bank.

Post office and telephones

Post office on Dimokritoú between E.
Venizélou and 4 Septembríou.
OTE, telephones and fax, on Kondiláki,
straight uphill from the National Bank.

Hospital

South of the Ayios Nikólaos road on the
outskirts of town, ☎ 28430 24312.

Shopping

There is a useful *períptero* (kiosk) in
Plateía Iróon Polytekhníou and a big
supermarket next to the bus station,
opposite the Archaeological Museum
which stocks a particularly good range
of Cretan wines. (To visit the local wine
cooperative which has a retail outlet, see
p 265.)

The main shopping street in the town
is Kornárou, one block up from the
waterfront. Apart from tavernas and
travel agents you will find a bookshop, a
shop selling Cretan spices, herbs and
other local produce, and (at 148) *Sitian
Arts* which specialises in high class
locally made craft work of all descriptions; this has a second outlet at Ayía
Photiá on the Zákros road.

History

Archaeologists have found signs of a Neolithic presence dating back to the
fourth millennium BC (Final Neolithic with similarities to the Neolithic of the
Dodecanese archipelago) at various points around the bay. In Minoan times

there was settlement on the hill at Petrás 1km east of the modern harbour (p 271). There have been major excavations at this site in recent years, with exciting results. The Siteía Archaeological Museum displays the new material with up-to-date background information.

The Greco-Roman period is not well documented; a town of Eteía is mentioned by the 6C Greek geographer Stephanos of Byzantium but without a precise location. There has certainly been a settlement on the present site of Siteía since the First Byzantine period, before the 9C Arab conquest.

The Genoese were briefly in control here early in the 13C, and are known to have strengthened existing fortifications during the confused period after the sack of Constantinople (1204) by the Christian armies of the Fourth Crusade. Under Venetian rule Siteía flourished as a fully walled city; the Kazárma, now restored at the top of the town, is one of the forts of this wall.

The Venetian city was twice damaged by earthquake and frequently by Turkish raids until, in 1539, it was sacked by the famous Turkish corsair, Khair-ed-Din Barbarossa. When the Turks blockaded the city in 1648, the Venetians forcibly evacuated the reluctant population to safety inland. The walls of the *kastro* held out for three years, but the town was left utterly destroyed and lay in ruins for two centuries. In 1870 the Turkish authorities decided to establish an administrative centre here. The town was rebuilt, but now little more than its regular street-plan survives.

Erotókritos

Siteía is proud of its association with the Hellenised Venetian family of Kornaros, distinguished in the spheres of art and learning. Its most famous member is Vitzéntzos Kornáros, who was born in the neighbourhood in 1533. He was the author of the 16C epic poem, *Erotókritos*, which is acknowledged as one of the supreme achievements of Cretan literature.

The story came originally from a medieval French romance popular throughout Europe as an archetypal example of idealised courtly love. Kornáros probably came across it in an Italian version. The principal characters of the tale are Princess Aretusa, daughter of Herakles, King of Athens, and Erotókritos, the son of one of his courtiers. Within the stylised conventions of the epic-romantic poem Kornáros constructed a huge work of 10,000 rhymed 15-syllable lines which allows space for philosophical digressions, descriptions, the analysis of emotions and reflection on underlying meanings often only thinly disguised.

The poem may be understood on many levels. The theme of national pride was a powerful unifying force wherever Cretans gathered, and *Erotókritos* often helped to keep hope alive during the centuries of foreign rule. It was important in this context that the poet had used and developed the Cretan dialect.

Many Cretans are said to have memorised the whole poem; numerous verses and quotations with the effect of an instantly recognisable coded language became part of everyday speech as well as the basis for folk songs, recitations and theatrical programmes. It is difficult to exaggerate the power of the work in earlier times, or the regard in which it is still held today throughout Greece, a regard often compared with that for the plays of Shakespeare in the Anglo-Saxon world.

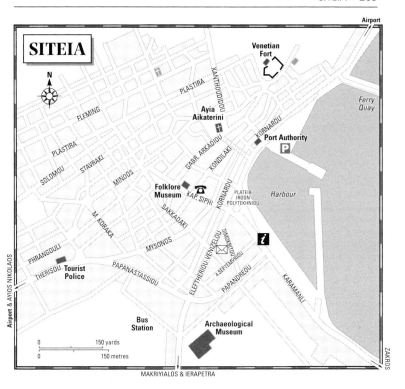

Archaeological Museum

● The museum is away from the seafront near the bus station at the start of the road south across the island. Open Tues–Sun 08.00–14.30, closed Mon, ☎ 0843 23917.

The building is attractively designed around a central court. The material from this eastern end of the island is arranged chronologically and each of the four sections is introduced with helpful background information.

Prominent inside the entrance is the remarkable chryselephantine statuette of a male, or *koúros*, from Palaíkastro (p 279), in characteristic pose with the left leg slightly forward. At least eight pieces of hippopotamus ivory were carved separately and fitted together with dowels; a ninth piece forms an ivory pommel from a missing dagger. A rectangular ivory peg behind the face fits a cavity in the serpentine head. Eyes (not restored) of rock crystal were worked at the back, apparently to take an iris, perhaps a small stone. The scraps of gold seem to have belonged to foot coverings, bracelets and the typical Minoan belt.

A free-standing case contains **Neolithic** material from Pelekitá, a cave on the seaward slope of Mount Traóstalos, north of Zákros, and a display of stone axes.

The **Bronze Age** material begins, left of the entrance, with finds from the cemetery of Ayía Photiá, where more than 250 tombs dating from the Prepalatial period were excavated. Experts note the strong Cycladic character of many of the artefacts emerging from this Early Minoan context; the frying-pan

The Palaíkastro kouros

shapes (also well represented in the Ayios Nikólaos Museum) are a local variation of a type characteristic of the Early Bronze Age in the Cyclades and on the Greek mainland. From the same site there is a good exhibit of obsidian pressure blades.

Next come votive terracottas from Petsophás above Palaíkastro and other Minoan peak sanctuaries (mountain-top shrines). A large proportion of the known sites of this type are located in eastern Crete.

The adjacent free-standing cases contain material from tombs on the offshore islet of Mókhlos and the Minoan settlement on the island of Pseíra, both sites along the coast west of Siteía. A stirrup-jar is a good example of the Neopalatial Marine Style of pottery, and the stone vases are of outstanding quality.

The finds from the current excavations at **Petrás** (east along the bay from Siteía) are exciting much interest in the archaeological world; a note in the free-standing case of exhibits gives an account of the discoveries. Among the Neopalatial material (in cases against the wall) is a display of artefacts from the Minoan town of Palaíkastro. The horns of consecration in stone are shown with a pottery rhyton for ritual use which has the same motif in its decoration. There are also two examples of a *kérnos*, one in clay (four cups) and one in stone (two cups).

The next section is devoted to the **palace of Zákros** but in the corner there is a well-preserved wine-press from the Late Minoan I country house just outside the modern village of Ano Zákros. The equipment was found with a pithos inscribed in Linear A (now in the Zákros room in the Herákleion Museum). The rest of this section illustrates various aspects of life in the Minoan palace. The exhibit of Linear A script is a reminder of the palace's administrative function. Giant pithoi emphasise the importance of storage and distribution in the palace economy. (Some large pots show signs of burning from the great fire which finally destroyed the palace c 1450 BC.) There is a selection of Minoan cooking pots and basins and then the cases showing the fine wares, including a good display of spouted jars. There are lamps and stone offering-tables, and a free-standing case brings together objects associated with Minoan cult practices: horns of consecration, double-axe stands, some of the *kérnos* vessels and also a scorched alabastron, a further reminder of the final conflagration.

The **Geometric and Archaic section** has material from cemeteries in the area and a display of Daidalic terracotta heads and figurines, a chance find during roadworks in the centre of modern Siteía. Daidalic sculpture also came from an Archaic sanctuary at Roússa Eklissiá in the hills behind the bay.

The last section is devoted to the **Hellenistic and Roman periods** when there were major settlements in the area, such as Xerókambos, south of Zákros, and Itanos at the northeast corner of the island. There is an intriguing display covering the small island of Kouphonísi (p 294) off the southeastern corner of Crete, where a flourishing settlement seems to have owed its existence to the preparation of dye (a purple or deep crimson) extracted from a gland in the shell-fish *Murex trunculus*.

Folklore Museum

• Siteía's excellent Folklore Museum is five minutes on foot straight uphill from the plateía, on the right-hand side halfway up Kápetan Síphi. Open Tues–Sat 09.30–14.30, and, Tues only, again 17.00–20.00, ☎ 28430 22861.

This ethnographic collection was started a quarter of a century ago by the Vitséntzos Kornáros Educational and Cultural Society of Siteía. After many vicissitudes it is now established in an attractive and well-restored period house.

The interiors are particularly well arranged, with traditional Cretan furniture and equipment. The collection concentrates on the domestic crafts of weaving, embroidery, lacemaking and woodcarving, exhibiting both the products and the equipment used to make them. In the bedroom the antique bedhangings of hand-spun and woven silk are as fine as any you will see on the island.

The museum society encourages the continuation of craftwork and the traditional skills in the Siteía community, and tries to keep for sale a supply of contemporary work, usually pieces following the old designs.

East of Siteía

The main road east from Siteía peters out at the archaeological site of the Minoan palace at **Zákros** (p 282). By the direct way it is 50km, but a recommended circular route (c 70km) takes in the fortified monastery of **Toploú**, the famous palm-fringed beach at **Vái**, the Minoan harbour at **Palaíkastro**, and the site of ancient **Itanos**, a powerful city-state in Greco-Roman times.

Travelling by bus

There are bus services from Siteía to Toploú and Vái, and to Káto Zákros (via Palaíkastro) for the palace site.

The Zákros road runs east out of Siteía along the shore. At **Petrás**, on the hill at the end of the bay, archaeologists have been uncovering since 1985 a major Minoan settlement which was exploiting this sheltered stretch of coast in the Bronze Age. The Minoans established two safe harbours either side of the little point here and their settlement covered the entire hill behind. There is as yet, despite the signs, no public access to the site, but material from it is instructively displayed in the Siteía museum.

There was Final Neolithic (c 3500 BC) occupation (with interesting similarities to the Neolithic of the Dodecanese archipelago) at various points on this bay.

The earliest occupation dates back to the Prepalatial (Early Minoan IIB) period. Protopalatial Petrás is known to have traded with other parts of the island and around the Aegean, but the settlement was at its most formidable in Neopalatial times.

On the plateau at the top of the hill was a large building with palatial-style architectural features, a shrine on an upper floor and storerooms where at least 40 pithoi were found. The west slope of the hill was artificially terraced to take roads and two-storey houses, with at the foot of it on the seaward side a fortification wall of monumental construction with large square towers; the wall is preserved in places to a height of 3.5m.

An impressive list of artefacts retrieved from the site includes hundreds of vases (as well as the large pithoi), metal objects, terracotta figurines and a wine press. Potters' marks were detected on some of the vases and other clay objects. The find of a well-preserved Linear A tablet pointed to the existence of an administrative archive.

The site was abandoned in Late Minoan IA following destruction by earthquake (perhaps associated with the volcanic eruption on Théra); only a small part of the hill was reoccupied in the Postpalatial period.

The first village eastwards on the coast road from Siteía is **Ayía Photiá**, where you pass the *Taverna Panorama*, popular for its traditional Cretan cooking. Opposite the taverna is a branch of the *Sitian Arts* craft centre, whose main shop is in Siteía. Around Ayía Photiá there is an important **archaeological area**, although (despite Ministry of Culture signs past the Hotel Maresol) nothing is officially accessible to visitors.

The excavation in 1971 of a large cemetery of the Early Minoan period (EMI-II, first part of the third millennium) on the rise near the sea found evidence for more than 250 tombs, with multiple burials and a rich variety of grave offerings with bronze and stone artefacts as well as pottery which can be seen in the museums of both Ayios Nikólaos and Siteía. These artefacts showed an unusual degree of Cycladic influence which may point to a colony here.

Some of the graves were simple shallow pits, but most were a primitive form of chamber-tomb. The rock-cut tombs were closed with an upright blocking slab, and many of the distinctive tall pedestalled cups came from small paved antechambers for the cult of the dead.

On the low hill 150m to the west archaeologists uncovered a large (18m x 27.5m) fortified rectangular building with 37 rooms arranged in units which communicate only with a primitive central court. The settlement is dated to a late phase of the Prepalatial period (Middle Minoan IA); nothing like it is known elsewhere in Crete at this time.

At a junction 12km from Siteía the direct road to Palaíkastro and Zákros runs straight on, but the recommended route takes the left turn (signed) to the fortified monastery of Toploú. Out to sea are the **Dionysádes** group of islands, interesting to ornithologists as a breeding ground for the rare Eleonora's Falcon (p 276).

Toploú

Once a solitary feature, a small fortified monastery on barren upland, Toploú has been partially transformed into an ecclesiastical museum with café and shop, and an enthusiastically restored windmill, and has become a regular stop on tours of eastern Crete. The monastery church houses an icon painted in the 18C by a member of the Kornáros family of Siteía which is one of the masterpieces of Cretan art. The monastery is open 09.00–13.00 and 14.00–18.00. Out of season you may be fortunate enough to enjoy it in tranquillity.

Toploú, the Turkish name for the monastery (derived from a cannon installed by the monks in Venetian times as a defence against pirates), has effectively replaced the earlier dedication to the Panayía Akrotiriáni, the Virgin of the Cape. There are records of a 14C church in the locality dedicated to Ayios Isídoros (hence Cape Síderos) and this may have been the original nucleus of later Venetian buildings which have undergone frequent restoration. The Akrotiriáni monastery was fortified at the end of the 16C.

During its chequered history as one of the most influential monasteries on Crete, Toploú acquired great power and wealth, with dependent churches and monastic foundations scattered across the island; it is still a major landowner in eastern Crete. The monastery endured many acts of destruction and plunder by, among others, the Knights of St John of Malta in 1530 and the Turks in 1646, as well as severe earthquake damage in 1612. The monks kept to a tradition of support for the Cretan national cause, and suffered accordingly. During the Second World War the monastery operated an underground radio transmitter, and for this the Abbot Silignákis was executed in the notorious Ayiá jail near Khaniá.

The main entrance is by the Loggia Gate into a reception and workshop area, and then on into the monastery proper through an easily defended double doorway with a massive door operated by a wheel mechanism. The cloister houses (right) a small museum and (left) the bookshop.

At the heart of the monastery is a diminutive cobbled court with a well in the corner. On three sides of the court the monks' cells, the abbot's quarters, and a big refectory are built into the walls which rise to battlements and a tall Italianate bell-tower reconstructed in its present form in 1836. On the fourth side is the double-naved **church**. The visitors' entrance is now through the museum but here in the court the façade attracts attention.

To the left of the main doorway four stone slabs are let into the church wall. One is a relief of the Virgin with Child, Our Lady of the Cape. The two central inscriptions record the pious labours of the Abbot Gabriel Pandógalos who restored the monastery after the 1612 earthquake with financial help from the Venetian senate.

The slab at door level preserves a fragment of an inscription dating to 132 BC known as the **Arbitration of Magnesia**. This city of the Roman Empire in Asia Minor had intervened in a series of territorial disputes between Itanos and first Praisós, then Ierápytna (modern Ierápetra). A central issue in the dispute was the control of the Temple of Diktaian Zeus at Palaíkastro. This inscribed slab was brought to Toploú from Itanos. It was in use as an altar table in the cemetery chapel across the road from the monastery when, in 1834, it was noticed by the English scholar and traveller, Robert Pashley, who suggested its present setting.

The **museum** in the cloister houses icons (15C–18C), manuscripts, and other ecclesiastical treasures of Toploú. One 15C icon is an example of the type known as the *Odiyítria* (the Virgin 'showing the way').

In the monastery church the older of the two naves (the northern one) is dedicated to the Panayía Akrotiriáni, with the southern one to Ayios Ioánnis Theológos, the Evangelist (feast days respectively 8 and 26 September). Frescoes of scenes from the gospels recently uncovered in the older part of the church are dated stylistically to the 14C. The small room on the north side was used in the past by women attending the services.

On an stand between the two altars is the portable icon entitled ***Lord, thou art great***, portraying 61 densely painted scenes each inspired by a phrase from the prayer of the Great Benediction used in the Orthodox liturgy on the feast of Epiphany. Two inscriptions in the lower part of the icon establish the artist, Ioánnis Kornáros, the date, 1770, and the donor, Demétrios, with his wife and children. The prayer begins: 'Great art Thou, O Lord, and marvellous are Thy works, and no word suffices to hymn Thy wonders.' The 6C Patriarch of Jerusalem, Sophronios, kneels to the right of Eve with the text open before him to begin the prayer which is often attributed to him but is more likely to have been composed by Basil the Great, one of the three Cappodocian fathers of the church. The four central themes, from the lowest level upwards are: the ***Descent into Hell***, the ***Mother of God enthroned between Adam and Eve***, the ***Baptism of Christ*** and the ***Holy Trinity surrounded by the Heavenly Hosts***. The intricate organisation of the subordinate scenes, with narrative derived from both the Old and New Testaments, followed a tradition dating back to the time of the Palaiologan emperors before the fall of Constantinople.

In the **cloisters** at the back of the courtyard there is now exhibited an archive of engravings covering a wide range of subjects connected with the history of the Orthodox church in the eastern Mediterranean, and aspects of monastic life including the artistic skills of the monks. The final section deals with the contribution of the monasteries to the long stuggle for the liberation of Crete ending with episodes from the time of German occupation during the Second World War.

The palm trees at Vái

The palm was a decorative motif in Bronze Age art and the grove at Vái was known already in Classical times. The species was first described (4C BC) by Theophrastus, a pupil of Aristotle who made a particular study of natural science and botany.

Phoenix theophrasti greuter is a distinct species closely related to the date palm, although its fruit is smaller, dry and unpalatable. You may be told that this species is restricted solely to eastern Crete, but apparently this is not so. *The Making of the Cretan landscape* (see Recommended reading) points out that these palms are found at many places around the coast of Crete, even if not in such a well-established condition as at Vái. Far from being brought to the island by the Arabs the tree is almost peculiar to Crete, though it does occur occasionally elsewhere around the Aegean, on Rhodes and some other islands, and on the coast of Turkey. Remains have been found in Pleistocene levels of the volcanic ash on Théra where the tree still grows wild.

From Toploú you can return to the direct road for Palaíkastro and Zákros, or continue on the circular route to the coast at Vái.

The road out to the east coast from the monastery of Toploú continues for 6km across uncultivated upland, empty except for the windmills of a wind farm. The project is controversial, not least because of the hazard to birds using this migration corridor. At a T-junction turn left, and after 1km right, signed for the beach at **Vái**, which is famous for its grove of tall palm trees whose trunks can reach a height of 10m.

Offshore rocks shelter a sandy beach at Vái but the days when this was an idyllic place to spend a day are hard to imagine. Because of its exotic reputation Vái attracts disproportionate crowds of visitors. There is a charge for (strictly regulated) parking, and coaches and snack bars dominate the scene. You may like to leave a vehicle out on the coast road and walk in to see the trees, preferably early or late in the day.

Itanos

The coast road continues north a further 3km to the site of ancient Itanos at **Erimoúpolis** (meaning the deserted place). There is a choice of small bays for swimming, either just by the car park or at the end of a track along the site fence to the south.

In Greco-Roman times this was the site of the harbour city of Itanos, one of the most influential ruling cities over a long period at this eastern end of the island, with territory stretching to the south coast including the island of Kouphonísi (Classical Levkí). The anchorage was sheltered from the prevailing northerly winds by Cape Síderos (the Cape Samonion of antiquity where a temple of Athena was consecrated by the Argonauts). The offshore islet of Elása (which also has ancient remains) reinforces the protection.

The site was explored at the end of the 19C and again soon after the Second World War but the results have never been fully published. In the mid-1990s excavation began again. Apart from investigating the urban area the main aims were to clarify the topography of its harbour and to survey the surrounding territory for evidence of habitation and features such as terrace systems, enclosures, rural sanctuaries and the road network. One interesting discovery to the south of Vái is a group of quarries for pink marble.

There was evidence for Minoan occupation in this area (from a Neopalatial country house south of the Greco-Roman site), but it is not known exactly when the city of Itanos was founded. According to a story in Herodotus (IV 151) it was flourishing by the 7C BC. There is a fine 5C silver coinage, indicating the prosperity which continued through to the Early Byzantine period. At least four temples are recorded from Classical times. Around 260 BC Itanos asked for Ptolemaic support against neighbouring Praisós, and an Egyptian garrison was established here, apparently without prejudice to the city's independence. Until the end of that century, and briefly again 50 years later, Egypt seems to have welcomed the opportunity to influence Aegean affairs, and eastern Crete was a convenient base for the recruitment of mercenaries. With the defeat of Praisós by Ierápytna (modern Ierápetra) c 155 BC, that city became the chief rival of Itanos, especially over the control of the prestigious temple of Diktaian Zeus at Palaíkastro, but it took 20 years to settle this frontier dispute. The treaty known as the Arbitration of Magnesia (see Toploú above) confirms that by 132 BC the Roman Empire was interested in the fate of Crete.

Itanos was a double acropolis site on two low hills linked by terracing. The eastern hill rises sheer out of the sea; the western one is marked by the ancient watch-tower and some fine Hellenistic terrace walling. The city spread on to the height beyond the bay to the south where a rampart is still visible in the south part of the ancient town. On the inland slope of the main eastern acropolis are the excavated remains of a **basilica church** of the Early Byzantine period. (It is likely that a much earlier predecessor on the site was a temple to Athena Polias, Athena as protectress of the city.) The basilica plan shows side-aisles extended to the limit of the main raised apse, and the central aisle has unusual small apse-like niches in its long walls. An atrium has been identified. The church was built partly of reused material, and the floors were paved with stone slabs. Several incomplete marble columns survive. A large block has carved decoration of circles filled with rosettes (one with a Greek cross).

Work is under way on the vast necropolis up the coast to the north of the ancient town, which includes a curious tripartite building known to the earlier excavators as the Grand Tomb. It seems that Itanos was almost continuously occupied from the end of the 8C BC through to the beginning of the Imperial period.

Cape Síderos runs north from the archaeological site, a desolate landscape out to the extreme northeastern point of Crete. Access is restricted on the last stretch on the approach to a military communications post. Ornithologists will be excited by the chance of spotting Eleonora's Falcon (*Falco eleonaorae*) from the well-established breeding ground on the islet of **Paximáda**, the northernmost of the Dionysádes group northwest of the cape.

Eleonora's Falcon

In the 1970s a census established that 56 colonies breeding around the Aegean sea (less than 3000 breeding pairs) represented two-thirds of the world population of these birds. Eleonora's Falcon winters in Madagascar and returns to the Aegean from early April to mid-May, ranging widely across Crete. Egg-laying is delayed until the end of July so that hatching a month later coincides with an explosion in the insect food supply, and before their own flight south the young can be fed on small birds already migrating. The colony begins to depart in the second half of October.

Palaíkastro

From Itanos to Palaíkastro follow the road south, past turnings for Vái and Toploú (also for Siteía). Soon the view ahead frames a prominent flat-topped hill at the edge of the sea, known as **Kastrí**; the Minoan harbour town at Palaíkastro lay on the coastal plain on the far (south) side of the hill. As the road from Vái nears the coast there is access at several points to a long (1.5km) stretch of beach on **Kouremónos** bay, with some of the best swimming in the area and a windsurfing school. At Palaíkastro's busy plateía where three roads meet, you rejoin the direct Siteía–Zákros route. The village and the surrounding area increasingly cater for visitors.

Practical information

Tourist information

A tourist information desk, ☎ 28430 61546, operates from the office of the telephone services (OTE) on the village street heading from the centre towards Siteía. Open daily 09.00–22.00, except Sunday 10.00–13.00 and 18.00–21.30, it offers currency exchange and help with finding accommodation as well as with a wide range of queries about the locality. You can refer to a large-scale map of the area on the wall.

Where to stay

C *Hellas* (13 rooms), ☎ and fax 28430 61240. On the village plateía, open year round.

C *Marina Village* (32 rooms), ☎ 28430 61284, fax 28430 61285. In the olive groves between the village and the archaeological site.

C *Castri Village* (47 studios and furnished apartments), ☎ 28430 61100,

fax 28430 61249. High above the coast road with a superb view over the Koureménos bay, fully booked for wind-surfers in July and August but for the rest of the season a comfortable base for exploring the region. Suitable for wheel-chair access.

There are many rooms and studios to rent, well advertised in Palaíkastro and along the coast. In case of difficulty consult the tourist information office.

Eating out

There is a good choice of tavernas around the village plateía including one below the *Hotel Hellas* and, nearby, the *Itanos*. Down at the beach near the archaeological site the waterside *Taverna Khiona* is one of the most popular in the neighbourhood, for fresh fish as well as for its location on the rocks; it will be crowded on summer weekends.

A small **Folklore Museum** in a restored village house, is signed near the tourist information office, open during the summer months 09.00–13.00 and 17.30–20.00 (closed Mondays).

The archaeological site

The coastal plain of Roussolákkos to seaward of Palaíkastro, has a long history of occupation in antiquity. Archaeologists have uncovered, among other features of interest, the evocative remains of an important Minoan town.

To find the site you leave the plateía towards Zákros. After 150m a by-road to the left (signed for Hotel Marina Village) leads in 2km to the excavations just in from the beach. Across a bridge over the stream-bed you turn left skirting the hamlet of Angathiá. The asphalt gives out at the hotel turn but keep straight ahead to arrive at the shore with the waterside tavernas to the left, on the south side of the flat-topped promontory of Kastrí. A track continues, circling inland round the base of the hill, to the Koureménos beach on the north side.

The scramble up **Kastrí** (from behind the tavernas) is worthwhile if only for the view. Offshore are the Grándes Islands. On a clear day you can make out Kásos and Kárpathos, stepping-stone islands to the east towards Rhodes. This was the notorious Kásos channel, a gateway to the Aegean Sea from Allied bases in North Africa. Through it the British Mediterranean fleet risked its warships during the 1941 battle of Crete under threat from Stuka dive-bombers based at the German-held airfield on Kárpathos.

Excavations on Kastrí have revealed walls (still visible) dating to Early Minoan

III and Late Minoan IIIC, that is early in the Bronze Age and at the very end of it, times of trouble when the defensive potential of this hill was of paramount importance.

> The Minoan settlement at Palaíkastro was investigated by archaeologists from the British School at Athens in the first decade of the 20C and again in the 1960s. The current programme began in 1983.
> There was evidence for occupation in the area from the Neolithic to the end of the Minoan period, with a continuing cult of Diktaian Zeus from Geometric down to Hellenistic and Roman times. Some of the earlier excavations on the coastal plain have been filled in again and levelled, but enough was left uncovered to illustrate the layout of a sizeable Minoan town, in particular a stretch of the paved 'main street' bordered by drains with along it the ground-floor plans of elaborate builidngs of the Neopalatial period.
> Palaíkastro was a town on a grander scale and architecturally more elegant than Gourniá, but if, as has always seemed likely, there were palatial quarters here comparable with those at Gourniá, they have remained tantalisingly elusive. Evidence from a recent geophysical survey points to a new area of interest, adjacent to the sanctuary of Diktaian Zeus, but any hypothesis can only be confirmed by excavation.

South along the coastal track from the Kastrí hill the guardian's hut 100m inland is a landmark for the site which is partly fenced but open every day. The shore here is now an area of salt-flats where pools in early spring attract wading birds on migration but in Minoan times this was the location of the main harbour; there would have been shelter on the other side of the hill from the occasional southerly gales. The excavated town inland of the hut occupies a stretch of land known locally as Roussolákkos (the red pit).

The most recent programme of archaeological work has been taking place on the seaward side of the 'main street' (see plan). The foundations of the excavated buildings here are aligned on a paved and walled **harbour road** which widens at one point to a space resembling a miniature **plateía**. Lacking the characteristics of Minoan domestic architecture the complex is understood as a group of public buildings, though their function is still open to debate.

Building 1 was a large Neopalatial (LMIA) structure with massive foundation slabs, still in situ, designed to carry the cut sandstone blocks probably to a height of two storeys. (This grand edifice was succeeded by a less imposing building of LMIII date, possibly a bench sanctuary of the type seen at Knossós in the Shrine of the Double Axes.) Diagonally across the 'plateía', under protective shelter, the Neopalatial phase of **Building 5** has unusually well-preserved mudbrick walls faced with mud plaster; they subdivided an existing colonnaded area. There was evidence for a storage system and pots still containing burnt seeds were retrieved. This building had its own well. Beyond an alley on its southern side, and a formidable wall, an area was left open and entirely unoccupied at the height of the Minoan period; it may have been a garden.

A branch of the harbour road turns south (under the wall of Building 5), towards the later **Building 7**. Interesting finds here, in Neopalatial levels, were a Linear A inscription on a pithos rim, and fragments of a plaster tripod offering-table decorated with narcissus in the fresco technique.

The most spectacular find from the recent excavations is a chryselephantine statuette of a young male, roughly one-quarter life-size. This was recovered in innumerable fragments during three seasons of digging, from the gravel surface of the open 'plateía' area and from Building 5 which is now regarded as its context; there is speculation about an urban shrine. The figure (known as the *Palaíkastro Koúros*, p 270) is presumed to have cult associations, and taking account of the much later temple on the site (see below) it is tempting to suggest links with the worship of the Cretan-born Diktaian Zeus. Fragments of ivory and gold leaf discovered in 1987 built up the torso and arms; the next year systematic sieving recovered scraps of neck, eyebrow, ear and then came a finely carved grey serpentine head that fitted neatly into a rectangular dowel at the back of the ivory face; this was completed by the finding of rock crystal eyes. In 1990 ivory legs joined ivory feet. The cult figure seems to have been deliberately vandalised when the town was destroyed at the end of the LMIB period. Now the restored statuette, in characteristic votive pose with left leg set forward, is prominently displayed in the Siteía Museum.

South of Building 5 is an area which has a frontage on the paved 'main street' of the 1903 excavations. **Building 6**, as it is now known, had a monumental entrance just off this street which led into a paved central courtyard. Two column bases on its south side indicate the remains of the colonnade which would have surrounded the court. Through the colonnade to the west there was a large paved room, with characteristics of the Minoan hall; the typical pier-and-door system of partition here was unusual in that the piers were given cut bases of mottled green serpentine. This was a well-appointed building with evidence for decorated plaster (a vetch design) and on the downhill side it was supported by a massive terrace wall. Tests below the Neopalatial levels found eggshell ware in the Kamáres style indicating earlier (Protopalatial) occupation, and a carefully built cupboard (sealed by later reconstruction after an earthquake) which had contained stacked cups and bowls suggesting that the building had been used for feasting. Following evidence for several phases of construction within the Neopalatial period came the intriguing discovery that the building was systematically dismantled before the end of the LMIA period. The site was cleared of walls, columns and paving slabs. Even where a scrap of the colonnade remains, a huge foundation stone was left partly levered out of the ground when the work was apparently interrupted. All this took place shortly before the area was covered with a layer of volcanic ash from the LMIA eruption of Théra.

After that, from Late Minoan IB, the plot was an open area with two wells sunk at this time which can still be seen. The central one reached a depth of 9m, stone-lined to 2.20m, with a subterranean cave and water source. It is large enough for several individuals to draw water simultaneously which suggests that it probably served a community rather than one household. The excavation of both wells produced a number of important artefacts and a valuable chronological sequence illuminating the history of the town. A second find of volcanic ash came from a drain along the north side of the main street.

The 'main street' of the 1903 excavation, running northwest–southeast, is paved with irregular blocks of limestone and schist, and bordered by drains. Recent tests established that this surface dated from the Postpalatial period and that the street had been remade several times before that. The one contemporary with the Neopalatial buildings had been a carefully constructed narrow paved way which recalled the Royal Road at Knossós.

The early excavators left visible a crossroads on their main street and the foundations of the houses immediately around it. On the south side, opposite the more recent excavations, **House Δ** has a grand ashlar façade 40m long, with a wide doorway midway along it. A main hall is marked by four column bases round a large slab.

East of the crossroads **House B** lies on the seaward side of the street; the entrance, across a large threshold block, is at the east end of the façade, where there is evidence for a staircase to an upper storey just inside the doorway. The porticoed court ahead may have been a walled garden. It led left into a peristyle hall with central impluvium and an adjacent lustral basin. The finds from this house, which included a Linear A tablet and superb Marine Style vases believed to be products of a Knossós workshop, were in keeping with the standard of the architecture, emphasising the wealth and importance of its owner. (See Herákleion Museum, Room IX, and the Bronze Age section of the Siteía Museum.) Across the street **House Γ**, with another wide entrance (under an olive tree), lay in the angle of two town streets.

In this area, just beyond where the 'main street' now disappears under the fill, the early excavators identified the site of the **Temple of Diktaian Zeus**. It was already known, from a fragment of a 2C BC inscription that came from Magnesia in Asia Minor (see also Touploú), that control of this sanctuary was a cause for dispute between the city-states of eastern Crete. The temple building had been completely demolished, but remaining architectural fragments dated back to the 6C BC, including sections of a clay *sima*, a waterspout with a chariot scene in relief. Scattered pieces of an inscribed limestone slab of the 3C AD recorded part of the Hymn to Diktaian Zeus, an invocation used in re-enacting the dance of the Kourétes who according to legend had protected the infant Zeus after his birth in the Diktaian cave (p 240). Both *sima* and inscribed slab are in Herákleion's Archaeological Museum (Room XIX on the ground floor); together they offer evidence of the longevity here at Palaíkastro of this cult of Zeus, at least during historical times.

As you leave the site you can pass (at the Kastrí end of the exposed section of the main street) a separate excavation (1962) known as **House N**, dating to the last years of the Neopalatial period (LMIB). From the street entrance (on the north side) a broad passage leads to an inner hall with staircase to an upper storey. Miniature horns of consecration and two pyramidal double-axe stands (like those in the Corridor of the Storerooms at Knossós) had fallen from above, suggesting a shrine on the upper floor. The large main room at the back may have been a dining-room, for a pantry in one corner produced nearly 400 cups, many stacked inside each other as they had fallen from shelves, as well as large jars and a tripod cooking pot.

To the Peak Sanctuary of Petsophás

Conspicuous to the south of Roussolákkos is the steep hill of Petsophás (215m). On its summit the Minoans established an open-air sanctuary which was first explored by the British in 1903 and then fully excavated in the 1970s by the Greek archaeologist Cóstis Daváras. Tucked against the rocks on the summit the walled precinct contained a small shrine with plaster benches. A great quantity of votive offerings was found, mainly human and animal fragments in clay, but also horns of consecration and Linear A inscriptions on stone offering-tables; examples are shown in both Ayios Nikólaos and Siteía museums.

For the climb to Petsophás, the time-honoured route follows a *kalderími* along the contour of the hills behind the archaeological site, starting (signed) from Angathiá (see above). To join this well-worn path after visiting the Roussolákkos excavation look for the landmark along it of a tin roof (which covers a well) on the red earth to the south up the hillside; a short-cut to the path should be signed from the site. Steadily gaining height the *kalderími* skirts the summit of Petsophás across the southern flank. At the highest point on the shoulder strike out to the right, less than five minutes to the peak. The sanctuary site overlooks the sea.

To the Minoan palace at Káto Zákros

This expedition to the remote site on the east coast 30km south of Palaíkastro is one that few who make it regret; for the site opening hours see p 283.

From Palaíkastro the Zákros road leaves the coast and winds for 20km across sparsely inhabited, windswept hills. A new track down to the sea at **Karoúmbes** is still rough, but (with the **Khokhlakiés Gorge** and the coastal path back to

Palaíkastro) is recommended to serious walkers. Just before Adravásti, a minor road, right, offers (see below) an alternative return route to Siteía.

In historical times the settlement at **Ano** (upper) **Zákros** must have prospered because of its plentiful supply of spring water; a sign in the plateía rightly suggests a walk up to the water source. Nowadays the village caters for visitors to the excavated Minoan palace at **Káto** (lower) **Zákros**, which is 9km further on a good road down to the coast; in summer the two buses a day from Siteía continue to the archaeological site.

Where to stay

C *Zakros* (24 rooms), ☎ 28430 93379, a long-established unpretentious hotel on the plateía in the upper village provides a base for exploring this extreme eastern end of the island. Open all year.

There are also rooms for rent and tavernas around the plateía. The seasonal accommodation on the sea near the Minoan palace is described below (p 287).

The walk through the gorge to the archaeological site

The traditional route on foot is down a spectacular gorge following the river which flows into the bay at Káto Zákros. Caves in the gorge were used for burials during the Early and Middle Minoan periods, hence the local name, the **Pharángi ton Nekrón** (Gorge of the Dead). This is now the final stretch of the E4 walking route from one end of the island to the other, and the 6.5km path through the gorge provides a fitting climax to the walk. (Early in the year and after storms the water levels may make the gorge impassable. If in doubt enquire in the upper village.)

In the plateía in the upper village, opposite the Hotel Zákros, a large-scale plan of the area shows a choice of three approaches to the gorge. Serious walkers will join the direct path as it leaves the village (signed with the yellow E4 diamonds, needing between one and two hours). Anyone with a vehicle will note that there are several points where they can explore the river bed and the upper part of the gorge (for example using the dirt track out of the village for part of the way, or stopping along the regular road to the coast) before driving the long way round for a view from the valley floor at sea-level where the Minoans built their palace.

The road down to the palace from Ano Zákros is signposted from the central plateía. Just out of the village it cuts through a country house or farmstead of the Neopalatial (LMI) period where in 1965 a wine press and a pithos inscribed in Linear A were found. The wine-making equipment is well displayed in the Siteía Museum, and the pithos is in the Zákros room at the Herákleion Museum. The road passes a signed viewing point above the old *kalderími* down to the gorge.

Above the sea the road turns left, to make the final approach to the palace along the coast from the south. Looking back, further south, two islets mark Xerókambos, and way beyond, 4km offshore (visible only on a clear day) is the island of Kouphonísi (p 294). Soon the palace excavation comes into view ahead. The Zákros bay provides the best protected harbour on this coast, and was well placed for trade with Egypt, Cyprus and the Levant. Exotic imports such as elephant tusks found in the palace debris and an adapted Egyptian jug indicate that the Minoan civilisation exploited this trading advantage.

The mountain to the north, beyond the bay, is **Traóstalos** (515m), site of an important Minoan peak sanctuary. Recent surveys have shown that in Minoan times all approaches to this bay except the main gorge were blocked by walls, and guarded by a series of watch-towers linked by a road laid out to serve this defensive system rather than for normal access to the palace. The research, which is echoed in findings in several other parts of the island, has encouraged a reappraisal of the traditional assumptions about a Pax Minoica and a land free from strife.

History of the site

The town site at Zákros was investigated by British archaeologists at the beginning of the 20C. However, the spectacular nature of the finds continuing to be unearthed locally, including gold objects, gave grounds for suspecting an undiscovered palace, and in 1962 the eminent archaeologist Nikolaos Platon and the Greek Archaeological Society decided to explore again and immediately met with success. Work on the site has continued each year since then but the results are not fully published. It appears that Zákros, like so many other Minoan sites, suffered a sudden and terrible catastrophe at the end of the Late Minoan I period which caused the buildings to collapse and burn. The inhabitants had time to escape, but though there was some rebuilding in the town area, the palace was afterwards left largely undisturbed, neither restored nor looted. Consequently the excavators found evidence of exceptional interest throwing light on the functions of dedicated areas of a Minoan palace, as well as a range of artefacts of exceptional quality even by Minoan standards. Room VIII in Herákleion's Archaeological Museum and a large section in the Siteía Museum are devoted to the Zákros material.

The palace at Zákros occupies flat land on the floor of the river valley. The sea level has risen here since Minoan times and early in the year the site is often partly under water. The harbour town was terraced over the lower slopes of three hills surrounding the palace, with narrow streets cobbled and stepped where necessary as at Gourniá. The excavators have recognised some larger houses or palace dependencies. Two of the hills form a low ridge to the north and the third is marked by the modern church of Ayios Antónios to the south. The most accessible sector of the town is on the slope immediately to the northeast of the palace.

Zákros was inhabited in Prepalatial times. It has been noted that the town comes right up to the palace, suggesting that this was a harbour town in existence before the palace rather than one that was planned or grew up around it. The palace remains now visible are chiefly of the Neopalatial (LMI) period, similar in plan to the other Minoan palaces though much smaller, but traces of an older palace have been encountered, including evidence for a central court and features by the main entrance gate and beneath the west wing. The main axis of the town, the harbour road (see plan), dates to this Protopalatial period.

• **Access to the palace site** Open 08.00–15.00 daily except Mon and public holidays all year, and usually longer, until 19.00, in high season (late June–Oct). If in doubt, check at the site or at the tourist information office in Ayios Nikólaos or Siteía. The site entrance is signed 300m inland (with room to park) along the road from the beach towards the foot of the Gorge of the Dead. On the way you pass the original guardian's hut at the northeast corner of the excavations which now marks the exit from the site.

From the ticket office you are directed to the south end of the Central Court past workshops and a well (**16**). It makes sense, however, to begin the tour using the old paved Minoan road that led up from the harbour towards the palace, and for this you need to make your way across to the hut by the site exit to start with your back to the sea.

If you prefer first to study the excavation of the buildings round the court, and later, as you leave the site, the Harbour Road and the Minoan entrance with adjacent features, you can start in the northeast corner of the court (**4** on plan, and see Central Court section below).

The harbour road

The Minoan road (see plan) was paved in a contrasting pattern of blue and white stones. On the south side of it the archaeologists were able to investigate features from the Protopalatial period. Under a protective roof the outline of a **metal-working furnace** is preserved in the form of a horseshoe-shaped smelting chamber with four air ducts; remnants of the ore were still in situ.

The road continues ahead into the town, but the principal **entrance** to the palace (**2**) is obliquely left through what was a covered gateway, now marked by a large limestone threshold block. You descend to the northeast court by a stepped ramp where the excavator compared the regular central slabs to a strip of ceremonial carpet. Some original fragments remain. The roofed area here is a **lustral basin** (**3**) with a bench, and column bases for a portico on its north and west sides. (Its proximity to the entrance suggests comparisons with a similar feature near the North Entrance at Knossós.)

The Central Court

You pass between two **pillars** (**4**) into the Central Court, which is laid out on a northeast–southwest alignment differing very slightly from that found at the other three palace sites. (Notably it is not on the precise north–south alignment of the town.) At just a little over 30m x 12m this court is only about one-third the size of the Central Court at Knossós. The façades of the surrounding buildings were in ashlar masonry incorporating vertical and horizontal timber beams as in the other palaces; the squared blocks came from a quarry at Pelekitá, 5km up the coast towards Palaíkastro. The conspicuous square stone in the northwest quadrant of the court has been interpreted as the base of an altar.

The West Wing

The **entrance** (**5**) from the court to the West Wing is across the massive threshold block in line with the altar base. An anteroom with a slender central column led to a square room understood as a reception lobby, and distinguished by a floor area with a central square of red tiles. A staircase behind led to a second storey. South of the lobby was a paved and colonnaded **light-well** (**6**), with crazy-paving set in red plaster; the floor drained from the northeast corner. Found in pieces in this light-well were a chlorite bull's head rhyton and the much illustrated *Mountain shrine rhyton*. This exquisitely worked stone vase (originally covered in gold leaf) contributes pictorial evidence of the greatest importance for an understanding of the Minoan peak sanctuaries; it is prominently displayed in the Zákros room in the Herákleion Museum.

The same light-well lit the north end of the large **hall** (**7**). This was designed with central columns and the space was made versatile by the pier-and-door

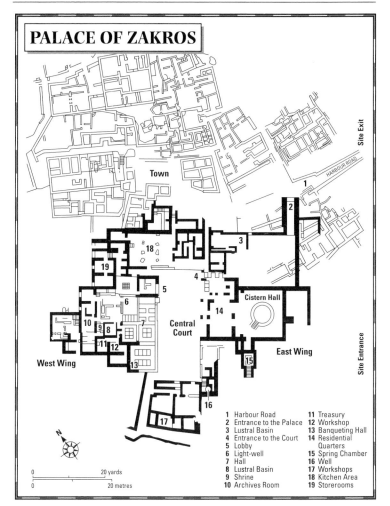

PALACE OF ZAKROS

Town

Site Exit

HARBOUR ROAD

Central
Court

Cistern Hall

East Wing

Site Entrance

West Wing

N

1 Harbour Road	11 Treasury
2 Entrance to the Palace	12 Workshop
3 Lustral Basin	13 Banqueting Hall
4 Entrance to the Court	14 Residential
5 Lobby	Quarters
6 Light-well	15 Spring Chamber
7 Hall	16 Well
8 Lustral Basin	17 Workshops
9 Shrine	18 Kitchen Area
10 Archives Room	19 Storerooms

0   20 yards

0   20 metres

(*polythýron*) partition wall characteristic of Minoan architecture. There were traces of wall paintings, and decorative panelling in the floor was framed by narrow strips of stucco originally painted red. These frames survived but, intriguingly, the material they outlined did not, with no trace of stone, nor archaeological evidence for wood.

This main hall communicated with the banqueting hall (**13**) to the south, but also, in conjunction with the entrance lobby (**5**), controlled access to the inner areas of the west wing where religious, administrative and economic functions can be deduced from the architecture and artefacts uncovered.

Immediately to the southwest of the light-well is a **lustral basin** (**8**) with eight steps down into it. Next to it (west) at the heart of the complex was the central **shrine** (**9**), with a ledge built into a niche across from a low bench. Nothing was found on the ledge, but on the floor were fine clay rhytons and pedestalled cups. Behind the shrine was an **archives room** (10) where record tablets had been kept in bronze-hinged wooden chests stored on wooden shelves. Most of the tablets had been crushed but 13 were recovered, some inscribed in Linear A. This combination of the provision for ritual and for the safe-keeping of administrative records was integrally associated with a labyrinthine arrangement of workshops and pot stores.

Immediately south of the shrine was the **treasury** (11) equipped with eight clay chests, now partially restored. This room was found unplundered, the chests tightly packed with fine vases, larger pots on the floor and probably on the chest lids as well; more pots had fallen from an upper floor. This treasury held some of the finest Minoan stone vases yet known (see exhibit in the Zákros Room at the Herákleion Museum). They included chalice shapes and jugs, and the exquisite rock-crystal rhyton with bead handle and collar, which had been crushed into more than 300 fragments. A vase of porphyritic rock from Egypt had been adapted for pouring by the addition of a Minoan bridge-spout. With these vases were also bronze double axes, fine stone mace-heads, and artefacts in ivory and faience.

In this same sector of the palace, but in a room over the storerooms and workshops, were kept valuable raw materials. Among the debris of the collapsed upper storey the excavators found six bronze ingots and three large elephant tusks (also displayed in the Herákleion Museum).

Next to the treasury is a **workshop** (12), the grouped flat stones perhaps forming a support for a craftsman's bench, and in the storeroom immediately to the south were found 15 pithoi, storage for agricultural produce.

Returning to the Central Court you pass the room (13) named the **banqueting hall** on account of the large number of drinking vessels found in the debris; the walls were decorated with a frieze of painted stucco and the room connected through a triple doorway with the main hall to its north.

The East Wing

Across the court the East Wing (badly damaged through the years by cultivation and flooding) was designated by the excavator as the residential squarters, to correspond with the two-storeyed private apartments found in the other palaces. Behind a pillared and colonnaded verandah two **main rooms** (14) connected through multiple doors. The northern room opened on to a light-well on the east side, but especially interesting behind the bigger room to the south is the **cistern hall**, a large area with a central basin or pool, built to retain spring water at a standard level. The substantial wall of the cistern was lined with plaster, and eight well-preserved steps led down to it. The floor of the hall slopes inward for drainage, and column bases suggested that the area may have been at least partially roofed. The water came from the **spring chamber** (15) immediately to the south, with its built well for the fountain which must have constituted one of the main supplies for the palace. It is thought that in Minoan times drinking water was obtained from the wells (which now produce a slightly saline water) in addition to cisterns. Clearly the control of water was always a problem at Zákros. For much of the year archaeologists now rely on pumps to prevent these structures being submerged.

At the southeast angle of the central court is another stone-lined **well** (16). From it in 1964 came a conical cup containing olives perfectly preserved in the water for more than 3000 years. On exposure to air they shrivelled within a very few minutes. The nearby buildings included workshops (**17**) for faience, rock crystal, ivory and scent.

At the other (north) end of the central court is the **kitchen area** (**18**) of the palace, north of the west wing. The six rugged column bases are taken to indicate structural support for a dining room above. The staircase is on the eastern side, and to the west the **storeroom block** (**19**) would also have had grander rooms above. It is worth walking up the stepped streets of this sector of the town to the upper levels for the splendid bird's-eye view of the palace excavation.

From Ano Zákros a dirt road (sometimes very rough in places but well signed thanks to local initiative) runs south, down to the coast, 10km to **Xerókambos**. There is a fine long beach (with developments already under way, tavernas and a few rooms to rent) and another striking gorge.

Towards the far end of the beach an ancient site has been excavated dating to the Hellenistic period (4C–1C BC). Archaeologists believe that these are indeed the remains of the small walled city described in the mid-19C by the British naval surveyor, Captain T.A.B. Spratt. You can circle back inland, past a restricted military area, to the plateau of **Zíros** (p 292) and the archaeological site of Praisós or the main route south across the island from Siteía. Zíros is on the E4 walking route.

On the road north from Ano Zákros to Palaíkastro an alternative return route to Siteía (30km by minor roads) runs through deserted country where the strikingly red earth is a rich hunting ground for wildflower enthusiasts. The off-the-beaten-track road turns off after **Adravasti** (signposted Karýdi 8km) and climbs to a plateau where in spring you may find the distinctive *Tulipa cretica* with open, star-like flowers. Karýdi is at the centre of a network of upland roads, including those to Khandrás (a good place to make use of the E4 footpath) and the site of Praisós, or across the Siteía–Ierápetra main road.

You can turn right in Karýdi for Mitáto, Krionéri, Roússa Eklissiá and a descent, especially beautiful in the evening light, to the coast 3km east of Siteía.

To Praisós and the south coast

The main road from Siteía to Ierápetra (60km) crosses the island to reach the south coast at the resort area of **Análipsi** and **Makriyialós**. The unspoilt countryside on both sides of the main road offers touring motorists and walkers based in Siteía a number of short excursions. Those whose primary interest is archaeology can visit some excavated sites of country houses or farmsteads of the Minoan period, and (20km from Siteía) the remote upland site of the ancient city-state of **Praisós** where Minoan traditions seem to have survived long after they had been superseded elsewhere on the island.

There is an alternative route across the island using minor roads from **Piskoképhalo** along the sparsely populated foothills of **Mount Ornó** and through **Khrysopiyí** to join the south coast road west of Makriyialós (24km from Ierápetra). Both roads south are crossed by the E4 long-distance footpath.

Travelling by bus

There are eight buses a day from Siteía to Ierápetra, and one to Néa Praisós which is otherwise 5km on foot from the stop on the main road in Epáno Episkópi.

The main road to the south coast leaves Siteía from the junction (signposted Lithínes) in front of the Archaeological Museum. After 2km, at **Manáres**, it cuts awkwardly through the (signed) excavation of a Minoan building, the remains of a large Neopalatial (Late Minoan I) country house that was terraced into the hillside and looked out eastwards over a fertile river valley. The staircase at the northern end of the site gave access to the upper level. The lower part, which included storerooms, was protected by massive stone blocks, possibly as an embankment against a wider river below.

An inconspicuous crossroads in **Piskoképhalo** (3km from Siteía) offers a choice of short detours, one in each direction, both circling back to Siteía. This is also the start of the back road through Khrysopiyí and Stavrokhóri across to the south coast.

Káto Episkopí and Zoú

A left turn in Piskoképhalo leads (in 1km) to Káto Episkopí and its 11C church. The road continues (less than 5km) to the excavation of another LMI country house, at Zoú, and back to the coast by Stavroménos and Roússa Eklissiá or on (for a longer c 40km round-trip from Siteía, perhaps with some roads still unsurfaced) through the upland village of Karýdi.

The Byzantine church of **Ayii Apóstoli** is signed off to the right in the village of **Káto Episkopí**. The final approach through narrow streets is easiest on foot. This tiny cruciform church with a dome on an octagonal drum and angled apse is now in use as a cemetery chapel, but it was built as an episcopal church soon after the island had been reclaimed for Byzantium from the Arabs.

The well-engineered Karýdi road first follows the river-bed, then crosses it and climbs into a side valley. The site at **Zoú** is up the right bank of the road cutting (250m before the stretch where the village is below the road left). As at Manáres, the house looked out over the fertile and cultivated land on which its economy would have depended. Beside the quite well-preserved entrance at the far (south) end of the façade is a small room with a stone bench; two deep pits nearby suggest storage of grain. This Minoan farmhouse had its own pottery kiln.

The village of Zoú is noted for its plentiful spring water which is now part of the Siteía supply. Just beyond the site the road sweeps left to cross the head of the valley towards Stavroménos. On foot here you could cut across to Roússa Eklissiá, but the road continues south and east across still unfrequented uplands to Sítanos and (18km from Zoú) Karýdi above Zákros. These uplands are renowned for their rich variety of wild flowers in spring including Crete's endemic tulips. On country roads you can make your way south to Praisós or return to the north coast through Roússa Eklissiá.

The Akhládia valley

From the Piskoképhalo crossroads on the main route south from Siteía, the minor road branches right to **Akhládia** past the excavation of a Minoan house or farmstead, also a well-preserved example of a Postpalatial (LMIII) tholos tomb.

After c 2km both are conspicuously signed along recently improved tracks.

You come first to what is known as **House A** at Akhládia where you see the massive foundations of a Neopalatial building (constructed in MMIII, destroyed in LMI) which was part of a small settlement stretching south and west along a low hill. In Neopalatial Crete the most sophisticated architectural practices seem to have been followed even in fairly remote settlements.

The approximately rectangular house had 12 rooms, with a main entrance in the centre of the **southeast façade**. The main hall was through double doors on the left of the entrance passage with a group of storerooms across the passage right. Three column bases remain along the axis of the hall which opened on to an area with a stone bench at one corner. At the back, against the northwest façade, a cupboard and utensils in a small room suggested a kitchen.

The tholos tomb (at **Platyskinós**) is signed on the cross-country tracks and also from a right-angle bend nearly at the village of Akhládia. The tomb, which was excavated during and shortly after the Second World War, dates from c 1300 BC (LMIIIB) during the period of Mycenaean control of the island. At the end of the *dromos*, or sloping approach, the two uprights of the low rectangular doorway support a massive lintel. The circular chamber is built of large stones, with the horizontal courses corbelled inwards to a keystone at the centre of the roof. Opposite the entrance a small doorway against the natural rock was found blocked by two walls; it has been compared with the false door provided for the spirit of the deceased in Egyptian tombs. The tomb had been robbed (the hole in the roof is the robbers' entry) but three *lárnakes* remained, one decorated with the double axe, horns of consecration and a griffin. The lid of another was shaped like the back of a bull, including head and tail at the gable ends. The finds from the tomb, including pots and a stone lamp, were destroyed during the war.

Before the village of Akhládia, a circular route recommended especially to walkers uses an unsurfaced road through **Kimouriótis** (signed right, rough in places) to cross the valley and join (3km) the main north coast road 6km from Siteía. On the banks of a stream shaded by plane trees you find Kimouriótis, a cluster of traditional stone-built houses with cobbled yards close to a church and a spring. A decade ago the hamlet was all but deserted, but there is now an attempt to bring it to life again.

The minor road south continues through Akhládia and then across empty uplands; the whole route is rewarding for wildflower enthusiasts. From **Khrysopiyí** or **Dáphni** walkers can enjoy stretches of the E4 long-distance path. There is a stiff climb west to a viewpoint on the way over to **Oreinó**; eastwards the path is less demanding. Eventually the road drops to wooded streambeds around **Stavrokhóri** and into pine trees below the village, reaching the south coast in **Koutsourás**.

Heading south from Piskoképhalo you can cross the island on the main Ierápetra road, or turn east to the archaeological site of Praisós and to the **Zíros** plateau. At the beginning of the village of **Epáno Episkopí** a left fork (signed) is the start of the country road to the east. However, if you made the detour to the Byzantine church of the Orthodox bishop at Káto Episkopí you may like to continue into the village here to compare the western-influenced architecture of the church built (at a later date) for his Latin equivalent. This was the seat of the Catholic bishop of Siteía under Venetian rule, at least by the early 16C, when Turkish raiders and independent corsairs were a constant threat to the coast.

You loop right uphill off the main road to pass the tall, slender basilica church of the **Panayía**, its construction overcoming an awkward slope. A plaque on the west façade was carved for Bishop Gaspar Vivianus. The Italianate bell-cote, pointed arches and details of the stonework and the doorway all emphasise the contrast with the typical Byzantine domed cruciform plan at Káto Episkopí.

Praisós

From the fork on the north side of Epáno Episkopí the Zíros road descends into the fertile valley of the Pantélis stream below the hilltop on which the ancient city lay, and then climbs to the modern village of **Néa Praisós** c 20km from Siteía.

From the plateía the road is signed downhill to the site. After c 2km you pass, left, a low rocky hill that is the city's so-called Third Acropolis, and half left ahead is the First Acropolis, distinguished by a network of terrace walling. Beyond some ruined buildings (remains of a Venetian village) there is a gate and signed footpath to the centre of the site.

History

Praisós flourished from the Archaic to the Hellenistic periods and is of particular interest because ancient authors regarded it as the city of the Eteocretans (true or original Cretans) who were probably survivors of Minoan stock. They were one of the five peoples of Crete listed in the *Odyssey* and their inscriptions using the Greek alphabet but for a non-Greek language form one of the most intriguing finds from this site. It has been suggested that the language may be related to Linear A.

The area was first investigated in the late 19C by the Italian Frederico Halbherr (known for his work at Górtyn), who found the first inscriptions, then by the British School at Athens and later by the Greek Archaeological Service. A survey has been in progress since 1995.

Praisós spread across three hills known respectively as the First, Second and Third Acropolis; this last is also referred to as the Altar Hill. Where the path meets the saddle, a little uphill right on the slopes of the First Acropolis and looking across to the Second, are the remains of a Hellenistic house dating from the 3C BC. This building has always been known as the Almond Tree House, for the tree which hung over it at the time of the excavation.

There were Neolithic finds in a cave 500m to the north of the site. There is evidence of Minoan activity in the neighbourhood, for example at the so-called Megalithic House of Neopalatial date excavated c 800m southeast of the acropolis hills. The clearing of various cemeteries which included scattered chamber tombs produced material dating from LMIII and through to the Hellenistic period. Only one of the tombs is visible, near the road 200m south–southeast of the Third Acropolis. The archaeologists at Praisós looked for continuity from a Bronze Age settlement, but found that the city of the Eteocretans was built mostly on the natural rock and had no earlier remains beneath it.

It is known that the Praisians had many contacts (both peaceful and warlike) with the neighbouring Greek cities of Ierápytna (modern Ierápetra) and Itanos. A major cause of dispute with Itanos in the extreme northeast of the island was the question of control of the important temple of Diktaian Zeus

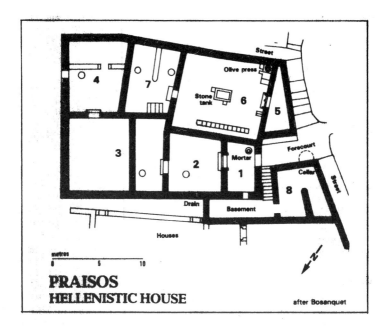

PRAISOS
HELLENISTIC HOUSE

after Bosanquet

at Palaíkastro. At one stage in the Hellenistic period the Praisians even shared citizenship with Ierápytna, but between 145 BC and 140 BC their city was destroyed by Ierápytna, and was never reoccupied.

An easy path leads round the western flank of the **First Acropolis** to the saddle between two peaks where the ancient city lay. On the summit of this acropolis scant remains of the foundations of a temple can be made out, and on the south side of the **Second Acropolis** (at the further end of the saddle) rectangular cuttings show where houses were built into the slope in the Hellenistic period with rock-cut shelves and alcoves. These two hills were enclosed by a defensive wall which can still be traced in places. Looking across a broad gully the **Third Acropolis** or Altar Hill (outside the circuit wall) is identified as a flat-topped wedge formation, approachable with ease only from this direction. The Eteocretan inscriptions were found on this hill. On the summit a primitive altar with rock-cut steps and ashlar masonry marked a sanctuary frequented, as the offerings prove, from the 8C (Geometric period) to 5C BC. Interesting terracottas among these offerings included large painted figurines of lions. By around 400 BC the temenos wall probably enclosed a small temple.

The excavation of the **Almond Tree House** on the north slopes of the First Acropolis offers a good understanding of a substantial house or perhaps a community building dating from the 3C BC. The outer walls are of ashlar masonry with exact joints finished with lime mortar. The house is built on a terrace on the steep hillside, the upper wall making use of the native rock and the lower being carried down as a strong retaining wall. Water spouts act as drains through this lower wall. Traces of cobble paving remain but the usual flooring was native rock or hard clay. The roof was tiled.

The house, designed to fit into an existing street plan, is entered from a shallow-stepped street. A forecourt leads to a **vestibule** (1) before the main front door into the **living quarters** (2–4); wide doorways and substantial stone jambs are a feature of the architecture. The doors turned on pivots as did the windows which were fitted with wooden shutters.

The principal living-room seems to have been at the northeast corner, enjoying the coolest aspect of the house. (Walls unshaded on the plan are part of alterations to the original design.)

From the forecourt there is also an entrance to three rooms of a different character at the back of the house. A triangular **vestibule** (5) led to a large **room** (6) with an olive press in one corner, and in the centre a stone vat presumably for the storage of oil; it is fitted to take a wooden lid, and could have been lined with lead. There are the remains of a stone platform that ran round the walls of this room. Next door was a **storeroom** (7) which contained numerous pithoi, one with a projecting spout flush with the base for the drainage of liquids. The stone stairs are part of the lower flight of a staircase to the upper floor; the upper flight was of wood.

From the forecourt, eleven steps lead down to a **basement room** (8) with a small rock-cut cellar in the rear wall. There was probably a room above with a door from the forecourt.

From Néa Praisós the road continues towards the Zíros plateau. After 5km, just before Khandrás, the romantic ruins of the medieval village of **Voilá** are spread along the hillside to the left of the road. A by-road (left and right before you are abreast of the village) leads to a Turkish fountain at the start of what was the main street. The ruins are dominated by the 15C double-naved church of Ayios Yeóryios, and a tower of the Turkish period; the decorative carving on its doorway includes an inscription dated 1742.

In **Khandrás** one road joined for a while by the E4 walking route keeps left to **Zíros**, across a plateau (at 600m) which has become one of the most highly regarded wine-growing areas of Crete. Zíros has the church of Ayía Paraskeví (left of the through road) which preserves in the arch above the door the latest dated fresco painting on the island (1565). The road ahead is restricted by military installations, but the E4 sets off north of them on its penultimate stretch across to Zákros.

From Khandrás you can continue in a westerly direction (through **Arméni**) back to the main Siteía–Ierápetra route. Outside Arméni you will notice the imposing three-aisled church of Ayía Sophía, all that remains of a monastery of the Venetian period.

You pass at **Etiá** the ruined walls of a 15C villa, one of very few reminders surviving on Crete of the grand country houses of the Venetian period. This one was highly praised by Giuseppe Gerola in his early 20C study of the island's Venetian monuments. He attributed the building of the villa to a member of Venice's De Mezzo family.

Writing an account of his travels on the island in 1856 Captain Spratt described a castellated Venetian villa combining strength, luxury and taste. 'It has a vaulted basement, like a fortified tower, with well-constructed second and third stories above, and displays some architectural effect throughout. In the upper part were five windows in front, and in the lower, one on either side of a handsome entrance, approached by a flight of steps ascending from a paved courtyard, around which were the servants' dwellings and outhouses.'

When the Turks occupied Crete the house was appropriated for one of their high officials. It was vandalised by the rebels in the 1828 Revolt while being used as a refuge, and again in 1897. This time materials were taken by the Christians to build their village church. The house fell into ruin and the remains were rescued by the Greek archaeological authorities. Spratt's 'vaulted basement like a fortified tower' is what you see today.

You emerge on to the main road at **Pappayianádes** (20km from Siteía by the direct route). This road across the island now climbs southwest to the watershed and then runs below the large village of **Lithínes**, the scene of heroic events during the time of Turkish rule, now an attractive place to explore on foot. A one-way system takes you up to park in the plateía in front of the main village church. Past the east end of it, 50m downhill, is **Ayios Athanásios** (15C–16C) which has contemporary ceramic plates embedded in its south façade. A parallel street out of the plateía leads to a church dedicated to the **Panayía** which is known for its fine icons. The key is held by the *papás*.

As you continue southwards the Libyan Sea is soon in view and you reach the coast at Análipsi.

A detour, less than 10km to the east on the surfaced coast road, takes you to the dramatically sited **Kapsás monastery**, built on a cliff edge just beyond the mouth of the Perivolákia gorge. There was probably a predecessor here in Venetian times, but the present buildings (apart from modern intrusions) mostly date from the mid-19C. The much earlier **grotto church**, now the north aisle dedicated to Ayios Ioánnis Prodrómos (the Baptist) was enlarged by the addition of a second aisle dedicated to Ayía Triáda (the Holy Trinity). The carved wooden iconostasis was installed at the same time. All this was achieved by an eccentric (some say saintly) character, a monk named Yerondoyiánnis, whose remains are still revered in the church.

Swimming is from patches of rocky pebble beach between clusters of hothouses. In summer this stretch of coast is taken over by campers.

From Análipsi a well-made road climbs 4km inland to the village of **Pevkí** (a place-name reflecting the wealth of pine trees in the locality).

At the end of the Bronze Age there was a refuge site here exploiting the relative security of one of the pinnacles in the hills above the village. This area is recommended especially to walkers who do not feel entirely confident about striking out into the wilds of Crete. A path inland from Análipsi up the gorge from Aspros Pótamos to Peukí, and others through the wooded country around this village, have been carefully signed, with display boards setting out alternative routes, walking times, and what to look out for along the way.

The taverna *Eleni* in Pevkí is a popular destination for anyone exploring whether by car or on foot.

Makriyialós

From Análipsi the main road turns west. The cliffs of the extreme southeastern corner of Crete as well as the island of Kouphonísi are still in view but in the foreground ahead are the heights of Thryptís north of Ierápetra.

Análipsi runs into Makriyialós and a long strip behind the bay has suffered at the hands of developers. To swim find the tamarisk-lined **Diaskári beach**, to the east where the main road from Lithínes comes down to the shore.

Where to stay and eating out

White River Cottages, Aspros Pótamos (13 furnished apartments), ☎/fax 28430 51120, signed from the coast road 1km back from the sea, a cluster of traditional Cretan houses refurbished to modern standards in a garden setting towards the foot of the Pevkí gorge.

For the odd night on a touring holiday there are plenty of **studio rooms** advertised behind the beaches, or above tavernas in the coves as you travel the coast road west.

There are beach tavernas all along this stretch of coast; the one on the **Diaskári beach** (see above) is pleasantly secluded. In the evening many people make for **Koutsourás**, 3km west of Makriyialós, where there is a good choice of places to eat. *Porphyra* in Makriyialós maintains a high standard and is deservedly popular.

The **Minoan country house** at Makriyialós was excavated in the 1970s for the Greek Archaeological Service and produced finds of the highest quality, some featuring in the display in Room III of the Ayios Nikólaos Museum.

The site is signed from the coast road 400m west of the new harbour quay and the same distance inland (driveable). The stream just to the east would have provided shelter for boats.

The ground plan of the house (damaged by modern farming activity before excavation) had similarities with those of the Minoan palaces, with a miniature version of a monumental west façade and of a central court and west court connected by a passage. The main entrance was probably on the villa's north side, but the central court also had an entrance from the east, and there may have been a walled east court. In the central court the excavator identified an altar and a bench shrine. A remarkable sealstone from this site is carved with a scene of a ship carrying an altar, flanked by a palm tree and an adoring female worshipper, suggesting marine associations for the Minoan goddess.

Kouphonísi

From the harbour of Makriyialós there is a daily boat trip during the summer season (weather permitting) to the uninhabited island of Kouphonísi, 4km offshore to the southeast; you should enquire at the ticket office on the quay.

The island (2km x 4km) is now a treeless place where the winds have eroded the soil and created great sand-dunes.

There is evidence for settlement dating from the Early Bronze Age. The remains of a considerable Roman town include a small stone-built theatre and Kouphonísi is known to have been a port-of-call on the trade routes from Rome to Egypt and Asia Minor. (The Greek Archaeological Service began excavating here in 1976.) In Venetian times it seems probable that Kouphonísi was protected as a rabbit warren. There are rabbits here today though they do not occur wild on mainland Crete.

Kouphonísi and the 'purple trade'

From the mollusc *Murex trunculus* the islanders extracted a dye valued by the Mediterranean textile industry for what was known as the 'purple trade', though the colour of the Tyrian purple prized by Phoenicians, Greeks and Romans, and associated with Roman emperors, was more exactly a deep crimson. The excavations uncovered vast numbers of murex shells and interesting evidence for dyeing installations. The murex had been exploited during the Minoan period by the relatively simple process of crushing the shells but the Romans developed more sophisticated methods of harvesting the shells and processing the precious fluid from the glands in order to produce strikingly bright colours; from each gland only a few drops of dye were obtained. (The process is well explained in the Siteía Museum exhibit where there is also a good photograph of the Roman theatre.)

From Makriyialós the road follows the coast for more than 25km. Easy access to this stretch of shore has only come about within the last 20 years, and has been followed by piecemeal development of varying quality largely aimed at the cheaper end of the tourist market.

At first the road passes a number of rocky coves where in spring the mountain streams flow down to the sea. From **Mávros Kólymbos** there is a scenic road 10km up to Oreinó on the slopes of the Thryptís mountains, a route specially recommended to flower enthusiasts and birdwatchers. Just to the east of it the **Daskári gorge** (though still recovering from a serious fire a few years ago) is being promoted as a habitat for butterflies. Walkers can climb the gorge to a chapel and then cut across to the Oreinó road.

Out of season you will find peaceful beach tavernas and well-advertised rooms to rent along the rocky shore (for example, in the hamlet of **Galíni** and the cove of **Ayía Photiá**). Then the coastal plain opens out behind a long beach with upmarket resort accommodation (as well as two camping sites) as you approach the town of Ierápetra (p 249).

RÉTHYMNON PROVINCE

The city of Réthymnon on the north coast gives its name to the *nome* or province which separates the territories of Herákleion and Khaniá and reaches to the south coast where the island narrows to the west of the Bay of Mesará.

The advantages of this province as a base for visitors include the civilised pleasures of the old Venetian city at the heart of modern **Réthymnon** as well as the beautiful and largely unspoilt countryside of the **Ida mountain range** and the **Amári valley**. The valley shelters many medieval churches decorated with wall-paintings in the Byzantine tradition and can be approached conveniently from either coast. The road up to **Anóyia**, for the high plain on Ida and the cave sanctuary of Zeus, starts from the north between Réthymnon and Herákleion.

The drive from coast to coast within the province takes little more than an hour but anyone interested in archaeology will want to stop at the Postpalatial cemetery at **Arméni**. The main north–south road runs through **Spíli**, a delightful place to visit or to use as a base for a longer stay inland.

On the south coast **Plakiás** is a good choice for a relaxing holiday, for swimming and walking, with two spectacular gorges and the star attraction of the **Préveli monastery** in the immediate neighbourhood. Plakiás is also within comfortable reach (with private transport) of the Amári valley, the Minoan sites around Phaistós and the mountainous region of Sphakiá (in the province of Khaniá). For climatic reasons the south coast is a good choice at either end of the season. In October the Libyan Sea is noticeably warmer than the Aegean, and the weather, which can be insufferably hot and windy in midsummer, is likely to remain milder than on the north coast.

The magnificent 12km beach to the east of Réthymnon is being developed, a little more each year, as a strung-out, unplanned resort area. There are a number of comfortable hotels but a lot else that is less desirable (and not traditionally Cretan in character) in between. To enjoy the flavour of Réthymnon to the full many visitors prefer to stay in the Old City.

Elsewhere the province's coastal resorts have evolved from former fishing villages. The process began later here than in some of the eastern parts of the island and on the whole has resulted in relatively small-scale and sensitive development.

From any part of the province, but from the north coast villages in particular (Pánormos, Balí) as well as Réthymnon itself, it is feasible to make a day-long expedition to the Minoan sites of Knossós and Arkhánes near Herákleion, as well as to view the unique collection of Minoan antiquities in Herákleion's Archaeological Museum.

Walkers who choose the province of Réthymnon for a holiday can expect to be rewarded. A large proportion of the province consists of sparsely populated mountains. There are possibilities for walks at any level of fitness or competence. Walkers should consider the northern foothills of Mount Ida or the Amári valley, both served by branches of the long-distance footpath route E4, as is the wooded country south and west of Réthymnon. Much of this hinterland is now crossed by asphalt-surfaced minor roads, to the advantage of touring motorists in search of birds and flowers on routes off the beaten track. In the south of the province the coastal paths have much to offer.

The **Arkádi monastery**, in the hills behind the north coast, is a monument of major architectural interest, with a history which makes it a place of pilgrimage for Cretans. Visitors to the island who are interested in Crete's long struggle against foreign rule will surely want to fit Arkádi into their itinerary.

Réthymnon

The city of Réthymnon, third largest town on the island, is the capital of its *nome* as it formerly was of the equivalent Venetian province. It houses the arts faculties of the University of Crete with a lively student population drawn from all over Greece, and prides itself on its reputation as the intellectual and cultural capital of the island. There is a small but highly regarded Archaeological Museum, a Historical and Folklore Museum beautifully arranged in an old Venetian building, and the Kanakákis Centre for Contemporary Art with a good record of wide-ranging exhibitions.

Réthymnon (see plan) is dominated at its western end by a great Venetian fortress built on a headland. The houses of the old city used to huddle under the massive walls of the fort, above and around an inner harbour. There have always been problems with the harbour because of a tendency to silting which has made it unsuitable for large vessels even with constant dredging. Nowadays fishing boats tie up at its quays which are lined by popular tavernas looking across to a splendid lighthouse (built originally by the Turks) and, beyond the breakwater, to the berth for the Athens ferries. The surrounding buildings mostly date from Turkish times. Relics of the city's Venetian and Turkish past are increasingly appreciated, and a programme of conservation is underway.

The new town stands behind a long sandy beach running eastwards from the harbour. Piecemeal resort development along the shore road has produced block after block of tavernas, bars and rooms to rent. Further east, beyond the town boundary, this sandy beach is one of the most important of the Mediterranean nesting sites for the endangered loggerhead sea turtle (*Caretta caretta*) (p 57).

Practical information

Travel and transport
By air

Réthymnon is about halfway between Herákleion and Khaniá airports. Taxi fares are displayed at both airports; for either journey expect to pay around €50.

By public transport you need to transfer from the airport to the city centre of Herákleion or Khaniá and then use the long-distance bus service to Réthymnon. The last buses (in summer) on the route leave at 20.30; both journey times are about an hour.

Olympic Airways, Dimitrakáki 6, near the Municipal Gardens, ☎ 28310 24333.

By sea

The Khaniá firm of *ANEK* runs an overnight service every night except Christmas Eve between Piraeus and Réthymnon. The booking office is at Arkadíou 250 (the harbour end across from the ferry quay), ☎ 28310 29221, fax 28310 55519. Piraeus booking office ☎ 21410 97410.

By bus

You arrive in Réthymnon at the bus station on the seafront at the west end of the town. For information, ☎ 28310 22212.

Town buses serve the hotels and beaches in both directions along the coast approximately hourly between 07.00 and 21.00. The route runs along Koundouriótou and past the Municipal Gardens.

By car

For a short visit to Réthymnon the car park alongside the Municipal Gardens (ticketed, free on Sundays) is convenient and does not involve negotiating the narrow streets of the Old City.

To park near the harbour leave the north coast highway at the traffic lights on the bypass (the first junction if you are approaching from the west). Then keep to the coast road, turning left along the sea past the bus station. The walls of the fortress will loom above you, but continue until the ferry quay is in sight; at the time of writing there is parking on both sides of the road. The big new car park at the end before the ferry quay, is subject to flooding during storms. Here you are on the west side of the Venetian harbour, and steps or a ramp lead up to the entrances to the

Fortétsa and the Archaeological Museum.

Approaching the town on the through road from the east you can turn down (at traffic lights for the crossing with Khortátsi) for Plateía Iróon and parking along the beach road near the tourist information office (see below); in high season you may have to leave a vehicle some way from the centre.

Taxi ranks

Plateía 4 Martýron, between the Municipal Gardens and the Porta Guóra, and in Plateía Iróon behind the beach.

Tourist information

The tourist information office is on the seaward side of El. Venizélou (see plan), ☎ 28310 29148. Open Mon–Fri 08.00–14.30.

Police

Tourist police, next door to the information office, ☎ 28310 28156. Open Mon–Sat 08.00–22.00; Sun 08.00–14.30.

Police station on Plateía Iróon Politekhníou, under the walls of the fort (not to be confused with Plateía Iróon behind the town beach).

Travel agencies

ANSO Tours, Arkadíou 295, ☎ 28310 57751.

Cretoise Tour Agency, Arkadíou 137, ☎ 28310 29791.

Ellotia Tours, Arkadíou 161, ☎ 28310 51981.

Odeon Travel, Palaiológou 25, ☎ 28310 57610.

Walking and mountaineering

The Happy Walker, an organisation for guided walks, has an office at Tombázi 56, ☎ 28310 52920; open Sun–Fri 17.00–20.30, closed Sat. The street is to the right just inside the Guóra gate from Plateía 4 Martýron into the old part of town. A Dutch couple takes small parties walking on the traditional paths and

tracks of the Réthymnon countryside. There are six different walks scheduled each week (finishing with a taverna lunch) and others, more demanding, by arrangement. The programme is designed to be informative about places of historical interest as well as the natural environment and the present-day life of rural Crete.
Ellinikós Oreivatikós Sýllogos (EOS), the Greek mountaineering society, has a branch at Dimokratías 12, ☎ 28310 23666; open only on Tues evenings, from 21.00.

Where to stay
Old City

B *Fortezza* (54 rooms), Melissinou, ☎ 28310 5555, fax 28310 54073. A up-market hotel on Melissinoú in the heart of the Old City, tucked under the walls of the Venetian fortress.

B *Ideon* (86 rooms), Plateía Plastira, overlooking the ferry dock, ☎ 28310 28667, fax 28310 28670, email: ideon@otenet.gr. A well-run, recently refurbished hotel up on Plateía Plastíra overlooking the ferry dock; suitable for wheelchair users.

If for a short visit you prefer accommodation away from the congestion of the Old City there are two hotels on Moátsou, a wide street running east from the Municipal Gardens, in the new part of town but convenient for the centre.

B *Liberty* (24 rooms), Moátsou and Prevelaki, ☎ 28310 55851-3, fax 28310 55850, email: liberty@ret.forthnet.gr. On Moátsou at the junction with Preveláki; open all year.

B *Olympic* (64 rooms), Moátsou 42, ☎ 28310 24761, fax 28310 2490. Next door to Hotel Liberty; open all year.

C *Kyma Beach* (35 rooms), Plateía Iróon, ☎ 28310 55503-4, fax 28310 27746. On Plateía Iróon, overlooking the beach near the tourist information office.

C *Park* (10 rooms), Leoph. Ig. Gavriil 9, ☎ 28310 9958. On the main through road opposite the Municipal Gardens.

A number of traditional buildings in the narrow streets under the fortress have been converted to **self-catering apartments**.

A *Palazzo Rimondi* (27 apartments), H. Trikópi, ☎ 28310 51289, fax 28310 26757, email: rimondi@otenet.gr.

A *Veneto* (13 apartments), Epimenidou 4, ☎ 28310 56634, fax 28310 56635.

For **studio rooms** to rent make for Plateía Plastíra overlooking the ferry quay where *Seeblick*, *Lefteris* and others are rightly popular. *Pension Anna* is in an attractive location close under the walls of the fortress on the stepped street, Katekháki. The tourist information office keeps an up-to-date list of inexpensive accommodation.

Beach resort hotels

Along the 12km beach to the east of town newly developed settlements offer a large number of hotels in various price categories, some especially suitable if you are looking for a self-contained base (perhaps for a family holiday) in the western half of the island.

A scheduled town bus service connects the hotels with the centre. If a self-contained beach resort hotel best suits your requirements, you should take advice from a travel agent at the planning stage and especially at peak times try to arrange bookings well in advance.

A *Rithymna Beach* (556 hotel rooms and bungalows), ☎ 28310 29491, fax 28310 71668, www.grecotel.gr, email: sales_rb@rb.grecotel.gr. At Adele, 5km east of the city centre, under Grecotel management this is one of the longest established resort hotels on the island and one of the best, providing all the facilities expected at this level.

A *Creta Palace* (370 rooms and bungalows), ☎ 28310 55181, fax 28310 54085, www.grecotel.gr, email sales_cp@cp.grecotel.gr. At Misíria, a

newer addition to the Grecotel chain
may be preferred because it is nearer the
city centre and in a tidier stretch of
development.

Youth hostel

45 Tobazi St, ☎ 28310 22848, email
yh_rethymnon@yahoo.com.

 ### Eating out

Most first-time visitors will
make for the tavernas lining
the quay of the Venetian harbour. The
day's catch of fish may be the deciding
factor in a choice between them but
Cretans consider that the *Knossos* keeps
up standards as well as any.

Up on Plateía Plastíra, conveniently
near the Archaeological Museum and
the Fortétsa, you can find good *mezédes*
at all times of the day within sight and
sound of the open sea.

Just behind the Venetian harbour,
Taverna Alana on Salamínos is in a
more sheltered position, with tables in
an attractive garden in summer.

Odós Vernárdou has *Minares*, *Old
Town* and *Kamára* close together, with
others neaby.

Taverna Veneto, round the corner in
Epimenídou, is a special experience both
for food and ambience; unlike some of
the others it is open all year round.

Banks

All the major banks are on Leoph. P.
Koundouriótou, the main through road.
The main branch of the *National Bank*
(with cash machines and automatic
currency exchange) is at the junction
with Dimokratías, with the *Commercial
Bank* diagonally across the road.

Post offices and telephones

The **central post office** is on Moátsou,
east from the inland end of the
Municipal Gardens; open Mon–Fri
07.30–20.00, Sat 07.30–14.00. In
summer a subsidiary office operates
(reduced hours) from a cabin at the east
end of the beach.

OTE for telephone and fax,
Koundouriótou 28, open Mon–Fri
08.00–20.00, Sat 08.00–15.00.

Hospital

Trandalídou, one block inland from the
Municipal Gardens, ☎ 28310 27491.

Public lavatories

At both ends of the town beach (by EOT
and the excursion boat quay).

Shopping

The stroll from the Pórta Guóra along
Ethnikís Antistáseos, turning down
Soulíou, taking in Palaiológou before
the length of Arkadíou should please
the most enthusiastic shoppers with a
range of possibilities from market stalls
to good quality stores for leather goods,
jewellery, textiles, specialist food shops
(products of Crete) for old postcards and
mementos of Crete, and (at Soulíou 43)
second-hand books.

On I. Petykháki, between the Loggia
and the sea, is the *International Press*
bookshop (one of the best stocked in
western Crete for tourist purposes), with
a jeweller next door to it on the seafront.

History

Archaeologists have evidence for a Minoan presence in the Réthymnon area,
at least in the Postpalatial period, from a chamber tomb in what is now the
southern part of the town. Modern Réthymnon occupies the site of Greco-
Roman Rhíthymna (a pre-Greek name). This city-state is known from ancient
texts and inscriptions and from its coinage, but the physical remains must lie

hidden under later buildings, most probably around the castle hill. In 1229, soon after the Venetians took control of the island, there is reference to a small fortified settlement known as Castel Vecchio which in 1307 was made the capital of one of four provinces and the seat of a rector (*rettore*) or governor. The harbour became a port of call on the Venetian trade route to the east.

In the 16C, with increased threat from the Turkish fleet under the piratical Khair-ed-din Barbarossa, there was an attempt to extend the fortifications, but in 1571 Turkish raiders were still able to loot and set fire to the town. Two years later the ambitious new fortifications for the Fortétsa on the Palaiókastro headland were begun. The compulsory service required to construct this enormous project caused great hardship to the inhabitants of the Cretan countryside, as well as consolidating their hatred of the Venetian rulers.

Despite all the harsh privations, the town flourished during the middle years of Venetian rule. This was a period of artistic and literary distinction when the fall of Constantinople (1453) brought about the movement of Byzantine scholars and painters to enrich the traditions of Crete which they and others carried westwards with them to Venice.

Márkos Mousoúros, a citizen of Réthymnon, was among the Cretan intellectuals who travelled to Venice. He was influential with Aldus Manutius in setting up (in 1490) the famous Aldine printing press to publish the Greek and Latin classics; this activity brought him into contact with the scholar Erasmus. Zakharías Kallérgis, also from Réthymnon, started (in 1493) the first wholly Greek publishing house in Venice; later he moved his business to Rome where he lodged in the same palazzo as the artist Raphael.

In 1646, when the triumphant Turkish army reached Réthymnon, the defenders withdrew into their fortress but were forced to surrender after only 23 days. The city became one of the three seats of government set up under Turkish rule. In 1897 (as part of the Great Powers' (p 50) move towards the autonomy of Crete) Réthymnon was occupied by Russian troops, a largely amicable arrangement from the point of view of the Christian population because of the affinity between the Greek and Russian Orthodox churches. In 1913 came the long awaited union with Greece and at last the Greek flag flew from the fortress walls.

The Old City

The **Municipal Gardens**, in a central position on the main thoroughfare, Leoph. P. Koundouriótou, are a convenient landmark (with a car park nearby) for the start of a walk through the old part of the city. The gardens were laid out over the former Muslim cemetery after the Turks left for Anatolia in 1924, at the time of the exchange of Greek and Turkish populations. A popular (and well advertised) wine festival is held here annually, in late July and early August.

From the northeast corner of the gardens cross the main road and walk downhill under the arch of the old gate known as the **Pórta Guóra**, after the Venetian rector Jacopo Guoro in charge of the construction in 1566–68. This was the main gate in the circuit of fortifications of which little else remains. The gate now leads into a scene far removed from modern commercial Réthymnon. If you explore the Old City you will find that a number of Venetian house façades (and especially the doorways) have survived, sometimes in passages or picturesque alleyways off the narrow main streets, while overhanging wooden balconies with iron supports and the occasional minaret are a reminder of Turkish times.

The street ahead through the Pórta Guóra is lined with colourful shops. A little way down you will notice on the left an elaborate church doorway, with an inverted acanthus motif carved on the keystone of the arch. The doorway was probably a later alteration to the simple single-aisled basilica with wooden roof which is all that remains of the Franciscan friary that stood here. The University of Crete has acquired the derelict building and there are plans to restore it.

A right fork (Soulíou) leads directly to the harbour but to the left the street widens into Plateía T. Petykháki. In summer the plateía becomes a shady open-air café with a good choice of tavernas and bars. There is now no indication that this was the western side of the Venetian piazza which extended from here to the sea, but remains of a priory, the ornate Rimóndi fountain, the restored loggia, still hint at the style of the important buildings which surrounded the piazza on three sides.

On the left as you reach the plateía the **Odeion**, or concert hall, has a 17C doorway dating from its days as the Latin church (Santa Maria) of the Augustinian religious house. The Turks converted the church into the **Nerátze mosque**, replacing the timber roof with cupolas and the bell-tower with a minaret, but the original doorway remains. The round-arched entrance, with an elongated corbel as a keystone, is supported by a pair of pillars with simple capitals. This doorway, flanked by pairs of half-columns with tall pedestal bases and Corinthian capitals, follows a design of the Italian Renaissance architect, Sebastiano Serlio, renowned for his influential treatise, *Architettura* (Venice, 1537).

You can walk on past the splendid minaret and along Vernárdou, but before that you will not want to miss (at the far end of the plateía) the richly decorated **Rimóndi fountain** built for the Venetian piazza in 1626 by another of Venice's rectors, Alvise Rimondi. Four short Corinthian columns frame elaborate lion-head waterspouts. An Italian engineer, assessing the city's defences at the height of the Turkish threat, expressed more confidence in Réthymnon's supply of drinking water from this fountain than in its fortifications or harbour.

Ahead (north) Mesologíou would lead you directly to the Kanakákis gallery (p 308) but if you extend the walk you will circle round to it, and to the fortress and the Archaeological Museum uphill from it.

Doubling back to the Odeion you can turn into **Vernárdou** which in summer offers a choice of atmospheric tavernas (p 300).

At Vernárdou 28–30, the much admired Historical and Folklore Museum (p 307) is housed in another restored Venetian mansion which makes an ideal background for the interesting and well-arranged collection.

Continuing along Vernárdou you find yourself in the plateía in front of a church built towards the end of the Venetian rule on the island (another **Santa Maria**, in this case Mary of the Angels, referring to the Annunciation), which was converted to a mosque with a minaret (soon reduced to a stump) and altered again when reconsecrated as a church in 1917. You can walk north towards Melissinoú and climb the stepped Katekháki to the Venetian fortress and the Archaeological Museum (see below). Turning right on Melissinoú, which becomes Salamínos, you pass the Kanakákis gallery on the way towards the Venetian harbour. If you cut through, along Arabatzóglou, parallel to the way

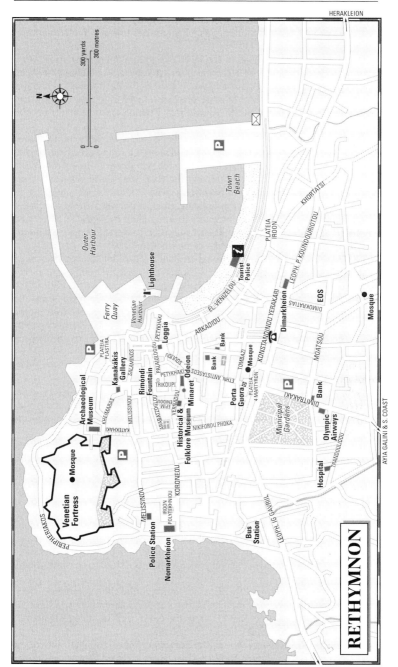

RETHYMNON

HERAKLEION

KHANIA

AVIA GALINI & S. COAST

300 yards
300 metres

N

Outer
Harbour

Town
Beach

Ferry
Quay

Venetian
Harbour

Lighthouse

PLATEIA
IRON

KHORTATSI

LEOPH. P. KOUNDOURIOTOU

DIMOKRATIAS

EOS

Mosque

Tourist
Police

EL. VENIZELOU

KONSTANDINOU YERAKARI

Dimarkheion

MOATSOU

ARKADIOU

Bank

PLATEIA
PLASTIRA

Loggia

PETYKHAKI

PALAIOLOGOU

TOUDOU

TOMBAZI

Mosque

Bank

SALAMINOS

Kanakákis
Gallery

Rimondi
Fountain

Odeion

PETYKHAKI

ETHN. ANTISTASEOS

VERNARDOU

Porta
Guora

PLATEIA
4 MARTYRON

Bank

DIMITRAKAKI

Archaeological
Museum

KHEIMARAS

MELISSINOU

ARABATZOGLOU

TRIKOUPI

Historical &
Folklore Museum

Minaret

NIKIFORDU PHOKA

Municipal
Gardens

Olympic
Airways

TRAANDOULIDOU

KATEHAKI

Venetian
Fortress

Mosque

Hospital

PERIPHERIAKOS

MELISSINOU

IRON
POLYTEKHNIOU

KORONEOU

Police Station

Nomarkheion

Bus
Station

LEOPH. IG GAVRIIL

you came, you will find yourself back at the Rimóndi fountain. From Plateía Petikháki in front of the fountain, Palaiológou heads towards the harbour and the town beach.

The **Venetian Loggia** (built in the mid-16C, given a flat roof in a 17C alteration) stands at the corner of Palaiológou and Arkadíou. The building has been carefully restored in recent years and is now used by the Archaeological Receipts Fund to sell high-class replicas of museum pieces as well as a range of illustrated guides to Crete published by the Ministry of Culture. Open Mon–Fri 08.00–17.00, Sat 09.00–14.00.

The Loggia was square in plan, elegantly symmetrical, with round-arched window openings and on each side the central arch forming an entrance with steps. The cornice rests on 22 corbels along each side above a defining moulding. Internally four pillars supported the wooden roof beams, and wooden corbels were carved with a decoration of acanthus leaves.

At the time of Venetian rule this building, then on the waterside at the corner of the piazza, would have been used as a meeting place by people of power and influence, for both business and pleasure purposes. Under the Turks it did a spell of duty as a mosque; the minaret was demolished in 1930.

The Loggia faces on to **Arkadíou** where some elegant buildings are in use as high-quality shops and travel agencies. Though the sea came in this far in earlier times there is now an outer block of buildings, many opening through to the beach road (E. Venizélou). If you turn left along Arkadíou (north from the Loggia) it takes you to the lively café-bars of **Plateía Plastíra**, overlooking the quay for the Athens ferry. The plateía extends along the coast, set back a little above the rocky shore, and is a place to look for rooms to rent or an informal (*mezédes*) meal.

Down to the east of the ferry quay is the picturesque Venetian harbour used by fishing boats and lined with romantically situated fish tavernas.

From in front of the Loggia you can cross Arkadíou into the short street **I. Petykháki**, and, past the International Press bookshop, come out at the quay for excursion boats, with the Venetian harbour to the left, and to the right the long town beach on the outer harbour.

Here, behind the beach, the resort takes over, with a diving club and then a long row of café-bars and souvenir shops. This is not a place for a memorable meal, but if you want to watch the world (and the traffic) go by you could follow the example of Cretan families who patronise the *Taverna Samaria*.

Venetian fortress

The formidable main gate into the enceinte is on the east side, opposite a free-standing bastion which now houses the Archaeological Museum. You can approach from the coast or from inland of the Venetian harbour. From the shore road west of the ferry quay (with car parking) there is a short steep climb, clearly signed to the Fortétsa.

From the Old City around the Rimondi fountain find Odós Salamínos which becomes Melissinoú (with a useful off-street car park). From here you have the choice of the stepped street Katekháki, or the easier walk uphill on Kheimáras, past the Kanakákis art gallery just out of Salamínos.

The Venetian fortress, known as the **Fortétsa** (from the Italian *fortezza*), is open 08.00–20.00 (in winter 10.00–16.00). There is a good Ministry of Culture illustrated guide on sale. The imposing fortifications offer vantage points for splendid views of the surrounding coast and countryside. A major programme of conservation and (where possible) restoration of the buildings inside the fortress has been under way for several years.

> Begun in 1573, the fort was a response both to damaging pirate raids and to the growing threat of Turkish intervention from the seas around Crete. The plans were drawn up by the Italian engineer, Sforza Pallavicini. The building took ten years to complete and the cost was enormous, with islanders from a wide area dragooned into forced labour. The immense ramparts (a circuit of 1307m) still stand, with their intriguing loopholed battlements, circular guard turrets and four great bastions on the vulnerable landward side.

The long, barrel-vaulted passage through the ramparts was designed to accommodate large scale movements of wheeled traffic or cavalry, and the recess above the gateway at its outer end would have held the familiar symbol of the lion of St Mark. There were two minor gates in the defences: the sea gate allowed access from small boats by a stairway in the rocks but, as it turned out, when the Venetians were besieged by the Turks severe storms prevented the landing of reinforcements.

The building to the right of the gate was an artillery magazine. Behind it, near the Ayios Nikólaos bastion, is the church of **Ayios Theódoros Trikhinás** (the epithet referring to the wearing of garments of animal hair) which was dedicated in 1899 to mark the withdrawal of the Turks from Crete.

In the lower ward, away to the left of the entrance, a deep well is reached by a sloping subterranean passage which may have been part of a defensive scheme for countermining. (You will notice an open-air theatre below the Ayios Ilías rampart where a festival is held every August.) The fortress depended largely on cisterns for its water supply and there are many examples of the remains of these structures.

The chief landmark in the centre of the enclave, near a lone palm tree, is the recently restored **mosque of Ibrahm Han** occupying the site of the Venetian cathedral church. The conversion took place in 1648 after the fall of Réthymnon to the Turks. The huge dome rests on eight supporting arches. The prayer niche or *mihrab* on the southeast side indicated the direction of Mecca. South of the mosque there is now a modern chapel.

At the north edge of the enclave, above the sea, are the remains of a large storeroom complex, with barrel-vaulted rooms, some of them below ground. It is on the record that these were designed for products such as wine, oil, vinegar and cheese (underground) with less perishable products like wheat and honey above ground.

Finally to the west, by the salient, is the (partially reconstructed) grand residence for the councillors, law enforcement officers under Venetian rule. The Turks added a bath-house.

As the Turkish menace increased in the 17C, there were misgivings (justifiable as it turned out) that the ramparts should have been surrounded by a moat, and that a harbour unable to take the Venetian galleys would prevent reinforcement in times of emergency. In 1645, after the town had been overrun by a large Turkish force, the great fort held out for only 23 days.

Archaeological Museum

The museum occupies the pentagonal free-standing bastion opposite the main gate of the Venetian fortress; this was built by the Turks as an additional defence. The bastion, restored in 1990, provides a single space with the effect of an atrium at its centre, ☎ 28310 54668. Open Tues–Sun 08.30–15.00 (16.00 in the summer season); closed Mon.

The exhibits, from sites all over the province of Réthymnon, are arranged clockwise round the room and chronologically, from the Neolithic to the Roman periods. The intention of the display is to inform and educate the visitor about the context in which the objects were found, and their significance in understanding the ancient people and places of the region. Thus the excellent labelling in both Greek and English gives a definitive framework of dates, and the introduction to each section, assuming no previous knowledge, supplies annotated maps of the sites.

The **prehistoric section** starts on the left wall as you enter with Late Neolithic and Early Minoan material from cave sites; this is one of the most comprehensive exhibits of finds from those times in any of Crete's museums, and includes (as well as pottery) clay and stone figurines and obsidian, bone and stone tools. Material from the important excavation of the Protopalatial settlement at Monastiráki (in the Amári valley) is deservedly allocated two cases. The archive of clay sealings discovered at this site has contributed to the understanding of administrative aspects of the economy during the early years of the Minoan palaces. Representative finds include a clay model of a sanctuary and an incised stone *kérnos*.

The peak sanctuary at c 850m near the summit of Mount Vrýsinas overlooks Réthymnon. The votive offerings excavated from the high rock clefts are typical of finds at such sites, often figurines of worshippers and domestic animals, in this case cattle. There is also a rare example of Linear A script incised on a stone altar. A peak sanctuary at Atsipádes in the south of the province has been the subject of detailed study in recent years and some material from that site is now on display.

The next cases hold groups of material from **Postpalatial** (LMIII) **tombs** all across the province, with the one at Mastambás confirming occupation in the immediate neighbourhood of modern Réthymnon.

From the Postpalatial cemetery at Arméni, south of Réthymnon, comes an outstanding display of **grave gifts** which accompanied the burials; of special interest (note the curator's comment) are a reconstructed boar's tusk helmet and the examples of Linear B script. Clay burial chests (*lárnakes*) positioned nearby include some from Arméni. Their painted decoration which ranks among the finest artistic achievements of Postpalatial Crete uses the octopus, bulls, birds and *agrímia* (Cretan wild goats) in a ritual hunting scene, as well as the double axe, sacred horns of consecration and tree-of-life motifs.

Among other material from the end of the Bronze Age (and the succeeding Subminoan period) there is exquisite **jewellery** from a chamber tomb at Pangolokhóri, a little east of Réthymnon, and figurines of the '*psi*' and '*phi*' types, so-called because their stylised shapes recall those letters of the Greek alphabet. Widely scattered at this period across the eastern Mediterranean, they are an indicator of a Mycenaean presence. In the same case are two tall bell-skirted goddess figurines, with characteristically raised arms; one was found also at Pangalokhóri.

The section of the display dealing with sites dating to the historical period begins with an outline of the important excavations by the University of Crete at the city-state of Eléftherna in the foothills of Mount Ida. From the Geometric and Archaic cemetery known as Orthí Pétra is displayed pottery, including an important series of miniatures, also human and animal figurines and a tripod table for offerings. The following cases contain artefacts from other regional sites flourishing at various times in the Archaic, Classical, Hellenistic and Roman periods. There is one group from the tomb of an athlete (at Stavroménos), another, with bronze figurines, from a ship wrecked off Ayía Galíni.

A case of **coins** includes examples from the Classical to the late Imperial period, from various mints both on Crete and the mainland. There is a good exhibit of early (Hellenistic and Roman) **glass** with a mould-blown flask and superb core-formed *amphoriskoi*. With this technique the glassmaker shaped on a metal rod a core (of clay or sand with an organic binder) to fit the inside of the body of the vessel. The core then had a trail of glass wound around it, or it might be dipped in molten glass.

Terracottas include Archaic heads and animal figurines, notably from Axós; the Daidalic style is well represented. There are also moulds used in the manufacturing process. One section of wall is devoted to inscriptions and nearby are grave steles from Eléftherna and Stavroménos (the same athlete's tomb). The display concludes with 4C BC red-figure pottery, both imported and from local workshops.

The museum has a number of large-scale sculptures, most of them of Roman date, all clearly labelled. A 1C AD relief of Aphrodite from the city-state of Lappa (Argyroúpolis) is composed of joined fragments which came to light at an interval of over 50 years, in 1910 and 1964.

Historical and Folklore Museum of Réthymnon

Vernárdou 30, ☎ 28310 23398. Open (summer) Mon–Sat 09.30–14.00, reopening Wed and Fri 18.30–20.30; closed Sun and public holidays.

The museum is housed in a restored Venetian mansion. It was founded in 1973 by local people as a private, non-profit-making operation. On the ground floor cases contain historical material, documents and mementoes of a broad spectrum of Réthymnon's public and professional life.

Upstairs the collection, amassed to preserve evidence of a rapidly disappearing world, is of considerable importance for the study of the social history of Crete, but the exhibits will also delight and inform anyone coming fresh to the subject. The displays in the elegant, spacious area are designed to the highest standards, with each section annotated. The exhibits cover a wide range of the crafts of Crete: all aspects of weaving, the various styles of embroidery, lace-making, potting, basket making, woodcarving and working in copper. The museum deals with traditional methods of agriculture in greater detail than elsewhere on the island. There is comment on the pioneer women involved in developing the economic and employment potential of some of these crafts.

Anyone considering buying bags, rugs, embroidered garments or other craftwork as souvenirs or gifts will have a chance here to absorb their traditional Cretan character before the influence of tourism and mass production made itself felt.

Kanakákis Centre for Contemporary Art

On Kheimáras, just off Salamínos and on the way up to the fortress. Open Tues–Sat 10.00–14.00 and 18.00–21.00, Sun 10.00–15.00; closed Mon; www.rca.gr. The centre was established in 1992. The nucleus of the permanent collection is the work of the Réthymnon artist Leftéris Kanakákis (1934–85), but the gallery also has a good reputation for mounting special exhibitions on Crete and for hosting others, in connection with a wider cultural network, from all over Greece.

The private collection amassed during the 20C by the late Eléni Frantzeskáki, and bequeathed in part to the municipality, used to be housed in a gallery across the street from the Kanakákis Centre but was closed indefinitely in 2000. The work of this self-taught Cretan artist was inspired by the traditional folk motifs that she collected all over Greece. Her beliefs in the role of women in society and the importance of the emerging ecological movement were ahead of her time in Crete. Visitors with an interest in period textiles should enquire about the collection at the tourist information office.

East of Réthymnon

Travelling by bus

There is an excellent bus service on the New Road route from Réthymnon bus station through to the harbourside in Herákleion.

To Pánormos and Balí

Leaving Réthymnon, join the bypass and head east, following the north coast highway (officially the New National Road). Readers who would like to visit the **war memorial to Australian forces** engaged in the 1941 Battle of Crete will need to watch for a slip-road at the Stavroménos junction which is signed (not too conspicuously) for Herákleion by the Old Road. Continue east on the Old Road and 1km off the highway the memorial is set back right, at the end of an avenue. It commemorates the courage of Australian servicemen and also honours those who fought alongside them 20–30 May 1941, Cretan civilians as well as Greek and British soldiers. Under a relief carving of defenders confronted with descending parachutists is a record of what was then the Australian Imperial Force. Two antique field guns add a historical perspective.

For Pánormos return to the north coast highway. Continuing east close to the shore, you approach the end of the coastal plain and the main Australian battleground. The airstrip here was one of the major objectives of the German airborne invasion which in May 1941 launched the battle for Crete. During the first wave of attack over this beach 161 German transport planes were recorded in the sky at one time (see *Crete: the Battle and the Resistance* in Recommended reading, p 58).

After the bridge over the River Yeropótamos you climb to a headland and leave the Réthymnon bay behind. 2km further on, at a turning inland, a good road runs up the river valley 7km to Pérama on the Old Road. On the seaward side of this junction is the village resort of Pánormos.

Pánormos

A decade ago this was a backwater except during the two hottest summer months when mainland Greeks arrived to enjoy the breezes of the Aegean Sea undisturbed by crowds of foreigners. Out of season Pánormos is still not over-crowded, partly perhaps because of the limitations of its beaches, but it is growing fast as a harbour village which can aim to appeal to discerning tourists.

Where to stay and eating out

B *Villa Kynthia* (5 rooms), ☎ 28340 51102, fax 28340 51148; one of the most exclusive small hotels on Crete, in a merchant's house dating from the end of the 19C, now lovingly converted.

C *Panormo Beach* (31 rooms), ☎ 28340 51321, fax 28340 51403. There is inexpensive accommodation on the village street and near the quay. *Captain's House*, a waterside taverna, also has apartments to rent.

There are a number of popular tavernas on the village street and down near the fishing boat quay.

AutPanormo Car Rental, ☎ 28340 51297, open 09.00–13.00 and 18.00–21.00, a small agency at the oblique crossroads in the village as you turn down to the harbour, will help with accommodation in case of difficulty.

Pánormos has played a part in the history of this stretch of the island's coast. The harbour was important from Venetian times until the early 20C as a trading centre for the surrounding area. When road communication developed between Herákleion and Réthymnon, commercial traffic moved away to these two major ports and inland to Pérama on the traditional route between them.

The ancient site of Pánormos, of which very little is known, extends over the low ridge to the southwest, inland of the highway and above the narrow coastal plain. Coins from here in the Herákleion Museum cover 1000 years from 1C BC–9C AD. On the crest of the ridge, with extensive views to the south across the island, are the excavated foundations of the Early Christian basilica of **Ayía Sophía**. The approach is signed left on the way down into the village (a ten-

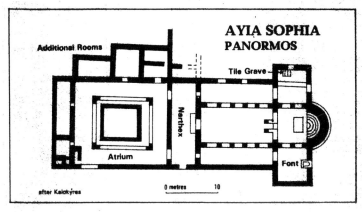

AYIA SOPHIA
PANORMOS

Additional Rooms

Tile Grave

Narthex

Atrium

Font

after Kalokýres

0 metres   10

minute walk, and possible by car). Keeping left at a fork you pass under the highway and the site is straight ahead, 150m uphill. Alternatively, drop down off the main road, inland, 400m west of the turning for Pérama (just before a guard rail protecting an underpass) and then proceed uphill.

The basilica, dated to the early 6C, was excavated in 1948. The three-aisled church ended in a triple transept and single apse, and the nave was divided by stylobates of four Ionic columns. Under the chancel floor was a small container filled with bones, presumably a foundation offering.

There were no mosaics, and the floors are of slabs or pebbles, but architectural fragments such as capitals and details from the screen were of high quality. West of the narthex there is an atrium which originally had a Corinthian colonnade around the central cistern. The function of the rooms along two sides of the atrium is uncertain but the one nearest the narthex may have been the original baptistery before a horseshoe-shaped font was installed in the south transept. The tile grave in the north transept is known from inscription to be the tomb of a minor cleric, Theodoros.

Balí

10km beyond Pánormos (c 35km from Réthymnon, 45km from Herákleion) with stunning views of the coast below, you can leave the highway for the resort village of Balí. This name is derived from the Turkish word for honey but in Classical times the sheltered bay was the site of *Astále*, seaport of Axós, a city-state inland on the slopes of Ida. Venetian maps kept alive the earlier name (sometimes Atále), as does the beautifully situated monastery of Ayios Ioánnis (see below), which is signed on the inland side of the main road.

As well as offering an attractive and comfortable base on the coast, Balí is well-placed for exploring this area of the island. You can get inland on to the Old Road, the old Herákleion–Réthymnon route along the foothills of Mount Ida, either up the river valley from Pánormos to Pérama or on a fine new road which climbs steeply from Sísses. Inland of the Old Road you have access to all the expeditions suggested east of Réthymnon, including to Anóyia and the high plain of Ida. Herákleion, with its outstanding Archaeological Museum, and the nearby Minoan palace site at Knossós are less than an hour away. The area is serviced by the E4 long-distance walking route.

Where to stay and eating out

B *Bali Beach* (63 rooms) ☎ 28340 94210, fax 28340 94252. This comfortable hotel is located above a diminutive private beach on the east side of the harbour cove.

C *Ormos Atalia* (33 furnished apartments), ☎ 28340 94171, fax 28340 94400. Overlooking the cliff path west of the harbour.

The harbour is lined with places to eat. On the west side of the cove *Taverna Panorama* is long-established and its traditional Cretan cooking is rightly popular.

High above the harbour, inland of the western cliff path, the food at *Valentino* is usually worth a visit.

At the extreme western end of the village coast road, above the Karavostásis cove there are still, for the time being, a few (coveted) **studio rooms** to rent and a couple of traditional tavernas. For *Sunrise Rooms* ask at the welcoming *Karavostasis taverna* on the way down the steps.

Mýthos Tours (☎ 28340 94450, fax 28340 94451), next door to the Hotel

Bali Beach, will provide all the usual assistance. The agency runs its own studios and apartments, handles currency exchange and arranges the hire of anything from a rowing boat to a yacht.

The road down to Balí passes a long stony beach and after more than 1km of small-scale development climbs to a white chapel. Here the harbour comes into view tucked under the headland on the west side of the bay and partly protected from the prevailing summer wind (*meltémi*). The resort is spread over, and up behind, several small coves. At the heart of the village the haven of the original fishing settlement is now surrounded by tavernas, many with accommodation above. It offers in high season every type of watersport, and is visited daily by excursion boats from Réthymnon. From the chapel the road winds on down to the quay. (There are places to park before the road becomes an alleyway.)

For a contrast to this organised holiday activity, walk for ten minutes on the cliff path west from the harbour, past a colony of crag martins, to the most westerly and most appealing of Balí's coves. Or you can drive, turning left to loop inland (signed to Evíta beach and various rooms to rent) instead of carrying on right, past a minimarket, down to the harbour.

This loop to the west comes to an end above **Karavostásis cove** where the swimming from off-shore rocks is as good as any on Crete, especially when the beach clears towards evening. In autumn the headlands here are a vantage point for birdwatchers as flocks on migration circle before tackling the hills behind.

The monastery of Ayios Ioánnis of Atále

The monastery, hidden 500m into the hills above the highway, is signed on the western side of the main exit for Balí. (Allow more than half an hour for a walk from the village.) Its opening times are Sat–Thurs 09.00–14.00 and in summer also 16.00–19.00; closed Fri.

Tradition associates the monastery's foundation with a hermit from across the valley to the east, and the evidence suggests a date in the first half of the 17C. In an isolated position for most of its existence (until the building of the New Road in the 1960s), the monastery played an important part in the island's long struggle for freedom from Ottoman rule. It commanded the route from the hidden landing-place below, through the Kouloúkonas hills to the Milopótamos valley on the way to the Cretan stronghold of the Ida range. After mainland Greece achieved independence in 1821, there are many tales about this lifeline to and from the outside world, including loss of life from bombardment of the bay by Turkish ships.

The monastery was attacked during the 1866 revolt but escaped complete destruction. The Italian scholar Giuseppe Gerola came here at the beginning of the 20C and noted the Venetian architectural detail on the parallel buildings linked by arches, and also the roofed main entrance with a 1635 inscription. But the monastery fell into decline, was deserted in 1941 after the German invasion, and stood empty until 1983 when the abbot and monks began work to bring it to life again. The garden that they planted on the approach, and lovingly tend, has already acquired some maturity.

This is a double-naved church with two dedications both (unusually) associated with St John. Feast days are celebrated on 24 June (for his birth) and 29 August (his martyrdom by beheading). Wall-paintings have been uncovered and dated to the first half of the 17C. From the terrace where cypress trees partly hide a fine church bell cast in Trieste in 1884 there is a memorable view of the coastline.

Continuing eastwards on the highway towards Phódele (p 187), soon after the turn for Sísses you enter the province of Herákleion; it is a further 20km to the outskirts of the city. For the easiest route to the Minoan palace of Knossós, see p 100.

To the northern foothills of Mount Ida

Determined motorists will be able to get an impression of this part of the island and visit its most interesting or picturesque features during the course of one long day, but others may enjoy spending more time exploring the unspoilt countryside. The northern route of the long-distance footpath E4 crosses this territory, passing the Arkádi monastery and the Eléftherna ridge on its way to the ascent of Mount Ida. There is simple accommodation in Anóyeia and Axós.

Three suggested itineraries are described separately below. The first runs southeast from Réthymnon to the important monastery of Arkádi. The second uses the Old Road east from Stavroménos, and through Margarítes (a village with a long tradition of pottery making) to Eléftherna, the spectacular upland location for a city-state dating back to the Archaic period. The third itinerary explores east from Pérama and the cave of Melidóni, which can be reached either along the Old Road or from Pánormos on the north coast highway. From the delightful village of Axós (within easy reach of the Sedóni cave and the Discuri monastery) you climb to Anóyia high on the slopes of Mount Ida, at the start of the ascent to the Nída mountain plain and the cave sanctuary of Zeus.

To the monastery of Arkádi

The monastic church at the centre of a serene courtyard is one of the most distinguished architectural monuments on the island, but it is as a place of pilgrimage to a symbol of freedom that visitors of Greek descent come to Arkádi from all over the world, and it is the heroic sacrifice of 1866 that is remembered and celebrated during the visit.

Travelling by bus
There is a convenient bus service from Réthymnon bus station.

The monastery is less than 20km inland from Réthymnon. There is a choice of well maintained though sometimes narrow roads up from the coast, or you can approach from the hinterland, from Eléftherna (p 315). The traditional and still most used route turns off the Old Road in Plataniás 4km east of the centre of Réthymnon signed Adele (or a little further east on the Old Road, signed Piyí). Approaching Réthymnon from the east on the New National Road watch for a sign for Arkádi in the suburban settlement of Adelianós Kambós. You join the traditional route in Loútra.

From the coast up to Piyí the road runs through great groves of ancient olive trees. 1km beyond Piyí, church enthusiasts can make a short (1km) detour to the Byzantine church of **Ayios Dimítrios**. A by-road right is signed to the village of the same name 1km beyond Piyí. Where the houses begin, continue on foot, keeping right past the whitewashed village church and on downhill c 200m to find the cross-in-square domed Ayios Dimítrios. The building is tentatively dated to the end of the Second Byzantine period, around the time of the arrival of the Venetians on the island. Externally, decorative arches echo the barrel-vaulting of the cross-arms and are emphasised by patterns executed in tiling. Similar patterns are repeated on the domed drum (restored 1971) which is lit by eight arched windows separated by slender columns. Inside the church the four columns under the dome are completed by Corinthian capitals reused from a building of the Early Christian period. From the 14C phase of wall-paintings only one full-length figure of a saint is preserved, but there is also evidence for earlier fresco decoration, probably contemporary with the 12C construction.

After Amnátos the road runs above a gorge to climb to uplands where the **Arkádi monastery** comes into view.

The annual festival on 9 November commemorates a heroic episode during the 1866–69 uprising against Turkish domination. As the headquarters of the revolutionary committee of Réthymnon, the monastery was besieged by an overwhelming Turkish force. The rebel defenders of the monastery under the leadership of the Abbot Gabriel, together with 600 women and children who had taken refuge with the monks, chose death rather than capture or surrender. They waited till the enemy smashed down the west gate, and then blew up the gunpowder magazine, killing themselves and at the same time many hundreds of Turks. The museum on an upper floor in the courtyard proudly exhibits relics of this inferno.

News of the tragic events of 1866 spread across Europe by means of reports from, among others, the American consul in Khánia. Victor Hugo wrote an emotional letter to a Trieste newspaper; Garibaldi expressed his sympathy with the Cretans as 'brave children of Ida'. Money was raised by European liberals and philhellenes for a supply ship, the SS *Arkadi*, in an attempt to break the Turkish blockade of the island. J.E. Hilary Skinner, reporter for the London Daily News, sailed with the ship on one mission, and wrote afterwards about the dangerous voyage delivering arms and supplies to southern anchorages guarded by the enemy fleet, and returning sick and wounded Cretans to be nursed on the Greek mainland (free since 1821). Commemorative plates, said to be made on the island of Sýros in the Northern Cyclades, now shown in the monastery museum, are decorated with a frieze of the *Arkadi* and her sister ship, the *Panhellenion*.

Much of the monastery that you see today originated in the 17C, though the main gateway into the courtyard was rebuilt to the original design after the 1866 destruction. The chief architectural interest lies in the ornate 16C west façade of the double-naved church dedicated to the Metamorphósis (Transfiguration of Christ) and to the Emperor Constantine, Ayios Konstantínos, and his mother, Ayía Eléni. The two-aisled design is reflected in the twin pediments of the façade, which are unified by a tall bellcote (with an inscription dated 1587). In the colonnade below, the pairs of Corinthian columns are evenly spaced, forming three equal bays in which the two doors serve the aisles, and the

Monastery of Arkádi

conventional central doorway is converted into a niche. Thus the Corinthian order was adapted to the double-naved Orthodox church.

On the north side of the courtyard the old refectory, pitted with bullet holes, and the roofless gunpowder storeroom, scene of the drama of 1866, are melancholy places. There is a fine view from the adjacent east gate or from the walls above; you look southeast towards the peaks of Mount Ida.

60m outside the main west gate (known as the Réthymnon Gate) is the ossuary for those who died, with the customary display of skulls. Nearby there is a small tourist pavilion café, open only erratically in summer and for the anniversary festivities.

It is worth walking back 300m below the monastery. Where the modern road up from Réthymnon crosses the stream-bed a narrow bridge (still well-preserved) carries the date 1685.

The road northeast from Arkádi leads (c 10km) to the site of ancient Eléftherna (see below). You could return to the north coast through Virán Episkopí, or continue to Margarítes and Pérama. These uplands are good walking country. Allow c 2 hours between Arkádi and Eléftherna.

To Margarítes and Eléftherna

Setting out from Réthymnon you take the New National Road which runs east for c 10km behind the long beach until signs indicate the Old Road to Herákleion. You pass the Australian war memorial (p 308) before Virán Episkopí. On the edge of the village there are remains of two ancient churches which enthusiasts may consider worth the short detour. **Ano** (upper) **Virán Episkopí** lies 1km off the main road (signed from a side-road, right, which is the shortest way to Eléftherna).

The chapel of Ayía Eiríne is built into the ruins of a 10C–11C basilica. There was another earlier church on the site which replaced a temple thought to be dedicated to the goddess Díktynna (from the evidence of a milestone recording road repairs paid for on her behalf). In medieval times the settlement was surrounded by a wall.

Continuing from Ayía Eiríne downhill (c 1km) and turning left at a T-junction you will find at a picturesque spot by a bridge over a stream the abandoned 14C domed basilica church of Ayios Dimítrios. (The builders reused an antique column and Ionic capital.)

Returning to the T-junction you continue ahead directly back to the main road to turn right for Margarítes.

Margarítes

The turning off the Old Road south, inland, for Margarítes (5km) and on to Eléftherna is 2km on the Réthymnon side of Pérama.

Margarítes is a village of potters and is much visited for this reason. It remains an attractive place perched on the edge of a hillside overlooking a wooded gorge with extensive views and cafés on the upper plateía from which to enjoy them. The ruins across the valley are the nearly deserted village of Káto Tripódos.

If you decide to stroll the length of Margarítes you can leave a vehicle when you reach the tree-shaded lower plateía. Every second shop is competing to draw attention to its pottery, local glass and other craft work. To find a potter specialising in the large storage jars or *pitharia* you have to continue beyond the top end of the village. A short distance along the Eléftherna road a workshop is set back on the left. During the summer months you are likely to find work in progress on these vessels which have altered little since Minoan times.

Three of the Byzantine churches in Margarítes preserve remains of wall-paintings: **Ayios Ioánnis Pródromos** (John the Baptist), **Ayios Ioánnis Theológos** (John the Evangelist) and **Ayios Yeóryios** (St George). You will probably notice the signs, but otherwise ask.

Eléftherna

Ancient Eléftherna (also transliterated Eleútherna) was one of the most important of the Dorian city-states and flourished from the 10C BC to medieval times. Its acropolis occupied a near impregnable spur rising steeply between two streams. A brief visit will suffice to give a sense of the place but to explore the whole site and the surrounding unspoilt countryside you could spend most of a day at Eléftherna. A walk on the acropolis might be extended down to an important cemetery of the Early Iron Age, or out north to a well-preserved Hellenistic bridge. In the valley below the steep east slopes of the acropolis, there are recent excavations of a Roman villa and an Early Christian basilica as well as a curious Byzantine church (see below). The E4 route crosses the site, so the steepest stretches of the footpaths have been improved, but at the time of writing Eléftherna is still far removed from the main tourist track.

You find the site from the hamlet now known as Arkhaía (ancient) Eléftherna approaching either from Margarítes (see above) or alternatively from the Arkádi monastery. On the way in from Margarítes, Roman remains are signed right (see below), but for the acropolis at the centre of the site keep on to the T-junction where the lane to the right (signed) leads in 200m to an isolated taverna which now straddles the approach to ancient Eléftherna. From the car park you walk north out on to the ridge, with the acropolis ahead.

The approach to the neck of the promontory was by a rock-cut road equipped with drains, along a saddle which forms a natural causeway not much more than 3m across. Where the causeway widens to allow a miniature courtyard the surface is worked to imitate paving stones. At the acropolis end of the saddle the ruins of a massive tower still stand to a height of 8m; it is thought to date to the late Roman or early medieval period.

ELEFTHERNA

(after Spratt)

History

The site was visited in the mid-19C by the British naval surveyor Captain T.A.B. Spratt who left a detailed description supported by a sketch plan. He drew attention especially to the defended approach to the acropolis, to the huge cisterns and to two ancient bridges, one of which still survives.

The archaeologist Humphrey Payne (husband of Dilys Powell, the film critic and author of *The Villa Ariadne*, see Recommended reading) investigated the site in 1929. It was known that the city had put up strong resistance before being overrun by Quintus Caecilius Metellus (Creticus) during the Roman campaign of 67 BC. He was credited with softening the city walls with vinegar to make them easier to breach. However, the city went on to thrive again under Roman rule. Payne noted massive walls from the Classical period repaired in Roman times, but did not come upon anything that intrigued him sufficiently to warrant further work.

The site of Eléftherna was left more or less undisturbed until 1984 when the University of Réthymnon began a major programme of excavation and study. This has clarified various periods in the city's long history which begins with evidence for Early Minoan settlement.

An important cemetery of the Early Iron Age, known as Orthí Pétra, has been located on the now heavily cultivated valley floor, c 100m in from the western stream. Excavation has added considerably to knowledge of the funerary practices of that time.

The ancient city spread down both the east and west slopes of the acropolis and across the western valley as far as the present-day village (known simply as Eléftherna) on the hill beyond the Kholopotá stream. From the ruined tower guarding the approach to the acropolis you can find the cemetery excavation in about 20 minutes. A longer walk, to the surviving Hellenistic bridge, follows the west (left) flank of the acropolis with access to the excavations on the summit, and then drops down to the north to the stream-bed. It involves a stiff climb on the return. You could allow between one and two hours for this expedition, especially in spring when the flowers on the terraced slopes are a distraction. At the time of writing the two routes are not officially linked; you may be able to find a way along the terraces between the higher path and the (roofed) cemetery excavation but the owners of the land do not encourage such initiatives.

To the cemetery of Orthí Pétra From the tower on the acropolis the old *kalderími*, with some sections still paved, keeps to the west slope of the hill. When it bends sharply left you can follow it for the Early Iron Age cemetery in the valley. On the way downhill after the bend you pass almost immediately a huge complex of **rock-cut cisterns** supplied by an aqueduct thought to be Roman, though the cisterns are probably earlier. The aqueduct brought water from a spring on the other side of the hill. There are two groups of three cisterns divided by rock pillars some 3m square. Each cavernous group measures c 40m x 25m with an average height of over 5m.

The steady descent continues. Near the bottom where the main track starts uphill again, half left, you take a narrow but well-worn path to the right. (There may be splashes of red paint.) Soon you arrive at a T-junction with ruined buildings ahead. Turn right and heading for a group of tall cypress trees follow the path back parallel to the stream, less than ten minutes to the site. Part of the excavation is roofed for protection but you can see quite well through the fence.

Orthí Pétra (meaning upright stone) is the traditional name for this locality. The archaeologists found the area damaged by cultivation and by a paved Roman road winding across it, and they had to disentangle the confusion created by superimposed use, continuous at least from the 10C to the 6C BC, to arrive at a detailed chronological picture of the funerary enclosure.

Apart from simple inhumations (usually of children) in a pithos or amphora, there were rectangular stone enclosures with a complex mixture of burial practices associated with both inhumation and cremation, probably reflecting family, clan and class traditions.

The work here included the study of pyre construction. The results confirm the record of events such as the cremation of Patroclus, friend of Achilles, described by Homer in the *Iliad* and also painted on Greek vases. The pyre might be built in a rectangular trench up to 1m deep, but on a layer of stones to provide draught. In a grid-iron pattern of tree trunks and branches, analysis has identified pine, cypress and olive wood. The body, sometimes elaborately clothed, was laid on the pyre with personal belongings, jewellery, perfume jars or weapons. It is estimated that the fire reached a temperature of 900° C and lasted a considerable time. It was eventually quenched with water, presumably from the nearby stream, and a mound of stones might be piled over the spot, though sometimes the bones were first retrieved, cleaned and interred in an amphora.

During the 1990 excavation season intriguing discoveries, with further connections between this Early Iron Age material and the accounts of Homer, suggested that human sacrifice had been part of the ritual associated with one of these pyres. The evidence assembled included a 30cm iron knife found near the neck of the victim (whose head was missing), a whetstone, presumably used to sharpen the knife, and a jar which could have held water to moisten the whetstone.

Analysis of the grave gifts and the evidence for ritual feasting on the site point to the connections between Eléftherna and other communities not only on the island but also abroad (the Greek mainland, Cyprus, the Phoenician coast and Egypt). Among the many exquisite finds in gold, crystal, faience, bronze, glass and pottery, there are four tiny (5cm) ivory heads which demonstrate carving of exceptional quality. They are thought to have come from wooden figures covered in gold leaf. There is an excellent display from Eléftherna in the Réthymnon Archaeological Museum.

An important Archaic statue (a male torso in the Daidalic style exhibited in the Herákleion Archaeological Museum, Room XIX) was an earlier find from the site. Now fragments of sculpture from Orthí Pétra, one with well-preserved painted decoration and another carved from local limestone, are throwing further light on Crete's contribution to the development of Greek sculpture.

Hellenistic bridge The recommended walk to the Hellenistic bridge sets off north (marked by E4 signs) along the flank of the acropolis from the hairpin bend above the cisterns. There are several points where you can get up on to the summit ridge of the acropolis to examine the recent excavations. One path, protected by a makeshift gate, leads to the fenced excavation of a large structure of the Early Christian period (recognisable by its quatrefoil plan). This was built on the site of a sanctuary that flourished in Archaic and Hellenistic times; from the quantity of inscriptions found the sanctuary is believed to have been of central importance to the city. The adjacent three-aisled basilica is easily identified. Down the hillside from these excavations, on the eastern side of the acropolis, archaeologists have traced the remains of ancient fortifications. Back along the ridge (south) a chapel to Ayía Eiríne was built into the ruins of either a basilica church or an earlier sanctuary.

The E4 path leads down the northwest slope of the ridge. The hillside is an undisturbed habitat for wild flowers and in spring the banks of the stream at the bottom are carpeted with the endemic cyclamen (*C. creticum*). You turn right to follow the stream-bed, with one short rise in the path, watching for the approach to the triangular-arched bridge below you. The Romans used the surrounding cliffs for rock-cut tombs.

The eastern side of the acropolis The easiest approach to the stream on the eastern side of the acropolis hill is from the Margarítes end of the Arkhaía Eléftherna hamlet where an unpaved road (signed to antiquities) descends into the valley. After 1km on a left-hand bend, look right for a curious double church. The domed, cross-in-square **Sotíros Khristós** (Our Saviour Christ) dates to the 10C, the Second Byzantine period, and has 12C frescoes (preserved only in the dome). The church was built over the foundations of a 6C basilica, and reused material from it. The basilica is believed to have been the episcopal church of ancient Eléftherna during the First Byzantine period. Then, towards the end of Venetian rule (16C), the 10C Byzantine church had joined on to it (probably to accommodate the Latin rite) the barrel-vaulted, pitched-roof structure dedicated to Ayios Ioánnis.

The track continues north along this eastern flank of the acropolis until (after 1km) a guardian's hut indicates the location of a recent programme of excavations. Below (right) are the remains of a **Roman villa** (2C–4C AD) and beside it a **basilica** of the First Byzantine period. These were built on the massive artificial terraces (dating back to the Hellenistic period) noted as a 'fine Hellenic platform' by Captain Spratt. A *kalderími* still leads down to a cistern near the stream where foundations of pillars are all that survives of the ancient bridge that crossed it.

From Arkhaía Eléftherna you can drive (3km) round to the village of Eléftherna. The road soon affords a fine retrospective view across the valley to the ancient site marked by the ruined tower and chapel on the acropolis. An open-air sanctuary was investigated in Eléftherna; nothing remains to visit but the excavation produced large quantities of terracotta figurines both human and animal, and also features of architectural interest from the Classical period.

Through the village you pass after 3km a turn for the monastery of Arkádi (p 313). If you continue ahead here towards the coast (keeping left in Skouloúphia) you will join the Herákleion–Réthymnon Old Road in Virán Episkopí 10km west of Pérama.

Pérama on the Old Road between Réthymnon and Herákleionflourishes as the busy commerical centre of a properous agricultural region. The direct route to Anóyeia (see below) sets off from here east towards Herákleion, but first there is the opportunity for a short detour to the Melidóni cave.

The cave of Melidóni

6km northeast of Pérama and at a height of 220m this cave would be worth a visit purely as a spectacle, but it is also a site of historic interest where Cretans keep alive the memory of an atrocity during the struggle for independence.

In Pérama take the Pánormos road but across the river bridge keep right and follow signs for Melidóni. From the village (with shaded tavernas round the plateía) you bear left to climb for 2km to the cave. There are views across the Mylopótamos valley to the Ida mountain range.

The cave is open (by local initiative) all day every day. Outside a café you will be asked for a contribution in return for a sketch plan of the cave. The rocky terrain may be slippery so sensible shoes are recommended.

The path to the cave, marked by a small church, leads up (3 minutes) to a hollow in front of the arched entrance far removed from the activity down below. The main cavern measures 40m x 50m and up to 25m in height. The huge stalagmites and stalactitic columns have been artistically lit to stunning theatrical effect with a special frequency system which avoids damage to the environment.

Tradition held that the Melidóni cave was the site of a Classical sanctuary dedicated to Hermes Talaios. Several seasons of rescue excavations during the last decade have confirmed that the cave was frequented on a regular basis from the Final Neolithic period until Roman times. There were levels rich in Minoan (Neopalatial) pottery with traces of ash and charcoal which may be associated with cult activity.

In historical times, at least from the 15C onwards, early travellers came here to admire a natural wonder. The cave is now revered, and a place of pilgrimage for Greeks, to commemorate the dead of an atrocity that took place in 1823. Three hundred and forty Christian women and children and 30 armed men who had taken refuge in the cave were trapped by a Turkish force under the ruling Pasha of the time. When the Christians refused all demands to surrender, the entrance was blocked up and a great fire lit to suffocate them. The bodies were left where they fell. The Christian community decided that no tomb nobler than the cavern could be devised and therefore the burial service was read over the victims where they lay.

The Englishman Robert Pashley, travelling on the island less than 15 years after this tragic event gives a graphic description of the piles of skulls and bones in the inner chamber, 'so thickly scattered that it is almost impossible to avoid crushing them as we pick our steps'.

Pérama to Axós

For Anóyeia from Pérama the direct route follows the Old Road along the Mylopótamos river valley and only leaves it east of Mourtzaná (c 8km from Pérama) to climb through Garázo towards the foothills of Psilorítis (Mount Ida) and the village of Axós.

Parallel to this road is an easily accessible stretch of the E4 walking route. This takes you near the village of Episkopí (also reached by road from Mourtzaná). In the middle of the village are the ruins of an episcopal church built under Venetian rule, perhaps as early as the 13C, in the Byzantine style but for bishops of the Latin rite. The ruins (including scant remains of frescoes) were conserved and rescued from further decay in 1960. The E4 continues past the Dioscuri monastery and on up a stream-bed to Zoniána for the Sedóni cave.

An alternative road between Pérama and Axós, carrying less traffic, loops inland into the hills from the eastern edge of Pérama meandering between villages dominated by mountain views. The uncultivated stretches of countryside are a hunting ground for botanists. Near Zonianá, shortly before the junction with the road through Axós, you pass the spectacular Sedóni cave. 4km from Pérama, on the edge of Khouméri, readers interested in church architecture could detour to **Kalamás** where the domed cross-in-square Byzantine church of **Ayios Yeóryios** (formerly the seat of a bishop) dates back to the 11C. A narthex was added at the beginning of the 12C and at a later date the building was enlarged again with an outer narthex in the form of a miniature three-aisled basilica. Eleventh-century frescoes have survived in the groin vaults of the main church, and the inner narthex has three early 12C martyrdom scenes.

Moní Diskoúri can be reached from Livádia or from the Garázo–Axós road. Open daily 09.00–12.00 and 16.00–21.00. The association with the Dioscuri (the twins Castor and Pollux, according to one tradition the sons of Zeus) is not fully understood but it is suggested that there may have been continuity from a sanctuary here in antiquity. The monastery flourished during Venetian rule, but now a small-scale foundation has been brought back to life within the last decade.

This is an idyllically peaceful spot. The lovingly tended monastic chapel is dedicated to Ayios Yeóryios, and outside the precinct the Byzantine church of Ayios Ioánnis Pródromos (the Baptist) has remains of frescoes which include a panel showing the Venetian donors of the work. On the summit of Ida the chapel of

Timiós Stavrós, the Holy Cross, belongs to this monastery.

Beyond Zonianá, signed left, is the **Sedóni cave**. Open daily April–October 09.00–18.00; reduced hours during the winter; guided tours only. This is the most spectacular cave on Crete that is easily accessible to tourists, and has accordingly suffered from the pressures of commercialism. On the positive side, wooden walkways already 300m long and planned to penetrate much further into the hillside provide access to the astonishing spectacle of the labyrinth and the specialised ecological interest of its micro-environment. The cave has been investigated by archaeologists who found evidence for Late Neolithic occupation and usage in Roman times, as well as some Late Minoan III material.

Axós is a delightful village, beautifully sited clinging to a high ridge. From Zonianá you descend into the village where three roads meet. Here the picturesque cross-in-square church of Ayía Eiríne with a central dome on blind-arcaded drum was a 14C addition built as a narthex to an earlier single-naved chapel. (For keys see below but this church's frescoes are in poor condition.)

Beside the church a track (signed) leads uphill for 400m to the site of ancient Axós, a city-state which flourished in the Archaic and Hellenistic periods. Little of the city survives above ground, but the extensive view and the frescoes in a cemetery church (**Ayios Ioánnis Pródromos**) make the 5-minute walk worthwhile. (The keys for both the above churches are held at a house immediately across the road from the start of the track.)

The city-state occupied a north–south saddle between two hills with the steep acropolis to the south (to the right as you approach) and extended down the northeast slope. On the saddle the cemetery church is built into the central nave and apse of an Early Christian basilica leaving some remaining fragments of a mosaic floor still visible. The church of Ayios Ioánnis has two phases of fresco decoration preserved (early 14C and early 15C); in the sanctuary densely painted scenes from the life of its patron saint, the Baptist, are the later work.

On the extreme top of the acropolis (reached by an old path from the cemetery church) a **temple** of the Archaic period, possibly dedicated to Apollo or Athena, was excavated by the Italians at the end of the last century. The massive temple platform can be distinguished most easily at the extreme south of the summit of the hill, now overlooking the many circular threshing floors of the modern village in the valley below. A magnificent bronze helmet in the Herákleion Museum, with cheek-pieces in the form of winged horses, came from this site. The Greek Archaeological Service has recently resumed work here.

The Anóyeia road climbs southeast from Axós soon passing the derelict Second Byzantine period church of Ayía Paraskeví which incorporates older material including fragments of columns.

Where to stay and eating out

There are quiet rooms to rent next to Ayía Eiríne, but for tavernas take the road left downhill to the plateía, which is often lively in the middle of the day. Here, under a plane tree beside a fountain, is *Taverna Plátano* (the Greek name for the tree), also a good place to ask about accommodation.

Anóyeia

Anóyeia occupies a commanding position at 730m in the northern foothills of Mount Ida, at the start of the (22km) road up to the Nída mountain plain where in antiquity a cave sanctuary was associated with the cult of the Cretan Zeus. Although in the province of Réthymnon, Anóyeia is geographically closer to Herákleion, c 35km on a quiet country road through the delightful village of Týlissos where three excavated Minoan houses are of considerable archaeological interest (p 189).

The large village of Anóyeia is laid out with two distinct centres, one along an upper road on the way in from Herákleion, with a plateía set back from it, and the other around the little plateía downhill on the slope below, which is where you will arrive from Axós. The two levels are linked by passages and steps. This is a village with a tradition of weaving; many of the houses have their own looms, and brightly coloured local products are everywhere for sale. There is a tourist information centre on the left of the road in from Herákleion within sight of the turning signed for the cave. Anóyeia is often busy during the day with coach tours from the coast.

Travelling by bus

There is a bus service to Anóyeia, five times a day from Herákleion and twice a day (early morning and mid-afternoon) from Réthymnon.

Where to stay and eating out

Several of the places advertising **rooms for rent** have magnificent views of Ida. *Hotel Aristea* is the best known, in the upper village, signed off the through road, with the *Aris rooms* nearby. *Manouradiana rent rooms* are left of the road from Herákleion.

The **tavernas** are mostly geared to lunches for tourist groups but there is a *psistariá* for grilled meats on the lower plateía. *Taverna Skalomata*, started by a much-admired *lyra* player whose home is in Anóyeia, is recommended by knowledgeable Cretans. It is a short distance up the road to the Idaian cave. The same customers patronise *Taverna Mikhail* at **Sisarkhá**, a hamlet c 4km out of Anóyeia on the road to Herákleion.

Anóyeia in 1944

Anóyeia has a long history as a centre of resistance and revolt, and bitter experience of the consequences. In the last century the village had to recover from devastation in August 1944, towards the end of the Second World War, when it was burnt to the ground by the German army of occupation, and any male inhabitants left behind or caught within a radius of 1km were executed. A proclamation listing the crimes cited by the occupying forces to justify this act of reprisal included the accusation that Anóyeia was centre of English espionage as well as a refuge for partisan (Resistance) bands. The Resistance fighters had shot the German commander of a small local garrison who had provoked a confrontation in the village, perhaps more by accident than design. When the first German column with punitive intent was ambushed with considerable loss of life, revenge was inevitable. The proclamation went on to state that the village had sheltered, earlier that year, the captors of General Kreipe whose kidnap (p 121) and spiriting away to North Africa by Allied agents with Cretan support had humiliated the German High Command. The Kreipe story has become accepted in folk memory as the principal reason for the dreadful retribution.

The story was probably more complex than that. Reprisals were usually intended as a rapid response to intimidate the local population but Anóyeia did not suffer until more than three months after the kidnap.

Anthony Beevor in *Crete: the Battle and the Resistance* (see Recommended reading) concludes that lingering humiliation was only one element influencing the Germans as, in August 1944, they faced defeat. What was then the main Herákleion–Khaniá road (the Old Road) running below Anóyeia was vital to the orderly withdrawal of their forces. The trigger for the destruction of the village, perhaps the final straw, was the threat of local unrest which immediately preceded it.

Mount Ida and Idaian cave

Dominating the view south from Anóyeia is Mount Ida, in Greek *Psilorítis* (from *psilós*, high or lofty), at 2456m the highest peak on Crete. The Idaian cave sacred to Zeus is at an altitude of 1540m and 15 minutes on foot above the mountain plain of Nída; this name is a corruption of the Greek *stin Ida* meaning at or in Ida.

The road into the mountains (which starts from the Herákleion end of Anóyeia) has been asphalted all the way (20km) to the high plain, partly to cope with access to a new observatory and a ski slope. A major excavation of the Idaian cave has recently been completed. The cavern is not in itself a spectacle to compare with Melidóni or Zonianá; its importance lies in its associations with a cult of Zeus, and in its history as a place of pilgrimage from far afield since ancient times.

• **Idaian cave** Open in the summer 09.30–16.00, daily except Mon. **Taverna Idaion Andron**, a café-bar below the cave (open in summer but only at weekends in winter), has simple accommodation. You can enquire ahead about availability at the **Stavrakis** taverna in Anóyeia, ☎ 28340 31141.

There are time-honoured routes from the mountain plain of Nída to the summit of Mount Ida (and on to Phourphourás in the Amári valley) or south over the shoulder to the Kamáres cave, but even with the arrival of the E4 these are expeditions only suitable for fit and well-equipped long-distance walkers. For further information consult the **Greek Alpine Club** (EOS) in Herákleion or Réthymnon (pp 65, 299) or the tourist centre in Anóyeia.

The 20km climb to the Nída plain is particularly recommended to wild-flower enthusiasts as the snow recedes in late spring and early summer. There is intensive use of the high summer pastures for great flocks of sheep and goats, and you will pass the *mitáta*, the round stone-built huts where for generations the shepherds have lived with their flocks in summer and made cheeses from their milk. (Nowadays the use of vehicles has reduced their isolation.) The age-old method of roofing these huts in stone with a true corbelled vault has been cited in connection with the unsolved problem of roofing the great circular Bronze Age tombs of the Mesará, not one of which was found intact.

9km into the climb on asphalt from Anóyeia, a dirt road comes in from the east (left). At this junction (at a height of nearly 1200m) an unusually well-preserved Minoan building was discovered in 1983. The site is known as **Zóminthos** after the nearby spring which has retained this pre-Hellenic name, one of the few certain survivals on Crete of a Bronze Age place-name. From the road you can see only some formidable Minoan masonry, but excavation has uncovered a large (54m x 37m) Neopalatial building (LMIA, c 1600 BC). Despite signs of damage caused by earthquake and a fire, walls stand up to 2.2m in places and the north façade includes two windows and a doorway to the height of the lintel. There was some wall plaster in situ. On a shelf in a small niche in one room were a terra-cotta bull rhyton and three vases. Fallen debris, which included burnt timbers and broken pots, confirmed the existence of an upper storey. The potter's work-shop (though apparently not part of the original design) was of interest because it contained a wheel, appropriate bronze tools, a built pit for the preparation of the clay and a large quantity of vases which seemed to have been stacked accord-ing to type.

In Minoan times the complex would have stood near a good source of water at the meeting of major routes on this approach to the Ida mountains; the route from the east would have been the shortest way from the palace at Knossós to the cult centre of the Idaian cave. The Minoan building is interpreted as some sort of station along the way. You can nowadays walk eastwards, towards a river gorge, in complete solitude, but perhaps not for much longer since roadworks have started at the Krousónas end, above the convent there.

15km from Anóyeia there is a turn to the new **observatory** on the summit of **Skínakas** at 1750m (which is 1000m above the tree line). This is a demanding walk or a short but exciting drive, requiring a clear day, c 4km on a narrow strip of asphalt. The final stretch is not recommended to sufferers from vertigo. The reward is a view of magnificent scenery with the Nída plain far below and the wall of Psilorítis to the south and west, a perspective elsewhere restricted to those who can make the ascent on foot.

Beyond the turning for the observatory the mountain plain (at c 1400m) opens out ahead, often with shepherds at work. The asphalt ends at the signs to the ski-slope but for the *Taverna Idaion Andron* (which does duty as a tourist pavilion) and for the cave you keep left round the edge of the plain. Above the track, right, as the snow recedes in late spring, are predictable sheets of moun-tain flowers including crocus and chionodoxa (*Chionodoxa cretica*), which is recorded on Mount Ida at the end of the Venetian period.

The search for endemic plants brought early travellers to the island, and Mount Ida was one of the first areas to be explored. The French botanist Pierre Belon climbed the mountain three times in the mid-16C. Today's visitors with an interest in the environment of the high mountains and their distinctive plants can consult Rackham and Moody's *The Making of the Cretan Landscape* (see Recommended reading).

From the taverna you can walk (10 minutes) or drive up a rough track to the **Idaian cave**. The guardian waits in the upper car park or at quiet times watches for visitors from below. From the open ground in front of the cave you have a bird's eye view of the plain.

The entrance to the cave, with (left) a large fallen rock roughly shaped into an altar with a step round it, leads to a steeply sloping first chamber. At the lowest level two side-chambers are formed (right and left). Ahead and at a higher level (8m higher) is a narrow inner chamber with stalagmites, which yielded impor-tant material for the archaeologists.

The cave was first investigated in 1885, and was immediately recognised as a highly important Iron Age sanctuary. In the 1950s the Greek archaeologist Spyridon Marinatos demonstrated that the Idaian cave was much frequented in

The Idaian cave and the cult of Zeus

There are several versions in Greek mythology of the story of the birth and early life of the god Zeus who had to be protected from his jealous father Krónos. Rival versions on Crete involve both the Psykhró cave on Mount Díkte and the Idaian cave, and if the Diktaían cave (p 240) is accepted as the traditional birthplace, then Zeus grew to manhood among the shepherds here on Ida.

The Idaian cave is associated with cult activity from early times, probably as early as the end of the Prepalatial period (Middle Minoan IA). The number of significant votive offerings increased in the Neopalatial period, and quantities of animal bones associated with ash and carbon suggested animal sacrifice and cult meals. Recent work has shown that cult practices continued without interruption from the Postpalatial (Late Minoan III) into the Geometric period. Offerings in the cave reached a peak in the 8C–6C BC; it is noted that they came from men as well as women and indicate that both warfare and fecundity were primary concerns.

By historical times the sacred cave was an accepted place of pilgrimage. The 6C BC Greek philosopher and teacher Pythagoras is said to have visited the sanctuary, with the Cretan poet and prophet Epimenides whose birthplace was Phaistós. In the 4C BC the Greek botanist Theophrastus (who did not himself travel to Crete) heard that it was the custom to hang votives on a tree at the entrance to the cave. Judging by the huge quantities of material retrieved over recent years by archaeologists, these pilgrimages continued through the Hellenistic and Roman periods into the 5C AD. Among this later material was a plaque naming Idaian Zeus. The Cretan Zeus died and was reborn and this distinctive concept connected with the annual cycle of vegetation, allied to stories of birth, marriage to a goddess and death, and the emphasis on his youth, are all elements of the myth peculiar to Crete.

With the degree of continuity in the archaeological record demonstrated at this site, these elements are likely to be of Minoan origin, though with the male god of the later Greek religion taking over the dominant position. It is widely accepted that a Minoan concept was central to the cult here on Mount Ida that was held in repute throughout the Classical world.

Minoan times, and probably for cult purposes. He brought out a variety of terracotta and bronze figurines, wine jugs and basins, as well as numerous objects in gold and ivory (see Herákleion Museum, Room XII). Tripod cauldrons, characteristic offerings in the great Geometric sanctuaries of mainland Greece, were found in numbers only exceeded at Olympia and Delphi.

Outstanding among the finds were ceremonial bronze shields from the Orientalising period c 750–650 BC (Herákleion Museum, Room XIX) and a bronze drum portraying Zeus between two attendants, the Kourétes. It is thought that a guild of metalworkers from the Near East, established on Crete, was responsible for these remarkable pieces.

The programme of excavation and study from 1982, directed by Professor J.A. Sakellarákis, has been one of the most ambitious and thorough projects on Crete in recent years, and has confirmed that this is the richest sanctuary known on the island. The whole cave has been meticulously examined, and structures such as walls and hearths identified. There is confirmation of Final Neolithic use of the cave in the fourth millennium and further evidence of cult activity developing in Middle Minoan times. Many unusual cult objects continue to appear among the votive offerings. Tests in the previously undisturbed deposits led to the discovery of a complete bronze shield (similar to those described above) decorated with sphinxes and griffins; this is particularly important because for the first time the exact find place of one of these shields has been recorded.

Among the extraordinary quantities of finds of exceptional quality were pieces of 8C–7C BC ivory objects from the Near East, with some important North Syrian material. Cretan ivories include a superb pin carved in a Janus-arrangement of two female heads, and part of a plaque in the Daidalic style, with the figure of a woman, perhaps a Mistress of Beasts. From the Geometric period (c 750 BC) there were ivory seals carved with a design of man and horse. There were also fragments of large statues in both bronze and terracotta; one painted terracotta head had an inlaid faience eye. Jewellery includes a gold pendant in the shape of a female head, and a gold appliqué of two warriors. The many rings included Hellenistic and Roman examples, these with engraved bezels. More than 1000 Roman lamps are a poignant reminder of the last generations of regular pilgrims.

A horizontal sculpture entitled *The Partisan of Peace*, is in sight from the terrace of *Taverna Idaion Andron* (where an article about it is available for interested visitors to consult). If you decide to walk across the plain for a closer look, it helps to take a bearing on its northern boundary before you continue down to the flat ground. You will notice a number of swallow-holes which help to drain the land in spring. Ornithologists will be excited by the number of songbirds on the plain as well as by the possibility of birds of prey soaring above Mount Ida.

The sculpture was created by a German artist, Karen Raeck, who has spent many years in the locality. As an assemblage of the stone boulders of Crete, her work is both a memorial reflecting Second World War heroism and a moving gesture of reconciliation to the people of Anóyeia. It depicts a figure, perhaps a partisan, a resistance fighter, stretched out on the ground. The suggestion of a shepherd's cloak carries the hint of an archangel's wing.

South of Réthymnon

To Spíli and the south coast

The province's main road across the island leads in 60km to Ayía Galíni, 36km to Plákias. On the way south you may want to stop at the principal feature of archaeological interest along this route, the Late Minoan III cemetery of **Arméni**. On a short excursion from the north coast you can turn off the beaten track into the hills above **Goulediáná** where an Early Christian basilica has been excavated, or explore the wooded countryside west of Arméni, through **Kástellos** and up to **Ano Maláki**, returning by the Old Road down to the highway. For walkers the Arméni cemetery is on the route of the E4, here running east towards the Minoan peak sanctuary near the summit of Mount Vrýsinas (858m) or west through woodlands to pass conveniently (for a circular return to the north coast) near the Old Road bus route (Episkopí–Réthymnon) at **Kaloníktis**.

In **Spíli** tourists stop to admire the unusual fountain and perhaps sample the choice of tavernas, but the village is also recommended as a place to stay if you are looking for an inland base for a few days. In nearby **Lambíni** there is a well-preserved former episcopal church (with remains of frescoes), an especially fine example of Byzantine church architecture. From Spíli a good road climbs east through a mountain pass into the **Amári valley**.

The road continues south to the popular coastal resort of **Ayía Galíni**, but if your destination is the Bay of Plakiás, the nearby **Préveli monastery** or the coast road west to the mountains of Sphákia (in the province of Khaniá) you must branch off to the west shortly before Spíli. You have a choice of two routes: the first (signed for Selliá) through the **Kótsiphos gorge**, best for the road west, and the second, 3km further south, through the even more spectacular **Kourtaliótikos gorge**, best for the monastery. For **Plakiás** you can use either road but the first is more direct.

Travelling by bus

There are good bus services from Réthymnon to Spíli, Ayía Galíni and Plakiás.

The Minoan cemetery at Arméni

From the centre of Réthymnon the main road climbs inland with fine views back over the fortress on the headland. You can join the Spíli road from the bypass. After 8km, at the crest of a long hill, you come to the Arméni cemetery on the right, back from the road, half hidden in a grove of oak trees. Open 08.30–15.00 daily except Mon.

The Cretan archaeologist Professor Y. Tzedákis began excavating here in 1969 and across the 4-hectare site has uncovered a remarkable series of more than **200 rock-cut tombs** dating to the Postpalatial period, 14C and 13C BC. The rock here is a fairly hard conglomerate, an unusual choice for a burial ground. The Minoans built a road across the cemetery, with branches leading off it. Now a circular path leads you round the site to the most interesting tombs; in spring the enclosure resembles a wild garden.

With the exception of one tholos the tomb architecture ranges from chambers little larger than niches to elaborate chamber tombs with an internal pillar or column and a bench round the wall. The rectangular or semi-circular burial chambers are approached by a *dromos*, a passage, sloping and sometimes stepped, down from ground level. (In a few cases, only the *dromos* seems to have been completed.) The burials ranged from a single inhumation without grave gifts to examples of multiple use with successive burials on the floor and also in clay chests or *lárnakes*. A selection of these chests is displayed in the Archaeological Museum in Réthymnon, as are some of the most outstanding of the gifts accompanying the burials. They include decorated pots, stone vases, vessels, tools and ornaments in bronze, sealstones and jewellery. A quantity of broken pots (both fine and cooking wares) noted on a small paved area linked to one *dromos* by a channel suggested cult practices. One special find, uncommon on Crete, was the covering for a helmet of a type described by Homer; it consisted of 60 plates cut from boar's tusk. (A similar helmet is displayed in the Herákleion Museum, Room VI.)

Evidence of workshops and kilns needed for the production of clay *lárnakes* has been found near the cemetery. The lively painted decoration has thrown new light on artistic standards in Postpalatial Crete. Continuing study of the human remains (over 500 skeletons) is contributing to knowledge of the physical appearance and health of the people who were buried here.

The oak trees in the grove at Arméni are the deciduous valonia oak, *Q. macrolepis*, rare on the island except in this area, easily identified by its huge acorns and acorn-cups.

The main road continues south through woodland to the village of Arméni.

A detour above Gouledianá

From the main Réthymnon–Spíli route take the cross-country road 2km south of Arméni signed for Karé, which leads over gentle, wooded hills to join (after 11km) the main road from Réthymnon to the high valley of Amári. Along this road a short detour into the uplands above Gouledianá is recommended.

This was the site of the ancient city-state of **Phálanna**, though almost nothing is left above ground. You can climb, by car or on foot (less than 2km), to an isolated plateau where the remains of a 5C–6C **basilica** have been excavated. The road into the hills starts (sharp right) at the far end of Gouledianá up a well-watered valley. You emerge on the rocky upland at the ruins of the deserted village of **Onythé** still preserving indications of the old vernacular architecture of the island. In the middle of the little plateau watch for signs left on to a track, which ends at the site.

The basilica, excavated in the 1950s, is built on a downward slope from south to north. The narthex, entered down three steps from a porch, has rooms at its north (downhill) end, probably for a baptistery, and to the south there may have been an atrium. Polychrome mosaics of elaborate geometric designs (no longer on view) helped to date the building to the late 5C–early 6C. Much of the chancel and apse had been destroyed by a later chapel, but a collection of small bones deposited in a pit sunk into the chancel floor is interpreted as a foundation offering, similar to that found at Pánormos east of Réthymnon.

The height to the north is **Mount Vrýsinas** (858m) where the Minoans established a peak sanctuary. In the 1970s archaeologists excavated from deep crevices in the rock a rich variety of votive material; an interesting selection is on display in the Réthymnon Archaeological Museum. The best approaches to the sanctuary are along the E4 walking route from Arméni or by tracks south of Roussospití.

Continuing south on the Spíli road you climb gently into a broad cultivated valley. 10km beyond Arméni the first of three turnings for Plakiás (p 331), this one signed for Selliá, diverges right beside a cemetery chapel. For the second turning, which is also the direct way to the Préveli monastery, continue 2km to a turn into Koxaré (signed for the monastery and Asómatos). For Plakiás go left downhill from the fork through Mýrthios (tavernas with view, the objective of a popular

3km evening walk up from the coast) and just beyond the village (signed Plakiás) turn right down to the bay. Selliá is at the start of the coast road west to Rodákino, and on to Khora Sphakíon (p 386) in the province of Khaniá.

2km south of the turning to the Préveli monastery, noted above on the main Réthymnon–Spíli road, a recommended detour left (of less than 2km) to **Lambíni** takes in the 14C church of the **Panayía** on a rise commanding the valley and the district of Ayios Vasíleios (St Basil) of which it was formerly the episcopal church. (You can also reach the church from Mixórruma, 5km north of Spíli.) The key is held at the house across the road and just beyond the church, and members of the guardian's family are eager to provide access.

This is a large 14C church (dedicated to the Assumption of the Virgin, feast day 15 August) with a central dome and a three-aisled and cruciform plan; an unusual feature is that the east arm of the cross is longer than the west one. Externally the transverse vaults are emphasised by decorative recessed arches, while the dome rests on a blind-arcaded drum. A plaque by the memorial in the precinct tells of a Turkish atrocity in 1827 when the congregation was burnt to death in the church.

Evidence for two layers of frescoes has been uncovered, dated to the end of the 14C and beginning of the 15C. The older style survives in the sanctuary and on the north wall at its western end. A panel in the church provides commentary on the ecclesiastical setting and the architecture, and details the remaining wall-paintings.

Spíli

30km from Réthymnon, Spíli lies on a steep hillside that is well-watered and fertile all the year round. This is a bustling centre for the inhabitants of the surrounding countryside (two banks, post office, chemist, good bakeries and tavernas competing to serve traditional Cretan food), but it manages to remain a delightful village where the inhabitants make it their business to welcome visitors. For a brief stop the plateía is beside the only right-angled bend on the long through road. It has a picturesque (and much photographed) **fountain** with a row of 19 lions' head spouts, and several cafés (offering local yoghurt and honey) from which to contemplate them.

In the hot weather Spíli makes a cooler and less hectic base than the coastal resorts, and is a good starting point for exploring the Amári valley and the western foothills of Mount Ida. For walkers the southern route of the E4 passes through the village. Motorists can make an easy day trip to the Minoan palace of Phaistós.

Where to stay and eating out

The *Green Hotel* (12 rooms), ☎ 28310 22225.http://server2042.virtualave.net/green-hotel/. Located on the right-hand side of the main street on the way in from Réthymnon, this is a small, family-run business with a great reputation, so that it is a matter of luck whether there is a room free at short notice, especially in April and May which are popular months for wild flower enthusiasts.

There are several **rent room** establishments in Spíli, most of them well advertised on the through road. You could try *Herakles*, next to the hotel, quieter than more central places, or *Horizon Apartments* at the start of the road over to the Amári valley.

Tavernas tend to concentrate on their daytime customers but *Costas*, on the left a little before the fountain as you approach from Réthymnon, flourishes in the evenings (and offers a choice of organic local wines from the barrel). Above the taverna are comfortable modern **rooms to rent**.

At the southern end of the village, by the start of the side-road to Mourné, the cemetery chapel of **Sotíros Khristós** (Our Saviour Christ) has the remains of late 14C wall-paintings. On the north wall there is a good example of Ayios Mamás, protector of shepherds, portrayed, according to the usual convention, with a crook and a young goat over his arm.

The early 14C frescoes in the church of Ayios Yeóryios in the village of **Mourné** are worth the 4km detour for enthusiasts. The decoration includes traditional scenes from the martyrdom of St George.

South of Spíli the main road follows an empty valley between Mount Kédros (1777m) to the north and Sidérotas (1162m) to the south. Minor roads across uncultivated stretches of hillside give access to beaches at **Ayía Photiní** and **Ayios Pávlos**. The road south approaches the coast alongside the broad watercourse of the River Plátys which runs into the sea east of Ayía Galíni.

Ayía Galíni

This picturesque village around and up behind a narrow harbour was the first holiday resort to be developed on the south coast. There is plenty of accommodation at the less expensive end of the market, but in high season this may be solidly booked from abroad, and visitors need to be able to enjoy the exuberant nightlife. The rocky beach at the mouth of the Plátys has a long-established camping site. Boats run daily to more attractive local beaches, including Ayios Pávlos and the Préveli beach (p 336) and to the Paximádia islands; details are advertised along the quay.

Out of season Ayía Galíni has much to offer as a base for a few days on a touring holiday. You can get to the Minoan palace of Phaistós early in the day before the coach tours arrive from the north. You are within comfortable reach (15km) of the southern end of the Amári valley and the monasteries along the slopes of Mount Ida beyond Kamáres (p 177).

Birdwatchers will find plenty to interest them around the Ayía Galíni harbour and the areas of reed-bed at the river mouth. From the village you can take the coastal path east (where the cliffs are now netted to discourage nesting by swifts) or the road round to a rough track down the west bank of the river (turning before the signs for camping). Further afield the path follows the shore of the Mesará Bay, south as far as Kómmos (p 161).

Inland of Ayía Galíni the minor road down from the village of Mélambes (at a height of 600m) offers the reward of stunning views of the island's southern coastline. If you arrive by bus you will be set down when you reach the lower village, before the streets narrow prohibitively. Most are dedicated to pedestrians but the main street takes cars down to the harbour front for parking (small charge).

Travel agency

The *Monza tourist agency* (☎ 28320 91004, fax 28320 91035), across the road from the bus station, will change money, rent cars and bikes, offer suggestions if accommodation is difficult, and is a mine of information about the resort.

Where to stay and eating out

The majority of hotels in Ayía Galíni are geared to package holidays booked from all over Europe and beyond. The independent traveller looking for relatively peaceful accommodation might try the following near the top of the old village.

Up the hill on the wide bend above the bus terminus there is an attractive group of buildings which includes two small hotels, C *Fevro* (49 rooms), ☎ 28320 91275, fax 28320 91475 and C *Glaros* (33 rooms), ☎ 28320 91151, fax 28320 91159, smothered in flowers, and the purpose-built **rent rooms Kriti**.

There are innumerable places where you can eat, some on the harbour, but you will find better food down the pedestrianised streets which in summer are a solid mass of tavernas and café tables. To enjoy traditional Cretan cooking find *Taverna Onar* up a flight of steps from the harbour plateía.

Plakiás

The shortest way across from the Réthymnon–Spíli main road follows a valley running west through Ayios Vasíleios. In Ayios Ioánnis it turns south to pass through the **Kotsiphós gorge**, from which you emerge to a spectacular view of the Pláka bay. In July and August especially, the prevailing north wind, the *meltémi*, is funnelled through this gorge, and the beach at Plakiás suffers accordingly. Before Selliá you go left through Mýrthios and just beyond the village turn right (signed for Plakiás) down to the bay.

Plakiás has expanded very successfully from a cluster of houses around a primitive quay at one end of a long tamarisk-shaded beach into a small-scale holiday resort. The new centre is by the harbour, now home to a dozen or so fishing boats and one or two motor launches for local excursions and a twice-daily boat service to Préveli beach. Across the way is a post office caravan, the office for the bus company, a tourist agency, useful shops and a laundromat. The nearest bank is in Spíli. On the road behind the beach east of the harbour there are two long-established small hotels (*Livikon* and *Lamon*), useful for the odd night but otherwise in a noisy location. The village and nearby beaches have a variety of more attractive places for a longer stay (see below).

Plakiás is highly recommended for a walking holiday of the less demanding variety, but it can also make a good base for day-long excursions, for example to the Amári valley (via Spíli), to the mountains of Sphakiá (p 383) or the Minoan sites at Phaistós, Ayía Triáda and Kommós.

The village's long sandy beach stretches east from the harbour around the bay, but there is also good swimming in the less developed coves along the coast in both directions. Two kilometres west of the harbour, where the coast road runs out at the far west end of the Pláka bay, the steeply shelving Soúda beach is a popular, and often relatively sheltered, place to swim.

Travelling by bus

Services include reasonably frequent buses between Plakiás and Réthymnon,

a limited service to Ayía Galíni via Spíli, and in the high season to the Préveli monastery and Sphakiá.

Travel agency

The tourist agency *ANSO*, set back 50m from the harbour front behind a highly visible bakery-cum-café, will change money and help with most holiday requirements. It arranges car and bike hire, access to water sports and diving, coach excursions to many tourist attractions and organised walks.

Where to stay

C *Ammoudi* (29 rooms), ☎ 28320 31355, fax 28320 31755. With a restaurant, in a delightful setting 200m back from the shore in the second cove to the east of Plakiás.

C *Horizon Beach* (26 rooms), ☎ 28320 31476, fax 28320 31154. Past the harbour on the western edge of the village. On the coast road towards the Horizon Beach hotel you pass a choice of inexpensive **rooms to rent**, most of them attached to tavernas, all within easy walking distance of the centre and the main beach.

C *Phoenix* (18 rooms), ☎ 28320 31331, fax 28320 31831. 2km west of the village above the rock shelf before the Soúda beach. Close by are the **studio rooms** to rent of the *Pension Soúda Mare*.

C *Plakias Bay* (28 rooms), ☎ 28320 31215, fax 28320 31951. Outside the village, on a rise at the furthest east end of the long sandy beach.

C *Souda Mare* (17 rooms), ☎ 28320 31931, fax 28320 31763. 2km west of the village above the rock shelf before the Souda Beach. Close by are the **studio rooms** to rent of the Pension Soúda Máre.

Youth hostel

☎ 28310 32118, fax 28310 3139, www.yhplakias.com, email info@yhplakias.com.

Eating out

One of the best places to eat classic Cretan taverna food is the family-run *Gio-Ma* which also enjoys a beautiful location right on the sea, on the west side of the quay so that the sheltered terrace has a romantic sunset view along the coast to the end of the bay.

For fish go to *Korali* (in the block opposite the harbour) and take the owner's advice on what is fresh; he has his own boat.

To the west under the cliffs at the **Soúda beach** there are two simple waterside tavernas, *Delphini* and *Galini*. At Mýrthios high (200m) uphill by a path from the harbour, *Taverna Panorama* and others either side of it, all with fine views from their terraces over the coast, are popular for their good food at the end of an evening walk.

East from Plakiás, either on foot along the coastal track or by road, there are several coves to explore. Start towards Mýrthios but keep right for the coast road towards Levkóyia and the Préveli monastery; the turnings for the coves are signed. **Damnóni** has a holiday village on the hillside, which means a crowded beach in summer, but in mid-season the tavernas can be recommended. **Ammoúdi** is a narrow cove with tamarisks lining a stream bed, an idyllic setting as long as further development can be resisted. From **Levkóyia**, a side-road (perhaps still unsurfaced for part of the way) leads in 4km down to **Skinária beach** with a café-bar, *Libyan Star*. In spring, flower enthusiasts have uncultivated roadsides to explore, and near the sea the stream-bed is lined by reeds which give shelter to birds. The *Paradise Dive Centre* based in Réthymnon, ☎ 28310 53258, may be operating from this beach in high summer.

The country immediately inland from Plakiás is beautiful and unspoilt. Lance Chilton's *Ten Walks in the Plakias Area* and his map should be available in the village. An inland path climbs directly up the stream-bed as far as the **Kótsiphos Gorge**. You can walk in c 2 hours to the Préveli monastery (see below) via Levkóyia and Giannoú; enquire about a bus for the return, or the ferry boat from Préveli beach way below the monastery, or arrange to be picked up by a taxi.

With private transport (even a bicycle) or using the Spíli bus, the short expedition to the **Kourtaliótiko Gorge** is highly recommended. If you enjoy tranquillity try to avoid weekends when groups or family parties are more likely to make the descent; you can usually tell from the cars at the top whether to expect a crowd.

From Asómatos follow the road curving left to run high above the gorge. There are several designated places to park for a closer view, but about midway along this section watch for one where railed steps set off into the ravine; they take you down to the stream-bed and the white chapel (hidden till you are upon it) of Ayios Nikólaos. The story is that the local saint, Nicholas the Kourtalióte, struck the rock (like Moses) and seven springs gushed forth. This is a particularly beautiful spot with water cascading over rocks. Readers with an interest in birds or wild flowers and plants in general are unlikely to be disappointed. In front of the chapel there are tables and benches set up for the annual celebrations of the saint's day, but convenient at other times for a picnic. The river here soon joins the Megapótamos to reach the sea at Préveli Beach (see below) through the lower gorge. The travel agency *ANSO* in Plakiás organises half-day walks (for guided groups) between Ayios Nikólaos and the sea.

The monastery of Préveli

At least from the second half of the 17C there were two monasteries associated with the name of Prévelis, an influential local family. The two were distinguished as *káto monastíri* (the lower monastery) and *píso monastíri* (the monastery behind, to the rear). Today the lower monastery is deserted but the function of the romantic ruins can be deciphered. The monastery behind, nearer the sea, now usually referred to simply as Moní Préveli, is open daily in summer 08.00–13.30 and 16.00–19.00 and, along with the palm-fringed beach far below it, ranks high among the tourist attractions of Crete.

Whether you approach from Plakiás or the Spíli direction you turn south on the edge of the village of Levkóyia for the last 6km to the monastery. Walkers from Plakiás can use a short-cut down from Yiannioú but will miss an especially beautiful stretch of the river and the ruined lower monastery which overlooked it. The Kourtaliótis, fed by the springs of the gorge, has been joined by other streams and this last stretch before the sea is known as the Megapótamos (literally the great river). This is one of the few rivers on Crete which flows year round. After 2km you pass a narrow, steeply arched bridge in the Turkish style, with an inscription recording that it was built for the monks in 1850 by Manólis Drandákis from Réthymnon. 500m further, staying on this same (right) bank of the river, the ruined Káto Préveli monastery lies below the road left. You can get a bird's eye view where the road climbs and bends left with the roofless buildings spread out below, but if you want a closer look stop at the end of the recently planted olive grove running up from the river, and approach by the remains of the original *kalderími* along the lower side of the ruins.

History

It seems that from a cluster of small religious communities of the Venetian period, some of whose frescoed chapels (all locked) are still scattered about the slopes of the valley, two monasteries emerged to flourish under Turkish rule. They profited from their relatively isolated position and *stavropegiac* status, which meant that they were answerable directly to the Patriarch of Constantinople and enjoyed a degree of protection under the Islamic rulers of Crete. They grew to be wealthy institutions and were influential as a focus of Greek learning and education through clandestine schools.

The monks of Préveli were deeply involved in support for the cause of Cretan independence. During the 1866 rebellion the monastery was an important link in the chain of relief operations. The fast steamship, the *Arkadi*, evading the Turkish fleet, brought in from the free Greek mainland guns and ammunition (and boot-leather) for the insurgents and evacuated the wounded as well as some women and children. The reporter J.E. Hilary Skinner wrote of an anxious wait with the monks on the beach at Préveli.

In 1941 the monastery was in the forefront of caring for Allied forces left behind on the island after the naval evacuation and then, as before, the monastic community suffered because of its involvement. In July that year Lt Cdr Francis Pool, who had worked for Imperial Airways on Crete before the war, was landed by submarine at Préveli beach. His mission was to organise the evacuation of Allied soldiers stranded after the Battle of Crete, and to relieve the suffering islanders of the added burden of caring for them. He made contact with the elderly Abbot Agathángelos Langouvárdos, a formidable man 22 stone in weight and in Antony Beevor's words 'fearless and enchanting'. The monastery became a gathering point for the escapees. The evacuation did not go smoothly but Pool left at the end of August, reputedly with a record for the number of people ever packed into one submarine. The abbot had to go into hiding himself before his eventual evacuation to Cairo where he swore in the new Greek government in exile. He did not live to see Crete again.

The ruined Káto Préveli monastery

The *kalderími* along the side of the remains nearest the river leads to the main entrance for the monastery courtyard and the church dedicated to Ayios Ioánnis Pródromos (the Baptist). You pass a spring chamber next to the abbot's quarters where the fountain has an inscription commemorating the 19C abbot Agathángelos. Inside the courtyard the kitchen is on the left with a huge chimney which conducted heat to the rooms above. To the right of the entrance, a main hall on the first floor of the abbot's quarters overlooks the west end of the single-naved church, rebuilt in the 19C after destruction by the Turks.

The oldest remaining buildings are two vaulted chambers beyond the east end of the church, one to house an olive press, the other a stable. In the 1821 fire, 14,000kg of oil contributed to the scale of the blaze. The monastery overlooks fertile river valley land, and the ruined warehouses and workshops are a reminder of the husbandry which was an integral part of the self-contained monastic life.

Káto Préveli was devastated by the Germans in 1941, after the evacuation which followed the Battle of Crete, and the monastic community never recovered.

Píso Moní Préveli

The monastery built by Abbot Prévelis in the 17C was hidden from piratical raids in the hills nearby. He dedicated the new foundation to Ayios Ioánnis Theológos, the Evangelist, and moved to it the monastery's valuable library. The modern road continues the climb up to this second monastery. Round the last corner the splendid buildings come suddenly into view. The 19C traveller, naval surveyor Captain Spratt, enthused over 'this paradise of Crete, in one of the most happily chosen spots for a retreat from the cares and responsibilities of life!'

Moní Préveli has been restored as a historic monument preserving the history of the religious foundation. Outside the gates are a cemetery chapel and an ossuary in the shape of a church. Abbot Prévelis built on a hillside and you will notice the terracing and the vaulted support devised to cope with this problem of the different levels. There is a fine view over monastery lands to the Libyan Sea.

The monastic **church** is a substantial double-naved building unified by a simple west facade with bell-tower, which was completed (as a replacement for the original church) in 1837. This was the time of the interim administration of Crete by the Egyptians. The principal interest of the interior of the church is that it has survived substantially unaltered since it was built. The two naves (dedicated to St John and to the Annunciation) are linked by the splendid carved iconostasis which was designed to incorporate icons (Old Testament subjects) from an 18C phase of redecoration of the previous church.

Across from the west façade is a two-storeyed building (in the neo-classical style) for formal reception or ceremonial use. Dating from the beginning of the 20C these rooms were hurriedly prepared to receive in 1903 the new high commissioner for the independent Cretan state. Picturesque older buildings include (opposite the west doors) the original bakery with a huge oven said to be capable of turning out 800 loaves a day.

The uphill side of the precinct is lined with two-storeyed cells. In the lower courtyard stone steps lead down to a fountain fed by a spring where an inscription (in palindromic form) dated 15 June 1701 translates: 'cleanse my transgressions, not merely my face'. On either side were a long stable and a workshop for making beeswax candles, and behind is an underground chamber, a naturally insulated cold store.

The vaulted stable has recently been turned into a small **museum** displaying icons and other ecclesiastical treasures, as well as vestments illustrating the local tradition of fine embroidery on silk. The exhibits contribute substantially to an understanding of the two centuries (17C and 18C) when this monastic institution was at the height of its influence and importance.

From later times a pair of silver candlesticks (case on the right-hand wall) were a gift from the British government as a token of gratitude at the end of the Second World War. A commemorative plaque in the courtyard provides further tribute.

Préveli beach

Picturesque Préveli beach, where the Megapótamos flows along a narrow palm-fringed valley and then through a miniature lagoon behind a sandbank before the sea, has become too well-known for its own good. It attracts visitors in overwhelming numbers. The awkward scramble down the cliff used to impose some limitation but now boats bring day-trippers from Plakiás and Damnóni, and from

Ayía Galíni, to a primitive café and its sunloungers and umbrellas all along the shore. In summer there are campers but no facilities for the disposal of rubbish. The authorities have made considerable efforts but the problems defeat them and sadly (except perhaps early in the year) the magic of this place has not survived.

If you want to take a look at the beach there are two options (apart from a boat trip), both requiring a degree of fitness and agility. On the last stretch of the approach to the monastery a track drops down to a conspicuous car parking area on a flat expanse of clifftop, from which a path (taking less than 15 minutes) zigzags down the cliff.

The route down the left bank of the Megapótamos is much less used. You can drive down the river valley to the sea, where there are two or three tavernas, and walk the cliff ledges 10 minutes west to the Préveli beach. Depending on the season's water levels, you can join an organised walk for the lower reaches of the river. Apply to the *ANSO* travel agency in Plakiás.

To drive to the sea return, north of the ruined monastery, to the 19C bridge over the Megapótamos. Using the modern river crossing, you turn on to the unsurfaced but viable track along the far bank of the stream. Soon another simpler but still picturesque bridge (1852) crosses the tributary (Bourtzoukós). At a chapel (right) the traditional route keeps to an old path following the river but with a vehicle you continue the slow descent signed occasionally for the tavernas.

From the cove the walk of ten minutes involves a scramble unsuitable for sufferers from vertigo, and at one point a primitive ladder. The path west along the rocks brings you to a viewpoint above a zigzag drop. You have a bird's eye view of the cluttered sandbank with the beautiful palm-fringed river behind it.

West of Plakiás

From Mýrthios and through Selliá the road runs west high above an empty but inaccessible coastline. The Levká Ori, the White Mountains, begin to dominate the view ahead. The village of **Rodákino** (15km from Mýrthios) is still relatively unspoilt by organised tourism and is recommended as a base. There are a number of places offering accommodation; the *Rent Rooms St George* are signed just off the coast road towards the sea. The beach, from which the kidnapped German General Kreipe and his captors were finally evacuated by submarine to Egypt in the Second World War (p 121), is 2km below the main road down a stream bed which promises well for birdwatchers. There are tracks along the coast and a serious walk on a branch of the E4 over to the remote village of **Alónes** in the sparsely populated central uplands.

The coast road enters the province of Khaniá and continues, inland of Frangokástello, to Khóra Sphakíon, the principal village of Sphákia (p 383).

Amári valley

The Amári valley lies southeast of Réthymnon across the centre of the island, between the eastern slopes of Mount Kédros (1777m) and the steep west flank of the mountain range of Ida (rising to 2456m). The valley is an area of great natural beauty still undisturbed by commercial development. Especially in springtime a visit is recommended to wild flower enthusiasts. This is one of the richest areas of the island for frescoed Byzantine churches. The invaluable *Byzantine*

Wall-paintings in Réthymnon by Ioannis Spathakis is available locally. Antiquities of various periods have been excavated at **Sýbritos**, **Monastiráki**, **Vizári** and **Apodoúlou**.

The Department of Byzantine Antiquities has been working to arrange easier access to buildings for which it is responsible. Where there is a sign to a church of historical interest you now have a good chance of finding it unlocked during the day, or otherwise a keyholder is available nearby.

Those with specialist knowledge will have planned their itinerary, but tourists with a general interest, on a day's expedition, might go up to **Thrónos** where, in the centre of the village, the Byzantine church is built into the pavement of an Early Christian basilica. It is then a short walk or drive to the little church of Ayios Ioánnis below **Kalógeros**. The road into the village of Amári from the west passes near **Ayía Anna** (with the earliest dated frescoes on the island). In the southern half of the valley, **Apodoúlou** has Ayios Yeóryios hidden beside a path down the hillside. In the centre of the village of **Ayía Paraskeví** the Byzantine church of the Panayía has well-preserved frescoes, good examples of what came to be known, when it spread across Greece and further afield, as the Cretan School of painting. On the way north you pass beside the road a picturesque ruined church (all that remains of a monastery at **Phóti**). In **Méronas** the Panayía is an architecturally interesting church with wall-paintings in reasonably good condition.

The opportunities for walking in the region have been revolutionised by the E4, which traverses the valley. The main route takes serious hikers on one of the traditional ascents (up from **Phourphourás**) to the summit of Ida, but there are also subsidiary paths (which should continue to be marked) to offer a variety of less testing routes across the valley and the lower slopes around it.

You can walk from Spíli to Yerakári by road, or take the E4 on one of its loops (south) exploring **Mount Kédros**. There are easier stretches to the village of Amári, and on past the Minoan site at **Monastiráki** and the **Lambiótes** frescoed church, perhaps ending at the excavation of an Early Christian basilica beside the new reservoir below Phourphourás.

Travelling by bus

There is a limited bus service from Réthymnon to the village of Amári but hiring your own transport for this expedition will bring particular rewards.

Where to stay

There are recommended hotels inland within easy reach of the valley, at **Zarós** (p 175) and in **Spíli** (p 329), which also has numerous places which rent rooms. For lovers of mountains it is now possible to find simple accommodation high up in the Amári valley, catering for climbers and walkers wanting to get to know off-the-beaten-track Crete. Look for suggestions in the villages of Thrónos, Phouphourás and Yerakári.

Most tourists exploring the valley make a day excursion from a base on the north coast. The main route up to the Amári valley leaves the Réthymnon bypass stretch of the north coast highway and climbs southeast for 25km to Apóstoli at the head of the valley. You can also approach from other directions. From the west a new road runs over a pass, 10km from Spíli to Yerakári; halfway along it, an area of upland meadows crossed by a meandering stream is well-known to flower enthusiasts in the spring. From the south of the island you turn off the coast road between Ayía Galíni and Tymbáki, signed for Apodoúlou.

Wherever you reach the valley the roads allow a circuit of it (c 70km) and the minor roads and tracks offer plenty of opportunity to leave the main route in search of unspoilt countryside.

Khromonastíri and the Mýli gorge

At the start of the main road up to Amári, just after it leaves the Réthymnon bypass, there are signs right for a detour (9km) to Khromonastíri, a village with two interesting Byzantine churches of early date.

The road runs parallel and to the west of the Mýli gorge named for the water-mills along the stream which, though now derelict, supplied flour to the Réthymnon area for several centuries. Researchers have found evidence for around 30 mills, but sadly buildings and traces of machinery are all beyond repair. Very soon a fork left (asphalted nearly to the river-bed) leads to rustic signs for the path at the lower end of the gorge. The road inland passes (right, after 2km) an imposing single-naved basilica church which (rebuilt in the 19C) must have dominated the Khalévi monastery, a foundation of the early 17C.

Down on the stream-bed there are two deserted settlements, Káto (lower) Mýli and Páno (upper) Mýli; the modern successor is signed above the road (right). Continuing past that turn, you watch for a rustic sign and a flight of steps down to the chapel of **Ayios Ioánnis** with (left, halfway down) a gateway to the ruins of a 16C mansion. This was used by the Venetian official who supervised operations here in order to tax the millers.

Keeping right after the chapel you find a bridge over the stream to **Páno Mýli**, a romantic spot (sometimes with a café-bar open). Then a path follows the stream (past the chapel of the Five Virgins) to **Káto Mýli**. Here you can climb back to the road, near the Khaleví church, or continue on the path to the bottom of the gorge (emerging near the bypass as noted above).

As you approach **Khromonastíri** the road runs straight with the village and its modern church in view ahead; on this stretch a track (left) is signed to a Byzantine church, the abandoned **Ayios Eftýkhios**, dating to the Second Byzantine period, is interesting both on account of its architecture and for the remains of 11C frescoes that are among the earliest uncovered on the island. It is possible to drive down the track, but many will prefer the walk of less than 2km. There is no problem about access to the church which lies below the track (right) with a smallholding close by it.

Inside, a magnificent *Pantokrátor* looks down on a building strongly evoking former glories. The nave, without parallel on the island, consists of five bays with the central one raised to form a cross-arm and surmounted by the dome. The 11C frescoes, preserved only in the sanctuary, are in the flat linear style still influenced by the conservative artistic traditions of the Macedonian dynasty in Constantinople. The Christ of the *deisis* composition was flanked by the Virgin and St John the Baptist; the extant apostles include St Peter. Very few examples of frescoes from the Second Byzantine period (961–1204) have survived on Crete but this locality has two churches preserving some 11C work.

If on returning to the road you continue straight through Khromonastíri you pass, near the end of the village, the shell of a mansion, the **Villa Clodio**, which was built by a wealthy Réthymnon family of Venetian origin as their country house, and then, under Turkish rule, appropriated by a local *aga*. Recent repair work has halted the building's decay.

For the church of the **Panayía** in the locality known as Kerá you continue, following signs, for 1km, along a concrete-surfaced road which ends with the church in view. The intriguing (and carefully restored) building is the result of several phases of construction. The original 11C domed, single-naved church had apses in the north and south walls, an unusual design on Crete. In the 14C a taller narthex was added, with an opening between columns giving the effect of an extended nave. The side-chapel and bell-cote were later additions. The 11C fresco decoration survives only in the sanctuary where there is an incomplete *deisis* composition. The remaining scenes are 14C work; in the apse on the south wall the figure of St Anne holds the Virgin, portrayed not as the child but as an adult looking out at the world with arms raised in blessing.

The road up to the Amári valley

From the turning off the Réthymnon bypass the Amári road soon begins to climb into the hills through groves of ancient olive trees. At 6km there is a fine view of one of the Khromonastíri churches, Ayios Eftýkhios, on the wooded hillside across the valley (right). In the distance to the southwest, the highest peak, with a white chapel on its summit, is Mount Vrýsinas (585m) where one of the richest Minoan peak sanctuaries was discovered.

After 8km you pass the village of **Prasiés**, attractively situated along a streambed and still retaining buildings from its Venetian past. On the through road, the cemetery church of the Panayía has some of the 14C frescoes preserved in good condition. Ask for the key at the *kapheneíon* near the bridge over the stream.

Above the village the road crosses a ridge (and the northern route of the E4) and a wide valley opens out ahead. Cliffs at a bridge before a sharp left-hand bend are worth a stop for birdwatchers. About 5km further, where the road enters the district of Amári, a large reservoir fed by the Stavromána river and its tributaries should begin to attract birds on migration.

A turning (right) off the main Amári valley road takes you through beautiful country to Pantánassa and (9km) **Patsós**. At the bottom of the gorge north of Patsós there was a spring sanctuary, in use intermittently at least from the Late Minoan period to Roman times, with a cult of Hermes Kranaíos. A track goes to the gorge, for the chapel of **Ayios Antónios**, but you may prefer to walk (c 30 minutes from the village).

The shrine, by springs c 40m southwest of the chapel, occupied a shelf at the front of the rock-shelters where evidence was found for rituals involving burnt sacrifice. Votive offerings included bronze figurines of worshippers and of animals, with reference to human fecundity suggested by an embracing couple and numerous nude females. Among the cult paraphernalia there were horns of consecration, offering-tables and a double axe. The main period of use was at the very end of the Bronze Age and during the Early Iron Age, but finds from the Hellenistic and Roman period include an altar with an inscription referring to Hermes Kranaios.

The main road gains height, zigzagging up the river valley. A conspicuous memorial, carved with the heroic figure of a moustachioed warrior of the wartime Resistance commemorates a local battle in September 1944 in the last weeks of the German occupation. The trigger was an ambush of German lorries by two factions of Resistance fighters. The operation which, with the end of the war in sight, contravened the advice of Allied liaison officers, left many dead on both sides.

At the watershed beyond the memorial, **Apóstoli** has a handsome church dating to the Venetian period. Steps lead to its terrace and magnificent views of Ida and (further left by the communication mast) the site of the Greco-Roman city-state of Sývritos (see below).

This valley forms one of the natural routes between the north and south coasts of the island, and yet sometimes, especially after the Venetian conquest and during the Nazi occupation, it has served as a remote refuge. The number of war memorials shows that the refuge was not always secure.

The villages of the Amári valley

1km beyond Apóstoli the road from Réthymnon arrives at a T-junction in **Ayía Photiní** and the valley opens out ahead. At the junction you have a choice. The main through road keeps left, along the eastern slopes of the valley. The right fork leads directly to the villages on the slopes to the west. From either route you can turn off to the principal village of Néfs Amári. The two roads converge south of Apodoúlou, offering a complete circuit of c 70km. The directions below assume that you turn left in Ayía Photiní and drive the circuit clockwise.

After 1km **Thrónos** is signed left, uphill. On the way into the village, off to the right, is the big family-run *Taverna Aravanes* with rent rooms enjoying stunning views to the south.

In the middle of the village the frescoed church of the **Panayía** (dedicated to the Assumption of the Virgin) is built into the foundations of an Early Christian basilica. The frescoes are of two periods, dated stylistically to the early 14C (only in the sanctuary) and the late 14C–early 15C. An interesting comparison is possible because the scene of the *Presentation of the Virgin* has survived from both periods: on the north wall of the sanctuary, and on the north side of the vault of the nave (western bay, lower register). The panel with the *Transfiguration* (south side of the vault) has a graffito date 1491.

The Kephála hill above Thrónos was known to be the site of ancient **Sývritos**.

During the last decade a Greek-Italian excavation campaign investigating the Classical and Hellenistic remains has confirmed the occupation of the site back to Late Minoan IIIC (12C BC, contemporary with the refuge sites at Karphí and the Kástro of Kavoúsi in the east of the island) with evidence for continuous use of the area through to historical times.

The Greco-Roman city-state flourished at least from the 5C BC into the Early Byzantine period; among the portrayals on the notably fine coinage are Dionysos and Hermes. The city spread over this hill where the village has grown up, and down the slopes to Ayía Photiní, with a cemetery at Yéna in the valley below. Probably the basilica site under the church of the Panayía was always one of its focal areas.

A 10-minute walk will take you up to the summit of the acropolis, a climb strongly recommended not least for the splendid view. From the village street just beyond the church a ridged concrete slope leads up (left) to a *kalderími* along the flank of the hill. Watch (right, before the modern road) for a stretch of the ancient city wall and opposite it turn left to climb again. From here the built path leads to the summit. Parts of the site are fenced and work is still in progress. A stretch of paved road is easily identified with, beside it, on a south-facing terrace, a monumental building which would have dominated all this fertile, wooded and well-watered Amári valley.

Sývritos must have owed its prosperity at least in part to its apparently unchallenged position on an important trade route. In Greco-Roman times the city's harbour was at Soulía, around the river mouth at present-day Ayía Galíni.

For **Kalógeros** you can take the loop road (passing a café-bar with another fine view) but the little frescoed church of **Ayios Ioánnis Theológos** (the Evangelist), below the village, is most easily found from the main valley road.

Turn off the main road at the sign for the village. Opposite two minor roads coming in together from the left, you take a track off to the right (probably signed). After c 2km one fork of the track drops steeply downhill right and the church is in sight. Leave a vehicle and walk (300m) past a hermit's grotto associated with the founding of the church in the cliffs left. The old church door has for some time been without a lock. An inscription dates the frescoes to 1347. In the *deisis* composition in the sanctuary, Christ is flanked by the Virgin Mary and as a special honour to the church's patron saint, by St John the Evangelist. The scene is repeated on the south wall of the church.

Back on the main road and 1km along it, you will notice, standing solitary and picturesque in a field (right) the tiny domed and cruciform church of **Ayía Paraskeví**. This was a chapel of the Khortátzis family, one of the distinguished families of the Byzantine aristocracy; it contains a family tomb as well as fragments of frescoes. The chapel is likely to be locked but you can get an impression of it through glass in the door. The date of the building is uncertain but some scholars connect the inscription on the wall-painting above the tomb with Yeóryios Khortátzis and one of the 13C uprisings against the new Venetian rule. In later times the church belonged to the monastery standing in the angle of two roads 1km further south.

The former **Moní Asomáton** was a foundation dating back to the Second Byzantine period, before the arrival of the Venetians. It flourished particularly in the 18C and 19C, amassing great wealth despite Ottoman control of the island secretly supporting Hellenic education and the struggle for Cretan independence. The monastery was dissolved in 1930 and the place has become an agricultural research centre.

Buildings from the monastery's Venetian past (much altered over time) stand alongside those of the modern farming activities, and a huge ancient plane tree provides summer shade. Liturgical furnishings from the former monastery chapel are displayed in the Historical Museum in Herákleion.

From the junction both roads to the right (west) will take you to the village of Amári but the one beside the monastery's old boundary wall climbs through **Monastiráki**, where an important archaeological excavation by the University of Crete has been in progress since the 1980s. The site occupies a low hill on slopes below the village. The way to it is well signed but the streets are narrow (narrower still if you take a wrong turning) and you may prefer to walk. Open Tues–Sat 09.00–18.00 (10.00–14.30 in winter); Sun 09.30–14.00; closed Mon.

Work here has uncovered a settlement of the Middle Minoan II period, contemporary with the First Palace at Phaistós. The evidence for monumental architecture with two storeys and the extensive workshop and storage blocks point to the palatial character of the complex. The most significant finds of that time were two separate archives of seals which connect Monastiráki with Phaistós and are contributing to a fuller understanding of the administrative and economic organisation of Protopalatial society. The settlement was destroyed c 1700 BC by earthquake damage and fire.

Monastiráki has two Venetian churches of interest to specialists. Downhill from the plateía (bell-cote in view from the central memorial) is the church of the **Arkhistrátigos** (Michael the Archangel), with an elaborately carved doorway and a frescoed scene of the *Assumption of the Virgin*. Uphill, at the top of the village, the apse of the partly ruined church of **Ayios Yeóryios** has a well-preserved *Platytéra* (Virgin with Child symbolising the Incarnation), which is said to have been influenced by the art of portable icons.

The road continues the climb to Amári, officially Néfs Amária to distinguish the main village of the district. In April, around the hamlet of **Opsígias**, the fields are colourful with wild tulips and lupins. On the outskirts of Amári the church of **Ayía Anna** preserves the remains of frescoes, not in good condition but the earliest dated by inscription (1225) yet known on Crete. Opposite the district police station a surfaced road (signed) turns back into the valley (in the direction of Moní Asomáton crossroads) and after less than 1km the church is on the left. Ayía Anna was built as a double-naved monastery church, which explains the filled-in arches along its south wall.

Amári is a picturesque place for a stroll. Visitors like to climb the clock tower for the view. The village is on the route of the E4.

From Amári there is a choice of surfaced roads across to the west, to Méronas or to Kardáki.

If you are continuing the full circuit of the valley you will return to the main road south, perhaps cutting across through **Lambiótes**. Here a signed track will bring you (less than 1km) to the church of the Panayía, with remains of elegant frescoes dated to the second half of the 14C, said to be particularly good examples of the stylistic influence of the Palaiologan revival.

In **Platánia** (across the valley road and 2km uphill beside a mountain stream) another church dedicated to the Panayía, signed on the village street, has 14C–15C frescoes, although only the lowest register is preserved.

Downhill (west of) **Vizári** was the site of a large Roman town. Most of the stony remains would alert only an expert to its past history, but there is an interesting excavation of the ruins of an Early Christian basilica, one of the best preserved on the island, with walls up to 4m high in places.

On the approach to the village from the north watch for the sign Límni (ΛΙΜΝΗ), to the recently constructed reservoir. Birdwatchers will want to make the (500m) detour but the track to the water is also the way to the basilica excavation.

The three-aisled **basilica church**, excavated in the 1950s, is tentatively dated to the late 8C or early 9C, shortly before the Arab conquest. Two Saracen coins were found in destruction debris. The aisles are separated by two raised stylobates for colummns. The architectural design is unusual in that the side aisles end in small apses of their own. This plan is seen at an earlier date in Bulgaria and Syria but no other example is known from Crete before the time of the Arab conquest. Not many architectural fragments were found, apart from two complete mono-lithic columns, but there is evidence for the screen across the central aisle, mounted between small columns and providing a spacious chancel. In the south aisle in front of the apse is a stepped font built of tile and cement; the floor of the central aisle was also tiled.

The building of this large church may reflect the wealth of the relatively pro-tected Amári valley at the end of the First Byzantine period, at a troubled time in the eastern Mediterranean when the island's coastline was frequently harassed by foreign raiders.

Phourphourás is one of the traditional starting points for the ascent of Mount Ida. Now the eastward route of the E4 goes to the summit (2456m) and infor-mation boards indicate an eight-hour climb. You can stay in the village and enjoy the choice of walks, as energetic or as gentle as you wish. Rent rooms *Simantiras* over a big café are signed on the lower road; turn down by a supermarket before buildings belonging to the Orthodox church.

South of the village the Byzantine church of **Ayios Yeóryios** is signed left of the road. 14C frescoes of the saint cycle are dominated by a formidable *Pantokrátor*.

Soon after Phourphourás, at a crest, the Libyan Sea comes into view, and in the distance the Mesará plain and the Asteroúsia mountains. This southern half of the valley is sparsely populated. You could cut across westwards through Ayios Ioánnis but readers concentrating during this expedition on frescoed churches will not want to miss out the villages of Apodoúlou and Ayía Paraskeví.

Approaching **Apodoúlou** there is a sign for **Ayios Yeóryios** which has mid-14C frescoes by Ieréas Anastásios. You can reach the church by car from the vil-lage but here it is only 5 minutes on foot below the road; at water-troughs on the path the *kalderími* turns back to your right along the contour, and Ayios Yeóryios is soon in sight down the hillside. The scenes on the north wall from the leg-endary life and death of the saint include a well-preserved figure on horseback opposite the entrance. Left of the altar the unknown donor makes the offering of his church.

Across the road (signed on the last bend before the village) steps in the bank indicate a Late Minoan III **tholos tomb**. A *dromos* cut into the hillside leads to the entrance where the lintel is still in situ. The excavator found the tomb plun-dered, but four clay *lárnakes* had survived, one with a scene of lamenting figures.

At the entrance to the village are the partly ruined remains of a solidly built **19C mansion**, an uncommon survival on Crete. This is a house with a history. During the disturbances of 1821 associated with the achievement of indepen-dence for mainland Greece, a young girl from Apodoúlou, Kalítza Psaráki, daughter of a local official, was abducted from the village by Muslims and sent to the slave market in Alexandria. She was freed by an Englishman, Robert Hay, an antiquarian travelling in Egypt, and in 1828 became his wife. When the couple returned to Crete, to the great delight of her family, they built this house in her home village.

In the village a minor road (signed for Ayios Yeóryios and the Minoan settle-ment of Apodoúlou) starts awkwardly downhill. You circle right for the frescoed church described above, but for the excavation keep left, 2km down into the valley, and the fenced site will be on your left. A Neopalatial complex (first explored in the 1930s) included an area for cult activity with gold and bronze double axes and a clay bull's head rhyton among the finds. A stone rhyton and a libation table were inscribed in Linear A. In the 1990s Greek and Italian archaeologists began new work at the site. Remains at the south end belong to a larger complex of Protopalatial (MMII) date. The amount of storage space is impressive, but the quality of some of the masonry and a find of painted plaster suggest that this was more than just an agricultural settlement.

Beyond Apodoúlou the road divides. The left fork follows the southern slopes of Ida to Kamáres and on to Zarós (province of Herákleion). Just off this road **Vathiakó** has yet another church dedicated to **Ayios Yeóryios**, this one with remains of two phases of fresco painting, of 13C date except in the western bay (14C). The right fork takes you down to the south coast; it is less than 10km to Ayía Galíni.

For the circuit of the Amári valley follow this road south for c 3km before turning back, acutely right (signed Ayía Paraskeví) to begin the long climb north. At this lower end of the valley there are groves of fine old olive trees as far as the eye can see.

In **Ayía Paraskeví** the Byzantine church of the Panayía stands on a rise (right) in the centre of the village just before the large modern one. (The key is held at one of the white houses behind the old church.) The elegant frescoes, dated 1516 by inscription, are not complete but they include in the apse a well-preserved *Platytéra* (Virgin with Child facing out into the world, symbol of the Incarnation) and on the west wall a good panel of the donor (a priest) and his wife. The particular interest of these wall-paintings is that both the technique and the peaceful, inward-looking nature of the compositions mark a highly developed phase of the Cretan School of painting.

After the village of **Ayios Ioánnis** the scenery becomes grander. You cross the Plátys river which runs into the sea near Ayía Galíni. The medieval bridge is preserved to the right of the modern one. This is an idyllic spot at any time of year and a stop is strongly recommended.

Then the road climbs above the olive-tree zone to a series of high villages along the slopes of Mount Kédros. There are fine retrospective views of the southern coastline, and across the Amári valley the dramatic wall of Psilorítis (Ida). **Ano Méros** has a well-sited café, *psistariá O Stinos*, with a terrace from which to enjoy these views.

The **war memorials** in these villages along the western slopes, from Meronás south to Khordáki, are a legacy of a week in August 1944 when nine of these villages were systematically razed to the ground by German soldiers. 164 inhabitants of the villages were shot dead (43 from Yerakári alone). Allied liaison officers watched helplessly from their cave hide-outs on Mount Ida as day after day, one after another, the villages burned. There was perhaps an element of reprisal by the Germans for the activities of the Resistance fighters but historians have concluded that the chief military purpose at this late stage of the war was to neutralise an area of guerrilla strength which threatened the German army's imminent withdrawal west from Herákleion to Khaniá.

Beyond **Kardáki** you pass, in a picturesque setting opposite a fountain and a spreading oak tree, the ruined church of **Ayios Ioánnis Theológos**, all that remains of the monastery at Phóti. The architectural scheme, the result of two building phases, can still be appreciated though the building is open to the elements and the frescoes have suffered accordingly. It is unusual to find a dome on a narthex. Remains of frescoes are dated late 13C in the original single-naved church, 14C–15C in the narthex. The old stone road can still be made out behind the church.

In **Yerakári** the new road over the pass to Spíli sets off to the west opposite the war memorial, as does the E4. On the main street there is a **café-taverna** with rooms to rent presided over by Kyría Déspina, renowned for her enthusiasm for delicious home-made produce. She runs the Cretan equivalent of a cottage industry with traditional recipes using local ingredients, especially the cherry crop, for jams, preserves, and alchoholic beverages and herb teas. The accommodation is simple but you will come away with insight into the traditional life of the valley.

If you continue on the (winding) road north to **Elénes** (or take the short cut on foot on the E4) the double-naved church of **Ayios Nikólaos** has frescoes of the mid-13C, painted in a conservative, even backward-looking style not long after the Venetians took control on the island.

In **Méronas** the ochre-coloured church of the **Panayía** is towards the end of the village, on the right of the road. The keyholder lives on the same side, a few houses before the church. The saddle roof unites the three internal barrel vaults of the three-aisled basilica church (with the south nave a later addition). It is interesting that architectural details reflect the influence of Venice, although the church belonged to the family of Kallérgis, Cretans with a strong aristocratic Byzantine tradition; their coat of arms appears carved on the exterior and painted on the interior of the church. The frescoes are dated stylistically (though not with unanimity) to the mid-14C. There are a number of unusual features in the decoration of this church. In the sanctuary of the central aisle the Hierarchs officiate as is customary but the portrayal of the Christ Child representing on the altar the elements of the Eucharist is rare on Crete. It is also unusual to find the Virgin in the *deisis* scene holding a scroll which marks her as interceding with Christ on behalf of mankind. At the west end of the church the scenes from the life of the Virgin are all that survive from the complete set illustrating the 24 stanzas of the great *Akathistos Hymn to Mary*, a part of the Orthodox Church's Lenten liturgy. The same cycle is preserved complete at Roústika (p 346) and at Valsamóneros (p 176) but otherwise found in only a handful of the island's churches.

A further 3km brings you to Ayía Photiní and the junction for the main road down to Réthymnon.

West of Réthymnon

From Réthymnon to Khaniá the direct route west (c 60km) on the north coast highway (New National Road) follows the shore of the long bay as far as (c 20km) **Yeoryioúpolis** where you enter the province of Khaniá. Then the road cuts across inland of Vámos to arrive at Soúda Bay on the approach to Khaniá. **Vrýses** (at 26km) is the start of the route south across the island to the district of Sphakiá. The Old Road meanders inland from Réthymnon through wooded countryside to (c 20km) Episkopí and returns to the coast at Yeoryioúpolis.

South from the Old Road there are recommended excursions into the relatively unfrequented hills overlooking the coastal plain, to **Roústika** for the monastery of **Prophítis Ilías** and an important frescoed church in the village, to the great springs at **Argyroúpolis** and to the 11C frescoed church of the former monastery of **Myrioképhala**.

Travelling by bus

The buses between Réthymnon and Khaniá run frequently by the New National Road, and twice daily on the Old Road via Episkopí and Vámos.

The Old Road to Roústika

The main road through Réthymnon meets the western end of the bypass at a major junction with traffic lights. Here the Old Road diverges inland. After 10km watch for a turning left for **Roústika**, 5km. The monastery of **Prophítis Ilías** (Elijah, feast day 20 July) is signed on the southeast edge of the village with superb views back to the coast. Two 17C bells hang in the bell-cote of the domed three-aisled church. The monastery was founded towards the end of the Venetian period. It acquired power and wealth under Turkish rule, with privileged status in that the abbot was responsible directly to the Patriarch in Constantinople with minimum interference from the local political administration. Nevertheless, the monastery was involved in the struggle for freedom and the buildings did not escape damage during that time. Some fine 18C icons have survived.

In the picturesque village the double-naved church of the **Panayía and Sotíros Khristós** (Christ the Saviour) has frescoes in the north aisle (dedicated to the Panayía) which are dated by the donor inscription to 1381–82. Some of the iconography reflects strong western influence. On the triumphal arch over the sanctuary in Byzantine churches the Holy Trinity is habitually symbolised by a fresco of the Feast of Abraham; here in its place at Roústika is a powerful scene known as the *Throne of Mercy*, with the crucified Christ held by the enthroned God the Father, the Holy Ghost between them represented as a dove. Yet in contrast to this and other treatments unconventional in Byzantine terms, the Panayía nave preserves one of the few complete cycles of the *Hymn to Mary*, the great 24-stanza Akathistos prayer sung only once a year in the Lenten liturgy of the eastern church (see also Valsamóneras, p 176, and Méronas, p 345).

From Roústika for Argyroúpolis (see below) and Myrioképhala you can continue across country through Ayios Konstantínos.

By the New Road to Yeoryioúpolis

On the coastal highway, 3km beyond the junction with the Old Road, you cross the Yeráni bridge. Below, near the sea, is a cave (signed but not open to the public) only discovered in 1967 during road building. The **Yeráni cave** was in use as a sanctuary during the Neolithic period, and finely worked Late Neolithic bone and obsidian tools from it are exhibited in the Archaeological Museum in Réthymnon. From Pleistocene levels investigated in the cave came a find of bones of the dwarf giant deer, one of six species of deer known at that time but destined to become extinct.

The Levká Ori (White Mountains) are in view ahead. The road runs for 10km parallel to a fine sandy shore; there are frequent access points, and though new developments are springing up in several places, parts of the beach are still relatively deserted. The bay is not always as innocent as it appears in calm weather, and even strong swimmers should be wary of unexpected currents. The highway crosses several reed-fringed river-beds which, early in the year, may interest bird-watchers.

After the Petrés river a side-road sweeps up (3km) to Episkopí on the Old Road, a useful short cut if your destination is Argyroúpolis. (Approaching from the west you would use the Old Road and the bridge over the highway to Lake Kournás from Yeoryioúpolis at the end of the bay.)

Argyroúpolis

Arriving in the village from Episkopí on the Old Road, you pass left the turn for the way over from Roústika (signed to Káto Póros). Very soon there is a choice of routes. Keep straight ahead for the plateía in the upper village and the road on to Myrioképhala, or fork right (signed for Así Goniá) to the lower level where a waterfall is channelled from the springs.

Where to stay

There are three sets of **rent rooms**— *Morpheus*, *Agnantema*, and *Arkhaia Lappa*—along the road inland from the plateía past the folklore museum in the upper village.

The settlement of Argyroúpolis grew up on the site of ancient **Láppa**, one of the powerful city-states of western Crete in Greco-Roman times, with its harbour of Amphýmalla in the corner of the bay now occupied by the resort village of Yeoryioúpolis. Láppa was destroyed in the Roman invasion in 67 BC. Afterwards forces from Láppa aided Octavius at the battle of Actium and were rewarded with permission to rebuild their city, which then flourished until it was finally destroyed by the Saracens in the 9C. Its successor, Argyroúpolis, became an important centre and the Cretan aristocracy built houses here during the period of Venetian rule. Continuous occupation has meant that only vestiges of Láppa are left above ground. The remains of a bath house near the springs and the Roman necropolis north of the city (see below) hint at its former importance.

The village occupies a fine position above the Mouséllas river valley, looking back to the sea from the wooded eastern foothills of the White Mountains. Visitors come here from across Crete (especially for Sunday outings) as well as from abroad to admire the force of nature in the perennial spring which emerges from a cliff of conglomerate rock, with a main outlet through a cave chapel. In modern times, the water which supplies the city of Réthymnon has been directed past numerous taverna terraces (and souvenir stalls). Below the road are the remains of a Roman aqueduct among great plane trees and lush vegetation with includes many aquatic plants. A side-road (signed beyond the springs) leads down to one of the most attractive of the tavernas (*Palaios Mylos*, the Old Mill). The speciality of local trout is advertised opposite the turning.

To the right of the downhill track there are the ruins of other mills (one a rare model apparently used for the process of fulling cloth) and the oval building of what may be the main **baths** of Roman Lappa.

Back at the springs a picturesque *kalderími* climbs past the little cave church and on steeply uphill to the village, the route for fetching water in earlier times.

The road to the upper village continue from the fork on the approach from Episkopí to arrive at a plateía in front of the elegant church of **Ayios Ioánnis** and a war memorial; the dates 1912–18 are a reminder of Greece's participation in war in the Balkans. The plateía gives a bird's-eye view of the pitched roofs typical of the mountain villages of western Crete.

In recent times there has been a move by the community to interest visitors in the long history of the village. Under an archway at the entrance to the plateía, a **shop** advertising local herbs and avocado beauty products acts as an information centre, selling books and maps and providing a free plan of the village. The frequently updated publication *Local Explorer* may be available and is recommended.

Leaving the plateía past the church you come to the **Zographáki folklore museum** on the left of the road with a fascinating collection based almost entirely on the possessions of one extended family. There is no charge but plenty of local products for sale to help finance the operation.

To visit the **necropolis** (a recommended ten-minute walk) return towards the north coast past the road to Así Goniá, and turn right as for Káto Póros. Halfway down the first hill you cross a well-trodden *kalderími* (which walkers may have picked up on a bend above the Así Goniá turning). Leave a vehicle and follow the path, the remains of the old Roman road, downhill to the cemetery. You come to the church of the **Five Virgins**, built among the numerous rock-cut Roman tombs. The path continues downhill to a fountain harnessing a source of water from the rocks with beside it a plane tree of great age, believed to be one of the oldest on the island. This is an idyllic spot.

The country south of Argyroúpolis is a little-known part of Crete, but the sparsely cultivated and unfenced uplands repay exploration, especially for wildflower enthusiasts and birdwatchers. The area is now crossed by a north–south branch of the E4 which links the main route along the spine of the island with the south coast trail. From **Alónes**, a stretch (only of interest to serious long-distance walkers) follows the time-honoured track over the coastal hills down to Rodákino (p 336).

The road inland from Argyroúpolis continues 12km into the hills to **Myrioképhala** (at a height of 500m). For the former monastic church of the Panayía follow signs downhill until the street widens under spreading trees in the middle of the village. The monastery was founded at the beginning of the 11C by the Cretan evangelist Ayios Ioánnis Xénos, who is known to have brought furnishings for it from Constantinople.

The domed, cruciform church (with narthex added in the form of a single-nave chapel) has Second Byzantine period frescoes that are among the earliest on the island. Fragments contemporary with the building are preserved in the dome, sanctuary and south cross-arm, as well as four scenes from the Passion of Christ in the west cross-arm which are later (end of 12C) but in the characteristic linear style and still predating Venetian rule on the island. They include a memorable rendering of **Christ's entry into Jerusalem** handled as a triumphal scene.

To Así Goniá

From the turning on the way into Argyroúpolis from the coast, a beautiful road climbs 6km to the west into the foothills of the White Mountains (in the province of Khaniá) to Así Goniá, home village of George Psychoundakis, author of *The Cretan Runner* (see Recommended reading). This road runs below Argyroúpolis, passing famous waterfalls from the springs which supply Réthymnon's water.

The ancient festival (*paneyíri*) of the blessing of the sheep, is still celebrated here on St George's Day (23 April unless this falls in Holy Week). If you can visit Así Goniá on that day aim to arrive at least by mid-morning. All the shepherds are dressed in their traditional best. Each of the local flocks is penned nearby and then, one flock at a time, the sheep are milked as they are driven past the priest alongside the church during the religious ceremony of blessing. The milk is distributed so that all those present can share in the special occasion. Afterwards the shepherds set off into the mountains towards the summer grazing, and on the hillside across the valley the slow procession of flocks, with intervals between them as they feed along the way, is an unforgettable sight enhanced by the distant sound of sheep bells.

Así Goniá is on the E4 but the shepherds' track across empty uplands towards Kallikrátis and the mountains of Sphakiá is not yet suitable for hired cars.

Back in Argyroúpolis you can return to the coast at Yeoryioúpolis, by way of the village of Kournás (on a short stretch of unsurfaced road) and the only freshwater lake on the island (p 383) or directly to Réthymnon from Episkopí.

KHANIÁ PROVINCE

The commercial city of **Khaniá** on the north coast, a thriving centre for the whole province, has grown up around what is left of a historic walled city and its picturesque Venetian harbour. The port for large ships is 5km to the east at **Soúda** on one of the most spectacular natural anchorages of the Mediterranean. A glance inland shows the close relationship between the town and the mountains, which are snow-capped for more than half the year.

Khaniá is an ideal base for those who enjoy city life. Visitors who prefer to stay on the coast, a comfortable half-hour's drive from Khaniá, might consider the coastline south of the gulf of Soúda; for example **Kalýves** or the village resort on a beautiful cove at **Almyrída**, or, maybe, even at **Yeoryioúpolis** near the border with the province of Réthymnon (but only outside the summer season, because the resort has long ago outgrown the charm of its peaceful river location). In Hellenistic times the city-state of **Aptéra**, above Kalýves, commanded the sheltered water of Soúda Bay. The climb to the site is rewarded by spectacular views, and a major programme of excavation is currently adding to the already known features of historical interest.

Readers interested in Byzantine churches will want to visit two near Yeoryioúpolis (at **Máza** and **Alíkambos**) which have early-14C fresco decoration by the admired artist Ioánnis Pagoménos, and should also explore the **Stýlos** area inland of Aptéra towards the White Mountains, as far as **Kyriakosélia**.

The cape jutting out to the northeast of Khaniá, known as the **Akrotíri**, is principally visited for two monasteries of the Venetian period and a walk to the romantic ruins of a third near the sea. In spite of its proximity to the city, the cape can still offer uncultivated countryside as a hunting ground for flower enthusiasts, especially for orchids in the spring.

The western end of Crete is the part of the island least affected by mass tourism, and is still an area of largely unspoilt natural beauty. More often than not the view is dominated by the peaks of the mountains known as the **Levká Ori** (White Mountains) rising to 2453m above sea level.

The one area of the White Mountains that does attract visitors in great numbers is the **National Park of Samariá**. The trek down the **Gorge of Samariá** to the Libyan Sea starts from the high mountain plain of **Omalós**. There is comfortable accommodation on the plain if you want to spend more than a day enjoying this environment where the silence is broken only by sheep bells. For visitors hoping for a chance sighting of a lammergeier, the rare bearded vulture, this is the place to be.

For accommodation on the coast west of Khaniá, it is best to look beyond Plataniás, perhaps as far west as the charming village of **Kolymbári** lying behind a small fishing harbour and within sight of the important monastery of the Panayía Odiyítrias, **Goniá**. Walkers will enjoy exploring the **Rodopós**

peninsula and off-the-beaten-track country to the south, around the rotonda church at **Episkopí**. The old-fashioned country town of **Kastélli Kisámou** has gradually adapted itself to tourism, impelled by the increase in traffic arriving at its expanding harbour on the car ferry service from the Greek mainland. The only disadvantage of a holiday base this far west is that a visit to the major Minoan sites of central Crete will involve the added distance beyond what is already from Khaniá nearly two hours on the road.

The whole province of Khaniá is recommended to anyone looking for a walking holiday. Expeditions with a guided group can be arranged in Khaniá. The long-distance walking route, the **E4**, starts from the ferry harbour west of Kastélli. At this western end of the island it has a network of branches taking in both mountain and coastal territory. A first stretch climbs gently to the site of ancient **Polyrrhínia**, scenically (and botanically) a good beginning.

The far west coast remained isolated until quite recent times. Now the road the road system is improving fast, from **Phalásarna**, worth visiting both for the archaeological site and beautiful beaches, down to the monastery of **Khrissoskalítissa** not far short of the idyllic beaches of **Elaphonísi**.

To explore the White Mountains from the southeast, you could stay down in the south in or around **Khóra Sphakíon**. The district of **Sphákia** is even now a relatively self-contained community where tradition and history still have a marked influence on modern life, and the inhabitants value memories of a troubled but heroic past. There is one road which climbs a short distance into the high valleys, and a coastal path at the foot of cliffs where the mountains drop sheer to the sea. Otherwise a boat service runs west under the mountains serving the former fishing settlements along the coast which have come back to life to meet the needs of tourism.

The southwest of the island, the district of **Sélinos**, is an area of gentle contours in the foothills of the mountains, and of valleys wooded with plane and sweet chestnut trees. Here are many of the island's churches with interiors preserving remains of fresco paintings in the Byzantine tradition. From 1204 the artists lived under the colonial rule of Venice, and sometimes demonstrated that they were aware of the art of their Catholic masters, but they usually worked strictly within the eastern tradition.

It is possible during a long day's excursion from the north coast to get a worthwhile impression of Sélinos, perhaps to visit some of the churches, or to walk from Soúyia to the sanctuary of Askleipos at **Lisós**. To explore in any depth it is necessary to spend a few days in the area, preferably at **Palaiókhora** (at the western end of the route of the south coast boat service). Although still essentially a village, on a neck of land between two splendid beaches, it offers the amenities of a small coastal resort.

Khaniá

Khaniá, a place-name correctly in the plural, Ta Khaniá (and also transliterated Haniá and Chaniá) is the administrative capital of its *nome* (province), the second city of Crete and the flourishing commercial centre for the western end of the island. It houses the highest judicial authority, the Court of Appeal, and the Art and Architecture departments of the University of Crete.

The modern town was laid out in the late 19C and early years of the 20C. At its heart, what remains of the earlier walled city around the harbour, and the Kastélli hill rising above it, manages to retain some of the charm of its Venetian and Turkish past. Sufficient hints of this past have survived despite the severe damage caused by German bombing in 1941 followed by haphazard reconstruction and, in more recent times, the conflicting demands and economic pressures of tourism. Now enlightened efforts to preserve historic features and integrate them with development are making a welcome impact.

Khaniá is a place to visit outside the main summer season. In spring and autumn you can enjoy the café life on the waterfront, explore the narrow streets of the old town with their specialist craft shops, and browse alongside the local inhabitants in the big cruciform covered market which for many people is one of the particular delights of Crete. The Battle of Crete, 23–30 May 1941, is commemorated on the Sunday of that week with church services and parades; the Greek Tourism Organisation in Khaniá should have details.

The city is rightly proud of its museums. Just inland from the outer harbour the **Archaeological Museum**, handling material from all over the province, exploits to memorable effect the setting of a former Venetian friary church. Nearby a collection of **folk art** is arranged in a charming old Cretan house. The **Historical Museum**, located in the modern town, provides insight into the long struggle for freedom from foreign rule, and also contains the Archives Collection of Crete. Nearby is the **War Museum**. The **Maritime Museum**, housed in the fort known as the Firkás, overlooking the harbour entrance, has attractive exhibits of the Venetian and Turkish periods, and draws many visitors to its rooms devoted to the German invasion during the Second World War. In a church behind the fort the recently established **Museum of Byzantine Antiquities** is making a contribution particularly valuable because public access to such collections is rare on Crete.

Néa Khóra beach is 15 minutes west on foot from the fort of Firkás, past the yacht harbour. From Plateía 1866 local (blue) buses are marked Kalamáki or Galatás and run every 15 minutes. Long-distance buses (green) running west by the coast road are sufficiently frequent for a beach day at, for example, **Ayía Marína** or **Plataniás**. They also serve the recommended beaches at **Stavrós** and **Kalathás** on the Akrotíri.

Practical information

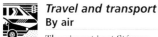

Travel and transport
By air

The airport is at Stérnes, 14km east of the city on the Akrotíri.

For flight information ☎ 28210 63264 or 28210 63171.

Charter flights are met by coaches but in recent years there has been no public bus service between the airport and the centre of Khaniá. It is worth checking the current position.

Taxis operate from a well-organised rank at the airport displaying a notice of fares to all the most likely tourist destinations. To the centre of Khaniá allow about € 11.

Olympic Airways' town terminal is at Tzanakáki 88, opposite the Municipal Gardens, ☎ 28210 57701-3.

Aegean Cronus Airlines, Eleftheriou Venizelou 12, ☎ 28210 51 100, fax 28210 51 222, www.aegeanair.com.

By car from the airport

With a car hired at the airport you have a choice of routes, either into the centre of Khaniá or, for all other directions, through Soúda to the north coast highway. Leaving the airport bear left round the end of the runway. Turn right at the T-junction on the main Sternés–Khaniá road. 5km along it an awkward fork downhill left is signed to Soúda and (7km) the New National Road. At Soúda you can go left towards Réthymnon or right for the Khaniá bypass and destinations west of Khaniá. Keeping to the main road into Khaniá you continue until it drops down with fine views over the city and the bay to a T-junction on the coast road. Here turn left, cross a dual carriageway and keep straight ahead to arrive in the commercial centre of Khaniá. On your right will be the landmark of the big cruciform covered market. For car parking, see below.

By car from other parts of the island

Approaching Khaniá from the east, the New National Road runs high above Soúda Bay. Halfway along the bay you pass a sign for Soúda (the ferries) and the Old Road. 2km further watch for a second slip road to Soúda. Despite the signs for Khaniá ahead (8km staying on the bypass) the city centre is more easily negotiated if you leave the highway here. At the end of the slip road turn left and continue along an avenue of euca-lyptus trees until you come to a one-way street system which leads (signed *kéntro* high up on lamp posts) straight ahead into Tzanakáki and on down to the dual carriageway in front of the covered market in the centre of Khaniá.

Approaching from the west on the old coast road there is no problem. If you are on the New National Road, turn off at the junction signed for Omalós and head for the coast road to follow signs for the centre of Khaniá. A dual carriageway becomes a one-way system for the through road, Kydonías, across the inland side of Plateía 1866.

Parking

Parking near the waterfront is not easy. All the harbour quays are closed to cars from the end of March until October (except 07.00–11.00 or for authorised access, for example to hotels), and strict controls are enforced in the Old City under threat of the removal of number plates and a substantial fine. Tourist status does not provide immunity.

There are meter bays in Plateía 1866 opposite the taxi rank (handy for the tourist information office), and on the east side of the covered market. Near the stadium on the road in from the airport there is an official car park on its seaward side, about five minutes' walk from the market. You should also find street parking places, especially outside business hours. If you are approaching Khaniá from the west, turn down towards the sea just before (or as soon as possible after) the start of the one-way system which uses Kydonías. Towards the eastern end of the tree-shaded beach road (Aktí Kanári) you can park under the city walls, except at the extreme end where space is clearly reserved for residents, and walk round to the outer harbour.

By sea

Car ferries from Piraeus dock at Soúda about 6km east of the city. There is a year-round nightly service run by the

ANEK shipping line. For port information at Soúda ☎ 28210 89240. For the car ferry service from the Peloponnese, see under Kísamos (Kastélli Kisámou).

Taxis meet the boats, or the frequent bus service from Soúda will set you down in front of the covered market in the centre of Khaniá.

ANEK, Plateía Soph. Venizélou, ☎ 28210 27500-4.

By bus

The bus station for long-distance services (**green buses**) is on Kydonías, at the southwest corner of Plateía 1866, ☎ 28210 93306, 28210 93052. There is a good service east to Réthymnon and Herákleion with a dozen departures daily (fewer on Sundays). For the route west to Kísamos (Kastélli Kisámou) ask at the bus stations for details of stops on the coast road, or the express service using the New National Road.

Local buses (including those on the Soúda route) are **blue**; their stops are on the main through road outside the market and in Plateía 1866 (with huts for tickets and information). Buses marked Kalamáki or Galatás are useful for beach expeditions.

Tourist information

The tourist information office nera Plateía 1866 closed indefinitely in 2003. Until new arrangements are made the best advice is to speak during morning hours to a temporary information office run by the Municipal Authority, ☎ 28210 36204 or (switchboard) ☎ 28210 92000, or consult the tourist police.

Tourist police

Iraklíou 23, ☎ 28210 53333. Open all day. Apokorónou (the road out to Soúda) becomes Iraklíou at the end of the one-way street system.

Travel agencies

Canea Travel Bureau, Tzanakáki 28,

near the main post office, ☎ 28210 24780.

Diktynna, Ayíou Márkou 6, at the eastern end of Kanevaro, ☎ 28210 41458.

Interkreta, Plateía Eleftherías 2, ☎ 28210 27222; with a branch office in Palaiókhora.

Kyriakakis Travel (Kyr), Khátsi Mikháli Yiánnari 78, at the corner of Khalidón, ☎ 28210 27700.

Omalos Travel, Plateía 1866, ☎ 28210 97119, 28210 96717.

Alpin Travel, Boniáli 11–19, in the Hermes office complex at the Apokorónou end of the street, 2nd floor of Building C, ☎ 28210 50939, ☎/fax 28210 53309. Specialises in organised hiking in the mountains of Sphakiá.

Mountain climbing

The *Greek Alpine Club* (Ellinikós Oreivatikós Syllogós, EOS) Tzanakáki 90, ☎ 28210 44647. Open only 19.00–22.00 as the premises are staffed by volunteers. The club operates the Kallérgis and Volikás refuge huts in the White Mountains.

Where to stay

Many visitors prefer rooms with harbour views, but the Khaniá seafront can be very noisy at night, especially around Plateía Elef. Venizélou on the outer harbour.

Hotels

A *Amfora* (21 rooms), Parodos Theotokopoúlou 20, ☎ 28210 93224, fax 28210 93226; classed as a traditional hotel in a converted mansion.

B *Doma* (25 rooms), Leoph. Elef. Venizélou 124, ☎ 28210 51772-3, fax 28210 41578; to the east of the Koúm Kapí suburb just before the airport road turns inland from the coast. (The seaview rooms have double glazing to cope with traffic noise.) One of the city's most elegant hotels, in a restored neo-classical building, retaining the feel of a museum of the history of 20C

Khaniá. Breakfast room and snack-bar on the top floor.

B *Minoa* (20 rooms), Tzanakaki 23, ☎ 28210 27970, fax 28210 27973, email: minoa@cha.forthnet.gr. This attractive hotel is equipped to welcome wheelchair users.

B *Porto Veneziano* (57 rooms), Akti Enosseos, ☎ 28210 27100, fax 28210 27105, email: portoven@otenet.gr. A particularly well-run modern hotel in a photogenic location at the eastern end of the Inner Harbour.

B *Rodon* (32 rooms), Akrotiríou 92, ☎ 28210 58317, fax 28210 56821. On the edge of Khaniá, halfway down the last hill to the coast on the road from the airport. Convenient for independent travellers for the night of arrival or departure. Swimming pool.

C *Amphitriti* (16 rooms), Lithinón 31–33, ☎ 28210 56470, fax 28210 52980. On the Kastélli hill, with the advantage of balcony views looking down on the Outer Harbour to be set against the inevitable background noise.

C *Astor* (36 rooms), El. Venizélou, On the main through road just east of the covered market, ☎ 28210 55557, fax 28210 55558. A simple no-nonsense establishment offering an economical base in a central location.

C *Kriti* (98 rooms), N. Phoká 10 at the junction with Kýprou, ☎ 28210 51881-5, fax 28210 41000, www.grecian.net/kriti, email: hotelkriti@grecian.net. Recently refurbished and modernised to high standards of comfort, with swimming pool.

Traditional hotels and apartments

In recent years there has been a move to restore and modernise Venetian and Turkish buildings within the Old City, classifying them as traditional hotels and traditional apartments. Many visitors seem to enjoy the old-world atmosphere, and to be prepared if necessary to pay a premium for it.

B *Casa Veneta* (14 furnished apartments), Theotokopoúlou 55–57, ☎ 28210 90007, fax 28210 75931. Relatively simple accommodation (partially air-conditioned) at realistic prices.

B *El Greco* (16 hotel rooms), Theotokopoúlou 47–49, ☎ 28210 90432, fax 28210 91829/95566.

These two are the most easily accessible, at the coast road end of Theotokopoúlou and not too far from a parking area. Theophanoús, on the harbour side of Zambelíou, has *Contessa*, *Porto del Colombo* and *Casa Delfino* (popular furnished apartments). On the way to these, up Theotokopoúlou, are *Kapetan Vassilis* and *Palazzo*. In the high season this type of accommodation is likely to be fully booked. In the low season apartments may be unoccupied and available at a substantial discount on the official price. Without a booking, allow time to explore on foot.

Rent rooms

Khaniá offers a great number of rooms for rent; the **Topanás** quarter behind the Outer Harbour (p 363) is suggested as an atmospheric place to start enquiries. The *Anemones* rooms and *Pension Orio* on Theophanoús or any of the three *Ifigenia* establishments will suggest alternatives if they have no vacancies.

The **Koúm Kapí** district to the east of the Inner Harbour, or along Síphaka on the Kastélli hill, are generally quieter areas.

 ## Eating out

Local advice is to avoid the tavernas on the Outer Harbour (along Aktí Koundourióti towards the Firkás) where the pressure of popularity has led to the lowering of standards and a limited menu. These places can be useful for a coffee or ice-cream, or a drink with *mezédes* during a stop to enjoy the splendid views.

To eat well in waterside surroundings, walk from Plateía El. Venizélou towards the Inner Harbour.

Monastiri, behind the Mosque of the Janissaries, is a taverna *oúzeri* with a good reputation for fish but also for a spread of *mezédes* sufficient for a meal.

Mathios and **Dinos**, side by side and owned by the same family, are on the main Inner Harbour quay towards the eastern end of Aktí Enóseos, where the fishing boats tie up.

Karnayio is set back from this quay in the corner of Plateía Katekháki, on the western side of the main group of Arsenals; it values its upmarket reputation and serves a wide range of traditional Cretan meat and fish dishes at reasonable prices, but vegetarians can also eat well here.

Taverna Fortezza is across the harbour (with a free ferry service), on the breakwater which ends at the lighthouse. The setting in the partly restored bastion is special, and a charcoal grill produces simple food.

Akroyiali and **Katofli** are well known fish tavernas on the beach road near the little yacht haven of Néa Khóra, ten minutes west on foot from the Firkás Outer Harbour.

At times of the year when the weather is less favourable, or just as a change from the waterside tavernas, the following are usually reliable and are popular with Cretans.

Anaplous, Síphaka 37, offers classic Cretan cooking alongside a good wine list.

Pavsilypon, Siphaka 19, is a good alternative.

To Pigadi tou Tourkou (The Well of the Turk), K. Sarpáki 1, is patronised for its exotic Anatolian and Middle Eastern dishes.

Tholos, Ayión Déka 36, is conveniently near the archaeological museum.

Ela, at the top of Kondiláki, a street of tavernas which runs inland from the Outer Harbour, has a particularly good reputation for meat dishes.

Banks

National Bank of Greece, Plateía Soph. Venizélou; cash machines and automatic currency exchange.

Commercial Bank, Khátsi Mikháli Yiánari 40–42.

Bureau de change, Plateía El. Venizélou, open till 22.00.

Post office and telephones

Central post office, at the market end of Tzanakáki, open 07.30–20.00, currency exchange 07.30–14.00. In the tourist season a subsidiary (for both mail and exchange) operates from a caravan in Plateía Mitrópolis in front of the modern cathedral.

The *OTE*, the **telephone company** headquarters for phone, fax and email services, is next door to the main post office. Open Mon–Sat 07.30–22.00, closed Sun and holidays.

Hospital

☎ 28210 22000, on the outskirts of town near Mourniés.

History

Most scholars agree that Khaniá lies on the site of ancient *Kydonía*, though the conclusive proof for this has not yet been established. Kydonía was founded according to legend by Kydon, a grandson of King Minos; the place-name (ku-do-ni-ja) occurs in the Linear B tablets of Knossós, and is familiar from many ancient literary sources.

Since the 1960s, extensive excavations on the Kastélli hill (p 361) overlooking the harbour have confirmed the existence of an important Bronze Age settlement dating back to the Prepalatial (Early Minoan II) period, mid-3rd millennium BC. Despite severe damage caused by fire in Late Minoan I this site continued to flourish after the 14C BC destruction of Knossós, and it is generally agreed that the centre of Mycenaean power was transferred here after the decline of Knossós. Modern habitation makes it difficult to prove the existence of the presumed palace, but the architecture uncovered and the range and quality of the finds demonstrate that the culture was undoubtedly palatial in style.

The Kastélli hill has been inhabited without interruption since the Bronze Age. There was Early Iron Age (Geometric period) occupation, and Kydonía played a prominent part in the politics of the Classical and Hellenistic city-states. It minted coinage from the 5C BC, and by the 2C was the leading city in western Crete. It fell to the Roman commander Metellus early in the campaign of 69 BC but went on to flourish throughout the period of Roman rule, and in the first Byzantine period became the seat of a bishop. Evidence for an Early Christian basilica church has recently come to light beneath the remains of the Venetian cathedral on the Kastélli hill.

The etymology of the name Khaniá is uncertain, but it may have derived from the place-name Alkania (known from an ancient inscription) associated with Velkhanos (Hephasitos, the Roman Vulcan), the god of fire, and its use in the arts. During the Venetian occupation Khaniá was rendered as La Canea.

When Crete was ceded to the Venetians after the Fourth Crusade (1204) they had to contend with the Genoese who were the first to take control around Khaniá. After Venice finally established supremacy in 1252 the new building included a cathedral, a rector's palace and a theatre on the Kastélli hill, by then known as the Castel Vecchio. The surrounding walls were consolidated by the mid-14C (partly on the line of earlier Byzantine fortifications) and consisted of straight sections of wall interrupted at intervals by small polygonal towers.

The harbour below the Kastélli became a centre of trade and an important base for Venice's fleet in the eastern Mediterranean. The dockyard grew to provide 17 *arsenali* for building and repairing the galleys.

By the mid-16C the threat of raids by Turkish corsairs such as the notorious Khair-ed-din Barbarossa compelled Venice to fortify the whole town. These new walls formed a rectangle parallel with the coast strengthened by four bastions, subsidiary bastions and a great moat up to 50m wide which ran along the line of what are now the streets Skalídi and Khátzi Mikháli Yiánnari. (The Roman theatre, still in existence in 1583, was demolished to provide building material for the fortifications.) The architect of the fortifications was Michele Sanmicheli from Verona. He was also responsible for the great walls of Candia (Herákleion), but these at La Canea were the less successful for in 1645 the city held out against the Turks for only two months.

The second half of the period of Venetian rule (after the sack of Constantinople in 1453) brought about improved relations between the native Cretan and Venetian communities. The threat from the east meant that the Venetians needed the support of the local population, and therefore adopted a more liberal religious policy. The Cretans began to look on Venice as a valued protector. La Canea prospered both materially and culturally at this time, within the sphere of European influence. In the early years of the 17C gifted icon-painters active in the city were aware of the work of Flemish engravers in the field of iconography, and in some cases adapted accordingly the traditions of the Cretan School. When the forces of the Ottoman Empire drove the Venetians from the island many of these artists went with them to work in Venice or the Venetian-dominated Ionian islands.

Under the Turks Khaniá became the seat of a *pashalik* but after the middle of the 19C the island was governed from the site of the former rector's palace on the Kastélli hill. The English scholar Robert Pashley, who landed at Khaniá in 1834, was impressed by its peaceable nature, for by this time over three-quarters of its population professed the Moslem faith. However, from the viewpoint of the movement for unification with the newly independent Greece it was from this city that the heroic uprisings originating in the mountainous hinterland were ruthlessly repressed.

The Turkish occupation ended in 1898. The interested European powers (Britain, France, Italy and Russia) installed Prince George of Greece as high commissioner, and Khaniá was made the capital of a semi-independent Cretan state. It remained the capital city after union with Greece in 1913 when the Greek flag at last flew from the walls of the Firkás at the entrance to the harbour. In 1971 this status was transferred to Herákleion, the geographical and commercial centre of the island.

The modern town

For a short visit the priority is usually to explore the Old City within the line of the Venetian walls (see below), but if you are spending time in the Khaniá region you will need to find your way about the streets of the new town outside the walls as well.

A useful starting point to orientate yourself is on the southern (inland) side of the municipal market (*agorá*), a cruciform covered building which was constructed in 1911 and is now one of the landmarks, and one of the major tourist attractions, of Khaniá. The market was built on the line of the 16C Venetian walls at a point where a bastion had to be levelled to make room for it. The dual carriageway, Khátzi Mikháli Yiánari (see plan), runs past the market.

Outside the entrance to the market's southern arm you are standing in a paved open space (officially **Plateía Soph. Venizélou**) back from the busy main road. On the far side of the road the modern commercial town begins. Immediately across from the municipal market is the National Bank, and just into Tzanakáki the post office and the telephone company office (*OTE*). Along this street are travel agencies, car-hire firms and the Olympic Airways office, but also the Municipal Gardens with a pleasantly shaded café.

The main road will take you west from the market, past a little plateía commemorating the Battle of Crete to the focal **Plateía 1866**, green with trees and shrubs. There are stops for local buses and a major taxi rank here, and some metered car parking. On the east side of the plateía is the National Tourist Office and on the inland side, on Kydonías, the regional bus station.

North of the plateía, back across the main road, Khálidon will take you into the Old City and downhill past the Archaeological Museum to the Outer Harbour.

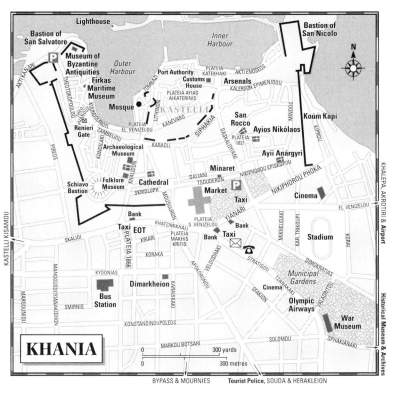

KHANIA

Lighthouse
Bastion of San Salvatore
Inner Harbour
Bastion of San Nicolo
P
Museum of Byzantine Antiquities
Outer Harbour
Firkas Maritime Museum
Port Authority
PLATEIA KATEKHAKI
AKTI ENDSEOS
Customs House
Arsenals
KALERGON EPIMENIDOU
Mosque
PLATEIA AYIAS AIKATERINIS
KASTELLI
Renieri Gate
PLATEIA EL. VENIZELOU
San Rocco
PLATEIA 1821
Kóum Kapi
Archaeological Museum
KARAOLI
SIPHAKIA
DASKALOIANNI
Ayios Nikólaos
Ayii Anárgyri
Schiavo Bastion
Folklore Museum
Cathedral
SKRIDLOPH
Minaret
DALIANI
TSOUDERON
NIKIPHOROU EPISKOPOU
NIKIPHOROU PHOKA
Market
P
Cinema
EL. VENIZELOU
Bank
Taxi
Taxi
Taxi EOT
KHATZIMIKHALI
PLATEIA S. VENIZELOU
YIANARI
Bank
Bank
Bank
Stadium
KRIARI
PLATEIA MAKHIS KRITIS
KORAKA
PLATEIA 1866
STRATIGOU
Municipal Gardens
KYDONIAS
Dimarkheion
Cinema
Bus Station
Olympic Airways
War Museum
KONSTANDINOUPOLEOS
0   300 yards
0   300 metres
MARKOU BOTSARI
SOLOMOU
SPHAKIANAKI

BYPASS & MOURNIES   Tourist Police, SOUDA & HERAKLEION

From the market to the harbour

The **covered market** (at its best in the mornings) has much to offer anyone shopping for Cretan specialities. There is a choice of café-bars and simple tavernas where you can watch the world go by.

To walk directly from the market to the harbour, you leave from the aisle leading west, past the piles of freshly landed fish. Outside this western exit vegetable stalls spill out on to the pavement. At the bottom of a flight of steps there is an excellent café patisserie, *Zakharoplasteion Kronos*.

Turn right here, and then left into **Skrídloph**, a street lined with shops selling leather goods where most tourists make at least one visit if only to browse. You can find bargains, but nowadays you also need to check carefully if you want articles that are made locally.

Skrídloph leads into **Khálidon**, the direct route down to the harbour from Plateía 1866. (To the left there is a good bookshop.) If you cross obliquely over Khálidon you will find a well-preserved stretch of the 16C fortifications. This is the **Schiavo bastion**, reinforced by the (circular) subsidiary **bastion of Lando**. The main water supply for the Venetian city was brought in near this point by an aqueduct from the springs of Perivólia to the south towards Thériso. The main gate into the city (the Réthymnon Gate) was a short distance to the east.

Khálidon passes a big open plateía in front of the 19C **cathedral** dedicated to the Presentation of the Virgin but also known as Trimártiri after the church which is thought to have stood here in Venetian times. The cathedral was completed by special dispensation under the Turks only in 1860; its character was intended to reflect influences from the by then liberated Greek state. Beside the road the multi-domed structure was once a Turkish bathhouse.

Across the road the **Cretan house Folklore Museum** is reached through an alleyway leading to a courtyard in front of the Roman Catholic church. Here, up a staircase covered with tumbling plants, you find a collection representing all the folk arts of Crete (both indoors and outdoors), lovingly arranged in the rooms of a typical old Khaniá house. Open 09.00–13.00, 18.00–21.00; out of season evening opening only may be the rule. For enquiries ☎ 28210 90816.

A visit is recommended to anyone hoping to take home from the island some good quality textiles; here you can get a feel for the traditional fabrics, designs and craftsmanship. The two women friends whose project this is are often at work on commissioned orders.

On the same side of the street a short distance towards the harbour, the Archaeological Museum (p 364) is housed in a former Venetian friary church. Khálidon ends at Plateía El. Venizélou on the Outer Harbour.

The Outer Harbour

Plateía El. Venizélou (formerly Syntriváni) on the Outer Harbour of the Venetians is the setting for the social life of the town. Khálidon comes down to the waterfront here and the quays to either side are lined by picturesque old buildings given over to cafés, bars and tavernas.

Café life around the plateía begins at breakfast time. There is an excellent bookshop, with foreign-language books and newspapers (and next door to it a currency exchange bureau). On summer evenings the plateía is a fine place to watch or join the *vólta* as people turn out to stroll and chat, parading to and fro along the quays after the heat of the day.

To the west you look along to the Venetian fort at the entrance to the harbour known today by the Turkish name **Firkás** (barracks) and now housing the Maritime Museum (see below). Across the harbour entrance, at the end of the mole which protects the Inner Harbour, is the splendid **lighthouse** with suggestions of a minaret in its design. The original Venetian lighthouse was reconstructed by the Egyptians during their brief spell on the island in support of the Turkish administration (1832–40).

The Kastélli hill

Overlooking both harbours is the Kastélli hill. The city of Khaniá grew up here and evidence has been uncovered for settlement dating back to the Bronze Age. There are traces of a circuit of defensive walls from the time of the Hellenistic city-state of Kydonía until the Venetian citadel outgrew them in the 19C. In Venetian times the hill was crowned by the cathedral or *duomo* which occupied the site of an Early Christian basilica church.

The corso of the Venetian city is now **Kanebáro**, running straight over the hill (east–west) through the centre of the walled city. The Venetians lined both sides of their corso with palazzi. At the end of the first short street to the left (Lithinón) the coat of arms of the Venetian archives is preserved and the doorway (no. 45) has an inscription recording its construction in 1624. (Three blocks are transposed indicating that the craftsman did not understand Latin.)

Here, with commanding views of the harbour, stood the palazzo of the Venetian governor. Only hints of this building have survived, with the remains of walls, arches, doorways, a vaulted passage and enclosed courtyard incorporated into later buildings. The Turkish *pasha* ruled from an elaborate wooden building using the same foundations but this was burned down in 1897.

At the far (eastern) end of Kaneváro was the Arcade of San Marco and the nunnery of Santa Maria dei Miracoli, now indicated only by ruins. (The *Pension Monastiri* in Odós Ayíou Markoú retains some of the atmosphere of the place.) Much of the city on the Kastélli that survived after the departure of the Turks in 1898 was damaged beyond repair by the German bombardment of 1941. Modern houses are often built into the remains of old structures.

The excavations on Kastelli hill

Despite the signs of archaeological activity all over this area, there are obvious difficulties about investigating prehistoric levels beneath densely populated urban Khaniá. One extensive excavation important for an understanding of Minoan Kydoniá has been possible in **Plateía Ayías Aikaterínis**, the location of the former Venetian cathedral, halfway along Kaneváro on the left walking up from the Outer Harbour. The work has been the result of Greek collaboration with the Swedish Archaeological Institute.

Many of the most interesting exhibits in the museum on Khalidón come from this site which is not yet open to the public but can be viewed quite well from outside the fence. At the height of the Minoan period (LMI) the excavation here shows many features of palatial-style architecture. Two-storey houses had carefully constructed façades. There were light-wells, and the pier-and-door (*polythýron*) arrangement (with walls made up of several doors giving sophisticated flexibility to room spaces), also paved floors and a drainage system. Two streets led to an open plateía. There were storerooms with large pots, and the find of a large number of loomweights indicated an area for weaving.

When these buildings were destroyed by fire (as were so many other Minoan sites across the island around the middle of the 15C BC) many fragments of tablets inscribed in Linear A, accidentally preserved in the debris, pointed to a well-developed system of administration. The existence of a palace at Khaniá at this time is generally accepted.

Although by far the most impressive architectural remains on the Plateía Ayías Aikaterínis site were of this LMI period, parts of the settlement were reoccupied after the fire destruction. It is known that the settlement here at Kydonía continued to flourish in LMIII, with a strong Mycenaean presence, and probably reached the height of its power. **Linear B tablets** from levels dated to c 1300 BC, the first excavated on the island outside Knossós, were a find of major importance for an understanding of western Crete in the Late Bronze Age. The tablets indicate a centralised administration and most probably a palatial centre here on the hill at this time.

Small pieces of the jigsaw of prehistoric Kydonía keep coming to light all over the Kastélli hill. On the southeast side of the hill, in the Splántzia district, there is a Minoan 'lustral basin' (not currently open to the public), a subterranean structure designed for ritual purposes, and a familiar feature of Minoan palatial architecture. This example, tentatively dated to the end of the Middle Minoan period, is remarkably well preserved. The walls and a supporting pillar at the foot of the staircase down to the paved floor were painted to imitate marble.

Stretches of the old walls of the historical period are best seen on the way back to the Outer Harbour along **Síphaka** (which becomes Karaóli-Dimitríou) inland of and parallel to Kaneváro. In some stretches it is possible to identify in the foundations the dressed blocks which probably belong to the Hellenistic wall. The Byzantines incorporated ancient building material from Greco-Roman Kydonía (finally destroyed during the Arab invasion) and both they and the Venetians reused in their ramparts recognisable fragments such as column drums, architrave blocks, even capitals, so that precise dating is difficult.

The Inner Harbour

A walk around the foot of the Kastélli hill can start from the busy plateía (El. Venizélou) at the waterfront end of Kaneváro. To the east along the quay is the **Mosque of the Janissaries** constructed in 1645, the year in which the Turks captured the town from the Venetians. Severely damaged by Second World War bombing, the building was partially reconstructed soon afterwards but during the last decade it has again been in the hands of restorers.

On the Kastélli hillside above the mosque the ancient city wall is still formidable below the foundations for the rector's palace. The quay leads round to the Inner Harbour of the Venetians. An exhibition centre for the craftwork of the region is tucked into the hillside, and in the summer season you pass on the waterfront a hut staffed by volunteers from the *Sea Turtle Protection Society of Greece* (STPS) keen to spread information about the society's work and the urgent need for it on Crete (p 57).

On the south side of the Inner Harbour and at its far end you will notice vaulted structures, the remaining *arsenáli*, shipsheds from the Venetian dockyard. Here, on a sloping shore, the galleys were built or repaired, each vault holding one ship. Nine survive, in two groups, comparable with those at Herákleion but in a better state of preservation. Beyond the first group there is a glimpse inland of the unconventional outline of the Dominican church of Ayios Nikólaos. The Customs House, recently restored, overlooks Plateía Katekháki.

The Venetian fortifications guarded the harbour from the northeast with the **Sabbionara bastion** at the edge of the sea. The ruined Sabbionara Gate here (the name indicating sand in Italian) was altered in Turkish times. The Gate of the Sand became **Koúm Kapí** in Turkish and the district east along the waterfront has retained the name. Out on the long mole forming the northern protection for the harbour is the recently restored **bastion of San Nicolo**, with a ruined chapel beyond which the mole ends at the lighthouse.

Back at the Sabbionara Gate you can follow the eastern stretch of the defensive wall along the Koúm Kapí shore. On Saturday mornings you will find a flourishing outdoor market here. The flea market is nearest the harbour, with the produce stalls up Kýprou. On the promontory at the end of the Koúm Kapí bay the coast road passes a small park before the Hotel Dóma).

If you make your way inland behind the Hotel Porto Veneziano (overlooking the Inner Harbour of the Venetians) in the direction of the big church of Ayios Nikólaos, you will discover the area known as **Splántzia**, with the maze of narrow streets which is one of the most picturesque corners of Khaniá.

Ayios Nikólaos, the church of a Dominican priory under the Venetians, was transformed by the Turks into the Imperial Mosque of Sultan Ibrahim, and still retains both bell-tower and minaret (damaged and reduced in height); the additional balcony on the minaret testified to the importance of the city's principal mosque. The building only become an Orthodox church in 1918. The tall galleried nave (much restored) has a coffered ceiling.

In front of the church is **Plateía 1821** with convenient pavement cafés. This is the centre of the Splántzia district which was a Turkish enclave under the occupation. The plaque in the middle of the plateía records that an Orthodox bishop was executed by hanging from the plane tree during the 1821 revolt which led to the independence of mainland Greece. At the west end of the square is the little double-aisled Venetian church of **San Rocco**, no longer in use but recently restored. Below the cornice on the west façade is a Latin inscription: 'Dedicated to God the Great and Mighty and to the Divine Rocco. 1630'. The saint was believed to offer protection from the plague prevalent at the time.

Two blocks further south from the plateía (on Nikiphórou Episkópou) the 16C **Ayii Anárgyri** (the Holy Poor) contrived to remain an Orthodox church under both Venetians and Turks. It served for a time as the Orthodox cathedral and still flourishes as a place of worship. Its iconostasis (1837–41) incorporates a work depicting *Ayios Kharálambos* (with three martyrdom scenes in the lower register) signed 'by the hand of Viktoros', a 17C painter. You will also find two icons, a *Dormition of the Virgin* and a *Last Judgement*, painted in 1625 by Ambrosios Embaros, a priest-monk from Khaniá whose work is said to show the influence of Flemish engravers. Continuing west you soon find the landmark of the municipal market.

From Plateía El. Venizélou to the Firkás

Parallel to the Aktí Koundourióti (the southern quay of the Outer Harbour lined with bars and tavernas) a picturesque narrow street, **Zambelíou**, runs west from the harbour plateía below the Kastélli to the **Topanás quarter** at the northwestern corner of the Old City. Past the first crossing, the shell of a palazzo, with a crest and Latin inscription high up on the façade, is a relic of Venetian times. The ruins now shelter one of the many tavernas along this street. (Further along it the *Taverna Tamám* is housed in former Turkish baths.)

Kondiláki runs inland, uphill. It is nowadays lined with places to eat, but under Turkish rule this was the Jewish quarter around the synagogue and the district is still known as **Evraikí**.

Just as Zambelíou starts to climb some steps, a right turn leads to the **Renieri Gate**, with a Venetian family's coat of arms and a memorial inscription of 1608. Through the gate (in Theophanoús) is the once elegant Renieri chapel, locked and long overdue for restoration. Beyond it, on the left, the vaults of the Venetian armoury have been restored and put to use.

This corner of the old town lies only just behind the hectic bustle of the harbour quay, but there are many picturesque rooms and apartments to rent at various price levels. The steps on Zambelíou lead round to **Theotokopoúlou** where many of the old buildings have been discreetly modernised to provide accommodation for visitors. Anyone looking for higher quality, specifically Khaniot, souvenirs will enjoy this area which has become a marketplace for local craftsmen.

You reach the waterfront at the bottom of Theotokopoúlou and the street opens out to what was the **Bastion of San Salvatore** which defended the harbour entrance on the western side (a recommended vantage point at sunset). The sea gate was here, both it and the bastion taking the name of the friary church on the right-hand side, newly restored and since 1998 housing Khaniá's **Museum of Byzantine Antiquities** (see below).

Opposite (west of) what remains of the friary's cloister you will notice a solidly constructed building with steps to the upper entrance (now a laboratory for the conservation of antiquities). This was built as the gunpowder magazine and its Turkish name (Top Hane) persists in this **Topanás** area of Khaniá.

The unsympathetic building high up further west, intruding on the line of the fortifications, was built after World War II as the state-owned Xenía hotel. The planning authorities have intervened to ensure that it does no further environmental damage. Above it there is a good view of the western wall and moat; the athletically inclined can follow the wall to the mid-16C Schiavo-Lando bastion (near the top of Khálidon; see above).

The Venetian fort facing the harbour on this western side (where the basin could be closed by a chain across to the lighthouse) is still known by its Turkish name as the **Firkás**. On 1 December 1913, on the little tower at the seaward corner of the fort, the Greek flag was hoisted officially for the first time on the island to celebrate Crete's long-awaited union with Greece; the ceremony is repeated on state occasions and annually on that day. Nowadays the upper level of the fort is used as an open-air theatre for drama productions in summer, and exhibitions of Cretan dancing are a regular event. The Firkás houses the Maritime Museum of Crete (see below).

If you follow the coastline westwards, away from the harbour entrance, you are walking towards the **Néa Khóra** district, past the yacht haven, 15 minutes to the town beach and two well-known fish tavernas.

Archaeological Museum

Open Tues–Sun 08.30–15.00, including public holidays; closed Mon; ☎ 28210 53033. The museum is at the harbour end of Khálidon, housed in one of the largest Venetian churches on the island, once part of a Latin monastery of St Francis. The building is crudely constructed, with a vaulted nave and narrow side-aisles, and with the peculiarity that the high altar was at the west end. In the adjoining garden to the north a Turkish fountain and the base of a minaret survive from the basilica's days as the Mosque of Yusuf Pasha.

The exhibits, with excellent labelling in English as well as Greek, build up a picture of archaeological discoveries across this western end of Crete. Material is regularly added from work in progress.

Artefacts of the **Prehistoric period** (Late Neolithic and Bronze Age) are in the first part of the building as you enter. The chronological sequence begins on the left and circles clockwise to the cases behind the ticket desk. The Late Neolithic material comes from a number of cave sites across the region. Some of the artefacts dated to the Early Minoan period (third millennium BC) indicate the strength even at this time of the relationship between Crete and the Cycladic islands of the Aegean.

There is Neopalatial material (**Case 7**) from a Minoan country house at Nerokoúrou on the flat ground south of Soúda Bay; the excavation was interesting because it was the first in this part of Crete of a type of building familiar further east on the island.

The most important Minoan site is in Khaniá itself, in Plateía Ayías Aikaterínis on the Kastélli hill above the harbour (see above) and material from this excavation is informatively displayed along the left wall. The fire which destroyed the buildings of the Neopalatial period (c 1450 BC) accidentally preserved an archive of tablets inscribed in Linear A, a find which pointed strongly to the existence of a palace in Neopalatial times.

In **Case 11** is a remarkable **seal impression** (widely illustrated and known as the Master Impression) of a god or ruler dominating a great building which is topped by horns of consecration; set in a rocky landscape by the sea the building can be interpreted as a city, a sanctuary or a palace.

Clay pyxis with a scene of a man playing a lyre, from a chamber tomb near Aptéra

The discovery in 1989 of tablets inscribed in Linear B, until then known on Crete only from the palace at Knossós, confirmed that the settlement on the Kastélli went on to flourish as a centre of power during the Postpalatial time of Mycenaean domination, at least until the 13C BC. The tablets, which preserve an early form of the Greek language, recorded the existence of a sanctuary to Zeus and Dionysos even during the Bronze Age.

You will notice inscribed fragments of stirrup jars dating from this period. A study has traced the movements of these jars (used to transport liquids) and the pattern that emerges points to the Khaniá area as the centre of an extensive trade network across the island and to the mainland around Mycenae.

The conspicuous **clay burial chests** (*lárnakes*) include a bathtub shape decorated with stylised octopus motifs from the Bronze Age cemetery at Khaniá (in an area of the new town where excavation is only occasionally possible). Against the walls are examples of pithoi that were used for storage but also for burial purposes.

If you cross the nave to the cases to the right of the entrance (behind the bookstall) the material displayed comes from cemeteries in and around Khaniá dating from the **Postpalatial period** (LMIIIA–B, c 1400–1200 BC). Much of the **pottery** was the product of a local Kydonía workshop, with a distinctive fine clay and slip. An outstanding example from this workshop is the extraordinary **pyxis** (no. 2308) which portrays (in a scene of religious significance denoted by horns of consecration and double axe motifs) a man playing a lyre to birds; the piece came from a chamber tomb near the Kiliáres river below Aptéra. Pottery from this same workshop has been found as far away as Cyprus and Sardinia, further confirming the evidence for trading activities at this time between western Crete and other parts of the Aegean world.

You turn to the side-chapel at a lower level, towards the garden, for **Minoan gold jewellery** and **sealstones**.

The **Iron Age** exhibits begin on the left (south) wall in the main body of the church (**Case 23**) with finds chiefly from cemeteries of the Geometric period. The later material (Archaic to Roman) associated with the city-states of western Crete is displayed in or near the rear side-chapels across the nave. These cases repay a close inspection; there are interesting terracotta figurines, a **clay model of a temple** from Phalásarna, intricate pieces of Hellenistic and Roman gold jewellery, also a good display of early glass.

One central case contains the museum's collection of **coins**, dating from Classical times to the Venetian period. In another there are numerous offerings brought to a rural sanctuary at Tsiskianá, Sélinos, where (4C BC–2C AD) the cult of Poseidon was practised. These bull figurines were substitutes for the customary sacrifice to Poseidon of black and white bulls.

The museum shows some striking **mosaic floors** rescued from Roman houses uncovered during building operations in modern Khaniá. By coincidence Poseidon features again here, with the nymph Anemone, as does Dionysos (with Ariadne on Náxos) whose name first occurred on the Linear B tablets (see above) unearthed on the Kastélli hill, with mention of a sanctuary at Kydonía.

Statuary (Hellenistic and Roman copies of Classical models) and stele collection are exhibited near the Roman mosaics. Among the figures are an *Asklepios* from Lisós near Soúyia, *Diktynna with hound* from the Diktýnnaion sanctuary on Cape Spátha, and dominating the far end of the building the *Philosopher of Elyros*, a heroic Roman copy of a Greek orator.

Historical Museum and Archives of Crete

This museum is at Sphakianáki 20, one block south of the Municipal Gardens, in an area of late 19C villas which became the setting for the social and political life revolving around Crete's first high commissioner (1898–1906), Prince George of Greece. Open Mon–Fri 09.00–13.00; ☎ 28210 52606.

The collection of historical records held here is considered second in importance in all Greece only to those of Athens. The museum exhibits are arranged on two floors, but the upper floor has been closed for several years (telephone well ahead of time for special permission for access). The display is designed primarily for serious students of Cretan history, but much of the material (old photographs, maps, contemporary comment from abroad) will interest any visitor wanting to know something of the foundations on which modern Crete is built. Translation of the labels is a little haphazard.

On the **ground floor**, the room to the right of the entrance is devoted to the politician and statesman **Elefthérios Venizélos** (1864–1936), Khaniá's most distinguished citizen of modern times. Exhibits are connected with the penultimate stage (1896–98) of the struggle for Cretan independence in which he played a leading part. A Greek force was sent to support the Cretan Revolutionary Assembly, and despite the initial ambivalence of the Great Powers, the Turks were finally compelled to withdraw from the island. It still took until 1913 to achieve union with Greece.

The majority of the items on display are related to Crete's long struggle against the Turks, and they illuminate the spirit of those engaged in it as much as the events themselves. Chronologically they begin with a *portrait of Daskalo-yiánnis*, leader of the 1770 Sphakiot rebellion. There is a series of portraits of the 19C regional commanders; their proud bearing and formidable weaponry proclaim their deadly earnest. An imposing collection of bishops is a reminder of the close involvement of the Orthodox church. Thomas Backhurst Sandwith, the

British honorary consul for Crete 1870–85, was an observer known to have been sympathetic to the Cretan cause.

On the staircase to the upper floor a 16C cupboard elaborately carved with hunting scenes is a rare survival on the island of Venetian furniture of this quality. **Upstairs** the theme of resistance to invaders is extended to resistance to the Germans during the Second World War. The museum's historical collection includes a great number of rare antique maps and topographical engravings, with several of Venetian Khaniá (La Canea) but also including a view of Herákleion showing the great Latin church of the Franciscans dominating the city skyline from the hill where the archaeological museum now stands. Complementing the engravings and early photographs the folklore collection preserves a wide range of traditional Cretan costume.

War Museum

The War Museum is at Tzanakáki 1, on the corner with Sphakianáki at the inland end of the Municipal Gardens. Open Tues–Sat 09.00–13.00; ☎ 28210 44156. Permission required for photography.

The War Museum of Khaniá is a department of the principal one in Athens. The collection here successfully complements those of the Maritime Museum and the Historical Museum and Archives here in Khaniá, as well as the Historical Museum in Herákleion.

Emphasising the Cretan dimension, the exhibits cover the struggle for the island's independence from Turkish rule, leading first to autonomy and finally in 1913 to the much desired union with Greece. Attention is drawn to the part played by Cretans in Greece's 20C wars in the Balkans and Asia Minor, and during the Second World War. At that time the Cretan division was marooned in the north of the country as the Germans advanced into Macedonia, and therefore to enduring regret was not available to defend the homeland.

Maritime Museum of Crete

The museum is housed in the Firkás (see above). Open Tues–Sun 10.00–16.00 in the main summer season (otherwise until 14.00); closed Mon and public holidays; ☎ 28210 91875.

An excellently presented museum, it covers the history of seafaring and its effect on the island of Crete from the period of the Venetian occupation up to the 20C. A visit to the upstairs rooms is vital for anyone with an interest in the World War II Battle of Crete. There is a long-term plan to move this section to a purpose-built museum in the village of Galatás, already the home of the New Zealanders' war memorial (p 373), but fund-raising for the project is not yet completed.

Museum of Byzantine Antiquities

This museum is housed in the restored church of the Franciscan friary of San Salvatore behind the Firkás at the waterfront end of Odós Theotokopoúlou. Open Tues–Sun 08.00–14.00, closed Mon; ☎ 28210 96046. An excellent illustrated leaflet (from the Archaeological Receipts Fund) sets the historical background and has a plan of the layout of the exhibits which are drawn from the collection of the Department of Byzantine Antiquities in Khaniá.

This is a valuable addition to the museums of Crete for visitors interested in the island's culture in Byzantine and post-Byzantine times.

The friary church is believed to date back to the 15C; the original domed chapel with apse was extended to the west in the following century, and then towards the end of the Venetian period space was added through the archways on the northern side. The Turks converted the church to a mosque.

The collection is displayed and explained in the best modern manner within the chronological framework of the Byzantine and post-Byzantine periods in the province of Khaniá. The First and Second Byzantine periods cover 330–1204 AD with a break for the years (824–961) of Arab rule. After the debacle of the Fourth Crusade (1204) the island became part of the Venetian empire but the Cretan population adhered to the culture and ideals of Byzantium.

To the right as you enter the church, there is a display of architectural fragments and inscriptions. A fine 6C **mosaic pavement** from Kísamos (present day Kastélli Kísamou) is immediately noticeable. The section covering wall-paintings will be especially useful for visitors to the island coming new to the subject, and in the oldest part of the church there are some important icons. Pottery and a good collection of coins rounds off the display.

The Akrotíri

This is the name (the word for 'cape' in Greek) which is given to the hilly land mass jutting out to the northeast of Khaniá and protecting the anchorage of Soúda Bay. Two important monasteries out on the cape date back to the time when the Venetians were in control of the island. A short walk by an old path takes you down to the romantic ruins of a much earlier foundation and a hermit's cave near sea-level, the burial place of one of the most revered Cretan saints, Ayios Ioánnis Xénos, St John the Stranger.

On the west coast of the cape small-scale holiday settlements offer good swimming at **Kalathás**, **Tersanás** and at the end of the road at **Stavrós**. Because they are close to the city the beaches (none of any great length) may be crowded, especially at weekends.

South of Stavrós the countryside is indiscriminately dotted with summer bungalows, but continue to an enclosed bay, dramatically overlooked by a cliff where the final scenes of the film *Zorba the Greek* were shot. There are tavernas close to the fishing boat quay.

The spectacular **cave of Lerá**, halfway up Zorba's cliff, was frequented in Neolithic times and there is evidence for a cave sanctuary from the end of the Bronze Age through to the Hellenistic period. (Finds from the cave are exhibited in the Archaeological Museum in Khaniá.)

To swim in the open sea you can walk or drive on a good coastal track a short distance west of the main cove to find the **Blue Beach** complex (also signed straight on at a bend on the approach road to the village). There is a pleasant taverna and bar here, and modern studio apartments usually booked from abroad may have vacancies outside the high season.

The monasteries of the Akrotíri

The Ayía Triáda monastery (16km from Khaniá) can be reached directly by the main road to the airport, or by minor roads across the central upland area of the

Akrotíri which is countryside enjoyed by walkers and, according to the season, a recommended hunting ground for wild flowers.

Travelling by bus

The bus service from Khaniá to Khordáki passes within 2km of the Ayía Triáda monastery, but the timetable is not designed for tourists. Walkers may be able to use this service for the out ward journey and then from the monasteries continue on foot west (c 5km) across to **Khoraphákia** (with a good taverna) for the return to Khaniá using the Stavrós bus service or a taxi.

By car you will approach the Akrotíri either from Khaniá or from the north coast highway round the head of Soúda Bay, past the Commonwealth War Cemetery. You leave the centre of Khaniá on El. Venizélou, signposted for the airport and Akrotíri. On the left at the top of the long climb up from the bay (c 5km) are the graves of the eminent Cretan-born statesman Elefthérios Venizélos and his son Sophoklés. Signs lead you by a one-way system to parking on the hill of Prophítis Ilías. The **Venizélos tomb** is impressive in its simplicity.

Elefthérios Venizélos, born in Khaniá in 1864, was prominent in European politics for nearly four decades, and is honoured as one of the architects of the modern Greek state.

On the hill of Prophítis Ilías in 1897, while the Turks were nominally still in control of the island, the Greek flag was raised by Cretan insurgents. This gesture took place in the teeth of an international naval bombardment (by ships of the Great Powers) ostensibly designed to defuse a tense situation between the Greek and Turkish nations.

There are popular summer tavernas and bars on the hill, through the gate at the lower end of the cemetery, with a fine view over the Bay of Khaniá to Cape Spátha where in Roman times the eye would have been drawn to the light on the marble columns of the temple of Díktynna.

If you are using the main airport road, running high above Soúda Bay, you may like to stop at the convent of Ayios Ioánnis Pródromos (the Baptist) near Korakiés where the nuns exhibit the weavings and embroidery for which they are noted; their recent work is for sale. Below on the bay the **Commonwealth War Cemetery** (p 373) is 2km away, down the road signed for Soúda. Elsewhere access to this north shore of the bay is restricted because of military installations.

For the monastery of Ayía Triáda keep on the airport road until you pass the end of the runway. Turn left at the next T-junction, and almost immediately (signed in Greek) right and then left again.

For the cross-country route from Venizélos graves to the monasteries take the side-road signed for (1km) **Kounoupidianá**. In the angle of two roads in the middle of the village there is the popular *psistariá Mítsos* (a rotisserie, open evenings only). Keep left at this fork and on the far side of the village pass the left turn for the Stavrós road up the western side of the Akrotíri.

Continue ahead through **Kambáni**. The uncultivated areas along this winding road shelter many species of wild flowers including (in spring) several varieties of orchids. Soon you are guided by signs for Moní Ayías Triádas, the monastery of the Holy Trinity. After the junction with the road from the airport, turn left again. The Khordáki bus stops at this corner.

In 1km a cypress avenue, right, marks the approach to the monastery. For the festival of Trinity Sunday this is a place of pilgrimage from far around.

The Ayía Triáda monastery

Although officially closed between 14.00 and 17.00, the arrangement is at the discretion of the monk or guardian on duty. Inside the gate a gift shop sells books and souvenirs, including olive oil and wine from monastery lands.

The church dominates a courtyard planted with orange trees that scent the air for much of the year; both these and the numerous cypresses were noted by a visitor from abroad at the end of the 17C. Rain is the only source of water for the monastery and the cisterns are beneath its courtyard.

This massive multi-domed church, consecrated in 1634, was built by two brothers from the Venetian Zangaróli family who had adopted the Orthodox faith. The monastic foundation, still associated with their family name, was probably in existence before their time. One of the brothers had studied Byzantine church architecture on Mount Athos but the façade here, reinforced by half-engaged Doric columns, reflects the Venetian influence, as does the imposing main entrance (dated by the inscription 1631); the campanile in its present form was a later addition.

Two plaques on the church, one either side of the main west door into the narthex, commemorate the contribution of the brothers, one of whom did not survive to see the completion of his work. The plaques are identical in content, but one is written in Latin, the other in Greek. The church's central dome was not finished in 1634 and with troubled times ahead it remained that way for nearly two centuries.

During the great revolt against the Turks in 1821 there was severe damage to this whole structure. During the interregnum of more lenient Egyptian rule, permission was obtained in 1827 for restoration which produced more or less the building that stands today. The last decade has seen major refurbishment.

The monastic buildings round the courtyard accommodate a small **museum** which sometimes displays interesting icons. There was a college of the Orthodox church here in the 19C and the monastery played an important part in the running of schools in Khaniá for the preservation of Greek culture. It is still a wealthy and influential foundation with a fine library.

The Gouvernéto monastery

It is 4km from Ayía Triáda to the second, more isolated, monastery (officially closed 12.30–16.30) known as Moní Gouvernétou after a nearby settlement which vanished long ago. A dirt road sets off north from the Ayía Triáda car park (at a right-angle to the end of the cypress avenue) and soon turns right to join the direct (surfaced) road. Across the uncultivated upland you start to climb through a narrow passage into the wild northeastern corner of the Akrotíri.

The foundation of the Gouvernéto monastery is thought to date back at least to the first years of the Venetian occupation, and perhaps to the 12C when pirates were ravaging the coast of Crete and an inland position offered relative safety. The history of the monastery is bound up with that of its predecessor, the Katholikó, the ruins of which are hidden in a ravine near the sea (a recommended walk, see below).

The plain exterior wall of the Gouvernéto quadrangle, on the model of a fortress with square towers at the corners, hides the richly decorated façade of the **cruciform church** dedicated to Our Lady of the Angels (Kyría ton Angélon), celebrating the feast of the Presentation of the Virgin.

The building of this church was started in 1548 but not completed, and only acquired its final form in the 19C after damage during the 1821 revolt. The striking relief carving of the bases of the six columns set into the church façade dates to the Venetian period and is most unusual for Crete, as is the ground-plan of the church.

One of the side-chapels is dedicated to the Ayii Déka, the Holy Ten (Crete's Christian martyrs under the Persecution of Decius in 250). The other commemorates the revered local saint (active c 970–1027, canonised 1632), Ayios Ioánnis Xénos, St John the Stranger, sometimes known as Ermítis, the hermit, because tradition has it that he died shut away from the world in the cave down at the Katholikó. The Feast Day of St John is 7 October, and the vigil here at the Gouvernéto on the previous evening begins one of the great religious festivals of western Crete.

St John the Stranger

St John (Ayios Ioánnis Xénos) was an influential evangelist, devoted to the task of re-establishing the Christian faith and reorganising monastic institutions at the time when the army of the Byzantine empire had recovered the island after more than a century of Saracen domination.

Ioánnis was born in Sívas in the Mesará but his work is best known in western Crete. He is credited with founding the monastery of the Panayía at Myrioképhala (p 348), in the hills southwest of Réthymnon. He visited Constantinople and brought back sacred vessels, books and icons as furnishings of the monastic life. He is also associated with the history of the Katholikó, perhaps consolidating what had been an anchorite community occupying the many caves in the hillside.

The walk to the ruins of the **Katholikó** (40 minutes, steep in places) starts from the Gouvernéto. The well-built path drops away past a memorial on the rise beyond the monastery. After 10 minutes you pass a first cave with a chapel at its entrance and inside it a stalagmite said to resemble a bear. The cave was originally sacred to Artemis, venerated here in the form of a bear (*arkoúda* in Greek). The Christian chapel was dedicated to the Panayía (Virgin) Arkoudiótissa.

The ancient path continues downhill and becomes a long flight of rock-cut steps; on a bend the Katholikó ruins are suddenly in view. They lie on either side of a wide bridge across the bed of a dried-up stream, between cliffs from which the unmistakable notes of the blue rock thrush are often heard.

In the cliff at the bottom of the stairway, level with the bridge, a rock-cut chapel marks the entrance to a passage leading to a spectacular cave chosen for the burial place of St John. (The passage and cave are often perilously slippery underfoot.) A 10-minute walk down the river-bed leads to the rocky shore. It is possible to swim from an ancient rock-cut slipway.

The Katholikó monastery on the Akrotíri near Khaniá, from Pashley, Travels in Crete, *1837*

East of Khaniá

The New National Road east from Khaniá runs within easy reach of the Commonwealth War Cemetery at the head of Soúda Bay, a Minoan excavation at Nerokoúrou and the site of Aptéra, a city-state of the Greco-Roman period in a stunning position overlooking the anchorage of Soúda Bay.

If you use the Old Road from Khaniá to Soúda (p 374) you can visit the historic monastery of **Khrysopiyí**. Open 08.00–12.00 and 16.00–18.00. The turning inland (3km from Khaniá) is signed to Maláxa but two side-roads fork off here: the right-hand one takes you down an avenue of eucalyptus to the walled convent. (Turn left to park round the back.) This is a flourishing and progressive establishment, home to more than 20 nuns.

The Khrysopiyí monastery was a 16C foundation. It is dedicated to *Zoodókhos Piyí* (the Virgin as the Fount of Life). Because of repeated damage in the 19C the buildings have no great age but the whole is immaculately cared for and you will feel welcomed to a self-sufficient world. Some of the younger generation of nuns run a computer project concerned with ecclesiastical publishing. Others produce professional copies of traditional Byzantine icons, and these are for sale.

Maláxa (see above-noted signpost) is a 14km climb, mostly on a well-engineered road but through uncultivated country which will appeal to wildflower enthusiasts. The village is on an escarpment which has played a part in the defence of the anchorage at the head of Soúda Bay during many periods of its history. The views are stunning and there are tavernas and cafés from which to enjoy them. This is a popular summer evening's excursion from Khaniá; you can return on a circular route using the road between Stýlos and Aptéra.

For the **Commonwealth War Cemetery** continue on the Old Road, past the Maláxa turning, towards Soúda. Pass the slip-road up to the New National Road and turn left (signed for the airport) on to the road round the head of the bay. After c 2km you cross the river running into the bay. (There is a track beside it down to the water, a spot where egrets and sometimes night herons may be seen.) Just before the turning to the war graves two tavernas sit side by side, in an attractive setting along the shore.

The cemetery, beautifully planted and tended, occupies a superb position at the head of the bay. It contains the graves of 1527 men (862 British, 446 New Zealanders, 197 Australians, 22 from other Commonwealth countries) who were killed in the last ten days of May 1941 during the Battle of Crete. There is a brief account of the campaign just inside the cemetery gate (see also p 52). An annual commemoration service is held on the Sunday at the start of Battle of Crete week. In 1963, 19 First World War burials were transferred here from the consular cemetery, along with 51 others dating back to 1897.

John Pendlebury

Among the graves (10E) is that of John Pendlebury, the English archaeologist shot by the Germans on 22 May 1941. For five years from 1929 Pendlebury continued the work of Sir Arthur Evans on the Minoan palace at Knossós. He is remembered for a legendary series of travels on foot throughout even the wildest parts of the island, searching for evidence of Crete's past and along the way winning the friendship and respect of very many Cretans. In 1939 he published *The Archaeology of Crete*. At the outbreak of war Pendlebury joined the army and was sent back to Crete as a member of British Intelligence to coordinate preparations for its defence. He was captured, and met his death in mysterious circumstances during the German attack on Herákleion. After the war the people of Herákleion held a memorial service for him; an address given by the eminent Greek archaeologist Nikólaos Pláton included the eulogy: 'Dear friend, Crete will preserve your memory among her most sacred treasures. The soil which you excavated with the archaeologist's pick and enriched with a warrior's blood will shelter you with eternal gratitude.'

Minoan excavation at Nerokoúrou

The village of Nerokoúrou is at the southern edge of the flat country south of Souda Bay. You can reach the village from Mourniés or Maláxa, or from the stretch of the Khaniá bypass between the Mourniés junction and the western of the two slip-roads for Soúda. The turning into a local road south (indistinctly signed) is beside a garden centre and opposite a vehicle repair works (with a notice for the Steam Company of Khaniá).

For the Minoan excavation, a surfaced track from the eastern end of the village runs north, back in the direction of the highway, and bends round partly ruined buildings reoccupied as a farmstead; a Venetian chapel in the courtyard suggests an original monastic use. Very soon the road straightens out again towards the highway and the site is on the right, fenced but usually accessible.

In the 1970s a Greek-Italian team of archaeologists investigated the foundations of a country house of the Neopalatial period (Middle Minoan III–Late Minoan I). The northern sector of the house had been damaged by bulldozers but the report noted a quality of architecture, in design and in the careful choice of materials, that is comparable with the houses of the same period in the towns and countryside of central Crete. (In the west of the island at the time of the excavation this was still an unusual discovery.)

It makes sense to view the excavation from the south, with your back to the mountains. In the first phase the area nearest to you was an open space with a paved and stone-lined cistern at its west side. A large hall opened northwards, with an entrance between columns; the bases for pillars along the right-hand wall suggested a possible balcony. Beyond (in the damaged section) there was evidence for at least one of the pier-and-door partitions so characteristic of the finest Neopalatial architecture. Coloured limestone slabs were used for paving and light-coloured limestone, carefully dressed, for column bases and door jambs. In the second phase the open area was walled to make a light-well (or miniature court). Later the access between columns was blocked and the outside space used for storage before the whole building was destroyed in Late Minoan IB.

Finds from the site are on display in the Archaeological Museum in Khaniá.

Soúda Bay

Along the stretch of the New National Road running high above the Bay of Soúda there are several designated viewpoints. This superb natural harbour is one of the largest in the Mediterranean, sheltered from the prevailing winds by the hills of the Akrotíri peninsula. There is a Greek and NATO naval base here so the notices forbidding photography should be taken seriously.

The fortress on the island of Soúda, towards the far shore at the harbour entrance, was built by the Venetians to guard the narrows, and did not surrender to the Turks until 1715, 46 years after the fall of Candia (Herákleion). In 1941 the anchorage played an important role, first during the evacuation of the Allied Expeditionary Force from the mainland of Greece, and then in supplying the garrison during preparations for the Battle of Crete, though by this time the shipping crowding the bay was at the mercy of the Luftwaffe which had undisputed command of the air.

The ancient site of Aptéra

In the Greco-Roman period this city-state controlled the entrance to Soúda Bay from two ports, on the land either side of it, with the powerful walled city on the heights to the south looking across to the Akrotíri. This is a vast site, with scant remains from a long period of time scattered on a plateau surrounded by defensive walls.

For the 3km climb to the site take a turning well signed from the highway c 10km from Khaniá. Keep left in the hamlet of Megála Khoráphia, a centre for holiday accommodation in converted traditional houses; at the crossroads three tavernas compete for custom. The road climbs through the settlement of **Metókhi**. This west side of the city was the cemetery area where rescue excavations find tombs from Geometric to Roman times.

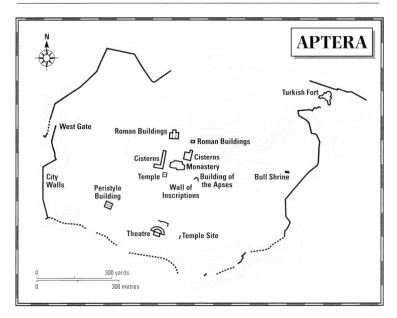

The name Aptéra has been recognised on Linear B tablets but it seems that the Minoan settlement lay to the south towards Stýlos (p 377). Evidence for habitation here on the plateau dates back to the 8C BC, the Late Geometric period, but the city-state flourished in the Hellenistic period (when it minted its own coins) and on into Roman and Early Byzantine times. It was damaged by earthquake in the 7C AD and destroyed by the Saracens in 823 AD.

The fortification circuit at Aptéra, parts of which date back to the 4C BC, was nearly 4km in length, and walls up to 2.8m thick still stand in places to a height of 3m. On the approach a Ministry of Culture notice marks the position of Aptéra's **West Gate** (see plan) and alerts you to the present major programme of work by the Department of Antiquities of Western Crete. The West Gate was set within overlapping walls of polygonal masonry. It was further protected by one square bastion on the outer wall and a second to the south allowing a line of fire straight into the gateway passage. You should find that as a result of the excavation there is access here to a new path ahead uphill (probably on the line of the ancient road), offering a short-cut on foot to the guardian's hut at the centre of the site.

The asphalt road continues the climb up to the plateau and then divides. Wild flower enthusiasts will enjoy this upland which is also rich in bird life. Go left for the remains of a mid-19C Turkish **fort** with stunning views of the coast. Aptéra is said to take its name (Wingless One) from the Sirens who, defeated in a musical contest by the Muses, plucked off their wings and so drowned in the bay below, forming the islets.

If you continue straight on at the fork, the road ends at the guardian's hut. Here the centre of the site is fenced but open 08.30–14.30 daily except Mondays.

Inside the fence are the much restored buildings of the former **monastery of Ayios Ioánnis Theológos** (the Evangelist). This was founded in the late 11C, the Second Byzantine period, to meet the need for the preaching of the Christian gospel on Crete after more than a century of Arab control. Monks arrived from the Dodecanese island of Patmós, where the monastery of the same dedication commemorates the tradition of the writing there of the last book of the Bible, the *Revelation of St John the Divine*.

Just inside the fence, before you come to the monastic buildings, a small **double-cella temple** was excavated by German archaeologists in 1942. Built of clamped ashlar blocks and without a central communicating door, the temple would have been dedicated to a pair of divinities. The original excavators dated it 5C–4C BC but some experts prefer 2C BC. Just to the east of it a wall of inscriptions (fragments of the decrees of an ancient city dated to 2C BC) was recorded by the English scholar Robert Pashley in 1834. The wall, which would have formed part of an important public building of the Hellenistic period, was cleared in the 1860s but by the end of the century the blocks had disappeared. Also east of the monastery a remnant of masonry with three internal niches is known as the Building of the Apses; of Roman construction, this was probably also part of a public building.

The remains of two large cistern complexes in the fenced area could date back to the Hellenistic period but major reconstruction can be attributed to the Romans. A large L-shaped building, on the left before the monastery, catches the eye but it is worth walking north (five minutes) out of the monastery grounds by a path past the chapel which will loop round to a remarkable **triple cistern**, divided by two rows of massive stone-built pillars and impressively vaulted. In early summer the vaults echo with the noise of nesting birds, and the endemic *petromarula* (rock lettuce) cascades over the arches.

Two further temples are recorded from this site. One, investigated after the Second World War and dated to the 1C BC, was named the **Bull Shrine**, on account of figurines found nearby. It stood at the east side of the site where the defensive walls are particularly well preserved. The other was to the south near a small **theatre**, now little more than a hollow in the ground with traces of seating but interesting because of the unusually early date of its construction, before the Roman conquest.

West of the theatre, recent archaeological work has brought to light another building of Hellenistic date, designed around a Peristyle Court, altered in the Roman period and eventually destroyed by a major earthquake. Column bases and many sections of columns are preserved.

To find the excavation start along the new track from the guardian's hut towards the West Gate. Pass the first olive grove on the left and use the next gap in the wall (left) to pick up the perhaps indistinct path. Work at Aptéra continues, so easier paths and more signs can be expected. The current guardian is enthusiastic about his site, and is happy to point visitors to what they want to find.

Kyriakosélia and Stýlos

From Megála Khoráphia (see p 374), a minor road leads south (inland) 6km to Stýlos, and on into the wooded foothills of the White Mountains to the church of **Ayios Nikólaos** at **Kyriakosélia**, comprehensively decorated with early 13C wall-paintings and one of the most romantically situated Byzantine churches on the island. *Byzantinisches Kreta* (still the definitive work on these buildings, see Recommended reading) ranks this among the foremost examples of Byzantine architecture on the island.

The road runs across open country well worth the attention of wild flower enthusiasts. 3km from Megála Khoráphia the **Minoan settlement** of **Stýlos** (above the road left) may be the predecessor in the area of the Early Iron Age site at Aptéra. The settlement is believed to date from Early Minoan times to the end of Late Minoan III. Before the settlement you pass (just off the road) a well-preserved LMIII **tholos tomb** with stone-lined *dromos* and vaulted circular chamber. Watch on the left for an olive grove, fenced and gated, where the Ministry of Culture sign for the tomb is hidden in the hedge, and then find the only overgrown patch of ground among the well-tended trees. Further along the road rusting metal cabins mark the stopping place for the excavation of the settlement. A path, uphill right, leads in three minutes to a Minoan kiln (now roofed for protection), dated 14C–13C BC.

As the road starts to descend the long hill before the village of Stýlos you catch a glimpse of a solitary Byzantine church (domed and cruciform) hidden deep in the cultivated valley below left. (A turning right is signed 8km across empty countryside to Maláxa overlooking Soúda Bay, p 374.)

The partly-ruined church of the **Panayía Serviótissa** is all that remains of a monastery founded in 1088 by monks from the island of Patmós (as at Aptéra, above). This is an archetypal cross-in-square church with dome on octagonal drum; the short detour to it, on foot (less than 15 minutes) or in a vehicle, is strongly recommended. Continue almost to a bridge across the river-bed where a surfaced road sets off left through the orange groves back towards the church. It very soon forks. The church lies in the triangle this creates; it is more easily spotted if you keep left.

At the beginning of the village of Stýlos the little double-naved church of **Ayios Ioánnis** has recently been investigated by specialists from the Department of Byzantine Antiquities in Khaniá. There are the remains of early frescoes (1271–80) in the northern aisle and the southern one is painted in the elegant, aristocratic style of the early 15C. Nowadays the church is usually locked and the key held by the guardian at Samonás.

Just beyond the church several **tavernas** under plane trees beside a shallow cascade on the **Kiliáris river** (here fed by great springs) offer an excuse for a pause in the expedition.

At the southern end of the village a road which forks right uphill will climb (with fine retrospective views of the north coast) 5km to **Samonás**. The key for **Ayios Nikólaos** is held at a house on the left at the far end of the village street, just before it turns sharply left. The guardian or his wife will accompany you the further 3km (a short stretch perhaps still unsurfaced) to the church now isolated at Kyriakosélia in a remote valley wooded with cypress, plane trees, olives and figs.

Ayios Nikólaos is a single-naved church of three bays built in the late 11C or early 12C (with an early 20C addition in the form of a chapel at the west end). The central bay is raised to take the dome supported on an elegant drum lit by eight slender arcaded windows. The interior is densely painted with **frescoes** dated 1230–36. At this time the Venetians were just introducing colonial rule and the rites of their western church in the city of Candia, but these wall-paintings in this remote part of the island seem to be entirely unaffected. They continue in the strictest traditions of Byzantine style and iconography, under the influence of the aristocratic Komnenian style which emanated from Constantinople during the previous century.

St Nicholas, one of the heirarchs or fathers of the church, was a 4C bishop of Myra in Asia Minor. Narrative scenes from his life portray him as a worker of miracles, concentrating on the legends of his precocious piety. Here the cycle begins on the walls of the central bay (under the dome) and continues at the same level in the western one. St Nicholas also figures as the fourth hierarch in the apse (on the southern side).

If you are the sole visitors you will need to take the guardian home but the road continues past the church, climbing into the White Mountains, 3km (surfaced) to a T-junction on the edge of **Ramní**. Here you can go left for the return to the coast through **Néo Khorió**. Turning right you would climb a further 3km to **Karés** at a height of 500m. Beside a memorial shaded by a huge plane tree in the plateía of the Revolutionary Assemblies 1821–66 the road ends. An old stone-paved *kalderími* leads on enticingly into the mountains.

The coastal villages of Kalýves and Almyrída

Below Aptéra, on the promontory level with the entrance to Soúda Bay, the north coast highway passes a massive Venetian fort, a military installation still known by its Turkish name, Itzedin. Under the infamous rule of the Colonels (1967–74) it held political prisoners. The main road drops down to the River Kiliáres and then, beautifully planted with cypress, tamarisk, mimosa and oleander, cuts across inland of Vámos to Vrýses (p 384) and Yeoryioúpolis.

After the Aptéra turning and just before the fort (c 14km from Khaniá) a sign marks an awkward turn left to Kalýves and Vámos. On this road, in the hamlet of **Kalámi**, an *oúzeri* perched above the great bay is a popular place to watch the sunset. The road crosses the Kiliáris as it nears the sea through an area of reeds and bamboo which is often rewarding for birdwatchers.

Kalýves is a pleasantly old-fashioned village which retains a life of its own as well as welcoming visitors and providing some resort facilities. The original houses are strung out along the waterfront at the eastern end of a long sandy beach looking across Soúda Bay to the hills of the Akrotíri.

The village centre, with church and plateía, is before the mouth of a little river (the Xidás) where decorative boats, lit at night, are a distinctive feature. Further east there is more sandy beach (with water sports) and, tucked under the cliff, the fishing boat harbour. Modern development is concentrated on the hill here above the harbour.

The helpful **Troulitaki** travel agency is on the village's main street, west of the plateía, next to the post office. Along the continuation of this street, between the plateía and the river, the wine merchant, **Kava**, stocks a particularly good range of Cretan wines.

Where to stay and eating out

C *Hotel Kalives Beach* (62 rooms), ☎ 28250 31285, fax 28250 31134, email: kalbeach@otenet.gr. A well-run hotel picturesquely located at the mouth of the Xidás. Suitable for wheelchair users.

There is a good choice of inexpensive accommodation but it is heavily booked in summer. **Dimitra & Anni** and **Mana** are **rent room** establishments side by side, a five-minute walk from the centre on the western approach along the sea.

To the east there are numerous blocks of **studio apartments** such as *Maistrali apartment* attached to the taverna below.

Taverna Maistrali, on the beach east of the river, keeps to a high standard year after year. For simpler places head for the beach along the western approach to the village. There is an economical *psistariá* (grill) where the main street meets the plateía. *Koumandros*, near the river mouth, is known for serious traditional cooking and its indoor dining room is a good alternative out of season, or when the north wind blows.

Inland from Kalýves it is 7km on the direct road to Vámos, or you can meander through Almyrída and Gavalokhóri, an attractive village with an interesting folkore museum.

Almyrída, 4km east along the coast from Kalýves, overlooking an attractive combination of coves and an offshore islet, is growing every year as a resort village to accommodate visitors. On the way in you pass the site of an excavated triple-transept **basilica church** where a high-quality mosaic floor probably dates to the early 6C.

Where to stay and eating out

A *Dimitra* (36 rooms), ☎ 28250 31956, fax 28250 31995. A small resort hotel set back from the shore.

B *Almirida Bay* (49 rooms), ☎ 28250 31650, fax 28250 31751. Also back from the shore, geared to families. Out of the holiday season there may be rooms available.

For inexpensive accommodation you could look at *Almirida Beach rooms and studios*, but there is plenty of choice. In season there will be bookings a year ahead, but out of season supply exceeds demand and many places close early in October.

The agency *Flisvos Tours*, on the waterfront, tries to keep track of available accommodation.

Almyrída has built up a reputation for the **fish tavernas** along its beach. At the western end *Dimitri* is long-established and reliable, and further east near the windsurfing station *Taverna Pharos* (with rooms) is popular, but each in the row has its own specialities.

Almyrída makes a good base for gentle walking and for visiting the inland villages where projects are in hand to revive traditional crafts such as the silk industry and lace-making. The Gavalokhóri folkore museum (see below) is a 3km climb up from the coast. You can walk, or drive, east to **Pláka** high above the sea (with café-bars popular for enjoying the view in the evening light) and on, out to **Cape Drépano**, across classic *phrígana* country for botanists. The road is closed just before you reach the lighthouse.

Vámos

The village lies north of the main Khaniá–Réthymnon road where it passes Vrýses (c 30km east of Khaniá) and the start of the route south over the mountains to Sphakiá. Vámos is a large village where layout and architectural surprises still hint at former glories; under Ottoman rule this was the centre of administration for the Apokóronas district.

Until recently the region was scarcely mentioned in guidebooks, but now this locality, which has long been a summer refuge for mainland Greeks and Cretans from the towns, is being discovered by foreign visitors looking for an escape from mass tourism and exclusively beach activities.

Travelling by bus

There is a limited bus service through Vámos using the Old Road between Khaniá and Réthymnon.

The Vámos cooperative

A cooperative recently established in the old part of the village by the people of Vámos has grown into a successful venture based on strong ecological convictions. Devoted to preserving the best elements of the traditional Cretan lifestyle it has taken the lead in promoting sustainable tourism. The cooperative's agency, *The alternative traveller*, is near a crossroads on one of the main streets at the north end of the village, ☎ 28250 23250, fax 28250 23250, www.travel-greece.com/crete/xania/vamos. The Vámos office handles accommodation in apartments and cottages which are modernised village houses, as well as car rental and cur-

rency exchange, and is a mine of information about every type of local activity. It can recommend organised walks and introductions to a range of Cretan crafts and country or cultural pursuits.

Where to stay and eating out

Parthenayoyeio (meaning the 'Old School for Girls') is a guest house (8 spacious rooms) in a renovated 19C building within a walled courtyard. Breakfast is taken in the café of the nearby art gallery looking across empty countryside between the White Mountains and the sea.

At the crossroads a taverna, *Sterna tou Bloumosiphi* (Bloumosiphi's cistern), serves traditional food from a wood-fired oven. It is run by the local enterprise, as is a shop concentrating on regional products, to be found a short distance down the street beside the taverna, towards the guest house.

You may find yourself in Vámos from Kalýves or Almyrída on the coast but if you are driving between Khaniá and Yeoryioúpolis on the New National Road the direct route turns north off the parallel Old Road from the western end of the village of Vrýses. (Local traffic uses slip roads as short cuts off the highway, one signed to the Vámos Health Centre.) Nearly at Vámos you pass the partly ruined former monastery of **Karýdi** below the road left; it is closed between 13.00 and 16.00 and on Sunday open only for the afternoon hours. Accommodation for the use of clergy is being restored and the church of Ayios Yeóryios (in a picturesque courtyard with fine views over the countryside towards the mountains) is again playing a part in the life of the neighbourhood.

Gavalokhóri

This is an attractive and well-kept village, just north of Vámos, with bougainvillea and jasmine tumbling over the houses. You can leave a vehicle below the war memorial in the little plateía which is overlooked by a taverna garden. Across the way the **Women's Cooperative for Agrotourism** (☎ and fax 28250 22038), dedicated to keeping old crafts alive, is a focus of activity, organising demonstrations and displaying products for sale. It is also a valuable source of advice about local accommodation.

Downhill from the plateía the **Gavalokhóri Historical Folklore Museum** is one of the best arranged and most interesting on the island. Open daily (summer) 09.00–20.00, ☎ 28250 22625. Telephone for out-of-season hours.

A visit is especially recommended to anyone interested in the silk industry or the ancient *kopanéli* method of lacemaking. The collection is housed in as good an example of traditional domestic architecture as you are likely to be able to visit on Crete. Clearly demonstrating the function of the arch (*kamára*) in its typical construction, the house dates back to the Venetian period, with alterations in Turkish times. Both it and the various sections of the exhibition are enriched by explanatory text and illustrations.

Signposts lead you on a stroll around the the edge of the village to a partially excavated **Roman cemetery**, to wells said to date from the 11C and to ruins of the Venetian period.

To Yeoryioúpolis

The New National Road, which has left Soúda Bay below Aptéra (see above) to cut across inland of Vámos, comes down to the sea again 35km from Khaniá at Yeoryioúpolis. The long bay of Réthymnon opens out ahead and the coastal village is reached by awkward sliproads near a bridge carrying the Old Road to Episkópi.

As you approach Vrýses (p 384), 5km before Yeoryioúpolis, side-roads are signed for local traffic but there is no mistaking the conspicuous junction where the Vrýses–Yeoryioúpolis stretch of the Old Road runs under the highway. A **bridge** from the Hellenistic period is hidden just on the Vrýses side of the underpass (behind a chapel). Vrýses is at the start of the road south over the mountains to Sphakiá. In the arc immediately south of the big junction a short detour, strongly recommended, takes in two Byzantine churches with frescoes by the admired 14C artist Ioánnis Pagoménos.

From the junction the slip-road leading up to the highway towards Réthymnon has a large sign right for **Máza**. **Ayios Nikólaos** in the plateía at Máza is a fully decorated church with the well-preserved frescoes dated by inscription to 1326. The patron saint is portrayed flanking Christ in the sanctuary (in the *deisis* composition). The single nave is densely painted with the Christ cycle, and in the lower register (starting on the north side) scenes from the life of St Nicholas. Specialists will notice that Pagoménos places the *Feast of Abraham*, signifying the Holy Trinity in Orthodox iconography, in the eastern bay (north side, lower register) rather than, as is customary, on the triumphal arch above the sanctuary, where he has the scene of the *Mandylion*, Christ's image imprinted on a shawl.

At the end of Máza go left before a turning right for **Alíkambos** and then keep right through that village, c 4km in all. (On foot there is a short-cut from Phílippos, but if the church is locked you will have to walk up to the village to ask for the key.) Down the hill from Alíkambos you come to an acute hairpin bend left, where tucked away on the right is a spring still used by shepherds to water flocks. A plaque records that the surroundings of the Venetian fountain were restored by the community in 1998. The valley is alive with birds and, rewardingly for enthusiasts, they fly up to the spring to drink.

Opposite the fountain an old stepped path leads down to the church, hidden in a graveyard shaded by an oak and a bay tree, and looking out over orange groves in the valley, altogether an idyllic spot.

The church of the **Panayía** (celebrating the Assumption of the Virgin on the 15 August) is decorated with a fine series of frescoes dated by inscription to

1316, ten years earlier than those at Máza but also by Ioánnis Pagoménos. Pagoménos painted the frescoes in the nave; those in the sanctuary by a different hand date from later in the 14C.

On the north wall of the nave, next to the iconostasis, is the *Virgin with Child* (*Odiyítria*), with a *Baptism* scene above. The saints Demétrios and Yeóryios are on horseback as is customary, with the Emperor Konstantínos (Constantine the Great) and his mother Eléni opposite. Rather indistinct on the upper register of the vault (south side) there is a fine *Nativity*. Donor and inscription are found on the west wall.

Apart from these two examples in the district of Apokóronas, Pagoménos's work is more familiar in the extreme southwest of the island, inland of Palaió-khora, where a number of churches can be visited.

Approaching **Yeoryioúpolis** from the west you are recommended to leave the highway at the Vrýses junction and use the Old Road, a pretty route which follows the river valley and passes a marshy area known as the *almyró* (from the Greek word for saline). Yeoryioúpolis is named after Prince George of Greece, high commissioner for Crete (1898–1906), who built a shooting lodge here.

Nowadays many types of waterfowl, glossy ibis among them, appreciate this terrain, making it a rewarding area for ornithologists. In addition to the meandering river and salt marshes, Lake Kournás is only a short distance inland.

Yeoryioúpolis was until recently a small fishing settlement at the mouth of the Vrýsanos river, a beguilingly peaceful place shaded by eucalyptus trees and sheltered by Cape Drépano from the prevailing winds of summer. However, in recent years the combination of beach, lake and river has been exploited by the tourist industry in a rather drastic way. A village resort has been created and the character of the place is now epitomised by a miniature train, which connects the new settlements along the spectacular beach with the lake as well as climbing as far as Vámos, and by expeditions in pedal boats up the river.

This said, the season for beach life at Yeoryioúpolis does not get fully under way until late May. Around Easter the village can provide a base for walking inland into the hills around Argyroúpolis (p 347) or out on the cape; for birdwatchers, flocks on migration sometimes rest here waiting for the right weather for the next stage northwards. Lance Chiltern's *Six Walks in the Georgioupolis Area* (with map and plant list sold separately) should be obtainable locally (see Recommended reading, p 58).

Travelling by bus

The frequent Khaniá–Réthymnon service stops on the main road leavel with the village, less than five minutes on foot from its central plateía.

Where to stay and eating out

C *Drossia* (12 rooms), ☎ 28250 61326; fax 28250 61636. This hotel is located in the quieter part of the village near the river; some central heating for visits early in the year.

Egeon and *Eleftheria*, are well-run blocks of **studio apartments** overlooking the river (on the left at the bridge).

During the summer there are innumerable places to eat. Even in the year you can rely on finding two or three snug tavernas around the plateía, for in the evenings they will be feeding local people and at weekends Cretans out from the towns.

Website

See www.georgioupoli.net for general information on the area.

Lake Kournás, the only natural freshwater lake on Crete, is 3km inland, reached by turning off the stretch of the Old Road between Yeoryioúpolis and Episkópi. The lake, picturesquely surrounded by hills, is fed by springs and measures 65 ha, with a depth of 50m at the deeper southern end.

There is holiday activity in summer, especially at weekends and several places to eat attractively located overlooking the lake from the east, but out of season a footpath part of the way round the shore in both directions from the access road is little used except by fishermen. Black-necked grebe are among the birds to be expected here; the lake's terrapins are best seen at the south end near the pumping station. A path (marked in some years) climbs due west from the lakeside path soon offering fine views into the clear depths. This was a traditional route over to Alíkambos.

The modern road continues past the lake, climbing (and out of season offering a recommended walk) 4km to the village of **Kournás**. To visit the church of **Ayios Yeóryios**, with 12C frescoes, watch for a popular taverna where the main street forks towards the end of the village. The key is held here and it is best to leave any vehicle and go the last 150m uphill on foot.

The church's layout is unusual in that it consists of four dissimilar chapels set side by side. It was originally painted throughout (including on the unifying west wall). Only tantalising fragments of decoration are preserved but there is compensation in the quality of the surviving work. This church merits a mention in the new Byzantine Museum in Khaniá as an important example of wall-painting of the Second Byzantine Period. This was a time when religious art on Crete was strongly under the influence of the style prevailing in Constantinople then ruled by the Komnenian dynasty of emperors. One wide sanctuary area has a well-preserved *Communion of Apostles* illustrating this influence. The striking portrayal of the patron saint, *St George*, is conspicuous on the arch between the two chapels to the south.

Leaving Kournás you can continue on country roads through Kástellos into the province of Réthymnon to arrive at Argyroúpolis (p 347).

South of Khaniá

Sphakiá

It is 40km across the island from Vrýses (which is roughly equidistant between Khaniá and Réthymnon on the north coast highway) to Khóra Sphakíon, the principal village of Sphakiá and the most easterly port-of-call of the south coast boat service (p 411).

This is a beautiful drive across the eastern foothills of the **Levká Ori** (White Mountains). The expedition is feasible as a day trip, but anyone who can spend time in the south to explore the mountainous hinterland of Sphakiá will be well rewarded. There is accommodation in and around **Khóra Sphakíon** and **Frangokástello**, as well as in the coastal settlements reached only by boat or on foot. The long-distance walking route, the E4, incorporates a number of the ancient paths, formerly the traditional road system of the region. With your own transport you can continue from Frangokástello east along the coast into the province of Réthymnon.

Travelling by bus

There is a bus service across the island to Khóra Sphakíon three times a day in summer from Khaniá, with guaranteed connections in Vrýses with Réthymnon.

Along the coast east from Khóra Sphakíon there should be at least one daily bus in the tourist season (Easter to mid-October), but the schedule alters annually.

Vrýses

Vrýses used to have a reputation as one of the more beguiling villages on Crete. Two streams meet here at a shallow cascades and local yoghurt with honey is a speciality of the tavernas under the plane trees beside the bridge. A monument commemorates the success of the 1897 revolt and the setting up of the constitutional commission which would at last establish autonomy for Crete. But nowadays the village's popularity as a staging-post for coach tours can be overwhelming, and many visitors will not stop for long before embarking on the climb through the southern part of the district of Apokóronas over the shoulder of the White Mountains to Sphakiá.

Within the first 5km you pass close to the two churches with frescoes by Ioánnis Pagomémos at Mazá and Alíkambos (p 381), each only 2km off the main route; watch for Byzantine Antiquities signs.

The main road south climbs steadily into the increasingly rocky scrub of these eastern ranges of the White Mountains. You gain height up a valley, often crossing the older, more direct, mule track, and reach (10km from Vrýses) the miniature upland plain of Krápi. *Lekanopédio* on the sign means a plain in the shape of a basin.

The easiest natural route into Sphakiá from the north coast followed the ravine of Katré leading out of this basin and Cretan folk-memory enshrines many heroic ambushes and rearguard actions against Turkish armies here at the frontier of the Sphakiot stronghold. On the modern road signposts note the pass.

Soon, at the ridge, the mountain plain of **Askýphou** (at a height of 730m) comes into view. The 19C traveller Robert Pashley described the plain as 'so surrounded by lofty mountain-summits that it has somewhat the appearance of an large amphitheatre'.

The settlements occupy the raised ground around the patchwork field-system which is dominated from a conical hill by a ruined castle, one of two forts built by the Turks to subdue the local population and control the routes crossing the plain. The villagers grow vines and cereals. In *The making of the Cretan landscape* (see Recommended reading) Rackham and Moody note that the plain is watered by wells from a shallow water-table. They draw attention to the pattern of fields turning gradually into terraces that follow the lie of the land and suggest that study of the hedgerows here will reward readers with ecological interests. They make special mention of the beautiful quince trees (*kydoniés* in Greek).

Askýphou figures often in the legends of the Cretan struggle for freedom from foreign rule. During the insurrection of 1821 (when the Greek mainland was near to gaining independence) a major pitched battle was fought here between Turkish forces and bands of mountain warriors; it resulted in a resounding and bloody victory for the Sphakiot forces which is still related in poetry and song.

In ancient times Askýphou was at a crossroads on the route from coast to coast. Traditional mule-paths (*kalderímia*) climbed west into the high pastures of the Levká Ori, southwest to Anópolis (p 388) and east over to Así Goniá (p 349). Now the rough tracks following these routes (bulldozed for the shepherds' vehicles) can be spotted from the plain. They are recommended to walkers and birdwatchers in search of the solitude of Cretan mountains. The E4 comes down to the plain from the high mountain spine to the west, and then (with alternatives as far as Asphéndou) crosses empty uplands eastwards to Así Goniá.

The main road follows the western edge of the plain before climbing out of it. At the top of the pass the narrow side-road, left, also used by the E4, is signed 8km to Asphéndou. The surface is not yet suitable for normal hire cars all the way to Así Goniá but the first stretch (maintained for the telecommunications station) offers a chance to turn off the beaten track; very soon there is a glimpse of the Libyan Sea. For Khóra Sphakíon the main road continues south to Imbros where the long descent begins.

The traditional mule track kept to the eastern wall of the spectacular gorge running south from the settlement of **Imbros** (sometimes written Nímbros, implying the preposition *stin*, at or in).

A walk down the Imbros gorge

The ancient route through the ravine down to Komitádes near the sea is now a popular, well-signed walk. You can get down to the valley floor from the Imbros plateía but the official entrance is at the southern end of the village. Watch for a café with a large rustic sign (with detailed information) and the E4 diamond on a telegraph pole. There is room to leave a vehicle if you plan to use a bus or taxi to return to this point; or you can get here by bus from the south coast. Allow c 2 hours for the 7km walk.

From **Komitádes** (p 392), where there are several café-tavernas, you will need to call a taxi, or be prepared to walk or hitch a lift at least for the 2km to the T-junction on the main road south (see below).

The modern road from Imbros towards the coast twists along the precipitous cliffs with the gorge below left. During four days and nights at the end of May 1941, 12,000 weary Allied soldiers, survivors of the Battle of Crete (see p 52), withdrew to the coast by this narrow road (not then complete) or on foot down the gorge. Various experiences of this retreat were vividly described in many post-war accounts (see Recommended reading).

The road emerges high above the Libyan Sea, with superb views of the coast. The large island directly south is Gávdos (p 417), the most southerly inhabited point in Europe. To the east, down by the shore, you can make out the walls of the Venetian fortress of Frangokástello, and beyond that are the Paximádia islands in the Bay of Mesará backed by the coastal range of the Asteroúsia mountains above Léndas.

At the foot of the vertiginous (850m) descent you will reach a T-junction on the south coast road marked by a café-taverna. To the left it is 11km to Frangokástello (past Komitádes at the foot of the Imbros gorge), and the right branch leads in 4km to the thriving harbour village of Khóra Sphakíon.

Khóra Sphakíon

This picturesque harbour village is, as its name implies, the chief settlement of the district of Sphakiá. The harbour's current prosperity depends on the great number of foreign tourists brought here by the well-known attractions of the walk down the Gorge of Samariá an hour away by sea to the west. From late afternoon on, the boats put in from Ayiá Rouméli at the foot of the gorge, and from May until October (the months when the walk is permitted) the village is at times overwhelmed by people and coaches. However, it is still possible to enjoy a stay in Khóra Sphakíon provided you are not expecting complete tranquillity. In the evening the coaches leave for the north coast resorts, and then the harbour regains its charm.

Where to stay

Xenia (12 rooms), ☎ 28250 91490/91202, fax 28250 91491. A small hotel flourishing under new management, beautifully situated on the rocks near the old western quay.

Otherwise outside the busiest season there should be a choice of accommodation in decent **rooms** above the waterfront tavernas. For a quieter location walk uphill inland from the Xenia; the block known as *Hotel Stavris* (at the top end of the street with the bakery noted above) has rooms with fine views of the sunset along the rocky coast. Just outside the village to the west, the **Ilingás cove** has modern rooms above a popular taverna.

Eating out

On the harbour waterfront *Livikon*, *Samaria* and *To Limani* are long-established tavernas and remain careful of their reputation. Greek customers eating fish are the best recommendation.

Taverna Illingas, a 10-minute walk west in the cove of that name offers an escape from the bustle of the village centre.

In the 18C there was a substantial town here, guarded by a castle, the ruins of which survive. At that time the mountainous stronghold of Sphakiá was fiercely independent, with a coastline that sheltered a fleet of 40 merchant ships.

A great rebellion in 1770 led by Ioannis Daskaloyiánnis (John the Teacher) from Anópolis, resulted in savage repression by the Turks, and although the Sphakiot people took a leading part in the struggle for freedom all through the 19C the region never regained its former economic strength.

During the Second World War the harbour played a vital part in the 1941 evacuation of defeated Allied troops from here and from the Ilingás beach just to the west. In a heroic operation on four consecutive nights ships of the Royal Navy came north from Alexandria to rescue nearly 10,000 men, exhausted at the end of the battle on the north coast and the retreat through the mountains.

On the way to the ferry quay an inscribed stone commemorates the operation, and above on the hillside, on the approach to the village from the east, another memorial with an ossuary completes the story by honouring the Cretans who gave their lives to support this operation.

The road down into the village ends behind the waterfront at an open space which does duty as a plateía. The tourist coaches leave from here at the end of the day. The plateía has a few parking spaces (regulated by an attendant) and the bus ticket office is here, also a post office, the *OTE* (telephone company) and along one side café-bars and souvenir shops. The agency **Sphakia Tours** is a source of help and advice. A water taxi is advertised for hire from one of the tavernas on the harbour front.

The harbour has expanded along the eastern shore with a new ramp for the car ferries and room under the cliffs for both short-term and long-term car parking. Parking tickets are sold at a kiosk on the waterside before you reach the ferry quay. Here you will notice the inscribed stone commemorating the 1941 evacuation (see above).

From the bus stop in the old plateía you can walk on into the village along the old harbour frontage, or alternatively parallel to it one block inland where you come immediately to a bakery, renowned across the island for its pies in the Sphakiot style made with the local *misíthra* cheese (*mizithrópites*). The shop beyond the bakery sells other local produce such as cheese and yoghurt from the mountains.

The waterfront is packed with café-bars and tavernas, several of which serve traditional Cretan dishes (with a good choice for vegetarians) as well as the local fish.

Khóra Sphakíon makes a good base for exploring the region, either with a vehicle or on foot. The Khaniá bus sets walkers down at the upper end of the Imbros gorge (p 385) or you can investigate the lower stretch of it by starting inland from Komitádes near the sea. Further east is the coastline (with sandy beaches and attractive places to eat) below the walls of the castle of Frangokástello.

From Khóra Sphakíon a road climbs northwest to Anópolis and towards the remote mountain country above **Arádena** and **Ayios Ioánnis**, or to a number of gorges and ancient paths leading down to the sea.

Serious (long-distance) walkers can make the descent from Ayios Ioánnis to the picturesque Byzantine chapel of **Ayios Pávlos** on the seashore, or alternatively reach the same spot by the coastal path (E4) west from Khóra Sphakíon to Ayía Rouméli. It is possible to use the coastal boat service (see below) in one direction for less demanding expeditions. *Crete: The White Mountains*, by Loraine Wilson, is invaluable for anyone planning a walking holiday in Sphakiá (p 383).

The south coast boat service

Khóra Sphakíon is at one end of the route for these ferries which now operate from a base at Palaiókhora (p 411) near the southwest corner of the island. The service grew up as a haphazard affair using the traditional fishing boats or caiques, but a larger type of modern ferry designed to carry vehicles came into service more than a decade ago. A reliable schedule can be expected, subject to weather conditions. The current timetable, which may change every month, should be available at all major tourist information offices across the island as well as locally.

The first priority is to move large numbers of walkers from Ayiá Rouméli at the foot of the Samariá Gorge to Khóra Sphakíon or Palaiókhora, but the boats put in to Loutró and Oúyia, and at least once a day it should be possible to travel the whole route in either direction. Ferries also supply the island of Gávdos (from

Palaiókhora). During the high season (between mid-June and mid-September), there are day-trips from Khóra Sphakíon to Gávdos, two hours away.

Anópolis and Arádena

A fine asphalt road sweeps northwest up from Khóra Sphakíon c 12km to **Anópolis** in a high valley running east to west under the White Mountains. This and the plain of Askýphou are the historical heartlands of Sphakiá where traditions and local customs have a particular value. The men of the region still wear the distinctive Sphakiot costume of black shirt and trousers or breeches with tall leather boots.

Travelling by bus

Only one bus a day serves the community, coming down from the mountains in the early morning and returning to Anópolis in the late afternoon.

Where to stay

The spread-out village of Anópolis (at a height of 600m) has grown from a loose amalgamation of six hamlets. There are a number of simple rooms to rent. Consult **Sphakia Tours** in Khóra Sphakíon if you want to telephone ahead. In the first hamlet where the road levels out at the top of the climb (before a good bakery) you pass two blocks of rooms almost opposite each other. *Panorama* is appropriately signed. For a more central location continue 1km to the plateía for rooms above the café-taverna *Platanias*.

Websites

A general website for the area is www.sfakia.com. The Sphakia Survey, an archaeological project, has a website at www.sphakia.classics.ox.ac.uk

Anópolis was the birthplace of the legendary Ioánnis Daskaloyiánnis (John the Teacher) who was martyred by the Turks as the leader of the 1770 rebellion; his statue stands in the plateía at the western end of the village.

Above the village, to seaward, are the unexcavated remains of the city-state of Anópolis which flourished in Greco-Roman times. From afar you can distinguish on the skyline the church of Ayía Aikateríni, which, with the adjacent tower, is at the centre of the site. The village plateía is the starting-point for the walk (20 minutes) up to the church. The lane south from the plateía becomes the old stone-built mule path or *kalderími* up over the hill and on down to the coast, but now the bulldozer has carved out a rough track for vehicles as far as the church at the crest; the site lies immediately to the west.

Great quantities of stones mark collapsed buildings and traces of strong fortification walls can be detected. The city commanded the route between the upland plain and its harbour of Phoenix, modern Loutró; the descent to the coast, stepped in places and still a well-worn path, zigzags down the near-vertical slope to the sea below. This is a demanding walk downhill (c 90 minutes) and a very stiff climb uphill; the reward is a vista of stunning coastal views. From Loutró you can return to Khóra Sphakíon by the coast path or by boat.

From the plateía in the centre of Anópolis a surfaced road continues across the plain 3km to Arádena and on to Ayios Ioánnis. Leave the statue of Daskaloyiánnis on the left, and just out of the plateía fork left in front of a *kapheneíon* (also the bus stop). The dirt-track to the right climbs c 14km into the White Mountains. Its surface soon becomes unsuitable for normal hire cars, but this is a route into the mountains for serious walkers. Anópolis is one of the established starting-points for the climb to the summit of **Pákhnes** (2453m); anyone planning this expedition should consult the *Greek Alpine Club* (EOS) or *Alpin Travel* in Khaniá (p 354).

About 2km from Anópolis, past the turn for the hamlet of Livanianá, you get a first view of **Arádena** with the 14C church of **Mikhaíl Arkhángelos** tranquil on the edge of one of Crete's most dramatic gorges. At this point for many centuries travellers have descended by the path snaking down into the ravine to arrive at the church on the far side, but in 1986 the gorge was spanned by a great steel bridge, financed by the internationally successful Vardinoyiannís family. The bridge was built as a gift to the village of Ayios Ioánnis from which the family originally came. As well as ensuring the future of an isolated community it has opened up access to the high mountain pastures for shepherds' trucks. A colony of crag martins is often active in the gorge below the bridge.

Romantics may like to negotiate the gorge by the old path to savour the obsolete road system of Sphakiá. Strike off the modern road 500m short of the bridge (at one of the points where telegraph wires cross the road) to pick up the track towards the well-maintained, stepped descent. This detour should be rewarding for botanists; from March to May *Tulipa saxatilis* blooms deep in the gorge.

The almost deserted village of Arádena occupies the site of the Greco-Roman city-state of Aradén. The domed, cruciform Byzantine church is built into the central nave and apse of an Early Christian basilica. The mid-14C frescoes include scenes from the Christ cycle in the vaulting, and the donors with the archangel in the north cross-arm. Unfortunately the church is usually locked.

To Ayios Ioánnis

The surfaced road continues on the far side of the bridge 5km to Ayios Ioánnis. It runs through woodlands where the scent of pine trees fills the air. The Cretan pine *Pinus brutia* was originally an Asian tree which has spread into Europe only as far as the heel of Italy and scattered locations in northern Greece. It is the common tree of the southern slopes of the White Mountains and is found in similar situations on some other mountain ranges across the island; elsewhere on Crete it scarcely occurs. The gentle ascent across the wooded slopes offers occasional views ahead to the high mountains or seaward to the foot of the Arádena gorge and out to the islands of Gávdos and Gavdopoúla. Walkers would be unlucky to encounter much traffic.

At the beginning of the village you come to a café-taverna, *O Ioannis*. Along a path, left below the road, there are two **frescoed Byzantine churches** (dedicated to Ayios Ioánnis and to the Panayía) both decorated in the 14C. Ask about keys at the taverna.

Past the taverna a dirt road circles the village to set off into the high mountains across the bare lower slopes of Pakhnés. Walkers heading for Ayiá Rouméli need to turn to seaward, to join the ancient route (now waymarked) with stretches of paved *kalderími* still preserved, which drops down to the coastal path. At the coast you join the E4 and turn west for the Byzantine chapel of Ayios Pávlos (p 392).

Loutró

A walk of c two hours from Khóra Sphakíon may be combined with the boat trip to or from Loutró. The footpath along the cliffs follows the route of an ancient way. The marked path, nowadays the coastal branch of the E4, is well maintained, but this is an expedition for reasonably agile walkers and during bad weather rock falls cannot be ruled out.

Set out along the road to Anópolis which follows the coast past the Ilingás cove. After 3km, on the first hairpin bend, with room to park if required, the path drops away from the road and runs west along the coast. The second chapel in sight marks your destination. **Sweetwater Beach**, midway between Khóra Sphakíon and Loutró lies at the foot of perpendicular cliffs and is sheltered and calm for swimming in all weathers except for a strong southerly wind. You pass a number of fine caves at the back of the beach, one reputedly a refuge for the legendary Sphakiot leader Daskaloyiánnis. (A café-bar on a pontoon has diluted the former romantic isolation of this beach and excursion boats from Khóra Sphakíon visit during the season.)

Where to stay

B *Porto Loutro* (15 rooms), ☎ 28230 91444, fax 0823 91091.

> Loutró, in the shelter of a promontory and an island, is the only natural year-round harbour on Crete's south coast. The location has been exploited all through history. On the promontory between two anchorages are scanty remains of the ancient city of Phoenix, the harbour town in Greco-Roman times for Anópolis in the hills above. (No systematic excavation has yet been carried out.) St Paul's vessel was making for safety here (Acts 27.12), from Kalí Liménes, the Fair Havens of the New Testament, east of the Mesará bay, until sudden unfavourable winds carried it south of Gávdos and on to shipwreck on Malta.
>
> In the 18C this was the winter harbour of Sphakiá, and the home port of craft large enough to trade as far as Smyrna (modern Izmir) and Alexandria. The only route inland is a near vertical ascent of more than 700m on the ancient path to Anópolis, and perhaps for this reason the importance of Loutró gradually declined in favour of Khóra Sphakíon.

Two decades ago Loutró was virtually deserted, but then came a move to reinvigorate the settlement. The quay was rebuilt and the monochrome houses behind the shingle beach began to be inhabited again. The word got about, and this exceptionally beautiful bay, still accessible only by boat or on foot, gained a reputation as an escapist paradise, with tavernas and rent rooms to meet the demand. Now the ferry arrives several times a day from Khóra Sphakíon. New apartments have been inserted among the original buildings and these feature in the brochures of tourist agents abroad. Water-taxis and canoes are for hire to reach isolated beaches further west, and purists complain that the village is transformed by a coat of white paint not at all characteristic of the traditional Cretan coastal settlement. But in the evening when the daytime visitors have left, and especially outside the main summer season, this is still an idyllic spot.

The long-distance coastal footpath continues west past the foot of the Arádena gorge to Ayiá Rouméli.

Ayiá Rouméli and the National Park of Samariá

Ayiá Rouméli has grown from a hamlet of fishermen's huts on a sheltered beach to a modern village providing for the tens of thousands of tourists each year who make the trek down the Gorge of Samariá from the mountain plain of Omalós. It is well provided with tavernas and rooms for rent (p 400). The main beach is crowded after midday.

The boat journey along the coast from Khóra Sphakíon to Ayiá Rouméli takes about an hour, and the timetable should allow 4 or 5 hours for exploring the lower part of the **Gorge of Samariá**. (If you want to catch one of the last boats, book for the return journey when you arrive.) The gorge is protected within a strictly controlled area designated as a National Park; access is normally permitted from May to mid-October, with discretion on the part of the authorities during two weeks at either end of that period.

The excursion into the gorge from this southern end (advertised by the island's tour operators as 'Samariá the Lazy Way') can give no hint of the awe-inspiring scenery surrounding the first descent from the Omalós (p 398) but a walk of little more than an hour early in the day up the stony river valley of the Tarraíos will bring you to the much illustrated feature known as the **Iron Gates** (where the rock walls 750m high narrow to a passage no more than 3.5m wide). You can enjoy the environment of this lower part of the gorge before the steady stream of those walking down from the top begins to arrive.

Before you reach the southern entrance to the National Park (where you will see posted a number of regulations which it is wise to observe) you pass through the ruins of the original village of Ayiá Rouméli. Here the little church of the **Panayía** is built into the remains of a 5C–6C basilica with walls still standing up to 3m in places. Fragments of the basilica's mosaic floor survived. During the Second World War German archaeologists found here a much earlier pebble mosaic showing the head of Apollo. This suggested a sacred building predating the basilica, probably the Hellenistic temple to Apollo.

The level ground at the bottom of the gorge was the location of ancient **Tárra**, a small independent city of the Greco-Roman period. In 1959 the site was investigated by American archaeologists with the help of specialists from Corning Museum of Glass.

The city's cemeteries on the eastern side of the stream have been excavated and were found to date from the Classical to Late Roman periods. Some of the finds, including glass artefacts, are on display in the Archaeological Museum in Khaniá. Despite the existence of a considerable quantity of burnt glass waste at Tárra which pointed to a manufacturing site nearby, no conclusive evidence for this could be found within the city boundaries.

According to mythology Apollo and Artemis visited Tárra for purification rites after the killing of Python at Delphi. Certainly a cult of Apollo Tarraíos was practised here. There is another legend that while at Tárra Apollo made love to the nymph Akakallis (daughter of Minos and Passiphaë) in the house of the Cretan seer Karmanor, winner of the first musical contest at Delphi. Minos disapproved and banished his daughter to Libya but the union produced Kydon, credited with the founding of Kydonía, modern Khaniá.

From Ayiá Rouméli you can walk the coastal path (E4) in either direction. To the east it follows the shore to the Byzantine church of Ayios Pávlos (see below) and to the west it runs high above the sea towards the cove at the foot of the **Kládos gorge**.

Ayios Pávlos

A recommended expedition (with opportunities to swim in peace) follows one section of the well-marked path which is an attractive feature of this coastline. This particular walk sets off along the coast to the east from Ayía Rouméli and in a little over an hour you come upon Ayios Pávlos, a domed, cruciform chapel of the Second Byzantine period. Its 10C–11C origins are associated with Ayios Ioánnis Xénos, a revered evangelist of western Crete. Remains of frescoes are tentatively dated to the 13C. One local tradition associates the spring beside the church with baptisms administered by St Paul.

There is now a café on a pontoon on the beach and regular visits by excursion boats from Loutró.

Beyond Ayios Pávlos the E4 path continues east, keeping close to the shore all the way to Loutró. A *kalderími* climbs (waymarked) into the mountains to the village of Ayios Ioánnis (at a height of 750m) on the way to Arádena and Anópolis (p 388), a route popular with serious long-distance walkers. It should be possible to contact a taxi in Anópolis if required for the last stretch down to the coast; ask at any *kapheneíon*.

East from Khóra Sphakíon

The coast road east takes you to Frangokástello, and on into the province of Réthymnon. After 40km, just beyond Selliá, you can turn down to the sea for Plakiás and the Préveli monastery. Continuing east from Selliá, through the Kotsiphós gorge, you join the main Réthymnon–Ayía Galíni route north of Spíli.

The E4 walking route keeps close to the road as far as Rodákino, and then strikes north for the stiff climb across unfrequented hill country to Alónes.

Travelling by bus

In the tourist season there should be at least one bus a day across the province boundary (running from Khóra Sphakíon to Ayía Galíni) and at Selliá or Plakiás you will link up with the more frequent Réthymnon service to the south coast villages and resorts.

The coast road offers a highly recommended scenic drive. It has been upgraded in recent years but care is still needed, especially after bad weather, as the terrain tends to be unstable in places. At the province boundary, after Skalóti, a 2km stretch may still be unsurfaced.

Just past the turn inland for Askýphou, the church of the Panayía (below the road to the right) is all that remains of the **Thymianí monastery**. On the 29 May 1821, 1500 Sphakiots gathered here to proclaim revolt against the Turks in conjunction with the struggle for freedom on the Greek mainland. There the struggle resulted in independence (1831) but the Cretan uprising was crushed.

5km from Khóra Sphakíon, below the village of **Komitádes**, the church of **Ayios Yeóryios** has frescoes by Ioánnis Pagoménos, one of the few artists known by name among those who decorated Crete's Byzantine churches. This is his earliest known work, dated by inscription to 1313. The little church was sadly neglected for many years but the fresco remains are sufficiently preserved to reward the enthusiast.

The road bends left in front of the Komitádes village church and you can leave a vehicle beyond it. To find Ayios Yeóryios (10 minutes below the village) take the signed path round the church wall and head downhill, past (right) a white chapel. Turn left on to a side path which bends right downhill towards the sea. Watch for the arched doorway (half hidden left) of the narthex of Ayios Yeóryios.

On the far side of Komitádes a group of café-tavernas marks the southern end of the Imbros gorge (p 385). On a footpath marked by blue arrows it is less than 15 minutes to the point where the walls of the ravine begin to close in.

The coast road links a series of villages along the slopes at the back of the plain. The path into the scarcely visited gorge behind **Ayios Nektários** may interest those looking for birds or specialised plants.

11km from Khóra Sphakíon a turning seaward is signed to (3km) Frangokástello. (There is another approach road, 4km further on east through **Kapsodásos**, for those travelling in the opposite direction.) The western approach to the fort is not visually improved by the scatter of concrete buildings, but these do include agreeable tavernas with rooms for rent.

Frangokástello

The **Venetian fort** of Frangokástello dominates a small marshy bay with a fishing boat haven and a picturesque lighthouse tower at the western end of a good sandy beach. Rackham and Moody (see Recommended reading) urge the visitor to try to imagine the 'lonely magnificence' in which the fort stood until the 1970s. The high walls are rectangular in plan, with square towers at the corners; the southwest tower is larger than the others, forming a guardhouse for the seaward-facing main gate adorned by the Lion of St Mark and a Venetian coat of arms. The interior now preserves only the skeleton of the original buildings.

The sea here is shallow for a long way out, making it suitable for children (with above average temperatures early and late in the season) but there is also deeper water around the harbour channel. A traditional-style beach taverna is sited near a freshwater spring. Another more secluded bay lies ten minutes' walk to the east along the track above the shore, past the ruined double-naved church, a relic of the monastery which stood on the point.

Where to stay and eating out

The most desirable places to stay at Frangokástello are right on the shore; west of the castle, near the lighthouse, the tavernas *Flisvos* and *Korelli* rent out comfortable rooms. Behind them the Artemis is close to the castle and with an easy path to the beach. *Babis and Poppi*, on the approach from the west, remains open for most of the year.

In the mid-14C a petition urged Venice to protect this coast from pirate raids, but the castle built as a response must have served a dual purpose, at the same time strengthening the Venetian hand against the rebellious stronghold of Sphakiá. Frangokástello was built in 1371 and appears always to have been an isolated fort without nearby settlement. The fortress was at first called by the name of the nearby Venetian chapel of Ayios Nikítas (see below) but it became known to the Cretans as Frangokástello. ('Frankish' is still used as a generic term for all western Europeans.) In 1770 the Sphakiot leader, Ioánnis Daskaloyiánnis, gave himself up to the Turks here, before the inevitable brutal execution in Khaniá.

One of the fiercest and bloodiest battles of the **Cretan uprising of 1821–30** took place here on the plain. Early in 1828 Khátzi Mikhális Daliánis, an adventurer from Epirus in northern Greece, had landed at the Cretan stronghold of Gramboúsa (at the northwest tip of the island) with a small force of 600 men and 100 cavalry. He arrived to campaign in Sphakiá, and in March captured the great fort of Frangokástello. Turkish troops were sent south from Khaniá to counter the threat. Disregarding experienced local advice that he should withdraw to the safety of the mountains Daliánis ordered a heroic last stand at the fort against a vastly superior force. The Cretans were massacred, losing 385 men, and Daliánis was killed, but it is claimed that in the dawn mist on the anniversary of the battle (18 May) each year a phantom army returns to dance on the plain; the optical phenomenon is known locally as *drossoulites* (dew shadows).

400m northeast of the fort, on the direct way back to the main coast road, you pass the **Ayios Nikítas chapel** built over the sanctuary (bema) of the smallest Early Christian basilica yet known on the island. The remains of a polychrome mosaic survived.

The route continues east towards **Skalotí**. The coastal plain peters out, and the road runs high above the Libyan sea, with narrow strips of cultivated land and the occasional glimpse of a beach far below. **Rodákino**, 27km from Khóra Sphakíon and in the province of Réthymnon, is a relatively unspoilt settlement (p 336).

Khania to Thériso

This attractive village, 17km south from the centre of Khaniá, lies (at a height of 580m) either side of a watercourse in a circular depression in the foothills of the White Mountains. A dramatic background of peaks is snow-capped for the first half of the year. The road from the coastal plain climbs beside a stream, through the **Gorge of Thériso** described (in *The Making of the Cretan Landscape*, see Recommended reading) as 'lush, winding and shadowy, with endemic plants growing all over its walls as in a botanic garden'.

The excursion, by car, bus, or on foot, can end at one of the village's traditional tavernas (crowded at weekends) beside the channelled stream.

Thériso takes pride in the part it played in the last phase of the struggle for *enosis*, Crete's union with Greece, and remains a place of pilgrimage for Greeks. At the start of the 1905 rebellion the Cretan commander Elefthérios Venizélos set up his headquarters and established a caretaker government here in his mother's home village. The Cretan forces succeeded in ridding the island of the high commissioner, Prince George, hated because he had become increasingly authoritarian and had not advanced the Cretan cause. Venizélos went on to play a prominent role in government in Athens and in 1913 Crete became part of Greece.

The start of the road from Khaniá to Thériso cuts through the city's southern outskirts, not always well marked. Take the road heading west from Khaniá towards Kastélli which becomes a double carriage-way. You need an inconspicuous side-road left, signed at traffic lights (100m before the major turning for the Omalós plain). At a T-junction turn right. Keep as near as possible straight on, to pass over the new bypass, and then after 1km the Thériso road forks left into the village of **Perivólia**. At a meeting of five roads you continue ahead left (usually signed) to a crossroads where the Mourniés road comes in from the left.

If you are approaching from the Khaniá bypass you should leave it at the junction for **Mourniés**; the village was the birthplace of Elefthérios Venizélos and his family home (on the main street opposite the community offices) is preserved as a small museum. Beyond the village turn right (below a large cross on the hillside ahead). At the crossroads with the main route inland (see above) you turn left towards Thériso.

You pass (above the road, left) the church of **Sotíros Khristós** (the Saviour), **Ayios Dimítrios, Ayios Kharálambos** and **Ayía Anna**, noted as an architectural curiosity, with four parallel naves built in three phases (dates uncertain). The road then runs for 6km through the picturesque gorge, offering a specialised environment which botanists will be keen to explore. Among the endemics growing here, *Aristolochia cretica*, with dark maroon pipe-shaped flowers, is found scrambling in the undergrowth not far off the road. Stopping on the narrow road is not always easy so if possible avoid the traffic at weekends and public holidays.

The road through the gorge emerges in an upland valley with the village ahead. There are signs (left) to the building, also preserved as a museum, which housed the headquarters during the 1905 rebellion.

Above Thériso a narrow road (unsurfaced part of the way) climbs out of the valley into foothills 3km to the hamlet of **Zoúrva** where a café-bar is well sited for the spectacular mountain views focused on the red roofs of the splendid Byzantine-style church at Lákki on the way up to the Omalós plain. The road (now surfaced) descends to the big church of the Panayía on the edge of **Mesklá** (p 397) and below it (in summertime) a taverna beside the mountain stream.

The Omalós plain and the Gorge of Samariá

The **Omalós plain**, 40km inland by car or bus from Khaniá, lies at a height of 1100m among the mountains of Crete's most impressive range, the **White Mountains** (Ta Levká Ori in Greek). There is an alternative approach from the western corner of the island, which makes a circular route possible (p 397).

The village of **Mesklá**, along a stream in the foothills on the way up to the mountain plain (and with an early 14C frescoed church) is a 20km drive from Khaniá. This shorter excursion can include the Ayiá reservoir for birdwatching or the ruins of two Byzantine churches nearby.

A day up on the plain can be handled as a simple excursion, to enjoy the spectacular mountain scenery with its specialised flora and bird-life, and to view the approach to the **Gorge of Samariá** which the 19C British naval surveyor, Captain Spratt, described as a 'yawning chasm' descending direct from the pass into this 'magnificent and picturesque' gorge.

The 17km trek through the gorge to the south coast at Ayía Rouméli is feasible as part of a day's round-trip from any of the north coast tourist centres, but it is a major expedition that needs careful planning (p 400). From the beach at Ayía Rouméli ferries of the south coast boat service take walkers east to Khóra Sphakión or west to Palaiókhora where public buses or tour coaches complete the journey back over the mountains to the various starting points. A less demanding alternative to this expedition is to arrive by boat at Ayía Rouméli to explore just the lower stretches of the gorge.

Travelling by bus

There are four buses a day from Khaniá to Omalós, including an early morning service with connections from resorts all along the north coast between Ayios Nikólaos and Kastélli Kisámou. One bus a day turns off to Mesklá which is otherwise a 5km walk from the main road stop in Phournés.

The Ayiá reservoir

From Khaniá you take the coast road (or the New National Road bypass) west towards Kastélli Kisámou, but on the outskirts of town turn off left for Omalós. An avenue of eucalyptus soon gives way to scented groves of citrus trees behind reed windbreaks. This broad, fertile valley is watered by tributaries of the River Kerítis. During the 1941 Battle of Crete it was known as 'prison valley' on account of the prison at Ayiá. This was one of the main landing zones for German paratroopers as part of the attack on Khaniá, then the capital of the island.

About 7km from the north coast highway there is a glimpse right of the **Ayiá reservoir** which, with its adjacent reed-beds, is now one of the most rewarding wetland areas on the island for birdwatchers. (The place-name Ayiá, accented in this way, probably derives from the Arabic word for water.) The reservoir is most easily viewed from the dam at its southern end.

At the entrance to the village of **Ayiá** a modern church is set back behind trees and a wall on the right-hand side of the road. For the dam take the next turning right (signed for Kyrtomádos). Three great springs which supply the drinking water for Khaniá are located to the right of this side-road. Soon you cross a small bridge over the river and turn right down a signed track leading to the dam. Marsh harriers hunt over the reedbeds which provide shelter for a great variety of water birds, both resident and on migration.

A ruined episcopal church

To visit the ruins of an episcopal church, turn off the main road as for the reservoir, but after 100m fork left. After a further 300m turn right, and along this narrow track the ivy-clad walls are in view ahead to the right, opposite well-tended orange groves. The area is known locally as **Episkopí**. In the Second Byzantine period and throughout the Venetian rule this church was the seat of the Orthodox bishop of Kydonía. It is dedicated to the **Panayía** (Virgin Mary) though there are old associations with Konstantíos and Eléni, the first Christian emperor and his mother.

The Byzantine church was built over one dating from Early Christian times. This has not been excavated, but it seems to have been a substantial structure with narthex and atrium. After the Arabs were driven from the island (in 961) by the forces of Byzantium under Nikephóros Phokás a great building programme was required to replace the churches destroyed during more than a century of Saracen occupation. For the new episcopal churches the sites of the pre-Arab basilicas were often favoured.

The walls of the 10C/11C church still stand to above window height in places, preserving some of the brickwork round the arches. This was a three-aisled basilica divided by two colonnades, each of three columns, with the pair to the west marble, the others granite. Material from its predecessor is incorporated, for example in the lower courses of the north wall. The tall (50cm) column bases may have been adopted so that the columns of the Early Christian basilica could be reused for its loftier successor.

The main road south from Ayiá arrives (after 3km) at a wide intersection opposite a memorial to partisans killed by the Germans. For the high plain of Omalós you keep straight ahead, but this is the junction for the road to the west of the mountains across the island to Soúyia (p 405). You could turn right here to make the short (2km) detour to the romantic 14C church of **Ayios Ioánnis** near Kouphós, now abandoned but still a fine example of typically Byzantine cross-in-square architecture; some important frescoes are preserved.

The Soúyia road crosses the Kerítis river to **Alikianós** but keeps left to skirt the village. For the church you turn off, right, into the village and almost immediately keep right at a fork following signs for Kouphós. (You will notice, right, the tiny cruciform church of Ayios Yeóryios dating from the early part of the Venetian period. The building was restored following war damage which destroyed its admired frescoes.)

After 1km on the Kouphós road the church of **Ayios Kyr Ioánnis** (Holy Master John) is hidden on the right in an orange grove.

In the First Byzantine period there was a basilica here, dated to the 6C; there are records of a mosaic floor depicting deer, peacocks and vases similar to the one at Soúyia. A church dedicated to the Panayía (Zoodókhos Piyí, the Virgin as the source of life) was founded in 1004, after the end of the Arab domination, by Ayios Ioánnis Xénos (p 371). That church was destroyed, but its successor followed soon afterwards and the association with Crete's St John was preserved in the dedication.

The cross-in-square plan of the 14C church (restored in 1971) has the west cross-arm wider than that of the east end; the narthex was added later. The design of the apse is most unusual for Crete, and is said to show the influence of Constantinople. The dome was supported on three columns (the southwest one restored) and a single square unadorned pillar. The capitals of the two northern columns are of an early 6C type, probably reused from the Early Christian basilica.

The surviving frescoes, tentatively dated to the 15C, are of particular interest as illustrations of an early phase of the Cretan school of painting. The best-preserved scenes are: the *Virgin with Child* (*Platytéra*) in the apse with the *Ascension* and *Pentecost*; in the south cross-arm (on its west wall) *Ayios Pandeleímon*, and in the same position in the north cross-arm *Demétrios*; opposite, in a niche, *Ayía Paraskeví*. Left of the main west door is a worn portrayal of the *Archangel Michael*.

From the war memorial (see above) you continue on the main road south 4km towards Omalós to the village of Phournés.

To Mesklá

On a right-hand bend a turning left is signed (5km) for Mesklá. The minor road, tree-lined and scented by orange groves, runs up the fertile valley of the Kerítis. On foot you can take the old track which follows the river-bed; fork right downhill 100m after leaving the main road.

On the edge of Mesklá, just across a bridge and on a long right-hand bend, a track on the left leads uphill (100m) to the frescoed church of the **Metamórphosis Sotírou** (Transfiguration of the Saviour). The frescoes, very worn in the sanctuary but better preserved in the nave, include a fine *Transfiguration* in the arch on the south wall. Right of this is the donor inscription dated 1303 and with the artists named as Theódoros Daniél and his nephew

Mikhaíl Venéris. The figure below the inscription is Leontios, patron saint of the donor the monk Leontios Khossákis. (The painting of the narthex is by a different hand, with a graffito 1471 on the south wall.)

The houses of Mesklá are strung out up one side of the street beside the river. The war memorial here carries a long list of names, including those of a group of about 30 described as 'missing in Germany' during the Second World War.

It is known that there was a Greco-Roman city on the slopes above the valley, but its identity is still disputed. At the top of the village the big modern church of the Panayía overshadows the old 14C chapel with the same dedication, which is built into the foundations of a 5C–6C basilica. The remains of its mosaic floor have been removed to greater safety. It seems that on the same site there was an earlier building, a temple of Aphrodite.

A simple taverna takes advantage of the terrace below these churches overhanging a meeting of streams. The unsurfaced road beside the stream leading on into the hills, over to **Thériso**, is strongly recommended as a walk (p 394).

From Phournés, the main Omalós road crosses the Kerítis river and leaves the valley, climbing in great zigzags. The land is terraced for olives and the view steadily increases in grandeur.

Lákki, 25km from Khaniá, is a superbly sited mountain village with trim red-roofed houses picturesquely dispersed in tiers over the hillside. There are rooms to rent on the through road.

The climb continues across bleak stony uplands and the air is scented by aromatic plants. For a while the mountains appear in the distance to the left. Then, across a saddle, the road turns towards them, and reaches a pass.

A little beyond the pass a plaque 'From your comrades in the National Resistance 1941–45' records the death in a German ambush on 28 February 1944 of the New Zealander, Sergeant Dudley Perkins, and a Cretan companion. Perkins had escaped from the island in 1942 but in 1943 returned as an undercover agent. He operated with a band of guerrilla fighters in the Sélinos district in the southwest of Crete. Their exploits, and his personal bravery in support of his comrades, have become part of Cretan folklore. The story is well told in Antony Beevor's account (see Recommended reading).

The road climbs yet higher. The stunted trees are surrounded in the season by mountain flowers. At the crest the plain comes into view and you descend steeply to the settlement of **Omalós**.

The Omalós plain

At an average height of nearly 1100m the plain is roughly triangular with the distance along each side being nearly an hour's walk. From each of the three angles a pass leads out through the encircling ring of mountains, so that the plain forms a natural focal point for the traditional routes through the Levká Ori. Snow lies till March, leaving behind as it recedes sheets of the crocus (*C. sieberi*), tulips (*T. cretica*) and other rarities. The land drains by a system of sinkholes; Rackham and Moody (see Recommended reading) describe the main one as a 'formidable swallow-hole, a fearsome cavern among limestone boulders at the bottom of a gully cut through some 10m of silt'. The plain remains green into early summer. It is too high for olives, but some cereals are cultivated by the villagers from Lákki and from Ayía Eiríne (over the pass to the west) who have shared property rights to the plain since Venetian times. After St George's Day (23 April) great numbers of sheep and goats are grazed up here, and the plain is alive with the sound of their bells. The main branch of the E4 long-distance footpath crosses the plain on its way east to the highest peaks of the White Mountains. It provides a number of walks in the neighbourhood, of varying degrees of difficulty.

Where to stay

The settlement of **Omalós** at the northern edge of the plain, regularly inhabited only during the summer months, consists of a cluster of tavernas with comfortable **rooms to rent**, for example the old-established *Samaria* or the *Levka Ori*. Two small modern hotels are popular with visitors who like to make an advance booking.

C *Neos Omalos* (26 rooms), ☎ 28210 6735/67269, fax 28210 67190.

C *To Exari* (24 rooms), ☎ 28210 67180, fax 28210 67124.

This accommodation can be recommended for an early start on the walk through the gorge of Samariá, or as a base for exploring the surroundings of the Omalós. Subject to weather conditions, food and rooms are now available over winter weekends.

Cretan leaders met on the Omalós in May 1866, and protested to the ruling sultan against harsh new taxation; their approaches to foreign consuls and the declaration by Sphakiá of union with independent Greece, precipitated the ill-fated 1866–67 Cretan revolt. Where the Khaniá road comes down to the plain you notice a chapel on a knoll to the left; beside it is the house and grave of Khátzi Mikhális Yiánnaris, one of the great rebel leaders of 19C Crete. He survived to become president of the Cretan Assembly which in 1912 at last achieved for the island the long-desired union with Greece. The chapel of **Ayios Pandeleímon** was built in gratitude for his deliverance from a Turkish prison where he had prayed to the saint to intervene on his behalf.

Crossing the Omalós plain

Leaving the settlement you join the road across the plain. To investigate the sinkholes, or walk to the western pass, take the right fork, but the main (surfaced) route keeps left. As you near the rising ground on the far side, a road branches off right to encircle the plain clockwise. It is heading for the western pass out of the Omalós and eventually connects in c 15km with the direct Khaniá–Soúyia road, north of Ayía Eiríne (p 403).

Just beyond that turning you come to a dirt road left (with E4 signs) which leads to the Kallérgis mountain refuge at 1680m; this is 5km, steadily uphill, c 75 minutes on foot. The chukar, the Cretan partridge, is not uncommon on these slopes, drawing attention to itself by noises in the undergrowth resembling a farmyard hen.

The **Kallérgis refuge** (30 beds), ☎ 28210 33199, is run by the Greek Alpine Club (*EOS*; see practical information for Khaniá or Réthymnon, or consult *Alpin Travel* in Khaniá, ☎ 28210 50939/53309). From the hut it is a serious expedition of 7 hours to the summit of Pákhnes (2452m). Psilorítis (Mount Ida in Réthymnon province) is higher at 2456m, but the Levká Ori are a formidable range, with ten peaks over 2000m.

National Park of Samariá

44km from Khaniá you reach the end of the road at the pass of **Xylóskalo**, Greek for 'wooden stairway'. The original steps for the old *kalderími* were constructed from tree trunks. This is the start of the precipitous descent to the now deserted village of Samariá, and the path through the gorge to the sea.

The tourist pavilion here, dramatically sited at 1227m overhanging the precipitous descent, consists of a café with stunning views from its terraces. Below it there is a new exhibition centre (opening hours unreliable). A nearby souvenir shop has books and maps, including *The Gorge of Samaria ... and its plants* by Antonis Alibertis which identifies plant habitats along the way.

The whole area around the gorge is a national park, well cared for and strictly regulated for the protection of flora and fauna. Since it was established in 1962 the project has earned a number of European awards relating to conservation and ecological principles. One of the world's rarest trees, *ambelitsiá* or *Zelkova cretica*, grows on the slopes above this southeast corner of the plain; at this end of the island it is the traditional source of wood for shepherds' crooks. The White Mountains are the last territory where the Cretan wild goat (*Capra aegagrus creticus*), known on the island as *agrími* or *kri-kri*, is still to be found in its natural habitat; its conservation was one of the motives for establishing the National Park.

- **Access** to the gorge (open every day 06.00–15.00) is usually permitted from the beginning of May but in some years up to two weeks earlier. This depends on the volume of melting snow in spring, and is at the discretion of the rangers (enquire at a tourist information office or a reliable travel agency or ☎ 28210 92287, the Forest Directorate). You will not be allowed to embark on this walk when the river at the bottom of the gorge, which has to be crossed many times, may be above knee height or affected by flash floods. The park is closed again at the end of October and the regular boat service from Ayiá Rouméli also ceases. If you arrive in the afternoon (between 15.00 and sunset) you will be allowed to take the path down for the first (very steep) 2km or so, as far the Neroutsikó spring.

- Various important regulations are proclaimed on a notice at the entrance to the park, alongside an excellent large-scale plan. It is forbidden to spend the night inside the restricted area. There is a small charge for entry and the ticket should be retained for surrender on leaving; it is part of the rangers' safety checks.

Where to stay

The coastal village of Ayiá Rouméli has many simple rooms to rent.

Aghia Roumeli (9 rooms), ☎ 28250 91241, fax 28250 91232, is convenient for an advance booking.

From below the Xilóskalo tourist pavilion there are also two alternative paths, both climbing into the mountains and early in the walk offering good vantage points for anyone on the look-out for birds of prey. One, signed from the car park, heads east on a direct route to the Kallérgis mountain refuge. The other, starting behind the tourist pavilion, gains height along the slopes of Mount Gíngilos, requiring a little over an hour to the water trough at the Linoséli spring. Serious walkers with experience in mountains can continue to the ridge of the Linoséli col and (given a good head for heights) tackle the scramble to the summit of Gíngilos (2080m), or even continue to the peak of Volakiás (2115m) overhanging from the south the route down to the gorge.

Sideróportes, the Iron Gates pass, the narrowest point in the Gorge of Samariá, from Pashley, Travels in Crete, *1837*

Walking the gorge of Samariá

Though many tens of thousands make the 17km trek each year from the Omalós plain to Ayiá Rouméli on the Libyan Sea, this ought to be treated as an expedition for the reasonably fit who are in the habit of walking at home. Fatal casualties are not unknown, usually caused by unpreparedness or disregard for regulations, and many tourists ruin several days of their holiday by walking the gorge in unsuitable footwear or insufficiently protected from the sun.

This said, the expedition properly planned is one of the major tourist adventures that Crete has to offer. There are a number of ways of tackling it, and, where there is a choice, the advantages of starting at first light to avoid the crowds, as well as the midday heat, cannot be too strongly emphasised. The all-inclusive round-trip conducted tour using coaches, offered by agencies from places as far afield as Ayios Nikólaos, will suit many people; the guides iron out all logistic problems. For those who prefer an independent approach, the early bus from Khaniá does not arrive until an hour after the first walkers have set off and in view of the return by a circular route, a car is no help unless the party happens to include a willing driver. A taxi (Khaniá to Omalós) is one possibility; a fare might be arranged in the region of 40 euros and this allows arrival to coincide with the opening hour for the park.

Some readers may choose to take the bus up the plain the day before the walk, to spend the night in the settlement of Omalós. In the early morning there is no organised transport to the start of the descent into the gorge; to be ahead of the buses you must be prepared to walk (5km), though you may be able to get a lift locally or from the first taxis up from the coast as they start the return journey.

You should allow between five and seven hours to enjoy the walk. In most places when you are actually walking along this trail you need to pay attention to the terrain underfoot. Provision for carrying drinking water is essential. There are a number of well-signed springs along the way (see plan at the entrance) where resting places have been organised with benches and tables (and toilets).

Ayiá Rouméli has tavernas and many rooms for rent, and also a good, usually crowded, pebble beach. Most people leave by boat for Khóra Sphakíon, some for Palaiókhora. Latest departure times may vary according to season and it is a good idea to buy boat tickets as soon as you arrive at the coast. The summer practice has been for the 17.00 boat to Khóra Sphakíon to connect with the 18.00 buses on to Khaniá, with a guaranteed connection at Vrýses for Réthymnon.

Everyone who undertakes this formidable walk remembers the excitement of the first precipitous descent, from a height of 1200m, down the 'wooden staircase' of Xylóskalo, and the drama of the scenery dominated right by the rock face of Gíngilos. There is an overpowering smell of pine. This is one of several widely-separated areas on the island where the Cretan pine, *Pinus brutia*, is well established. As the rising sun strikes the surrounding peaks there is the chance of eagles or vultures, including the rare bearded vulture or lammergeier, soaring above them, though the experts suggest mid-morning, with the increase in the warm thermal air currents, as the most promising time of day. More predictable as you continue the steep descent is the long-established colony of crag martins before the Neroutsikó spring.

The path continues to descend in sweeping bends, from pines into deciduous trees. Far down at the bottom it joins the stream-bed of the Tarraíos which will run into the sea at Ayiá Rouméli. First you notice the course of a seasonal torrent, then a spectacular waterfall (forming a tributary from the east, from the region of the Kallérgis refuge). Nearby is the second of many springs, Ríza Sykiás, and then, right of the path, the chapel of **Ayios Nikólaos** overshadowed by some of the finest cypresses on the island. The sound of running water increases as a background to birdsong. The rare peony *P. clusii* flourishes in damp areas beside this path; indigenous to Crete, it flowers a creamy-white in late May and early June. After another spring you climb briefly to a high path along the contour, in dappled shade, before at the 6km mark rejoining the widening river-bed.

The walls of the gorge increasingly dominate the scene as you reach the deserted village of **Samariá**. After many centuries as a naturally defended refuge at the heart of the Sphakiá region, Samariá saw its inhabitants rehoused at the coast soon after the park was established in 1962.

The broad valley floor makes a popular halfway stopping place but you can also cross by a bridge into the village now partly restored as a base for the park rangers. An organised resting site has picnic tables and toilets. (The waiting donkeys and a helicopter pad are a reminder of the occasional rescue operations.)

Five minutes beyond the village, to the east across the stream-bed and romantically situated at the foot of a steep cliff, is a little Byzantine church with the date 1379 above the door and remains of frescoes. The church's dedication **Osía María**, Blessed Mary the Egyptian, was corrupted (as Sía María) to the name for the village and gorge.

The deepest and narrowest part of the gorge is ahead. At first the path is shaded and a breeze may be blowing up from the south coast. In summer the river-bed here is dry, but earlier in the year and after the second of two springs, Kephalovrysiá (the great springs), you will be glad to use the stepping stones for the many crossings of the stream. Near the chapel of **Aphéndis Khristós**

(Christ the Lord) on the left of the path, cold air issuing from clefts in the rocks has given rise to the suggestion that this was the site of the oracle of Apollo recorded in legend. The chapel signals the approach to the Sideróportes or **Iron Gates**, in fact a series of three narrow (3–4km) passes out of the gorge, the last between vertical cliffs towering to a height of 600m.

As you leave the National Park there are cafés before you continue through the ruins of the original village of Ayiá Rouméli. Left of the path is the little Byzantine church of the **Panayía** built into the remains of a 5C–6C basilica. This probably stood on the site of a Hellenistic temple belonging to the city-state of Tárra which occupied this lowest stretch of the river valley in Greco-Roman times. For further details of the church and the scant remains of the city turn to p 391. You complete the walk to the welcome of the modern settlement of Ayiá Rouméli on the Libyan Sea.

Across the island to Soúyia

The main road south across the island to Soúyia, 70km from Khaniá, runs at first through the orange groves of the coastal plain, and then climbs across the western flank of the White Mountains before the descent to the Libyan Sea.

You set off inland as for the Omalós plain (p 398). After about 10km, where a war memorial overlooks a wide junction, the Soúyia road turns off right. It crosses the broad river-bed of the Kerítis and keeps left, skirting the village of **Alikianós** to head for the mountains. (For a recommended 2km detour to visit the Byzantine church of Ayios Kyr Ioánnis near Kouphós, you must turn into Alikianós, p 397.)

On the main Soúyia road, **Skinés** is one of the commercial centres for the citrus trade of the region. Soon after **Khliaró** the orange groves peter out, and the road begins to gain height following a narrow river valley into the wooded foothills of the White Mountains. You cross the river and reach the head of the valley, but through **Néa Roúmata** and **Prasés**, and on past **Sémbronas** (620m), the long climb continues. The forested hillsides are particularly beautiful in autumn as their colours change to red and gold. Finally, not far short of 40km into the drive, the road reaches the pass across the spine of the island where you have extensive views ahead as well as back to Khaniá and the north coast. There is room to pull off the road.

A turning to the left, along the ridge, is signposted to Omalós (10km). This dramatic road, adequately maintained for tourist traffic but still needing careful driving, runs through a wild and beautiful landscape to the western pass out of the Omalós plain, and then down to join the main road across it (p 399). The pass is marked by a white chapel. At the fork near houses down on the plain (and near a pond which during the migration times is often a worthwhile stop for birdwatchers) you keep right for the head of the gorge of Samariá, left for the settlement of Omalós and the main road down to Khaniá.

South from the pass, the Ayía Eiríne valley, narrowing to a gorge, stretches away to the sea. The area of the **Ayía Eiríne gorge** has been declared a nature reserve. A branch of the E4 follows the gorge path, and there is signed access to it from the northern end of the village of Ayía Eiríne on the Soúyia road. On the well-tended trail (provided with a café and toilets) it is c 8km from this point (allow three hours) to the bridge south of Moní which carries the side-road up to Koustoyérako (see below). Here the E4 rejoins the regular Khaniá–Soúyia road, 5km from the coast.

The Soúyia road turns southwest away from the gorge, and the descent begins. By a chapel on a ridge above Epanokhóri comes the first sight of the Libyan Sea. The road drops through **Prinés** and **Tsiskianá**. Here the excavation in the 1980s of a rural shrine dedicated to the worship of Poseidon yielded large numbers of terracotta figurines of oxen; a selection of them fills a case in the Archaeological Museum in Khaniá. Beyond Kambanós, **Marália** clings to the hillside in tiered rows tucked below the road. After a long bend, a big modern church with clerestory is conspicuous on a saddle far ahead. This marks the site of Elyros, once one of the largest and most powerful of the Greco-Roman city-states of southwest Crete.

At a T-junction just below the church (57km from Khaniá) the Soúyia road turns left. A café-bar on the hillside benefits from the view down to the far-off sea. The road to the right at this junction leads into the village of Rodováni, then through Teménia to **Anisaráki** (for frescoed churches, see excursions from Palaiókhora p 413) and (after 18km) Kándanos on the main Khaniá–Palaiókhora road. This cross-country road has been widened and realigned and has opened up a remote area of the Sélinos hills offering an alternative route between Khaniá and Palaiókhora.

Elyros

On a promontory of the hillside above this T-junction, the ruins of Greco-Roman Elyros were rediscovered in the early 19C by the English scholar Robert Pashley. The modern church of the **Panayía** is built on the site of a 6C basilica near its centre; in the First Byzantine period this was the seat of a bishop. In 183 BC Elyros is known to have joined an alliance of 31 Cretan city-states with Eumenes II, King of Pergamon, a celebrated city of Asia Minor and for a while capital of the Roman province of Asia.

A large Roman statue found here and named '*the Philosopher of Elyros*' is a striking exhibit in the museum at Khaniá, but little archaeological investigation has yet been carried out. Cisterns can be identified, the theatre is known to have been located near the basilica, but only scattered stretches of walls remain above ground. The ancient city flourished until the Saracen invasion. A detour up to the modern church is worthwhile for the panoramic view.

Elyros controlled the valley running down to one of its harbours at Syía (modern Soúyia); the other was at **Lisós** (see below), a recommended walk or boat trip from Soúyia.

Moní

Below the village of Moní, the church of **Ayios Nikólaos** has the remains of frescoes by Ioánnis Pagoménos dated by the donor inscription to 1315; its free-standing campanile, believed to be contemporary, is unique on the island. One of the first houses, just beyond a fountain on the left, keeps the key of the church which is left of the road, hidden by trees in summer. You can drive down a track from the turn-off 800m back, around the curve, or take the footpath (ten minutes) starting from the guardian's house.

The single-naved church has an addition across its west end which, curiously, could only be entered from the nave. Pagoménos painted the frescoes in the original church; what remains (which includes some scenes from the Christ cycle) is dominated by a larger-than-life portrayal of the patron saint on the south wall. In the arch Nicholas is consecrated bishop (of Myra in Asia Minor). Frescoes in the annexe are by a different artist.

Two kilometres beyond Moní a minor road left crosses the river and climbs east, 8km into the mountains to **Koustoyérako**.

Here, in 1943, a German platoon was preparing to execute the women and children huddled on the village plateía who had concealed the whereabouts of their menfolk involved with an Allied wireless transmitter and an arms drop for the Resistance movement. But the men of the village were hidden on the slope above, and from 400m their leader shot dead the German machine-gunner at the start of a stirring rescue operation.

The episode is vividly described in *The Cretan Runner* by George Psychoundákis (see Recommended reading). The abandoned village suffered accordingly, but was later rebuilt.

From the top of the plateía a *kalderími* sets off east into the mountains (c two hours) to the village's summer pastures on Mount Akhláda. Koustoyérako is on the E4, here a stretch between the coastal path at Soúyia and the heart of the White Mountains. Not far above the village a left branch of the traditional routes leads serious walkers north to the western pass into the Omalós mountain plain.

Soúyia

The main road reaches the coast at the remote village resort of Soúyia which is tucked under the White Mountains on their western side. The settlement at the mouth of a seasonal river benefits from a good stretch of tamarisk-shaded beach with a small harbour under the cliffs at its western end. The community of fishermen has expanded in the last two decades to make a living from tourism, but despite road improvements and new harbour works for this regular port-of-call on the **south coast boat service** (p 411), there is still an end of the road atmosphere about Soúyia. For some this is its chief appeal.

With private transport Soúyia is a comfortable return journey from the north coast in one day. There should be time for the walk or taxi boat trip to the nearby cove of Ayios Kýrkos, site of the coastal city of **Lisós** renowned in Greco-Roman times for its sanctuary dedicated to Asklepios, god of healing (see below).

Travelling by bus

The limited service across the island from Khaniá may enforce an overnight stay.

Travel agency

The agency *Roxana Travel* (☎ 28230 51362) at the bottom of the main street should be able to help with all the usual enquiries from tourists and to help if required with finding accommodation.

Ask here about the regular long-distance ferry services and local excursion boats and water taxis.

Where to stay

In high summer Soúyia will be lively and crowded, and the eastern end of the beach given over to campers, but for the rest of the tourist season there should be a good choice of **studio rooms** to rent, with or without self-catering facilities.

Look first along the shore towards the river-bed.

C *Poikilassos* (9 rooms), ☎ 28230 51342, fax 28230 51185. A long-established, family-run hotel, one block back from the sea.

C *Santa Irene* (16 apartments), ☎ 28230 51342, fax 28230 511820, email: travel@nanadakis.cha.forthnet.gr. A comfortable modern development on the beach road.

A dozen or so **tavernas** are in competition along the road behind the beach; several have simple **rooms** attached.

Walking

Many visitors who enjoy walking find that Soúyia makes a good base. The traditional coast path is now incorporated in the E4. The marked trails can offer either a brief escape into empty countryside or energetic long-distance hiking along the cliffs in both directions from the village. From Koustoyérako in the hills behind Soúyia, a mountain track heads north over to the Omalós plain at the head of the gorge of Samariá.

The harbour town of **Syía** flourished here in antiquity, serving the important city-state of Elyros (see above) until its destruction at the time of the Arab invasion. In subsequent periods there is no record of use except as a supply port during the various periods of struggle against foreign rulers, and then in recent times as a haven used by fishermen from the villages back from the coast.

Modern Soúyia has grown up on the site of Syía. Traces of tile- or stone-faced concrete remains of the Roman city can be made out on the east side of the river-bed. The sea level was higher in antiquity, and the harbour lay to the west of the river mouth, protected by a mole.

On the raised beach at this end of the village, a modern church is built into the foundations of a 6C basilica; its polychrome mosaics, which until 1986 could be seen both inside and outside the modern chapel, have been removed to the safety of the Archaeological Museum in Khaniá. They are considered the finest of this date yet known on the island; the design includes the type of vase known as a *kanthoros*, and tendrils of ivy leaves, deer and peacocks, one of the symbols of immortality.

Lisós

The expedition to the site of Greco-Roman Lisós, on the cove of Ayios Kýrkos west of Soúyia, is a walk of something over one hour, or a short trip by excursion boat or water taxi. The outward journey by water and the return on foot (avoiding if possible the midday heat) is a popular choice.

Lisós was famous for its temple dedicated to Asklepios, god of healing, and his daughter Hygieia. For two centuries (1C BC–1C AD) the sanctuary and its medicinal springs attracted pilgrims in search of cures. Many inscriptions were found in the sanctuary, including one in honour of Tiberius, but (surprisingly) none recorded a successful cure.

The city-state was prominent by the 3C BC when it joined the League of the Oreíi (the people of the mountains) and it seems to have flourished until it was abandoned during the 9C Saracen occupation.

From Soúyia the walking route is well marked as this stretch of the E4 strikes inland from the harbour, 500m west of the settlement, where a narrow gorge leads into the mountains. After c 20 minutes watch on the left side of the stream-bed for a cairn and signs indicating the path which, built for the first stretch (and afterwards where necessary) snakes straight up the cliff. It then continues to climb through trees on the pine-scented hillside. From the crest you cross a broad stony upland and the little bay of Ayios Kýrkos comes into view far below. The tri-angular valley hemmed in by steep cliffs was the site for the ancient city. Two chapels are useful landmarks on the valley floor: **Ayía Panayía** near the shore, and inland, towards the apex of the triangle, **Ayios Kýrkos**. The outline of the theatre can be distinguished, just on the seaward side of it. The precipitous descent is by a built path down to the back of the cove to arrive near the site of the sanctuary of Hellenistic and Roman times.

From a boat you land on the east side of the bay just below the church of Ayía Panayía which has built into its wall a fragment of an Asiatic sarcophagus with Medusa head.

Recent survey work suggests that since the sea level was higher in antiquity, the 1.5m wide wall 150m northwest of the present beach is part of the old har-bour mole. The survey also located stretches of ancient roadways across the site associated with access to the Asklepieíon.

On the terraces up the western slopes of the valley the **Roman necropolis** consists of a great number of built, barrel-vaulted tombs, rectangular in plan and equipped with niches; 118 have been identified. This is a tomb type so far known on Crete only from three sites in this locality (the other two are at Soúyia and at Lasaía on the bay of Kalí Liménes).

Modern pathways guide you to the various features of the site. The central one leads to Ayios Kýrkos. You pass the guardian's premises and then, keeping right, arrive at the excavated remains of the sanctuary.

The **Temple of Asklepios** was built against the cliff on the northeast side of the valley where a perennial spring flowing out of the rock provided the essential therapeutic waters. The sanctuary site is fenced but usually accessible. If the gate is locked, the guardian nearby, along the path into the valley, may be available with a key. Otherwise you can view fairly well from a vantage point on the slope above.

The remains, excavated nearly half a century ago, are of a small Doric temple of the Hellenistic period dedicated to Asklepios and Hygieia. The construction was of ashlar blocks except for the east wall where the rougher masonry may be earlier, or designed for added strength against the hillside. The cella has a door-way at the south end, with two steps up to it, and on the far wall is a marble podium for the cult statues. In the northwest angle a stepped bench with a hole in it could be a libation channel or a pit for Hygieia's sacred snake. A low bench or kerb surrounds the remains of a good-quality **mosaic floor** of 1C AD date on which panels of black and white geometric designs include the remains of a large maze inlaid with polychrome birds, a goat and a feline. The excavators uncovered a pit dug through the mosaic, which contained about 20 fragmentary statues, including the *headless Asklepios* in the Khaniá Museum. The buildings of the sanctuary collapsed at the beginning of the 2C AD but this pit may have been the work of fanatical Christians who completed the destruction of the temple (using material in the walls of their new churches) and defaced its remains with their symbols.

It is still possible to distinguish that in front of the temple there was a small paved forecourt with low walls on its south and west sides. From a narrow stoa on the south side of the temple a flight of steps led down to the sturdily constructed fountain fed (by pipes beneath the temple) from the sacred spring.

The coastal path continuing west to Palaiókhora starts up a cleft at the back of the valley, left of the ravine formed by the seasonal stream from the hills behind.

Khaniá to Palaiókhora

The direct route follows the coast road west for 20km to Tavronítis, then climbs into the hills to Kándanos, before descending to the south coast at Palaiókhora 77km from Khaniá. The unspoilt country around Kándanos and south towards Palaiókhora, the district of Sélinos, is particularly rich in churches preserving Byzantine fresco decoration. Examples along the route are noted during this drive across to the south coast, and more detailed information is given in the excursions starting from Palaiókhora (see below).

For a day trip there are alternative return routes to the north coast using the Khaniá–Soúyia route (p 403) or taking the slower roads northwest from Palaiókhora to Míli for Topólia and Kastélli Kisámou.

Palaiókhora is a large resort village that welcomes considerable numbers of visitors but is still a comfortable, relaxing place to stay and convenient for exploring this corner of the island. It is the base for the ferries of the south coast boat service which operate a tourist schedule to Ayiá Rouméli (for the Gorge of Samariá) and to Khóra Sphakíon, as well as supplying the island of Gávdos, a two-hour sea journey away and the southernmost inhabited point in Europe.

Travelling by bus

There are buses to Palaiókhora from Khaniá (3 times daily, duration of trip 2 hours) and also from Kastélli Kisámou.

The New National Road runs west from Khaniá along the narrow coastal plain. This was a crucial battleground during the 1941 German invasion of Crete (p 52). In the middle of the village of **Tavronítis**, you turn inland for Kándanos and follow the west bank of the broad river bed up a fertile valley. **Voukoliés** is a market centre with a big plateía shaded by plane trees. The road climbs to a ridge with panoramic views. Around **Kakópetros** the hillsides are densely wooded, but soon the landscape becomes wilder. Above the village there is a monument to a patriot hanged by the Germans in 1944, and then a final glimpse (right) of the north coast and the Bay of Kísamos. The road climbs to a pass before the descent to **Kándanos**.

A stretch of the old road here (signed for Spína) leads down left into a gorge, the scene in May 1941 of a heroic delaying action involving the local population against a German motor-cycle detachment which was pushing south after the capture of the Máleme airfield to secure Palaiókhora. The force was held up for two days by men of the Cretan Resistance movement and afterwards, in reprisal for the death of 25 German soldiers, Kándanos was utterly destroyed.

The village was rebuilt after the war and now flourishes as the administrative centre of the district of Sélinos. On the approach (to the left behind a low wall) there are waterworks given by a German group as a post-war act of reconciliation.

Between Kándanos and Palaiókhora readers interested in Byzantine churches may want to take this chance to visit one or more of the examples noted here. (For further details turn to the route from Palaiókhora to Kándanos and Teménia, p 412.) The first detour to be considered is to **Ayios Mikhaíl Arkhángelos**, **Kavalarianá**, now a cemetery church and usually unlocked by day, which preserves much-admired fresco decoration by Ioánnis Pagoménos. Beside the waterworks wall on the approach to Kándanos a surfaced side-road climbs (less than 2km) to the church; this makes a recommended walk, with the promise of wild flowers in spring.

From the centre of Kándanos, before the big plateía, a turning left (signed for Teménia) offers a second detour off the main route, 3km to Anisaráki, to visit four easily accessible frescoed Byzantine churches.

From Kándanos the main Palaiókhora road continues south. Soon there is a right turn for **Strovlés**, 10km across country on the way to Míli. This provides access to the extreme west part of the island (district of Kísamos) and also makes possible a circular drive from Palaiókhora taking in frescoed Byzantine churches in Sklavopoúla (p 416) and Sarakína.

Staying on the main route south you pass (signed immediately below the road) the church of **Ayios Yeóryios**, **Plemeniana** (see below), which has early 15C wall-paintings. The road begins to follow the valley of the Kakodikiános river which runs into the sea close to Palaiókhora. At **Kalithéa** there are (as the place-name says) fine views out to the west over the valley, and café-bars from which to enjoy them.

There are two interesting frescoed churches above Kakodíki. The church of the Panayía in the village of **Kádros** can be included in the same detour, but if time is short this church with exceptionally well preserved frescoes is less than 1km off the main road; access is usually straightforward. A little further south on the main road a conspicuous sign on the river side points to the 14C cemetery church of **Sotíros Khristós** (Christ the Saviour).

The road crosses the river and a gradual descent for the last 8km brings you down into Palaiókhora.

Palaiókhora

Palaiókhora sits on the narrow promontory jutting out into the Libyan Sea where in 1279 the Venetians built a fort and named it Castel Selino. Today the *phroúrion* or fort is little more than a shell of restored walls; the enceinte provides fine views, especially of the grand mountains to the east, but a better idea of the walls of the fort is obtained from the beach or the old part of the village below.

The location is the secret of Palaiókhora's particular attraction. As a small holiday resort it can offer two long beaches of entirely different character. The east-facing one is the original village beach where the fishing boats used to be drawn up on the pebbles, sheltered from the prevailing wind. Here traditional tavernas and simple rooms for rent first attracted visitors from the populated areas of the north coast to enjoy the extended southern summer. Excursion boats still leave from the old harbour quay here. The shoreline south, under the fort, is a popular stroll, with a taverna-bar (*Fortezza*) overlooking the coast.

Across the promontory the sandy beach faces west, fringed by tamarisk trees along the bay towards **Cape Kriós**. The beach has always been popular with campers, though nowadays they are not encouraged, but it has also proved ideal for tourist development on a modest scale, with some small hotels as well as many blocks of studio rooms and self-catering apartments. The organised bathing beach here flies the 'blue flag' for its cleanliness rating and many types of watersport are available during the high season.

Palaiókhora's enlarged modern harbour out at the tip of the promontory (500m beyond the fort) is the home port for the south coast ferry service. There has been some progress in establishing a marina for visiting yachts.

Walking in spring across the empty ground along the western shore on the way out to the harbour, anyone interested in the wild flowers of Crete will notice clumps of the small pinkish flowers of the delicate asphodel *A. fistulosus*. The authors of *Flowers of the Aegean* (see Recommended reading) suggest that this is the asphodel of the Elysian Fields, the home of the dead in Greek mythology, since the stronger-growing common asphodel seems too coarse for that locality.

Arriving in Palaiókhora from the north you find yourself in the main street, **Venizélou**, running down the centre of the promontory and directed into a one-way traffic system. On summer evenings Venizélou is closed to traffic and crammed with tables to turn it into a lively open-air café. The other street of consequence, **Kontekáki**, crosses the promontory at its narrowest point, at right-angles to Venizélou, from the quay on the east side to the sandy beach on the west.

Travelling by bus
The bus station is at the inland end of Venizélou. The service on the Khaniá route allows walkers to explore the unspoilt hill country back from the coast. When the Gorge of Samariá is open a bus leaves Palaiókhora at 06.00 for the Omalós plain and Xylóskalo, the northern entrance to the National Park (p 400).

Tourist office
The excellent tourist information office run by the local community is halfway down Venizélou. Open daily except Tuesday, 10.00–13.00 and 18.00–21.00, ☎ 28230 41507. It can provide a detailed plan of the village and much helpful advice about accommodation, boat schedules, walking routes and boat excursions. You may find a 1998 monograph by Nicolaos Pyrovolakis entitled *Paleochora: a look back into the past*, a work full of local knowledge and insight.

Travel agencies
Selino Travel ☎/fax 28230 42300 is on Venizélou, opposite the municipal

information office, catering for all the usual requirements (car, scooter and also bicycle hire, coach tours, help with self-catering accommodation).

Intercreta Tours, ☎ 28230 41393, fax 28230 41050 on Kontekáki, near the quay on the east beach, is best for specialist enquiries about boat trips, including excursions in search of dolphins.

Where to stay and eating out
B *Hotel Elman* (23 furnished apartments), ☎ 28230 41414, fax 28230 41412. A modern establishment on the west beach, popular for family holidays.
C *Aris* (25 rooms), ☎ 28230 41502, fax 28230 41546, www.paleochora-holidays.gr. On the southern edge of the original village, towards the harbour; with garden and some sea views.
C *On the Rocks* (12 rooms), ☎ 28230 41713, fax 28230 41735. Below the castle walls with sea views to the east; suitable for wheelchair users.
C *Pal Beach* (58 rooms), ☎ 28230 41512, fax 28230 41578. At the harbour end of the west beach.

C Rea (14 rooms) ☎ 28230 41307, fax 28230 41605. A family-run hotel tucked away in a garden setting between the west beach and the main street (Venizélou), ranked by many regular visitors as one of the most delightful hotels in this corner of the island.

There are well-signed **rooms to rent** in the village and above the tavernas along the pebble beach, also many self-catering apartments on the west beach. In case of difficulty consult the tourist information office (see above). Out of the village the coast road west to Koundourás has simple rooms, well-signed, often attached to tavernas.

The official **camping site** is 1km east on the Anýdri road.

Eating out

In the search for good tavernas Palaiókhora's east beach usually offers quieter alternatives to the massed tables in Venizélou.

Galaxy, halfway along the beach road, has a special reputation for well-cooked fish.

O Anikhtos is a simple *psistariá* for grilled meats; it is at a crossroads on the inland stretch of Venizélou towards the bus station.

Taverna Grammeno, 3km west behind the beach of the same name, is highly regarded for its traditional Cretan food, perhaps at the end of an evening walk (with taxi home); by day it operates as a beach café-bar.

The Third Eye, one block inland from the west beach, is a taverna specialising in vegetarian food, making it a rarity on the island. It is run by a Greek-New Zealand couple. From the centre set off west on Kontekáki and watch for signs left and then right towards the sea.

Banks

There are three on Venizélou. The *National Bank of Greece* is a short distance north of the tourist information office.

Post office and telephones

The **post office** is centrally placed along the road behind the west beach, north of Kontekáki.

OTE for telephone, fax and email is almost next door to the information office on Venizélou.

The south coast boat service

Palaiókhora is at the western end of the route to Soúyia, Ayiá Rouméli (for the Samariá gorge), Loutró and Khóra Sphakíon (p 386). Weather permitting this is usually a reliable service, though the schedule can vary confusingly according to season; it is much reduced in April and October and functions only for local needs in winter. The timetable is published on a monthly basis, starting around Easter, and should be available from major tourist information offices on the island. Enquire locally about day-trips from Palaiókhora, for example, to Elaphonísi or Lísos.

Travelling light and using buses and boats you could make a circular tour from the north coast, with an outward journey down to Khóra Sphakíon and the return north from Palaiókhora (or vice versa) with overnight stops where the ferry calls in between. In high season you may want to book rooms before you set out on the boats; see the sections on where to stay under each harbour village and in case of difficulty consult a tourist information office or a local travel agency.

West out of Palaiókhora polythene hothouses are grouped along the narrow coastal plain but the Koundourás road allows easy access to the shore which is part sand part rocks. **Grámméno beach**, after 3km, is a good stretch of sand. *Taverna Grammeno* on the roadside behind it is deservedly popular.

The coast road ends at the beach below **Cape Kriós** (cold) named for the cold springs in the sea, refreshing in the heat of summer. The time-honoured coastal path climbs high along the cliffs; now it is part of the E4 trail. It will take serious walkers to Elaphonísi (p 434) but before setting out consult Palaiókhora's tourist information office about route maintenance. An early morning bus to the end of the road shortens the expedition and you can plan to catch a ferry for the return.

To Anýdri and Prodrómi

The Anýdri road runs east along the coast before climbing inland beside a stream and up a wooded gorge. This is a popular walk of 6km from Palaiókhora, especially in spring when the road is quiet and the terrain along the way rewarding for wild-flower enthusiasts. The church of **Ayios Yeóryios**, **Anýdri**, preserves an outstanding set of frescoes painted in 1323 by Ioánnis Pagoménos.

Beyond the village an unsurfaced road continues across empty countryside passing after a further 8km a frescoed church near Prodrómi on a circular return route to Palaiókhora through either Teménia or Azogirés. Before **Prodrómi** long-distance walkers can take a track right, signed to Lisós, to join the coastal footpath (E4), turning east for the ancient site (p 406) or west for Palaiókhora.

In the middle of Anýdri Ayios Yeóryios is signed below the road, right. Walk downhill past a *kapheneíon* to a path running right where the red-roofed, double-naved church is in view overlooking the valley to the sea.

The north nave is densely painted with scenes from the *Christ cycle* and the miraculous *deeds and martyrdom of St George*. The patron saint is the third figure in the deisis scheme in the apse, and the portrayal on a white horse dominates the north wall of the central bay. (The remains of frescoes in the south nave dedicated to Ayios Nikólaos are the work of a different artist.)

Continuing towards Prodrómi botanists will recognise the shrubland known as *maquis* or *garigue* (and to Cretans as *phrýgana*) with its own specialised plant life which includes orchids. For walkers there is little shade.

North of Prodrómi a modern church is conspicuous on a mound. Ahead, above the road left, there is an isolated single-naved church; its apse has a distinctive zigzag plaster moulding. Watch for a bend with a track heading uphill. (Approaching from the opposite direction the building is hidden until you have passed it.)

This church of the **Panayía**, **Skaphídia**, celebrating the Presentation of the Virgin, has wall-paintings dated by inscription on the west wall to 1347. The frescoes, carefully restored, are of high quality though tantalisingly incomplete. The artist named as Joachim is thought to have been influenced by Pagoménos.

One kilometre further uphill you arrive at a T-junction; the ancient site of Hyrtakína is ahead on the horizon. To the left an unsurfaced road (signed to Asphendilés) will take you through Azogirés, directly back to Palaiókhora. Right is Teménia, and a former monastic church. These places are visited along the route from Palaiókhora to Soúyia via Kándanos (see below).

Palaiókhora to Kándanos and Soúyia

This excursion will take you across unspoilt country 40km to Soúyia (p 405) with time to visit the ancient site of Lisós (p 406). For those interested in the frescoed Byzantine churches of Sélinos the route passes within reach of many of them. For an introduction to these churches you could consider short detours to Kádros and to the church decorated by Ioánnis Pagoménos at Kavalarianá outside Kándanos.

Travelling by bus

The Khaniá service is convenient for walkers who want to go exploring off the main road between Palaiókhora and Kándanos.

Azogirés is a popular walk 6km off the bus route. From the stop in Kakódiki it is 2km uphill to the unsurfaced tracks which will take you south along the hillside, reassuringly parallel to and overlooking the river valley, between the churches of Astratigós and Kádros; there you can drop down to the main road for a bus back to Palaiókhora. If you choose to alight in Kándanos, Mikhaíl Arkhángelos, Kavalarianá is a 2km walk from the northern outskirts of the village, and from the centre it is 3km on a side-road to the churches of Anisaráki. On foot there is a possible short-cut between the two roads.

With private transport you leave Palaiókhora on the Kándanos road to the north. After 3km you cross the river and the cemetery church of **Sotíros Khristós**, with mid-14C frescoes, is signed below the road left. Soon after this comes the turn for a (6km) detour to Azogirés which could take in the village museum, a former monastic church and a dramatically sited cave signed left on the way into the village. (The descent into the cave is only for the agile; consult the tourist information office in Palaiókhora.)

For **Kádros**, which is 1km above the main road, you need to watch for the turning 7km north of the river bridge. (If you pass the turn you can circle back along the hillside from Kakódiki.) Near the top of the strung out village of Kádros, a little beyond the last *kapheneíon*, a footpath leads right, downhill, to the church of the **Panayía**. The dedication here is to the Nativity of the Virgin (feast day celebrations on 8 September). When the church is shut the key is kept at the nearby house (over a stile beside a gate).

This church has a well-preserved set of frescoes dated to the second half of the 14C; in the apse Mary is portrayed as the *Panayía Eléousa* (the Virgin of Mercy) with the *Dormition* on the west wall. The nave has scenes from the Christ cycle (with a memorable *St Symeon* in the Presentation panel beside the Crucifixion along the upper register on the north side).

The frescoed churches above **Kakodíki** are most easily found from the main valley road. On the approach to the village the turn, at an acute angle uphill, is signed on a bend. The side-road climbs through olive groves, 1km to the prominent domed modern church of Ayía Triáda, Astratigós; beside it is the little Byzantine church of **Mikhaíl Arkhángelos**. The key is held by the priest who lives 250m further up the hill. Pass the gate to the church and keep left at a fork to the end of the track.

Mikhaíl Arkhángelos has frescoes dated to the first half of the 14C and a beautiful old wooden iconostasis. This is a single-naved church, but the nave is divided by pilasters into four bays (rather than the usual two or three). The original Byzantine chapel was altered and elaborated by the Venetians; a new door and window have damaged the frescoes on the south wall. Scenes preserved include the *Apostle Communion* below the *Pantokrátor* in the apse, and on the north wall, next to the iconostasis, a rare portrayal of the archangel mounted on a horse (see Plemeniána, below).

A little further south, at **Tselenianá**, is a church dedicated to **Ayios Isídoros**, with elegant frescoes dated by inscription 1420–21. From Astratigós keep right (south) along the hillside at the fork noted above. In less than 1km, just across a stream-bed (a ford in spring) the keyholder's house is in view down a track to the right; he will accompany you (700m further along the road) to the church overlooking the valley. These are the only frescoes on Crete dealing with themes from the life of the saint. Isídoros was martyred for his faith on the island of Chios during the reign of the 3C Emperor Decius who was notorious for his persecution of the Christians. The upper registers of the vault are devoted to the Christ cycle, but in the lower registers are: on the south side scenes of the baptism, imprisonment (behind a grille) and the beheading of Isídoros, and opposite, the saint's avowal of his faith before Numerius, commander of the Roman fleet, and the punishment of being dragged behind two Arab horses.

Kádros (see above) is 2km further south on the way back to the main road. If you turn right at the main road to continue north from Kakodíki you pass café-bars at **Kalithéa** (literally a good view) overlooking the river valley. Two kilometres further on the church of **Ayios Yeóryios**, **Plemeniána**, is signed, immediately below the roadway. Its frescoes, dated 1409–10 include a panel with one of the archangels mounted on a horse, a rare scene although a similar one was noted in the Astrátigos church (above).

The main Khaniá road continues into Kándanos (p 408). On the far side of the big village, the cemetery church of **Mikhaíl Arkhángelos**, **Kavalarianá**, preserves an exceptional set of frescoes painted in 1327–28 by Ioánnis Pagoménos. As the road sets off for Khaniá there are waterworks behind a low wall (right); a side-road here is the easiest approach.

The arrangement of the iconography is conventional in the apse and on the vault of the nave, except that on the south wall of the apse Pagoménos includes Ayios Títos, appointed by St Paul as the first bishop of Crete. The inscription with the date 1327–28 is on the south wall of the nave, flanked by the Emperor Constantine. Either side of the window below the inscription are the archangels, left Michael and right Raphael, and below them four figures in a donor panel. Between the two blind arches is the figure of the Cretan evangelist, Ayios Ioánnis Xénos. On the north wall the Archangel Michael as patron saint appears twice, once in the eastern blind arch and again above a second donor panel.

For Soúyia you turn east in the centre of Kándanos, at a sign for Teménia.

Anisaráki, strung out along the Teménia road 3km from Kándanos, has four Byzantine churches preserved with remains of interesting frescoes; all are signed from the road, and usually open during the day. **Ayía Anna**, below the road left at the beginning of the village, is built over an earlier church, probably a First Byzantine period basilica as the column fragments now lying outside suggest. The frescoes, dated 1462, depict scenes from the life of St Anne, mother of the Virgin Mary. A rare feature is an iconostasis in stone, fully decorated, with the two main panels depicting *Christ Pantokrátor* and *Ayía Anna holding the infant Mary*. On the south wall (near the west end) the donor is depicted, with inscription opposite.

For **Ayios Yeóryios** turn left 200m further along the modern road on to a track that leads to a group of houses. Five minutes on foot beyond them, keeping straight ahead, the little church is in view. Late 13C–early 14C frescoes include scenes from the life of the saint on the south side of the vault (martyrdom on the north side) and on the south wall the familiar portrayal on horseback, here between the Virgin (left) and Ayía Marína.

For the other two churches continue to the far end of Anisaráki where the street bends right and the church of the **Panayía** sits on a terrace to the left immediately above the road. Its relatively sophisticated architecture shows strong Venetian influence. The original doorway was in the south wall, and the *graffito* 1614 may be associated with the alterations. The late 14C frescoes are particularly well preserved, with the **Communion of the Apostles** below the **Virgin with Child** (*Platytéra*) in the apse, and the barrel-vaulting densely painted with scenes from the life of Christ.

On the (adjacent) higher terrace, the church of Ayía Paraskeví has frescoes dated stylistically to the first half of the 14C. The saint is depicted on the north wall, with Ayía Varvára.

South to Teménia

The cross-country road climbs steadily from Anisaráki through Vamvakádos and then to a crest. After 8km Teménia is delightfully situated at 700m on wooded slopes, especially attractive in the heat of summer. *Taverna Oikoteneiaki*, on the right-hand side as you approach the village, has a good reputation for traditional home-cooked food. Beyond the taverna there has been an attempt to establish rooms for rent; watch for signs off the road left on the way in, or ask in the village.

Above Teménia is the site of the city-state of **Hyrtakína** which flourished in the Hellenistic period. There are traces of walls in polygonal masonry, probably of a late-Classical or early-Hellenistic date, and Hellenistic houses have been excavated, as well as a 4C–3C sanctuary of Pan. A 1C AD statue of the god is in the Archaeological Museum in Khaniá.

At the far end of Teménia you keep left for the Khaniá–Soúyia road. (A right turn here leads back south, in c 15km, unsurfaced part of the way, through Azogirés to Palaiókhora.) A chapel is conspicuous on a hill left, and then right of the road a sign points to the former monastic church of **Sotíros Khristós** at the end of a short track, raised on a mound but partly hidden among oak trees. A torch is useful for the interior.

Architecturally this church possesses a special charm derived from the material used in its construction and its curious plan, unique on Crete. The original single-naved chapel (tentatively dated to the 13C) has a miniature version of a cross-domed church added on to its west end (probably in the 14C); reached by a shallow flight of steps, this takes the place of a conventional narthex. The frescoes, preserved only in the original nave, were perhaps painted as late as the 17C. The scenes from the Christ cycle, sadly incomplete, include the subject (rare on Crete) of the **Interrogation of Christ by Pontius Pilate**. See one panel on the north side of the vault (western bay, lower register) and a second on the west wall (below the **Entry into Jerusalem**), where the unexpected female figure behind Christ is interpreted as Pilate's wife.

Continuing east from the church another minor road right leads back to the coast through Prodrómi and Anýdri (p 412). For Soúyia continue through Máza to Rodováni and the junction (at a well-sited café-taverna) with the main

Khaniá–Soúyia road. For the site of ancient Elyros on the hillside here and the descent to Soúyia, turn to p 404.

Palaiókhora to Sklavopoúla

Northwest from Palaiókhora improvements to the road system have opened up this remote corner of the island. There is a choice of routes (offering a circular drive) for a short expedition of c 20km to Sklavopoúla which combines visits to a number of frescoed Byzantine churches with exploring countryside off the beaten track. At suitable seasons both routes will reward a search for wild flowers. From Palaiókhora the more adventurous road (the westerly one) keeps west along the coast as far as Koundourás and then takes you north (across empty hillsides with wide views) on an unsurfaced but well-engineered road to Ayii Theódori, and on to Sklavopoúla. (Do not be tempted to cut across west to Elaphonísi unless you have been advised by the information office in Palaiókhora that roadworks are completed. Some maps are ahead of the road builders.)

The faster route climbs from Palaiókhora to join a beautiful river valley to Voutás and then turns west into the hills. From Voutás you could continue north to Strovlés and Míli (p 409) which is on the direct route between Kastélli Kisámou and the extreme southwest of the island, the monastery of Khrisoskalítissa and the renowned beaches of Elaphonísi.

You leave Palaiókhora on the road westwards that runs parallel to the village's west beach towards Koundourás, and turn right inland on the road to Voutás and Míli (signed). 8km inland, by a bridge below the village of Kondokiníagi, there is a short detour, 3km right, to the little frescoed church of **Mikhaíl Arkhángelos** at **Sarakína**. The side-road climbs beside the stream-bed, passing a monument (erected in 1986) to commemorate a battle in 1897, the last year of the Turkish occupation, in which 150 Turks, withdrawing to the coast to leave the area, were massacred by Christian forces.

At the meeting of two streams the church is hidden in undergrowth at the end of a paved footpath ahead right. The stone iconostasis (a rare feature, as at Ayía Anna, Anisaráki) is painted with icons of Christ and the Panayía Eléousa (the Virgin of Mercy); the wall-paintings are dated stylistically to the second half of the 14C. Ahead in the village, the church of **Ayios Ioánnis** has remains of frescoes (dated 1341–49).

For Sklavopoúla you continue north, on a beautiful stretch beside the main river, to **Voutás** where, for the river crossing you take a side-road left. Just out of the village the old bridge is preserved, to the right of the modern one. Anyone with an interest in Byzantine fresco paintings could turn off the road, left, for three churches close together on the outskirts of Voutás. Watch for signs for the old churches and the hamlet names: Ayios Ioánnis Khrysóstomos (dedicated to one of the hierarchs of the eastern church) outside Khasí; Ayios Yeóryios in the partly deserted settlement of Azogirés, and Ayía Paraskeví in Kýtiros. The frescoes are dated respectively to the mid-14C, to the second half of the 13C (later phase an the east wall) and by inscription to 1372–73.

The road from Voutás to Sklavopoúla, narrow but surfaced, climbs until the valley opens out. Still climbing you pass Kalamiós, and 8km from Voutás arrive in **Sklavopoúla** to look out from a height of 640m across cultivated hillsides to the distant sea. The place-name is often said to indicate settlement by Slav mercenaries left behind by the Byzantine commander after the reconquest of the island for Christendom in 961, but the words for Slav and slave may have been confused.

Tourists come to the village to admire its three frescoed churches. Left of the road on the way in is **Ayios Yeóryios**, an unusually tall building. (The keyholder lives in the cluster of houses down the slope below the school playground.) After reconstruction only part of the original church remained, but it preserves wall-paintings from two different periods superimposed in some places, inviting interesting comparisons. The earlier work, easiest to study in the sanctuary, is dated by an inscription above the window to 1290–91. The frescoes of the second phase, dated stylistically to the end of the 14C, dealt with the life and martyrdom of Saint George (upper register, north wall). Below from west to east are Theódoros and Yeóryios (on horseback), and Mikhaíl Arkhángelos.

The other two frescoed churches are close together below the village. From the plateía and a conspicuous modern church in the centre, continue steeply downhill for 400m and turn back left, again downhill, to parking for the lower village. Walk on into the old village street, up some steps and through a roofed passage, past a partly ruined tower of the Venetian period. (If keys are needed, the guardian lives beside the tower.) Where the houses stop the *kalderími* continues ahead but the two little churches are on the left, above the path.

The first you come to (usually unlocked) is dedicated to **Sotíros Khristós**, Christ the Saviour. The remains of 14C frescoes (with scenes from the Christ cycle) are sadly fragmentary. Beside them, on the north wall, there survives a panel with the (defaced) donor Partzális among trees and with his church in the background. (Scraps of an earlier phase of painting can also be identified.) On the south wall, with the military saints on horseback, are graffiti of 1422 and 1514.

Immediately above on the hillside is the little church dedicated to the **Panayía** (Virgin Mary), densely painted with fresco decoration in a much better state of preservation. (For the key see above.) The frescoes are dated stylistically to the late 14C–early 15C (graffito 1518); art historians value them as an important link in the development of what became known as the Cretan School of painting. The decoration of the apse shows the fathers of the Church with the sacrificial lamb on an altar, and (unusually) the instruments of the crucifixion foreshadowing that event. The vault of the nave is painted with a well-preserved set of gospel scenes. Here again the north wall has a panel with the donor and the model of his church.

The island of Gávdos

Ferries from Palaiókhora run a regular supply service to Gávdos, which lies c 30km south of the coastline of Sphakiá. The island, c 9km x 5km in extent, is the most southerly point of Europe that is inhabited all the year round. Gávdos is tentatively identified with Ogygía where, according to Homer, Odysseus lingered for seven years bewitched by Calypso.

Getting there

The Palaiókhora service runs twice a week, weather permitting, to the little harbour of Karavés, and more often in summer. With a call at Soúyia, the schedule may give little time on the island. In the high season there are ferries from Khóra Sphakíon, and the shorter journey time of two hours allows a longer stay.

There are four small settlements with only primitive electricity and transport, and less than a hundred people, engaged in farming, fishing and tourism, make their home on Gávdos. A visit is recommended by Rackham and Moody (see Recommended reading) to anyone sympathetic to the old-fashioned Cretan way of life, as well as to botanists interested in the endemic flora.

If you plan to stay overnight or longer, consult the Tourist Information Office in Palaiókhora; **Karavés** has a few rooms to rent for the adventurous, as does **Kastrí**, the main village in the centre of the island. The majority of visitors opt for a day trip and a half-hour walk from the harbour to swim off the beautiful sands of Sarakíniko bay, where there are simple beach tavernas.

With archaeological evidence for occupation dating back to the Neolithic period, the island was in Greco-Roman times a dependency of the city of Górtyn. A headless statue of a woman (probably 2C AD) presented to the British Museum in 1865 by the surveyor Captain T.A.B. Spratt RN came from a site on the northern cape.

The ship carrying St Paul on his voyage to Rome was driven past the island, then known as *Clauda*, by the fierce north wind, Euroclydon (Acts 27, 12), which had prevented landfall in the safe winter harbour of Phoénix, modern Loutró, directly to the north.

Gávdos seems to have flourished as the seat of a bishop during the last years before the Arab conquest, but then, located on one of the Mediterranean sea lanes, became known as a pirate lair. The island remained vulnerable in Venetian times; fortification was discussed but not implemented. During Sphakiá's struggle against Ottoman rule Gávdos served as a refuge. In the 20C, before World War Two, it was briefly a place of exile. There are dreams for the future; see the beautifully illustrated *Gavdos*, subtitled Travelogue in Time and Space, by I. Alexiadou-Sgouraki, available locally.

Visitors with time to walk the island comment that it is surprisingly densely wooded; it is more than half covered with land juniper, lentisk and Cretan pine. The terrain rises to 350m, with sheer cliffs in the southwest attracting rain and mist. The southern tip runs out into a spine ending in three great sea caves, a romantic conclusion to inhabited Europe.

West of Khaniá

Khaniá to Kastélli Kisámou

Kastélli Kisámou (officially renamed Kísamos but still known locally as Kastélli) is a small harbour town 40km west of Khaniá, the commercial and administrative centre of this rural and relatively isolated region west of the White Mountains. In recent years, partly as a result of an improved ferry service between its harbour and mainland Greece (the Peloponnese), the town has begun, in a small-scale way, to cater for tourists and it now makes a practical base for exploring the extreme west of the island.

If you are planning a day-trip to Kastélli you may want to leave time to explore the site of ancient **Polyrrhénia** 7km inland from the town (p 427).

The fishing village of **Kolymbári**, halfway to Kastélli, is tucked into the shelter of the Rodopós peninsula at the western end of the Bay of Khaniá. This is a very agreeable place to spend a few days, to enjoy exploring the peninsula or the off-the-beaten-track hill country to the south. The important **Odiyítria monastery** at Goniá, on the edge of the village, and the intriguing Byzantine rotonda church at **Episkopí** will reward interested readers.

Travelling by bus

There is a good bus service from Khaniá to Kastélli. Khaniá city buses (p 354) to the villages of Kalamáki and Galatás can be used for the beaches on the western edge of town.

The recent extension of the north coast highway, the New National Road, west of Khaniá is complete except for a short stretch behind Kolymbári. On the old road which follows the coast along the Bay of Khaniá there is haphazard ribbon development on a modest scale as far as Plataniás. This development offers accommodation and beach taverna meals, but also noisy bars and discos. Self-catering apartments, often advertised as studios, are here replacing the traditional Cretan rooms to rent and there is the occasional larger hotel geared to package holidays. The road, lined with tourist agencies and souvenir shops, and often crowded with pedestrians, is not one to drive in a hurry.

You can travel west from the city continuing from the bypass on the new highway, and then take the exit cutting down to the coast at Plataniás. Both roads follow the coastal plain which in 1941 was the scene of a German airborne invasion from bases in Attica (see below). On the old road 4km west of the city a turning inland is signed for **Galatás**. Here, as the Allied forces began the retreat, New Zealand troops fought a heroic rearguard action on 21 May 1941. In the plateía at the inland end of the village, simple marble pillars form a memorial to those killed in the battle. A religious service is held here annually on the Sunday in Battle of Crete week.

After the Galatás turning the road runs close to the shore along the bay. The beach here is not wide, but long stretches of good sand (with sun loungers and umbrellas) alternate with rocky outcrops. The prominent offshore island of Ayii Theódori is one of several reserves for the Cretan wild goat, the *agrími*.

Plataniás is a large village, 11km from Khaniá, which has spread from its flat-topped hill to cater for tourism along the shore. Beyond, the scene remains more rural and unspoilt.

13km from Khaniá the road crosses the River Plataniás, fed from the White Mountains (through Mesklá and Alikianós) by the Kerítis and lesser tributaries. A minor road inland along the west bank cuts across to Ayiá (p 396) on the Omalós road; the signs are for Vrýses, but keep left at a fork to follow the river. The area is recommended to bird-watchers who should bear in mind that the rare Eleonora's falcon breeds on some of the offshore islands not far away.

After Plataniás the coast road winds on through groves of orange and tangerine trees and around Easter the scent of blossom is overpowering. The reappearance of tourist develoment indicates that you are approaching **Máleme**. The airfield (now a military base) which played a decisive part in the German airborne attack in 1941 is beyond the village on the seaward side of the road, but before this there is a left turn for the **German war cemetery** (signposted in Greek and German); it lies less than 2km inland on the rising ground. A schematic wall map illustrates the sombre facts of the Battle of Crete, 20 May–1 June 1941. 6580 Germans were killed, including those missing at sea, and there are 4465 well-tended graves on the hillside here.

The Máleme cemetery lies at the end of a north–south ridge running out from the White Mountains. This was Hill 107, a vital tactical position in the battle for what was, at that time, the civilian aerodrome for Khaniá. The bird's-eye view of the coast from the cemetery helps to bring alive the written accounts of the battle.

200m down the road below the cemetery a **Late Minoan** (LMIIIB) **chamber-tomb** was excavated in 1966. There is a sign on a bend with a path east for 100m along the terraced hillside. This tomb has an exceptionally long (13.8m) *dromos*, a lined passage leading to a rectangular chamber with corbelled roof. The doorway is designed with a relieving triangle behind the upright slab above the heavy lintel. The tomb had been robbed, but two interesting seals are recorded; one in bronze, perhaps originally covered with gold leaf, showed a cow suckling her calf, and the other in agate was carved with *agrímia*.

The main road continues past the airfield to the bridge over the broad stony river-bed of the Tavronítis; on the right are the remains of the wartime Bailey bridge which continued in use for some 30 years. Birdwatchers can walk or drive (1km) down the west bank (first skirting the works buildings) to the reed-beds behind the shore. When the river is fed by the melting snows the water forms a small lagoon at the river mouth which often shelters wading birds on migration.

The village of **Tavronítis** is a busy centre for the fruit growers of this narrow coastal plain. Here you would turn inland to Kándanos if you were crossing the island to Palaiókhora on the south coast. Continuing west you approach the Rodopós peninsula which forms the western limit of the Khaniá bay. In the angle formed by peninsula and bay the red-painted dome of Moní Kerás Goniás (literally the monastery of Our Lady of the Corner) stands out ahead on the rocks above the shore.

Kolymbári

The Kolymbári crossroads (23km from Khaniá) is a bustling place where bus stops, a taxi rank, tavernas and bars serve primarily the needs of Cretans on the move between the interior of the island and the towns. From Khaniá the main road bears half-left uphill for Kastélli, but a 1km detour to the right leads down into the village and the monastery just beyond it. You come first to a war memorial in an open space serving as a plateía. There is access here to the long pebble beach stretching back along the bay. Ahead, at the far end of the plateía the narrow, tamarisk-lined village street backs on to the little harbour, with room to park down on the quay.

Travel agent

Antiliá, ☎ 28240 22961, in the plateía, will help with visitors' problems including accommodation. Ask here about boats to the **Meniés cove**.

Where to stay

B *Chryssana* (43 rooms), ☎ 28240 22812, fax 28240 22811. A modern hotel set back from the beach in a garden where the local river runs into the sea; a 5 minute walk into the village. Suitable for wheelchair access.

E *Dimitra* (24 rooms), ☎ 28240 22244. Long-established, perhaps still old-fashioned, but right behind the harbour with views along the coast to the monastery.

There are plenty of **rent rooms** and **studio apartments** in the village (heavily booked in the high summer season). Start opposite the war memorial where *Minerva* has seafront studios.

Eating out

Argentina in the main street is a well-known fish taverna, long popular for outings from Khaniá on summer evenings and for Sunday lunch. *Diktynna*, almost opposite, on the harbour side of the road, is an alternative also with a reputation for good fresh fish. In good weather a cluster of seafront tavernas level with the war memorial competes for custom. *O Mylos*, a café-bar in a converted mill overlooking the harbour, contributes to the holiday atmosphere.

The Goniá monastery

Open 08.00–12.30 and 16.00–19.00 daily, except Saturday when open afternoons only. The monastery is dedicated to the Odiyítria, the Virgin as Guide to Salvation, and celebrates the Feast of the Assumption (15 August).

The monastery was founded in 1618 by a monk from Cyprus, with the help of the Zangaróli family, Venetians who had adopted the Orthodox faith (also associated with the Ayía Triáda monastery on the Akrotíri (p 368). The first cruciform church, completed in 1634, was severely damaged by Turkish forces when they landed nearby 11 years later, at the start of their final assault on Crete. However, the monastery obtained a stavropigiac charter, which put it under the direct authority and protection of the Patriarch in Constantinople, so the church could be rebuilt (1662). (The side-chapels and narthex are 19C additions.) The church school here played an important part in the preservation of Greek culture. The monastery's rich library was burned at the time of the 1866 rebellion; certain treasures, including a 17C codex, were saved.

Tradition links the origins of the monastery, at least by the early years of the Second Byzantine period if not before, with the church of Ayios Yeóryios, Meniés, close to the site of the Greco-Roman sanctuary of Díktynna, north along the coast towards the tip of the Rodopós peninsula. The monks are thought to have moved from that remote spot to the greater safety of Kolymbári; the ruins of their 13C monastery survive on the hillside above the present-day one.

Goniá monastery, from Pashley, Travels in Crete, *1837*

The Odiyítria church, restored after damage during the German occupation, stands at the seaward end of a courtyard. The refectory, at the northeast corner, has a classical doorway embellished with baroque volutes, and from the terrace behind the church there is a fine view of the Bay of Khaniá and the White Mountains. The cannonball in the wall of the south apse is a memento of the Turkish bombardment.

The monastery possesses one of the most important collections of **icons** on Crete. A monk is usually on hand to open the small museum across from the church where some of them are on view, with ecclesiastical valuables and historical documents. The icons include a superb *Crucifixion* by Konstantínos Palaiókapas (dated 1634, the year of the completion of the original church); in the treatment of background buildings and landscape, and the realistic anatomy, this work is said to show the influence of Italian art.

Outside the handsome west gate is a fountain (1708). Its inscription translated reads: 'Most delicious Spring of water bubbling up for me; Water, for all creation, the sweetest element in life.' There are steps beside the fountain to a gate and a steep path up the herb-scented hillside which leads in five minutes to ruins of the monastery's 13C predecessor with remains of frescoes in the chapel. The gate is usually locked; ask the guardian monk about access.

The modern complex above the shore just beyond the monastery is the Orthodox Academy of Crete.

The Rodopós peninsula and sanctuary of Díktynna at Meniés

A formidable peninsula, named after the village on its spine, extends north from Kolymbári out to Cape Spátha (ancient Tityros). Nowadays the peninsula is populated only by shepherds and goatherds but in antiquity a great temple, dedicated to the goddess Díktynna, stood high on the cliffs above the cove of Meniés Rodopoú near the cape.

Almost nothing remains to indicate the former glories, mentioned with admiration by many writers, but the isolated cove is a romantic spot with good swimming. It faces southeast, sheltered from the prevailing wind of summer and is visited by excursion boats from Kolymbári and sometimes from Khaniá. Enquire about excursions or hiring a boat in Kolymbári, on the quay, at the Taverna Díktynna or at the travel agency Antiliá (see above). (If possible compare prices; private hire is not cheap.) On the way up the coast the boat passes the cave of **Ellinóspilios**, one of the few known Neolithic sites of western Crete with evidence for both habitation and burial; sherds of pottery were found at the back of the 100m-deep chamber.

The peninsula is good walking country. A spectacular coast road along the cliffs north of Kolymbári leads to Aphráta, 4km beyond the monastery. A narrow road continues (keeping right) down to the sea, with a steep drop through a ravine to the narrow rocky bay. In suitable weather there may be a boatman to ferry you the short distance north to Ellinóspilios (see above).

The cave (exploration suitable only for specialists) can be reached on foot. You start out from Aphráta on the beach road but fork left after 500m signed for the church of Ayios Konstantínos which offers a possible circuit anti-clockwise to Rodopós, but a track, right, leads to the cave. Wildflower enthusiasts will enjoy the uncultivated hillside, the typical *phrýgana* of much of the Cretan terrain.

From Aphráta there is a longer return route to Kolymbári, through Astrátigos and Aspra Nerá, with more fine views.

Walking on the Rodopós peninsula

For the direct road to the village of Rodopós, you need to get on to the (signed) Old Road 1km west of Kolymbári, rather than the new highway, and then watch for a turning right. It is 6km to the village and 17km further to the sanctuary of Díktynna on a shepherds' track, unsurfaced after the first few kilometres and not suitable for the average hired car. The track runs north up the spine of the peninsula before it bends right towards the sea for the descent to the Meniés cove. Before the long bend east you may notice raised stretches of the paved Roman road to the sanctuary. After the long bend you see, in a hollow (right), the old church of Ayios Yeóryios, Meniés, beside a ruined medieval tower. This is the church associated with the origins of the Goniá monastery (p 421).

This off-the-beaten-track countryside is recommended to botanists and bird-watchers. Take provisions, including water, and remember that there is very little shade. For a shorter walk there is a branch left from the main track (about 6km from Rodopós) to the church of Ayios Ioánnis, Yioní, halfway up the west side of the peninsula. An annual pilgrimage takes place here for the feast of St John (29 August); babies to be named John are brought for baptism from all over western Crete. A footpath back down the west coast of the peninsula is way-marked for a circular return route ending in Rodopós.

The Diktýnnaion

The Diktýnnaion was the most important religious sanctuary in western Crete during the Roman period. Control over it brought great prestige to a city-state and was fiercely contested, especially between Kydonía and Polyrrhénia. The wealth of the sanctuary financed public works programmes.

The cult of the Cretan goddess Díktynna, related to that of Britomártis (a pre-Hellenic name meaning 'sweet maiden'), was to some extent a survival of the worship of the Minoan mother goddess. There were cult centres in Athens and the Peloponnese (and Marseilles), but Díktynna was especially venerated in the west of Crete. The name may be connected with Mount Díkte but the Greek historian Strabo proposed that *diktyon* was the fishermen's net which is supposed to have saved the goddess when she leapt into the sea to escape the unwelcome attentions of Mínos. Like the Greek goddess Artemis, Díktynna was a huntress and the deity of nature, the wild countryside and mountains. Her sanctuary on Cape Spátha was guarded by hounds which the Cretans claimed to be as strong as bears.

The sanctuary lay on either side of the water-course that runs into the cove where the excursion boats land. There are remains of Roman buildings on the north side of the beach (the statue of **Hadrian** now in Khaniá museum came from one of them), and traces on the south side of the stream-bed of a bridge which may have served also as an aqueduct.

The great temple stood on the high promontory to the south of the cove; it would have been visible from far away. German archaeologists excavated here in 1942, only to find that the site had been systematically looted and robbed. The platform, measuring 55m by 50m, had supported a peripteral temple. This was built of limestone and surrounded by columns using both blue and white marble, and it stood in a court paved in marble with stoas on three sides. Now only some ashlar blocks of the terrace and a few architectural fragments survive. This temple is tentatively dated to the 2C AD. There was certainly an earlier building on the site, and probably a Doric predecessor just to the west of it.

South of the terrace are the remains of four Roman cisterns which had a total capacity estimated at 400 cubic metres. Between the temple and the cisterns stood a stepped altar of white marble, and beside this, at the southwest corner of the temple, there was a small circular building which may perhaps have been a treasury. The statue, **Díktynna with hound**, one of the most striking exhibits in the Khaniá museum, was found at that spot in 1913.

To Spiliá and Episkopí

From the Kolymbári crossroads, take the minor road inland to Spiliá. Soon a turning signed for **Marathokephála** leads to a cave in the hills above the village which is a popular place for Cretan outings. A chapel in the cave is dedicated to the Cretan saint, Ayios Ioánnis Xénos (p 371). The feast day is celebrated here on 7 October.

Past the turning for the cave the road south continues 3km to **Spiliá**, one of the most delightful villages in this part of the island, with an interesting frescoed Byzantine church. There is a pleasant stroll of less than ten minutes from the prominent modern church, bearing left at the bottom of the flight of steps up to it, and following signs past a fountain and out to the edge of the village, to the tree-shaded old church dedicated to the **Panayía**. By car continue south through the village and watch for a sign right.

The frescoes (torch useful), dated stylistically to the 14C, with *graffito* of 1401, are cited as an early example on the island of what is known as the Cretan School of painting (p 95). Two important icons have been removed from the church for security reasons.

The minor road runs on south from Spiliá towards Episkopí. After 2km **Ayios Stéphanos** is signed right. A path (five minutes) follows a bank that is smothered in cyclamen in spring, to a tiny frescoed church, dating back to the 10C, the time of the restoration of the Christian faith after the Arab occupation.

1km further, turn right for the village of **Episkopí**. The intriguing church of **Mikhaíl Arkhángelos**, of particular architectural interest, is beautifully situated (before you reach the village) on the slopes of a wooded valley.

This church became the seat of the bishopric of Kísamos during the Second Byzantine period. Essentially a rotunda is provided with an apse and enclosed in a (more or less) rectangular building; the rotunda rises to a stepped dome consisting of five concentric rings. The design is unique on Crete and has few exact parallels in Byzantine architecture. (The only comparable building on the Greek mainland is Ayios Yeóryios at Thessaloníki.)

There have been various theories about the architecture of Mikhaíl Arkhángelos. Evidence for a mosaic floor dating back to the 6C (Crete's First Byzantine period) suggested that the present church was built over the foundations of an Early Christian basilica. A major investigation carried out by the Khaniá Service for Byzantine Antiquities supports the view that the rotunda itself dates to the 6C and may have been the original church on the site, with later (post-Arab) adaptations. Frescoes have been uncovered from at least three periods. The earliest detected fragments date from the 10C, with two phases of wall-painting during the 12C.

From Episkopí it is possible to continue south to Delianá and cut across to the Palaiókhora road north of Kándanos (p 408).

West from Kolymbári

The New National Road cuts across the neck of the Rodopós peninsula and descends to run parallel to the sandy shore of the Bay of Kisamós which is sheltered by the two formidable capes, Voúxa and Spátha. The winding Old Road across the peninsula takes you through a natural gap in the hills until the coastal plain is suddenly in view. Down on the plain by either route you pass, hidden between the two roads, the evocative remains of the **Villa Trevisan**, a country house built c 1500 by Crete's Venetian rulers. To find it from the new highway turn inland at the first broad crossroads towards Koléni. When you come to the Old Road go right and watch for a sign right into a side-road; then, nearly back at the highway, the villa comes into view.

Villa Trevisan, from Monumenti Veneti nell'Isola di Creta *by Giuseppe Gerola*

Kastélli Kisámou

The place-name Kastélli Kisámou refers to the castle of Kísamos built here by the Genoese freebooter, Enrico Pescatore, as part of his attempt after 1206 to challenge Venice's claim to the island. In the mid-20C, to avoid confusion, in particular with Kastélli in the Pediáda district, the name officially reverted to Kísamos, after the city-state that flourished here during the Greco-Roman period. However, locally the traditional name persists.

Kastélli is a convenient stop on a touring holiday. The little town still has an air of preoccupation with regional business rather than with visiting foreigners, but the improvement in the car-ferry service from Greek mainland ports in the Peloponnese and the near completion of the New National Road from Khaniá have increased its popularity with tourists, and the trend will surely continue. Kastélli's harbour is the official starting-point for the E4 footpath.

On the way in from Khaniá, the traditional centre of town, **Plateía Tzanakáki**, is signed right, on a one-way system along Skalídi, the old main street which branches off at an angle from the broad through road (Papayiannáki). The plateía (with some parking) is more than 500m back from the sea, where a straggle of modern buildings lines a long beach of sand and scattered rocks. One short block inland from the central plateía, the through road widens into a second open space, **Plateía El. Venizélou**, recently landscaped with shrubs and seats, and sculpture by local artists. Everything that the passing tourist is likely to need is around or close to these two plateías. A small folklore museum on the beach road preserves the fast disappearing material remains of the traditional Cretan way of life.

Travel and transport
By bus

There is a decent service from Khaniá. The bus station is in the central Plateía Tzanakáki; for information about local services ☎ 28210 220305.

By ferry

The Khaniá shipping line *ANEK* has taken over a twice-weekly service (May–October) to the island of Kýthera, the nearby mainland (Peloponnese) ports and on to Piraéus for Athens. Check with the *ANEK* office on Skalídi, ☎ 28220 22009.

The newly enlarged harbour is 3km west of the town. There is a café-bar by the ferry quay and taxis meet the boats.

Travel agencies

Kissamos Travel, ☎ 28220 23740, fax 28220 23460, is at the western corner of Plateía El. Venizélou, ready with a helpful approach to all the usual tourist requirements such as accommodation, car hire and out-of-hours currency exchange.

Kheroukhakis Travel, ☎ 28220 22655, fax 28220 23464, on Papayiannáki east of Plateía El. Venizélou, deals with boat tickets both for the ferry service to the mainland and for local excursions to

Bállos beach and the ruined Venetian fortress on the rock of Gramvoúsa (p 429).

Where to stay

B *Helena Beach* (40 rooms), ☎ 28220 23300. In a quiet location on the western edge of the town. Convenient for ferry passengers.

B *Hermes* (27 rooms), ☎ 28220 24109, fax 28220 22093. Uphill as you travel west from the centre, with good views. Suitable for wheelchair users.

C *Peli* (29 rooms), ☎ 28220 23223, fax 28220 22343. In an attractive garden on one of the roads west from the centre of town; also with good access for wheelchair users.

There is a growing number of well-advertised **studio apartments**, especially along the beach road, as well as traditional rooms for rent in the town. At the distant eastern end of the beach, the *Taverna Galini* has modern studio apartments to rent. In the centre, overlooking Plateía Tzanakáki, the lively taverna-bar *Kastro* has pleasantly old-fashioned rooms open year-round; known as the Hotel Kástro this is a long-established institution.

At the eastern end of the Bay of

Kísamos, where the road comes down from the hills there are two popular **camping sites**, *Camping Mythyma* and *Camping Nopigia*.

Eating out

Along the coast towards the harbour you pass the sheltered anchorage for fishing boats and yachts. This is a popular place to eat, either at the lively taverna and bar named the *Captain*, or (more secluded and right on the water) at *Taverna Katerina*. Otherwise there is an ever-increasing choice of beach tavernas grouped together (many specialising in freshly landed fish) to the east of the river mouth, reached by the road from the central plateía out to the sea.

A **bakery**, on the inland side of Plateía Tzanakáki, near the bus station, is popular for its cheese or spinach pies.

Wherever you choose to eat at this extreme western end of the island the local **wine**, whether in carafe or bottled under the label of Kissamos, is likely to be made from the *roméiko* grape. The stock is believed to have been brought to the island by the Venetians, but from vineyards in mainland Greece rather than from Italy. The modern winegrowers are proud of the blueish red colour of their wine, the traditional *mavro*, black, wine of Crete, as well as of its high alcohol content (up to 14 per cent proof).

Banks

The National Bank of Greece with all facilities is on the eastern corner of Plateía El. Venizélou. There are several others nearby along the main through road (Papayiannáki).

Post office and telephones

The post office and the *OTE* for telephones, fax and email are close together on Papayiannáki near the National Bank.

Hospital

The medical centre is signed inland of Plateía El. Venizélou.

Ancient Kísamos, one of the two harbours of the inland city-state of Polyrrhénia, became an independent city itself only in the 3C AD, but then gradually superseded Polyrrhénia. It was the seat of a bishop until the Saracen occupation (9C), and later a thriving Venetian settlement, fortified in the 16C. There are eye-witness accounts from early travellers of impressive ancient remains, but, as at Khaniá, the existence of the modern town impedes archaeological investigation of the site. Construction work sometimes makes it possible to excavate on a limited scale, and gradually details of the Roman town are being pieced together to improve knowledge of public buildings and individual houses. Some fine panels from mosaic floors are displayed in Khaniá's Museum of Byzantine Antiquities. The loggia in the central plateía (Tzanakáki) in Kastélli is designated as a local archaeological museum but despite refurbishment it has for some time functioned only as a storeroom for finds from the district.

Polyrrhénia

This recommended excursion is to a hilltop stronghold 7km inland, the location chosen for a city-state which flourished from Archaic to Roman times. There has been little systematic excavation but the site offers spectacular views of western Crete and is renowned for the added interest of its spring flowers.

By car the road is signed inland off the town's main through road (c 250m from the eastern end of it). The more direct E4 footpath sets off parallel to it on the side nearer the town centre; ask to be shown the starting point if necessary.

Travelling by bus

The bus leaves Kastélli for the once-a-day return journey in the early afternoon, so without private transport a walk in one direction, or a taxi (from the rank in the plateía) are the usual alternatives.

The country road climbs inland through olive groves with a view of dramatic rock formations ahead, and ends near a ruined tower at the foot of the village. Water gushes from fountains fed by the springs which made this a favoured spot in antiquity. Both cobbled streets ahead lead to the ancient site (ten minutes on foot). On the one to the left (steep only briefly) after 150 paces take the upper track to the left. At the top of the village turn left on to a dirt track which winds round (right) to the landmark of a church. Or nowadays you can drive from the fountain on a track to the *Taverna Acropolis* and walk on uphill to the same church. Here, on a relatively level shoulder of the hill, the church of **Ayii Patéres** (the Holy Fathers) is built over the foundations of a large Hellenistic building, probably a temple. The lower courses of its massive walling now support the cemetery. A Latin inscription is built into the wall of the church.

The ancient city of Polyrrhénia lay on the slopes around the church and down to the village, with the acropolis, and its secondary spur, above to the northeast. Sherds indicate occupation from the Archaic (6C BC) to the Roman periods. The site was reoccupied in the late 10C and continued in use as a Venetian stronghold. Although its position was almost impregnable, on a steep hill surrounded by ravines, the city was also walled. The remaining fortifications, including towers, date from the Second Byzantine and the Venetian periods (best preserved on the north spur), but lie in part on earlier foundations, probably of Hellenistic walls repaired in Roman times. On the acropolis there were cisterns for water, but the town below was supplied from the abundant springs by rock-cut aqueducts.

From Kastélli Kisámou to the far west

The direct road south across the island (to the monastery of Khrysoskalítissa and the beaches opposite the islet of Elaphonísi leaves the north coast from the Old Road at Kaloudianá, 3km east of Kastélli, and follows the valley of the River Yíphlos which narrows (10km inland) to a dramatic **gorge** below the village of Topólia. Both gorge and village will appeal to walkers. The road continues through chestnut woods, over the watershed to Kepháli where there are distant views of the Libyan Sea.

The alternative is to use the scenic west coast road, and a circuit from Kastélli of a little over 100km, returning direct from Kepháli, would take in a visit to (16km) the site of ancient **Phalásarna** and the west coast road as far as Sphinári, where you turn inland to Kepháli. It is then 10km southwest down a wooded valley to one of the most picturesque sights on the island, the **Khrysoskalítissa** monastery, perched on a rock above the sea. Five kilometres further on an unsurfaced road are the **Elaphonísi** beaches. There are rooms to rent here and at the settlements down the west coast, as well as in Kepháli.

To remain in the south of the island you can turn east from Míli, north of Kepháli, to cut across to Plemeniána (p 414) on the Palaiókhora road.

Travelling by bus
From Kastélli there is a limited service to Phalásarna and Sphinári on the west coast, and in summer one bus a day to Khrysoskalítissa monastery and Elaphonísi.

For the circular route the road sets off west along the coast, past the harbour of Kísamos, but soon turns inland running southwest across the base of the **Gramvoúsa peninsula** that stretches away to the north sheltering the Kísamos bay.

On a rock off the peninsula's northwest tip the Venetians built a fortress in 1579 that held out against the Turks until 1692, 23 years after the surrender of Herákleion. The Gramvoúsa fortress later became a stronghold of piracy. In the 19C the Turks exploited its position to harass the short sea-crossing between rebellious Crete and the island of Antikýthera, by then a part of independent Greece. During the Battle of Crete in World War Two, Royal Navy ships based in Malta had to be put at risk against German naval and air forces in this same corridor on the western approaches to the island's main harbours.

The walk to Bállos bay
Kalyvianí at the base of the peninsula marks the start of a long expedition for serious walkers out to Bállos beach around a cove opposite the fortress of Gramvoúsa. (For details of boat trips see p 426.) The cove is sheltered by the **Tigáni** headland (shaped, as its name implies, like a frying pan), and is famed for its beach of strikingly pale sand. This is a 21km round trip; allow about 2½ hours on foot out to the cape, but you can take a vehicle at least 3km, sometimes further, on the first stretch. (There is also a west coast path from Phalásarna.)

Five kilometres from Kastélli an insignificant turning is signed right (beside a cement works) with a fork left to **Kalyvianí**. Taxis will go this far. Keep straight ahead through the village until a broad track branches downhill, right. There is room to park when the track deteriorates. The path, marked spasmodically with paint splashes, keeps to the eastern side of the spine of the peninsula, and gains height gradually to pass above several small watercourses. Long stretches of this walk are across bare hillside, but at a little over halfway a conspicuous clump of oleanders marks a welcome spring, and conceals the weathered blocks and pointed arch of the old Ayía Eiríni fountain. A climb brings you up on to a plateau; bear left across it, cutting off the narrow tip of the peninsula. Before the steep descent to the west coast bay, you can walk out to the edge of the perpendicular cliff. One islet is linked to the beach by a sandy spit, but offshore, just to the north, is the rock of **Gramvoúsa**, flat-topped except for a knob at its seaward end on which the Venetians built their fortress; the turreted walls of this isolated outpost still stand.

Phalásarna
Ten kilometres along the main road west from Kastélli, in Plátanos, you must turn off to the coast if you plan to visit the site of the Greco-Roman harbour

town of Phalásarna. At a fork at the beginning of Plátanos keep right for the signed turning. There is a short cut following arrows to Phalásarna beach but both routes join at a red-roofed church and the well-made road drops downhill 6km to the settlement. The panoramic view of the Bay of Livádi takes in a dense olive grove, and polythene hothouses glinting behind a long sandy beach, one of the finest on the island; there is access at several points. The archaeological site is below Cape Koutrí at the northern end of the bay and then the Gramvoúsa peninsula stretches away into the distance. Piecemeal development for tourism has begun on this remote west-facing stretch of coast and is set to continue.

Where to stay and eating out

Out of season there should be no problem about accommodation. The *Phalasarna Beach* apartments dominate the settlement at the northern end of the sandy bay where paths take you down to the shore. The blocks of **studio rooms** to rent increase in number every year.

C *Plakurés* (25 rooms), ☎ 28220 41581, fax 28220 41781. This recent addition, with taverna, is useful for anyone who likes to book in advance.

The long-established *Taverna Sunset* is tucked away on the seaward side of the new settlement, with uninterrupted views. The service is friendly and there are rooms to rent above the terrace level.

The unsurfaced road leaves the new buildings behind and crosses the protected archaeological area. You pass on the left (just beyond the last hothouses) the so-called rock-cut throne which has been the subject of much speculation. One suggestion is that it served as a speaker's podium. Keep on until you come to a guardian's hut below the chapel of Ayios Yeóryios on the headland. The track curves away to the right to the cove beyond, but a footpath left from the hut leads to the centre of the ancient site.

Phalásarna, the most westerly city-state of Crete, was at the height of its power in the Hellenistic period (4C–3C BC), although sherds of 6C black-figure Corinthian pottery found in the cemeteries (and now on display in the Khaniá Archaeological Museum) testify to earlier occupation. For a time Phalásarna was the west coast port of Polyrrhénia (p 427).

The city was mentioned by ancient geographers especially for its 'enclosed' harbour. The Englishman Captain T.A.B. Spratt, on a Royal Navy survey expedition in the mid-19C, was the first to realise that, owing to an alteration in the sea-level, this enclosed harbour was high and dry c 100m inland (see plan). Spratt left an invaluable record of the upstanding remains of the city walls which he supposed had surrounded it.

The acropolis of the city-state lay to the north of the harbour on the headland of Cape Koutrí which drops sheer into the sea. (There is now a rough path up from the east above the chapel of Ayios Yeóryios.) Remains on the higher summit may belong to a temple of Diktynnaion Artemis; the other known temple, dedicated to Apollo, was probably down by the harbour. The city spread on to the slope below the headland. The promontory was crossed in the Hellenistic period by a fortification wall (still preserved in places). The city's cemeteries were chiefly on the rising ground inland.

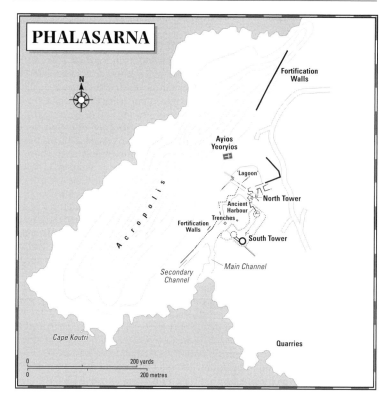

Archaeological investigation at Phalásarna has been conducted since the early 1980s by the Greek Archaeological Service, and since 1986 there has been collaboration with American archaeologists from their School of Classical Studies in Athens. A 1986 geophysical survey confirmed the existence of an artificial harbour with surrounding defence walls very much as they had been planned in 1860. Recent excavations have demonstrated that tectonic displacement occurred in the late 5C AD, raising this coast 6–9m above the present sea level.

The artificially excavated **harbour basin**, roughly rectangular, measuring 100m x 75m, is now a flat area filled with earth, but the original construction had been connected to the sea by a natural opening in the rock enlarged to form an entrance channel 10–12m wide. At some point in antiquity passage was deliberately obstructed with large blocks of stone. A secondary, shallower, channel diverged from the main one to reach the sea 100m further north; it may have had a desilting function or served as a dock for small boats. Both channels can still be traced; it is estimated that the harbour could take vessels needing a depth of 1.2m.

The harbour was defended by stretches of the city wall, and by four towers and a mole. To the southeast of the harbour there is a deep tank or cistern, and clear evidence for quarrying the quartz-rich sandstone blocks from which the city was built. The **South Tower** (excavated 1986–87) turned out to be a formidable for-

The 'throne' of Phalasarna, from Pashley, Travels in Crete, *1837*

tification built in the second half of the 4C BC, circular in plan (not square as Spratt had supposed), with massive foundations built of ashlar sandstone blocks in isodomic style, without mortar, and strengthened by an internal arrangement of quadrants deliberately filled with rubble. At one place eight courses of its external wall are preserved, to a height of 4.5m. The excavators draw attention to the architectural design of the base of the tower by which the diameter decreases above a rounded moulding three courses (1.65m) from ground level. This structural feature is common in Greek military architecture but not on harbour towers, and had not previously been uncovered on Crete. To the west of the tower two parallel walls with moat between are interpreted as a protective sea wall. Another unusual feature is the cistern which was bonded into the northwest side of the tower and, intriguingly, had its plastered interior treated with a black paint. This cistern (now roofed for protection) would have provided a secure water supply for defending forces, but may also have facilitated the swift resupplying of ships.

The rectangular **North Tower** dating back to the 4C BC was reconstructed in late Hellenistic times. In antiquity there was a second basin to the north of this tower which was at first thought to have been a small inner harbour, but it is awkwardly limited by walls and its function remains uncertain.

In Hellenistic times the menace of piracy from vessels based in Cretan waters is well documented. Faced with the lack of evidence for commercial harbour activities, and with the obviously defensive works and hints of military structures around this enclosed port the excavators have put forward the hypothesis that the city-state of Phalásarna sheltered a pirates' lair. When the Romans invaded Crete in 67 BC one of their aims was to reduce the menace of piracy from bases on Crete, and the blocking of the entrance channel into the harbour here may have played a part in campaign.

The west coast road

From Plátanos the road sets off south towards (8km) Sphinári. Soon, at the turn for Lusakiés, the E4 walking route joins the coast road as you climb to a fine view over the bay back to Phalásarna and Cape Koutrí. This scenic road was engineered more than a decade ago to open up this stretch of the west coast. Upgrading has continued and the asphalt surface is virtually complete but still this is not a road to drive in a hurry. It winds high above the sea, with the as yet undeveloped coastline spread out below and a number of tracks down to it clearly visible, while others point invitingly into the hills. Oleanders are beginning to hide the scars left by the roadworks.

Sphinári, 35km from Kastélli, is a small village 800m inland of a pebble beach, with a choice (in the village and on the sea) of tavernas and rooms for rent. The road south turns inland climbing to **Ano Sphinári**, and on through lightly wooded country. You emerge on to a corniche road with stunning views back along the coast. The next village with access to the sea (2km down a gorge) is **Kámbos**, also with tavernas and a few rooms for rent; the houses are strung out along a wooded stream and a *kalderími* following it into the hills leads over the watershed in the direction of **Sirikári** a route recommended to walkers. In spring all this region is a delight for its profusion of wild flowers (cyclamen, lupins and other rarer finds to please the specialist), but with the relatively cool, damp, west coast climate the season may be as much as two weeks behind the rest of the island.

Before Keramotí the view opens out ahead, down the coast to the southwestern corner of Crete over the narrow plain behind the indent of the Stómio Bay to Moní Khrysoskalítissa, gleaming white and picturesquely elevated on a rock above the sea. The unsurfaced coastal track is in sight all the way (c 15km) to the monastery and several (sometimes rough) side-roads are signed down to it. On the main road you continue past **Keramotí** and **Amigdalokepháli**, and then turn inland to the village of **Kepháli**, beautifully situated high above a wooded valley, looking down to the distant sea. There are a number of simple tavernas and some rooms to rent; start at the *Taverna Polakis* (with rooms above) where you can take advice about access to some of the Byzantine churches roundabout. One on the southern edge of the village, **Metamórphosis tou Sotiroú** (the Transfiguration of the Saviour) has wall-paintings dated to 1320.

From the eastern end of the village a road (widened and improved but perhaps still not surfaced all the way) runs down the river valley to the coast and (11km) Moní Khrysoskalítissas. Two kilometres down the hill **Váthi** has two frescoed churches to interest enthusiasts; both may be locked, but ask about keys at the *kapheneíon* on the right in the little plateía. The church of **Ayios Yeóryios** (in the village, signed to the right from the plateía) has frescoes dated by inscription 1254. Scenes in the upper register of the vault were inexpertly reassembled during repairs to the roof. In the apse some of the original sketches can be traced.

In the fields immediately below the road, a few minutes south of the village (with a path signed left) the church of **Mikhaíl Arkhángelos** has early 14C frescoes, notably the *Fall of Jericho* and the *Presentation in the Temple*. The paintings in the apse are later 14C work.

The road, with the E4 path following the same route, continues beside a stream overhung by sweet chestnut and plane trees. About 7km from the turn in Kepháli there is a new bridge over the stream and when there is much water coming down from the hills it is best to cross to the other bank here. Otherwise you can keep straight ahead (signed for Stómio) to emerge on the bay. To the right, below a gypsum quarry, are the ruins of the deserted village of **Stómio**, its fate bound up with the coastal trade. Turn left towards the **Khrysoskalítissa monastery**, nowadays allocated for nuns though few remain.

The monastery is open 08.30–12.00 and 15.00–19.00. The first church here was built inside a grotto. Now the double-naved church is dedicated to the Panayía Khrysoskalítissas, the Virgin of the Golden Stair; *khrysós* is gold in Greek and *skalí* a stair. Ninety steps lead down to the sheltered cove to the south of the pinnacle on which the church is built, and it is said that only those without sin can recognise the one stair that is made of gold. The present monastic buildings are of no great age but the panoramic view from the terrace is worth the climb.

Scattered concrete buildings have not increased the romance of this remote spot but rooms to rent at the taverna to the south of the monastery enjoy an extremely satisfying view of it.

The recently improved road continues 5km further south to a long tamarisk-shaded beach of pale sand sheltered by the **Elaphonísi islands** just offshore; this is generally agreed to be one of the most idyllic spots on Crete. (Avoid high summer unless you enjoy crowds.) There are sunloungers with umbrellas and makeshift refreshment stalls at the centre of the beach but otherwise, in both directions, an expanse of dune empty except for summer campers. The main island, with deep water swimming beyond it, is reached by wading across a narrow channel. Outside the high season there is likely to be a choice of rooms to rent above the tavernas back from the beach; *Taverna Elaphonisi* is near the end of the road. A ferry boat runs day-trips from Palaiókhora, and there are buses from the north coast as well as tour operators' coaches bringing custom to the tavernas, but in late afternoon peace returns. However, there is reason to fear future development so the extraordinary natural beauty and sense of isolation may not survive for much longer.

For long-distance walkers a shepherds' track climbs inland towards Sklavopoúla but the E4 route swings east following the time-honoured coastal path to Palaiókhora.

To return northwards you can retrace the route as far as Kepháli and there turn right (signposted for Khaniá). After 5km you pass through the attractive village of **Elos**, the centre of a wooded region where sweet chestnuts are a commercial crop. A chestnut festival is held here annually in October. 4km beyond Elos, just before Míli, you pass the junction (signed right for Strovlés) for cross-country roads to Palaiókhora. The direct route would take you east to Plemenianá on the main road near Kándanos. Another climbs in a loop into the wild and unspoilt hill country of the southwestern corner of the island, and over the watershed to a fertile valley of orange groves, and Voutás; for the excursion from Palaiókhora to Voutás and the churches of Sklavopoúla see p 434.

The main road from Kepháli to the north coast continues to **Míli** through the chestnut woods. You follow the Typhlós river, which runs through the dramatic **Gorge of Topólia**, to the east of the village, but as the valley narrows you notice, to the right of the road at **Koutsomatádos**, *Taverna Panorama* (with rooms to rent), overhanging the path into the gorge at the start of a 7km walk down to the sea.

The road enters a tunnel before the village of Topólia, but before that there are signs, left, for the cave of Ayía Sophía. A 15-minute climb brings you to a chapel at the entrance to a lofty cavern known for its spectacular stalactites; the cave was frequented from Neolithic to Roman times.

Topólia is a particularly pleasant village in a fine setting, and a stroll around it is recommended as part of a short excursion from the Old Road along the north coast. The Byzantine church of **Ayía Paraskeví** is signed downhill from the main street.

The road continues towards the coast down the river valley to Kaloudianá where you turn left for the last 5km to Kastélli Kisámou, or a junction with the New National Road for the return to Khaniá.

Glossary

abacus a flat block crowning the capital of a column

agorá public square or marketplace

aryballos small ovoid or round pot usually containing perfumed oil

ashlar square-cut stone in regular courses of masonry

askós a vase shape derived from the traditional form of a wineskin, equipped with handle and small opening for pouring; often in the shape of an animal or bird

atrium forecourt of a Roman house

ayios (m.), **ayía** (f.), **ayii** (m. pl.) **ayiés** (f. pl.) Saint(s)

basilica originally a colonnaded hall for Roman civil administration; later a three-aisled church (with apse or apses), the nave separated from the side-aisles by columns which supported the central raised roof (clerestory)

bema the sanctuary of a Byzantine church

breccia a conglomerate rock

cavea seating area of a theatre

cella enclosed sanctuary at the centre of a temple

deisis iconographical composition of petition or intercession with Christ between the Virgin Mary and (usually) St John the Baptist

demotic the vernacular Greek langauge, as opposed to *katharevousa*, formal academic Greek

dimarkheíon town hall for adminstration of the *dímos* or municipality

distaff an implement used in spinning

double axe a tool with a blade on either side of the central shaft, also for ceremonial use and occurring frequently as a cult symbol

exedra semicircular (sometimes rectangular) recess with seats

faience in antiquity, the product of fusing granular quartz or sand with an alkali, which was then coated with an alkaline glaze

fibula pin to fasten clothing, ornamental as well as practical

firman decree from the Ottoman government

fresco wall painting executed while plaster still wet

gorgoneion mask of the gorgon

gypsum an easily worked limestone used for Minoan palatial-style buildings

heroön funerary monument, a shrine to honour a hero

horns of consecration stylised bulls' horns, a cult symbol modelled in stone or plaster, also shown in frescoes on the eaves of buildings

hýdria three-handled vessel for carrying water

iconostasis screen adorned with icons in Orthodox church separating the sanctuary from the main body of the church

isodomic masonry with each vertical joint placed over the centre of the stone in the course below

kálathos a deep bowl with two handles at the flaring rim

kalderími a paved road dating from before the modern era

kérnos cult vessel with a number of small receptacles

kouloúra Greek word meaning round and hollow, hence a pit

koúros the Greek word for a youth, adopted to denote the sculptural representation of a standing figure of a young male

krater large two-handled bowl for mixing liquids, associated with ceremonial drinking

lárnax, (pl.) **lárnakes** clay coffin(s)

lékythos one-handled vase with narrow ovoid body and tall narrow neck

libation liquid offering to a deity

lustral basin small sunken room in Minoan architecture associated with purification and cleansing

martyrion a building commemorating the death of a martyr

mégaron in Greek, an imposing hall. The Mycenaean megaron was rectangular with a central hearth, and a single entrance through the porch at one end

meltémi the prevailing north wind of midsummer in the Aegean

narthex a shallow porch extending the width of a church

nomarkheíon centre of provincial administration (for the *nome* or province)

obsidian a natural glass occurring in restricted volcanic areas

odeíon a small roofed theatre, usually for musical performances

Odiyítria the Virgin Mary pointing to the Christ Child held on her left arm as the way of salvation

oinóchoe a wine jug with narrow neck and round or trefoil mouth

orthostat stone slab set vertically

Panayia the All Holy Virgin

Pantokrátor Christ, the ruler of all things, portrayed holding a Bible and in the act of blessing

peristyle colonnaded court resembling a cloister

phýlax, or **phýlakas** guardian, here of antiquities

píthos, (pl.) **píthoi** large pottery jar(s) for the storage of oil or grain; also used for inhumation burial

Platytéra representation of the Virgin and Child as a symbol of the Incarnation

polythýron Greek for many doors, used for a Minoan hall partitioned by walls of multiple pier-and-door openings

pronaos porch as entrance to a temple

propylon, or **propylaeum** columned ceremonial gateway

protome model of part of an animal or human body as applied to pottery vases

prytaneíon the assembly hall of the ruling council of a Greek city-state

pýxis small lidded box in pottery, stone, ivory or metal

rhyton vessel designed for the pouring of libations

sacral knot Minoan cult symbol modelled as for a band of cloth, looped and knotted with the loose ends fringed

scarab beetle-shaped seal

skyphos cup with two horizontal handles at the rim

sphyrelaton technique sheet bronze hammered on a wooden core and pinned

steatopygous fat-buttocked

stele stone slab, often with sculptural decoration as a marker for a grave

stirrup jar a pottery vessel with stirrup-shaped handles from shoulder to false neck and the spout on the shoulder

stoa a free-standing colonnaded portico

temenos a sacred precinct

thólos circular vaulted building

votive offering any object offered to a deity

Index

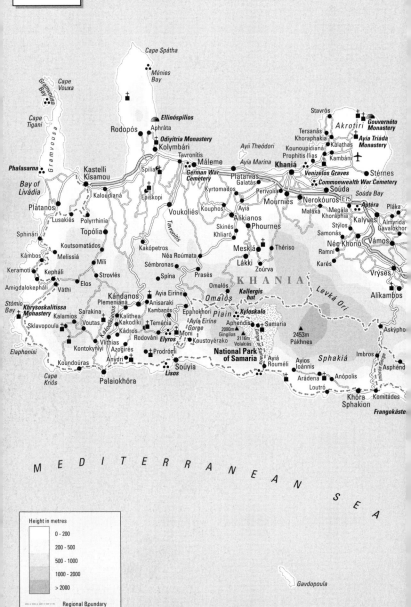

CRETE

Cape Spátha

Ménies Bay

Cape Vouxa

Cape Tigáni

Gramvoúsa Bay

Ellinóspilios

Rodopós

Aphráta

Odiyítria Monastery

Kolymbári

Tavronítis

Ayii Theódori

Máleme

German War Cemetery

Stavrós

Akrotíri

Gouvernéto Monastery

Tersanás

Khoraphákia

Kalathás

Ayía Triáda Monastery

Kounoupidianá

Prophítis Ilías

Kambáni

Phalásarna

Kastélli Kísamou

Spília

Plataniás

Ayía Marína

Khaniá

Kámbos

Galatás

Venizélos Graves

Stérnes

Bay of Livádia

Kaloudianá

Episkopi

Kyrtomados

Perivólia

Commonwealth War Cemetery

Soúda

E75

Soúda Bay

Aptéra

Pláka

Plátanos

Polyrrhinia

Voukoliés

Kouphos

Ayiá

Alikianós

Mourniés

Nerokoúros

Megála

Khoraphía

Almyrida

Lusakiés

Topólia

Skínes

Phournés

Maláxa

Stylos

Kályves

Gavalokhór

Sphinári

Koutsomatádos

Melissiá

Kakópetros

Khliaró

Mesklá

Thériso

Samonás

Néo Khorió

Vámos

Kámbos

Keramoti

Mili

Néa Roúmata

Lákki

Zoúrva

Ramní

Kepháli

Elos

Strovlés

Sémbronas

Prasés

KHANIA

Karés

Vrýses

Amigdalokepháli

Váthi

Spína

Omalós

Levká Ori

Alíkambos

Stómio Bay

Khrysoskalítissa Monastery

Kalamios

Kándanos

Plemenianá

Ayía Eiríne

Omalós Plain

Kallérgis hut

Askýpho

Sklavopoula

Voutas

Sarakína

Kalithéa

Kambanós

Epahokhóri

Xyloskalo

Samariá

Imbros

Asphénd

Kakodíki

Temenía

Ayía Eiríne Gorge

Aphéndis

2080m

Volakás

Kádros

Rodováni

Moni

Gingilos

2116m

2453m

Pákhnes

Sphakiá

Imbros Gorge

Kontokyníyi

Azogirés

Koustoyérako

National Park of Samariá

Ayios Ioánnis

Anópolis

Komitádes

Koundoúras

Anydri

Pródromi

Ayía Roúmeli

Aradena

Elaphonísi

Cape Kriós

Souyia

Lisos

Palaiokhóra

Loutró

Khóra Sphakíon

Frangokáste

MEDITERRANEAN SEA

Gavdopoula

Height in metres

0 - 200

200 - 500

500 - 1000

1000 - 2000

> 2000

Regional Boundary

Main roads

E4 Walking route

Airport

Monastery/Church

Places of historical interest

Cave

Gavdos

Sarakiniko Bay

Kastrí

Karavés

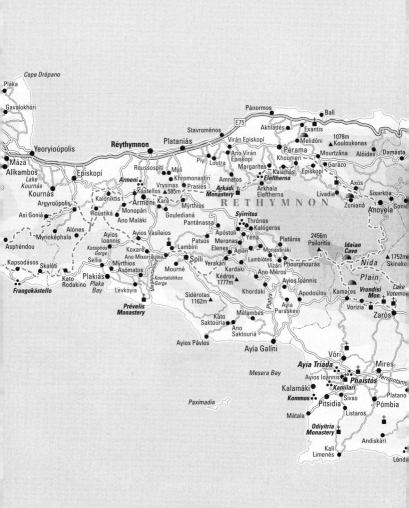